ABRAHAM LINCOLN

The Sangamon Edition
VOLUME FOUR

The White House in '61; statue of Jefferson in the foreground

Photograph by Brady, from the L. C. Handy studios

Carl Sandburg

ABRAHAM LINCOLN

The War Years – II

VOLUME FOUR

The Sangamon Edition

CHARLES SCRIBNER'S SONS

New York 1944

CONTENTS

33. DRIFTING—MURFREESBORO—"OLD STARS"   3
   Adam Gurowski – Karl Marx – Portrait of Ormsby MacKnight Mitchel

34. FINAL EMANCIPATION PROCLAMATION '63   8
   A New Year's Day both merry and solemn – A single act becomes a titanic tradition

35. "MORE HORSES THAN OATS"—OFFICE-SEEKERS   28
   Many seekers and callers see the President – They wear him

36. FOREIGN MEDIATION—BUTLER   66
   England – Pope Pius IX – Greeley – Napoleon III – "Old Cock-Eye" – The question of Negro troops

37. HOOKER—CHANCELLORSVILLE—CALAMITY   74
   Portrait of Hooker – Thad Stevens says to kill or exile all slave-holders

38. VICKSBURG—GRANT, LIQUOR, AND LINCOLN   105
   Porter's loyalty and McClernand's ability questioned – Is Grant losing or winning? – Lincoln studies Grant

39. DEEP SHADOWS—LINCOLN IN EARLY '63   122
   Portrait of Clement Laird Vallandigham – Wilbur Fisk Storey – J. Wesley Greene – C. Chauncey Burr – Defamation – Horatio Seymour – Habeas corpus – Secret societies – Vallandigham arrested and banished – Negro troops – Frederick Douglass – Cotton-traders – "The Shoddy" – The National Bank Act – Lincoln's reputation at its lowest point – Greeley seeks a candidate to replace him in '64 – The furtive movement to impeach the President – Congressman Albert Gallatin Riddle defends him – "A woman spy in the Executive Mansion" – Lincoln reads aloud the pamphlet *How a Free People Conduct a Long War* – An unknown marksman shoots at Lincoln on horseback

40. THE MAN IN THE WHITE HOUSE   207

Pennsylvania Avenue motley – Lafayette Square and the Jackson statue – Assassination safeguards against Lincoln's wishes – The President familiar with his guards – Sketch of Gurowski – The President's office and methods of work – A light sleeper – "A total abstainer" – Handling correspondence – Observers report his individual handling of scores of callers – Serious and light matters among telegraphers at the War Office – Varied impressions of Mrs. Lincoln – The family embarrassments of public life – Lincoln anecdotes of matrimony – The boy Tad his father's favorite companion – Other children in the White House – Public receptions and "levees" – Noah Brooks – The Soldiers' Home grounds and summer cottage – The terrific multicolored Washington scene, gaudy and bawdy – Nathaniel Hawthorne and Walt Whitman write impressions of it – A series of observers give sketches of the Lincoln they saw and heard at close range – Tom Thumb and his bride call at the White House – Lincoln's keen interest in inventions, science, abstractions – Remarkable letters, a long droll one to the King of Siam – What Lincoln recited or read aloud to companions – Talk with Louis Agassiz – Hawthorne's *Atlantic Monthly* article and deletion of passages the editor considered unfair – The President's growth during two years of office – Lincoln sometimes termed the first All-American President – White House phantoms

41. GETTYSBURG—VICKSBURG—DEEP TIDES '63   334

Portrait of George Gordon Meade – How the news of the two mid-'63 victories came to the White House – Lincoln's perplexity and gloom over the failure to destroy Lee's army – Alexander Hamilton Stephens seeks peace negotiations at Washington and is rebuffed – New York draft and race riots – Draft enforcement that summer – Vallandigham appears in Canada and addresses his followers in the United States – The President's "stump-speech" letter to Conkling

42. LINCOLN AT STORM CENTER   389

Sherman advises a policy of terror – North Carolina leans to peace – The President's Mexican policy – Missouri and Kansas radicals call at the White House – The President replies to their demands – Postmaster General Blair assumes roles – The race question seethes – Frederick Douglass reports his interview with the President – Lincoln transfigured among myth-making Negroes

43. CHICKAMAUGA AND ELECTIONS WON '63   420

Stanton and Lincoln prepare for Chickamauga by sending 23,000 troops from Virginia to Tennessee – The news of Chickamauga dribbles into Washington – Lincoln's strange letter to McClernand – Portrait of George Henry Thomas – Meade and Lee fail to grapple – The President at political risk enforces the draft and calls for more troops – Vallandigham a candidate for Governor of Ohio – Unionist victories at the November polls

44. LINCOLN SPEAKS AT GETTYSBURG   452

Edward Everett accepts the invitation to be orator of the day – The condition under which Lincoln prepares "a few appropriate remarks" – The wedding of Kate Chase – Initial point of the Union Pacific Railway fixed – The journey to Gettysburg and the ceremonies

45. EPIC '63 DRAWS TO A CLOSE   477

Lookout Mountain – The President's '63 message – James Russell Lowell's remarkable analysis and estimate of Lincoln in the *North American Review* – Wendell Phillips again lampoons Lincoln – The Vatican stands neutral – World-wide folk tales and foreign opinion favor the North – Robert J. Walker and Henry Ward Beecher in England – Russia favors the North – The Reverend Henry Fowler's appraisal of Lincoln – '63 in retrospect

46. GRANT GIVEN HIGH COMMAND '64   535

Attempts to set up Grant as candidate for President – He repudiates them – Congress creates the rank of lieutenant general – The President appoints Grant, who goes to Washington for his first meeting with Lincoln

47. WILL HIS PARTY RENOMINATE LINCOLN?   555

Congress and politics in early '64 – Isaac N. Arnold the lone Congressman openly favoring a second term for Lincoln – The popular trend with Lincoln, though party leaders in Senate and House hold aloof – Orestes Augustus Brownson and Horace Greeley belittle Lincoln – Other possible candidates for President – Anna Elizabeth Dickinson and Wendell Phillips for, then against, Lincoln – Beecher wavers – A hymn of hate – Portrait of August Belmont – McClellan proposed as the Democratic-party candidate – Lincoln appraised by metropolitan and country editors – Francis Bicknell Carpenter begins his White House residence, painting Lincoln and the Cabinet – The dying Lovejoy

48. CASH FOR WAR–ALMADEN–HARD TIMES   600

Jay Cooke phenomenal at selling United States bonds – Cotton speculators and corrupt contractors – War fortunes – Labor strikes – High prices and cheap money press on the poor

49. CHASE THIRSTS TO RUN FOR PRESIDENT   624

The Pomeroy Secret Circular – Lincoln's humor and patience with a rival in his Cabinet – Welles resents the call for a campaign-fund contribution

LIST OF ILLUSTRATIONS

The White House in '61 *frontispiece*
Lincoln as Brutus haunted by the ghost of Caesar—in a *Punch* cartoon 9
Sketch of Negro cabins 11
The pen with which Lincoln signed the Emancipation Proclamation 17
The letter of George Livermore concerning the pen the President sent 17
Early draft of the Emancipation Proclamation signed by Lincoln 19
General and Mrs. Nathaniel Prentiss Banks 20
Ormsby MacKnight Mitchel 20
John Alexander Logan 20
Oil painting of Abraham Lincoln, by W. T. Matthews 21
Photograph of Lincoln, October 3, '61 21
A broadside picturing Lincoln bestowing emancipation on slaves 24
Harper's Weekly cartoons a jubilant freed Negro 27
Manacles gone out of use 28
Abraham Lincoln, November 15, 1863. Photograph by Gardner 52
Charles Anderson Dana 53
Thomas Thompson Eckert 53
Edwin McMasters Stanton, Secretary of War 53
Punch cartoons Lincoln and Jeff Davis at billiards 67
Lincoln beheads generals and Cabinet members—in a *Leslie's* cartoon 81
Joseph ("Fighting Joe") Hooker 84
Federal field hospital at Savage Station, Virginia 84
Army of the Potomac scouts 85
Vanity Fair cartoons New York editors failing to get Lincoln's ear 101
A harassed Chief Magistrate is cartooned as suave and ironic 112
Clement Laird Vallandigham 116
Samuel Sullivan ("Sunset") Cox 116
Erastus Corning 116
Martin Kalbfleisch 116
William Marcy Tweed 116
Horace Greeley 117
William Lloyd Garrison 117
The usually friendly *Harper's Weekly* savagely pillories Lincoln, Stanton, Halleck 123

The English cartoonist Matt Morgan presents the aerial Lincoln 129
Leslie's caricatures Old Man of the Sea Welles riding Sinbad Lincoln 133
Volck draws Lincoln playing "a pleasant comedy"—of death 140
An envelope cartoon of Lincoln as a comet—up among the stars 203
Lincoln indorses Lamon as "entirely reliable, and trust-worthy" 205
The White House from Lafayette Square 212
Lincoln, "the thinker" 212
The War Office daily visited by Lincoln 212
Relief map (1861) of Washington, the Potomac, and Virginia 213
Willard's Hotel, "the conversational capitol" 213
Plans of the first and second floors of the White House 215
Nicolay sends the *Washington Star* a "notice" 219
Closing part of a letter John Hay wrote for the President 220
The Lincoln family pastor writes a recommendation for a chaplaincy 223
Lincoln writes a card introducing "my friend T. J. Carter" 229
Chiropodist Zacharie gets a recommendation signed "A. Lincoln" 230
The President serves as social secretary to his wife 235
John George Nicolay 244
John Hay 244
The White House; front portico and roadway 244
A section of the East Room in the White House 244
The President's cousin Dennis Hanks 245
The newlywed "General" and Mrs. Tom Thumb 245
The eminent tragedian John McCullough 245
The ex-slave Sojourner Truth 245
Mrs. Lincoln writes in behalf of Kentucky horses for the army 248
Leslie's sketches White House guests in crinoline 251
Ladies and costumes at a White House reception 257
A card of invitation to dinner at the White House 258
The President signs thanks for white rabbits presented to Tad 262
The President writes an order for a Navy sword for Tad 264
Robert T. Lincoln telegraphs, his father writing "Charge to me" 266
Print of the Soldiers' Home 270
Print of the President's cottage at the Soldiers' Home 271
Willie and Tad Lincoln with Major Lockwood Todd 276
William ("Willie") Wallace Lincoln 276
Julia ("Julie") Taft Bayne at sixteen 276
"Holly" and "Bud" Taft 276
Earliest known photograph of Tad 277

The boy has grown 277
Tad with a sword and in colonel's uniform 277
James C. Welling edits Lincoln's rhetoric 307
Lincoln. Photograph by Gardner in early '63 308
Lincoln. Photograph by Brady, probably late '63 308
Robert Todd Lincoln, Harvard student 308
Mary Todd Lincoln, in mourning garb after Willie's death 308
The President's reception room 309
A handbill sounding alarm over Lee's invasion of Pennsylvania 337
The Roman Catholic Bishop of Buffalo beseeches his flock to keep
   the peace 365
Punch cartoons Lincoln as instigator of race riots 367
U.S.A. Government transportation for "one drafted man" 369
The New York draft riots cartooned in *Leslie's* 371
George Gordon Meade 372
Oliver Otis Howard 372
William Starke Rosecrans 372
John Adams Dix 372
Archbishop John Hughes 373
Bishop Matthew Simpson 373
Henry Ward Beecher 373
A bullet-pierced, lifesaving New Testament 373
Harper's Weekly presents a fat contractor and a lean soldier 374
Inequity between exploiters and the enlisted man cartooned in
   Harper's Weekly 376
Harper's Weekly puts a current draft joke into a cartoon 378
Tailpiece—Rusty weapons 389
John McAllister Schofield 404
Lincoln, February 9, '64. Photograph by Brady 404
Ben Butler at his headquarters 404
David Hunter 404
George William Curtis 405
Bayard Taylor 405
James Russell Lowell 405
John Bright, M.P. 405
James Longstreet 436
John Singleton Mosby 436
Joseph Emerson Brown 436
John Cabell Breckinridge 436

Pierre Gustave Toutant Beauregard   436
Braxton Bragg   436
Nathan Bedford Forrest   436
Colonel and Mrs. John Hunt Morgan   436
James Ewell Brown ("Jeb") Stuart   436
Ambrose Powell Hill   436
Daniel Harvey Hill   436
James Alexander Seddon   436
Lincoln, two of five photographs made November 15, '63   437
Lincoln, two of four photographs made in early '64   437
Lincoln's letter regarding honor and blame "if Gen. Meade can now
    attack"   439
Edward Everett   468
Lincoln in '63. Photograph by Brady   468
Lincoln about the time of the Gettysburg speech   468
Andrew Gregg Curtin   468
Lincoln. Photograph eleven days before the Gettysburg speech   469
Drafts of an early passage in Gettysburg Address, showing revisions   470
Drafts of a later passage in Gettysburg Address, showing revisions   471
Lincoln's attitude toward John Bull cartooned in *Harper's Weekly*   513
Punch sees American President and Russian Czar as sinister friends   523
Punch cartoon covers Tory fear of co-operation between the U.S.A.
    and Russia   524
Harper's Weekly cartoons Lincoln telling Seward to use "Russian
    Salve"   525
The honor medal voted General Grant by Congress   546
Ulysses Simpson Grant, Lieutenant General   548
Charles Sumner   549
Charles Francis Adams, Sr.   549
Nathaniel Hawthorne   596
Wendell Phillips   596
Mr. and Mrs. Gerrit Smith   596
The chamber of the United States House of Representatives   597
Schuyler Colfax, Speaker of the House   597
Chauncey Mitchell Depew   597
The Treasury Building '61   628
Pontoon bridge and officials from Washington in carriage   628
Katherine ("Kate") Garniss Chase Sprague   629
The White House   655

Abraham Lincoln
THE WAR YEARS

ABRAHAM LINCOLN: The War Years

CHAPTER 33

DRIFTING—MURFREESBORO—
"OLD STARS"

> The Reverend Doctors Leacock and Goodrich, and Reverend Mr. Fulton, three Episcopal clergymen of the city of New Orleans, arrived in New York a few days since in the *Cahawba* as state prisoners, on the way to Fort La Fayette by order of General Butler. They refused to pray for Mr. Lincoln. Served them right. Everybody should pray for Mr. Lincoln. He surely needs the devout prayers of all the devout people of the country.—*Iowa Bugle*.

THIS item reprinted in the *Crisis* of Columbus, Ohio, joined an editorial discussion of the President's "wild and unbridled career." Editor Sam Medary invited him to gaze on "fields of slaughtered men, 150,000 sick and wounded in the hospitals, widows and orphans everywhere." Other editors and journals wished the President remorse on New Year's Day of '63.

The war would never end by a single event, by one great battle, Wendell Phillips was saying. It was too deep in its sources. "The great struggle in England between democracy and nobility lasted from 1640 to 1660, taking a king's life in its progress, and yet failed for the time. The great struggle between the same parties in France began in 1789 and is not yet ended. It will take ten or twenty years to clear off the scars of such a struggle."

Phillips voiced an element moving to power. "The South has not yet begun to play her last card. The moment she begins to feel exhaustion she will proclaim liberty to the negro . . . she will call the black into her ranks . . . by some proclamation of gradual emancipation."

The North was ready to go on with the war for a generation. The South would find a North untouched. "So much money," said Phillips, "that we have not to go abroad to borrow any, so much wheat that we could feed the world, such ample munitions of war that your traitor merchants smuggle them to Carolina; a traveller might journey through half the North, and if he neither spoke nor read English, he would never dream there was a war in any part of the nation."

Christy's blackface minstrels were performing to crowded houses. At one time four theatres in New York City were playing *Uncle Tom's Cabin* to crowded houses. Barnum announced exhibition of the world's heaviest woman, weighing one-fourth of a ton; the dwarf General Tom Thumb was outdwarfed by Commodore Nutt. The symphony orchestra of Theodore Thomas had played Wagner, Schubert, Meyerbeer, at New York concerts that year. Henry Thoreau with shattered lungs had passed on among his bequests an essay "On the Duty of Civil Disobedience" telling men their consciences were better guides than their governments, North or South. John Tyler and Martin Van Buren, former Presidents of the United States, had died, and the mourning was brief and perfunctory.

"The events are too grand and too rapid for Lincoln. It is impossible for him to grasp and to comprehend them," wrote Count Adam Gurowski in a published diary that set official Washington and the New York literati chattering. From the jug of a large ego Gurowski poured out opinions. He published Seward as "intriguer, imbecile," and much else, not mentioning his own dismissal as paid translator in the State Department.

"Great injustice was and is done to Mr. Seward," wrote Gurowski, "by the lying . . . rumor that he is often intoxicated. I am sure that it is not so. . . . Mr. Seward [has an] unhappy passion for generalizations. He goes off like a rocket. Most people hearing him become confused, understand nothing, are unable to follow him in his soarings, and believe him to be intoxicated."

"Poor Lincoln! I pity him; but his advisers may make out of him something worse even than was Judas, in the curse of the ages," wrote Gurowski. "Lincoln is a simple man of the prairie, and his eyes penetrate not the fog, the tempest. He begins now already to believe that he is infallible; that he is ahead of the people, and frets that the people may remain behind. Oh simplicity or conceit!"

Gurowski was a studied croaker, a crow cawing his omens. "The country is marching to its tomb, but the grave-diggers will not confess their crime. . . . O God! O God! to witness how by the hands of Lincoln-Seward-McClellan, this noblest human structure is crumbled. . . . The more I scrutinize the President's thus called emancipation proclamation, the more cunning and the less good-will and sincerity I find therein. I hope I am mistaken."

Gurowski considered the President as a storyteller. "In the midst of . . . death-giving news, Mr. Lincoln has always a story to tell. This is known . . . by all who approach him. Months ago I was in Mr. Lincoln's presence when he received a telegram announcing the crossing of the Mississippi by Gen. Pope, at New Madrid. Scarcely had Mr. Lincoln finished the reading of the dispatch, when he cracked (that is the sacramental word) two not very washed stories." In his first estimates Gurowski held Lincoln an excellent President for quiet times. "I still hope, perhaps against hope, that if Lincoln is what the masses believe him to be, a strong mind, then all may come out well."

In Europe the chief philosopher of the International Working Men's Association, the German Jewish scholar Karl Marx, wrote of Palmerston trying to bring England into war on the North: "He may possibly succeed in bringing it about, but not easily. He must have a pretext, and it does not seem to me that Lincoln will give him one." Marx read documents of events and men and deduced. "The anger with which the Southerners receive Lincoln's acts proves their importance. Lincoln's acts all have the appearance of illiberal stipulated conditions (or narrow formalism) which an attorney presents to an opponent. This, however, does not hinder their historic content."

Marx saw a Yankee "bourgeois" democracy riding into complete national power. "Like others I naturally see that which is repulsive in the Yankee movement. Nevertheless, the events there are world-shaking." The North was permitting the South to throw its entire fighting strength into the field, leaving the productive labor at home to be done by the slaves. "In my opinion this will take another turn. The North will finally carry on the war seriously and resort to revolutionary means and cast aside the domination of the border slave states. A single nigger regiment will have a remarkable effect on Southern nerves."

Marx also saw indications of radical changes in the relations of capital and labor to come as a result of the war. No miracles were to happen, yet forebodings haunted the ruling class of America "that the present society is no solid or crystal, but an organism of change and is constantly changing."

England prepared to junk her wooden navy. Young Henry Adams at the United States Legation in London took a world view of man, his discoveries and inventions up to 1862. He wrote to a brother in America: "I tell you these are great times. Man has mounted science, and is now run away with. I firmly believe that before many centuries more, science will be the master of man. The engines he will have invented will be beyond his strength to control. Some day science may have the existence of mankind in its power, and the human race commit suicide by blowing up the world. Not only shall we be able to cruize in space, but I see no reason why some future generation shouldn't walk off like a beetle with the world on its back, or give it another rotary motion so that every zone should receive in turn its due portion of heat and light."

On New Year's Eve, 1862, came telegrams to the War Department. One of the bloodiest battles of the war was opening at Murfreesboro, Tennessee, along Stone's River, between the Union army of Rosecrans and the Confederates under Bragg. The Confederates drove the right wing of the Union army back two miles, and Bragg sent a telegram of victory to Richmond on New Year's Eve. "God has given us a happy New Year," wired Braxton Bragg. The war news that Lincoln went to bed on that night was of men marching in rain, sleeping on wet ground, fighting through mud, the South having made the gains of the day. Two days more of maneuvering and grappling went on between 41,000 under Rosecrans and 34,000 under Bragg. They fought in the rain and fog of raw winter days of short twilights. On the second day horses could not take the artillery over the soaked and slippery ground.

One out of four men on the field was shot down, killed or wounded, or taken prisoner, the Union army losing 12,906 and the Confederates 11,739. Bragg retreated south.

Rosecrans, a Roman Catholic, had high mass celebrated in his tent, and attached to the close of his official report to the War Department the words from the mass: *Non nobis, Domine, non nobis; sed nomini tuo da gloriam*— "Not unto us, O Lord, not unto us; but unto thy name give the glory." Rosecrans saw three of his orderlies shot down. He was grazed by a cannon ball that took off the head of his chief of staff. Riding in the thick of the fighting, he was told of a general who had gone down. "Never mind, brave men must die in battle; we must seek results." The headless trunk of another general toppled near his horse's feet. Rosecrans rode on. News was brought of his friend General McCook, as lost. "We cannot help it; men who fight must be killed." Colonel Roberts fell from his saddle with three bullets in him. "Boys, put me on my horse again." They lifted him, but his breath was gone before he reached the saddle.

In a stretch of cedar timber the fighting Irishman, Phil Sheridan, commanded a division of 6,500 men that lost 1,700, including 70 officers, 2 of whom were brigadiers. The Virginian George H. Thomas emerged as calm and granitic, holding the left wing firm while the right was crumbling. A brigade of Southern troops plucked cotton from bolls standing in the fields and stuck them in their ears during a shattering artillery fire. "Dozens of horses were torn to shreds," said an eyewitness. A single shell crashed into three horses and piled them in one heap. Wounded men lay in pools of blood, frozen to the ground in changing weather. Hundreds of rabbits scampered between the battle lines, one advancing private calling: "Go it, cottontail! I'd run too if it wasn't for my reputation."

A staff man with Bragg told of that commander, nearing Tullahoma, meeting a mountaineer and asking him if he belonged to Bragg's army. "Bragg's army? He's got none. He shot half of them in Kentucky and the other half got killed up at Murfreesboro." General Bragg laughed and rode on.

And this huggermugger of smoke and steel, flame and blood, in Tennessee meant to the President far off in the White House one episode. The Union men of Tennessee would have easier going. The man power of the South was cut down by so many figures. Wendell Phillips was correct. The war would never be ended by any one event, any single battle. Also Phillips was correct—and Lincoln knew it—in the point that the war might go on twenty or thirty years, using up a generation of people. It was implied in Lincoln's warning against the contest's developing into "remorseless revolutionary warfare."

Lincoln telegraphed Rosecrans: "God bless you and all with you! Please tender to all, and accept for yourself, the nation's gratitude for your and their skill, endurance, and dauntless courage."

Besides mercilessly taking ordinary men by squads and platoons, the war picked off rare and special men. The name of Ormsby MacKnight Mitchel had come before Lincoln as a West Pointer who had graduated with Robert E. Lee, who had been admitted to practice law in Cincinnati while serving as chief engineer of the Little Miami Railroad, and had then held the chair of mathematics, astronomy, and philosophy in Cincinnati College. Mitchel toured Europe in 1842 for the equipment to make a great refracting telescope at Cincinnati in one of the first of the larger astronomical observatories of the country. He invented electromagnetic and other devices for measuring and recording the movements of stars. He originated an instrument that could detect one one-thousandth of a second of time. "During 1854-59 he made nearly 50,000 observations of faint stars." When the war opened he was at the head of two observatories, of international reputation in astronomy, perhaps the foremost stargazer of America.

As a brigadier general of volunteers, Astronomer Mitchel took 8,000 men of the Army of the Ohio into Alabama in early '62, destroyed railroads, locomotives, and rolling stock, burned bridges, fought small engagements, and reported on May 1, "All of Alabama north of the Tennessee floats no flag but that of the Union." Stanton telegraphed him, "Your spirited operations afford great satisfaction to the President." In one dispatch to Stanton, Mitchel described outrages by men in his own command beyond his control, "robberies, rapes, arsons, and plunderings, committed by lawless brigands and vagabonds connected with the army." He asked authority to give the death penalty. The authority was granted, but no one punished. The guilty were too many to shoot. A brigade had sacked a town, looted houses, violated women, and when citizens respectfully gave General Mitchel evidence of atrocities and asked protection and justice, he replied, "I cannot arraign before a court, civil or military, *a brigade*," and requested them to fix the guilt on "some individual officer or soldier under my command." His superior officer, General Buell, thought him a schoolteacher of mercurial temperament, and he resigned and went to Washington.

Lincoln had commissioned Mitchel a major general of volunteers and had plans for him to lead a Mississippi Valley expedition. But Halleck refused the necessary orders.

Then Lincoln had put the astronomer-warrior in command of the Department of the South at Hilton Head in South Carolina. There in the last of October of '62 he died of yellow fever. His nickname in the army was "Old Stars."

CHAPTER 34

FINAL EMANCIPATION PROCLA-
MATION '63

HORACE GREELEY occasionally sent letters to kindred spirits. One to Sumner from the office of the *New York Tribune*, August 7, 1862, read:

My dear Sir:
 Do you remember that old theological book containing this
 "Chapter I. Hell.
 Chapter II. Hell Continued."
Well that gives a hint of the way Old Abe *ought to be* talked to in this crisis of the Nation's destiny.
 Still, I comprehend the wisdom of not breaking with the Chief of the Republic in this hour of her fiery trial, and shall respect it. Only you must do all his puffing; for I can't help you. He's a bad stick.
Yours
Horace Greeley

Hundreds of letters in like tone had come to Sumner from antislavery men and women. The weeks drew on toward January 1, 1863, the day set for the second and final Emancipation Proclamation—and many doubted the President would issue the edict. His courage, they said and wrote, required bolstering, "puffing," as Greeley put it. Also the President was uncertain, "anomalous," as Senator Fessenden phrased it. He pursued a "serpentine course," according to one critical editor. He was under the spell of Seward, whom Lydia Maria Child in a note to Sumner set down as "a snake," "a crooked and selfish hypocrite," and more yet. George William Hill of Springfield, Illinois, wrote to Sumner thanking God there was a Sumner, adding, "The people cannot forget themselves and lose you and your counsel to the President."

Regularly Sumner visited the White House and out of his interviews with the President gave favorable reports to his correspondents. "You will be glad to know that the President is firm," he wrote to S. G. Howe on December 28, 1862. "He says that he would not stop the proclamation if he could, and he could not if he would." These words relieved Howe, who had written, "The President has set his face steadily Zionward, though he is as yet rather ashamed of his Lord." The Sumner cohorts wanted assurances from him, though they might waver as to his judgments. Alfred Horton, a Massachusetts follower, had thus wavered, saying November 23: "Some months ago I wrote you in regard to the position of President Lincoln. Apparently at that time he was not proving himself so true to the great cause of Freedom as you had given us assurance. I wish now to say that for one

BRUTUS AND CÆSAR.

(From the American Edition of Shakspeare.)

The Tent of Brutus (Lincoln). *Night. Enter the Ghost of* Cæsar.

Brutus. Wall, now! Do tell! Who's you?

Cæsar. I am dy ebil genus, massa Linking. Dis child am awful Inimpressional.

Punch of London considers this the statement of a dilemma

I am perfectly satisfied with his course and see that when you gave that assurance you knew more than we could divine."

John Jay of Katonah, New York, set forth to Sumner a theory of leadership: "The President is to be sustained by us as far as possible and we are not to throw away our influence over him and give it up to our opponents. Burke says the man who would lead a nation must oftentimes be content to follow. It is hard to do—but as far as it can be done consistently with our own integrity I think we should do it. Our turn to lead the President may be near at hand." E. George Squier of 13 East Thirty-eighth Street, New York, had no such view of leadership. "Sir! the air is thick with treason!" he wrote to Sumner. "We must send no more men to Washington. There are enough there if action is intended. Poor Lincoln, honest, hesitating, drifting, feeble-minded Lincoln—patriotic buffoon! it would be no great pity, if he were lugged off to Dixie, except for the name of it! This is no time for standing on the rigidities of etiquette."

After the battle of Fredericksburg, John Murray Forbes of Boston worried, and wrote to Sumner: "The main thing seems to me to be to reach the President *and that at once.* . . . The first of January is near at hand, and we see no signs of any measures for carrying into effect the Proclamation. . . . Will it do any good for a mixed deputation of laymen and clergy to go from here and from New York to try and influence him?"

George Livermore of Boston, who had published a formidable research on the authorities and precedents for using Negroes as soldiers, a paper he had read before the Massachusetts Historical Society that year, wrote to Sumner requesting him to buy a good pen for Lincoln to use in signing the Emancipation Proclamation, the pen to go to Massachusetts for "perpetual preservation." Livermore began his letter with "God bless Abraham Lincoln!" and closed with "God help Abraham Lincoln!"

Little Harriet Beecher Stowe did not join with friends, nor with her brother Henry Ward Beecher, in suspicions that Lincoln would put off or evade the proclamation. She urged Sumner, "Please do not forget to express to the President my suggestion that he recommend solemn religious services on that day." She heard inquiries. "Everybody I meet in New England says to me with anxious earnestness, 'Will the President stand firm to his Proclamation?' Brother Henry says—not so sure after all—it's far easier to slide down the banisters than to go up the stairs." And she interjected, as to slavery, "I expect to live to see this thing all down under foot yet."

The pioneer abolitionist agitator, William Lloyd Garrison, had drifted along with the grumblers against the President and then slowly changed as though he were getting a clear insight into the workings of Lincoln's mind on emancipation. To an English abolitionist, Professor Francis W. Newman, Garrison had written of Lincoln: "His freedom to follow his convictions of duty as an individual is one thing—as the President of the United States, it is limited by the functions of his office, for the people do not elect a President to play the part of reformer or philanthropist, nor to enforce upon the nation his own peculiar ethical or humanitary ideas without regard to his oath or their will."

At the yearly meeting of the Anti-Slavery Society of Massachusetts, Garrison had rebuked the slurs of Wendell Phillips on the President's motives, holding "it is not wise for us to be too miscroscopic" in finding fault with the President. And facing his fellow zealots, Garrison did a rather amazing thing. He presented a case for Lincoln almost as though it had come from the President's own lips, saying:

"Supposing Mr. Lincoln could answer to-night, and we should say to him: 'Sir, with the power in your hands, slavery being the cause of the

Negro cabins

rebellion beyond all controversy, why don't you put the trump of jubilee to your lips, and proclaim universal freedom?'—possibly he might answer: 'Gentlemen, I understand this matter quite as well as you do. I do not know that I differ in opinion from you; but will you insure me the support of a united North if I do as you bid me? Are all parties and all sects at the North so convinced and so united on this point that they will stand by the Government? If so, give me the evidence of it, and I will strike the blow. But, gentlemen, looking over the entire North, and seeing in all your towns and cities papers representing a considerable, if not a formidable portion of the people, menacing and bullying the Government in case it dare to liberate the slaves, even as a matter of self-preservation, I do not feel that the hour has yet come that will render it safe for the Government to take that step.' I am willing to believe that something of this feeling weighs in the mind of the President and the Cabinet, and that there is some ground for hesitancy, as a mere matter of political expediency."

Rumors ran in Washington that Lincoln on January 1 would withdraw, not issue, the Emancipation Proclamation. The Reverend Byron Sunderland, chaplain of the Senate, preached an antislavery sermon the Sunday before New Year's Day, and with a friend called on the President. Ushered into the Cabinet room, the short Dr. Sunderland looked up into Lincoln's face. "I have come, Mr. President, to anticipate the New Year with my respects, and if I may, to say to you a word about the serious conditions of the country."

"Go ahead, Doctor, every little bit helps," replied Lincoln. And as Sunderland told of it, he was too much in earnest to laugh with the President. He went on, "Mr. President, they say you are not going to keep your promise to give us the Emancipation Proclamation, that it is your intention to withdraw it."

"Well, Doctor," said the President, "you know Peter was going to do it, but when the time came he did not."

"Mr. President, I have been studying Peter," continued Sunderland. "He did not deny his Master until after his Master rebuked him in the presence of the enemy. You have a master, too, Mr. Lincoln, the American people. Don't deny your master till he has rebuked you before all the world."

The President was interested. His tone changed. "Sit down, Dr. Sunderland. Let us talk." The President was silent a moment, with an elbow on a table, gnarled hands closed over his forehead. He looked gravely at the Senate chaplain, who reported their talk:

" 'Doctor, if it had been left to you and me, there would have been no war. If it had been left to you and me, there would have been no cause for this war; but it was not left to us. God has allowed men to make slaves of their fellows. He permits this war. He has before Him a strange spectacle. We, on our side, are praying Him to give us victory, because we believe we are right; but those on the other side pray Him, too, for victory, believing they are right. What must He think of us? And what is coming from the struggle? What will be the effect of it all on the whites and on the negroes?' And then suddenly a ripple of amusement broke the solemn tone of his voice. 'As for the negroes, Doctor, and what is going to become of them: I told Ben Wade the other day, that it made me think of a story I read in one of my first books, Aesop's Fables. It was an old edition, and had curious rough woodcuts, one of which showed four white men scrubbing a negro in a potash kettle filled with cold water. The text explained that the men thought that by scrubbing the negro they might make him white. Just about the time they thought they were succeeding, he took cold and died. Now, I am afraid that by the time we get through this war the negro will catch cold and die.'

"The laugh had hardly died away before he resumed his grave tone, and for half an hour he discussed the question of emancipation. He stated it in every light, putting his points so clearly that each statement was an argument. He showed the fullest appreciation of every side. It was like a talk of one of the old prophets. And though he did not tell me at the end whether the proclamation would be issued or not, I went home comforted and uplifted, and I believed in Abraham Lincoln from that day."

Lincoln could have told Sunderland of how in the past month he, the President, tried personally to buy the freedom of one Negro. A little yellow boy had come into the camp of the 22nd Wisconsin regiment at Lexington, Kentucky, a beaten and starved creature. "He lived on black walnuts till the snow came, and he was obliged to seek shelter somewhere," said Colonel W. L. Utley. "He sought protection from several regiments, but could gain no admission till he came here." One Judge George Robertson came, hotly claiming, "He is my nigger but niggers lie." The boy told of belonging to a man in Lexington who had hired him out at $50 a year since he was five years old, his master taking all the wages; so he had run away. The boy stuck to his story through a furious cross-examination from Judge Robertson. On Colonel Utley's refusing to give up the boy, the Judge called the 22nd Wisconsin "a gang of nigger-stealers." He had been in Congress, said the Judge, was a Union man, was a friend of Lincoln, had written an essay against slavery, and he would take his case to the President. Lincoln wrote to Judge Robertson:

"Your despatch of yesterday is just received. I believe you are acquainted with the American classics (if there be such), and probably remember a speech of Patrick Henry in which he represents a certain character in the Revolutionary times as totally disregarding all questions of country, and hoarsely bawling, 'Beef! beef!! beef!!!' Do you not know that I may as well surrender the contest directly as to make any order the obvious purpose of which would be to return fugitive slaves?" But this reply Lincoln did not send. He laid it by for the files and wrote another, which read:

"A few days since I had a despatch from you which I did not answer. If I were to be wounded personally, I think I would not shun it. But it is the life of the nation. I now understand the trouble is with Colonel Utley: that he has five slaves in his camp, four of whom belong to rebels, and one belonging to you. If this be true, convey yours to Colonel Utley, so that he can make him free, and I will pay you any sum not exceeding five hundred dollars."

Judge Robertson refused this offer and sued in the United States District Court for possession of the yellow boy. Under Lincoln's eye came many like cases that brought home the difficulties ahead in redefining the status of the Negro. Thomas P. Dudley, an elderly clergyman in Lexington, a war veteran of 1812, wrote that he considered secession "an enormous and inexcusable heresy," but he was alarmed by "the improper interference of some of the officers and soldiers of the United States army with our slave property." Dudley's people had borne outrages; he feared bloody collisions between citizens and soldiers.

Browning in familiar talks with the President repeatedly urged that the preliminary Emancipation Proclamation had brought disaster. On December 31 he wrote: "Some days ago I said to Judge Thomas [B. F. Thomas of the Massachusetts Supreme Court 1853-59] that I thought he ought to go to the President and have a full, frank conversation with him in regard to the threatened proclamation of emancipation—that in my opinion it was fraught with evil, and evil only . . . and that I thought his opinion would have influence with the President—that he might possibly induce him to withhold or at least modify it. . . . He informed me to night that he had taken my advice, and had the talk but that it would avail nothing."

Browning lamented what was to come. "The President was fatally bent upon his course, saying that if he should refuse to issue his proclamation there would be a rebellion in the north, and that a dictator would be placed over his head within the week. There is no hope. The proclamation will come—God grant it may [not] be productive of the mischief I fear."

Thurlow Weed wrote to John Bigelow: "I labored earnestly with Mr. Lincoln against this proclamation. I struggled hard to keep our convention from going to the people on that issue. But all was in vain."

George Bancroft, the historian, at the White House found the President "turning in his thoughts the question of a slave insurrection." What should be his course if suddenly there came news of scores or hundreds of Southern masters, their women and children, slaughtered in their beds and their houses burned, in the style of the Nat Turner rebellion? In the draft of the proclamation he was writing, Lincoln inserted the words "I hereby enjoin upon the people so declared to be free to abstain from all violence, unless in necessary self-defence; and I recommend to them that, in all cases when allowed, they labor faithfully for reasonable wages."

Uprisings of Negro slaves would surely follow the impending proclamation, with murder and worse visited on the Southern people, several English journals predicted. The London *Times* was both hysterical and rhetorical. "When blood begins to flow and shrieks come piercing through the darkness, Mr. Lincoln will wait until the rising flames tell that all is consummated, and then he will rub his hands and think that revenge is sweet."

Congressman John Covode of Pennsylvania told of calling at the White House that last week of December to find the President in his office walking back and forth with a troubled face. As to whether he would issue the Proclamation, said the President: "I have studied that matter well; my mind is made up. . . . *It must be done. I am driven to it.* There is no other way out of our troubles. But although my duty is plain, it is in some respects painful, and I trust the people will understand that I act not in anger but in expectation of a greater good."

Harper's Weekly believed it significant that in a conversation at the White House with a New York banker, a leading Republican, the President observed it was "much wiser to do a thing than to talk about it."

Copies of the proclamation were handed Cabinet members on December 30. The next day at ten o'clock in the morning they went into session. Seward and Welles suggested minor changes. Chase argued that the slaves should be declared free in entire States, with no parts or fractions stipulated as not being included. Also Chase had brought along a complete draft of a proclamation he had written himself. He suggested to Lincoln a final paragraph to read: "And upon this act, sincerely believed to be an act of justice warranted by the Constitution, and an act of duty demanded by the circumstances of the country, I invoke the considerate judgment of mankind, and the gracious favor of Almighty God."

"You may not approve it," said Chase, "but I thought this, or something like it, would be appropriate."

"I do approve it," replied Lincoln. And he adopted it, leaving out one clause and adding that "military necessity" dictated the action.

Thirteen parishes in Louisiana, and counties in Virginia around Norfolk, were excepted from the proclamation. In those areas the slaves were not to be declared free. Blair argued that people long after would read and wonder why these parishes and counties were excepted; they were in the very heart and back of slavery, and unless there was some good reason, then unknown to him, he hoped they would not be excepted. Seward remarked, "I think so, too; I think they should not be excepted."

Lincoln replied. What he said was noted by John P. Usher, an Indiana man, First Assistant Secretary of the Interior, a week later appointed to take the place of Caleb B. Smith, who resigned to take a judgeship in Indiana.

"Well, upon first view your objections are clearly good," said the President, "but after I issued the proclamation of September 22, Mr. Bouligny of Louisiana, then here, came to see me. [John Edward Bouligny was elected to Congress as a National American from a New Orleans district, served from December 5, 1859, to March 4, 1861, and was the only Representative from a seceding State who did not leave his seat in Congress.] He was a great invalid, and had scarcely the strength to walk upstairs. He wanted to know of me if these parishes in Louisiana and New Orleans should hold an election and elect members of Congress whether I would not except them from this proclamation. I told him I would.

"No, I did not do that in so many words," continued Lincoln. "If he was here now he could not repeat any words I said which would amount to an absolute promise. But I know he understood me that way, and that is just the same to me. They have elected members, and they are here now, Union men, ready to take their seats, and they have elected a Union man from the Norfolk district."

Blair said, "If you have a promise out, I will not ask you to break it." Seward added: "No, no. We would not have you do that." Chase interposed, "Very true, they have elected Hahn and Flanders, but they have not yet got their seats, and it is not certain that they will." Chase was voicing the fear of Northern antislavery men that Southern Union men, sympathetic to slavery, would win added strength in Congress; he believed Congress might refuse to seat Hahn and Flanders.

Michael Hahn was Bavarian-born, a New Orleans high-school graduate, a lawyer who in politics had fought the Slidell faction in Louisiana, had done his best for Douglas for President in 1860, and favored gradual compensated abolishment of slavery. Benjamin Franklin Flanders, the other newly elected Congressman from New Orleans, was New Hampshire-born, a Dartmouth graduate, a high-school principal, and an editor and publisher in New Orleans; being an outspoken Union man, he had to leave that city early in 1862, returning when the Union army and navy captured it that year.

On Chase's saying that Hahn and Flanders were not yet seated and it was not certain they would be, Lincoln rose from his chair. He was not easy about the matter. Usher noted that he walked rapidly back and forth across the room; looking over his shoulder at Chase, he burst out: "There it is, sir! I am to be bullied by Congress, am I? If I do I'll be durned." This ended the discussion. The parishes and counties were to stay excepted in the Emancipation Proclamation.

That afternoon and the next morning, as Lincoln rewrote the entire draft of the proclamation, he took his time, went to pains to have the penmanship plain, clear, unmistakable, in a manner solemn and testamentary. He had told Sumner, "I know very well that the name connected with this document will never be forgotten."

The text was dry, strict, brief. Its sentences stood alone and sent out red runners against deep purple. It had no more poetry than an inviolable winter sunset that happens, is recorded as a finality. It performed, then vanished, as though enough echoes might join and band to take care of what came afterward.

On the morning of New Year's Day the high officers of the Government, the civil, military, and naval departments, the diplomatic corps in gold braid and official hats, arrived at the White House for the annual presidential reception. The carriages drove in on the half-oval roadway, the horses champed, the important guests were delivered at the door; the long porch of the White House, the sidewalk, and part of the lawn filled up with the multitude, bystanders and beholders, the people who look on. The President began handshaking and greeting. For three hours it was "How do you do?" "Thank you," and salutations, cordiality, bantering.

Seward and his son Fred, on that afternoon, walked over to the White House carrying Lincoln's own draft of the Emancipation Proclamation. Lincoln had left it with them for the State Department to engross duly. It needed one thing to be a complete document. The President must sign it.

They found the President alone in his office. The broad sheet was spread out before him on a table. He dipped his pen in an inkstand, held the pen in the air over the paper, and hesitated, looked around, and said: "I never, in my life, felt more certain that I was doing right, than I do in signing this paper. But I have been receiving calls and shaking hands since nine o'clock this morning, till my arm is stiff and numb. Now this signature is one that will be closely examined, and if they find my hand trembled they will say, 'he had some compunctions.' But anyway, it is going to be done."

And with that he slowly and carefully wrote the name of Abraham Lincoln at the bottom of the Emancipation Proclamation. It was a bold, clear signature, though "slightly tremulous," as Lincoln remarked. The others laughed at him, for it was better than he or they expected by way of handwriting from fingers squeezed and wrenched by thousands of hands that day. Then Seward signed, the great seal was affixed, and the document went into the archives of the State Department.

The pen of steel, with its end of the wooden holder slightly dented by

Pen (above) with which Lincoln signed the Emancipation Proclamation and (below) part of a letter of George Livermore informing Benton J. Lossing that the President had sent him the pen as requested by Senator Sumner

The President sent me the pen with which he signed the charter of freedom: I value it exceedingly. I hope some time to show it to you in my new library —

Lincoln's teeth, went to Senator Sumner for transmissal to George Livermore, who wanted it for "perpetual preservation" in Massachusetts archives.

The dry formal text of the document—the most exciting news matter telegraphed, mailed, published, heralded over the world that day and month, for all that it was dry and formal—read as follows:

BY THE PRESIDENT OF THE UNITED STATES OF AMERICA:

A Proclamation.

Whereas, on the twenty-second day of September, in the year of our Lord one thousand eight hundred and sixty-two, a proclamation was issued by the President of the United States, containing, among other things, the following, to wit:

"That on the first day of January, in the year of our Lord one thousand eight hundred and sixty-three, all persons held as slaves within any State or designated part of a State, the people whereof shall then be in rebellion against the United States, shall be then, thenceforward, and forever, free; and the Executive government of the United States, including the military and naval authority thereof, will recognize and maintain the freedom of such persons, and will do no act or acts to repress such persons, or any of them, in any efforts they may make for their actual freedom.

"That the Executive will, on the first day of January aforesaid, by proclamation, designate the States and parts of States, if any, in which the people thereof, respectively, shall then be in rebellion against the United States; and the fact that any State, or the people thereof, shall on that day be in good faith represented in the Congress of the

United States, by members chosen thereto at elections wherein a majority of the qualified voters of such State shall have participated, shall, in the absence of strong countervailing testimony, be deemed conclusive evidence that such State, and the people thereof, are not then in rebellion against the United States."

Now, therefore I, Abraham Lincoln, President of the United States, by virtue of the power in me vested as commander-in-chief of the army and navy of the United States in time of actual armed rebellion against the authority and government of the United States, and as a fit and necessary war measure for suppressing said rebellion, do, on this first day of January, in the year of our Lord one thousand eight hundred and sixty-three, and in accordance with my purpose so to do, publicly proclaimed for the full period of one hundred days from the first day above mentioned, order and designate as the States and parts of States wherein the people thereof, respectively, are this day in rebellion against the United States, the following, to wit:

Arkansas, Texas, Louisiana, (except the Parishes of St. Bernard, Plaquemines, Jefferson, St. John, St. Charles, St. James, Ascension, Assumption, Terre Bonne, Lafourche, St. Mary, St. Martin, and Orleans, including the city of New Orleans), Mississippi, Alabama, Florida, Georgia, South Carolina, North Carolina, and Virginia, (except the forty-eight counties designated as West Virginia, and also the counties of Berkeley, Accomac, Northampton, Elizabeth City, York, Princess Anne, and Norfolk, including the cities of Norfolk and Portsmouth), and which excepted parts are for the present left precisely as if this proclamation were not issued.

And by virtue of the power and for the purpose aforesaid, I do order and declare that all persons held as slaves within said designated States, and parts of States are and henceforward shall be free; and that the Executive government of the United States, including the military and naval authorities thereof, will recognize and maintain the freedom of said persons.

And I hereby enjoin upon the people so declared to be free to abstain from all violence, unless in necessary self-defence; and I recommend to them that, in all cases when allowed, they labor faithfully for reasonable wages.

And I further declare and make known that such persons of suitable condition, will be received into the armed service of the United States, to garrison forts, positions, stations, and other places, and to man vessels of all sorts in said service.

And upon this act, sincerely believed to be an act of justice warranted by the Constitution upon military necessity, I invoke the considerate judgment of mankind and the gracious favor of Almighty God.

In witness whereof, I have hereunto set my hand and caused the seal of the United States to be affixed.

Done at the city of Washington this first day of January, in the year [SEAL.] of our Lord one thousand eight hundred and sixty-three, and of the independence of the United States of America the eighty-seventh.

Abraham Lincoln

By the President:
  William H. Seward,
    Secretary of State

Salutes of a hundred guns were fired in Pittsburgh, Buffalo, Boston, after newspapers published the proclamation. At night in Tremont Temple, Boston, it was read before an abolitionist crowd that included the Negro members of the Union Progressive Association. Antislavery crowds held jubilation meetings, though some of the extremists said the document should have

The military, naval, and civil authorities thereof, will recognize and maintain the freedom of said persons.

And I hereby enjoin upon the people so declared to be free to abstain from all violence, unless in necessary self-defense; and I recommend to them that, in all cases when allowed, they labor faithfully for reasonable wages.

And I further declare and make known, that such persons of suitable condition, will be received into the armed service of the United States, to garrison forts, positions, stations, and other places, and to man vessels of all sorts in said service.

And upon this act, sincerely believed to be an act of justice, warranted by the Constitution, upon military necessity, I invoke the considerate judgment of mankind, and the gracious favor of Almighty God.

In testimony whereof, I have hereunto set my name, and caused the seal of the United States to be affixed.

Done at the City of Washington, this first day of January, in the year from our Lord, one thousand eight hundred and sixty-three.

[L.S.]

Abraham Lincoln

By the President
Willa H Seward
Secretary of State:

An early draft of the Emancipation Proclamation prepared for Lincoln's signature. In the final draft (later destroyed by fire) the word "witness" was substituted for the word "testimony" and the word "hand" for the word "name." From the original in the Barrett collection.

gone farther, was too moderate. Critics took much the same view as they did of the preliminary proclamation in September. The London *Times* in Europe and the anti-Administration press in general agreed with the *New York Herald:* "While the Proclamation leaves slavery untouched where his decree can be enforced, he emancipates slaves where his decree cannot be enforced. Friends of human rights will be at a loss to understand this discrimination. As a war measure it is unnecessary, unwise, ill-timed, impracticable, outside the Constitution and full of mischief." Other newspapers went farther, the *Ashland Journal* in Ohio saying, "We publish in another column the emancipation proclamation issued January 1st, 1863, by the tyrant and usurper." Increased tension was noted at performances of *Uncle Tom's Cabin* when the slave under the lash cries, "Mah body belongs to you, Massa, but mah soul belongs to God!" The *Richmond Examiner* spoke for much of the South in declaring the proclamation to be "the most startling political crime, the most stupid political blunder, yet known in American history," aimed at "servile insurrection," with the result that "Southern people have now only to choose between victory and death." Jefferson Davis in a message to the Confederate Congress assumed lofty ground: "Our own detestation of those who have attempted the most execrable act recorded in the history of guilty men is tempered by profound contempt for the impotent rage which it discloses."

Lincoln issued no statement nor argument to support the proclamation. He let the paper go forth for whatever it might do, sent it fluttering to the four breezes of a continent and a world. "It will undoubtedly do mischief to the slave interests; but how far it will help the efforts to put down the rebellion is yet to be tested by experience," said the *Philadelphia Public Ledger*. At a later time to a Border State governor and Senator the President gave his reasons, his curiously complete justification. "You ask me to put in writing the substance of what I verbally said the other day in your presence, to Governor Bramlette and Senator Dixon," he wrote to A. G. Hodges of Frankfort, Kentucky. Then he proceeded: "I am naturally antislavery. If slavery is not wrong, then nothing is wrong. I cannot remember when I did not so think and feel, and yet I have never understood that the presidency conferred upon me an unrestricted right to act officially upon this judgment and feeling."

His oath to follow the Constitution stood in the way of doing what he might personally want to do. Yet the time came when he had to reason with himself: "Was it possible to lose the nation and yet preserve the Constitution? By general law, life and limb must be protected, yet often a limb must be amputated to save a life; but a life is never wisely given to save a limb." He came to see that "measures otherwise unconstitutional might become lawful" rather than that he should "permit the wreck of government, country, and Constitution all together." He forbade Frémont, Cameron, Hunter, to issue proclamations or arm the blacks, because he did not yet think it an indispensable necessity. He had asked the Border States to buy the slaves' freedom with Federal Government money, and this offer was declined. "I

General and Mrs. Nathaniel Prentiss Banks

From the Barrett collection

Ormsby MacKnight Mitchel   John Alexander Logan

From the author's collection

One print of this photograph Lincoln sent to Mrs. Lucy
G. Speed of Louisville, Kentucky, autographed at Washington, D. C., October 3, '61

From the Barrett collection

Oil painting of Abraham Lincoln from life, by W. T. Matthews

was, in my best judgment, driven to the alternative of either surrendering the Union, and with it the Constitution, or of laying strong hand upon the colored element. I chose the latter."

The Emancipation Proclamation struck at property valued on tax books at nearly $3,000,000,000. If not retracted and if finally sustained by the Union armies in the field, the newly issued document would take from Southerners, by force and without compensation, livestock classified and assessed with horses, cattle, and mules, more than 3,900,000 head. The property value of these 3,900,000 and more chattels would be written off and erased if and when the Union armies won their objectives.

To those who shrank in horror from the act, Lincoln at a later time made his argument: "You dislike the emancipation proclamation, and perhaps would have it retracted. You say it is unconstitutional. I think differently. I think the Constitution invests its commander-in-chief with the law of war in time of war. The most that can be said—if so much—is that slaves are property. Is there—has there ever been—any question that by the law of war, property, both of enemies and friends, may be taken when needed? And is it not needed whenever taking it helps us or hurts the enemy? Armies, the world over, destroy enemies' property when they cannot use it; and even destroy their own to keep it from the enemy. Civilized belligerents do all in their power to help themselves or hurt the enemy, except a few things regarded as barbarous or cruel."

Down across the Southern States the word spread among Negroes: the "Linkum" Government at Washington had declared them free; if the Union armies won the war they would no longer be bought and sold. No longer would it be a crime to read, to be found with a book. Some of them had sung:

> Go down Moses,
> Way down in Egypt land.
> Tell old Pharaoh
> Let my people go.

In the days to come the Negroes would answer, or not, to the declaration that they were free.

As a metaphor of the hour Lincoln remarked: "We are like whalers who have been on a long chase. We have at last got the harpoon into the monster, but we must now look how we steer, or with one flop of his tail he will send us all into eternity."

Seward commented: "Sooner or later the proclamation will find and reach a weakness in every nook and corner of the insurrectionary region. The very violence with which it will be met, probably will, after a while, increase its efficiency." To Donn Piatt on the street Seward rebuffed compliments on his share in the proclamation by saying, "Yes, we have let off a puff of wind over an accomplished fact."

"What do you mean, Mr. Seward?"

"I mean that the Emancipation Proclamation was uttered in the first gun fired at Fort Sumter, and we have been the last to hear it. As it is, we show our sympathy with slavery by emancipating slaves where we cannot reach them, and holding them in bondage where we can set them free."

At a dinner Browning asked Seward why the Cabinet did "so useless and mischievous a thing as to issue the proclamation." And Seward gave an anecdote. A man raised a Liberty Pole in his village just after the Revolutionary War. His neighbors often asked whatever he wanted with a Liberty Pole. Wasn't he just as free without it as with it? And he always answered, "What is liberty without a pole?"

A piece of historic drama had been enacted. Some liked the play but would have preferred a different cast. The Ohio Brigadier James A. Garfield wished that Chase, who had dignity, could have appeared in the leading role. Garfield wrote that it was a strange moment in world history "when a second-rate Illinois lawyer is the instrument to utter words which shall form an epoch memorable in all future ages." Garfield was inadequate, however, compared with the London *Times*, which had a few remarks. "The vivacious and waggish President and his more sombre and sad belongings, his cabinet, his congress, and his riotous and exuberant press, have passed with clumsy confusion, changing as their leader changed, from attitude to attitude, from grimace to grimace, never being at any moment natural or true, but always being consistent in a certain uniformity of contortion." Thus the London *Times* spoke for its particular Tory and imperialist class, not voicing Great Britain and its people, however.

Where the stress lay was more adequately told by Henry Adams at London in a brotherly letter: "The Emancipation Proclamation has done more for us here than all our former victories and all our diplomacy. It is creating an almost convulsive reaction in our favor all over this country. The London Times furious and scolds like a drunken drab. Certain it is, however, that public opinion is very deeply stirred here and finds expression in meetings, addresses to President Lincoln, deputations to us, standing committees to agitate the subject and to affect opinion, and all the other symptoms of a great popular movement peculiarly unpleasant to the upper classes here because it rests on the spontaneous action of the laboring classes. . . . We are much encouraged and in high spirits."

Four weeks after the proclamation came out, young Adams wrote again from London to his brother: "I went last night to a meeting of which I shall send you a report; a democratic and socialist meeting, most threatening and dangerous to the established state of things; and assuming a tone and proportions that are quite novel and alarming in this capital. And they met to notify Government that 'they would not tolerate' interference against us. I can assure you this sort of movement is as alarming here as a slave insurrection would be in the South, and we have our hands on the springs that can raise or pacify such agitators." Not all the intrigue in the world could create such demonstrations of sympathy, young Henry Adams believed. "Where we have been friends, there we shall have support, and those who help us will do it of their own free will."

Adams saw "the old revolutionary leaven" of democracy working steadily in England. "You can find millions of people who look up to our institutions as their model and who talk with utter contempt of their own system of Government. Within three months this movement has taken a development that has placed all our enemies on the defensive; has driven Lord Palmerston to sue for peace and Lord Russell to proclaim a limited sympathy."

In his enthusiasm over the first results of Lincoln's boldest play since Sumter, Adams was overrating it. But there was a leaven working. The government heads of Great Britain would find it less easy to interfere with the United States or to lend the British Navy to the South.

Foreign Minister Earl Russell at London, in a note to the British Minister Lyons at Washington, wrote that in his lordship's dispatch of January 2, 1863, was found enclosed a proclamation of the President of the United States which appeared to be of a very strange nature. In five short paragraphs then Russell analyzed the proclamation. He did not like the proclamation. It was not a way to do. He seemed to be trying to guess what it was the somber, sober, and peculiar President of the United States was doing. If he was fighting a war, why not fight? If he was freeing the slaves, why free them here and there and not everywhere? "The proclamation *professes* to emancipate all slaves in places where the United States authorities cannot exercise any jurisdiction nor make emancipation a reality; but it does not *decree* emancipation of slaves in any States or parts of States occupied by federal troops. . . . There seems to be no declaration of a principle adverse to slavery in this proclamation. It is a measure of war of a very questionable kind. As President Lincoln has twice appealed to the judgment of mankind in his proclamation, I venture to say I do not think it can or ought to satisfy the friends of abolition, who look for total and impartial freedom for the slave, and not for vengeance on the slave owner."

No precedents were at hand to guide the British diplomatic chief at London, either as to the proclamation or in the matter of two public letters of the President of the United States, one addressed "To the Working-men of Manchester," the other "To the Working-men of London." It was not a custom for the ruling heads of nations to address letters to "working-men" in other countries.

Lincoln, however, had received addresses from bodies of workingmen in those cities giving him the hand of fellowship, and he replied. He would have a spirit of amity and peace prevail in the councils of "your Queen, who is respected and esteemed in your own country only more than she is by the kindred nation which has its home on this side of the Atlantic." The peace and friendship between the two nations he desired to make perpetual, though studious representations had been made that a government "which should rest exclusively on the basis of slavery" was likely to obtain the favor of Europe. Now had come these expressions against the sanction of slavery by European workingmen under severe trial. "I know and deeply deplore the sufferings which the working-men at Manchester, and in all Europe, are called to endure in this crisis. . . . Under the circumstances, I

cannot but regard your decisive utterances upon the question as an instance
of sublime Christian heroism which has not been surpassed in any age or in
any country."

At his home in Kentucky Joshua Speed told his wife of his talk with
Lincoln at the White House. They had discussed the proclamation before it
was issued, Speed saying he was opposed to it, while Lincoln "seemed to
treat it as certain that I would recognize the wisdom of the act when I
should see the harvest of good we would glean from it." Lincoln drew on
his memory, went back to the time in the early days in Springfield when he
thought of doing away with himself, saying in his gloom that he had "done
nothing to make any human being remember that he had lived," that his
heart's desire was to link his name with events in the interest of his fellow
man. He reminded Speed of that conversation twenty years earlier and said,
"I believe that in this measure [the proclamation] my fondest hopes will be
realized." Yet he had "been anxious to avoid it," he told Speed, and had
come to it by necessity. Speed mentioned certain Western Congressmen as
charging Lincoln with promising one action and performing another in regard to Negro freedom. Lincoln convinced Speed otherwise. Speed wrote:
"I never believed the charge, because he told me from his own lips that the
charge was false. I, who knew him so well, could never after that credit the
report."

A single act becomes a titanic tradition. From a contemporary broadside.

Around the world and into the masses of people whose tongues and imaginings create folk tales out of slender fact, there ran this item of the Strong Man who arose in his might and delivered an edict, spoke a few words fitly chosen, and thereupon the shackles and chains fell from the arms and ankles of men, women, and children born to be chattels for toil and bondage, ushered on their birthdays into the class with cattle, horses, sheep, livestock exchanged for money.

"It was well to delay the steamers at the wharves until this edict could be put on board," wrote Emerson. "It will be an insurance to the ship as it goes plunging through the sea with glad tidings to all people."

Some of the meetings in Northern cities lasted all night, with song, laughter, prayer, Negroes greeting the dawn kneeling and crying. Emerson read a new hymn to a Boston assembly:

God said, I am tired of kings,
    I suffer them no more;
Up to my ear the morning brings
    The outrage of the poor.

My angel—his name is Freedom,—
    Choose him to be your king;
He shall cut pathways east and west,
    And fend you with his wing. . . .

Think ye I made this ball
    A field of havoc and war,
Where tyrants great and tyrants small
    Might harry the weak and poor?

Pay ransom to the owner
    And fill the bag to the brim.
Who is the owner? The slave is owner,
    And ever was. Pay him. . . .

My will fulfilled shall be,
    For, in daylight or in dark,
My thunderbolt has eyes to see
    His way home to the mark.

Lincoln in an audience had heard Emerson: "Ideas are impregnable, and bestow on the hero their own invincibility. . . . Hitch your wagon to a star." The living issues coiled and tangled about his feet were not, however, to be set smooth and straight by any one gesture, or a series of them, in behalf of freedom. His authority, worn often as a garment of thongs, was tied and knotted with responsibilities. Nailed with facts of inevitable fate was his leadership. The gestures of stretching forth his hand and bestowing freedom on chattel slaves while attempting to enforce his will by the violence of armies subjugating the masters of slaves on their home soil, the act of trying to hold a just balance between the opposed currents of freedom and authority, raised up a riddle that gnawed in his thought many nights.

Others saw this snare. They glimpsed Lincoln's drift. Part of it was caught by J. W. Phelps, a Massachusetts man commissioned to enlist Negro soldiers in Southern States. In a letter to Sumner, Phelps wrote: "The rod of authority is mysterious and its ways past finding out. It has a goad to push forward and a hook to pull back and the hook seems to be used oftener and faster than the goad. The President tries to hide himself behind Congress; Congress tries to hide itself behind the people, and the people still want to worship the calf of their own cunning—like a simple girl they want to be a whore and virtuous too; they want slavery and liberty both. I can see no other way but for our regular constituted authorities to take the reins and go ahead. Our head must begin to *act*. . . . Our President must play the dictator, the King, decide for himself and do what is right. In no other way can he inspire enemies with dread and friends with confidence. I am convinced that moral considerations should have been placed before military necessity as a reason for the act of abolishing slavery. . . . But it is folly in times like these to speculate as to what individuals would or would not do. The President is a war President—commander-in-chief—and he must command. I cannot help but think he has ability enough if he decides to use it. And who can say his course has not been for the best?"

Those who cared to know Lincoln's view as to whether slave insurrections might spring up in the wake of his Emancipation Proclamation could read his Cooper Union speech of three years before. Then he believed to be lacking "the indispensable concert of action" requisite to insurrection, the slaves not having rapid communication; "nor can incendiary freemen, black or white, supply it. The explosive materials are everywhere in parcels; but there neither are, nor can be supplied, the indispensable connecting trains." A plot for an uprising could scarcely be devised and communicated to twenty individuals before some one of them, to save the life of a favorite master or mistress, would divulge it. This was a rule; the slave revolution in Hayti was not an exception to the rule, but a case occurring under peculiar circumstances. "Occasional poisonings from the kitchen, and open or stealthy assassinations in the field, and local revolts extending to a score or so, will continue to occur as the natural results of slavery; but no general insurrection of slaves, as I think, can happen in this country for a long time. Whoever much fears, or much hopes, for such an event, will be alike disappointed."

Lincoln had made that analysis in peacetime. Under war conditions lighted by a proclamation telling the slaves that they belonged to themselves and not to any masters, the Cooper Union analysis might have to be recast. Browning and others called on the President and found him hoping that what he had said three years before would hold good. He brooded over the hazardous, incalculable factor of bloody slave insurrections. Anything like the Negro revolts of Hayti would play havoc with political opinion in the North and in Europe.

To John Hay on November 24, 1863, Lincoln spoke as one who had studied slaves, their minds, their impulses, the conditions that produce mass revolts, the limits of oppression and exploitation that bring insurrection. Hay had brought in a *Baltimore American* editorial, "Shall the Gulf States Be Allowed to Retain a Remnant of Slavery?" The President "did not entirely agree" with the editorial, believing for himself "that the enormous influx of slave population into the Gulf States does not strengthen slavery in them." As a social engineer, an analyst of motives complicated and seething, a contemporary historian of masses of Negro workers, Lincoln meditated aloud for Hay:

"It creates in those [Gulf] States a vast preponderance of the population of a servile and oppressed class. It fearfully imperils the life and safety of the ruling class. Now, the slaves are quiet, choosing to wait for the deliverance they hope from us, rather than endanger their lives by a frantic struggle for freedom. The society of the Southern States is now constituted on a basis entirely military. It would be easier now than formerly to repress a rising of unarmed and uneducated slaves. But if they should succeed in se-

[JANUARY 17, 1863.]   HARPER'S WEEKLY.

CUTTING HIS OLD ASSOCIATES.
MAN OF COLOR. "Ugh! Get out. I ain't one ob you no more. *I'se a Man, I is!*"

cession the Gulf States would be more endangered than ever. The slaves, despairing of liberty through us, would take the matter into their own hands, and, no longer opposed by the Government of the United States, they would succeed. When the Democrats of Tennessee continually asserted in their canvass of '56 that Frémont's election would free the negroes, though they did not believe it themselves, their slaves did; and as soon as the news of Frémont's defeat came to the plantations the dissappointment [sic] of the slaves flashed into insurrection."

Soon the vivid Mrs. Chesnut wrote in her diary of her Uncle William's saying, "The men who went into the war to save their negroes are abjectly wretched," and her own view: "Neither side now cares a fig for these beloved negroes, and would send them all to heaven in a hand-basket, as Custis Lee says, to win the fight." From her husband came the news: "General Lee and Mr. Davis want the negroes put into the army. Mr. Chesnut and Major

Venable discussed the subject one night, but would they fight on our side or desert to the enemy? They don't go to the enemy, because they are comfortable as they are, and expect to be free anyway."

Of one of her butlers, Dick, whom as a boy she had taught to read, she wrote: "He won't look at me now; but looks over my head, scenting freedom in the air. He was always very ambitious. . . . He is the first negro in whom I have felt a change. Others go about in their black masks, not a ripple or an emotion showing, and yet on all other subjects except the war they are the most excitable of all races. Now Dick might make a very respectable Egyptian Sphinx, so inscrutably silent is he."

What gold money was in the house Mrs. Chesnut had sewed into a belt of wadded cloth: "My diamonds are there, too. It . . . can be tied under my hoops about my waist if the worst comes to the worst. . . . Lawrence [another house butler of faithful service] wears the same bronze mask. No sign of anything he may feel or think of my latest fancy. Only, I know he asks for twice as much money now when he goes to buy things."

"A great day," wrote Longfellow far North in Massachusetts on New Year's Day of '63. "The President's Proclamation for Emancipation of Slaves in the rebel States, goes into effect. A beautiful day, full of sunshine, ending in a tranquil moonlight night. May it be symbolical."

CHAPTER 35

"MORE HORSES THAN OATS"— OFFICE-SEEKERS

THE name of Fitz-John Porter had come often to Lincoln's desk. In May of 1861 he had commissioned Porter a colonel in the regular army, in August a brigadier general of volunteers, in July of 1862 a brigadier general in the regular army and a major general of volunteers. Porter was a fighter, had valor and skill on the battlefield, was the son of a naval commander, had passed through West Point.

On the basis of court-martial findings, however, Lincoln on January 21, 1863, wrote an order cashiering Porter, dismissing him from the regular service, and declaring him "forever disqualified from holding any office of trust or profit under the Government of the United States." The record of the trial ran 298 closely printed octavo pages.

"The President," said Porter's counsel, Senator Reverdy Johnson of Maryland, "should have taken time before approving of such a sentence to have examined it to find what it could contain to justify such a judgment. . . . The President's time, however, was perhaps so engrossed by matters which he supposed to be of more pressing national moment [as if anything was more important than justice] that it was impossible that he could have read it through carefully or at all" between January 12, when the record was placed in his hands, and January 21, when he pronounced Porter's doom.

Disobedience of orders and misbehavior in the face of the enemy at Second Bull Run, the charges against Porter, were denied by friends, who argued that only Porter's obstinate resistance at that battle had saved the Union army from a total rout. However, Porter had talked too much; officers who believed that injustice had been done him found his words to be "indiscreet and unkind" criticism of a superior officer. He had been rash with his mouth when an army hung in peril and fomented "the spirit that inhibits victory."

Lincoln presented no explanations, issued the order cashiering Porter, and let it go as an act deemed necessary for holding the Government intact enough to function. Porter claimed later that Lincoln changed his mind and admitted to W. A. Newell of New Jersey that the judgment was excessive. The secretaries, Nicolay and Hay, disagreed with Newell. Porter's counsel pointed to the War Department having published the Judge Advocate's review of the case and having scattered it broadcast over the land. "Almost simultaneously with its publication, three of the members of the Court were made Major Generals, all certainly most estimable gentlemen, and possibly competent soldiers, but with no claims to such promotion."

Between bitter factions in the army and the political parties, the Fitz-John Porter case was argued; it became a topic for Administration critics; it could be argued up or down. After his decree of doom for Porter, Lincoln kept silence on it. John Hay at a later time wrote in a confidential letter to Nicolay, "Porter was the most magnificent soldier in the Army of the Potomac, ruined by his devotion to McClellan."

A lower-rank officer came and read to Lincoln long arguments on why he should not have been cashiered from the service and why he should be restored. Lincoln heard him several times, saying the facts were such that he couldn't interfere. At their final meeting the man blazed out, "Well, Mr. President, I see you are determined not to do me justice." Lincoln quietly laid down a package of the man's papers, took the cashiered officer by the coat collar, marched him to the door of the room and out. "Sir, I give you fair warning never to show yourself in this room again. I can bear censure but not insult!" The ex-officer whined he must have his papers. "Begone, sir, your papers will be sent to you. I wish never to see your face again."

Sometimes Lincoln forgot, was reminded, and forgot again, an appointment promised. Robert L. Meade, son of Robert W. Meade, commanding the United States ship *North Carolina*, had for good reasons resigned from the naval academy at Annapolis in 1858, and the father wrote to Secretary Welles that when a Congressman called at the White House to ask for a commission in the Marine Corps for the young man, "Mr. Lincoln received him cordially, and assured him, with much earnestness, that he should be gratified, if a vacancy existed, that Mr. Meade should have it at once." The necessary papers were left with the President, "who, in his multifarious and more vital duties, lost sight of it, and when the papers were received by me, the endorsement thereon was without date and did not express the promise made." The father then called personally on the President, who signed an endorsement: "My wish is, that the prayer within be granted, in the case of the first vacancy not promised." Then five months had passed, and not hearing from the President, the father was taking the case to Secretary Welles.

A young fellow who had held a small job with one of the State legislatures came with plans to visit Richmond as a spy, get drawings of forts, learn the number of troops and guns. Lincoln asked how he would go. "As an organ grinder." So Lincoln gave him $150 to buy a hand organ and pay expenses. Weeks passed, and a report came from the young fellow, enclosing drawings and figures as to troop numbers in Richmond. Lincoln had him appointed second lieutenant, a reception was held in his honor, and a friend presented him with a sword and a uniform. Then came a Senator from the young fellow's home State with the information that he had never bought a hand organ, never been to Richmond; he had invented the drawings and numbers in his report, having been safe at home all the time. Lincoln withdrew the appointment.

Often came men of loyal party service who had contributed to campaign funds, had received promises, frequently indefinite, such as "You will be taken care of," from county chairmen and State leaders. For the President to meet and greet them was easier than to hand them equal and exact justice. John Hay told of some who had earlier presented their cards at the White House and gone away empty-handed. "Many of the visitors who presented so piteous a figure afterwards marched, with the independent dignity of a private soldier, in the ranks of the Union army, or rode at the heads of their regiments like men born to command."

Many called and few were chosen. "The numbers were so great, the competition so keen, that they ceased for the moment to be regarded as individuals, drowned as they were in the general sea of solicitation. When after weeks of waiting, one of them got access to the President, he was received with kindness by a tall melancholy-looking man sitting at a desk with his back to a window which opened upon a fair view of the Potomac, who heard his story with a gentle patience, took his papers, and referred them to one of the Departments, and that was all; the fatal pigeonholes devoured them."

Then as months wore on and the offices were filled, the White House was overrun by young men who wanted commissions in the regular army, credentials for raising regiments and battalions; officers seeking promotions or new assignments; men seeking contracts for supplies to the army and navy, commendations for newly invented rifles, cannon, munitions.

"Those around him strove from beginning to end to erect barriers to defend him against constant interruption," wrote Hay, "but the President himself was always the first to break them down. He disliked anything that kept people from him who wanted to see him, and although the continual contact with importunity which he could not satisfy, and with distress which he could not always relieve, wore terribly upon him and made him an old man before his time, he would never take the necessary measures to defend himself. In most cases he could do them no good, and it afflicted him to see he could not make them understand the impossibility of granting their requests." Senator Henry Wilson said he counseled, "You will wear yourself out," at which Lincoln smiled sadly. "They do not want much; they get but little, and I must see them."

The Republicans were new to power, many party workers not familiar with governmental machinery. They were breezy about their many errors in procedure, quick to ask why this or that could not be done, lacking the smoothness of the old and trained bureaucracy which had held sway in Washington for so many years. Lincoln's usual practice was to get the views of State delegations, Senators and Congressmen, before making appointments of importance for their States. Besides the political leaders in his Cabinet, who were in touch with their localities, the President gave ready hearing to such party men as Thurlow Weed, John W. Forney, Joseph Medill, old Frank P. Blair, various editors, lawyers, clergymen. Always, too, the governors of the States must have respectful hearing.

Governor Morton of Indiana wrote Lincoln that the Indiana delegation had named men to be appointed brigadier generals. Morton did not know who they were and had not been consulted. The President answered that the Governor had been hearing rumors, and asked him to telegraph recommendations. When the Governor at another time complained of two rumored nominations, Lincoln replied that they had not been made, adding, "The latter particularly has been my friend, and I am sorry to learn that he is not yours."

Part of the Cabinet friction ran back to jealousies over patronage. Early in the Administration, when the New York list of appointments was being made up, Welles had insisted that the Secretary of the Treasury and the Attorney General should be consulted on offices to be filled in their departments. Seward said he knew what was best for the party in his own State, and that, as he and the Senators were agreed on the list, the discussion could end. Welles urged the rights of the Secretaries. Lincoln decided the high department chiefs ought to be consulted, and the appointments were laid over.

Unless special conditions dictated, Lincoln seemed invariably to call in department and bureau heads for conference on selections for office. He wrote the Secretary of the Interior once to bring along the Commissioners of Indian Affairs and of the General Land Office. "I want the assistance of all of you in overhauling the list of appointments a little before I send them to the Senate." Not often was party harmony such that Lincoln could write as he did to Governor Sprague of Rhode Island, that the two Senators, the two old Congressmen, and one of the new ones, all and several, favored the same man for postmaster of Providence.

In some abolitionist circles they were not merely suspicious of any act or policy coming from Lincoln but they were sure he discriminated against them in his appointments. Emerson wrote of this in his journal: "He [Lincoln] thinks Emancipation almost morally wrong and resorts to it only as a desperate measure, and means never to put radicals into power. When he puts one into office, as Frémont, or Phelps, or Lane, he takes care to neutralize him by a Democrat or a Kentuckian who will thwart him."

Emerson on coming away from a White House visit, in which he had urged Lincoln to see that the slave-trader Gordon was well hanged, compared Lincoln to the hardheaded, circumspect, yet unafraid Samuel Hoar, a Massachusetts oak of a man "indifferent to fortune, either good or evil." George Luther Stearns, Frank Bird, and other Boston radicals came away from a session in which they had failed to budge Lincoln. "It is no use to disparage his ability," said Stearns. "There we were, with some able talkers among us, and we had the best position too; but the President held his ground against us." "I think he is the shrewdest man I ever met," said Frank Bird. "But not at all a Kentuckian. He is an old-fashioned Yankee in a western dress."

Lincoln let Seward have what he wanted in most consular appointments, occasionally having "some wish," such as moderate-sized consular posts for two painters who had done portraits of him at Springfield. Weed got from Seward an order appointing one of his organization workers to a consulate at Falmouth, England. The chief clerk of the State Department protested to Weed that it would mean the removal of an able official whose father had been appointed to the same post by President George Washington. Weed, who had a finer side to him, tore up the order of appointment for his own man.

A delegation called to present a paper reflecting discredit in the matter of appointments on Lincoln's old friend, Senator Baker. Lincoln took it in his hands, asking, "Is this paper mine to do with as I please?" The delegation replying, "Certainly, Mr. President," Lincoln laid the paper on live coals in the fireplace, watched it burn, and rose to say, "Good morning, gentlemen." When they had gone he told Senator Henry Wilson: "They did not know what they were talking about when they made Ned Baker responsible for what I had done or proposed to do. They told me that that was my paper to do with as I liked. I could not trust myself to reply in words, I was so angry. That was the whole case."

And Wilson noted further that Lincoln said: "If ever this free people, if ever this government itself, shall become utterly demoralized, it will come from this human wriggle and struggle for office; a way to live without work—from which complaint I am not free myself!" To one applicant eager for office Lincoln said: "There are no emoluments that properly belong to patriotism. I brought nothing with me to the White House, nor am I likely to carry anything out."

General Egbert L. Viele, while Military Governor of Norfolk, spent many hours with Lincoln on a steamboat, saw the President in somewhat relaxed and contemplative moods. He said to Viele one morning, as that rather sober and responsible civil engineer noted the talk: "If I have one vice, and I can call it nothing else, it is not to be able to say 'No.' Thank God for not making me a woman, but if He had, I suppose He would have made me just as ugly as He did, and no one would ever have tempted me. It was only the other day a poor parson whom I knew some years in Joliet came to the White House with a sad story of his poverty and his large family—poor parsons seem always to have large families—and he wanted me to do something for him. I knew very well I could do nothing for him, and yet I could not bear to tell him so, and so I said I would see what I could do. The very next day the man came back for the office which he said I had promised him—which was not true, but he seemed really to believe it. Of course there was nothing left for me to do except to get him a place through one of the secretaries. But if I had done my duty I should have said 'No' in the beginning."

> For weeks and for months he could get no sleep,
> For parties called on him, who for offices did seek;
> He was shook by the hands until they were sore,
> And had now more trouble than he ever had before.

Thus ran one of many verses in *Vanity Fair* to the tune of "Sweet Betsy from Pike." Other stanzas sung to the air of "Reuben, Reuben, I've Been Thinkin'," were as follows:

Good Mr. Lincoln,
I've long been thinkin'
How I can serve my country best;
And I've concluded
To do as you did
When you were living 'way out West.

You went Campaigning—
With little training
You entered on the field of strife;
But yours was civil,
While I'm a divil
That wants a military life.

You gained your wishes,
Your loaves and fishes,
Your Presidential chair of state;
May I not pray, then,
At some near day, then,
To have the same success with Fate?

With your position
A small commission
You easily might give to me;
As I can ride, sir,
And shoot beside, sir,
I'd like to join the cavalry.

Now, if you'll take me,
Good Abe, and make me,
Lieutenant, first, or second, say,
When in the saddle
I'll not skedaddle
But give Secesh the deuce to pay.

So, mighty Magnate,
Don't let me stagnate
In ease and idleness as now,
The while I'm knowing
That laurel's growing
To make a garland for my brow.

Please think it over;
I'll be in clover
If you a place for me can spare,
And that your glory
May fill Fame's story
Shall ever be my earnest prayer!

A Canadian ornithologist, A. M. Ross, working confidentially with Lincoln and Sumner on foreign and Confederate movements to the north, called with important intercepted mail. It was midnight and he apologized to Lincoln for the hour. Lincoln was in good humor. "No, no! You did right. You may waken me whenever you please. I have slept with one eye open ever since I came to Washington; I never close both except when an office seeker is looking for me." On another visit Ross noticed a young army officer rebuffed with good humor. "No! I can't do that. I must not interfere. They would scratch my eyes out if I did. You must go to the proper department."

The President walking down Pennsylvania Avenue with Ross, a pedestrian stepped alongside and thrust a letter into Lincoln's hand applying for an office in Wisconsin. Lincoln handed the letter back without reading it. "No, sir, I am not going to open shop here." Ross noted that Lincoln did it "in a most emphatic manner, but accompanied by a comical gesture which caused the rejected applicant to smile." As Lincoln went on walking with Ross he mentioned that no sooner was he elected than he became the prey of hundreds of applicants "whose highest ambition is to feed at the Government crib."

Having sold his New York newspaper, the *Courier and Enquirer,* to the *New York World,* James Watson Webb meandered into Lincoln's office; the least he could ask for would be a commission as major general. In below-zero weather in Wisconsin, Webb had fought Winnebago Indians. He was then a regular-army second lieutenant irregularly appointed by Secretary of State John C. Calhoun. Known as "Calhoun's scrub lieutenant," during seven years he fought two duels and narrowly escaped two more. Editing his Whig newspaper in New York, Webb started a daily horse express between New York and Washington, with relays of horses every six miles of the way, at a cost of $7,500 a month getting the Washington news twenty-four hours earlier than his rivals. Webb fought a duel with a Kentucky Congressman over unkind newspaper remarks, was wounded, was indicted by a New York grand jury for participating in a duel, pleaded guilty, was detained two weeks and then pardoned. In 1849 he was appointed Minister to Austria, but the United States Senate rejected his name.

Webb, however, had been ranked as major general in New York when serving as engineer in chief of the State, and now insisted that Lincoln should make him a major general of volunteers. He went away; Lincoln considered, sent Webb a commission as brigadier general, and got the commission back in the mail next day with Webb's notation: "Respectfully declined." Seward then sent to Webb an appointment as Minister to Turkey, which came back with Webb's notation: "Respectfully declined." Seward tried him again with an appointment as Minister to Brazil. This Webb accepted, though saying he would go to Brazil via Paris and dine with the Emperor Napoleon III.

In that case, suggested Lincoln, Webb might urge the Emperor not to interfere with the Union blockade of Southern ports. Webb later reported that he did so, and the Emperor said, "Tell the President that France will recognize the blockade." In Paris and Rio de Janeiro, on land or sea, however, Webb still believed that Lincoln should have appointed him major general, rating himself a grand strategist, having fought white men in duels and red men in frontier war.

Many outwardly bent on errands for others had hidden hopes. Doctor R. Shelton Mackenzie of Philadelphia requested, as twenty or thirty callers would do in a day, that he might have the President's autograph. Lincoln inquired, "Will you have it on a card or a sheet of paper?" The jovial physician answered, "If the choice rested with myself, I should prefer to have it at the foot of a commission." The point was neatly put; Lincoln smiled, shook his head, wrote a few pleasant lines, an ordinary autograph.

Nicolay and Hay often were able to send away satisfied the less persistent callers. A farmer-looking man appeared one day saying: "I am come here about the business of this war we are engaged in. I am commissioned from On High to take the matter in hand and end it. I shall take only 2,000 men, and shall go down South and get Jefferson Davis and other leaders of the rebellion and bring them here to be put in the lunatic asylum—because they are plainly crazy, and it is of no use to be fighting crazy men." Nicolay kept a straight face and talked it over with the man, who went away saying he would write the Governor of New York about it.

"An observer would have thought I was as crazy as the man himself," wrote Nicolay, "from the perfectly serious and natural manner in which he and I talked the matter over. Lunatics and visionaries are here so frequently that they cease to be strange phenomena, and I find the best way to dispose of them is to discuss and decide their mad projects as deliberately as any other matter of business."

From the barroom of Willard's Hotel to Lincoln's office, a notorious fixer made repeated trips asking a favor. On his final visit, according to William O. Stoddard, he came out of the office door "a large foot just behind him, suggesting to any naval constructor the idea of a propeller." Stoddard commented, "He was received from the first as a rogue, a wolf in sheep's clothing, but his criminal audacity went beyond the limits of patient endurance."

A young German count, vouched by the Prussian legation as of noble blood, seeking place in the army, was introduced by Carl Schurz. The count assured Lincoln that his family stood high; they had been counts for centuries. "Well," said Lincoln, "that need not trouble you. That will not be in your way, if you behave yourself as a soldier." The young count was puzzled and asked Schurz, as they walked away, what in the world the President could have meant by so strange a remark.

A young Ohioan called to thank Lincoln for appointment to a South American consulate. He was dressed as a dandy, "fit to kill," as slang of the day had it. But he was gloomy. He had met an acquaintance who said the insects of South America would bore holes clean through him before he had been down there a week.

"Mr. President, I can't say I'm so very glad of this appointment after all. Why, I hear they have bugs down there that are liable to eat me up inside of a week."

"Well, young man, if they do, they'll leave behind them a mighty good suit of clothes."

A place-seeker ushered into Lincoln's office took a chair at a table with Lincoln at the opposite end. "I listened to the requests of several men and women and saw that very few were granted," the newcomer noted. "Soon after I was seated, in walked several officers of the Spanish navy to pay their compliments to Mr. Lincoln. By some means they were directed to my end of the table and I saw that they took me for the President. Mr. Lincoln saw the same thing and hastily signaled to me 'go ahead,' and receive them. I rose, shook hands with each officer and exchanged a few words with them, which would, I suppose, have been appropriate, had I indeed been President. The moment their backs were turned I looked towards Mr. Lincoln. He was shaking with laughter. I thought now I had paved my way to win the position I had come to ask. I made up my mind to address the President in a new way and thus add to the hold I already had on him. So when my time came I stepped up to Mr. Lincoln and said, 'Sir, I have seen the annoyances to which you are subjected by so many requests for positions. Now if you will permit me to shake hands I will endeavor to smother my desire for a certain position which I had come to ask of you.'

"Mr. Lincoln jumped to grasp my hand and said, 'Sir, you are one man in a thousand. I am doubly indebted to you. You have been the means of conveying to those Spanish officers that the President of the United States is a very handsome man, and then you do not even ask an office. But,' he added, 'hurry home; you may repent.'"

Cabinet members protesting an appointment of a Democrat once received the reply: "Oh, I can't afford to punish every person who has seen fit to oppose my election. We want a competent man in this office."

And justifying the appointment of one particularly bitter opponent, the President said: "I suppose Judge —— did behave pretty ugly, but that wouldn't make him any less fit for this place, and I have scriptural authority for appointing him. You recollect that where the Lord on Mount Sinai was getting out a commission for Aaron, that same Aaron was at the foot of the mountain making a false god, a golden calf, for the people to worship; yet Aaron got his commission, you know."

The historian Bancroft entered one day to see Lincoln reading a paper handed him by a man sitting in a chair opposite, restless, of unsteady eyes. "Mr. Lincoln, still holding the paper up and without movement of any kind, paused and, raising his eyes, looked for a long time at the man's face and seemed to be looking down into his very soul. Then, resuming his reading for a few moments, he again paused and cast the same piercing look upon his visitor. Suddenly, without warning, he dropped the paper and stretching out his long arm he pointed his finger directly into the face of his vis-à-vis and said, 'What's the matter with you?' The man stammered and finally replied, 'Nothing.' 'Yes, there is,' said Lincoln. 'You can't look me in the face. You have not looked me in the face since you sat there. Even now you are looking out of that window and cannot look me in the eyes.' Then, flinging the paper in the man's lap, he cried, 'Take it back! There is something wrong about this. I will have nothing to do with it'—and the discomfited individual retired."

Occasionally the President moved in behalf of civilian rights taken away by military commanders, as when Halleck under date of January 21, 1863, wrote to Major General Grant at Memphis: "It may be proper to give you some explanation of the revocation of your order expelling all Jews from your department. The President has no objection to your expelling traitors and Jew peddlers, which, I suppose, was the object of your order; but as it in terms proscribed an entire religious class, some of whom are fighting in our ranks, the President deemed it necessary to revoke it."

Cameron called in behalf of a young man who had been a pest in applying for a consulate. "Where do you want to have him sent?" asked the President. The Pennsylvania leader stepped to a large globe of the earth, put an arm around it as far as he could reach, and said, "I do not know what my finger is on, but send him there." And, so it was told, he was accommodated.

A Hoosier one day was not in the least backward. On his leaving Lincoln wrote a memorandum:

> Today Mr. Blake of Indianapolis, asks
> 1. Captain Aiken be promoted.
> 2. Colonel William H. Blake of the 9th be promoted.
> 3. Colonel John W. Blake of the 40th be promoted.
> 4. That himself—James Blake—have something.

On the back of this paper Lincoln wrote "Submitted to the Secretary of War."

A brigadier general commanded four regiments, was rated four times as important as a colonel, could have more of the physical comforts, if he chose. The pressure was heavy for this rank. There were jests and quips about the brigadiers. A Midwest War Democrat asked appointment as a naval commander. Lincoln gazed at this prairie citizen, whose naval service had been limited to rowboats on the Scioto River, and inquired whether he had had experience as a sailor. "I never had, Mr. President, but judging from the brigadier-generals you have appointed in Ohio the less experience a man has the higher the position he attains."

A young brigadier with a small cavalry troop strayed into Confederate lines in Virginia and was captured. Receiving the report, Lincoln said he was sorry to lose the horses. "I can make a better brigadier any day, but those horses cost the government $125 a head."

The President dipped into ancient history and told Senator Wilson, as *Leslie's Weekly* published it for the country to read, that some of the generals reminded him of a joke. "A sarcastic Athenian gravely proposed in the public assembly that a decree should be passed declaring that asses were horses. The motion was voted down as ridiculous, when the proposer retorted, 'But this is the way you make your generals, dubbing with the title men who have learned nothing of war.'"

A New England woman on a hospital errand entered the President's office unnoticed by Lincoln and another man, who was handing Lincoln a paper. Lincoln read it carelessly and said, "Yes, that is a sufficient endorsement for anybody; what do you want?" The woman bystander did not hear the man's reply but later heard his sarcastic remark, "I see there are no vacancies among the brigadiers, from the fact that so many colonels are commanding brigades." At this, the President threw himself forward in his chair in such a way that she saw his "curious, comical expression." He was looking the man squarely in the face; and, with one hand softly patting the other, and the funny look pervading every line of his face, he said: "My friend, let me tell you something about that. You are a farmer, I believe; if not, you will understand me. Suppose you had a large cattle-yard, full of all sorts of cattle—cows, oxen, and bulls—and you kept killing and selling and disposing of your cows and oxen, in one way and another, taking good care of your bulls. By and by you would find out that you had nothing but a yard full of old bulls, good for nothing under heaven. Now it will be just so with the army, if I don't stop making brigadier-generals." The man was answered, tried to laugh, but the effort was feeble. The woman caller noticed, however, that Lincoln "laughed enough for both," in fact, laughed the man out of the room.

From a line of people at an informal reception came a shout: "Hello, Abe, how are ye? I'm in line and hev come for an orfice too." Lincoln recognized an old Sangamon County friend of his youth and told him "to hang onto himself and not kick the traces." They shook hands and after the reception Lincoln had to explain that his old friend could not handle the transactions in the office he wanted. The old friend worried, his lips trembled, and he sketched a world of personal history for Lincoln's understanding in saying, "Martha's dead, the gal is married, and I've guv Jim the forty." He moved closer and half whispered, "I knowed I wasn't eddicated enough

to get the place but I kinder want to stay where I ken see Abe Linkern."
And for a time he worked on the White House grounds.

On board a government steamer taking a party to Washington's home
at Mount Vernon, Seward told Lord Lyons and others that one day some
twenty place-hunters from all parts of the Union had taken possession of
the President's office "with bales of credentials and self-recommendations
ten miles long." And Lincoln joked them, said Seward, "though Mr. Lincoln
never tells a joke for the joke's sake; they are like parables, lessons of wisdom." One time, minding a mud scow in a bayou near the Yazoo, Lincoln
drawled, he read a story of a certain king who called the Court Minister,
said he wanted to go hunting, and asked the Minister if it would rain. The
Minister told him the weather would be fair, it would not rain, and he
could go hunting. The royal party on the way met a farmer riding a jackass.
He told the king to turn back, it was going to rain. The king laughed, went
on, and no sooner got started hunting than a heavy downpour of rain
drenched him and his party to their royal skins. The king went back to the
palace, threw out the Minister, and called for the farmer.

"Tell me how you knew it would rain."

"I did not know, Your Majesty, it's not me, it's my jackass. He puts his
ears forward when it's going to be wet, and back when it's going to be
dry weather."

The king sent the farmer away, had the jackass brought and put in the
place of the Minister.

"It was here," said Lincoln, "the king made a great mistake."

"How so?" asked some of his audience.

"Why, ever since that time, every jackass wants an office!" To which
the President added, "Gentlemen, leave your credentials, and when the war
is over you'll hear from me."

Thus the matter was published in odd corners of reputable newspapers,
which also alleged that Lincoln sometimes told of a young man who went
West and wrote back to his politician father: "Dear Dad: I have settled
at —— and like it first rate. Do come out here, for almighty mean men
get office here."

A young Republican lawyer from Bloomington, Illinois, William W.
Orme, law partner of Leonard Swett, had his request for a brigadiership
presented to Lincoln by Lamon. From the field in southwestern Missouri
he wrote to his wife of a letter from a brother in Washington. "He says
Lamon is at work with the President; and that Mr. Lincoln would make
the promotion at once if he could say in justification of himself that I had
distinguished myself in battle." In action later Orme did show gallantry and
the promotion came. Until he was appointed, however, Lincoln's old associates in law kept Orme's name before the President, reporting to Orme its
status, how the Senate returned to the President one batch of brigadier
appointments on the ground that by law no more could be appointed, how
the Senate had passed a bill to create twenty new major generals and fifty
brigadiers, Judge Davis writing to Orme: "There is nobody here to help

at all unless it is Hill [Lamon] and myself. Every other one has somebody that he wants. Trumbull will do nothing, Washburne growls all the time. The President has not asked my advice on any subject. When I have given any I have thrust it on him."

Again Davis wrote Orme of some Congressmen trying to create one hundred additional brigadiers instead of fifty: "We are going to try Mr. Lincoln again tonight to see if he will say what he will do in your case. I was to see him 3 or 4 times before Swett came. He would not promise what he would do. He has told Swett the same. We will try him tonight and telegraph result. I don't believe he will say what he will do, but we will try him. He says that he wants the bill to pass first so as to know how many generals he can appoint. Now says he, Davis you know I like Orme as well as you do and you would hesitate when you have a limited number to appoint as I have. I told him I would not hesitate a moment. The subject dropped and I left. Swett wants Hovey appd. There can't be two from Bloomington. Swett will yield in your favor. I am against Hovey anyhow, firmly and decidedly. Swett and I are in antagonism there."

These Illinoisans were well aware of what General Halleck had told a colonel who wanted promotion, who had letters vouching for his military fitness but no political recommendations. "To be frank with you," said Halleck, "with only such letters, your chances of promotion are about equal to those of the stump-tailed bull in fly-time."

In the matter of giving Lew Wallace of Indiana an army command, Senator Lane of Indiana called on Lincoln, who remarked to a later caller, "Halleck wants to kick Wallace out, and Lane wants me to kick Halleck out."

"Well, I'll tell you how to fix it to the satisfaction of both parties."

"How is that?"

"Why, kick 'em both out."

"No, that won't do. I think Halleck is a good man. He may not be—of course; I don't know much about such things. I may be a judge of good lawyers, but I don't know much about generals. Those who ought to know say he is good."

"Well, if you don't know, you ought to know; and if the people don't know that Halleck is a fool, they think they do, and it's all the same."

A Senator, on learning from Lincoln that Halleck had negatived proposed military changes, asked the President why he didn't get Halleck out of the way. "Well—the fact is—the man who has no friends—should be taken care of."

Odd luck befell men of the same name, as Colonel Addison Farnsworth of New York, wrote to Lieutenant W. T. Lusk in December of '62. "The other day Thurlow Weed was sitting with the President—Generalissimo Lincoln—when Colonel Farnsworth's card was sent in. Weed, supposing that the card represented this individual, remarked, 'By the way, Mr. President, my call on you was particularly in relation to Col. Farnsworth.' And then he 'put in' for me, leaving with the promise that my name should be sent in to the Senate immediately. Three or four days thereafter, to the astonishment of Mr. Weed, he saw an announcement in the papers that Col. Farnsworth of *Illinois* had been appointed a Brigadier! In fact, the Illinois Farnsworth secured his promotion at the expense of the New York Farnsworth. Mr. Weed and others are now pushing the thing for me, but as every Col. in the army is now an applicant for a Brigadier-ship, I am not disposed to rely solely upon the aid and influence of politicians. That letter from Burnside would fix the thing at once. In the event of my promotion, you can rely upon the Lieut. Colonelcy. Keep mum on the subject. . . . I am getting better—leg improving a little. Great excitement here among ye people in relation to Fredericksburg affair. Don't be surprised to hear in a few days that 'Old Abe' has been forced to abdicate or change his cabinet."

Welles brought dispatches to Lincoln regarding a naval officer, and noted in his diary that the President said promptly: "Dismiss him. If that is your opinion it is mine. I will do it." The dismissed officer later had his case pleaded in a memorial from important citizens of Maine, with an earnest letter from Senator Fessenden. "The President read it through," wrote Welles, "and said no one could be dismissed or punished without bringing up a host of sympathizing friends to resist the unpleasant but necessary action of the Government, and make the victim a martyr. Said he would do nothing in this case unless I advised it."

When Welles stepped out of the naval sphere into the military, however, the President was not so quick to agree. Stanton was Mars and Welles was Neptune, as Lincoln nicknamed them. The Secretary of the Navy presented the name of a man for brigadier general and noted it "was kindly received but no assurance given."

A father and mother came for help to get their two boys back home. They had tried other ways and the President was their last hope. The two boys, under age, had enlisted in the navy. The worst fault of the boys, said the parents, was their disobedience. Lincoln picked up a card and wrote to the Secretary of the Navy ordering their discharge on the point: "The United States don't need the services of boys who disobey their parents."

Often on one man leaving a place to which another would be appointed, a buzz and flutter ensued. "Hon Isaac Newton called at night to urge upon me to accept a position in the Cabinet as Secy of the Interior, in place of Secy Smith," wrote Browning in his diary on December 3 of '62. Eleven days later Browning wrote: "Mrs Lincoln sent her carriage this morning for me to go to Church with her which I did. The President did not go. After Church she rode with me to Capitol Hill. On our way down she told me the President was anxious to get Secretary Smith out of the Cabinet, and me in his place. That he was anxious to have Mrs Browning and myself in Washington, and the only thing that would prevent him offering me the place would be the fear of having it said he was giving everything to Illinois, but she thought he would do it—She knew he wished to." A few weeks later another than Browning was appointed.

In charge of the appointment branch of the Adjutant General's office at one time was James B. Fry, who noted of one day at the White House that Lincoln confided: "I have here a bushel-basketful of applications for officers in the army. I have tried to examine them all, but they have increased so rapidly that I have got behind and may have neglected some. I will send them all to your office. Overhaul them, lay those that require further attention before the Secretary of War, and file the others."

Fry went through the bushel basket, found the papers dotted with notes, comments, and queries by the President. One slip of paper he brought back to the President, remarking that he supposed the President would not care to have it in the official files. Lincoln had written: "On this day Mrs. —— called upon me. She is the wife of Major —— of the regular army. She wants her husband made a brigadier-general. She is a saucy little woman, and I think she will torment me till I have to do it." Fry recalled this notation at a later time when the little woman's husband was named a brigadier.

A high private from the rear ranks poured out his complaints to the President one summer afternoon as Fry came in, and Lincoln's reply ran, "That may all be so, but you must go to your officers about it." The private had the idea maybe the President hadn't heard him, and told his story two or three times more as the President sat and gazed out the south window on the Potomac. At last the President turned. "Now, my man, go away, *go away!* I can not meddle in your case. I could as easily bail out the Potomac River with a teaspoon as attend to all the details of the army."

A report having much useless language lay on his desk, the work of a congressional committee regarding a newly devised gun. "I should want a new lease of life to read this through," groaned the President. "Why can't an investigating committee show a grain of common sense? If I send a man to buy a horse for me, I expect him to tell me that horse's points—not how many hairs he has in his tail."

The case came of Billy Patterson, a Mississippi River pilot, smart at running past Confederate batteries, now asking captaincy of an old river boat sheeted with iron and mounted with two antiquated guns. A pompous examination committee had questioned him about English history and Oliver Cromwell, Billy Patterson snorting, "I don't know and don't care a damn who he was; I ain't hunting his job." The committee chairman wrote across the application "Not recommended—ignorant and insolent."

Friends took up his case, and Lincoln, it was related, wrote on the back of his application: "This seems to have become a sort of triangular contest between Charles Stuart, Oliver Cromwell and Billy Patterson. It is generally believed hereabouts that Charles and Oliver are dead. If the committee upon investigation finds this to be the fact, give the appointment to Billy Patterson."

A delegation of Baltimoreans semicircled the President one morning as a spokesman stepped out and read an address to the effect that while they believed implicitly in the honesty and the patriotism of the President, and so forth, they were ready to affirm that the person proposed to be placed in a certain office, Mr. So-and-So, was a consummate rascal and notoriously in league with the enemy. The speaker concluded, folded up his address, and stepped back into the semicircle. The President replied. He complimented them on their appearance and professions of loyalty, and so forth, but said he was at a loss what to do with Mr. So-and-So, as a delegation twice as large, just as respectable in appearance, and no less ardent in professions of loyalty, had called on him four days before, ready to swear, every one of them, that Mr. So-and-So was one of the most honest and loyal men in Baltimore.

"Now," said the President as Noah Brooks recorded it, "we cannot afford to call a Court of Inquiry in this case, and so, as a lawyer, I shall be obliged to decide that the weight of testimony, two to one, is in favor of the client's loyalty, and as you do not offer even any attempt to prove the truth of your suspicions, I shall be compelled to ignore them for the present." The delegation bade him good morning and put on their hats.

Donn Piatt wrote of once hearing Seward say that in the ability to manage saying No to office-seekers, the President "had a cunning that was genius."

Carl Schurz noted the President as saying once in a heavy hour, "I have discovered a good way of providing officers for this Government: put all the names of the applicants into one pepper-box and all the offices into another, and then shake the two, and make appointments just as the names and offices happen to drop out together."

In another care-laden hour, according to Schurz, the President pointed out to a friend an eager throng of office-seekers and Congressmen in an anteroom and spoke these words: "Do you observe this? The rebellion is hard enough to overcome, but there you see something which, in the course of time, will become a greater danger to the republic than the rebellion itself."

Both the gravity and the intricacy of this phase of the Government were presented by Gustavus Vasa Fox, Assistant Secretary of the Navy, in a letter marked "Unofficial" addressed to Rev. W. L. Gage, Portsmouth, New Hampshire, December 30, 1862. That Fox was rather strictly the working executive head of the Navy Department, with a reputation for straight dealing, gave his letter added weight to its reader. Fox wrote:

"I have not answered your last application because I hoped to have been able to assist you to the desired place. It is however most difficult during a Session of Congress to obtain an appointment of this kind without political influence.

"The members watch us very sharp, and having great power over all the Dep'ts of Government, generally get what they want. Mr. Ely the member of Congress from New York who was captured at Bull Run, and imprisoned at Richmond, sells appointments, and so openly, that it is notorious. Do you wonder that the wrath of God is upon us? I suppose you know that I was the principal person in bringing on this war, by persuading the Prest that Fort Sumter could be relieved, and the attempt was ordered by the Pres't.

but so late, that the surrender took place before the force arrived there.

"About the time I was doing this action, and having as I always have had, the full confidence of the Prest, Mr. Blair at my instigation nominated my father as Postmaster of Lowell. He is one of the old Congregational type of the New England puritan school—Republican in politics from the start. For what little I have done for my country I only asked this Appt. as my father is poor.

"It was refused by the Pres't because the M.C. from that district wanted another person, and yet that M.C. is opposed to the policy of the Administration. I mention this because I know you to be a good man, and an inside picture will open your understanding more than any declaration. I will try sincerely to help you."

In the matter of placing a certain brigadier general under the orders of Commodore Porter, the President's signature was required. Stanton opposed Fox's request to the President but, as Fox wrote to Porter: "Stanton lost his temper so we beat him. The cool man always wins. Let me impress upon you to be incontrovertibly right in case of a difference with the Army. The President is just and sagacious."

To the Reverend F. M. Magrath the President wrote in late '61 that having been "solicited by Christian ministers and other pious people to appoint suitable persons to act as chaplains at the hospitals for our sick and wounded soldiers," he felt the "intrinsic propriety" of such action but no law conferred on him the power to so appoint. If, however, such services were voluntarily performed, he would recommend that Congress make compensation the same for chaplains on hospital duty as in the army.

To Archbishop John Hughes of New York the President wrote in late '61 with the salutation "Right Reverend Sir" and beginning the letter: "I am sure you will pardon me if in my ignorance I do not address you with technical correctness." Though he could find no law authorizing his appointment of chaplains for hospitals, "yet the services of chaplains are more needed, perhaps, in the hospitals than with the healthy soldiers in the field." Therefore he had given "a sort of *quasi* appointment" to three Protestant ministers and "If you perceive no objection, I will thank you to give me the name or names of one or more suitable persons of the Catholic Church, to whom I may with propriety tender the same service." The President's personal touch with the Archbishop went into a closing sentence: "Many thanks for your kind and judicious letters to Governor Seward, and which he regularly allows me both the pleasure and the profit of perusing."

A note of the President to the Rev. Dr. A. Fischel in late '61 said that in several particulars the law as to chaplains was having attention and "I shall try to have a new law broad enough to cover what is desired by you in behalf of the Israelites."

Having talked with a widow about her two sons in the army, Lincoln wrote to Stanton to verify her statement that one of them was under arrest for desertion, unable to return to duty under a proclamation giving him that benefit. "Please have it ascertained if this is correct, and if it is, let him be discharged from arrest and go to duty. I think, too, he should have his pay for duty actually performed. Loss of pay falls so hard upon poor families."

The President noted points to jog his memory as to how matters stood in the revenue collectors' offices in two districts. "On something I said to Mr. Conkling, he did not get up recommendation of Mr. Blake. Says both are good men—Blake has never had anything. Orton has an office of $1200 in same district. Is for Blake. Says Orton could go to Seventh."

One pest of a politician, who might be called So-and-So, came often asking offices, suggesting removals and creation of new offices, and Lincoln, reviewing his day's routine to a friend, said that at night as the closing act of the day "I look under the bed to see if So-and-So is there, and if not, I thank Heaven and bounce in."

A dispute over a high-salaried Ohio postmastership brought several delegations to the White House, and papers piled high in behalf of two men about equally competent. One day, as the politicians told of the affair afterward, Lincoln was bored by still another delegation, more arguments, even more petitions. And he called to a clerk: "This matter has got to end somehow. Bring me a pair of scales." They were brought. "Now put in all the petitions and letters in favor of one man and see how much they weigh, and then weigh the other fellow's pile." It was done. One bundle weighed three-quarters of a pound more than the other. "Make out an appointment," said the President, "for the man who has the heavier papers."

The fearless strutter Cassius M. Clay was manifest and insistent. Browning at the White House one evening had his session with Lincoln interrupted by callers. "Cassius M. Clay & some other gentlemen sent in their cards. He [the President] was much annoyed—said to me he did not wish to see them, and finally told the servant to tell them he was engaged and could not see them tonight. I asked him what he thought of Clay. He answered that he had a great deal of conceit and very little sense, and that he did not know what to do with him, for he could not give him a command—he was not fit for it. He [Clay] had asked to be permitted to come home from Russia to take part in the war, and as he [Lincoln] wanted some place to put Cameron to get him [Cameron] out of the War Department he [Lincoln] consented, and appointed Clay a Majr Genl hoping the war would be over before he [Clay] got home."

Now Clay had come from Russia, was dissatisfied, wanted to go back to Russia. He "was not willing to take a command unless he could control everything—conduct the war on his own plan, and run the entire machine of Government—That could not be allowed." So now Clay was urging that he be sent back to Russia. "What embarrassed him [Lincoln] was that he had given him [Clay] his promise in writing to send him back if Cameron resigned"

Bayard Taylor, poet and author serving as secretary of the United States Legation at St. Petersburg, had nursed hopes of being appointed Minister to Russia and notified a Philadelphia friend in August of '62 that a letter from

Vice-President Hamlin reported Hamlin's interview with Lincoln in behalf of Taylor. "The reasons which I urged seemed to impress him favorably, and while he gave me no positive assurance of what he would do, I am confident he feels at least well-disposed." Taylor's failure to get the diplomatic post he so eagerly desired resulted in his writing to E. C. Stedman in February of '63 a letter not at all diplomatic.

After reciting his own qualifications, Taylor wrote: "On the other hand, a man who (entre nous) made the Legation a laughing stock, whose incredible vanity and astonishing blunders are still the talk of St. Petersburg, and whose dispatches disgrace the State Department that allows them to be printed, will probably be allowed to come back to his ballet-girls (his reason for coming) by our soft-hearted Abraham. Let the Government send a man who will not be laughed at—who has one grain of prudence and one drachm of common-sense, with a few moral scruples—and I shall gladly give up all my pretentions [sic] and go home. From my private correspondence, I know that Lincoln says Clay is not fit for the place, but 'he is an elephant on my hands, and I guess I shall have to give it to him!' "

Senators and Congressmen came to the White House with letters imploring offices for relatives soon to be married, for friends who were sick and had dependents. "I need the position for a living," wrote one to Sumner. "I have been unfortunate and poor." William Henry Fry of the *New York Tribune* asked Sumner to get him a diplomatic post, preferring the Russian mission. "I need more repose than I get (you know what night labors are on the *Tribune*)—and I am fit for the place." To Chase and other departmental heads, as to the President, came letters crying personal poverty as a basis for public office, in the tone of one: "God knows no one needs the appointment more than I do."

The President needed watching and reminders to make sure that he would do a thing he was inclined to do. Thus Carl Schurz in a letter to Sumner asked him to see that the President put Schurz on the next list of major generals; he was disappointed in not being among the latest announced and had called on the President. "I think he is inclined to send in my nomination tomorrow if he is reminded of it. . . . I want to press you to do this reminding. Will you? It will cost you only five minutes."

Behind a single application for office sometimes lay an odd mess of relationships. Seeking place as a revenue collector, Henry C. Bowen wrote to Senator Sumner, in part, as follows:

"Someone has been cutting out Mr. Beecher's editorials in the *Independent* and sending them to President Lincoln to prejudice him against me, and I have heard *directly* that Mr. Lincoln censures me severely. Now I am not responsible, at all, for the editorial opinions of the *Independent*, any more than you are—except in the *Commercial Department*. There I have full control. I desire to have the President set right in this matter and will you pardon the liberty I now take of sending to you the enclosed with the request that you place it personally in his hands—after reading and sealing. By granting me this favor you will place me under renewed obligations.

"When in Washington I have been invited to the President's house, into his family. Mrs. Lincoln has been to my house and the President just before his nomination, went with me to church in Brooklyn. I mention these to show you that the President has a right to feel sorely if he thinks, as he does, that I am untrue to him. Mr. Colfax when in the city last week, called at my house several times and while here, I, for the first time, heard of the President's feelings. Mr. Colfax said he would see him and explain matters fully but advised me to write him under cover to you and ask you to present the letter. I feel grieved as much as Mr. Lincoln and desire to be set right. . . . The names of the collectors will soon be sent in for confirmation and may I bespeak your friendly attention to my interest? . . . In regard to yourself I am happy to say that all connected with our paper agree perfectly. The article about you by Greeley was written at my suggestion."

Much water had passed under the bridge since the days when William Lloyd Garrison denounced the Constitution as "a covenant with death and a compact with hell." Now he had a Government and felt himself part of it. In a letter to Sumner on September 5, 1863, he requested "the situation of Assistant Paymaster in the Navy" for "my young friend, Mr. William Hovey (a worthy and very promising son of my lamented friend, the late Mr. C. F. Hovey)." It was an entirely decent and courteous letter, which closed: "This will be handed you by my son Wendell, who will call for any letter you may feel disposed to write." In the old days Garrison could not have done it. Now he had a Government.

A man appointed and then dismissed brought pressure to be put back. Senator Sumner submitted a resolution in December of '62 that the President be requested, "if not incompatible with the public interests, to communicate to the Senate any information in his possession showing why General Saxton has been removed from his command at Hilton Head." The President was quoted as telling a member of Congress who asked for a list of appointments: "Your demand illustrates the difference between the abstract and the concrete. When a bill is pending to create more army officers you take the floor and denounce it (although you dodge a vote on it) as a needless scheme to increase the power and tyranny of the Executive; but as soon as the bill becomes a law you come here and demand that all your brothers-in-law and cousins and nephews be appointed under it; your action in Congress is abstract, but in the Executive Chamber is concrete."

Lincoln telegraphed S. B. Moody at Springfield, Illinois: "Which do you prefer—commissary or quartermaster? If appointed it must be without conditions." The matter was personal; when a Congressman later wished to name a postmaster in Springfield, Lincoln said, "I think I have promised that to old Mrs. Moody for her husband." The Congressman demurred: "Now, Mr. President, why can't you be liberal?" "Mrs. Moody would get down on me." In some matters he was directly personal. He wrote that he knew nothing of charges brought against a Lieutenant Merryman. "I only wish to say, he was raised from childhood in the town where I lived, and I remember nothing against him as boy or man. His father, now dead, was a very intimate acquaintance and friend of mine."

Personal sentiments would govern. William Kellogg, Jr., quit the West Point military academy under demerit; if he had not resigned he would have been dismissed. His father, an Illinois Congressman, reappointed the boy. An investigation and report by General Joseph G. Totten disapproved of the boy's going back to West Point. Lincoln wrote the Secretary of War that the father was a friend of twenty years' standing. "This matter touches him very deeply—the feelings of a father for a child—as he thinks, all the future of his child. I can not be the instrument to crush his heart. According to strict rule he has the right to make the re-nomination. Let the appointment be made. It needs not to become a precedent." Thereafter Lincoln would have the rule that no resignation should be handed in by a cadet without express stipulation in writing that the resigning cadet would not take a re-nomination. The President meant no censure on General Totten and wrote, "Although I have marked this note *private* I am quite willing for him to see it."

Learning that Captain John A. Dahlgren, commanding the Washington navy yard, wanted his boy in the army, Lincoln wrote the Secretary of War: "I need not tell you how much I would like to oblige Captain Dahlgren. I now learn, not from him, that he would be gratified for his son Ulric Dahlgren, to be appointed a lieutenant in the Army. Please find a place for him."

A note to the official having the appointing power frequently had the expression from Lincoln "He is a good man," or "an old friend of mine," or in the case of Ward Hill Lamon "my particular friend." To Governor Curtin went a note: "The bearer of this, Edward D. Baker, is the son of my very dear friend Col. Baker, who fell at Balls Bluff." He disclaimed all wish to interfere with State troop matters but hoped Baker could be made a field officer in a Pennsylvania regiment.

To a Rhode Island Senator went a note about a girl from that State whose brother had been killed and her father made prisoner in the Peninsular campaign. "If you can be satisfied that her story is correct, please see if you can not get Mr. Secretary Chase or friend Newton to find her a place." Regarding Richard M. Corwine, who had served as Judge Advocate under Frémont four months without a commission, Lincoln wrote the War Department that his services had been valuable: "The meritorious ones ought to have commissions, nunc pro tunc, and an honorable recognition of them, and should also be paid." If a White House caller seemed honest and competent, Lincoln might begin a personal inquiry with a note such as one to the Secretary of the Interior: "George L. Pomeroy of Illinois, tells me he was a clerk in the Census Bureau, and has been removed. Will you please ascertain, and tell me the circumstances?"

The looks of a young fellow who spoke for himself had something and the President wrote Stanton: "Please see this Pittsburg boy. He is very young, and I shall be satisfied with whatever you do with him." Another note to Stanton inquired whether Second Lieutenant Alexander E. Drake of Company D, 2d Infantry, at Alexandria, was not entitled to promotion. "His wife thinks he is. Please have this looked into."

His friends among generals had the President's advice to stay away from that hotbed of politics and place-hunting—Washington. He wrote to Major General S. A. Hurlbut at Belvidere, Illinois: "You now stand well with the Secretary of War, and with General Halleck, and it would lessen you with both for you to make your appearance here. I advise you by all means to dismiss the thought of coming here."

A note sent to Wait Talcott was directly personal: "I have determined to appoint you collector. I now have a very special request to make of you, which is, that you will make no war upon Mr. Washburne, who is also my friend, and of longer standing than yourself." The President seemed to like Talcott, writing a note of introduction: "The Secretary of the Treasury and the Commissioner of Internal Revenue will please see Mr. Talcott, one of the best men there is, and, if any difference, one they would like better than they do me." One applicant carried away on Executive Mansion stationery Lincoln's attestation: "Whom It May Concern: Edward Hall, a Texas gentleman, is a very competent, faithful, and genteel man." For those who might not observe that Mr. Hall was "genteel" it was noted. Mr. Hall himself could read that he was of the gentility.

Murat Halstead of the *Cincinnati Commercial* sought men close to the President and tried to land a postmastership for a friend. As a poor loser, Halstead wrote his friend: "I use the mildest phrase when I say Lincoln is a weak, a miserably weak man; the wife is a fool—the laughing stock of the town, her vulgarity only the more conspicuous in consequence of her fine carriage and horses and servants in livery and fine dresses and her damnable airs. . . . Lincoln is very busy with trifles, and lets everybody do as they please. He is opposed to stealing, but can't see the stealing that is done."

In one letter referring to Lincoln as a "strong ass" bowed beneath burdens, Murat Halstead put the matter bluntly. "Chase was very earnestly your friend in the Post Office business. If Lincoln had been a man you would have had the Post Office. He yields not to the force with which an application is asked, but to importunity in the applicant. If Chase had to deal with a man acting upon principles that govern gentlemen there would have been no trouble. But he could not persist and insist and run up and down and—others did. So Chase had to give it up." Halstead retailed further information. "The way Chase manages Lincoln is to make him believe that he (Lincoln) is doing all things. The poor silly President sucks flattery as a pig sucks milk."

As Orpheus C. Kerr (Office Seeker), R. H. Newell of the *New York Mercury* wrote humorous sketches in which Lincoln appeared as garrulously but cleverly outgabbing the place-hunters. A Democrat having asked candidly for "any offices which you might have to dispose of," Honest Abe wiped the blade of his jackknife with his thumb, leaned over the arm of his chair, said he was reminded of a small tale from days when he was beating the prairies for clients in Illinois and knew a codger named Podger at Peoria. "His wife knew enough for all the rest of the family . . . a very good woman in her way. She . . . made my friend Podger so happy at home that he never dared to go away from home without her permission. Her temper was of [a] useful nature . . . and I don't think she ever called Job Podger an Old Fool except when company was present. If she had one peculiarity more than another, it was this: she was always doing something for Podger's sake."

Then came a horseplay yarn, long-spun, dwelling on what the unworthy wife did for her husband's sake, ending with the point that what this particular Democrat had done for the Union's sake was much like what Mrs. Podger did for her husband. "Immediately upon the termination of this wholesome domestic tale, the political chap sprang from his seat, smiled feebly at the ceiling for a minute, crammed his hat down over his eyes, and fled greatly demoralized." That Orpheus C. Kerr's sketches had a large number of readers, and were widely talked about, was an indication that the President had considerable sympathy in his difficulties with the patronage. That Kerr should present Lincoln as slicker in gab than any gabby applicant for office was to Kerr's readers a hilarious farce.

From a marble mantelpiece in a waiting-room of the White House Congressman Josiah Bushnell Grinnell took a copy of *The Orpheus C. Kerr Papers*, with its opening paragraph—"Though you find me in Washington now, I was born of respectable parents, and gave every indication, in my satchel and apron days, of coming to something better than this" and its narration that the family doctor, holding him as a six-months child, had chuckled: "How beautiful is babes! So small, and yet so much like human beings, only not so large. This boy will make a noise in the world yet. He has a long head, a very long head. . . . The little fellow has a long head, a very long head—and it's as thick as it is long," whereupon arose "some coolness between the doctor and my father after that, and, on the following Sunday, my mother refused to look at his wife's new bonnet in church."

Lincoln, entering to see Grinnell holding the book, said he must not be judged entirely by such nonsense. "I read it," Grinnell noted Lincoln as saying, "when my brain is weary . . . and I must be unbent. When a boy, the owner of a bow and arrow, I found one must let up on the bow if the arrow is to have force. Read Kerr and then pity me chained here in the Mecca of office-seekers. You flaxen men with broad faces are born with cheer, and don't know a cloud from a star. I am of another temperament. But, drop the book, and if the country will get up as much fever in enlistments as there is strife for the offices, the rebel leaders will soon have a collapse."

Months later when Grinnell called to ask promotion of a colonel to brigadier, Lincoln saluted him: "How is Iowa? With whom did you leave those few sheep [Grinnell had a few hundred] in the wilderness?"

"Not much, Mr. President, of shepherd David's wilderness—all prairie. Will you please tell me, how did you know I kept sheep?"

"I remember men by association, and know you a tariff man and sheep owner by a picture of one of your flock, in the United States Agricultural report. It was his Satanic majesty, clipping the hog, that founded the old proverb, 'Great cry and little wool'; but the war demand should make your sheep farmers very happy and patriotic."

Grinnell brought up the matter of advancing Colonel Elliott W. Rice, for gallantry at Donelson and other meritorious service, to brigadier. "What does Stanton say?" queried Lincoln.

"Nothing. Will not even look up the papers."

"Yes, I know the cases like yours are hundreds, and it disturbs him, even my hint that we may move up the boys and encourage enlistments. It is a very delicate question. Don't be impatient, but get on the right side of a very good officer."

Again Grinnell called and heard from the President, "Stanton was fairly mad on the suggestion of promotion by civilians or members of Congress."

"I base my claim on the recommendations of superior officers in the field."

"You get the facts, and quietly say the president hopes your request will be granted."

Once more Grinnell, who had traveled from Iowa to Washington on this special piece of business, came to Lincoln, whose greeting was: "Have you not gone home yet? Let us walk. I am weary and depressed by many things I cannot talk about." They walked. Grinnell renewed his points in behalf of the Fourth District of Iowa and the gallantry and number of her soldiers, Lincoln saying: "I cannot attempt to make Stanton over at this stage. You will win, if patient." They were back at the White House, the President nodding with doubt over the matter as he rested a hand on a doorknob. "Have you a slip of paper?" he suddenly asked in a changed tone. Then, according to Grinnell, leaning against a column of the porch he wrote: "Sir: Without an if or an and, let Colonel El[l]iott W. Rice be made a brigadier-general in the United States army. A. Lincoln. To E. M. Stanton, Secretary of War." They shook hands and Grinnell took the slip of paper over to the War Secretary, who had previously told him: "Your case is like thousands. What we want now is victories, not brigadiers," and on Grinnell's saying that he would regret having to resort to the President, "Get your request granted and I will resign."

To the War Secretary Grinnell now handed the slip of paper. "I will resign," said the War Secretary, crushing the paper and tossing it into a wastebasket. Grinnell lingered a moment, was turning to go when the War Secretary smiled, for the first time smiled into Grinnell's face, and said, "Wait, Mr. Grinnell, come over and take dinner with me." In due form the appointment was made later, and the man proved himself worth it. And Stanton did not resign.

Stanton at one point had told Grinnell: "We are in a crisis. I refuse, sir, to make a promise even to *consider* the wish of a civilian at this time." Lincoln understood what Stanton in many like cases was doing. He wrote to an editor who had complained of Stanton, a Democrat: "I wish to correct an erroneous impression of yours in regard to the Secretary of War. He mixes no politics whatever with his duties." When the pre-eminent Republican general, Frémont, was dismissed, Grinnell was speaking for himself and other Republicans as he laid a budget of grievances before the President for so freely appointing Democrats to army commands.

"Young man, forget your annoyances," said Lincoln. "They are only as flea-bites to mine. They are serious comedy, while I am in the focus of tragedy and fire. You folks up on the [Capitol] hill must aid me in placating those congenital Democrats whom we want to keep fighting for us if they will. We must coyly give rope if we have to make a short turn later. I remember of the New York 'Barnburners' it was charged that to get clear of the rats they burned the barn. We must put up with vermin intrusion to save the barn." Referring to recent good news, he added, "The croakers are getting hoarse, the spies scarce, the maligners well-known."

Grinnell came once with the specific grievance that a constituent of his, a clerk in the Interior Department, was being frequently insulted by another department clerk, "a real rebel," and the more bold in his insults because he had a brother, a member of Congress, whom the Secretary of War would be slow to offend. Grinnell noted: "As I opened my grievance, Mr. Lincoln laid his hand on my shoulder and said, 'Don't ask me to strike so low. I have to do with those whom I despise, for we are at war. Democratic aid we must have if possible, and I conciliate to avoid all friction. There is General McClernand from my state, whom they say I use better than a radical, and the devotees of Douglas I honor and praise often, as I would have promoted their chief had he lived. There is too much of mixing war and party in the field, when real fighting out of the trenches would better suit the case.'" Of the last point, noted Grinnell, "I knew he was alluding to McClellan."

David R. Locke, under the pen name of Petroleum V. Nasby, was writing sketches that had a national audience laughing at issues of the day. He flattened pompous patriots with his comic potshots:

> 1st. I want a offis.
> 2d. I need a offis.
> 3d. A offis wood suit me; there4
> 4th. I shood like to hev a offis.

Beneath Locke's mockery shone affection, and the President wrote to the satirist: "Why don't you come to Washington and see me? Is there no place you want? Come on and I will give you any place you ask for—that you are capable of filling—and fit to fill." Locke was interested. The President had read some of his writings and was so pleased that in a generous outburst he wrote that Locke could have "any place he asked for."

Then, as Locke analyzed it, after signing the letter the President saw that he was offering too much to a man he knew only through newspaper sketches, so the saving clause was added, "that you are capable of filling,"

Abraham Lincoln, November 15, 1863

Photograph by Gardner, from the Barrett collection

Charles Anderson Dana   Thomas Thompson Eckert

Edwin McMasters Stanton, Secretary of War

From the Barrett collection

and, to guard himself entirely, "that you are fit to fill," Locke did go to see Lincoln, but not to ask for a place. "He gave me an hour of his time," said the humorist, "and a delightful hour it was."

Almost in the tone of Artemus Ward, Lincoln told a well-dressed man who sought earnestly a pass to Richmond: "Why, my dear sir, if I should give you one it would do you no good. I have given McClellan more than two hundred thousand other passes to Richmond, and not a single one of 'em has gotten there yet!"

Not so gay was the handling of another well-dressed man of sixty years who asked merely that the President allow the use of his name for advertising a project in view. "No!" flashed the President. "No! I'll have nothing to do with this. Do you take the President of the United States to be a commission broker? You have come to the wrong place. There is the door!" The caller slunk away without a word.

A governor of a State entered Lincoln's office bristling with complaints as to his State quota and enforcement. He had seen Adjutant General Fry and then gone to Stanton for a session of loud angry words. Now he was going to have it out with the President. Fry in his office, and in charge of this special subject, sat for hours expecting orders from the White House or at least a summons to explain matters. He was surprised to see the Governor come in with a pleasant smile to bid good-by. Fry soon reached Lincoln, to ask what he had done with the Governor. "He went to your office in a towering rage. I suppose you found it necessary to make large concessions to him, as he returned from you entirely satisfied."

"Oh, no, I did not concede anything," Fry noted the President's explanation. "You know how that Illinois farmer managed the big log that lay in the middle of his field! To the inquiries of his neighbors one Sunday, he announced that he had got rid of the big log. 'Got rid of it!' said they, 'how did you do it? It was too big to haul out, too knotty to split, and too wet and soggy to burn; what did you do?' 'Well, now, boys,' replied the farmer, 'if you won't divulge the secret, I'll tell you how I got rid of it—I ploughed around him.'"

"Now," said Lincoln to Fry, "don't tell anybody, but that's the way I got rid of the Governor. I ploughed around him, but it took me three mortal hours to do it, and I was afraid every minute he'd see what I was at."

To a party leader or a State official the President would write or wire, "Please send me a nomination," or an indication of which office he had at his disposal. "I can give you collector, but not assessor," he wired Jesse O. Norton at Joliet, Illinois. "Which will you have for collector Ellsworth or McIntosh? Answer at once." He aimed appointments so far as possible to smooth, lubricate, and strengthen the Federal organization for carrying on the war. The exceptions were usually for the sake of a friend or a personal attachment. The *New York Tribune* had urged that postmasters be chosen by vote of the Republicans in any given district. Lincoln followed this rule in some cases, but the Union Democrats, the old-line Whigs, the antislavery factions, were often too much at loggerheads for it to be effective. To an appeal that he should unscramble a Missouri omelet he replied: "I appointed one whom I understood to be an editor of the 'Democrat' to be postmaster at St. Louis—the best office in my gift within Missouri. Soon after this our friends at St. Louis must needs break into factions, the 'Democrat' being in my opinion justly chargeable with a full share of the blame for it. I have stoutly tried to keep out of the quarrel, and so mean to do."

An Indiana delegation at the White House to win appointment for Judge Otto of their State as Assistant Secretary of the Interior carried away no promise from Lincoln. Congressman George Julian noted, "Otto was afterward appointed, but Mr. Lincoln then only responded to our application by treating us to four anecdotes."

The President's personal attention to so many of these cases brought the viewpoint Richard Henry Dana wrote to Charles Francis Adams early in '63: "He seems to me to be fonder of details than of principles, of tithing the mint, anise and cummin of patronage, and personal questions, than of the mightier matter of empire."

A letter to Postmaster General Blair in the summer of '63 went far in newspaper publication and discussion of it. The Lincoln opposition howled about it from many places; thousands of soldiers read it, forward and backward, for assurance. In two cases of postmasterships sought for widows whose husbands had fallen in battle, the President had indorsed them and now wrote:

"These cases occurring on the same day brought me to reflect more attentively than I had before done, as to what is fairly due from us here in the dispensing of patronage toward the men who, by fighting our battles, bear the chief burden of saving our country. My conclusion is that, other claims and qualifications being equal, they have the better right; and this is especially applicable to the disabled soldier and the deceased soldier's family."

At the time this letter went forth, William Johnston, a Cincinnati Republican, made a trip to Washington with a verbal message to Lincoln from Governor Tod of Ohio that care must be taken of the Democratic soldiers in the field, that the removal of McClellan was still a sore spot. "One bright moonlight night," said Johnston, "I saw a regiment of Pennsylvanians mostly, marching from the Capitol down Pennsylvania Avenue, yelling at the top of their lungs, 'Hurrah for Little Mac!' and making a pause before the White House they kept up that bawling and hurrahing for McClellan. I went to see Mr. Lincoln early next morning, and asked him if he had witnessed the performance on the previous night. He said he had. I asked him what he thought of it. He said it was very perplexing. I told him I had come to make a suggestion. I told him I would introduce him to a young man of fine talents and liberal education, who had lost an arm in the service, and I wanted him to tell one of his Cabinet ministers to give that young man a good place in the civil service, and to avail himself of the occasion to declare that the policy of the administration was, whenever the qualifications were equal, to give those who had been wounded or disabled in the service of the country, the preference. He said it was an idea he would like to think of, and asked me how soon I would wait on him in the morning. I said any hour; and I went at seven o'clock and found him in the hands of the barber."

While the barber lathered him, Lincoln told Johnston of a colonel killed at Vicksburg, his head carried off by a shell. "He was postmaster and his wife wants the place." And Lincoln asked whether the appointment of the widow would not be a good example in line with Johnston's idea. Johnston agreed, the papers were made out, and Lincoln wrote Blair the letter setting forth the policy involved.

Johnston took the letter for publication in the *Washington Chronicle* the next day, and also rode an ambulance to a camp of 7,000 convalescing soldiers near Washington, where Ohio men called for a speech. He quoted for them the old saying "Republics are always ungrateful," and added, "I can not vouch for the republic, but I think I can vouch for the chief man at the head of the administration." Then Johnston read Lincoln's letter and noted that "the boys flung their hats into the air, and made the welkin ring for a long while."

The short and simple annals of the poor reached the President in many forms. He shared with Brooks the reading of one letter which Brooks copied: "I take my pen in hand to aske yu about the munney cumming to me frum my husband Daniel Spielman who was a solger in the 2d Mariland Ridgment in cumpany C who was kill in a fite with the rebs last fal near Boonsborrow. I haint got no pay as was cummin toe him and none of his bounty munney and have borrered all what I lived on last winter and this summer toe. Now Mr President I can soe and cook and wash and du enny kind of work but I cant get none. See if you cant git me a plaice in one of your hospittles and I will goe rite toe work. But I dont want to leve my little gurl so I want to git a plaice what I can take her toe. I no yu du what is rite and yu will see tu me a pore widder wumman whose husband fote in your younion army Mr President." Had she been literate the widow would have been directly eligible to a post office. Her letter, wrote Brooks, "was sent by the President to the proper department of the Government."

Some cases Lincoln let go with a note to a department head, such as a line to Chase: "Please strain a point for him if you do not have to strain it too far." The President heard one White House caller through and then wrote to Hiram Barney, port collector at New York, of what the man told him: that he had served three months in the war, that he had a son who was a colonel in service, that he had a brother and a first cousin in the war. "His name is Patrick Murphy, and he now seeks employment in the Custom House. I shall be glad if you can find it for him." In a note for another New Yorker the President was more reserved. "This introduces C. Vanderbilt, Jr., son of the Commodore," he wrote the Quartermaster General. "He comes with a business proposition to you. Please give him a fair and respectful hearing, and oblige him if consistent with the service."

Off in Kentucky an old friend was worried lest someone lose place, and

Lincoln wrote to Mrs. Joshua F. Speed, "Mr. Holman will not be jostled from his place with my knowledge and consent." An editor printing government advertising had to be cared for, and Lincoln wrote Stanton: "I wish you would allow the 'Republican' (my paper as you jokingly call it) to be paid for advertising. The non-payment is made a source of trouble to me."

A man came wearing a colonel's uniform, though no longer a colonel, dismissed for drunkenness on duty. Lincoln knew him. The man had a record for valor in battle. He was seated. Lincoln drew his chair near and heard the story. The man wanted back his old rank and place. Lincoln listened. The man finished.

Lincoln stood up, too moved and uneasy to stay in his chair. He took the soldier's right hand in both his own. Then slowly, tears in his voice, he told the man: "Colonel, I know your story. But you carry your own condemnation in your face." They were hard words to say, Judgment Day words. Later in referring to the case Lincoln told James M. Scovel, "I dare not restore this man to his rank and give him charge of a thousand men when he 'puts an enemy into his mouth to steal away his brain.'"

A one-legged soldier on crutches asked for some kind of a job; he had lost his leg in battle. "Let me look at your papers," said Lincoln. The man had none; he supposed his word was good. "What! no papers, no credentials, nothing to show how you lost your leg! How am I to know that you lost it in battle, or did not lose it by a trap after getting into somebody's orchard?" The President's face was droll. The honest-looking German workingman, turned soldier, earnestly muttered excuses. Lincoln saw this was no regular place-seeker. Most of them came with papers too elaborately prepared. The chances were entirely in favor of any one-legged man having lost his leg in battle. "Well, it is dangerous for an army man to be wandering around without papers to show where he belongs and what he is, but I will see what can be done." Then he wrote a card for the man to take to a quartermaster who would attend to his case.

Senator Preston King introduced to the President one Anthony J. Bleecker, who at the President's request read aloud his own credentials that he was just the man for the job. Halfway through the documents Lincoln cried, "Stop! you are like the man who killed the dog," and told of a man knocking the brains out of a vicious animal and then going on with more clubbing. When a neighbor said, "You needn't hit him any more; the dog is dead," the man replied, "Oh, yes, I know that, but I believe in punishment after death."

Bleecker admitted he might be making too strong a case for himself and told of a good priest trying to convert an Indian to Christianity, quoting St. Paul, "If thine enemy hunger, feed him; if he thirst, give him drink." The Indian couldn't see it, but when the priest said, "for in so doing thou shalt heap coals of fire on his head," the Indian fell on his knees and called blessings on the head of his enemy. The priest interrupted the long prayer to say it was more than enough. But the Indian cried, "Oh no, father, let me pray! I want to burn him down to the stump." Bleecker got the job.

Discussing the requirements of an office-holder, Lincoln told of an Andrew Jackson Democrat who received a letter from the postal department denying his application for a post office because of his "proximity" to another office. The Democrat replied that his father had fought for liberty in the War for Independence, and he should like to have "the name of the scoundrel who brought the charge of proximity or anything else wrong" against him.

Another case was a Patent Office amanuensis who refused to answer strangers such simple questions as "Where is the Capitol?" or "Where is the President's house?" A visitor once accused him of ignorance and the amanuensis answered: "Stranger, I was turned out of the post office for knowing too much—I don't mean to offend again. I am paid for keeping this book. I believe I know that much. But if you find me knowing anything more, you may take my head."

Once a humble man came asking to be made doorkeeper to the House and Lincoln let him down and out without hurting his feelings. Their conversation, as published, ran as follows:

"So you want to be Doorkeeper to the House, eh?"

"Yes, Mr. President."

"Well, have you ever been a doorkeeper? Have you ever had any experience in doorkeeping?"

"Well, no—no actual experience, sir."

"Any theoretical experience? Any instructions in the duties and ethics of doorkeeping?"

"Um—no."

"Have you ever attended lectures on doorkeeping?"

"No, sir."

"Have you read any textbooks on the subject?"

"No."

"Have you conversed with anyone who has read such a book?"

"No, sir, I'm afraid not, sir."

"Well, then, my friend, don't you see that you haven't a single qualification for this important post?"

"Yes, I do." And he took his hat and left humbly, seeming rather grateful to the President.

On a problematic application for a position, Lincoln wrote, "I think after all, but am not sure, that he is a drunken loafer." He abolished a false weather prophet when a Mr. C. sent up a card, writing: "It seems to me Mr. C. knows nothing about the weather in advance. He told me three days ago that it would not rain again till the thirtieth of April or first of May. It is raining now and has been for ten hours. I cannot spare any more time to Mr. C." Or again for Nicolay to decipher was the scribble: "O.H.P. trying to resign an office which he does not hold."

On an application for a generalship with no indication of what rank the applicant preferred, Lincoln wrote across the back, "Major General, I reckon." The result of successive interviews with one applicant brought the memorandum: "Today I verbally told Col. Worthington that I did not think him fit for a colonel, and now, upon his urgent request, I put it in writing."

A Harvard College chum of Robert T. Lincoln, Henry M. Rogers, called at the White House one morning and a half-hour later wrote home: "I have to announce that I have just come from the presence of the Mighty Abraham. I arrived at the White House at 9.30, sent in my card and in two minutes was in 'Abe's' presence and alone with him. That was a piece of good luck. He asked me to be seated. I handed him Bob's letter, told the President what I wished, answered two or three questions as to my residence, age, etc., and seated myself by the fire, while he took the letter and a pen. After a few minutes he looked up and laughingly read this indorsement to me—

" 'Mr. Rogers wishes to be an Asst. Paymaster in the Navy. I know not whether there is a vacancy. The within shows that my son "Bob" has a high opinion of him. A. Lincoln.'

"Let me describe to you how 'Abe' looked. When I entered his room, he was seated by the fire in a very comfortable position, apparently very easy in mind and body. On my presenting my letter, he asked me to be seated, took his eyeglasses from his pocket, adjusted them on his ample nose, and slowly read the letter. He then asked me where I was from: said, 'I suppose you are within the required age—under 26.' I told him yes—I was 23. He then seated himself at his desk, seemed thinking how to write, began, and in two minutes read what I have already written. While I was there, Abe's barber came in to adorn and beautify him and I know just where the soap and razor are kept; when I become President I'll keep my soap and razor in the same place! Abe's raven locks were in extreme disorder when I left him; by this time he is probably quite decent. I wrote Bob Lincoln this A.M. thanking him for his letter and telling him the reception I had met with from his Papa. That I shall be obliged to wait a long while, perhaps, I cannot doubt; an appointment to a Massachusetts man is almost a miracle."

The atmosphere of bureaucracy and its difficulties was rendered in a burlesque exchange of courtesies between Lincoln and Stanton, reported as follows:

> Dear Stanton:
> Appoint this man chaplain in the army.
>   A. Lincoln

> Dear Mr. Lincoln:
> He is not a preacher.
>   E. M. Stanton

> Dear Mr. Stanton:
> He is now.
>   A. Lincoln

Dear Mr. Lincoln:
But there is no vacancy.
                                                E. M. Stanton
Dear Stanton:
Appoint him chaplain-at-large.
                                                A. Lincoln
Dear Mr. Lincoln:
There is no warrant in law for that.
                                                E. M. Stanton
Dear Stanton:
Appoint him anyhow.
                                                A. Lincoln
Dear Mr. Lincoln:
I will not.
                                                E. M. Stanton

The appointment of a military governor was sent to the White House with Stanton's signature immediately at the foot of the body of the text. After the President scanned it he asked the clerk who brought it, "Can you tell me whereabouts on this paper I am to put my signature?" The clerk couldn't, and began explaining how it might have happened that the paper was improper in form. Lincoln interrupted: "Take the paper back to the Secretary of War, with my compliments, and say that the President will promptly sign any *proper* commission that may be sent to him."

"He is a pretender, a humbug and a fraud," protested Stanton at one proposed appointment. "Did you ever in all your life see the head of a human being who so closely resembled that of a codfish?" The man won place but was later expelled for fraud and peculation.

When Judge Baldwin of California asked Lincoln for a pass through army lines to visit a brother in Virginia, the President inquired, "Have you applied to General Halleck?"

"Yes, and met with a flat refusal."

"Then you must see Stanton."

"I have, and with the same result."

"Well, then," drawled Lincoln, "I can do nothing; for you must know I have very little influence with this administration." In this case it was a pleasantry with Lincoln. The same remark to a soldier's widow, who asked for a sutler's appointment, was a sorry fact.

The Governor of Pennsylvania and others requested a month of additional time for recruiting a Philadelphia regiment. Lincoln joined his endorsements to the document, under which Stanton wrote, "There is good and valid reason for not extending the time, and the Secretary of War refuses to do it." Both Stanton and Lincoln under furious pressure were coming to understand each other. The Secretary sent an army officer back to the White House with a presidential order for reconsideration. Lincoln at his desk, with an office full of callers, saw the officer, stepped forward and took him to a corner of the room, where he heard that Stanton wished him to reconsider the order. "Stanton is careful and may be right," said the

President. "I was very busy when I examined the case, but I will take the papers, reëxamine, and by four o'clock this afternoon send them by messenger to your office." Before the hour he mentioned Lincoln had revoked his own order and approved Stanton's view.

Commenting to a Cabinet member on how he and Stanton got along, Lincoln said: "I cannot always know whether a permit ought to be granted, and I want to oblige everybody when I can; and Stanton and I have an understanding that if I send an order to him that cannot be consistently granted, he is to refuse it, which he sometimes does. And that led to a remark which I made the other day to a man who complained of Stanton, that I hadn't much influence with this administration, but expected to have more with the next."

When they discussed brigadier appointments one day, going over applications and recommendations, Lincoln said he concurred in about all that Stanton proposed. "The only point I make is, there has got to be something done that will be unquestionably in the interest of the Dutch, and to that end I want Schimmelfennig appointed."

"Mr. President, perhaps this Schimmel-what's-his-name is not as highly recommended as some other German officers."

"No matter about that. His name will make up for any difference there may be, and I'll take the risk of his coming out all right." Then with a laugh he spoke each syllable of the name distinctly, accenting the last: "Schim-mel-fen-*nig* must be appointed."

A speculator pressed for a pass through army lines and a Treasury license to buy cotton. He was steadily refused. "Few things are so troublesome to the government," Lincoln had remarked, "as the fierceness with which the profits in trading are sought." This particular trader brought influence to bear on Lincoln, who signed the permit requested and told the man, "You will have to take it over to Stanton for countersigning."

Later the trader came back, in a heat, telling how Stanton had torn to pieces and stamped his feet on the paper signed by the President. Lincoln put on a surprised look and asked the man to tell exactly how the Secretary had acted. Then, pausing a moment or two, he told the speculator, "You go back and tell Stanton that I will tear up a dozen of his papers before Saturday night."

Congressman Samuel Shellabarger asked Lincoln to transfer young Lieutenant Ben Tappan from volunteer to regular service, on staff duty, retaining his rank. Stanton favored the appointment, though army regulations forbade the procedure, and had only declined to act because he was an uncle by marriage of the Lieutenant. Lincoln told Shellabarger a story, observed that the army was getting to be all staff and no army, examined the papers in the case, wrote a brief statement of it, signed his name to a record of his stand in the case, in substance: "If the only objection to this transfer is Lieut. Tappan's relationship to the Secretary of War, that objection is overruled." Shellabarger noted: "This threw the responsibility of breaking the regulation on Stanton. We never heard anything more about the transfer."

A widow from Tennessee came to Stanton with papers regarding her only son, a college boy who had enlisted in a Confederate regiment and was taken North as a prisoner, with wounds. She asked the War Secretary to give him a release, on parole, from the hospital at Fort McHenry. He heard her as he worked at his desk, swung round in his chair, and pressed out the words: "So, *you* are the woman who has a son prisoner of war in Fort McHenry."

"I am so unfortunate."

"I have nothing to say to you, and no time to waste on you. If you have raised up sons to rebel against the best government under the sun, you and they must take the consequences."

The boy was only seventeen, had enlisted without her knowing it or saying Yes to it. She tried to explain this and was interrupted:

"I don't want to hear a word from you. I want you to go at once. I'll do nothing for you."

She left sobbing, later was told to try Lincoln, found him alone in his office. "Take this seat, madam, and then tell me what I can do for you."

He read the papers she handed him, turned somberly, and asked, "Are you, madam, the unhappy mother of this wounded and imprisoned son?"

"I am."

"And do you believe he will honor his parole if I permit him to take it and go with you?"

"I am ready, Mr. President, to peril my personal liberty upon it."

"You shall have your boy, my dear madam. To take him from the ranks of rebellion and give him to a loyal mother is a better investment for this government than to give him up to its deadly enemies."

He wrote an order for the release. "There! Give that to the commanding officer of Fort McHenry, and you will be permitted to take your son with you where you will; and God grant he may prove a great blessing to you and an honor to his country."

Stanton was often hard, and Lincoln saw that only a hard man could meet the crowds who filled the War Office from day to day. The newspaper correspondent George Alfred Townsend told of Stanton meeting the seekers:

"What do you want?" to a woman.

"I want a pass to see me husband in Camp X."

"You can't go. Next!"

"I want permission to copy the papers in the Smith court martial."

"What for?"

"To make an appeal."

"Come again tomorrow. I'll think about it."

"But—"

"Come tomorrow. (In a high key) Pass on! Next!"

"I want a pass to Y— to find the body of my son."

"Let me see your letter of recommendation . . . Yes! You will have it.

Stand aside there! What are you doing here?" (To an officer with a star on his shoulder straps—a General.)

"Why, Mr. Secretary, I thought I'd look in—"

"Go to your brigade! If I find you in this District within six hours I'll put you in the Carroll prison amongst the common deserters. Go! Next man."

The next man puts up a paper and says, "I want that!"

"That you shall have. Orderly, take him to General Townsend. Next!"

The correspondent who recorded this scene joined with Henry Ward Beecher and others in believing that the towering figure of the war was Stanton; the correspondent wrote: "The President jested, the Secretary of State gave dinners, the Secretary of the Treasury had ambition, the Secretary of the Interior was for himself. Stanton was the one man forever alive to the fact that bloody rebellion was to be gashed, stabbed, fought, humiliated, and, if need be, made a dreadful spectacle of retribution."

A plan for mingling Eastern and Western troops was urged on Lincoln by a committee headed by Lovejoy of Illinois. Lincoln wrote a note to Stanton suggesting a transfer of regiments. "Did Lincoln give you an order of that kind?" asked the Secretary.

"He did, sir," replied Lovejoy.

"Then he is a damned fool!" said Stanton.

"Do you mean to say the President is a damned fool?"

"Yes, sir, if he gave you such an order as that."

At the White House Lovejoy told what happened. "Did Stanton say I was a damned fool?" asked Lincoln.

"He did, sir, and repeated it."

The President was thoughtful. "If Stanton said I was a damned fool then I must be one. For he is nearly always right, and generally says what he means. I will step over and see him."

Noah Brooks wrote to the *Sacramento Union* of how one day in the office of the Superintendent of Public Printing he saw a tidy-looking young woman enter with a card signed "A. Lincoln" telling Superintendent Defrees: "The bearer, a poor girl, has a brother in our lines, as a prisoner of war, who wishes to take an oath of allegiance. Be good enough to look into the facts and report to me." From the tidy-looking young woman came a story that her brother was forced into Confederate military service early in the war, that he had been unable to escape to the Union lines, that she believed his claim that he was a Union man from the first and should be released on his taking the oath of allegiance. "The girl had been turned away by the surly officials of the War Department," wrote Brooks, "but had got access to the President, whose kind heart was at once enlisted, and he determined that justice should be done, so he sent the sister of the prisoner to the kindly Defrees, who likes to do a generous act."

Chase picked a man, Mark Howard, for revenue collector of the First District of Connecticut. Senator Dixon from that State brought the Senate to refuse confirmation. Chase, in something of a rage, urged Lincoln to send the name of his man to the Senate again, or wait till the Secretary picked another. Lincoln wrote to Chase that, "with a good deal of pain that it is adverse to your wish," he had concluded it was best to name Edward Goodman, recommended by one Senator and one Congressman from Connecticut. "I will thank you, therefore, to send me a nomination, at once, for Mr. Goodman." Chase on receiving this wrote out a stiff, dignified letter closing: "I respectfully resign the office of Secretary of the Treasury."

Before Chase could send the letter Senator Dixon called on him. "The result of our conversation," Chase wrote the President, "was an agreement to call on you as soon as practicable, and submit the matter to your further consideration. I do not insist on the renomination of Mr. Howard; and Mr. Dixon and Mr. Loomis, as I understand, do not claim the nomination of his successor." To this Chase added a little lecture on "the principle" which should be established "to secure fit men for responsible places."

Thurlow Weed told Leonard Swett that Lincoln kept "a regular account book" of his appointments in New York, "dividing favors so as to give each faction more than it could get from any other source, yet never enough to satisfy its appetite." In giving out offices or favors, the President had one guiding principle, as Swett saw it: "An adhesion of all forces was indispensable to his success and the success of the country; hence he husbanded his means with nicety of calculation. Adhesion was what he wanted; if he got it gratuitously he never wasted his substance paying for it."

Swett was speaking for himself and for many other old friends of Lincoln. "They all had access to him, they all received favors from him, and they all complained of ill treatment; but while unsatisfied, they all had 'large expectations,' and saw in him the chance of obtaining more than from anyone else whom they could be sure of getting in his place. He never wasted anything, and would always give more to his enemies than he would to his friends; and the reason was, he never had anything to spare, and in the close calculation of attaching the factions to him, he counted upon the abstract affection of his friends as an element to be offset against some gift with which he must appease his enemies. Hence, there was always some truth in the charge of his friends that he failed to reciprocate their devotion with his favors. The reason was, that he had only just so much to give away. 'He always had more horses than oats.'"

Late at night after a long talk with Lincoln at the Soldiers' Home on the quarreling political factions in Missouri and Kentucky, Swett was saying good-by. They were parting at the door as Lincoln said, "I may not have made as great a President as some other man, but I believe I have kept these discordant elements together as well as anyone could."

Charges came from various Republicans and army officers of New Mexico that the Territorial supreme court chief justice, Kirby Benedict, was not merely a tippler but a toper, unfit for the bench. Kirby was a Douglas Democrat appointed to the bench by President Pierce in 1853. Until then Benedict had for many years practiced law in Illinois, where Lincoln knew him as one of the best of storytellers, a literary artist, a rare bird of human fellowship. To the Republican politicians, the army officers, the New Mexico Territorial delegate in Congress, the President's reply to their charges was quoted: "Well, gentlemen, I know Benedict. We have been friends for thirty years. He may imbibe to excess, but Benedict drunk knows more law than all the others on the bench in New Mexico sober. I shall not disturb him." Usher Linder wrote of Lincoln "besieged" to appoint a Republican in place of Benedict and "Mr. Lincoln told them Benedict was too good and glorious a fellow for him to lay violent hands upon; that he could not find it in his heart to do so, and he wouldn't; nor did he."

The light and flavor of Judge Benedict's mind, which lingered with Lincoln, was in a remarkable death sentence pronounced by the Judge who said, in part, to the murderer: "José Maria Martín, it is now the springtime, in a little while the grass will be springing up green in these beautiful valleys, and, on these broad mesas and mountain sides, flowers will be blooming; birds will be singing their sweet carols, and nature will be putting on her most gorgeous and her most attractive robes, and life will be pleasant and men will want to stay; but none of this for you, José Maria Martín; the flowers will not bloom for you, José Maria Martín; the birds will not carol for you, José Maria Martín; when these things come to gladden the senses of men, you will be occupying a space about six by two beneath the sod, and the green grass and those beautiful flowers will be growing above your lowly head."

Senate and House in March of '63 took action, approved by the President, which swept out of existence the Circuit Court of the District of Columbia, its judges, its powers. In its place Congress and the President put a new tribunal, the supreme court of the District of Columbia, with four new judges appointed by the President, and sitting as chief justice David Kellogg Cartter of Ohio, one of the strategists who had led in nominating Lincoln for President at the Chicago convention of 1860. The District lawyers, almost to a man, remonstrated. A formidable minority in Senate and House clamored that if the judges of the old court were treasonable and corrupt they should be impeached; it was a new and tyrannical way of removing judges hostile to an Administration. Only by 19 to 16 votes did the act pass the Senate, winning in the House by 86 to 59. The majorities who jammed through the bill, with short shrift in the House for several anxious debaters, wanted in the long shadows of the Capitol building a court beyond suspicion of loyalty to the Union. The accusations of treason directed at the old court, of sympathy with secession and with slavery, had been heard too long, they said. So they legislated the old court out of business, authority, and salaries—and put in a new court that satisfied them as to loyalty.

The finely tested loyalist Senator Thomas H. Hicks of Maryland demurred. "Do not attempt to break in on our judiciary system that has been tried for so long a time and worked well." And Senator Henry Wilson of Massachusetts countered as to the chief judge of the old court, "I believe his heart is sweltering with treason," Senator Sumner holding it "notorious" that disloyal officials and a disloyal population in the District were obstructing the Government. Senator Ira Harris of New York pointed to all sorts of patchwork that Congress for many years had carried on as to this "complicated, incongruous" court, and how there was one vacancy on the bench of the old court, another judge was entirely superannuated, and the new court would actually displace only two judges. The bill passed the House on March 3, 1863, and on the same day Nicolay brought notice that the President had "approved and signed" the bill.

Lamon suggested to Lincoln that he appoint their old friend David Davis of Bloomington, Illinois, to the office of Commissioner of Patents. This met instant refusal—early in the Administration.

When Justice McLean of the Supreme Court died late in 1861, friends of Davis moved to place him on the high bench. Old Eighth Circuit lawyers became active. Swett spoke for him personally to Lincoln. Lawrence Weldon wrote to Lamon: "Why not David Davis, especially when he was so instrumental in giving position to him who now holds the matter in the hollow of his hand? Dear Hill, if justice and gratitude are to be respected, Lincoln can do nothing less than to tender the position to Judge Davis. I want you to suggest it to Lincoln." Hawkins Taylor, an Iowa delegate to the Chicago convention which nominated Lincoln, wrote to the President: "I will say that in my honest opinion, with every opportunity of knowing, that but for the *extraordinary* effort of Judge Davis, you would not have received the nomination at the Chicago convention. I can say to you that I consider your nomination providential. It is due to yourself as well as to Judge Davis that you should tender him the appointment of Supreme Judge."

Letters of Judge Davis during this period held deep disgust at the President's appointments in general, one in particular bringing the comment *"De gustibus non disputandum est"*—"There is no disputing about tastes." Once Davis had written Lamon that he believed he would prefer a Federal district judgeship rather than to go on the supreme bench. "I know I could discharge the duties of the one satisfactorily, but am diffident about the other." Months passed, a year, a year and a half—and Judge Davis saw no move of Lincoln to appoint him. Meanwhile Secretary Cameron named Davis a member of the Board of Visitors to the United States Military Academy at West Point, also a member of a commission to investigate expenditure and fraud in Frémont's army in Missouri.

On the last day of the October term of court in 1862 Davis notified the members of the McLean County bar to meet him in the old courthouse at Bloomington. He spoke to them: "My official connection with the people and bar of this circuit is about to terminate. The President has tendered me an appointment as Associate Justice of the Supreme Court of the United States which I shall accept, although distrustful of my abilities to discharge the duties of the office."

Davis called the roll on the little group of lawyers who during so many years had been chums and boon companions. Three had become judges, two of them United States Senators, one wounded and two killed in battle, one President of the United States.

Davis went on to Washington, where he wrote in a letter, "Mr. Lincoln is very kind, but care worn."

CHAPTER 36

FOREIGN MEDIATION—BUTLER

AS early as September of '62 the two dominant men of the Government of Great Britain had agreed that if the Union Army lost again to Lee they would offer mediation, hoping to step in and umpire the difficulty. As umpires they would like to swing recognition of the Confederacy. If that failed, they would go ahead anyhow and recognize the Confederacy.

This private concert of the suave Russell and the cynical Palmerston was in Russell's note of September 17, 1862, to Palmerston: "I agree with you that the time is come for offering mediation to the United States Government with a view to the recognition of the independence of the Confederates. I agree further that in case of failure, we ought ourselves to recognize the Southern States as an independent State."

Then the hope and intention of the two grim and crafty statesmen, who wished to lend the British Navy to the Davis Government, went glimmering when Lee's army was thrust back at Antietam, followed by Lincoln's preliminary Emancipation Proclamation, which added heat and power to a massed British public opinion that Russell and Palmerston had to consider.

"We may wait a while and see what may follow," the cynical Palmerston wrote to the suave Russell.

Raymond of the *New York Times* wrote in his diary one evening in January, '63, that on the way to Albany he had for a fellow passenger Horace Greeley, who said that he, Greeley, would bring the Government to foreign mediation. The plan, as Greeley arranged it with the French Minister at Washington, was for Switzerland, as a neutral nation, to conduct an arbitration.

Pope Pius IX, it was known at this time, favored mediation by an unimportant smaller country "with no interest in diminishing the power of the United States."

"You'll see," Greeley prophesied as he and Raymond journeyed to Albany, "I'll drive Lincoln to it."

Already Greeley had published articles in the *Tribune* urging that this scheme would end the war, implying too that the people of the North would welcome such an action. However, when Emperor Napoleon III in February did send to the United States Government a proposal for a conference aimed to reconcile the warring sections in America, the plan was promptly declined by President Lincoln. Seward, as Prime Minister of the United States, sent a note to the French Foreign Minister with a long polite argument making clear that his Government could not enter into diplomatic discussions while putting down an armed insurrection.

Again *Punch* of London sees Lincoln worried and losing the game while Jeff Davis is smiling and winning—the English journal's tone being in agreement with that of defeatist Horace Greeley in the *New York Tribune*

The Senate joined with declarations that the United States was grappling with an unprovoked and wicked rebellion which sought the ruin of the Republic that it might found a new Power whose cornerstone should be slavery; while so engaged any proposal from a foreign government aiming to keep the Union fleets and armies from their objectives would be looked on as an unfriendly act. The President was requested to have these resolutions laid before foreign governments.

Thus while Greeley's activities had helped spread an impression that the Washington Government was on its last legs and ready to talk peace, the *Tribune* editor had intensified the issue and brought out declarations that cleared the air. Meantime Napoleon III granted a private audience to Minister Slidell of the Confederacy and gave assurances that M. Arman of Bordeaux, the largest shipbuilder in France, could go ahead and build four ironclad war vessels of the type of the *Alabama*, provided their destination be kept secret. The French Minister of Marine protested, was overruled by the Emperor, and reluctantly signed the order authorizing the building of the ships; thus Slidell wrote to the Confederate Secretary of State, Judah P. Benjamin, in the spring of 1863.

Before these ships were completed, however, Napoleon III ordered that they be sold to neutral countries; he declared he had learned that the ships were to be ironclad and armed, which would be a violation of the laws of war; so the vessels were sold to Prussia, Denmark, Peru—and Confederate hopes of more swift destroyers on the high seas went glimmering.

Bribery, spying, tampering with confidential clerks and messengers, were practiced by William L. Dayton, the United States Minister at Paris, or his agents, while deception and crooked diplomacy marked the course of the French Emperor and his Ministers, according to James D. Bullock, naval representative of the Confederate States in Europe, writing in explanation of his diplomatic failures.

Intervention in America was a leading topic of diplomatic conversations in Europe. Leaders in England and France who favored recognition of the Confederacy found Russia a hindrance. Late in '62 a personal letter from President Lincoln was transmitted to the Russian Foreign Minister, Gorchakov, at St. Petersburg, by Acting American Minister Bayard Taylor. Their conversation was published by order of Congress, though Lincoln's letter to Gorchakov was not made known.

"Russia alone has stood by you from the first, and will continue to stand by you," said Gorchakov. "Proposals will be made to Russia to join in some plan of interference. She will refuse any invitation of the kind. You may rely upon it, she will not change." From none of the Great Powers of Europe had the United States been able to win so positive a declaration. In this decision Russia was aligning herself against England and France, who had fought her so recently in the war in the Crimea. Also Russia had no such textile industries as England and France, suffering from cotton famine.

Across Europe ran two extremes of opinion, with many moderate views intermingled. The liberal John Bright of England favored a united country in America, sent a letter to the Chamber of Commerce of New York. Bright wished it known that "there is no other country in which men have been so free and so prosperous as in yours, and that there is no other political constitution now in existence, in the preservation of which the human race is so deeply interested." The conservative London *Dispatch* phrased its view: "The real motives of the civil war are the continuance of the power of the North to tax the industry of the South, and the consolidation of a huge confederation to sweep every other power from the American continent, to enter into the politics of Europe with a Republican propaganda, and to bully the world." Occasionally abroad the mystic cause of American Union blazed forth, as when the French author M. Pelletan in his work *La nouvelle Babylone*, bemoaning the degeneracy of the modern Parisians, paused to exclaim:

" 'The Americans of the North,' 'the Yankee,' the 'Clown,' the 'worshipper of the almighty dollar,' behold what he does when the slaveholding South, as if to fasten upon the negro the tyranny of climate, tears the bond of Union. For a simple metaphysical idea—the Union; for a dozen of stars more or less on a stripe of bunting, the American of the North offers upon the altar of his country his last man and his last dollar. He takes the rifle himself, ready to die for abstract justice. He learns the art of war, as the France of the Republic did under the fire of the enemy; he hesitates at first, he loses the battle at first; but be sure he wins the day at last. Do you know any grander spectacle—any fairer apotheosis of freedom?' "

An international world opinion favoring the North was Seward's steady objective. Often he brought to Lincoln's desk designs and schemes for approval on matters of broad policy. The President and his State Minister spent more and more time together, grew in respect and affection. "The President is the best of us," Seward had written to his wife. Often on Sunday mornings they had long talks, came nearer being cronies than any other two of the Cabinet.

Raymond wrote in his diary of a dinner and smoking party at Seward's house: "Of President Lincoln he spoke in the strongest terms of praise. With all his defects, he said, he seemed just the man for the crisis. Patient, capable of endurance, just and tolerant beyond example, he said that Providence had raised him up for this emergency as signally as He raised up Washington for the necessities of our struggle for independence."

Foreign policy overlapped domestic affairs and military conduct when a hullabaloo was raised in England and France over General Butler's order that any female insulting Union soldiers or officers or the American flag in New Orleans should be treated as "a woman of the town plying her vocation." Lincoln and Seward attached more weight to specific protests against Butler which came from foreign consuls in New Orleans and from the Dutch Minister in Washington. Taking possession of a metropolis filled with a hostile population, and bringing order, health, and obedience, gave Butler a conqueror's problem, including street mobs, which he threatened to clear away with artillery; a sanitation policy to combat yellow fever; burnings of property by unknown instigators; women who spit in officers' faces; spies; destitution; hoodlums yelling at him as "Old Cock-Eye."

Calling fifty slaveholders into the parlors of the St. Charles Hotel, Butler told them, "I am a Democrat, and shall always be a Democrat; and I tell you I will burn every house in the State of Louisiana, and put every negro's right hand upon every master's throat, before I will take down that [Union] banner and go home." Butler armed free Negroes, levied on rich secessionists for needs of the poor. He arrested and put on trial William Mumford, leader of Confederate patriots, who had climbed up on the mint, hauled down the United States flag, and torn it into rags with curses and jeers.

In answer to the défi that he would not dare hang Mumford, Butler erected gallows in front of the mint, in accordance with an old Spanish custom that a doomed man should die near the scene of his crime. The drop was sprung and the body dangled before the eyes of a large crowd, who had shouted until it was done that Butler would not dare do it. Three burglars dangled from rope ends, a gesture of Butler's to looters. He seized $800,000 of currency deposited in the office of the Dutch consul, claiming it was for purchase of Confederate arms; the Federal Government at Washington ordered the money returned to the Dutch. Amid a revel of corruption where newcomers from the North gathered large and small fortunes for themselves, Butler so managed that no accusation could be made to stick to him personally.

"I know of but one fault to be found with General Butler," wrote George S. Denison, a Treasury Department official, to Secretary Chase. "He has (in my opinion) been altogether too willing to permit his friends to make fortunes." Denison was in charge of matters connected with the raising of the blockade and the renewal of trade at New Orleans. He reported to Chase that Andrew J. Butler, a brother of General Butler, was in the city, and known as Colonel Butler, though he occupied no position in the army: "Government officers, citizens, and rebels, generally believe him to be the partner or agent of General Butler. He does a heavy business and by various practices has made between one and two million dollars since the capture of the City. . . . General Butler knows everything, controls everything, and should be held responsible for everything. . . . He has great ability, shrewdness, and activity, and industry, but he can never acquire a character here for disinterestedness."

Chase wrote to Butler about speculations and trading with the enemy by the General's brother Andrew J. Butler showed Chase's letter to Denison, who reported to Chase: "The General confidentially says that his brother's gains have been less than Two Hundred Thousand—that he has done only a legitimate business—that without being interested he assisted his brother at first with his (the General's) credit—and that Colonel Butler will close his business as quickly as possible and go home."

Removed from command of the Department of the Gulf and replaced by General Nathaniel P. Banks, Butler arrived off Cape Hatteras in January, '63. Met by a naval revenue cutter, Butler was handed a note from President Lincoln. It read, according to Butler: "I really wish to see you at the earliest moment. I am contemplating a peculiar and important service for you." At the White House when they met Lincoln was cordial, Butler reserved.

"Mr. President, will you please tell me for what acts of mine I am recalled from New Orleans?"

"I am not at liberty to tell you, but you may ask Mr. Stanton. I should be very happy to see you to-morrow for a consultation."

Butler went to Stanton, who would not tell; to Seward, who referred him to Halleck; to Halleck, who said the removal was "solely under the direction of the Secretary of State." Commercial reasons, Butler learned later, had led to his removal, Seward's circular to foreign Ministers noting that General Banks's administration in New Orleans would "relieve the condition . . . of uneasiness" affecting foreign powers.

Frederick Seward commented: "Claims and complaints at New Orleans, based upon interruptions and losses in trade, were numerous. Some were intricate and delicate, and even threatened to endanger friendly relations with European powers." Butler said he wished Seward or Stanton could have the courage to declare publicly, "General Butler has been recalled at the request of the Emperor Napoleon." He told Lincoln he would turn in his commission, quit the service.

The President asked Butler to put the commission back in his pocket, to go down on the Mississippi River, take command there, enlist, arm, and organize as many Negro troops as could be had. Butler urged to be put back at New Orleans. The President walked back and forth, gave an appealing look to Butler. "I cannot recall Banks." Butler said the removal of himself, a Democrat, replaced by Banks, a Republican, was a mistake to be blamed on Seward, who could not understand that Butler had higher reputation as an antislavery man than Banks. "The position that I have taken in my farewell address at New Orleans, which I shall stand by, will cause me to be looked upon as at the head, next to yourself, of the anti-slavery cause."

They parted with handshakes, the President saying, "You shall go where you please, General, but keep your commission." Butler went home to his family in Lowell, where he soon had a letter from Senator Sumner with a half-promise: "I . . . saw the President, who said that he hoped very soon to return you to New Orleans." Stanton wrote Butler that he too had seen the President, who hoped soon to return him to New Orleans.

And while Butler waited there in Lowell, Wendell Phillips in a speech inquired: "Why is General Butler idle? Who can tell? Abraham Lincoln can't; he says he knows nothing about it. [Laughter.] General Halleck can't; he says he knows nothing about it. William H. Seward can't; he says he knows nothing about it. One of the best generals in the service, the man who held the third city in the empire in his right hand like a lamb, that man comes home to the Capital, and cannot find a man in the Cabinet who will take the responsibility of saying, 'I advised his recall,' or will tell him the reason why he was recalled. [Three cheers for Butler.] Why is he, one of the ablest of the very few able men this war has thrown to the surface,— why is he idle?"

Admiral Farragut wrote home that it seemed to him a proper time for a milder system of administration in New Orleans. "But I am satisfied that Butler was the man to begin. Banks brought me an autograph letter from the President, and says the President told him to rely on my 'judgment,' 'discretion,' etc., and we are likely to get along very well."

Also while Butler waited at home and had no word from Lincoln, Chase's man Denison, at New Orleans, wrote that Banks was a conciliator, was losing the Union grip on the city, and Butler was the man needed. "In two weeks he could restore everything, but I do not suppose he will be sent here, for he is too earnest a man to suit Mr. Seward, and if placed in a high position, he might become dangerous as candidate for the Presidency."

Lincoln, however, did make a decision to return Butler to his old place. He wrote Stanton on January 23, 1863: "I think General Butler should go to New Orleans again. He is unwilling to go unless he is restored to the command of the department. He should start by the 1st of February, and should take some force with him. The whole must be so managed as to not wrong or wound the feelings of General Banks. . . . I think we cannot longer dispense with General Butler's services."

So definitely was Lincoln's purpose set to appoint Butler to the old command that he drafted a lengthy letter to inform General Banks in a kindly way that while Banks headed an expedition into Texas, Butler would take charge of the Emancipation Proclamation in Louisiana; for this work there was "no such man as General Butler," and "In beginning the peculiar work alluded to there should not be an hour's delay. Hence I send him at once." This draft of a letter to Banks Lincoln left undated. As time passed he did not send it to Banks. Nor did he appoint Butler to New Orleans again.

But the President's regard for the importance of the Massachusetts political General, who had by now somersaulted from his Breckinridge-proslavery position into the out-and-out abolitionist ranks, was shown in a curious personal credential that Lincoln wrote: "Major-General Butler, bearer of this, visits the Mississippi River, and localities thereon, at my request, for observation. The Military and Naval Commanders, whom he may meet, will please facilitate his passage from point to point, and make him as comfortable as possible during his stay with them respectively. I will thank them also to impart to him such information as they may possess, and he may seek, not inconsistent with the military service."

But this was not used. Butler did not go. Later the President was to find another niche for the rapidly reversible politician-warrior who had dramatized himself into the affections of the spotless Wendell Phillips.

In Missouri, Tennessee, parts of Virginia and North Carolina, where the Union flag again floated, new rulers held sway. Andrew Johnson had resigned from the Senate to become Military Governor of Tennessee, to live under threats from proved marksmen while trying to bring back a legislature, courts, and processes of law that had gone underground with the trampling of armies. "The archives have been desecrated," he reported, "the public property stolen and destroyed; the vaults of the State Bank violated and its treasures robbed, including funds gathered for the instruction of our children."

From Washington came word that the President believed Johnson had the constitutional power to appoint two Senators from Tennessee; Johnson decided not to use the power. Lincoln heard that Johnson was thinking of raising a Negro military force and he wrote Johnson not to dismiss the idea, as it would have weight coming from "an eminent citizen of a slave State." Johnson was able to do little with the plan, though Lincoln declared to him, "The bare sight of fifty thousand armed and drilled black soldiers on the banks of the Mississippi, would end the rebellion at once."

The argument over the President's authority to set up military governments in conquered areas went on in Congress, in the press, on platform and stump, on sidewalks, in homes and saloons, on railroad cars and steamboats. Thaddeus Stevens declared in February of '63 that the President had ordered men to be elected to take their seats in Congress, had also directed what kind of men should be elected, "which, perhaps, was right enough, or we might have been overrun by secessionists." Stevens inquired, however, as to why squadrons of cavalry had been sent to some counties in Virginia "to protect the ballot box and those voting" when it happened that "the secessionists attacked them and drove them off."

In such a case Stevens would have the President forget the Constitution: "I say that you cannot justify nine out of ten of the acts of the Government, or of our own acts here, if you consider the Constitution a valid and binding instrument with reference to those in arms in the rebellious States." To this Congressman Olin of New York added that in wartime in occupied territory, the President had the power to do what must be done. Necessity alone justified him. "Of that necessity," said Olin, "the President is alone the judge, as the commander-in-chief of the army."

Three Congressmen from the new State of West Virginia had welcome from Stevens. Cox of Ohio said they held their seats in violation of the Constitution, Stevens replying that the Constitution and martial law were not at war with each other. The two Congressmen elected from Louisiana, however, were objectionable to Stevens; he had said so when they were seated by the previous Congress; he said so again and pressed for rejection of their credentials; he did not wish to be discourteous, but would expel them; they were from a conquered province that had not extinguished slavery. Blair of Missouri said Stevens "takes very good care of his bantling," Stevens breaking in: "I take care of nobody. . . . I do not care much for anybody. . . . I call the gentleman to order."

The statements of testimony, arguments as to justice and procedure, bills of particulars, charges and countercharges, brought to the White House verbally or in writing would have filled many shelves and filing cases.

Without shift or modification of his original thesis, Thad Stevens held that the ruling class of the South must be killed off or driven out forever, and every Negro be given some such allotment as a mule and a 40-acre farm: "I advocated at the outset of the war, the arming of the negroes, the slaves of the rebels, as the only way left on earth in which these rebels can be exterminated."

Stevens predicted that within two years the gentlemen in Congress would adopt his view: "They will find that they must treat those States now outside the Union as conquered provinces and settle them with new men, and drive the present rebels as exiles from this country; for I tell you they have the pluck and endurance for which I gave them credit a year and a half ago, in a speech which I made, but which was not relished on this side of the

House, nor by the people of the Free States. They have such determination, energy and endurance, that nothing but actual extermination or exile or starvation will ever induce them to surrender to this Government."

Thus foreign and domestic affairs of a wide and kaleidoscopic character came under Lincoln's eye during early '63, toward the close of two years of war. In letters and speeches of the time were many guesses that the war would not end during Lincoln's Administration.

The hope of the President that he might find a 10 per cent of people in the Southern States who would take the oath of loyalty to the Union, and form a basis for reconstruction, was named "Lincoln's ten-per-cent plan." The oath itself never ceased to have both solemn and humorous phases. Newspapers in North and South enjoyed giving their readers an incident from the *Kentucky Daily Democrat* at Louisville. Near Nashville a dashing Southern girl was among women brought before General Rosecrans for the oath of loyalty:

"The bold, bright-eyed Juno in question objected to taking the oath, saying that her mother had taught her that it was wrong to swear; that her social education had instructed her that it was unladylike to swear; her sense of morality forbid her to swear, and swear she could and would not.

"The officer insisted that the lady must take an oath before she left his presence.

" 'Well, General,' said bright eyes, 'if I must swear, I will; but all the sin of the oath must rest on your shoulders, for I swear on your compulsion: G—d d—n every Yankee to h—l!'

"And the defiant beauty tossed her dark curls, and swept out of the presence unmolested."

CHAPTER 37

HOOKER—CHANCELLORSVILLE— CALAMITY

SO cool, so droll, was Seward at his best, writing to Bigelow amid the up-roar of early '63: "We are wearing through our contest here very well—according to present appearances. It is quite amusing to see ourselves laid aside and buried by our mourning friends in Europe, and enjoy most, the charitable obituaries that are pronounced over our remains. All the more so because we think we shall excite an agreeable surprise when we pronounce in the ears of the mourners the soothing assurance that we still live."

The Army of the Potomac in early '63 had lost—on the Peninsula, twice at Bull Run, and again in the slaughter at Fredericksburg. It had, however, kept enemy bayonets out of Washington and the Free States. And other Northern armies, with naval co-operation, had captured all the Confederate strongholds—except Forts Sumter and Morgan—on the seacoast from Fortress Monroe in Virginia to points in Texas. Rosecrans was marching close to the Alabama line, Grant was in Mississippi, Curtis in Arkansas, Banks at New Orleans.

The *Richmond Examiner*, reviewing the scene on January 20, 1863, said, "The pledge once deemed foolish by the South, that he would 'hold, occupy and possess' all the forts belonging to the United States Government, has been redeemed almost to the letter by Lincoln."

In this month, however, major generals of the Army of the Potomac talked about the Government's crumbling and a military dictator's being needed. "The loyal North," said *Harper's Weekly*, was "filled with sickness, disgust and despair" over "unequivocal evidences of administrative imbecility." Such massacres as that at Fredericksburg must not be repeated: "Matters are rapidly ripening for a military dictatorship."

A renewed play of commentary, a sharpened political activity, rose from extremist Democrats wholly against the war. Sumner wrote Franz Lieber in January: "These are dark hours. There are senators full of despair,—not I. The President tells me that he now fears 'the fire in the rear'—meaning the Democracy—especially at the Northwest—more than our military chances."

Burnside, under the weight of his command of the Army of the Potomac, was crumbling. He frankly said to the President that the Secretary of War and the General in Chief had lost the confidence of the soldiers, and he himself "ought to retire." To a letter from Burnside resigning as major general, Lincoln replied, "I do not yet see how I could profit by changing the command of the Army of the Potomac." And to show publicly his faith in Burnside the President told a *New York Times* correspondent, for publication: "Had Burnside had the same chances of success that McClellan wantonly cast away, today he would be hailed as the savior of his country."

Raymond of the *Times* visited the army, asked a Michigan colonel why Burnside was estimated so low among officers and men, and heard that it was because Burnside rated himself so low. This might be only the natural modesty of a truly capable man, Raymond suggested. Yes, said the colonel, that was true, but Burnside had not only *spoken* of his incompetency, but had gone before a congressional committee and *sworn* to it. This was extraordinary conduct. Burnside was peculiar in his integrity, in his unabashed admissions that he was a poor instrument for what was to be done.

When Burnside wrote for publication a letter taking all blame on himself for the Fredericksburg disaster, Lincoln told him that he was the first man found who was willing to relieve the President of a particle of responsibility. Then Burnside and Lincoln went to see Stanton, who delivered the chilly remark, "You have not published the letter which you promised the President you would publish."

And as Raymond of the *Times* gathered the incident: "General Burnside said that Stanton's rebuke made him angry. He told the Secretary this was wholly a private matter between him and the President—that he should do as he pleased about it. He then left the room. But soon after the President sent for him [Burnside], and told him the Secretary wished to see him. He returned and Mr. Stanton handsomely apologized." Stanton had learned that the letter was mailed and on its way to publication before his rebuke of Burnside.

Burnside planned a night attack on Lee's army. The pontoon corps would march to the river, lay bridges across the Rappahannock; the cavalry, artillery, foot troops, would follow, and smash Lee. Generals Baldy Smith and Franklin came to Burnside's tent and argued for hours that the enemy was too strong, their own troops not in fighting mood.

Burnside insisted, and on the night of January 20 as the army started rain began slowly, a wind came up, the rain turned to sleet, horses and wagons sank in the mud and were stuck for all night; men and mules failed to make headway with the pontoons, also with the unhitched cavalry steeds and the early morning ration of whisky ordered by Burnside for every man.

After breakfast at staff headquarters the next morning General Hooker talked with a newspaperman about how the commanding General was incompetent, the President and Government at Washington were imbecile and "played out," a dictator was needed and the sooner the better.

What with failure in the field, grumbling and mutiny among officers and men, Burnside was harassed and weary as he told Raymond on January 23, "I'm not going to resign." Instead of that he would go to Washington and lay before the President his orders for dismissal of Generals Hooker, Franklin, Smith, Sturgis, Woodbury, Newton, Cochrane; the President would approve the orders or he, Burnside, would resign as major general. That Hooker might raise a mutiny among his troops was suggested to Burnside, who replied that he would "swing him before sundown if he attempted such a thing."

Burnside telegraphed the President he would be at the White House the next day at one o'clock. He and Raymond left army headquarters for Falmouth at half-past eight at night in an ambulance. In mud and fog they lost the road, found it again, lost it once more, stumbled over dead mules and upset caissons, and in three hours had traversed the three miles to Falmouth. The special locomotive ordered by the General had left for other duty farther up the line; orders were telegraphed for it but it did not come.

Burnside and Raymond walked the railroad track, the General carrying a lantern. Two miles up the track, Burnside signaled the returning engine, which took them to Aquia, where they boarded a steamboat for Washington. They arrived at six in the morning.

Before nine o'clock Burnside, having interviewed the President, was at breakfast with Raymond at Willard's. He said his announcements to the President of the orders he intended to issue had come upon the President "like a clap of thunder, and the President was very doubtful as to the result." At half-past ten in the morning Burnside left for his army.

Raymond looked up Chase, and went with the Secretary and his "bright, lively, and agreeable" daughter to a White House levee that evening. "I found a great crowd surrounding Mr. Lincoln," wrote Raymond. "I managed, however, in brief terms, to tell him that I had been with the army, and that many things were occurring there which he ought to know. I told him of the obstacles thrown in Burnside's way by his subordinates, and especially of General Hooker's habitual conversation. He put his hand on my shoulder, and said in my ear, as if desirous of not being overheard, 'That is all true—Hooker does talk badly; but the trouble is, he is stronger with the country today than any other man.' I ventured to ask him how long he would retain that strength when his real conduct should be understood. 'The country,' he answered, 'would not believe it; they would say it is all a lie.'"

Burnside resigned, was persuaded to withdraw his resignation, was relieved of duty, and on January 25, 1863, the President ordered Hooker to the command of the Army of the Potomac.

Chase was pleased; so were members of the Committee on the Conduct of the War; so were many people attracted by his fighting quality and a touch of the dramatic and impetuous about Hooker. "Now there is Joe Hooker," Nicolay heard the President say. "He can fight. I think that is pretty well established—but whether he can 'keep tavern' for a large army is not so sure."

Welles wrote in his diary that he had at one time recommended Hooker to Lincoln but had since changed his opinion. "Who can take command of this army?" Lincoln had asked him months before. "Who is there among all these generals?" Welles had not expected that he, a navy man, should have such a question plopped at him, and had given offhand the name of Hooker. The President looked approving, but said, "I think as much as you or any other man of Hooker, but—I fear he gets excited," looking around as he spoke. Welles covered a retreat with remarking, "If his habits are bad, if he ever permits himself to get intoxicated, he ought not to be trusted with such a command." The appointment of Hooker being made, Welles wrote, "I am surprised at his selection."

Whether or not the President indirectly negotiated with McClellan to come to Washington was anybody's guess. Welles wrote in his diary: "Blair . . . tells me he visited McC. last winter with a view of bringing him here to take Halleck's place. The President was aware of his purpose. McC. assured him he had no Presidential aspirations; his desire was to be restored to his old military position. When B. returned from his successful mission to New York he found his plans frustrated, and the President unwilling to give them further consideration."

Stanton was not among those who had advocated Hooker. A War Department man said: "Stanton knew there were two Hookers in the same man. He knew one as an excellent officer, mentally strong, clever and tireless, and charming, even magnetic, in address. It was the other Hooker on whom he wished to take no chances." When Hooker was named, Stanton considered resigning, but stayed on and surprised Hooker by his ready co-operation.

Hooker himself had not played politics to win the appointment. How-ever, an observer on the inside at army headquarters, Charles F. Benjamin, noted: "There were men about Hooker who believed in, and hoped to rise with him, and these men were rich in personal and external resources of the kinds needed for the combination of political, financial, and social forces to a common end." Joined with these efforts was "the unselfish labor of earnest men" who believed in Hooker's fighting qualities, and who appreciated his freedom from undue attachment to McClellan.

The political manipulations in behalf of Hooker stood no chance against Stanton's complete disapproval of Hooker until, as Benjamin phrased it, "connection was made with a powerful faction which had for its object the elevation of Mr. Chase to the Presidency at the end of Mr. Lincoln's term."

The factors were delicate as a problem in chess. "Making every allow-ance for the strength and availability of Mr. Chase, as against Mr. Lincoln or any other civilian candidate, his friends did not conceal from themselves that the general who should conquer the rebellion would have the disposal of the next Presidency, and they were on the lookout for the right military alliance when they came into communication with Hooker's friends and re-ceived their assurances that, if it should be his good fortune to bring the war to a successful close, nothing could possibly induce him to accept other than military honors in recognition of his services. General Hooker there-upon became the candidate of Mr. Chase's friends. Hooker probably knew of these dickerings. Certainly Stanton did, through a friend in Chase's own circle."

Whether or not the event was another in which Lincoln's born sagacity had outrun Chase's cultivated intelligence, under the shift that took place "Mr. Chase found his situation as sponsor for the new commander embar-rassing. As a member of the Cabinet he could freely express his views with reference to any military question coming up for Cabinet discussion, and upon any matter introduced to him by the President he had fair opportunity of making a desired impression; but further than this he could not go with-out disclosing a personal interest inconsistent with his place and duty."

Lamon urged Lincoln to look well to the fact that there was a scheme on foot to depose him, and to appoint a military dictator in his place. Lincoln laughed and said, as Lamon quoted him: "I think, for a man of accredited courage, you are the most panicky person I ever knew; you can see more dangers to me than all the other friends I have. You are all the time exer-cised about somebody taking my life,—murdering me; and now you have discovered a new danger; now you think the people of this great govern-ment are likely to turn me out of office. I do not fear this from the people any more than I fear assassination from an individual. Now, to show you my appreciation of what my French friends would call a *coup d'état*, let me read you a letter I have written to General Hooker." He opened the drawer of a table and took out and read a letter which was sent to Hooker—

a letter dated January 26, 1863, not made public then but later published and widely discussed:

"General: I have placed you at the head of the Army of the Potomac. Of course I have done this upon what appear to me to be sufficient reasons, and yet I think it best for you to know that there are some things in regard to which I am not quite satisfied with you. I believe you to be a brave and skilful soldier, which of course I like. I also believe you do not mix politics with your profession, in which you are right. You have confidence in yourself, which is a valuable if not an indispensable quality. You are ambitious, which, within reasonable bounds, does good rather than harm; but I think that during General Burnside's command of the army you have taken counsel of your ambition and thwarted him as much as you could, in which you did a great wrong to the country and to a most meritorious and honorable brother officer.

"I have heard, in such a way as to believe it, of your recently saying that both the army and the government needed a dictator. Of course it was not for this, but in spite of it, that I have given you the command. Only those generals who gain successes can set up dictators. What I now ask of you is military success, and I will risk the dictatorship. The government will support you to the utmost of its ability, which is neither more nor less than it has done and will do for all commanders. I much fear that the spirit that you have aided to infuse into the army, of criticizing their commander and withholding confidence from him, will now turn upon you. I shall assist you as far as I can to put it down. Neither you nor Napoleon, if he were alive again, could get any good out of an army while such a spirit prevails in it; and now beware of rashness. Beware of rashness, but with energy and sleepless vigilance go forward and give us victories."

Not long after receiving the letter, Hooker stood with his back to a cozy fireplace in his log-and-canvas army hut. And looking quizzically at his only companion, Noah Brooks, newspaper correspondent, he said, "The President tells me that you know all about the letter he wrote to me when he put me in command of this army." Mr. Lincoln had read the letter to him, admitted Brooks. "Wouldn't you like to hear it again?" asked Hooker, drawing it from a pocket. Brooks told Hooker that he would enjoy the letter again, although he had been so impressed by its first reading that he believed he could repeat most of it from memory.

Hooker read, pausing to demur at one point: "The President is mistaken. I never thwarted Burnside in any way, shape or manner." Resuming the reading, Hooker's tone softened, and he finished the reading almost with tears in his eyes as he folded the letter, put it back in the breast of his coat, saying: "That is just such a letter as a father might write to his son. It is a beautiful letter, and, although I think he was harder on me than I deserved, I will say that I love the man who wrote it."

Then Hooker added, "After I have got to Richmond, I shall give that letter to you to have published."

A handsome soldier, Hooker looked warlike for those to whom war is color, dash, valor. Blond of hair, with wavy ringlets, with a flushed and rosy face, forty-nine years of age, he was tall, blue-eyed, had a martial air. A West Point graduate, brevetted captain for bravery at Monterey in the Mexican War, he was a farmer and superintendent of military roads on the West Coast when the war began. Calling at the White House after the first battle of Bull Run, and explaining his position on the war, that he was ready for service, and that he had been out looking over the scene of the Manassas rout, he said to Lincoln, "I was at Bull Run the other day, Mr. President, and it is no vanity in me to say I am a damned sight better general than you had on that field."

Hooker had a tongue. So many mentioned it. "Hooker is a fool, and always was, and that's a comfort," wrote one Confederate West Pointer to another—a report that probably came to Lee, measuring his new opponent. "Brave, handsome, vain, insubordinate, plausible, untrustworthy," were the hand-picked adjectives F. W. Palfrey used as to Hooker. They were all true but others were equally true, for he was at times, and at his best, precisely what Chase described him, "a frank, manly, brave, and energetic soldier." But Chase added the reservation "of somewhat less breadth of intellect than I had expected."

So often came a reservation in the judgments of Hooker. "He could play the best game of poker I ever saw until it came to the point when he should go a thousand better, and then he would flunk," said a cavalry officer. "Handsome and picturesque in the extreme, though with a fatally weak chin," said a general.

And yet time and again Hooker had led his division into slaughter where men fell by platoons and his lines held their ground. At Williamsburg on the Peninsula under McClellan he had 2,228 killed and wounded. The nickname came of "Fighting Joe" Hooker. Shot in the foot at Antietam, he stayed in the saddle on the field with his men till the fighting was over.

Having sat with Hooker through a dinner party, John Hay commented on one point: "Hooker drank very little . . . yet what little he drank made his cheek hot and red & his eye brighter. I can easily see how the stories of his drunkenness have grown, if so little affects him as I have seen."

A gay cavalier, easy, confident, nonchalant, in his talks with the President over his new command he was "cheery as a boy," Noah Brooks noted. With frequency the words came from him "When I get to Richmond" or "After we have taken Richmond."

Lincoln was near groaning as he said in confidence to Brooks: "That is the most depressing thing about Hooker. It seems to me that he is overconfident."

Hooker had a conference with Lincoln in the White House one evening the first week in March, Lincoln saying with his good-by, "General, we shall expect to have some good news from you very soon." Then the President had turned to a young New Jersey cavalryman, Sergeant J. M. Stradling. "What can I do for you, my young friend?" A permit was wanted to ride a steamer to Aquia Creek, and join up with the cavalry again, after

LINCOLN'S DREAM; OR, THERE'S A GOOD TIME COMING.

Having removed several important heads, Lincoln dreams of more to come to the block and the ax—as a cartoonist sees it in early '63 when Hooker is named to follow Burnside, McClellan, and McDowell, who met disaster

furlough. John Hay had written across a card: "To any steamboat captain going to the front, please give bearer transportation," which Lincoln signed and, handing it to Stradling, said, "If I have any influence with the steamboat captains, I think that will take you to the front."

The young Sergeant was about to step out of the room when Lincoln said to Senator Wade and two others: "Senator, we have had the head of the Army here a few minutes ago, and learned from him all he cared to tell. Now we have here the tail of the Army, so let us get from him how the rank and file feel about matters. I mean no reflection on you, Sergeant, when I say the tail of the Army."

The President then spoke of many men deserting that winter. There must be some good cause; the army was opposed either to him, to the generals, or to the Emancipation Proclamation, and he was very desirous of learning from the rank and file about conditions. "None of the Generals desert or resign, and we could spare a number of them better than we can spare so many privates." He asked the Sergeant to enlighten him on any of these points.

Stradling had been flustered at first, but now felt that the President wanted him to speak frankly, even if what he had to say was not pleasing. He began: "Mr. President, so far as I know, the Army has the utmost confidence in your honesty and ability to manage this war. So far as I can learn, the army had no faith in the ability of General Burnside. . . . He . . . fought his battles like some people play the fiddle, by main strength and awkwardness." Senator Wade asked if there was any excuse for such a blunder as Fredericksburg. Lincoln spoke up, "This is very interesting to me, so please go ahead." The Sergeant explained that the country was an open one, with no real mountains or rivers; both flanks of the Confederate army could have been turned. "Even we privates wondered why such an attack was made. General Burnside must have known of the sunken road, for we of the cavalry had been over this road with General Bayard in 1862, and he must have informed General Burnside all about it. If General Burnside had possessed any military genius, he would have flanked Lee out of that strong position, and fought him where he could have had at least an equal chance."

The President was talking with a man of the ranks, in somewhat the tone and manner he used with many of them, hundreds every month, and he said, as Stradling wrote it in a letter, and told it to comrades at mess and on the march: "What you have stated, Sergeant, seems very plausible to me. When General Hooker left us but a few minutes ago, he said, 'Mr. President, I have the finest army that was ever assembled together, and I hope to send you good news very soon.' That is just the language General Burnside used when he left me shortly before the battle of Fredericksburg. And such a disaster that followed still makes my heart sick."

The frank Sergeant, opening his mind and heart, said: "Mr. President, even privates when on the ground cannot help seeing and wondering why certain movements are made. I refer to the charges of General Hooker on our right. [Hooker had demurred against making these assaults but Burnside had insisted.] Our duty, however, is not to criticise, but to obey even if we get our heads knocked off. I have found that soldiers are willing to obey without hesitation and take the chances when they feel that their show is equal to that of the enemy."

"You have said nothing about how the soldiers feel towards the Emancipation Proclamation," suggested Lincoln.

"Mr. President, I approach the Emancipation Proclamation with great reluctance, for I know how your heart was set on issuing that document. So far as I am personally concerned, I heartily approve of it. But many of my comrades said that if they had known the war would free the 'niggers' they would never have enlisted, so many of them deserted. Others said they would not desert, but would not fight any more, and sought positions in the wagon train; the Ambulance Corps; the Quartermaster's Department, and other places, to get out of fighting."

The President, Senator Wade, and the other gentlemen must have wondered what they had before them in such a straightaway talker. So thought the Sergeant. But he went on: "I was born a Quaker, and was therefore an anti-slavery young man when I entered the army. When I was a boy I attended from two to three debating societies a week, and the slavery question was always under debate in one form or another. I had heard the question debated and helped debate it for two or three years before I entered the army, and was therefore a full-blooded abolitionist, and welcomed the proclamation with open arms. The issuing of the proclamation caused many to desert, no doubt, and the presence of General Burnside at the head of the army caused many others to leave."

Sergeant Stradling had finished his say. The President sat still a moment or two, then said: "Sergeant, I am very glad indeed to have had your views. I am glad to know how many of your comrades feel about slavery, and I am exceedingly glad you have mentioned the Emancipation Proclamation, for I shall take this opportunity to make a few remarks which I desire you to convey to your comrades.

"The proclamation was, as you state, very near to my heart. I thought about it and studied it in all its phases long before I began to put it on paper. I expected many soldiers would desert when the proclamation was issued, and I expected many who care nothing for the colored man would seize upon the proclamation as an excuse for deserting. I did not believe the number of deserters would materially affect the army. On the other hand, the issuing of the proclamation would probably bring into the ranks many who otherwise would not volunteer. After I had made up my mind to issue it, I commenced to put my thoughts on paper, and it took me many days before I succeeded in getting it into shape so that it suited me."

The President, during all of the conversation, Stradling noted, was a woebegone man. "He did not smile, and his face did not lighten up once." The President went on: "Please explain to your comrades that the proclamation was issued for two reasons. The first and chief reason was this, I felt a great impulse moving me to do justice to five or six millions of people. The second reason was that I believed it would be a club in our hands with which we could whack the rebels. In other words, it would shorten the war. I believed that under the Constitution I had a right to issue the proclamation as a 'Military Necessity.' I have faith that it will shorten the war by many months. How does the rank and file view General Hooker?"

A hard fighter, said the Sergeant. "The boys have great respect for him, as well as great faith in his ability."

"I thank you very much," said the President, with a handshake, "and I trust you will reach the front in the morning."

And Sergeant Stradling left the White House, slept on sacks of oats aboard the same steamer that carried General Hooker in its cabin that night. He wrote home of his visit to the Executive Mansion: "I was awful glad to get out, and when I did get away I felt as though I had been to a funeral. Senator Wade did smile once or twice, and so did the other two gentlemen who were present, but Lincoln did not even show the shadow of a smile. His long, sad and gloomy face haunted me for days afterward."

Slowly across weeks of February, March, April, the gloom of the Army of the Potomac changed toward gaiety. Hooker had found at the close of January that in round numbers 3,000 officers and 82,000 men of the ranks were absent; they were on the rolls of the army, but not answering roll call. Some were sick, wounded, on furlough. Others had run away. Homesickness, gloom, and a general feeling of uselessness had brought an average of 200 desertions a day during the winter; relatives and friends sent express bundles to their loved ones, citizen's clothing for escape. Under the new rule express trains were searched, all citizen's clothing burned.

A new regime operated. Steadily a sulky army became willing and eager to fight. It lay at Fredericksburg, a day's phaeton or buggy ride from Washington, so that important public men came for personal inspections, accompanied by their wives and daughters in crinoline.

Early in April Hooker said that under his command was "a living army, and one well worthy of the republic." He also rated it "the finest army on the planet." He had 130,000 troops against Lee across the river with 60,000.

The President kept in constant touch with the forging and welding of this new weapon for smiting the Confederacy, sending Hooker such communications as "Would like to have a letter from you as soon as convenient" and "How does it look now?" On April 3 he notified Hooker that he would arrive at the Fredericksburg camp on a Sunday and stay till Tuesday morning. "Our party will probably not exceed six persons of all sorts." They left the Washington navy yard in a little steamer, the *Carrie Martin*, with Lincoln, his wife, Tad, Attorney General Bates, Dr. Anson G. Henry, and Noah Brooks on board. A driving snow and heavy stormy weather forced them to anchor for the night in a little cove in the Potomac opposite Indian Head.

Brooks recorded that he could not help thinking "that if the rebels had

Joseph ("Fighting Joe") Hooker

Federal field hospital at Savage Station, Virginia, June 30, '62. These troops wounded at Gaines' Mill June 27, and their medical attendants, became prisoners of war when Confederates moved into this area

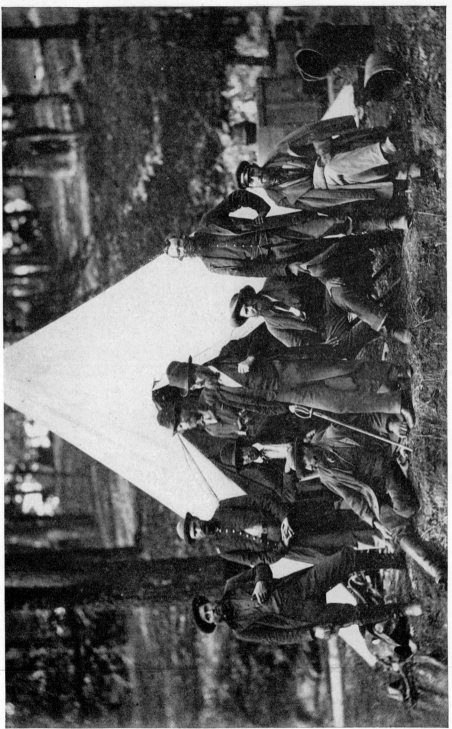

Army of the Potomac scouts

Photograph by Alexander Gardner, from the Gardner Album No. 1 in the Barrett collection

made a raid on the Potomac at that time, the capture of the Chief Magistrate of the United States would have been a simple matter; there were no guards, no precautions against a surprise."

Dr. Henry and Brooks sat up with Lincoln till long after midnight, telling stories, discussing politics and the war in a free and easy way. Dr. Henry had yawned, dozed, and gone to bed. Lincoln was alone with his tested friend, a newspaper correspondent to whom he made comments which Brooks could not think of publishing or of repeating in conversation.

Lincoln's voice dropped almost to a confidential whisper, saying, "How many of our ironclads do you suppose are at the bottom of Charleston Harbor?" This was the first intimation Brooks had that the long-talked-of naval attack on Fort Sumter was to be made that day. The President had been jocular and cheerful during the evening but now talked about possible defeat. He would not be encouraged by Brooks. "He went on to say," noted Brooks, "he did not believe that an attack by water on Charleston could ever succeed. He talked a long time about his 'notions' as he called them, and General Halleck's plans. He went off to bed saying, 'I have no faith in it. It is too late.'"

In the morning, April snow still falling, they arrived at Aquia Creek water front, lined with transports and government steamers unloading supplies for 130,000 men and 60,000 horses and mules. A crowd of army people cheered the arrival of the President, cheered again when his party was put on board a plain freight car with rough lumber benches, gay with flags and bunting. At the army camp a cavalry escort took the party to Hooker's headquarters. Lincoln insisted on going to the nearest hospital tent, stopping to speak with nearly every one of the sick and wounded, shaking hands with many, asking a question or two here and there, and leaving a kind word as he moved from cot to cot.

"More than once," noted Brooks, "as I followed the President through the long lines of weary sufferers, I noticed tears of gladness stealing down their pale faces; for they were made happy by looking into Lincoln's sympathetic countenance, touching his hand, and hearing his gentle voice; and when we rode away from the camp tremendous cheers rent the air from the soldiers, who stood in groups, eager to see the President."

At Hooker's headquarters Lincoln asked for "rebel papers," which came through the picket lines when the armies were not in action. He turned the pages, scanned the columns, finding no news as to Charleston. One day after searching through the *Richmond Whig* several times without coming across a paragraph which he had been told was in it, he was pleased to have a correspondent point it out to him. "It is plain that newspapers are made for newspaper men; being only a layman, it was impossible for me to find that." He read an editorial predicting that Charleston would never surrender. "If taken it will be only a heap of ruins." He telegraphed the full text of the editorial to the Secretary of the Navy.

Brooks mentioned to Lincoln one evening at headquarters after a day of riding at army inspection that the President was looking rested and in better health. "It is a great relief to get away from Washington and the politicians," was the answer. "But nothing touches the tired spot."

On another evening in Hooker's hut, according to Brooks, the President looked cautiously about, saw that they were alone, and in a half-jocular way took out from a pocket a small piece of paper and handed it to Brooks. On it were written the figures "216,718—146,000—169,000." Brooks studied the numbers with puzzled wonder, when the President explained that the first figures represented the sum total of the men on the rolls of the Army of the Potomac, that the second were those of the actual available force, and the last represented the numerical strength to which the force might be increased when the army should move.

"You can send that by letter to California, by and by, if you want," said the President. "It can't get back here in time to do any harm. But don't you ever let on that I gave you those figures. They'd hang me for giving information to the enemy."

Once in the course of a chat with Hooker, Lincoln said, "If you get to Richmond, General—" and was interrupted by Hooker: "Excuse me, Mr. President, but there is no 'if' in this case. I am going straight to Richmond if I live." Later in the day Lincoln remarked mournfully to Brooks, "It is about the worst thing I have seen since I have been down here." By letter and by word he had tried to impress on Hooker that the objective was Lee's army and not Richmond, that Richmond would be easy to enter at any time when Lee's army was not in the path.

An ambulance took Lincoln, Brooks, and army men for an eight-mile ride out to a corps review. Six mules pulled the ambulance over a rough corduroy road that jolted the passengers. At his wild mules the driver let fly volleys of oaths. Lincoln leaned forward, touched the driver on the shoulder, and said:

"Excuse me, my friend, are you an Episcopalian?"

The surprised driver looked around. "No, Mr. President, I am a Methodist."

"Well, I thought you must be an Episcopalian, because you swear just like Governor Seward, who is a church warden."

The driver stopped swearing. The ambulance plunged through jack oak and scrub pine. Lincoln pointed to stumps where an axman had done clever work, "a good butt"; or again to poor chopping.

Tad said he must see "graybacks," Confederate soldiers. Two staff men took Tad and his father on a frosty morning down to the picket line opposite Fredericksburg. They saw hills and a city war-swept, mansions and plain homes in ruins, farms desolated by shot, axes, wagon ruts, corduroy roads. Smoke rose from enemy campfires just above a stone wall where Burnside's men by thousands had weltered in blood. From a house that stood whole out of the wreckage floated a flag—the Confederate Stars and Bars. This was one of the few moments that Lincoln had gazed on that flag while it fluttered amid the protective bayonets of men ready for all sacrifice in order to make it an emblem of authority and dignity.

Two Confederate pickets stood near a tall chimney across the river, one wearing a light-blue United States Army overcoat. They yelled to Tad and his father derisively that the Yanks had been "licked" at Fort Sumter. A Confederate officer heard the yelling, came down to the riverbank, and looked across the river with a field glass. Whatever he made out through his glass and whether or not he saw and recognized the tall form of the President of the United States and Commander in Chief of the Northern armies, the officer struck an attitude of dignity, took off his hat, made a long sweeping bow, and retired. On the night before Lincoln's arrival at the Union camp, a Confederate picket on his side of the river had called out asking if "Abe and his wife" had come yet.

Tobacco, coffee, newspapers, and jackknives were being traded across the river between Confederate and Union pickets. They spoke good morning and saluted each other as "butternut" and "bluebelly." A Confederate officer sent across a photograph of himself for a West Point classmate in the Union forces. It was shown to Mrs. Lincoln, with its autograph and the notation "a rebellious rebel." She said that logically the inscription meant that the officer was a rebel against the rebel Government. Lincoln smiled and gave his view that the officer was determined everybody should know he was not only a rebel, but a rebel of rebels, "a double-dyed-in-the-wool sort of rebel."

An ambulance took the President and his wife one day suddenly into a settlement of hastily slung together shanties and tents on a hillside, a camp of colored refugees. The entire population of blacks and mulattoes swarmed out crying shrill hurrahs for "Massa Linkum." Mrs. Lincoln asked how many of "those piccaninnies" he supposed were named Abraham Lincoln.

"Let's see; this is April, 1863. I should say that of all those babies under two years of age, perhaps two-thirds have been named after me."

On horseback and wearing a high silk hat the President rode alongside General Hooker at troop reviews. The ritualism and pageantry, the pomp and circumstance of tribesmen and warriors, effects built up and developed across many centuries, were there: drums, trumpets, fifes, brass bands for tempo and rhythm, spick-and-span uniforms encasing men drilled to evolutions that would shape them into mobile units subordinate to a central mind and will.

From a reviewing stand the President, Hooker, and the staff watched 17,000 horsemen file past, the biggest army of men and horses ever seen in the world, said Hooker, bigger even than the famous cavalry body of Marshal Murat with Napoleon. Mud flew from the horses' feet. The ground was soft with melting snow. On the fringe of the cavalry cloud came Tad, in charge of a mounted orderly, his gray cloak flying in the wind like a plume. The infantry filed past the eyes of the President, four corps, 60,000 men, a forest of moving rifles and bayonets. Then came the reserve artillery force, some 400 cannon.

Zouave regiments in baggy red trousers, crack drill troops, marched and made a contrast. The President asked General Hooker if fancy uniforms were not undesirable because they made better targets, the General replying that these uniforms had the effect of inciting a spirit of pride and neatness among the men.

"It was noticeable," recorded Brooks, "that the President merely touched his hat in return salute to the officers, but uncovered to the men in the ranks."

Hour on hour in platoons and in company front, the Army of the Potomac, a sad army that had seen rivers of blood and anguish to the depths, marched by for the Commander in Chief in the reviewing stand, surrounded by his generals, the best choices that personal judgment and military traditions could give him. They sat in a chilly wind of late winter impinging on spring. They saw mustaches, whiskers, sideburns, Galways, and goatees, gilt braid and epaulets, endless brass buttons and polished rifle barrels. They saw color-bearers come past with shot-riddled flags, emblems with burnt holes in the silk and the language of lead and steel nicked and torn on the hickory staffs.

"The President, mounted upon a large bay had entered the field followed by a brilliant throng of generals, colonels and lesser officers," wrote the *New York Herald's* eyewitness. "The lancers with their fluttering pennants and a troop of orderlies galloped after. The troops marched upon the field with no confusion nor noise except the music of the bands, the tramp of the regiments and the brief orders of the officers. Hours slipped by and the dark blue masses on the plateau grew larger, the flags more numerous and the rattle of drums more bewildering. The artillery came out and the great guns that thundered at the heights of Fredericksburg pointed their muzzles over the white tents in the hollows; and the little rifle cannon drew up briskly beside them, as if proud of the work they did near Richmond, at Antietam and over the pontoons down by the river.

"The columns were all in line, the men waited and grew impatient; the horses, to amuse themselves in the cold, kicked each other's shins. The wind swept across the open country, stinging the fingers of the soldiers, playing mad pranks with caps, tugging at the flags upon the tall bending staffs as if impatient at the delay and the troops began to fall out one by one to bestir themselves into warmth.

"Suddenly a volume of smoke burst up from the right, followed by another and then another while the sullen boom of guns rolled across to the left, and announced the commencement of drama. The infantry bands burst into 'Hail to the Chief' and Mr. Lincoln turned his attention to the infantry review. While one corps was saluted and being saluted, the other rested upon their arms, while the rear ranks fell out and danced fantastic jigs in the cold to the rattle of drums in the distance. . . .

"Out upon a little swell of upland were crowded the President and his staff of generals, and over all the plain stretched the columns of the army. In the distance were the camps, the river, the spires of Fredericksburg and the frowning batteries beyond; behind, miles of mud-walled villages, long white-topped baggage wagons, and cannon on the hills. Now and then the sun came out and lighted up the field with flashes that seemed almost supernal, bringing glimpses of visions and splendor that vanished and seemed as a mirage. The sun danced on the bayonets and rifles and lingered in the folds of the flags; then the shadows drifted over the plains and melted away with the music.

"Steadily the tide of veterans surged onward. The front was lost in the winding valleys leading to the quiet camps and the rear still waited on the knoll, while the columns, one by one, continued to swing off and around before the President and lost themselves in the distance. The afternoon wore on and the regiments, like sea waves, swept after each other regularly as before; the wind grew restless, the sunbeams lost themselves among the soldiery and Mr. Lincoln sat wearily upon his horse, tired of the ceaseless tramp. The last regiment came, dipped its colors. A number of ladies remained and came upon the field in fanciful costumes. Now and then were glimpses of crinoline and curls in the ambulances and once in a while a fair equestrienne dashed along the plain to the admiration of young officers and to the envy of their less fortunate sisters. Artists were scattered about, pencil and portfolio in hand; newly fledged poets sought inspiration from the classic canteen and the knights of the quill played around the edges of the day. . . . The appearance of the troops was remarkable.

"The Chief Magistrate must have felt a thrill of pride as he looked over the sea of bayonets, the blue coats and the determined faces. . . . Now the regiments are filing into their distant camps, the sound of drums is feeble; the bands have lost their fullness of melody, the bugles peal out alone and stop suddenly as if startled at their insignificance. Out on the field, trampled smooth and hard, where the cannon stood and thundered their welcome to the President, a handful of boys play handball."

In the moving platoons that day were regulars, volunteers, conscripts, bounty men. From Boston, New York, Philadelphia, were sons of Daughters of the Revolution whose ancestors had fought ragged and shivering under George Washington from Valley Forge to Yorktown, and they were mingled in divisions with German, English, Scotch, Irish, Scandinavian, Jewish, Polish immigrants or children of immigrants, whose forefathers had fought with or against Bonaparte, Frederick the Great, Marlborough, Gustavus Adolphus, in decisive battles that had hammered out historic texts of the destiny of man.

In the 2d Division of the 11th Corps, Brigadier General Adolph von Steinwehr had in his command Colonel Adolphus Buschbeck, Major Alex von Schluembach, Colonel Patrick H. Jones, and Lieutenant Colonel Lorenz Cantador. At the head of the 3d Division rode Major General Carl Schurz with Brigadier General Alexander Schimmelfennig, leading Illinois, Ohio, New York, and Pennsylvania regiments. Colonel W. Krzyzanowski, whose nomination by Lincoln to be a brigadier had failed of approval in the Senate, headed a New York regiment. Youths who had left their classes at Harvard, Kenyon, Oberlin, Knox, and many other colleges were in the ranks; wild Irish from the sidewalks of New York, Bavarians and Prussians from St. Louis and Milwaukee. Green Mountain plowboys were there; farm hands from the cornfields and orchards of Michigan.

These platoons of regulars, volunteers, conscripts, bounty men, were marching for adventure and glory; for the country and the flag; for a united nation from coast to coast; for the abolition of chattel slavery; for the reason that they were drafted and there was no escape; or because they were paid a bounty of cash money. In a hundred soldiers picked at random might be a hundred different explanations of why they had gone to war and become individual, mobile units of the Army of the Potomac. They were young, so young, most of them in their early twenties, some in their teens—soft-haired darlings, yet many of them fierce cubs of war ready to earn with pride and contempt the crimson ooze known as the red badge of courage.

Lincoln that day gazed on his own boy eager to breathe war in all its phases. "Master Tad Lincoln, booted and spurred, rode bravely at the side of his father, followed by his dashing little orderly," wrote the *New York Herald* man. "And thereby hangs a tale. When the war broke out, a smooth-faced lad came down with the troops from Burlington, New Jersey, and with the rest went into the fights. General Kearny noticed him and made him his bugler, and all through the struggles on the Peninsula kept him at the front of the division. General Kearny fell but the bugler remained. Now he trumpets for General Sickles at the head of the corps, sports his sword belt and sergeant stripes with the air of a veteran, a favorite of the officers, an appointment to West Point hinted. Yesterday he accompanied Master Lincoln as inseparably as his shadow and after the review initiated him into the science of managing the lance. The boys are fast friends and ramble around like brothers."

What Mrs. Lincoln wore at the grand review was duly chronicled by the *Herald* man: "Her attire was exceedingly simple, of that peculiar style of simplicity which creates at the time no impression and prevents an observer from remembering any article of dress; not one in twenty gathered about could tell what she wore. A rich black dress with narrow flounces, a black cape with broad trimming of velvet around the border and a plain hat of the same hue composed her costume. A shade of weariness, doubtless the result of her labors in behalf of the sick and wounded in Washington, rested upon her countenance but the change seemed pleasant to her. The President wore a dark sack overcoat and a fur muffler while Master Lincoln scrambled about in a suit of gray."

Instead of a lean cob with a docked tail, the President should have sat "a fair-sized cavalry horse of which there were plenty," wrote William F. Goodhue of Company C, 3d Wisconsin Infantry, to his home folks. "Mr. Lincoln sat his cob perfectly straight, and dressed as he was in dark clothes, it appeared as if he was an exclamation point astride of the small letter *m*."

General Darius N. Couch rode to the side of the President, who was on horseback one reviewing day, and said as General Carl Schurz approached with his division, "Mr. Lincoln, that is General Schurz," pronouncing it *Shurs*, after the American fashion. Lincoln turned and said, "Not *Shurs*,

General Couch, but *Shoortz*." He did it pleasantly, and Couch was surprised that a Westerner should have the advantage of him in Teutonic pronunciation.

And Couch also told of the occasion: "It was a beautiful day, and the review a stirring sight. Mr. Lincoln, sitting there with his hat off, his head bent, and seemingly meditating, suddenly turned to me and said, 'General Couch, what do you suppose will become of all these men when the war is over?' And it struck me as very pleasant that somebody had an idea that the war would sometime end."

"The President has now reviewed the whole army, and expresses himself highly delighted with all he has seen," wrote Major General George Meade to his wife. "I have been making myself, or at least trying so to do, very agreeable to Mrs. Lincoln, who seems an amiable sort of personage. In view also of the vacant brigadiership in the regular army, I have ventured to tell the President one or two stories, and I think I have made decided progress in his affections. The other day, Major-General Stoneman came up to me and said he was very glad to hear I was so much talked of in connection with this vacancy."

Meade also spoke to the President about Major General Franklin's quarrel with Burnside over the meaning of an order at Fredericksburg, "Burnside thinking he was saying and ordering one thing and Franklin understanding another." As to Hooker and liquor, said Meade to the President, "Since I have been associated with him in the army I can bear testimony of the utter falsehood of the charge of drunkenness."

Rumors about the low morale of the Army of the Potomac may have been one of the reasons that led the President to visit the army. Charles Francis Adams, Jr., a cavalry officer of steady service with that army, son of the United States Minister to London, believed that Hooker "in no way and in no degree" represented the typical soldiership of America. "During the winter when Hooker was in command, I can say from personal knowledge and experience," wrote Adams, "that the Headquarters of the Army of the Potomac was a place to which no self-respecting man liked to go, and no decent woman could go. It was a combination of barroom and brothel." From the field Adams wrote to his brother Henry in London, as to Hooker: "I never saw him to speak to, but I think him a noisy, low-toned intriguer, conceited, intellectually 'smart,' physically brave. His habits are bad and, as a general in high command, I have lost all confidence in him."

Neither Meade nor Noah Brooks nor others who saw more of Hooker's headquarters than did Adams reported whisky and loose women as holding sway. Whatever Hooker's drinking habits had been in the past, they were not worrying Meade, whose habits and character were such that Adams would have liked to see Meade replace Hooker at the head of the army. Yet Adams was the kind of man who would have had some basis for writing his brother Henry that Hooker and Hooker's two favorite generals, Daniel Sickles and Daniel Butterfield, were men of "blemished character, humbugs, intriguers, demagogues," and under them the Army of the Potomac "sank to its lowest level." This may have mixed with the strut and brag in Hooker's words to Lincoln that there would be no "if" about his getting to Richmond, which brought Lincoln's mournful remark to Brooks, "It is about the worst thing I have seen since I have been down here."

In the Confederate army across the river horses were gaunt from lack of forage. Scurvy had begun to appear among troops lacking balanced rations. Cattle had arrived so thin that Lee asked to have them kept to fatten in the spring and that salt meat be issued instead. Through an unusually bleak and frigid winter some of Lee's troops had no blankets. Many wore coats and shoes in tatters. In subsistence and clothing it was known that the neighboring Union army was vastly superior. Valorous men were hungry, Lee directly implied in his patient letter of April 23, 1863, to the Confederate Secretary of War. "I am painfully anxious lest the spirit and efficiency of the men should become impaired, and they be rendered unable to sustain their former reputation, or perform the service necessary for our safety."

An evangelistic revival through the winter, in which religious leaders from Southern cities joined with chaplains, had brought thousands of converts and given a religious impress to the Army of Northern Virginia. Lee in many decisions strengthened morale. A private deserted on reading a letter from his distressed wife; on finding he had come home without leave, she sent him back to the army; a court-martial sentenced him to death; Lee confirmed the sentence of death and then got a pardon for the man. In a battle later this man at a cannon was to see all others on duty at that gun go down in withering fire and go himself last of all.

At a dinner party given by General Hooker, all the corps commanders were present, also Mrs. Lincoln. The President kept his talk on how to meet the enemy on the hills across the river. It interested him that the Confederates had shouted over the Rappahannock that day, "You have taken Charleston." But his business now was to leave one point unforgettable in the mind of Fighting Joe Hooker. He was speaking to this point in a side tent of the General's headquarters when General Couch, invited to discuss the Charleston rumor, stepped in.

As Couch recorded it: "My entrance apparently interrupted a weighty conversation, for both were looking grave. The President's manner was kindly, while the general, usually so courteous, forgot to be conventionally polite. The Charleston rumor having been briefly discussed, Mr. Lincoln remarked that it was time for him to leave. He stepped toward General Hooker, and said, 'I want to impress upon you two gentlemen in your next fight *put in all your men.*'"

Generals Schurz and Sickles accompanied the President back to Washington and to the White House, where they had dinner, then left for the army. On the way up-river Schurz held private conversations with Lincoln and again at the White House next day. After the company had gone Lincoln asked Brooks to go upstairs with him for a few minutes. He started up slowly and thoughtfully, then, turning around on the stairs, said, as Brooks later wrote it: "Did you notice how glum Schurz is? He is dissatisfied. Poor

Schurz! He seems never to forget that he is an adopted citizen of the country."

True it was "the Yanks were licked" at Charleston, dispatches told Lincoln. A fleet of ironclad vessels, long and carefully prepared, had failed to batter down Fort Sumter, and under fire from heavy shore batteries had retired somewhat crippled with one vessel sunk and two disabled. Because Charleston was a symbol, a starting-point of secession, many in the North hoped it could be taken; they had expected much; they would wait.

Some days after the attempt at Charleston, Welles received a dispatch he considered "not worthy" of Admiral S. F. Du Pont at Charleston: "He says he never advised the attack and complains of a telegram from the President more than of the dispatch from the Department." Lincoln's telegram to Du Pont read: "Hold your position inside the bar near Charleston; or, if you shall have left it, return to it and hold it till further orders. Do not allow the enemy to erect new batteries or defenses on Morris Island. If he has begun it, drive him out. I do not herein order you to renew the general attack. That is to depend on your own discretion or a further order."

This seemed a large order. Experts could debate it for hours and in the end its issue would hang entirely on personal factors, such as Gustavus Vasa Fox, Assistant Secretary of the Navy, who had never graduated from the Annapolis naval academy, favoring as a successor to Du Pont, Rear Admiral John Adolph Dahlgren, who was also not an Annapolis man. Lincoln had no particular acquaintance with Du Pont, while on the other hand he held a personal warmth for Dahlgren, and had once given a card to Noah Brooks concerning a naval appointment, saying to Brooks, "Here, take this card to Captain Fox—*he* is the navy department."

The failure at Charleston led to Admiral Dahlgren's relieving Admiral Du Pont in command of the South Atlantic blockading squadron. Welles recorded Lincoln as saying: "Du Pont, as well as McClellan, hesitates—has *the slows*. McClellan always wanted more regiments; Du Pont is everlastingly asking for more gunboats, more ironclads. He will do nothing with any. He has intelligence and system and will maintain a good blockade. You did well in selecting him for that command, but he will never take Sumter or get to Charleston. He is no Farragut, though unquestionably a good routine officer, who obeys orders and in a general way carries out his instructions."

Thus Lincoln was taking it as his duty to supervise personally fleets and squadrons at sea as well as armies and expeditions on land.

John Hay was sent to the South Atlantic squadron with dispatches and reported to Lincoln: "I was several times struck by the identity of opinion and sentiment between Admiral Dahlgren and yourself. You had repeatedly uttered, during my last week in Washington, predictions which have become history." Hay quoted Dahlgren: "The orders you have given me show how vast was the importance of my preserving this fleet for the work which I agree with the President in thinking the most momentous, the opening of the control of the Mississippi River."

"Write me often. I am very anxious," wrote Lincoln to Hooker a week after his visit to the army, in a letter saying he feared "another failure already" in the matter of a large cavalry expedition ordered by Hooker. The cavalry had traveled less than twenty-five miles in three days of fair weather, had sixty miles yet to go on the raid planned. "By arithmetic, how many days will it take him?" queried Lincoln. He thanked Hooker for maps, newspapers, and a letter which arrived April 28. "While I am anxious, please do not think I am impatient, or waste a moment's thought on me, to your own hindrance, or discomfort." He sent two telegrams to Hooker in the first week of May querying, "What news?" Hooker was letting no one into his secrets. "I heard him say," wrote Meade, "that not a human being knew his plans either in the army or at Washington."

One foggy night this spring of '63 Lincoln asked Brooks to walk over to General Halleck's headquarters. From a number of walking-sticks in a corner of the White House, Lincoln picked a heavy one, shod and tipped with historic iron bolts from that famous ship, the *Constitution*. He had not made a habit of using a cane, and as he took this one, according to Brooks, his voice dropped to a seriocomic and confidential whisper: "Mother [Mrs. Lincoln] has got a notion into her head that I shall be assassinated, and to please her I take a cane when I go over to the War Department at night—when I don't forget it."

Brooks felt a little nervous about Lincoln's caution even though Lincoln made fun of it. A man slouching in the fog and gloom of a building drew Brooks's notice. He could pay little attention to the President's chat; he was seeing an apparition. An hour or two later as they came back from Halleck's office, Brooks knew that inside of himself he was "positively scared" by the shadows of trees in the park.

Lincoln had noticed how Brooks was acting, and when they were safely back in the White House, said, "Now own up that I scared you by putting plots and assassinations into your head when we went out." Brooks confessed he was worried and shouldn't have thought of danger if it had not been mentioned. Lincoln laughed and said that was human nature, adding seriously: "I long ago made up my mind that if anybody wants to kill me he will do it. If I wore a shirt of mail and kept myself surrounded by a bodyguard, it would be all the same. There are a thousand ways of getting at a man if it is desirable that he should be killed. Besides, in this case, it seems to me, that the man who would come after me would be just as objectionable to my enemies—if I have any."

On May 1 Hooker had brought most of his army across the Rappahannock River, to a crossroads named Chancellorsville, for a frontal combat with Lee, while an army corps under General John Sedgwick had crossed the river at another point aiming to harass Lee, flank or rear. Hooker believed he had Lee in a tight box and issued an address: "Our enemy must either ingloriously fly or come out from behind his defences and give us battle on our own ground, where certain destruction awaits him."

Hooker attacked, Lee counterattacked, and Hooker ordered his men to fall back. "Just as we reached the enemy we were recalled," wrote Meade, while General Couch, second to Hooker in command, said: "Hooker expected Lee to fall back without risking battle. Finding himself mistaken he assumed the defensive."

Early the next morning Lee sent half his army under Stonewall Jackson on a march that took them till late in the afternoon, when they delivered a surprise attack that smashed the Union flank and rear. The next day Lee outguessed and outfought Hooker. With an army half the size of Hooker's, he so mangled and baffled the Union forces that Hooker called a council of his generals, of whom four voted to stay where they were and fight, two voted to retreat across the river. Hooker then ordered the retreat.

The white moon by night and the red sun by day had looked down on over 20,000 men who lay killed or wounded on the open farms and in the wilderness of trees, thickets, and undergrowth, the figures giving Union losses at 11,000, Confederate at 10,000, not including 6,000 prisoners captured by Lee and 2,000 by Hooker.

Numbers, however, could not tell nor measure the vacancy nor the Southern heartache left by the loss of Stonewall Jackson, shot by his own men, it was reported, as he was inspecting positions in the zone of fire. "You have lost only your left arm, while I have lost my right," mourned Lee to his dying lieutenant, who passed into a delirium calling the names of Old Testament warriors, pronouncing admonitions: "In washing the hands, have always in mind the cleansing blood of Calvary. Bear in mind in dressing, to be clothed in righteousness as with a garment." His wife and baby came to heal or to help. His mind roamed to the battlefield. "Tell A. P. Hill to prepare for action." Peace came after the storm and Stonewall Jackson went with a murmur—"Let us pass over the river and rest in the shade of the trees."

At the old brick mansion serving as headquarters, a cannon ball had broken a pillar against which General Hooker leaned, knocked him down, left him senseless a half-hour, dazed for an hour or more, while the battle lines rocked and tore on the second day. Under the puzzling maneuvers and swift stinging blows from Lee, Hooker had lost his nerve, disappointed his friends.

Always until Chancellorsville Hooker galloped, swore, and gave blow for blow. Now it was as though he would play chess and outthink an opponent. He had gone into battle with a good plan and dropped it when the enemy refused to do what he expected. He was sick with himself as he told Meade that he was ready to turn over the army; he had had enough and almost wished he had never been born.

Of course there was one large excuse for Hooker. Against him during the three days he had Lee, a genius with a chest of stratagems, whose gray and butternut battalions had given Hooker the impression they were retreating when they were flanking, seemed to be going when they were coming. Detachments executed a repulse on one front and swung to another to support attacking columns. While Hooker failed to put half his men into combat, Lee came near making one soldier count for two.

A curiously civilized warrior was Lee, pausing in this battle to listen to a Union prisoner declaring that his hat was stolen, Lee ordering a Confederate soldier to give back the hat. A staff officer noted: "I happened to be standing beside General Lee under fire and in full view of a very interesting episode of the fight. I was astonished when, in spite of the excitement natural to such a scene, he . . . began to converse with me about popular education of the future." More than he accomplished was asked of Lee by the *Richmond Enquirer* correspondent, whose account dated May 6 began: "It cannot be denied that we allowed the enemy to get off too easily. His whole force ought to have been captured." Again, as at Fredericksburg, Lee's army was too gashed and spent to follow up its hard-won victory.

News of what happened to Hooker was slow reaching the White House. "I this P.M. met the President at the War Department," wrote Welles on May 4. "He said he had a feverish anxiety to get facts; was constantly up and down, for nothing reliable came from the front. There is an impression, which is very general, that our army has been successful." At Cabinet meeting next day, "The President read a brief telegram which he got last evening from General Hooker, to whom, getting nothing from the War Department, he had applied direct to ascertain whether the Rebels were in possession of the works on the heights of Fredericksburg. Hooker replied he believed it was true, but if so it was of no importance."

Sumner came to Welles's office that afternoon, and from foreign affairs they shifted talk to the latest battle: "The President came in while we were discussing the subject, and, as is his way, at once earnestly participated. His suggestions and inferences struck me as probable, hopeful, nothing more. Like the rest of us, he wants facts; without them we have only surmises . . . doubt, uncertainty. He is not informed of occurrences as he should be, but is in the dark, with no official data, which confirms me in the belief that the War Department is in ignorance, for they would not withhold favorable intelligence from him, yet it is strange, very strange . . . the President strives to feel encouraged and to inspire others, but I can perceive he has doubts and misgivings, though he does not express them."

The next day Sumner came to Welles's office, raised both hands, cried, "Lost, lost, all is lost!" He had come direct from the President, "who, he said, was extremely dejected." Sumner could give Welles no particulars. Noah Brooks, however, was at the White House that day and found the President "anxious and harassed beyond any power of description," that while without any positive information Lincoln was certain in his own mind that "Hooker had been licked." He was only then wondering whether Hooker would be able to recover himself and renew the fight. He asked Brooks to go into the room occupied by his friend Dr. Henry, a guest, and wait for later news.

"In an hour or so, while the doctor and I sat talking, about 3 o'clock in the afternoon," wrote Brooks, "the door opened and Lincoln came into the room. He held a telegram in his hand, and as he closed the door and came toward us I mechanically noticed that his face, usually sallow, was ashen in hue. The paper on the wall behind him was of the tint known as 'French gray,' and even in that moment of sorrow and dread expectation, I vaguely took in the thought that the complexion of the anguished President's visage was like that of the wall. He gave me the telegram, and in a voice trembling with emotion, said, 'Read it—news from the army.'

"The despatch was from General Butterfield, Hooker's chief of staff, addressed to the War Department, and was to the effect that the army had been withdrawn from the south side of the Rappahannock and was then 'safely encamped' in its former position. The appearance of the President, as I read aloud these fateful words, was piteous . . . broken . . . and so ghostlike.

"Clasping his hands behind his back, he walked up and down the room, saying, 'My God! my God! What will the country say! What will the country say!'

"He seemed incapable of uttering any other words than these, and after a little time he hurriedly left the room.

"Dr. Henry, whose affection for the President was deep and tender, burst into a passion of tears. I consoled him as best I could, and while we were talking and trying to find a gleam of sunshine in this frightful darkness, I saw a carriage drive up to the entrance of the White House, and, looking out, beheld the tall form of the President dart into the vehicle, in which sat General Halleck, and drive off. Immediately after, an attendant came to tell us that the President and General Halleck had gone to the Army of the Potomac, that Mr. Lincoln would return next day, and would like to see me in the evening."

Rumors flew over Washington that the President and Halleck had gone to the front; Hooker would be put under arrest; Halleck would command; Stanton had quit; Lee had cut Hooker to pieces and was moving on Washington; McClellan was coming by special train from New York to command, while Generals Sigel, Butler, Frémont, on the shelf, would soon arrive. The bar at Willard's was crowded; men with their feet on the brass rail drank hard liquor and conducted a war that existed in their own minds.

A *New York Tribune* correspondent, John Russell Young, held confidential and never wrote for a newspaper a story he said came from a conversation with Stanton. Lincoln, according to Young's story, after crying that day, "My God! Stanton, our cause is lost!" had stood trembling, with sweat on his forehead, and after long silence had said, "If I am not about early tomorrow, do not send for me nor allow anyone to disturb me."

Young quoted Stanton: "Mr. Lincoln had fully made up his mind to go to the Potomac River, and there end his life, as many a poor creature—but none half so miserable as he was at the time—had done before him." And Stanton said he was afraid to leave Lincoln alone, told him to be brave, to lie down on a lounge, sleep, and then visit the army in person, which braced Lincoln as a tonic. Whatever actually underlay this incident which Young in after years related circumstantially to boon companions, Lincoln had a speaking acquaintance with despair that day and Stanton may have been a comforter, though it would have been a new role for Stanton.

The President on May 7 wrote to Hooker as though a good fighter had been sent reeling, wasn't hurt, and might make a swift comeback. "An early movement would . . . help," he wrote, asking if Hooker had in mind a plan wholly or partially formed. "If you have, prosecute it without interference from me. If you have not, please inform me, so that I, incompetent as I may be, can try and assist you in the formation of some plan for the army."

Lincoln's visit at the front was partly told by General Meade in a letter to his wife on May 8: "I was summoned to headquarters, where I found the President and General Halleck. The former said he had come down to enquire for himself as to the condition of affairs and desired to see corps commanders. He and Halleck spent a couple of hours, took lunch, and talked all sorts of things, but nothing was said of our recent operations, or any reference made to the future, nor was any corps commander called on for an opinion. The President remarked that the result was in his judgment most unfortunate; that he did not blame any one—he believed every one had done all in his power; and that the disaster was one that could not be helped. Nevertheless he thought its effect, both at home and abroad, would be more serious and injurious than any previous act of the war. . . . Since seeing the President, he [Hooker] seems in better spirits, and I suppose, unless some strong pressure is brought to bear from external sources, he will not be disturbed. For some reason they have prohibited bringing newspapers to camp, so that I am completely in the dark as to public opinion." And on May 10, "Couch, I hear, told the President he would not serve any longer under Hooker, and recommended my assignment to the command."

Lincoln's eye was on this very man who could write to his wife with such fine modesty the sentence "Hooker has one great advantage over his predecessors in not having any intriguer among his subordinate generals." Senators Wade, Chandler, Wilson, Doolittle, had come down, asked Meade no questions, and he had offered them no suggestions. However, General Couch felt that a statement should be presented to Lincoln by the generals. "I declined," wrote Meade, "to join Couch in a representation to the President, and I refused to join Slocum, who desired to take action to have Hooker removed. I told both these gentlemen I would not join in any movement against Hooker, but that if the President chose to call on me officially for my opinions, I would give them."

Meantime as many explanations of the repulse at Chancellorsville had been published as earlier were offered to solve the first Bull Run rout. "The failure at Chancellorsville has never been satisfactorily explained," wrote Welles. "Perhaps it cannot be . . . the President and Halleck are silent on this subject." While there was no such malice or partisan feeling as in the cases of Burnside and McClellan, the cry was general that Hooker was to blame.

When newspapers again sifted through to the army, officers read that the *Chicago Tribune* on May 23 called for Abraham Lincoln to take the field as actual commander. Under "Old Abe" the Army of the Potomac could be led to victory. "If he does not, who will?" Lincoln was seeking the answer. Meanwhile in passing weeks he sent in a kindly way his best counsel to Hooker, advice in the tone of his long letter which Hooker had said was like that of a father to a son.

Lee was carefully screening a movement that seemed to be aimed northward, possibly another invasion of Maryland. "I think Lee's army, and not Richmond, is your true objective point," wrote Lincoln. "If he comes toward the upper Potomac, follow on his flank and on his inside track, shortening your lines while he lengthens his. Fight him, too, when opportunity offers. If he stays where he is, fret him and fret him." To one inquiry from Hooker he replied that "so much of professional military skill is requisite to answer it" that it was turned over to Halleck. He could see, however, that it would be well for Hooker to stay on the same side of the Rappahannock if Lee crossed that river to fight. "I would not take any risk of being entangled upon the river, like an ox jumped half over a fence and liable to be torn by dogs front and rear without a fair chance to gore one way or kick the other."

On June 14 Lincoln queried Hooker: "If the head of Lee's army is at Martinsburg and the tail of it on the plank road between Fredericksburg and Chancellorsville, the animal must be very slim somewhere. Could you not break him?" On Lee's moving toward Harper's Ferry, Lincoln wrote to Hooker that it "gives you back the chance that I thought McClellan lost last fall."

The President was almost apologetic: "Quite possibly I was wrong both then and now; but, in the great responsibility resting upon me, I cannot be entirely silent. Now, all I ask is that you will be in such mood that we can get into our action the best cordial judgment of yourself and General Halleck, with my poor mite added, if indeed he and you shall think it entitled to any consideration at all." This, in a letter dated June 16, the President followed at ten o'clock at night with a telegram stating that Hooker was strictly under General in Chief Halleck: "I have not intended differently, but as it seems to be differently understood I shall direct him to give you orders, and you to obey them."

In no grandiose style Welles was writing in his diary on June 2: "Halleck . . . sits back in his chair, doing comparatively nothing. It worries the President, yet he relies upon Halleck. . . . No one more fully realizes . . . the vast consequences involved, than the President; he wishes all to be done that can be done, yet in army operations will not move or do except by the consent of the dull, stolid, inefficient, and incompetent General-in-Chief." A few days later Welles wrote that the Cabinet members were not informed of army movements: "The President is kept in ignorance and defers to the General-in-Chief, though not pleased that he is not fully advised of matters as they occur. There is a modest distrust of himself, of which advantage is taken."

This was Welles's own impression. He was not aware that Lincoln received a wide variety of scraps of information and often reserved to himself the replies to such telegrams as one to General Couch on June 28: "What news now? What are the enemy firing at four miles from your works?"

Welles wrote that he was puzzled no condemnation of Hooker came from Lincoln: "The President . . . has a personal liking for Hooker, and clings to him when others give way." Welles repeated this to Monty Blair when they met at a railroad depot: "Told him [Blair] of the conversation I had last evening with the President and the appearance of things at the War Department. It affected him greatly. He has never had confidence in either Stanton, Halleck, or Hooker. He fairly groaned that the President should continue to trust them and defer to them, when the magnitude of the questions is considered. 'Strange, strange,' he exclaimed, 'that the President, who has sterling ability, should give himself over so completely to Stanton and Seward.'"

Sumner came to see Welles and was emphatic that he could not agree with Chase in favoring Hooker, a "blasphemous wretch" who after crossing the Rappahannock toward Lee had exclaimed, "The enemy is in my power, and God Almighty cannot deprive me of them." Welles noted: "Whiskey is said by Sumner to have done the work."

As though he had it from Sumner, Welles made the entry in his diary: "The President said if Hooker had been killed by the shot which knocked over the pillar that stunned him, we should have been successful."

Hearing that Lincoln was going to give him command of the army, the able and valorous corps commander General John F. Reynolds hurried to the White House and told Lincoln he did not want command of the Army of the Potomac and would not take it. Then Reynolds spoke "very freely" to the President about Hooker. He went so far in his comment on Hooker that Lincoln spoke up in defense of that general. As Reynolds told it to Meade, "The President said he was not disposed to throw away a gun because it missed fire once; that he would pick the lock and try it again." Hooker would not be replaced, Meade surmised, because of two reasons: (1) the difficulty of finding a successor and (2) "the ridiculous appearance we present of changing generals after each battle."

As late as June 26, nearly seven weeks since the battle of Chancellorsville, Hooker had done nothing to fret or harass Lee, and Lincoln gave to Welles the first inkling that he might have to let Hooker go. Welles in his diary quoted the President: "We cannot help beating them, if we have the man. How much depends in military matters on one master mind! Hooker may commit the same fault as McClellan and lose his chance. We shall soon see, but it appears to me he can't help but win."

Chase visited Hooker in camp and wrote from Washington on June 20 to Hooker: "On returning from your headquarters, I called on the President and Secretary of War, each of whom seemed gratified by what I had to

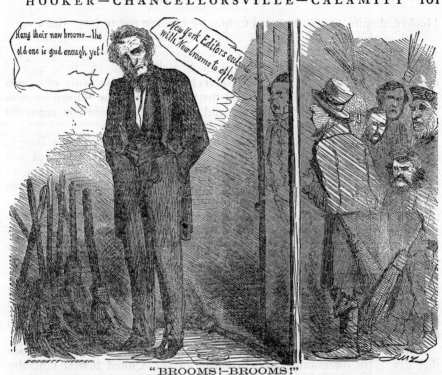

"BROOMS!—BROOMS!"

SHOWING HOW EACH OF THE PRESS GANG THINKS HE HAS A NEW BROOM THAT WILL SWEEP UP THE REBELLION QUICKER THAN THE OLD ONE—GENERAL HOOKER: BUT THE PRESIDENT DOESN'T SEEM TO "SEE IT."

Vanity Fair cartoons Lincoln's refusal to sweep Hooker from command, as loudly urged by Greeley, Bennett, Raymond, and others outside the door—termed "the press gang," each member with a broom

state. My conviction is strong that you will want nothing which can contribute to your success. . . . The President and Secretary of War both expressed admiration at the prompt celerity which has distinguished all your movements of troops." From the tone of this note it seemed as though Chase believed his plans for the retention of Hooker were going as smoothly as could be asked.

The War Department commentator, Charles F. Benjamin, in a long sentence struck the highlights and delicate shadings of the affair: "The friends of Mr. Chase considered that the fortunes of their leader were too much bound up with Hooker to permit of the latter's ignominious removal and, although the President had learned much that he did not dream of at the time he parted company with the War Department in the matter of appointing a successor to Burnside, the Treasury faction had grown so powerful that Lincoln could not consent to a rupture with it, and a temporizing policy was adopted all around, which General Couch, commander of the 2d Corps, nearly spoiled by contemptuously refusing to serve any longer under

Hooker, despite an abject appeal to him by Hooker not to leave the army."

While this political game went on across the weeks after Chancellors-ville, Lee rested his army, received new divisions of freshly conscripted troops, slipped away into the Shenandoah Valley, and by June 29 had crossed the Potomac, marched over Maryland, and had an army of 75,000 on Pennsylvania soil. Having learned that Lee had left the Rappahannock, Hooker broke camp with his army and moved it northward in scattered formation.

At Frederick, Maryland, a man in civilian clothes, riding in a buggy, begging, buying, and wheedling his way through straggling parties of sol-diers and wagon trains, arrived at three o'clock in the morning of June 28 and went to the tent of General George Gordon Meade, was let in after wrangling. He woke Meade from sleep, saying he had come to give him trouble. Meade said his conscience was clear; he was prepared for bad news.

A letter from General in Chief Halleck was put in Meade's hands, read-ing: "You will receive with this the order of the President placing you in command of the Army of the Potomac. . . . You will not be hampered by any minute instructions from headquarters. Your army is free to act as you may deem proper under the circumstances as they arise." Meade argued with General James A. Hardie, chief of staff of the Secretary of War, who had brought the order. He did not want the place. But every point he made had been anticipated.

Meade was ordered as a soldier to accept, which he did, issuing notice that day: "By direction of the President of the United States, I hereby assume command of the Army of the Potomac." He informed his officers and troops that he was obeying an order "totally unexpected and unso-licited"; they would have fatigues and sacrifices; it was with "diffidence" he relieved in command "an eminent and accomplished soldier."

Meade had grace of conduct and many reservations. "Dearest," he wrote his wife, "you know how reluctant we both have been to see me placed in this position. I had nothing to do but accept. I am moving at once against Lee. Pray for the success of my country."

Lincoln met his Cabinet on this same Sunday morning that Meade took command: "The President . . . drew from his pocket a telegram from Gen-eral Hooker asking to be relieved," noted Welles. "The President said he had, for several days as the conflict became imminent, observed in Hooker the same failings that were witnessed in McClellan after the Battle of Antie-tam—a want of alacrity to obey, and a greedy call for more troops which could not . . . be taken from other points." When Halleck refused to give him the force at Harper's Ferry, Hooker had "taken umbrage" and asked to be quit of his command. The names of Meade, Sedgwick, Couch, were sug-gested in a discussion of who should next take command.

"I soon saw," wrote Welles, "this review of names was merely a feeler to get an expression of opinion—a committal—or to make it appear that all were consulted. It shortly became obvious, however, that the matter had already been settled, and the President finally remarked he supposed General Halleck had issued the orders. He asked Stanton if it was not so. Stanton replied affirmatively, that Hooker had been ordered to Baltimore and Meade to succeed him. We were consulted after the fact. Chase was disturbed more than he cared should appear."

Welles was puzzled: "The President has been partial to Hooker in all this time and has manifested no disposition to give him up, except a casual remark at the last Cabinet-meeting." And Welles mused in his diary on whether it could be that the troop refusals had been intended to drive Hooker into a disgust that would make him ask to be relieved.

Welles in his sometimes innocent and inadequate diary entries fumbled a situation. In this one, Benjamin, on the inside of the War Department, came nearer hitting off the moment: "Hooker was so full of hope and energy that severe measures had to be resorted to in order to wring from him that tender of resignation deemed to be necessary to enable his supporters at Washington to keep on outward terms with the Administration. When it did come, the impending battle was evidently so close at hand that the Secretary of War was seized with the fear that, either by accident or design, the change of command to General Meade would not be effected in time to avoid the very contingency aimed at by the change. At the last moment, the President too became alarmed, and there was another conference at the Department to settle the means of insuring the transfer."

Chase, in a long polite letter to the President that day, intimated that trickery had been on foot in the ousting of Hooker. "There are two or three circumstances which perhaps I should have mentioned this morning," began Chase, then recited the circumstances which he had gleaned from his private investigation at the War Department. To his daughter Kate, Chase wrote: "What prompted the request [Hooker's] I do not know. I did not hear of it, nor of the appointment of Meade in his place, till Sunday, when, at a meeting . . . called for a different purpose, having no connection with Hooker's affairs, the President mentioned it to us."

From day to day, during the northward shift of the armies, Lincoln had been in the War Department telegraph office much of his time. He queried the operators often, "Where's Meade?" or, "What's the 5th Corps doing?" From the North came a clamor, a throng of suggestions. A. K. McClure of Philadelphia urged Lincoln to put McClellan again in command, which was also the wish of many business and professional men of New York and Philadelphia. Lincoln replied with two questions: "Do we gain anything by opening one leak to stop another? Do we gain anything by quieting one clamor merely to open another, and probably a larger one?"

On the steamer *Carrie Martin* one night on the Potomac just before Chancellorsville, Lincoln had told Noah Brooks, "I kept McClellan in command after I had expected that he would win victories, simply because I knew that his dismissal would provoke popular indignation and shake the faith of the people in the final success of the war." Weeks had passed and the rumor ran high that McClellan would again command. Brooks said he chanced to be in the family sitting-room at the White House one evening, with the President, Mrs. Lincoln, and several callers present, when a young woman blurted out, "Mr. President, is McClellan going to be recalled to the command of the Army of the Potomac?" The answer was evasive and good-natured.

But the conversation on McClellan continued, and soon Brooks was saying that as the President hadn't settled the matter, there might be something in the general suspicion that McClellan would be recalled. Lincoln, sitting near Brooks, gave him a hard look, spoke in an undertone: "And you too?" Brooks flashed back to the steamer conversation of weeks ago, apologized for lack of faith. Lincoln: "I see you remember the talk we had on the *Carrie Martin*."

Hooker went to Baltimore, as ordered, became impatient and went to Washington to ask for orders. There he spoke harsh words of his generals and contempt for Stanton and Halleck. He asked Noah Brooks what the President had said about him. "I hesitated," said Brooks, "but when he pressed for a reply, I said that Lincoln had told me that he regarded Hooker very much as a father might a son who was lame, or who had some other physical infirmity. His love for his son would be even intensified by the reflection that the lad could never be a strong and successful man. The tears stood in Hooker's eyes as he heard this curious characterization of himself; but immediately rallying, he said, 'Well, the President may regard me as a cripple; but if he will give me a chance, I will yet show him that I know how to fight.'" The next day Hooker was arrested on a War Department order for having visited Washington without leave, contrary to rules and regulations.

This, as Brooks said, was a most ungracious and needless bit of oppression. Hooker was released in a hurry. John Hay liked him; so did Lincoln, who remarked to Hay, "Whenever trouble arises I can always rely on Hooker's magnanimity."

The next great battle, it seemed to many, would be a duel between Meade and Lee, somewhere in Pennsylvania, at Philadelphia, Chambersburg, Harrisburg, perhaps Gettysburg. Welles pondered what Lee's men might do "should they cross the Susquehanna." So did Lincoln, the country, the press, the pulpit, the man in the street, the farmer in the field.

Lee would be missing Jackson, of whom a sweet fantasy was now told—that a legion of angels had left Heaven to bring him up home, but not finding him on earth, gave up their search, flew back to Heaven, and found that Jackson had "executed a swift flanking movement" and got to Heaven before them.

A soldier with both legs shot off was being carried to the rear in the recent fighting. And seeing a woman selling leathery-looking pies, he called out, "Say, old lady, are those pies sewed or pegged?" Lincoln told of it to Brooks.

Also there was a high private at Chancellorsville who had been through several campaigns with a crockery mug, from which he was drinking coffee as his regiment awaited action. A stray bullet, just missing the coffee-drinker's head, shattered the mug and left only its handle on his fingers. Turning his head toward the enemy, he growled, "Johnny, you can't do that again!" Lincoln told of it to Brooks. "It seems as if neither death nor danger can quench the grim humor of the American soldier."

Now the war had begun and had gone on. Now the war already had a considerable past. In a little wilderness clearing at Chancellorsville, a living soldier had come upon a dead one sitting with his back to a tree, looking at first sight almost alive enough to hold a conversation with the living. He had sat there for months, maybe a year, since the fight that gave him his long rest. He seemed to have a story and a philosophy to tell if the correct approach were made and he could be led into a quiet discussion. The living soldier, however, stood frozen in his foot tracks a few moments, gazing at the ashen face and the sockets where the eyes had withered—then he picked up his feet, let out a cry, and ran. He had interrupted a silence where the slants of silver moons and the music of varying rains kept company with the one against the tree who sat so speechless, though having much to say.

CHAPTER 38

VICKSBURG—GRANT, LIQUOR, AND LINCOLN

THE Southern Confederacy, worn ragged and bleeding, fighting at odds, still had stamina and resources. Lieutenant Colonel Fremantle of the British Coldstream Guards spent three months in the Confederacy, from the Rio Grande to the Potomac, in the early half of '63, being extended every courtesy, living with the main armies, talking with government chiefs; and Fremantle came to feel that the South could never be subjugated. He closed a 309-page book published while the war went on: "Even supposing that their extermination were feasible, as some Northerners have suggested, I never can believe that in the nineteenth century the civilized world will be condemned to witness the destruction of such a gallant race." The Confederate Secretary of State, Judah P. Benjamin, had told him their peace terms: "on a blank sheet of paper the words 'self-government.' Let the Yankees accord that, and they might fill up the paper in any manner they chose. All we are struggling for is to be let alone."

President Davis, though emaciated, was determined. Fremantle told of women he had seen in Davis's home State, left desperate by their husbands and brothers in the army, yet quiet and uncomplaining; Davis said with much feeling that he always considered silent despair the most painful misery to witness, in the same way that he thought mute insanity the most awful form of madness. While held to his Richmond office Davis yearned for the battlefields. "Walking home with Mr. Benjamin," wrote Fremantle, "he told me that Mr. Davis's military instincts still predominate, and that his eager wish was to have joined the army instead of being elected President."

Rhett, Yancey, Toombs, and other revolutionists who by agitation and direct action had swung the plunge into secession scored Davis for failures, for not getting more guns from Europe before the blockade went into effect; for not trading millions of available bales of cotton to England and France for gold, credit, and supplies; for mistaken appointments of generals; for not carrying the war into the North. Edward A. Pollard of the *Richmond Examiner* incessantly criticized in a nastily superior personal tone. The North Carolina and Georgia governors complained of injustice to their regiments, of despotism, interference with States' Rights in conscription decrees by the Richmond Government. Enlisted men had been drafted for the duration of the war. Murmuring arose that it was "a rich man's war"; all who owned twenty slaves were exempted; a planter with nineteen slaves, it was told, jubilantly welcomed a newborn pickaninny that saved him from going into the army. Drugstores had increased in some cities and towns because "apothecaries" were exempt.

Toombs had openly defied the government order that planters must put in food crops instead of cotton. The editor of the *Tuscaloosa* (Alabama) *Observer* declared that the planter raising cotton was meaner than the meanest Yankee: "Such a man would dig up the bones of his mother, and make dice with them to play for a counterfeit shin-plaster upon her tombstone."

Yet for all the difficulties, the ruling class of the South had common understandings, maintained a cohesion of forces and a more widespread loyalty, were less troubled by mixed bloods and breeds, than the more loosely allied ruling class of the North. "I always admired the South," commented Grant, "for the boldness with which they silenced all opposition and all croaking, by press or by individuals, within their control."

One question weighed heavily on the Richmond Government in the spring of '63. Would Grant take Vicksburg? If so the Mississippi River would pass wholly into Union possession. Lincoln had talked about such a result to Commander D. D. Porter, pointing at a map and saying, as quoted by Porter: "See what a lot of land these fellows hold, of which Vicksburg is the key. Here is the Red River, which will supply the Confederates with cattle and corn to feed their armies. There are the Arkansas and White Rivers, which can supply cattle and hogs by the thousand. These supplies can be distributed by rail all over the Confederacy. Then there is that great depot of supplies on the Yazoo. Let us get Vicksburg and all that country is ours. The war can never be brought to a close until that key is in our pocket. I am acquainted with that region and know what I am talking about. We may take all the northern ports of the Confederacy and they can still defy us from Vicksburg. It means hog and hominy without limit, fresh troops from all the States of the far South, and a cotton country where they can raise the staple without interference."

This, noted Porter, was Lincoln's comment before New Orleans had been taken and "A military expert could not have more clearly defined the advantages of the proposed campaign. Mr. Lincoln was, in fact, the one who, after the thing had been proposed to him, was most active in urging it on. The President would come in while McClellan and myself were discussing the matter and have his say."

Then New Orleans was taken; the navy delayed moving up to Vicksburg, lacking troops for land assault; and the Confederates had erected heavy batteries on the tall hills, adding near the levee a water battery of twelve guns which the Union sailors nicknamed "The Twelve Apostles." The ablest military engineers of the Confederacy gave attention to Vicksburg, and when they had finished President Davis termed it "a Gibraltar."

Captain Porter, when not yet a commander, had left the Southwest with "breakbone fever." While recovering at the Newport Club, Newport, Rhode Island, amid the sofas of a billiard room after merry dinner parties, Porter heard excited talk and profanity among groups of club members. "This is our usual evening's entertainment," an old member told him. "It is . . . the copperheads and radical republicans. Each is now bragging of his own general, and seems determined to bet him into the Presidency." A shout came: "I'll bet five hundred dollars General [McClellan] will be the next President!" A crowd surged toward Porter. And a little fellow whom Porter considered as having more money than brains, whose principal recommendation was a fine set of teeth, yelled, "Captain Porter, I bet General [McClellan] is the greatest general the world ever saw, and will be our next President." Porter joked him and the little fellow said he couldn't stand joking. "You can't stand drinking either," said Porter. "It has been too much for your weak head." In the words that followed the little fellow made claims for Stonewall Jackson, Porter replying, "I have heard some people assert that Stonewall Jackson is the hardest man alive to whip."

"Sir, you are talking treason—yes, sir, treason," blurted the little man. "I'll bet you two thousand dollars General [McClellan] will be the next President."

"Look here, little man, you have a good set of teeth, and my advice to you is to try and keep them in your mouth."

Friends took the little fellow away, Porter resumed a game of billiards; but the next morning his physician, a navy man, told him of ugly reports that he had used treasonable language. A telegram ordered him to Washington; the command of his ship was taken from him; he was ordered West on ironclad construction. He saw that he was being disciplined and discriminated against because some informer had sent word to Washington that he was talking like a rebel. He sought Lincoln, found him in company with Seward, and their talk, as Porter later wrote it, perhaps without strict accuracy, ran:

"What can I do for you, Captain?"

"Sir, I think of resigning and getting the merchants of New York to give me a suitable steamer, so that I may show the Navy Department how to catch the *Alabama*. That would suit my disposition better than superintending ironclads at St. Louis."

"They shall not do it," said Seward, jumping up. "I have not forgotten how you helped me to save Fort Pickens to the Union."

"Yes," said the President, "and got me into hot water with Mr. Welles, for which I think he has never forgiven me."

The President asked Porter to tell about the taking of the forts at New Orleans, afterward adding: "I read all about it, how the ships went up into line firing their broadsides; how the mortars pitched into the forts; how the forts pitched into the ships, and the ships into the rams, and the rams into the gunboats, and the gunboats into the fire-rafts and the fire-rafts into the ships. Of course, I couldn't understand it all, but enough to know that it was a great victory. It reminds me of a fight in a bar-room at Natchez, but I won't tell that now. It struck me that the fight at the forts was something like the Natchez scrimmage, only a little more so."

Porter gave his opinion that Farragut's management of the battle at New Orleans was the most important event of the war, and for it he had received merely a vote of thanks from Congress. "The British Government would have loaded him with honors and emoluments."

"How is that, Seward?" asked the President.

"I don't know anything about it. I am not the head of the Navy Department."

"No," said Lincoln. "But you don't mind running off with a navy-ship when it suits your purposes." He sent for Gustavus Vasa Fox, said good-by to Porter with, "You shan't go to St. Louis, you shan't resign, and you shall be at Vicksburg."

Porter returned to Newport to find a telegram from Welles ordering him to report in person at the Navy Department without delay. In Welles's office, the Secretary gave him two fingers for a handshake, Porter thinking, "I will at least be allowed a cell to myself at Fort Lafayette." Then Welles handed Porter a sealed document, which he opened to read that he was appointed commander of the Mississippi squadron for immediate duty. He mumbled to Welles, "There's a divinity that shapes our ends."

The Secretary congratulated Porter, asked him to dinner, the bureau officers shook hands with him, and he noticed the chief clerk smiled at him for the first time in weeks. "I had been 'selected by the President'!" he said to himself. "I had friends at court. Human nature is everywhere the same, even in the little semblance of a court which we try to maintain. Everyone notices when the President nods, and what it means, and the man who receives his approval is patronized at once. What a difference between this reception and the one two days previous! Then I was almost driven to resign. Now I was a flag officer."

Porter found Lincoln in fine humor; they talked of plans and Porter said

Vicksburg could earlier have been captured easily but was now a second Gibraltar, where the navy alone could do nothing.

"Well," said the President, "whom do you think is the general for such an occasion?"

"General Grant, sir. Vicksburg is within his department; but I presume he will send Sherman there, who is equal to any occasion."

"Well, Admiral, I have in mind McClernand." Porter did not know McClernand, which seemed to surprise Lincoln, who tried to give Porter McClernand's impression that McClernand had saved the day at Shiloh and was a natural-born general. Porter argued for Grant. "If you take troops from Grant and Sherman to give them to McClernand, you will weaken the army."

"Oh, no, I don't mean to do that. McClernand is to go to Springfield, Illinois, and raise troops there for the capture of Vicksburg. In the meantime you can prepare to coöperate with him." And the President gave Porter a note of introduction to McClernand. "I want you to talk the matter over with him before you leave Washington."

Porter looked up McClernand at his hotel and heard the General say he was under orders to enlist an army in Illinois and command it at Vicksburg, and would take Vicksburg in a week. Several weeks later at Cairo, Illinois, Porter told Grant what he had heard from Lincoln and from McClernand. Since then much had happened. McClernand had gone to Illinois and had raised an army corps. It was an able piece of recruiting work. An order from the War Department instructed McClernand to proceed to Illinois, Indiana, Iowa, and by volunteering or draft to organize troops to be forwarded south to points designated by General in Chief Halleck.

That the President and the War Department were taking good care of General Grant and keeping him in control was evidenced in a reservation that "when a sufficient force, not required by the operations of General Grant's command, shall be raised, an expedition may be organized under General McClernand's command against Vicksburg." Lincoln wrote an endorsement on the order that it was confidential but might be shown to governors when such showing was indispensable.

In sending John A. McClernand to the Midwest to raise troops Lincoln put into use elements at hand for war. The General was Kentucky-born, a Black Hawk War soldier, editor of the *Shawneetown Democrat*, then a lawyer in Springfield, Illinois, where he had been a steady Douglas ally for years. He was the sort of Illinois Democrat that Lincoln said he would rather deal with than an Eastern Republican, because he knew his Illinois man. McClernand had an extra-high opinion of himself, lacked humor, was loyal to the Union; as an old and tried Douglas man he could exercise persuasion with all the Midwestern Democrats whose hearts still held memories of the Little Giant as the greatest man since Andrew Jackson. McClernand had resigned from Congress, raised a brigade and commanded it at Donelson and Shiloh, giving a good account of himself in the fighting.

Lincoln, in giving Porter the impression that McClernand was a fighting general, may have expected that the Admiral would pass on that impression to McClernand. Lincoln welcomed one of McClernand's prestige, either political or military, as a helper; such helpers were scarce and should have every chance for distinction or glory. Thirst for military renown lay in McClernand's bosom. On the field later, when a small victory had been achieved by others under his command, he muttered like a peacock of Mars: "Glorious! Glorious! my star is ever in the ascendant!"

"McClernand was a merely smart man, quick, very active-minded, but his judgment was not solid, and he looked after himself a good deal," noted Charles A. Dana. "Mr. Lincoln also looked out carefully for McClernand, because he was an Illinois Democrat, with a considerable following among the people. It was a great thing to get McClernand into the war in the first place, for his natural predisposition, one would have supposed, would have been to sympathize with the South. As long as he adhered to the war he carried his Illinois constituency with him; and chiefly for this reason, doubtless, Lincoln made it a point to take special care of him."

From the fall of '62 till July 1 of '63 Grant performed with armies roundabout Vicksburg, marching them along the Yazoo River, the Yalobusha, the Tallahatchie, amid the miasma of swamps and the tangles of live oak and Spanish moss, digging ditches and canals, chopping wood, building bridges, throwing up breastworks, standing waist-deep in the mud of rifle pits, sleeping in soaked fields and slogging on through monotonous heavy rains, enduring plagues of malarial fever, measles, mumps, and smallpox. They became familiars of Five Mile Creek, Deer Creek, Eagle Bend, Moon Lake, Rolling Fork, the Big Sunflower, Muddy Bayou, the inlets and curves of the Mississippi River with its great sudden twist at the bluffs of Vicksburg, a city of 5,000 people two hundred and fifty feet above the river.

Grant's home-town Congressman, E. B. Washburne, wrote to Lincoln in May that Grant lacked style. "On this whole march for five days he has had neither a horse nor an orderly or servant, a blanket or overcoat or clean shirt. His entire baggage consists of a tooth brush." For weeks the army lived on the country, took the cattle, hogs, grain, supplies, from the farming sections where they were fighting. Mississippi citizens, seeing their food supplies running low, came to Grant asking, "What are *we* to do?" He replied his army had brought along its own food but Confederate cavalry had torn up the railroads and raided his supply depots; their friends in gray had been uncivil; men with arms must refuse to starve in the midst of plenty.

Grant slogged and plodded, trying a plan to find it fail, devising another plan, hanging to one purpose, that of taking Vicksburg and clearing the Mississippi. At one time Lincoln and Stanton had no word from him in ten days. His men marched one hundred and eighty miles; fought five battles, killed more than the enemy; took 6,000 prisoners, 90 cannon, in twenty days. Porter's ironclad gunboats ran the fire of the heavy shore batteries around the long U-bend of the Mississippi, took terrific pounding, lost coal barges and one transport, but came through with the armored flotilla safe.

Two other flotillas were put on the Vicksburg operation, cutting off that city from all lines of communication in three directions. Thus with the navy taking care of three sides by water and Grant's army moving on the fourth or land side, the Mississippi River was in control of Union forces aiming to make the temporary control permanent.

By keeping his plans to himself till ready for action, by hauling and hacking, by outguessing the enemy and making war according to plain facts developed from day to day, Grant made headway toward his one design. Of his men he wrote to the War Department at Washington, "Since leaving Milliken's Bend they have marched as much by night as by day, through mud and rain, without tents or much other baggage and on irregular rations without a complaint and with much less straggling than I have ever before witnessed."

The people in the North, fed by alarmist newspaper correspondents, expected any day to hear that Grant's army had been crushed between two Confederate armies outnumbering his own. Grant meantime took Jackson, the Mississippi State capital, destroyed railroads, bridges, factories there, ended with cooping up in Vicksburg the army of General John C. Pemberton.

Twice Grant had tried to storm his way into Vicksburg, and failing, had settled down to pick and shovel, advancing trenches, stopping food and supplies for the city.

The commander of Vicksburg, John C. Pemberton, was a favorite of President Davis, a West Pointer, a Mexican War veteran, an Indian-fighter, Pennsylvania-born and raised, a descendant of three generations of Quakers. His Northern birth was a liability; accusations arose in the South that he was plotting to sell Vicksburg to the North.

After Grant's second storming attempt, Pemberton made a short speech to his troops: "You have heard that I was incompetent and a traitor; and that it was my intention to sell Vicksburg. Follow me and you will see the cost at which I will sell Vicksburg. When the last pound of beef, bacon and flour, the last grain of corn, the last cow and hog and horse and dog shall have been consumed, and the last man shall have perished in the trenches, then, and only then, will I sell Vicksburg."

The weeks of May and June had dragged on with artillery and sharp-shooters sending soldiers and citizens into cellars, bombproofs, caves burrowed in the hillsides. Night and day guns of both armies howled, shell explosions tore the earth and air. This clamor, this pandemonium, had become a secondary factor not comparable to the silent one: starvation. Vicksburg's army would surrender when hunger said so.

For six months and more Grant, to many people in the North, seemed to be wandering around, stumbling and bungling on a job beyond him. He had outplayed enemy armies twice his own in number, far in the Deep South, a long way from home, with climate, mosquitoes, swamp fever of a stranger soil, ever a threat. Food, guns, powder, had to be hauled hundreds of miles to reach his men. The imagination of the North was slow at picturing what Grant was doing. What was a bayou or a jigger to any citizen of Chicago or Boston unless, like Lincoln, they had seen or felt one? The adventure sagged, came forward, sagged again.

"We have been to Vicksburg and it was too much for us, and we have backed out," wrote General William Tecumseh Sherman, Grant's right-hand man, to his wife in January of '63. And Sherman wrote again at the end of April: "I look upon the whole thing as one of the most hazardous and desperate moves of this or any war."

So crazily intricate became the layout that in early June Sherman wrote

MANAGER LINCOLN. "Ladies and Gentlemen, I regret to say that the Tragedy, entitled *The Army of the Potomac*, has been withdrawn on account of Quarrels among the leading Performers, and I have substituted three new and striking Farces or Burlesques, one, en-titled *The Repulse at Vicksburg*, by the well-known, popular favorite, E. M. STANTON, ESQ., and the others, *The Loss of the Harriet Lane* and *The Exploits of the Alabama*—a very sweet thing in Farces, I assure you—by the Veteran Composer, GIDEON, WELLES."
(*Unbounded Applause by the* COPPERHEADS.)

A subtle cartoon of the Chief Executive and his chosen department heads

home: "I don't believe I can give you an idea of matters here. You will read so much about Vicksburg and the people now gathered about it that you will get bewildered." In March he had written, "No place on earth is favored by nature with natural defense such as Vicksburg, and I do believe the whole thing will fail"; another plan would have to be worked on.

Thus often the very spectators on the spot felt desperate, and newspaper correspondents had good reason, at times, to send North stories of gloom and despair. Yet there were also malice and treachery in much of what the newsmen scribbled and mailed to their papers. Under their noses was an epic of mud, struggle, and blood; not one of them saw it and wrote it.

"So long as our camps are full of newspaper spies revealing each move, exaggerating our difficulties, success cannot be expected," wrote Sherman. He detested in his camp "some half-dozen little whipsnappers who represent the press, but are in fact spies, too lazy, idle, and cowardly to be soldiers."

Sherman arrested Thomas W. Knox, *New York Herald* correspondent, tried him by court-martial on the charge of writing letters for publication without submitting them to the commanding general. Knox was sentenced to stay outside of army lines. Sherman wrote his wife that it was more than he could stand to see correspondents repeatedly publishing information valuable to the enemy. "I will never again command an army in America if we must carry along paid spies. . . . I shall notify Mr. Lincoln of this if he attempt to interfere with the sentence of any court ordered by me."

In Washington a committee of newspapermen laid the papers in the Knox case before Lincoln, who remarked to Albert D. Richardson of the *New York Tribune:* "Oh yes, I remember you perfectly well; you were out on the prairies [of Kansas] with me on that winter day when we almost froze to death; you were then correspondent of the *Boston Journal.* That German from Leavenworth was also with us—what was his name?"

"Hatterscheit."

"Yes, Hatterscheit," said Lincoln, as Richardson recorded it. "By the way, [The President, motioning them to seats, settled down into his chair, with one leg thrown over the arm.] that reminds me of a little story, which Hatterscheit told me during the trip. He bought a pony of an Indian who could not speak English, but who, when the bargain was completed, said: 'Oats—no! Corn—no! Cottonwood—yes! very much!' Hatterscheit thought this was mere drunken maundering; but a few nights after, he tied his horse in a stable built of cottonwood logs, fed him with hay and corn, and went quietly to bed. The next morning he found the grain and fodder untouched, but the barn was quite empty with a great hole on one side which the pony had gnawed his way through! Then he comprehended the old Indian's fragmentary English."

On the same Western trip, Lincoln recalled, he was told of a little creek whose Indian name meant "Weeping Water" and felt that, as "Laughing Water," according to Longfellow, was "Minne-haha," the name of this rivulet should be "Minne-boohoo."

Then Lincoln told the committee he couldn't embarrass his generals in the field, though he would be glad to serve Mr. Knox or any other loyal journalist. He began writing, with pauses, a statement to whom it might concern, that Knox's offense was "technical rather than wilfully wrong" and the sentence should be revoked. "Now, therefore, said sentence is hereby so far revoked as to allow Mr. Knox to return to General Grant's headquarters, and to remain if General Grant shall give his express assent, and to again leave the department if General Grant shall refuse such assent."

This satisfied the committee, Richardson noting: "There was too much irresistible good sense in this to permit any further discussion. Reading it over carefully he handed it to me, and gave a little sigh of relief, said with earnestness: 'God knows I want to do what is right, but sometimes it is very difficult to determine.'" He spoke of naval and military matters, of anxiety as to what was happening to Union boats "upon narrow streams like the Yazoo, the Yallabusha, and Tallahatchie, not wide enough for a long boat to turn around in." He caught himself suddenly. "I am talking again! Of course, you will remember that I speak to you only as friends, that none of this must be put into print."

Doing justice as between Sherman and McClernand was not easy for Lincoln. Sherman was on the ground, had made a good record, and was Grant's choice for a division commander. Yet Lincoln arranged for McClernand to outrank Sherman. To his brother Sherman wrote in January: "McClernand has arrived to supersede me by order of the President himself. Of course I submit gracefully. The President is charged with maintaining the government and has a perfect right to choose his agents." To his wife Sherman wrote: "It was simply absurd to supersede me by McClernand, but Mr. Lincoln knows I am not anxious to command, and he knows McClernand is, and must gratify him. He will get his fill before he is done."

In due time as the months passed McClernand made minor errors, and finally a blunder so openly in violation of army regulations that Grant relieved him of command and put Sherman back in his old place. Only his loyalty to Grant seemed to have kept Sherman in service, for at the time Lincoln set McClernand over him, the newspaper clamor was sharp that Sherman was wasting precious lives of soldier boys through mismanagement. He wrote to his wife: "Painfully it begins to come home to the American people that the war which all have striven so hard to bring on and so few to avert is to cost us so many thousands of lives. Indeed I do wish I had been killed long since. Better that than struggle with the curses and maledictions of every woman that has a son or brother to die in any army with which I chance to be associated. Of course Sherman is responsible. Seeing so clearly into the future I do think I ought to get away. The President's placing McClernand here and the dead set to ruin me for McClernand's personal glory would afford me a good chance to slide out and escape the storm and trouble yet in reserve for us."

Yet Sherman stuck on with the army, held by affection and admiration for Grant, writing letters to his Senator brother that Grant was honest, able, sensible, and a hero, which sentiments reached Lincoln. If Grant should be relieved and McClernand put in his place, he couldn't serve under McClernand, Sherman wrote his brother. In his embitterment at the Government failing to recognize the stupendous efforts in the mud bottoms of the Mississippi he wrote, "It may be the whole war will be turned over to the negroes, and I begin to believe they will do as well as Lincoln and his advisers."

He was redheaded, lean, scrawny, this Sherman, with a mind of far wider range than usual in the army. One of the eleven children of a lawyer who served as judge of the supreme court of Ohio, when his father died he was adopted by Thomas Ewing, lawyer and famous Whig. An 1840 West Pointer, Sherman saw Indian fighting in Florida, studied law, was an adjutant general in California during the Mexican War, managed a bank in San Francisco, operated a New York office for a St. Louis firm, practiced law in Leavenworth, Kansas, and at the opening of the war was superintendent of the Louisiana State Military Academy at Alexandria. He had seen the United States and anxiety rode him about it; newspapers, politicians, the educated classes, were corrupt, blind, selfish, garrulous, to the point of tragedy.

"It may be, however," wrote Sherman, "that God in his wisdom wants to take down the conceit of our people and make them feel that they are of the same frail materials of mortality as the other thousand millions of human beings that spin their short webs and die all over earth. In all former wars virtues lost sight of in times of peace have revived, and to anyone who looked it is unnecessary to say that our governments, national, state, county and town, had been corrupt, foul and disgraceful. If war will change this, it will be cheaply bought."

At the opening of the war when Sherman had tried to impress Lincoln with the fighting capacity of the Southern people, saying he had lived among them and knew them, he was disgusted with Lincoln's reply: "Oh, I guess we'll manage to keep house." And Lincoln had been pleased at Sherman's saying he didn't want appointment to high rank; he would be a subordinate and perhaps work his way up while learning the art of war. He was a Midwestern man, at home with an Iowa farm hand or an Illinois college boy. The spare living of active service he accepted with humor. "A cavalry-soldier lent me his battered coffee-pot with some coffee and scraps of hard bread out of his nose-bag; Garland and I made some coffee, ate our bread together, and talked politics by the fire till late at night, when we lay down on straw saturated with the blood of dead or wounded men."

Riding up to a farmhouse in the path of conquest near Vicksburg, Sherman saw a dozen women sitting on the porch. One was the mother of a boy who had gone to school to Sherman at the Louisiana State Military Academy. She told him the boy was now an artillery lieutenant inside Vicksburg. "I then asked about her husband, whom I had known. She burst into tears, and cried out in agony, 'You killed him at Bull Run, where he was fighting for his country!' I disclaimed killing anybody at Bull Run; but all the women burst into loud lamentations, which made it uncomfortable for me. I rode away."

Sherman bemoaned the needless wreck and waste of war. When a dignified old plantation was burned and ruined near Grand Gulf, he blamed "the cursed stragglers who won't fight, but hang behind and disgrace our cause and country." An army should seize only what it needs to live on. "Of course I expect and do take corn, bacon, ham, mules and everything to support an army, and don't object much to the using of fences for firewood. But this universal burning and wanton destruction of private property is not justified in war."

Two Confederate majors at Vicksburg sent through the lines to Sherman a bouquet of flowers with compliments because he had refrained from firing on them the evening before when they were putting on a party. He was sentimental in April. "The trees are now in full leaf, the black and blue-birds sing sweetly, and the mocking bird is frantic with joy. The rose and violet, the beds of verbena and mignonette, planted by fair hands now in exile from their homes occupied by the rude barbarian, bloom as fair as though grim war had not torn with violent hands all the vestiges of what a few short months ago were the homes of people as good as ourselves."

Early in the war it had racked Sherman's mind that there was to be wholesale and organized slaughter by prolonged combat between his Northern people against others "as good as ourselves." He had paced to and fro in the hall of a hotel in Cincinnati mumbling to himself, and his high-pitched commentaries had earned him the nickname of "Crazy" Sherman among those who misunderstood.

Letters of Sherman to his wife and brother, as the war wore on, gave evidence he was anguished mentally by the cost in lives and money required to conquer the Southern people. He was the one Union general from whom would most naturally flow the remark "War is hell." For what seemed to him a just cause he would invoke terror. "To secure the navigation of the Mississippi River I would slay millions; on that point I am not only insane, but mad." Thus far only a few among important men knew in any degree the sincerity and the sensitively human quality of Sherman. Lincoln was yet to get acquainted with this lean, restless, hawk-eyed rider of war and apostle of conquest.

"I never saw such roses; and the other day I found a lily as big as a tiger lily, only it was a magnificent red." Thus Charles A. Dana, writing to a child at the North in a letter from Hankinson's Ferry on the Big Black River, with Grant's army in the Deep South. Dana's business, however, was not to tell children in the North about Southern red roses; his errand directly was to report to Lincoln and Stanton on what Grant, Sherman, McClernand, were doing. Dana had been Horace Greeley's managing editor on the *New York Tribune,* had revolted at Greeley's muddled, equivocal support of Lincoln, had resigned, later was given full credentials to travel with Grant's army, see everything, and report to the President and the Secretary of War. He had sent word to them that McClernand was no first-rate field officer, that

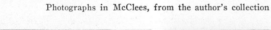

Clement Laird Vallandigham   Samuel Sullivan ("Sunset") Cox

Photographs in McClees, from the author's collection

Erastus Corning   Martin Kalbfleisch (above)
                              William Marcy Tweed

Photograph in McClees, from the author's collection   From the Meserve collection

THESE WERE TERMED "COPPERHEADS"

Horace Greeley

William Lloyd Garrison

TWO RADICALS, ONE AN OPPONENT, THE OTHER A SUPPORTER, OF LINCOLN

McClernand's delay in one movement had worried Grant, who "felt reluctant to remove McClernand, assigned to command by the President."

Stanton had conferred with Lincoln and telegraphed Dana on May 6: "General Grant has full and absolute authority to enforce his own commands, and to remove any persons who, by ignorance, inaction, or any cause, interferes with or delays his operations. He has the full confidence of the government . . . is expected to enforce his authority, and will be firmly and heartily supported, but he will be responsible for any failure to exert his powers. You may communicate this to him."

Dana reported three remarkable men heading the campaign, Grant, Sherman, and James B. McPherson, the last "thirty-two years old . . . a very handsome and gallant-looking man, with rather a dark complexion, dark eyes, and a most cordial manner," a natural engineer, having graduated No. 1 in his class at West Point. Dana noted that these three leading generals, all Ohio-born, had between them "utmost confidence," no jealousy nor bickering. "In their unpretending simplicity they were as alike as three peas." John A. Logan, the Illinois Douglas Democrat from far south in Illinois, Dana reported, was proving a heroic, brilliant, sometimes unsteady brigadier general, "full of generous attachments and sincere animosities"—few officers more effective and faithful.

Grant's home-town lawyer friend, now Assistant Adjutant General John A. Rawlins, Dana noted, gave himself no indulgence over Grant, "watches him day and night, and whenever he commits the folly of tasting liquor hastens to remind him that at the beginning of the war he gave him [Rawlins] his word of honor not to touch a drop." On a steamer trip up the Yazoo, Grant drank wine till he was too fuddled to make a decision as to how far up-river the boat should go, Dana ordering the steamer to return. "The next morning," wrote Dana, "Grant came out to breakfast fresh as a rose, clean shirt and all, quite himself."

A letter from Rawlins to Grant that morning said: "Tonight I find you where the wine bottle has just been emptied, in company with those who drink and urge you to do likewise. . . . You have the full control of your appetite and can let drinking alone. Had you not pledged me the sincerity of your honor early last March that you would drink no more during the war and kept that pledge during your recent campaign, you would not today have stood first in the world's history as a successful military leader. Your only salvation depends on your strict adherence to that pledge." What with Rawlins's watchfulness and loyalty, this wine drunk seems to have been the only one for Grant during the Vicksburg campaign.

Rawlins had almost an official status as a guardian of Grant in this one particular, for he had written Congressman Washburne, "I say to you frankly, and I pledge you my word for it, that should General Grant at any time become an intemperate man or an habitual drunkard, I will notify you immediately, will ask to be relieved from duty on his staff (kind as he has been to me), or resign my commission." So faithful was the watch kept by Rawlins over Grant that no distinct occasion ever arose that scandal-bearers could point to and say that drink had brought disaster.

Grant saw in Rawlins an unquestionable devotion and gave him wide sway. "He bossed everything at Grant's headquarters," wrote Dana. ". . . I have heard him curse at Grant when, according to his judgment, the general was doing something that he thought he had better not do. . . . Without him Grant would not have been the same man." Rawlins's pledge to notify Washburne when Grant became intemperate was not kept. But to the young woman to whom he was engaged to be married, Miss Mary Emma Hurlbut of Danbury, Connecticut, Rawlins wrote frankly of one occasion when he had to forego meeting her because he was held to the duty of keeping Grant sober.

He had hoped, wrote Rawlins, for a "moonlight-jewelled night" with "my dearest Emma" but "Matters have changed and the necessity of my presence here made almost absolute, by the free use of intoxicating liquors at Headquarters which last nights developments showed me had reached to the General commanding. I am the only one here (his wife not being with him) who can stay it in that direction & prevent evil consequences resulting from it. I had hoped but it appears vainly his New Orleans experience would prevent him ever again indulging with this his worst enemy. . . . That of which I have here written threatens to extend the time beyond that named for coming to you. This however I shall try and obviate by persuading the General to send for his spouse: if she is with him all will be well and I can be spared." It was Rawlins who detected that Grant away from his family was liable to spells of gloom that made him drink to forget his misery. It was Rawlins who persisted and managed till it became a custom for General Grant's wife, usually bringing the children, to visit him at headquarters, sometimes staying for weeks.

A steady stream of letters in the mail, and persistent callers at the White House, brought Lincoln the advice that for the sake of the country he must get rid of Grant. The tone of many of them ran like that of a letter of Murat Halstead, editor of the *Cincinnati Gazette,* to Secretary Chase. "How is it that Grant, who was behind at Fort Henry, drunk at Donelson, surprised and whipped at Shiloh, and driven back from Oxford, Miss., is still in command? Governor Chase, these things are true. Our noble army of the Mississippi is being wasted by the foolish, drunken, stupid Grant. He cannot organize or control or fight an army. I have no personal feeling about it; but I know he is an ass. There is not among the whole list of retired major-generals a man who is not Grant's superior."

On this letter Chase wrote an endorsement for Lincoln to read: "Reports concerning General Grant similar to the statements made by Mr. Halstead are too common to be safely or even prudently disregarded."

Among White House callers came one day John M. Thayer, a brigadier from Grant's army, who though a Nebraska man was for special reasons making a trip East. A secretary took his name in to the President and added, "Just from Vicksburg." And as Thayer told of this interview, Lincoln's first greeting was: "How does it happen that a man by the name of Thayer should have strayed way out to Nebraska? I thought all people of that name were Yankees and lived down roundabout Boston." Thayer was interested that Lincoln should be informed as to Thayers in general and himself in particular.

Lincoln told a doorman to let no one in without further orders, drew a chair alongside his own high-backed armchair and said, "Now sit down there and tell me all about Vicksburg." They talked an hour, Lincoln asking questions.

"General, you have a man down there by the name of Grant, have you not?"

"Yes, sir, we have."

And fixing an earnest and somewhat quizzical look on Thayer, Lincoln asked, "Well, what kind of a fellow is he?" Thayer replied that Grant was a real commander, popular with the army, making plans and throwing all his energies into their execution, going into campaigns with a fixed determination to win under all circumstances. Lincoln listened closely and then put the blunt question:

"Does Grant ever get drunk?"

"No, Mr. President, Grant does not get drunk."

"Is he in the habit of using liquor?"

Thayer said he had had many opportunities to observe Grant during two years of service. "I have seen him often, sometimes daily, and I have never noticed the slightest indication of his having used any kind of liquor. On the contrary, I have, time and again, seen him refuse to touch it. It has been charged in northern newspapers that Grant was under the influence of liquor on the fields of Donelson and Shiloh. The charge is atrocious, wickedly false. I saw him repeatedly during the battles of Donelson and Shiloh on the field, and if there were any sober men on the field, Grant was one of them. My brigade and myself gave him a Fourth of July dinner in Memphis in 1862. He, of course, as a guest, sat upon my right, and as wine and something stronger were passed around he turned his glass upside down, saying, 'None for me.' I am glad to bring this testimony to you in justice to a much maligned man."

"It is a relief to me to hear this statement from you," said Lincoln, "for though I have not lost confidence in Grant, I have been a good deal annoyed by reports which have reached me of his intemperance. I have been pestered with appeals to remove him from the command of that army. But somehow I have felt like trusting him, because, as you say, he has accomplished something. I knew you had been down there with him, and thought you would give me reliable evidence, for I have desired to get the testimony of a living witness. Your direct and positive declarations have given me much satisfaction. Delegation after delegation has called on me with the same request, 'Recall Grant from command,' as the members of the delegations were not willing their sons and brothers should be under the control of an intemperate leader. I could not think of relieving him, and these demands became very vexatious. I therefore hit upon this plan to stop them.

"One day a delegation headed by a distinguished doctor of divinity from New York, called on me and made the familiar complaint and protest against Grant being retained in his command. After the clergyman had concluded his remarks, I asked if any others desired to add anything to what had already been said. They replied that they did not. Then looking as serious as I could, I said:

" 'Doctor, can you tell me where General Grant gets his liquor?'

"The doctor seemed quite nonplussed, but replied that he could not. I then said to him:

" 'I am very sorry, for if you could tell me I would direct the Chief Quartermaster of the army to lay in a large stock of the same kind of liquor, and would also direct him to furnish a supply to some of my other generals who have never yet won a victory.' "

Lincoln handed Thayer a friendly slap on the leg, lay back in his chair, had a laugh, and resumed:

"What I want and what the people want is Generals who will fight battles and win victories. Grant has done this and I propose to stand by him. I permitted this incident to get into print, and I have been troubled no more with delegations protesting against Grant. Somehow or other I have always felt a leaning toward Grant. Ever since he sent that message to Buckner, 'No terms but unconditional surrender,' I have felt he was a man I could tie to, though I have never seen him."

The secretaries, Nicolay and Hay, noted that when overzealous people had accused Grant of intemperance, Lincoln's reply was, "If I knew what brand of whiskey he drinks I would send a barrel or so to some other generals."

The President was going the limit for a fighting general and wrote to Congressman Isaac N. Arnold as between good friends, "Whether Gen Grant shall or shall not consummate the capture of Vicksburg, his campaign from the beginning of the month up to the twenty-second day of it, is one of the most brilliant in the world."

At one time, Nicolay noted, Grant's standing had sunk so low with newspapers, politicians, and a large public that Lincoln remarked, "I think Grant has hardly a friend left, except myself." Lincoln and Stanton sent down a committee of three to observe Grant. They were Grant's home Congressman, the teetotaler E. B. Washburne, the hard-drinking Governor Yates of Illinois, who had given Grant his first regiment to command, and the moderate-drinking Adjutant General Thomas from the War Department.

"I carry in my bag full authority to remove General Grant and place whomsoever I please in command of the army," said Thomas to Commander Porter as they drank on the flagship a toddy Porter had mixed with a guarantee. "It will make you sleep like a top, and you won't feel the mosquitoes." Further along, Porter warned Thomas not to use the authority to remove

Grant. "The army and navy would tar and feather you and neither Grant nor myself could prevent it." The old General, chuckling from above a long nightshirt loaned him by Porter, queried, "Is it possible?" and gave the assurance: "I don't intend to do anything. We are delighted with all we have seen, so there will be no change."

Grant's own uncomplaining explanation of his unpopularity during early 1863 was simple: "Visitors to the camps went home with dismal stories to relate [of rain, mud, fever, measles, smallpox]; Northern papers came back to the soldiers with these stories exaggerated. Because I would not divulge my ultimate plans to visitors, they pronounced me idle, incompetent and unfit to command men in an emergency, and clamored for my removal. Not to be satisfied, many named who my successor should be. McClernand, Fremont, Hunter and McClellan were all mentioned in this connection."

The President having selected him for command, without his seeking it, Grant said he felt more free to follow his own plans through than if he had been appointed through personal or political influence. "With all the pressure brought to bear upon them, both President Lincoln and General Halleck stood by me to the end of the campaign. I had never met Mr. Lincoln, but his support was constant."

When in June Grant had at last penned Pemberton in Vicksburg and stood a chance of bagging the whole of that Confederate army, the tide of feeling about Grant began to change, so much so that Sherman wrote in a letter home: "Grant is now deservedly the hero. He is entitled to all the credit. . . . He is now belabored with praise by those who a month ago accused him of all the sins in the calendar, and who next week will turn against him if so blows the popular breeze. Vox populi, vox humbug."

During June, Grant's army, earlier numbering only about 40,000, was reinforced to 70,000 and more. The plantations of Jefferson Davis and his brother Joseph had been captured and supplies from them lent aid to the Union cause. A world audience was looking on and wondering how many days or months the siege might last.

The marching of Lee with 80,000 Confederate troops up into Pennsylvania, with Meade and the Army of the Potomac trailing him for battle, hoping to stop him, was a bold movement, partly made on the chance that the danger to Northern cities would cause Lincoln and Halleck to draw off troops from Grant to fight Lee. In such event it was believed that Pemberton might, as ordered by his superior, General Joseph E. Johnston, cut his way out of the seven miles of Union trenches encircling Vicksburg. Kirby Smith to the west had an army that might try coming to Vicksburg. At any time, too, Johnston eastward might get reinforcements, march to Vicksburg, and turn the siege into a battle. Johnston was rated by many as in military genius second only to Lee among living Confederate generals. The anxiety of the North was phrased: "Grant is a long way from home and anything can happen to him."

In hundreds of caves dug in the clay hillsides of the besieged city, women and children wondered how long till the end. One eyewitness told of seeing a woman faint as a shell burst a few feet from her. He saw three children knocked down by the dirt flung out from one explosion. "The little ones picked themselves up, and wiping the dust from their eyes, hastened on." Said another, "I saw one bright young bride whose arm shattered by a piece of shell had been amputated."

Yet these were minor incidents to the thousands whose daily monotonous menu of mule and horse meat with parched corn had run out in latter June. Pemberton, as he had said he would, killed the last dog for food. Then what? Then he fed the men of his garrison on rats, cane shoots, and bark. Some of the men standing in the firing trenches were wobbly on their legs. Pemberton was obeying instructions from President Davis to hold Vicksburg at all costs.

CHAPTER 39

DEEP SHADOWS—LINCOLN IN EARLY '63

> *Only they*
> *That come to hear a merry, bawdy play,*
> *A noise of targets, or to see a fellow*
> *In a long motley coat guarded with yellow,*
> *Will be deceiv'd.*
> —SHAKESPEARE, King Henry VIII

THE tragedies of Shakespeare took on deepening interest for Lincoln in the progressions of the war. Politics and war, plots and whispering, blood-soiled prospects moaned over, involved conscience offset with comic thrust and belly-bursting laughter; the same humanity whether riding an English stagecoach or a B. & O. passenger train, comrade greeting from a line: "In God's name what are you and how came you hither?" In the White House in winter and at the Soldiers' Home in summer John Hay heard "The Ancient," as he sometimes wrote of Lincoln, recite:

> For God's sake, let us sit upon the ground,
> And tell sad stories of the death of kings:
> How some have been depos'd, some slain in war,
> Some haunted by the ghosts they have depos'd;
> Some poison'd by their wives, some sleeping kill'd;
> All murdered: for within the hollow crown
> That rounds the mortal temples of a king
> Keeps Death his court; and there the antick sits,
> Scoffing his state, and grinning at his pomp;
> Allowing him a breath, a little scene
> To monarchize, be fear'd, and kill with looks,
> Infusing him with self and vain conceit

WAR DEPARTMENT

EVERY DAY
THIS WEEK
ONWARD TO
RICHMOND
BY A SELECT
Company of STAMP
GENERALS

COLUMBIA. "Where are my 15,000 Sons—murdered at Fredericksburg?"   LINCOLN. "This reminds me of a little Joke—"   COLUMBIA. "Go tell your Joke at Springfield!!"

Harper's Weekly, usually friendly to the Administration, pillories Lincoln, Stanton, and Halleck

> As if this flesh which walls about our life
> Were brass impregnable; and humour'd thus,
> Comes at the last, and with a little pin
> Bores through his castle walls, and farewell king!

In those months between Fredericksburg and Chancellorsville, in the weeks that saw Lee put an army of 80,000 into Pennsylvania, events swirled round the peculiar pivot where Lincoln moved, and put him into further personal isolation.

Death was in the air. So was birth. What was dying men did not know. What was being born none could say.

So often daylight seemed to break—and it was a false dawn—and it was as yet night.

When hope came singing a soft song, it was more than once shattered by the brass laughter of cannon and sudden bayonets preceding the rebel yell.

Said Howell Cobb of Georgia in early '63: "Only two things stand in the way of an amicable settlement of the whole difficulty: the Landing of the Pilgrims and Original Sin."

The first combat of Negro troops against white had taken place in the Vicksburg area when 1,000 enlisted Union black men defended Milliken's Bend from an attack of some 2,000 Confederates. The fighting was hand-to-hand mainly, and when the repulse was over, many were found dead with bayonet stabs and others with skulls broken open by musket butts.

"It is impossible for men to show greater gallantry than the negro troops in that fight," said General Elias S. Dennis, an eyewitness. Said another: "White and black men were lying side by side, pierced by bayonets, in some instances transfixed to the earth. Two men, one white and the other black, were found side by side, each with the other's bayonet through his body. It was a contest between enraged men. One took his former master prisoner, and brought him to camp. A rebel prisoner requested that *his own* negroes should not be placed over him as a guard."

As such news spread North it intensified agitation for and against the use of more Negro regiments.

In the deepening bitterness General John M. Thayer and others heard Lincoln say his main anxiety was in the North. "The enemy behind us is more dangerous to the country than the enemy before us." When the South Carolina secession convention had declared its reasons for leaving the Union, Delegate Dargan had said: "Not all the Northern people are hostile to the rights of the South. We have a Spartan band in every Northern State. It is due to them they should know the reasons which influence us."

Editor Rhett of the *Charleston Mercury* in early '63 pictured this "Spartan band" as reinforced. "The mighty rabble of New York and Philadelphia have caught up the cry raised by the Hoosiers of the North-west, and day by day the peace element grows stronger. The utterances which reach us show that there has been no lack of venal presses and unscrupuli politicians, shaping their course so as to share the rising fortunes of the anti-war movement."

The Richmond Government could not have planted a readier spokesman than it had in Congress at Washington in Clement L. Vallandigham, who could see George Washington as sadly looking down upon "us, the false, degenerate, and imbecile guardians" of the Republic. "He was a rebel. And yet we, cradled ourselves in rebellion, would now, forsooth, make the word 'rebel' a reproach." Vallandigham quoted Chatham, "My lords, you can not conquer America," and went on: "And you have not conquered the South. You never will. . . . War for the Union was abandoned; war for the negro openly begun, and with stronger battalions than before. With what success? Let the dead at Fredericksburg and Vicksburg answer."

The costly and bloody failure of the war, urged Vallandigham, was admitted by Lincoln in his two Emancipation Proclamations. "The President confessed it on the 22nd of September, solemnly, officially, and under the broad seal of the United States. And he has now repeated the confession." Could the war go on? "Whence the money to carry it on? Where the men? Can you borrow? From whom? Can you tax more? Will the people bear it? . . . Will men enlist now at any price? Ah, sir, it is easier to die at home. I beg pardon; but I trust I am not 'discouraging enlistments.' If I am, then first arrest Lincoln, Stanton, Halleck . . . and I will retract." More than 1,000,000 had been called to arms: "Seventy-five thousand first . . . then eighty-three thousand more were demanded; and three hundred and ten thousand responded. . . . The President next asked for four hundred thousand, and Congress . . . gave him five hundred thousand; and, not to be outdone, he took six hundred and thirty-seven thousand. Half of these melted away in their first campaign; and the President demanded three hundred thousand more for the war, and then drafted yet another three hundred thousand for nine months. The fabled hosts of Xerxes have been outnumbered."

Should the war go on? "I answer no—not a day, not an hour," shouted Vallandigham. He outlined a plan for the soldiers of both armies to fraternize and go home, while the governments at Washington and Richmond should not even negotiate a treaty of peace; the geographical unity and the old bonds and the former common flag would restore the old Union. "When we have done this, the welfare, peace, and safety of the African will have been best secured."

A peace man of shaded sincerity, Vallandigham of Dayton, Ohio, had the country's eye. His father, a Presbyterian minister, traced directly to a Huguenot driven out of France for religious convictions and settling in Virginia in 1690. His mother was Scotch-Irish. Teaching school at Snow Hill, Maryland, he studied at night; he practiced law in Columbus, Ohio, served in the State legislature, edited the *Western Empire* at Dayton, and, known as an extreme proslavery man, lost several campaigns for judge, lieutenant governor, member of Congress, declaring the abolitionists had given him "ten years of exclusion from office and honor at that period of life when honors are sweetest." He had supported the Douglas ticket in 1860, had served two terms in Congress, had failed of re-election in 1862 because of a strong Republican county added to his gerrymandered district.

Seven petitions for Vallandigham's expulsion had been received and read in the House of Representatives. A resolution had been moved for an inquiry into his loyalty by a House committee. But instead of his being gagged, at the close of an hour of his peace oration on January 14, 1863, when his time had expired no member objected to his proceeding another half-hour. They permitted him to lay down all essential points he had in mind. In his efforts it was evident he had studied the classics of oratory and of dramatic appeal, that he was not averse to language and had practiced with adjectives.

Vallandigham quoted the sustaining verse "The Lord is my shepherd," knowing there was a heroic isolation in his position. And yet, though he had faced mobs and hostility as fierce as Wendell Phillips had known, he lacked the simple words and the cool deliberation of Phillips. "Let New England heed," he warned the antislavery men, "else she, and the whole East, too, may learn yet from the West . . . that . . . *evulgato imperii arcano, posse principem alibi, quam Romae fieri*." Except for the word "alibi" few knew what he was talking about.

The war was not so much one of sections as one of different types of mind, held Vallandigham. "It is the old conflict of the Cavalier and the Roundhead, the Liberalist and the Puritan . . . upon new issues . . . of the Yankee and the Southron." The Roundhead "by a skillful use of slavery and the negro united all New England first, and afterwards the entire North and West, and finally set out to battle Celt and Saxon, German and Knickerbocker, Catholic and Episcopalian, and even a part of his own household. . . . Said Mr. Jefferson, when New England threatened secession, sixty years ago: 'No, let us keep the Yankees to quarrel with.' Ah, sir, he forgot that quarreling is always a hazardous experiment." Then followed Vallandigham's view that "popular uprisings" were in preparation in the North, civil war between the West and New England.

Tall, bearded, sonorous, he was; his self-righteousness gave him a personal exaltation; he was chosen to be the vocal instrument of absolute justice. "Perish office, perish honors, perish life itself; but do the thing that is right, and do it like a man. I did it. Certainly, sir, I could not doubt what he must suffer who dare defy the opinions and the passions, not to say the madness, of twenty millions of people. Had I not read history? Did I not know human nature? But I appealed to Time, and right nobly hath the Avenger answered me. I did not support the war; and to-day I bless God that not the smell of so much as one drop of its blood is upon my garments." He abhorred and detested the execrable maxim "All is fair in politics," and declaimed, "I had rather that my right arm were plucked from its socket, and cast into eternal burnings, than, with my convictions, to have . . . defiled my soul with the guilt of moral perjury."

Pretending candor, Vallandigham employed the innuendo. "I have spoken, and I would that my voice could penetrate that most impenetrable of all recesses, the precincts of the White House." His assertion was that the President kept secluded from the public. Having alleged, he passed on as though a fact had been established.

He sketched the war beginning. "The President elect left his home in February, and journeyed towards this capital, jesting as he came; proclaiming that the crisis was artificial, and that 'nobody was hurt.' He entered this city under cover of night and in disguise." On being sworn in, the President announced in the same breath that the platform of his party should be the law unto him; from that moment all hope of peaceful adjustment fled. "Hate sat enthroned, and the sacrifices of blood smoked upon every altar." Habeas corpus and the guarantees of personal freedom vanished. "The Attorney-General, first of all men, proclaimed in the United States the maxim . . . *Whatever pleases the President, that is law!*"

Vallandigham alluded to Athens, Rome, Carthage, English kings. "Of what possible avail was his [the President's] proclamation of September? Did the South submit? Was she even alarmed? And yet he has now fulmined another 'bull against the comet'—*brutum fulmen*—and, threatening servile insurrection with all its horrors, has yet coolly appealed to the judgment of mankind, and invoked the blessing of the God of peace and love!"

Vallandigham had a vision of "the gospel of peace" replacing "the gospel of abolition and hate." He became practical and specific. "Stop fighting. Make an armistice—no formal treaty. . . . Buy and sell. . . . Open up railroads. . . . Visit the North and West . . . the South. Exchange newspapers. Migrate. Intermarry. Let slavery alone. Hold elections at the appointed times. Let us choose a new President in sixty-four."

John A. Bingham of Ohio replied: "Strip these words of all disguise, and they simply mean to-day . . . this Government has no power to defend itself against armed rebellion and treason. . . . The gentleman stands here to denounce Abraham Lincoln . . . for issuing his proclamation of the 15th of April, 1861, after the walls of Sumter had been broken by the infernal enginery of treason, and the hand of the Almighty alone had saved its gallant defenders from perishing in its flames. . . . Sir, the gentleman . . . would have been eulogizing, instead of denouncing the present Executive of the United States, if, like his predecessor, instead of issuing that proclamation . . . he had crept through the avenues of the capital muttering, like a gibbering ghost, the silly words, 'the Constitution does not allow the coercion of a rebel State.' "

Thad Stevens rose to say that Vallandigham might be guilty of either treason or treasonable practices. "Any deputy provost marshal not skilled in these nice distinctions would be very likely to do great injustice by reporting the gentleman. [Laughter.]"

Vallandigham believed in peace and free speech—on occasion. Once he had used his right of free speech to write in his Dayton organ that the abolitionists, having brought on the war, aimed further to bring a horde of Negroes into Ohio to take bread out of the mouths of white laborers. This he followed with a reference to an antislavery speech by Moncure D. Conway in Dayton. "It seems to us that about three months in Fort McHenry, in a straight uniform, with frequent introductions to the accommodating institution called the town pump, and without the benefit of the writ of *habeas corpus*, would have a tendency to improve the gentleman mentally, and, for a while at least, rid the community of a nuisance."

Less sincere, more adroit and incessant, than Vallandigham was Wilbur Fisk Storey, publisher and editor of the *Chicago Times*, a broken-down newspaper which he had vitalized and made the voice of the extremist enemies of the Lincoln Administration. A Vermont boy, he had been printer's devil, typesetter in New York, and drifting West had edited Democratic newspapers at La Porte and Mishawaka, Indiana, in Michigan was postmaster at Jackson under President Polk, in two cities had run drugstores, had given eight years to building up the *Detroit Free Press*, earning $30,000 for himself, and in 1861 at forty-two had begun to give Chicago and the Middle West a morning paper that was gossipy, sensational, fearless, devious.

A tight-lipped, short-spoken man, his face whiskered except for the upper lip, Storey cultivated suspicion as a habit, looked men over with a cold glitter of eye, boasted he had no friends, and seemed to count that day lost which brought him no added haters. He illustrated the claim that men often threatened with death seldom die early. Into the news of the day and the editorial comment, he shot a phosphorescent and fascinating malice, possibly foretokening the future hour when he was to be paralyzed and legally adjudged insane.

During March of '63 the *Chicago Times* printed items accredited to its anonymous and apocryphal Washington correspondent. He was joining his effort with shadowy others who wished to impeach the President of the United States. Without giving a name, a date, a definite source of information, a shred of evidence, or a slight clue, this journalist gabbled with a responsible air in a lingo of finality. The President was an outrageous criminal who would be punished with impeachment, and soon—such was the gist of this news.

"I learn from a distinguished gentleman from New York," wrote the poisoned pen one day, "that there is a movement on foot in that city looking toward the impeachment of the President at the opening of the next session of Congress, in the manner provided by the Constitutional lawyers of the country, including two from the West, and is in the hands of men whose character for decision and firmness, as well as for courage, is a sufficient guarantee that they will carry it through. Every intelligent man is aware that the crimes committed by the Executive, and his utter inability to conduct the affairs of the nation, even in a time of peace, have furnished ample grounds for his impeachment; and every true patriot will rejoice to learn that he is to be brought to punishment. The first draft of the articles of impeachment is already drawn up. It embraces charges which if proved against Queen Victoria, would bring her to the untimely end of Charles I. The English people would not have endured the outrages on their rights to which the American people have patiently submitted. No English King would have dared to violate the English Constitution as our President has violated the Constitution of the United States."

Editor Storey, as one having full traditional freedom of the press, could have accurately and properly headed this Washington correspondence "Off with His Head!"

The Chicago Board of Trade and the Young Men's Christian Association began a boycott of the *Times* early in '63. The Chicago & Galena Railroad ordered its sale stopped on trains. General Hurlbut at Memphis and other

From the first ring, "Brag—Buncombe," the aerial acrobat Lincoln has moved through the second ring, "Paper money," has his left foot in "Emancipation" and his right foot about halfway toward "Utter Ruin." The English cartoonist Matt Morgan sees eye to eye with Congressman Vallandigham and Editor Storey.

commanders forbade in their military districts the circulation of Storey's newspaper.

Few newspapers in the Southern Confederacy were so generously sympathetic toward President Davis as the *Chicago Times*. When an old Mexican War acquaintance of Davis's, J. Wesley Greene of Pittsburgh, Pennsylvania, made his way to Richmond and returned North, the *Chicago Times* printed a four-column affidavit by Greene in which he told of interviews with Davis and with Lincoln. "I regard Mr. Davis as bowed down under a weight of tremendous responsibilities, and of almost overpowering sorrows," read the Greene affidavit. "I regard Mr. Davis as a man who this day needs, and I may say deserves, the sympathy of humanity in a pre-eminent degree. In heart, I do not believe him a rebel against the Constitution. . . . I think he has taken, and maintains at much personal discomfiture, the position he now occupies, with the sincere hope of navigating the hostile vessel and directing the course of the ship of state into a harbor where hostilities must cease, and from whence, a better understanding springing up, they may sally forth with the old flag unfurled to wave in every breeze and gladden every sea."

Thus Storey and the *Chicago Times* were trying to change impressions in the minds of the boys and men by thousands in the Board of Trade regiment, in Mulligan's Irish Brigade, and other commands, who had marched away singing "The Union Forever" and "We'll hang Jeff Davis to a sour apple tree." The *Times* printed the Davis peace terms as given, verbally, to J. Wesley Greene. Three times Greene had called on Davis and repeated the terms so that he would be sure to have them precisely correct when he later gave them to Lincoln in Washington. The terms in brief were: (1) general and unconditional amnesty for all political offenders; (2) restoration of all fugitive slaves; (3) each of the contending parties to be held responsible for its own debts.

By rail and on horseback Greene was escorted by Confederate officers to a point near Harper's Ferry, made his way home to Pittsburgh, wrote a letter to Lincoln saying he had been to Richmond, had talked with Davis, and "matters had transpired" which he believed, followed up, "would lead to a cessation of hostilities and the restoration of the Union." In reply came a telegram from Stanton inviting him to Washington.

Greene went on to the capital, handed Stanton letters of introduction from respectable citizens of Pittsburgh, was at once taken to the White House, waited five minutes outside Lincoln's office, and then was told to walk in where the door was open. "Mr. Lincoln was alone. He greeted me in an easy affable manner, and, on taking a seat near his table by his direction, he handed me my own letter to him, with the inquiry, 'Did you write that letter?' I replied, 'I did.' He then rang the bell, which was answered by a man whose business it is to wait near the door of the Executive Chamber for certain specific purposes. Mr. Lincoln told this man he would receive no more visitors that morning. On the man's departure, Mr. Lincoln requested me to tell him in detail as nearly as I could remember, everything touching on the matter hinted at in that letter. I commenced by saying that I had been guilty of some irregularity—perhaps impropriety—and hoped that the end would, in his judgment, justify the means. I then gave him all the details of my visit to Mr. Davis. Mr. Lincoln's first remark, made without a moment's hesitation, was, 'I see nothing objectionable in them.' I understood him to refer to the proposals of Mr. Davis, as I ceased speaking when I named them. I suppose that Mr. Lincoln saw at a glance the pleasure and eagerness with which I caught his reply; for he began immediately to modify the expression, in view, apparently, of certain contingencies; but the impression made upon my mind then was not removed by any subsequent remarks of Mr. Lincoln nor is it removed by anything I find in his message to Congress, namely: that, if left to the impulses and convictions of his own heart, and at liberty to do so, he would inaugurate a peace on the basis of those proposals."

Stanton arrived on Lincoln's summons. They questioned Greene, had him repeat the proposals he said he had memorized from the lips of Davis at Richmond. Lincoln said that would be all, but he would like Greene to stay at his hotel between the hours of four and six, on call.

At five o'clock a messenger came to Willard's and escorted Greene to the White House, where he was introduced to the Cabinet, examined as to his acquaintance with Davis. A discussion of the peace terms followed and became, said Greene, "enveloped in a cloud of embarrassing considerations." Inquiry rose as to why Mr. Davis did not pursue the course that he knew all along was open to him.

"Some little merriment was indulged in," said Greene, "in reference to Mr. Davis' views respecting the Emancipation Proclamation—the President in this taking the lead; Secretaries Seward and Welles being the only gentlemen who seemed to preserve the dignity of their position, and rightly to estimate the importance of the occasion. As for Mr. Stanton, a semi-fiendish vindictiveness came out prominently in every look, in every motion of head and hand, and in every word. It seemed to greatly please the President, because it flattered his vanity, and I thought I could read in his countenance that he deemed that proclamation a stroke of statesmanship that posterity would regard as the boldest and grandest conception of military strategy; the military necessity sunk into utter nothingness that which others might esteem its unconstitutionality. Never did the tones and bearings of a man appear before me in all my ideas of the despot whose only will is law, as did those of Mr. Lincoln on that occasion. I looked at him with the eye of an artist, and had I the ability to place on canvas my idea of the highest type of despot, I should paint Mr. Lincoln as he then appeared; because he presented to my mind all the characteristics of a man conscious that he was lording it over a free people. The very apparent self-gratulations of Mr. Lincoln were the signal or license for a little desultory and personal conversation among the several gentlemen. Mr. Lincoln dismissed me by saying that he wished to see me the next morning at his chamber, and very kindly offered to send an attendant with me to the hotel. This I declined. One or two of the gentlemen said they were going partly in that direction, but, without waiting for them, I bowed myself out."

The next morning, J. Wesley Greene had a brief interview with the President, in the evening, so his affidavit ran, met the Cabinet again, felt that they were less inquisitorial and incredulous of him. "I saw Mr. Lincoln, at his own request, three successive mornings afterward. He appeared to have no business with me, beyond that of seeing me, and asking some trifling questions in reference to something before said. I also saw Mr. Stanton each day, at his request, and his business seemed to be similar to that of the President. My calls on Mr. Stanton were made in the afternoon, by his appointment. That there was a concerted motive in timing these calls I was satisfied, but cannot say, or even guess, what it was."

Finally Stanton gave Greene transportation to Pittsburgh, continued the affidavit, and by order of the President $100 for services. "Mr. Lincoln dismissed me in a formal but friendly way, suggesting at the same time, that perhaps I had not better return to Pittsburg for a short time. He gave no reasons for this suggestion. Imagine as many as I may they are but imaginings at best. I omitted to say that the President, in dismissing me, requested to be kept advised of my whereabouts. My doubts of Mr. Stanton, and reawakened fears for my own safety, led me to use the order of transportation only from Washington to Baltimore. From that point I pursued my way by a zigzag course, and have not, as yet, seen proper to comply with the President's request, and advise him of my whereabouts."

Thus ended the affidavit of J. Wesley Greene, subscribed and sworn to in Cook County, Illinois, on December 9, 1862, and published in the *Chicago Times* and other newspapers. Thus a soiled dove of peace in the service of Editor Wilbur F. Storey failed in the mission he set out on and was generally taken to be an odd fisher in muddy waters.

The *New York Express* made outcry that the President had rejected an evangel of fraternal feeling. The *New York Tribune* replied that no message, no overture, "justifying a hope that any other than a Disunion Peace was attainable" had ever failed of the warmest welcome from Abraham Lincoln. "Witness the success of the arch impostor and swindler, J. Wesley Greene, who, on the strength of merely presenting himself as an emissary from Jeff Davis bearing proffers of reconciliation, was favored with repeated and confidential interviews with Mr. Lincoln and was sent on his way rejoicing with his pocket replenished. That the villain lies with regard to many of the incidents of the interviews is clear enough; but that they took place, substantially as he alleges, is undenied and undeniable."

Robert Todd Lincoln figured in several fabricated news items. Barefaced and unembarrassed, without basis or explanation, with no more emotion than might shade the frozen face of a brass monkey, the editors of the *New York Day Book*, the *Chicago Times*, and like party organs printed the one sentence: "The President's son, 'Bob,' as he is called, a lad of some twenty summers, has made half a million dollars in government contracts."

That was the item entire. How or where the President's son spent his

SINBAD LINCOLN AND THE OLD MAN OF THE SEA.
[From *Frank Leslie's Illustrated Newspaper*—May 3, 1862]

For months *Leslie's Weekly* carried editorial and cartoon attacks on Secretary Welles,
alleging the Navy Department incompetent and corrupt—though not convincing the
President of its own purity of motive

time or his money, or in what particular field of contracts he might have made $500,000, could not be told without at once confusing any political reader whose sympathies already inclined him to believe that the President was corrupt as well as despotic. The editors intended to do what they did.

Surrounding one viciously false item with strictly correct facts about fire, murder, hog and corn shipments, disasters at sea, they could snare the careless average reader into accepting the false item and spreading it by word of mouth.

The editors Fernando Wood and Wilbur F. Storey, when they could by this process create a vague, uneasy, primitive fear of something wrong, would refer to it as "public opinion."

Wood and Storey were clammy. Old Sam Medary, joined to them politically, was no buzzard but was a philosopher, a natural dissenter and protestant, whose weekly newspaper, the *Crisis* at Columbus, Ohio, presented the ancient Anglo-Saxon case for personal liberty as against the arrogance and presumption of authority. Born of a Quaker mother whose ancestors had crossed the sea with William Penn, he was in his editorials eloquently antiwar and consistently held Lincoln all wrong, on the premise that all wars are all wrong. Medary had personally thrown his help to Samuel F. B. Morse, inventor of the telegraph, in promoting that device, and now personally joined Morse in antiwar propaganda. A Buchanan appointee Governor of the Territory of Kansas, a veteran Jackson and Douglas Democrat, Medary was referred to as "The Old Wheel Horse of Democracy."

Sixty-two years old, bluff, gray-bearded, sincere Sam Medary could sit at his desk and keep up a running conversation with any visitor as his pen chased along writing an editorial. "Abe Linkin reminds us of a little anecdote we once heard, very foolish and no nub to it," he wrote. Or "A 'Loyalist' is one who acknowledges Abe Lincoln to be 'the Government.' If Abe Lincoln is the Government, with his army of official thieves, would it not be an act of patriotism to notify such a Government to skedaddle as soon as possible?" The President's course was "serpentine," said the *Crisis*.

A mob one night wrecked the print shop, smashed the editorial desks, and Editor Medary issued a number blaming soldiers from Camp Chase, egged on by the *Ohio State Journal* editor, whom he characterized as "dirty pup," "hired pimp," "daily associate of burglars," "gloating hyena"; the Republicans concerned were "idiots and knavish asses."

An open letter of the *New York World* "to the President of the United States" played on Lincoln's rural Midwestern surroundings, his status as a country greenhorn. "You have read, Mr. Lincoln, in the quiet shades of Springfield, where you passed so large a portion of your life in the unostentatious practice of the private virtues which gained you the esteem of your neighbors—in that tranquil retreat, sir, with the horror natural to an ingenuous mind, you have read of the Roman emperor who placed his edicts so high in the air they could not be deciphered by the keenest eye."

The *World* writer sought for masterly invective, withering satire, which would become an American classic, à la Junius. "Mr. Lincoln, you were educated a lawyer, and from the great amount of leisure you must have enjoyed in the intervals of your rural practice to qualify yourself, by fit studies, for your present exalted station, it is to be presumed that you are well read in the literature of your noble profession. Permit us to carry your mind back to those assiduous and ennobling studies." Then proceeded accusations that the President was polluting the fountains of justice instead of cleaning the Augean stables.

Many of the anti-Administration newspapers and periodicals were openly or impliedly proslavery. The *Old Guard,* published monthly by C. Chauncey Burr in New York, might have been edited from Richmond or Charleston and only by extremists of Southern viewpoint in those cities. The abolitionist preachers were going directly against the teachings of Christ and the Apostles, according to this periodical. Burr signed a long thesis, quoting the Apostle Peter, I Peter, 2 : 18, as saying: "Slaves, be subject to your masters with all fear; not only to the good and gentle, but also to the froward. For this is thankworthy, if a man for conscience towards God endure grief, suffering wrongfully." St. Paul, he said, had converted a fugitive slave, Onesimus, and sent him back to his master, Philemon, with a letter. From the time of Augustus to that of Justinian, there were in Italy 20,000,000 slaves to 6,000,000 freemen. Corinth, where Paul preached, was the chief slave market for Greece. "Though Christ and his apostles were thus surrounded with slaveholders, they never once denounced the institution then as a sin or the sum of all villanies."

Burr quoted I Timothy, 6 : 1: "Let as many servants as are under the yoke count their own masters worthy of all honor, that the name of God and his doctrine be not blasphemed." If Jesus and his Apostles lived in New York or Ohio in 1863, they would be denounced by the abolitionists as traitors and sympathizers with rebellion, though "Our Lord often refers to the institution of slavery to illustrate some great principle of duty. He always refers to it without a word of censure." In fact, "Many of our Lord's most beautiful parables are pictures of slave establishments."

Burr quoted Christ as saying, "The kingdom of heaven is like unto a man traveling into a far country, who calleth his own slaves, &c." He quoted Beecher in a Boston sermon: "We need more bloodshed. Blood is the wine of the nations. God feeds them on blood," and replied: "Then pour out your own purple current, ye snuffing, yelping bloodhounds. You are the leeches without bowels, that ever cry, *more!* You have dragged the blessed gospel of peace into a pool of blood, impaled humanity as in hell. The besotted throngs who have drunk of your spirit are nearer devils than men, breaking humanity to pieces on the anvil of death."

Burr inquired whether radical traitor Congressmen had coerced the President into a war of conquest. "If, as we have been told, this wretched man, the President, has been forced to proclaim against the Constitution, let him, by all means, be forced to re-proclaim in its favor. If rascals have compelled him to do wrong, let honest men compel him to do right." Otherwise, "Let us begin to prepare epitaphs of eternal shame for the tombs of

the traitors who dare lift up their hands, with Abraham and his fellow con-
spirators, against the Union and the Constitution."

Burr quoted Danton: "Room, there! Room in Hell for Robespierre!"
Over and again came this cry, published and circulated; Lincoln was a
Robespierre; in the near future he awaited sudden, violent death. Said the
Old Guard in a passage reprinted in many newspapers: "O Lincoln! O
Seward! O Stanton! Remember Robespierre, whose head rolled at last under
the very guillotine where he had caused so many innocent heads to roll
before! Remember and tremble!" Under the heading "The Lincoln Cate-
chism" were such points as:

Question. What is the Government?
Answer. Abraham Lincoln, Charles Sumner, and Owen Lovejoy.
Question. What is a President?
Answer. A general agent for negroes.
Question. What is Congress?
Answer. A body organized for the purpose of appropriating funds to buy Africans,
and to make laws to protect the President from being punished for any violations of
law he may be guilty of.
Question. Whom are the members of Congress supposed to represent?
Answer. The President and his Cabinet.
Question. What are the particular duties of a Commander-in-Chief?
Answer. To disgrace any general who does not believe that the negro is better than
a white man.
Question. What is the meaning of the word "law"?
Answer. The will of the President.
Question. Have the States any rights?
Answer. None whatever, except what the general government bestows.
Question. What is the *habeas corpus?*
Answer. It is the power of the President to imprison whom he pleases as long as
he pleases.
Question. Who is the greatest martyr of history?
Answer. John Brown.
Question. Who is the wisest man?
Answer. Abraham Lincoln.
Question. Who is Jeff. Davis?
Answer. The Devil.

After March 4, 1865, drawings and paintings would be put on exhibition
in Washington, C. Chauncey Burr predicted in the *Old Guard*, including
such pictures as: No. 1. A view of the Cave of Famine. A graveyard in the
distance with 400,000 graves; at the right 200,000 cripples, and on the left
an uncountable throng of widows and orphans. A remarkable picture—
dedicated to Abraham Lincoln. No. 2. Judas Iscariot in the act of betraying.
Dedicated to E. Stanton, Esq. No. 4. A group of gamblers quarreling. Dedicated to Republican contractors. No. 9. A white man embracing a Negro
wench. An immodest picture, dedicated to Charles Sumner. No. 10. The
Forty Thieves breaking into a Government treasury. Dedicated to friends
of the Administration. No. 18. Diplomatic dinner at the White House. His

Black Excellency the Minister from Hayti seated between Mrs. Lincoln and the charming Miss Chase. The seats of the rest of the diplomatic corps vacant.

One morsel of utterance from Lincoln was seized on. Editors and orators of the opposition hurled their strength at Lincoln's fragment in his inaugural address: "Suppose you go to war, you cannot fight always; and when, after much loss on both sides, and no gain on either, you cease fighting, the identical questions as to terms of intercourse are again upon you." Burr quoted this and observed that Lincoln was a Babylon-builder. "The passion-blinded Nebuchadnezzars in the British House of Lords scorned the warning words of the great and sagacious Pitt, when he thundered in their ears, 'My lords, you can not conquer America!' "

Demurrings arose also to Lincoln's progressions in styling the Negroes in 1859 "negroes"; in 1860, "colored men"; in 1861, "intelligent contrabands"; in 1862, "free Americans of African descent."

"A Washington Republican letter-writer says that Mr. Lincoln reminds him of Louis XIV," wrote Burr. "But he does not tell us why. Is it because Louis was a great tyrant and a great fool? Or is it because he was surrounded with pimps, plotters, rascals? Louis' flatterers really persuaded him that he was a great man, and they gave him golden medals, setting forth exploits never achieved. Perhaps Lincoln's flatterers, the contractors and the brave knights of shoddy, have persuaded him that he is a great man. Lincoln should have a medal representing himself as standing between a dungeon and a graveyard, holding a white man's skull on the point of a sword with a negro baby resting on his bosom. The Washington letter-writer is not to be laughed at for discovering parallels between a French Bombastes and an American Furioso."

Burr and other extremist editors in the North alluded frequently to Negro-blooded Republican leaders. "A western author has issued a pamphlet adducing evidence to show that Old Abe is 'part negro,' " wrote Burr. "Of the truth of his *facts* we know nothing. Hamlin and Sumner, to the scientific eye, show the presence of negro blood, but we cannot say the same of Old Abe. Nature, however, sometimes disguises herself so effectually as to elude even the quick gaze of science. On the whole we are not sure that it would not redound to Lincoln's honor to have it proved that he is part negro. For then, on the ground of a natural sympathy with his own race, we might find excuses for acts which we could never pardon in a white man."

Months passed with C. Chauncey Burr proclaiming tyranny in the land; his New York magazine circulated freely through the Federal mails, his personal exercise of free speech not hampered. "The crimes of the administration are all Mr. Lincoln's own. What is the sense in talking about the President's 'honesty' and 'good intentions'? Does he not know better than to *break* the laws he was elected to administer? Those conservative members of Congress who still profess to believe in his good intentions, should bring a resolution to remove him as an imbecile—an incapable executive."

Copperhead editors took it as grist to their mills that the *Economist* of London should say that "the smallest, weakest, and meanest set of men who ever presided over the policy of a great nation" headed the Federal Government. "The President means well, but he does nothing else well. He was not selected: he is 'the accident of an accident,' the inexplicable caprice of a forgotten caucus; no one knew much about him, and therefore scarcely anyone could object to him."

In the President's enjoining the people set free by the Emancipation Proclamation "to abstain from all violence unless necessary in self-defence," the *New York Herald* saw a dangerous firebrand. "An Irish student who witnessed from his room in old Trinity, a proctor being ducked in the college tanks, cried out with the gravest air, 'Boys, don't nail his ear to the pump.' Of the same solemn character is the injunction of Mr. Lincoln to the negro in his Proclamation." A black-face minstrel joke became common:

"Sambo, why don't you go for to be a soldier?"

"Well, suh, did yuh evah see two dogs fightin' ovah a bone?"

"Yes, I have seen two dogs fightin' over a bone, but what has that got to do with you?"

"Well, suh, you nevah see de bone fight, did you? I'se de bone!"

The *Metropolitan Record* of New York City began an article by saying that "the present unworthy successor of Washington, the Abolition President, Abraham Lincoln, has become a convert to spiritualism." Therefore the editor gave Lincoln a trial presided over by the ghosts of the Republic— Jefferson, Jackson, Clay, Calhoun, and Hamilton. The arguments closed with Lincoln's being convicted in phrases modeled from the Declaration of Independence: "He has erected a multitude of new offices, and sent hither swarms of officers to harass our people and eat out their substance. He has quartered large bodies of armed troops among us, deprived us of the benefits of trial by jury, taken away our charters, suspended our own Legislatures. He has incited domestic insurrections among us." And so on, with other charges. At their reading "a ghastly pallor overspread the face of the criminal at the bar, and as he looked upon the immortal document he trembled in every limb."

A verse screed of more than two hundred lines describing "The Devil's Visit to Old Abe" as imagined by the Reverend E. P. Birch of La Grange, Georgia, was much reprinted, somewhat in class with doggerel from an anonymous Baltimorean:

With a beard that was filthy and red,
His mouth with tobacco bespread,
Abe Lincoln sat in the gay white house,
Awishing that he was dead—
Swear! Swear! Swear!
Till his tongue was blistered o'er,
Then in a voice not very strong
He slowly whined the Despot's song;

Lie! Lie! Lie!
I've lied like the very deuce!
Lie! Lie! Lie!
As long as lies were of use;
But now that lies no longer pay,
I know not where to turn,
For when I the truth would say,
My tongue with lies will burn!

> Drink—Drink—Drink!
> Till my head feels very queer!
> Drink—Drink—Drink
> Till I get rid of all fear!
> Brandy, and Whisky, and Gin,
> Sherry, and Champagne, and Pop,
> I tipple, I guzzle, I suck 'em all in,
> Till down dead drunk I drop.

There were six more similar verses. Orpheus C. Kerr had the word "poickry" for it. A "Political Alphabet" made the rounds, of which the letters A and P had the following verses:

> A stands for Old Abe, who has made up his mind
> To yield to the pressure that crowds him behind;
> And to aid the Malignants in splitting the Nation,
> Has issued his mandate of Emancipation.

> P stands for Priests who in politics dabble,
> Exciting the fury and hate of the rabble;
> Inflaming the mind with fanatical vigor,
> To crush down the Saxon, and build up the Nigger.

Jinglers plumb disgusted with the Government took their pens in hand. The *Bangor Democrat*, way Down East in Maine, had a versifier who spilled sixteen stanzas of "A Plain Epistle to Uncle Abe" without stopping for breath, two reading:

> You're out of luck entirely, Abe,
>   The engine's off the track;
> The biler's bust, and there you are,
>   A sprawling on your back!
> The exciseman is at the door,
>   Contractors cry for pelf;
> You're blind and stupid, deaf and lame,
>   Not very well yourself.

> You want to free the darkeys, Abe,
>   At least, I so construe it;
> The difficulty seems to be
>   To find out how to do it.
> The way, dear Abe, is mighty dark,
>   And bothersome to see;
> I fear you'll have to give it up,
>   And let the darkey be.

The *New York Mercury* gave its readers a satire as "coming from a devotee in the city churches." Its closing lines read:

> O Abe! Save thy people and bless thy parasites!
> Govern them and increase their salaries forever!
> Day by day we puff thee,
> And we exalt thy name forever in the daily papers.
> Vouchsafe, O Abe! to keep us this day without a change of Generals!
> O Abe! have mercy on the army of the Potomac!
> O Abe! let thy mercy be upon us, as our trust is not in Stanton.
> O Abe! for thee have I voted, let me never be drafted!

A touch of nonsense and democracy was in shafts of sarcasm from the *Logan Gazette* in Ohio. "We suppose the Government was cut with a razor the other day when Seward wounded his hand. . . . If Lincoln should

The President and aides "play a pleasant comedy"—of death—in the view of cartoonist
Adalbert J. Volck of Baltimore

take the diarrhoea the Government would have to swallow burnt brandy or
some other astringent to regulate its bowels. . . . If Lincoln should get the
rheumatism, the Government would have to go on crutches. . . . When
Chase takes snuff the Government has to sneeze. . . . The Government is
about six feet high, has large feet and lank jaws, and used to maul rails when
it was young."

Both loyal and disloyal newspapers gave the case of a young trader
anxious to make some money by sending goods from Memphis down to
New Orleans. "Are you a loyal citizen?" asked the provost marshal.

"No, sir."

"You must take the oath of allegiance."

"Very well, sir."

And he was duly sworn, the marshal saying, "There, you have taken the oath. Do you know what that means?"

"Yes, sir. It means a padlock on my mouth and a bayonet in my rear."

The eminent scientist Matthew F. Maury, acting as a Confederate naval agent in Europe, wrote in the London *Times* in the summer of 1863 that elections in the South were a mockery, that Lincoln had ordered his generals "to let none vote but friends of Lincoln and the Union." The hostility to Lincoln resulting from martial law was bringing the war to an end. "Indeed, so straitened is Mr. Lincoln at this moment that his partisans are resorting to a desperate game. They are endeavoring to raise the war-cry against France and England, hoping thereby to rally the people to arms. Nay, more; there are rumors of a peace party in his Cabinet; and of a proposition there to revoke the Emancipation Proclamation and propose terms to the South."

This letter of Maury's was widely circulated internationally because of his distinguished name and career. An accident had lamed him for life when as a young lieutenant in the navy he had taken to study, written a worthy volume on *The Physical Geography of the Sea*, made original discoveries regarding ocean currents and the Gulf Stream, received the order of knighthood, medals, and honors from the leading European governments. A Virginian, he had resigned as head of the United States naval astronomical observatory and as chief of the hydrographic office when Virginia seceded. Now he was assuring Europe that in America the lower levels of society would soon be trumpet-tongued for peace. "To smother that voice, even now Mr. Lincoln has to keep an armed force not only in New York and Kentucky, but in Ohio, Indiana and other States. He is even now marching one up into Iowa, to put down there the cry for peace."

In New York City, Samuel F. B. Morse, who held the patents on the electric telegraph and had been knighted and awarded medals and honors from many nations, served as president of the Society for the Diffusion of Political Knowledge, a Peace Democrat organization sending forth showers of pamphlets under the slogan "Read—discuss—diffuse." To a brother-in-law Morse wrote that Lincoln was "weak," "vacillating," "illiterate," "a President without brains." Politely yet firmly the pamphlets of this society maintained that the President was completely mistaken as to habeas corpus, slavery, and the conduct of the war. "Sir, we can not acquiesce in your dogmas," was the way they put it. "Will you, Mr. President, maintain that because the writ of habeas corpus may be in suspense, you can substitute soldiers and bayonets for the peaceful operation of the laws?"

The chameleon Congressman James Brooks had built the *New York Express* into a paying newspaper which daily struck at the Administration. He had in effect endorsed secession and favored New York as a Free City out of the Union. Brooks's sea-captain father was lost in a shipwreck, and the eleven-year-old boy clerked, taught school at $10 a month, and worked his way through college, became Washington correspondent for the *Port-*

land Advertiser, started the *Express* in New York. A Harrison Whig in 1840, Brooks later joined the American (antiforeigner and anti-Catholic) party, in 1861 inviting himself into the Democratic party. In speeches and editorials he enjoyed quoting from Lincoln's inaugural address: "I have no purpose, directly or indirectly, to interfere with the institution of slavery in the States where it exists. I believe I have no lawful right to do so, and I have no intention to do so." The Society for the Diffusion of Political Knowledge published one of Brooks's speeches:

> Who created Abraham Lincoln the Government of the United States? Who elected him, a man of no better flesh and blood than the rest of us, to be the Government of thirty millions of people in the United States?
> *A Voice*—The people. [Cries of "No, no," "Put him out," "Let him be."]
> *Mr. Brooks*—The people! Never! [Exciting cheers.] Never, never did the people give him a majority of their suffrages. [Continued cheers.] He is a minority President, appointed by the operations of the Constitution in spite of the people of the United States. [Cheers.] A large majority of the people voted against him, and he was created President in and under that very Constitution he would overthrow by his proclamations. [Great and continued cheers.]

Brooks quoted from the Emancipation Proclamation: "The Executive Government . . . will recognize and maintain the freedom of such persons [Negro slaves] . . . in any effort they may make for their actual freedom," and commented: "I do not know that the President means to excite a servile insurrection. I will not impute to him the horrible intent of converting the Southern country into a Hayti or St. Domingo, with the 'Authority' of his army and navy to help, but I say, that the language is susceptible of that meaning, and such meaning has been given to it throughout the civilized world. [Applause.] When the 'Executive Government' thus addresses negroes or slaves, words ought to be used that negroes or slaves can not pervert into authority to burn, slay, destroy, without regard to condition, age or sex. [Applause.]"

The Lincoln opposition took pleasure in reprinting extracts from the official report of the Anti-Slavery Society's convention in 1862, as presented in the *Anti-Slavery Standard.* The Emancipation Proclamation had not yet been issued and Delegate Pillsbury gave the view: "Abraham Lincoln, formerly called the slave hound of Illinois, has increased and enlarged his former tendency." Mr. Stephen S. Foster submitted "there is no need to compare Davis and Lincoln, any more than any other two slaveholders." Lincoln, as a slave-catcher returning fugitive slaves to their masters, was worse than Davis, the slaveholder. "I would rather take my chances with Jefferson Davis at the last judgment than with President Lincoln."

With the purpose of making Lincoln seem to be a radical abolitionist, the Lincoln opposition often reprinted a genuine letter from Senator Sumner to a Boston antislavery friend, beginning: "Your criticism of the President is hasty. I am confident that, if you knew him as I do, you would not make it." Sumner gave cases of the President's repudiating actions such as turning the Union Army camps into hunting-grounds for fugitive slaves. "I have often heard from his own lips, that slaves finding their way into the national lines are never to be re-enslaved. This is his conviction, expressed without reserve."

Copperhead editors were pleased to publish statements of Sumner that he had found the President eager to emancipate the slaves of the District of Columbia, to acknowledge the independence of the Negro republics of Hayti and Liberia, and to carry forward the principles of the Declaration of Independence. Emancipation of the slaves in the District of Columbia was peculiarly the President's own proposition. "In familiar intercourse with him, I remember nothing more touching than the earnestness and complete-ness with which he embraced this idea. I say, to you, stand by the Adminis-tration. I wish that you really knew the President, and had heard the artless expressions of his convictions on those questions which concern you so deeply. You might, perhaps, wish that he were less cautious, but you would be grateful that he is so true to all that you have at heart. If I write strongly, it is because I feel strongly, for my constant and intimate intercourse with the President beginning with the 4th of March, not only binds me peculiarly to his administration, but gives me a personal as well as a political interest in seeing that justice is done him."

Sumner in this would not be taken literally by abolitionists in the mood of Lydia Maria Child. She quoted John Bright, "God is carrying on the revolution in America very *slowly*, that he may make emancipation *sure*," and added her own opinion: "Certainly, if the Lord wanted *slow* work to be done, He could not have employed a better hand than Old Abe."

A letter from Orestes Augustus Brownson to Sumner was not halfway in its judgment that failure and collapse would be seen under the Presidency of Abraham Lincoln. "I do not believe in Mr. Lincoln at all, and, to make headway against him and the Rebellion together is more than the United States can do. He is thickheaded; he is ignorant; he is tricky, somewhat astute, in a small way, and obstinate as a mule. Even the good measures that he is willing to adopt lose all their value by his adopting them out of season and in an unstatesmanlike manner. Is there no way of inducing him to resign, and allow Mr. Hamlin to take his place? My opinion of Mr. Lincoln is that nothing can be done with him, that no change in the Cabinet would make matters any better. He would damp the ardor of the bravest and most loyal man, and neutralize the efforts of the ablest and most accomplished statesman were they in his Cabinet. He is wrong-headed, the attorney not the lawyer, the petty politician not the statesman, and, in my belief, ill-deserving of the *soubriquet* of Honest. I am out of all patience with him. The war is not conducted as war, but subsidiary to his politics and to the cupidity of railroad-men, shipping masters, and contractors. . . . The Pres-ident in persisting in treating the Seceded States as States in the Union cre-ates all the difficulty there is in regard to the slavery question, and his policy in regard to compensation is rather pro-slavery than anti-slavery."

"Abe will do nothing decent till driven to it by a power which would move all the devils in hell," wrote F. W. Bird to Sumner, while J. M. Forbes of Boston inquired: "Can nothing be done to reach the President's ear and heart? I hear he is susceptible to religious impressions; shall we send our eloquent divines to talk to him, or shall we send on a deputation of mothers and wives, or can we, the conservatives of liberty, who have elected him, combine with Congress in beseeching him to save the country?"

Any affiliation of Lincoln with the radical abolitionist Owen Lovejoy was seized on by the opposition press. "The President," said Lovejoy in a Cooper Union speech, "is like a man driving a horse in the thills of a buggy, and leading another behind by a halter-strap. It is very awkward managing two horses this way, as I know from experiment. Now, the President knows that the horse Radical that he is driving can go ahead, for he has by him been taken in handsome style into the Executive chair; but he is a little afraid that this mettlesome charger cannot be trusted going down hill, otherwise he would let go of the old racka-bones that hobbles along behind. Now, I do not propose to dash ahead, so as to throw the President out, or break the carriage; but to go so steadily, that the Executive can be assured that he is safe with the Radical steed, down hill as well as up, and on level ground. . . . If the President does not believe all I do, I believe all he does. If he does not drive as fast as I would, he is on the same road, and it is a question of time."

Verse-writers welcomed by anti-Lincoln editors saw their hundreds of stanzas published, many similar in style and feeling to "The Serenade of the 300,000 Federal Ghosts," which was "respectfully dedicated to Old Black Abe" and told of "the long, long procession of hearses at thy gate." One stanza:

> Around thy bed we'll stand, at midnight's awful hour,
> And our wrongs and our country's into thine ear we'll pour,
> While headless trunks and gory breasts, fresh from the carnage there,
> Shall mingle all unheeding of the looks of blank despair.
> But mind not thou the slain, the day of ghosts they say is o'er,
> Yet we're coming, Father Abr'am, with three hundred thousand more.

More readable was "A Prayer" reprinted in Northern papers from the *Columbus* (Georgia) *Enquirer*. Found in the pocket of a captured Union soldier, written on a blank leaf of a religious tract, the lines ran:

> Our Father who art in Washington,
> Abraham Lincoln be thy name.
> Thy will be done at the North
> As it is in the South!
> Give us this day our daily
> Rations of crackers and bacon;
> And forgive us our shortcomings
> As we forgive our quartermasters
> And commissaries; for thine is the
> Power, the nigger, and the soldiers,
> For the term of three years, Amen.

Verses titled "The Heavy Curse" signed by "Toaster" were printed in Copperhead newspapers and in at least one Republican journal, which commented, "So far as we can learn, Mr. Lincoln still sleeps o' nights, just as if Toaster hadn't cursed him so heavily." Four stanzas read:

May Heaven's curses, dark and dire,
Commingled with Almighty fire,
Fall on your head and press you down
With dreadful torture to the ground!

On you may hell put forth its might,
And shroud your soul in endless night;
May this e'er be thy resting-place,
And that of all your cursed race!

May peace forever from you fly,
Pleasures fleet when they seem nigh,
And in their place may gnawing pain
Seize and rack your burning brain!

And if there be a curse more dire
Than hell with all its liquid fire,
Oh, may it in your soul e'en creep,
And hellish fiends their nightly orgies keep!

Doggerel titled "An Eagle for a Goose" was blunt as a maul and aimed at being serious with a modulated grimace. The key verses ran:

How changed—how strange is everything—
  We had a Union once—
A statesman for a President,
  But now we have a dunce.

We have no Eagle—change is there—
  Abe swapped our bird away,
We have no Eagle any more,
  Bald-headed, black or gray.

An Eagle once we had, a brave,
  A proud majestic bird—
And on the freedom-giving mount,
  His piercing voice we heard.

Abe swapped away our glorious bird—
  Got cheated like the deuce!
The talons for the web-foot went—
  The Eagle for the Goose!

A parody of "Johnny, Fill up the Bowl" could be sung by those who liked singing. One verse ran:

Abram Lincoln, what yer 'bout?
  Hurrah! Hurrah!
Stop this war! It's all played out—
  Hurrah! Hurrah!
Abram Lincoln, what yer 'bout?
Stop this war! It's all played out—
  We'll all drink stone blind—
  Johnny, fill up the bowl!

"Here is the latest joke," said the *Salem Advocate* in southern Illinois on May 28, 1863. "We commend it to old Abe, for he likes a joke and had rather indulge in one than to say his prayers. A well-dressed, smiling gentleman, named Cox, called at General Burnside's headquarters in the Burnet House in Cincinnati last week and desired to see the General. After delay he was ushered in. 'General Burnside,' said Mr. Cox, 'I have read your general order No. 38 and not wishing to violate it have called to get a permit.'

" 'You do well to observe the orders of the department,' said the General. 'You wish a permit?'

" 'Yes, sir,' said Mr. Cox, smiling obsequiously. 'I wish to get permission from this department to call Abe Lincoln an old miserable lying son of a b——, and to call his cabinet a thieving, corrupt set of scoundrels.'

" 'Do you wish to insult this department?' shouted the General.

" 'Oh, no, by no means,' said Mr. Cox, 'not for the world. I only want to express my opinions of these men, and if you will grant a permit I will do so. But if you refuse permission, why then you know, as I wish to obey the order No. 38, why you know, General, why I won't say it, that's all.' And Mr. Cox bowed himself out."

Under the heading "Lincoln Again in Doubt" the *Salem Advocate* said that someone sent President Lincoln an assortment of newspaper clippings and in speaking about them to a friend, Lincoln said: "I read this batch of editorials, and when I was through reading I asked myself, 'Abraham Lincoln, are you a man or a dog?' " The *Advocate* remarked, "Possibly he may be waiting to find out which side the Almighty is on."

The press was serving ideas in fricassee style, and when a Congressman said, "Mr. President, we have had Nigger served up to us three times a day regularly, dished up in every possible style," Lincoln, it was published, made a pun in replying, "The principal style, I think, was *free-cuss--ee.*"

More serious was a February sentiment of the *Louisville Journal*: "If Mr. Lincoln, gazing abroad throughout the whole country that he was elected to preside over, does not regret his election more than almost any other man in the nation, bitterly as millions regard it, he must be almost the weakest and worst man in the nation." In newspapers and in the *Congressional Globe* appeared Lincoln's Mexican War speech wherein he alluded to President Polk as "a bewildered and miserably perplexed man," with Lincoln's hope for Polk: "God grant that he may be able to show there is not something about his conscience more painful than all his mental perplexity."

The methods of newspapers came briefly into a talk of Lincoln's with Congressman John B. Alley of Massachusetts, who wrote of how John Quincy Adams hated Daniel Webster, refused to speak to Webster when they met. Yet when charges of corruption were brought against Webster, Adams went to a committee of investigators and begged them to admit only "proof of the most positive character" because "to taint his reputation would be an irreparable injury to the nation." Adams pointed to the chief glory and wealth of England as consisting "in the great historic names of which she was so justly proud." This, noted Alley, struck Lincoln into an exclamation: "How just, noble and patriotic such sentiments were—and oh! if the Press of this country could be made to inhale something of this spirit of patriotism and fairness—what would I not give?"

In Northern homes when children asked fathers and mothers, "Why did the war begin and why does it go on?" the Copperhead answer was the same as in the South, and fairly well gathered by Mrs. M. B. Moore in *The Geographical Reader for the Dixie Children*, published in 1863 in Raleigh, North Carolina: "In the year 1860 the Abolitionists became strong enough to elect one of their men for President," read the school primer. "Abraham Lincoln was a weak man, and the South believed he would allow laws to be made, which would deprive them of their rights. So the Southern States seceded, and elected Jefferson Davis for their President. This so enraged President Lincoln that he declared war, and has exhausted nearly all the strength of the nation, in a vain attempt to whip the South back into the Union. Thousands of lives have been lost, and the earth has been drenched with blood; but still Abraham is unable to conquer the 'Rebels' as he calls the South. The South only asked to be let alone. It would have been wise in the North to have said to her Southern sisters, 'If you are not content to dwell with us longer, depart in peace. We will divide the inheritance with you, and may you be a great nation.'"

Hate was wanted, more hate and deeper hate, also hate tempered and steeled harder, edged with finer cutting blades, according to one high adviser of Lincoln. Until the Union troops and their home neighborhoods had more of a thirst to kill the enemy, the North would lose, ran this counsel. The earnest and personally kindly General Burnside, after the Fredericksburg breakdown in morale, said to Congressman Julian, and could hardly have withheld the same view from President Lincoln: "Our men did not feel toward the rebels as they felt toward us, were not sufficiently fired by resentment." Burnside urged Julian "to breathe into our people at home the same spirit toward our enemies which inspired them toward us."

Cold with the revolutionary scorn that can kill and take joy in killing were the lines of mingled ice and fire in a poem printed in the *New York Tribune Almanac* for 1863. Hate was there for the F.F.V.—the First Families of Virginia. "Bone Ornaments" was the title and it read:

> Silent the lady sat alone;
> In her ears were rings of dead men's bone;
> The brooch on her breast shone white and fine,
> 'Twas the polished joint of a Yankee's spine;
> And the well-carved handle of her fan
> Was the finger-bone of a Lincoln man.
> She turned aside a flower to cull
> From a vase which was made of a human skull;
> For to make her forget the loss of her slaves
> Her lovers had rifled dead men's graves.
> Do you think I'm describing a witch or ghoul?
> There are no such things—and I'm not a fool;
> Nor did she reside in Ashantee;
> No—the lady fair was an F.F.V.

Into the roofs and walls of Southern homes fell Northern shells, scattering families southward, bringing the war to women and children. Fleets and armies had desolated Southern cities. Houses of several Main Streets stood mute as dried skulls. In the North many streams of life flowed on as if the war had never been heard of. While the rifles spat and cannon roared below the Ohio River in the spring of '63, announcement was made from New York of the publication of the sixteenth and concluding volume of the *New American Cyclopaedia*, a compendium of human knowledge under American direction, edited by George Ripley and Charles A. Dana, the whole costing more than $400,000.

The immortal Greek statesman Pericles and the plodding contemporary Abe Lincoln were stood alongside each other for comparison in an *Atlantic* article titled "Pericles and President Lincoln" by Henry M. Alden, who saw Greece of twenty-three centuries past split into Ionic and Doric sections seeking to frustrate and disembowel each other. "President Lincoln meets the same embarrassments . . . that Pericles met in his campaigns against Sparta; it was his coming into power that precipitated the violence of war; his determined action against all sympathizers with the enemy draws down upon him the intensified wrath of these sympathizers; the generals whom he sends into the field . . . are trammelled with political entanglements and rendered useless."

Lincoln, "the Baboon President," was "a low-bred obscene clown," according to the *Atlanta Intelligencer* in Georgia, while Robert E. Lee, according to the *Boston Transcript* in Massachusetts, had with his own hands flogged a slave girl and poured brine on her bleeding wounds. Each side played for hate. "The cruel and incredible barbarities of the rebels every day accumulate in horror," said *Harper's Weekly*. "They cut off the heads of our dead at Manassas; they boiled the bodies to get the bones more readily; they buried our brave brothers with their faces down; they swung their heads as trophies upon their homeward march." Almost the same sentences in Southern newspapers used the word "Yankees" instead of "rebels."

Ninety-six clergymen of all the denominations in the South signed an address *To Christians throughout the World*. Published in April of '63, it distinctly charged that President Lincoln by his Emancipation Proclamation intended to produce a general insurrection of slaves, which event "would make it absolutely necessary for the public safety that the slaves be slaughtered, and the history of that event would record the darkest chapter of human woe yet written." Old men had been put at hard labor with a ball and chain at their ankles; helpless women had been torn from their homes, jailed, and "fed on loathsome rations," according to a proclamation of Jefferson Davis, which also declared, "The President of the United States has by public and official declaration signified not only his approval of the effort to excite servile war within the Confederacy, but his intention to give aid and encouragement thereto."

Southern newspapers told of Yankee troops entering the home of ex-Governor Clark at Rocky Mount, North Carolina, taking from Mrs. Clark her jewelry, and saying it was military orders. With this was coupled an item in the *Savannah News:* "We learn from the *Philadelphia Inquirer*, the most sycophantic of Lincoln's lickspittles, that the betrothal ring ordered by ex-Governor Sprague for his intended bride, Miss Kate Chase, is a diamond solitaire, set in enamel, price $4,000."

These were mild allegations compared with the *Chicago Post* story of marines at Tensas Bayou finding skeletons of white officers who had commanded Negro regiments, and taken prisoner, "these officers had been nailed to the trees and crucified." Charred and partially burned limbs were "evidence" that other officers had been nailed to slabs of wood and given slow death from broiling. Less grim was the allegation that Southern soldiers taken prisoner, being asked what they were fighting for, replied, "We are fighting for the rich man's niggers."

The widow of ex-President James K. Polk at her Nashville home gave an interview reporting the head and heart of a perplexed and confounded woman. "I never was a secessionist, and I don't think I ever will be one. I said that Mr. Lincoln was constitutionally elected, and that that election should be acquiesced in by every true patriot. . . . I do not deny that my womanly sympathies are with the South, and that I often catch myself exulting over the success of the Confederate arms, but this is only when my reason is taken prisoner and my judgment temporarily suspended at the bidding of my prejudices. I was born in the South. My surroundings have all been Southern, my relatives, friends, and more than all. Is it, then, reasonable to suppose that 'in a moment, in the twinkling of an eye,' with the frosts of many winters upon my head, I can throw off, as I would a garment, all the affections, all the endearing associations, of a long life? No! no! this cannot be. Yet I long and pray for a restoration of my distracted country to its former peaceful and happy condition, for a restoration of the 'Union as it was.' "

"John W. Andrews exhibited a cross, the emblem of the sufferings of our blessed Saviour, fashioned for a personal ornament, which he said was made from the bones of a Yankee soldier," related newspaper correspondence from New Orleans. The Butler regime gave Andrews two years at hard labor.

Southern journals informed their readers of Yankee soldiers gambling with dice made from the bones of Confederate soldiers. The *Philadelphia Press* reported a Tennessee Union man who, having twice been drafted into the Confederate Army and having twice deserted, "was captured, carried off in the night, and actually crucified: spikes being driven through his hands and feet, thus fastening him to a tree and leaving him to a lingering and horrible death; gagged that his cries might not call anyone to relieve him, nearly a week elapsed before he was discovered; he was still alive but died the second day of his release." A Confederate prisoner at Camp Morton, Indianapolis, received a letter from a girl cousin, writing: "I will be for Jeffdavise till the tenisee river freaze over, and then be for him, and scratch on the ice

"Jeffdavise rides a white horse
Lincoln rides a mule,
Jeffdavise is a gentleman,
And Lincoln is a fule."

A war was on and the gates of Janus open. The *New York Tribune* chronicled John A. Tainter, of Hartford, Connecticut, dying and leaving $1,000,000 to his wife and two daughters, providing in his will that should either of the daughters marry a foreigner or the native of a Southern or slaveholding State, she would lose her interest in the property. The *Charleston Courier* printed a note from one of the matrons of South Carolina: "I propose to spin the thread to make the cord to execute the order of our noble President Davis when old Butler is caught and my daughter asks that she may be allowed to adjust it around his neck."

The *Louisville Journal* took note of several editors in the Confederate States fond of calling Mr. Lincoln "the Gorilla," and commented: "The Gorilla, as travelers tell us, is an animal that sits upon the branch of a tree, and when a man is passing under, seizes him around the throat, draws him up, and holds him suspended in the air till he is choked. Have our friends of the secession press some suspicion that Old Abe may haul them up to the limb of a tree?"

Propaganda roared and shibboleths were shrieked. The storm rose, let down, came back with higher hurricane howling. The masses of people of North and South stood as a landscape lighted by slogans. Prayers of white and gold lost their way in yells of red and black. Two contestants dug deeper for stronger hates.

A bird was brought to the White House, metaphorically speaking, and one man said it was a white dove of peace and another said it looked to him more like a hankering crow black as the ace of spades. Fernando Wood, become a Congressman, wrote Lincoln that the Southern States would send representatives to the next Congress if so permitted; he had been so advised by a well-informed authority. Lincoln wrote Wood, "I strongly suspect your information will prove to be groundless; nevertheless, I thank you for communicating it to me." If the South should send Congressmen to Washington, that would be the same as ceasing resistance to the Washington Government. "I say that in such case the war would cease on the part of the United States" and amnesty or full pardon would not be withheld. "I do not think it would be proper now for me to communicate this, formally or informally, to the people of the Southern States. My belief is that they already know it; and when they choose, if ever, they can communicate with me unequivocally." The President, however, did not think it proper to suspend military operations to try any experiments of negotiation. He would receive with great pleasure any exact information which Wood might furnish him. "While there is nothing in this letter which I shall dread to see in history, it is, perhaps, better, for the present, that its existence should not become public. I therefore have to request that you will regard it as confidential."

Nothing developed from this exchange of views, except that Wood gave his letter and Lincoln's to the newspapers for publication.

While the Confederate armies strode through the victories of Fredericksburg and Chancellorsville, several quiet and somewhat furtive movements aimed at peace by negotiation. Senator Powell of Kentucky brought to the Senate a resolution before the legislature of his State to provide "that a commissioner be appointed to visit Mr. Lincoln and those in power at Washington, and the Confederate government at Richmond, to settle our difficulties and bring about peace." The movement, vague in its peace terms, was suspect. Senator Powell said it was unjust that those who originated it were "harshly denounced."

New York Peace Democrats took on fresh activity with the inauguration of their new governor, Horatio Seymour, fifty-three years old, a man of inherited fortune who had gone into politics and followed it as a career, serving as Mayor of Utica, Speaker of the State Assembly, lieutenant governor, delegate to national conventions. Seymour shaved his face, wore a muffler of whiskers around his throat, had ringlets of hair circling a bald pate. Though his mouth and chin were all curves, he was utterly serious. "In common with the majority of the American people, I deplored the election of Mr. Lincoln as a great calamity," he said after the war began. "Yet he was chosen in a constitutional manner, and we wish, as a defeated organization, to show our loyalty by giving him a just and generous support." Seymour gave money and time to raising troops.

"We denounce the rebellion as most wicked," said Seymour, "because it wages war against the best government the world has ever seen." The months wore on. His campaign for the governorship approached. He called for closer Democratic organization to oppose the incompetents at Washington who would never save the nation, intimated that compromise measures could have prevented the war, demanded full freedom to criticize the Federal Administration. "The President holds his office, not by the will of the majority, but by the Constitution which placed him there by a vote of 1,800,000 against 2,800,000."

The Emancipation Proclamation, Seymour said on taking office, violated the Constitution; to free 4,000,000 Negro slaves, the North would require a military despotism. He was sincere and earnest toward political ends, his word on immediate issues usually dictated by his purpose of leading a party of opposition. He meant to hold his party together and eventually take control at Washington.

"I assure you that the Government, President, and every member of the Cabinet, Seward included, are firm in their purpose to press this war and to make no peace on any terms which severs the nation," wrote Edwards Pierrepont, eminent New York attorney, in January of '63 to Seymour. "I have never seen the President half as earnest."

Lincoln wrote to Seymour in March of '63 a letter so simple, so plain, and so openly friendly that Seymour was suspicious as he read: "You and I are substantially strangers, and I write this chiefly that we may become better acquainted. I, for the time being, am at the head of a nation which is in great peril, and you are at the head of the greatest State of that nation. As to maintaining the nation's life and integrity, I assume and believe there cannot be a difference of purpose between you and me. If we should differ as to the means, it is important that such difference should be as small as possible; that it should not be enhanced by unjust suspicions on one side or the other.

In the performance of my duty the coöperation of your State, as that of others, is needed—in fact, is indispensable. This alone is a sufficient reason why I should wish to be at a good understanding with you. Please write me at least as long a letter as this, of course saying in it just what you think fit."

Seymour sent a brother to Washington to convey assurances of loyal support and to protest against arbitrary arrests. Then after three weeks the Governor took his pen in hand and wrote Lincoln a reply. He had been delayed, busy with "public affairs" and "pressure of public duties." He had marked out a course for himself from which no one could turn him aside. "I am confident the opinions I hold are entertained by one-half of the politicians of the United States." He would show due deference and respect for the Administration at Washington, and "no political resentments or personal objects" would keep him from yielding support to all measures "within Constitutional powers."

At a later time Seymour said that when Lincoln wrote to him, he, Seymour, had reliable information of a conspiracy of leading Republicans to force Lincoln out of the White House. Also Seymour had heard of a movement to impeach the President. The President knew of these plotters, Seymour guessed, and was "anxious" to win Seymour for a friend in the crisis. Besides his letter to Seymour at this time, Lincoln sent Thurlow Weed to Seymour. But Seymour was suspicious of Weed too.

Weed's account (of which Nicolay and Hay were skeptical) ran that one evening in the White House the President said: "I have sent for you, Mr. Weed, to ask you to go to Governor Seymour and tell him what I say. Tell him, now is his time. Tell him, I do not wish to be President again, and that the leader of the other party, provided it is, in favor of a vigorous war against the rebellion, should have my place. Entreat him to give the true ring to his annual message; and if he will, as he easily can, place himself at the head of a great Union party, I will gladly stand aside and help to put him in the Executive Chair."

Weed said he was not surprised at this because he had long before heard the President say, "If there is a man who can push our armies forward one mile further or one hour faster than I can, he is the man who ought to be in my place." A *New York Tribune* editorial of March 25, 1863, noted that politically the war issue dwarfed all others: " 'Tell your brother,' said President Lincoln lately to the brother of a prominent Democratic aspirant to the Presidency, 'that he can not be the next President of the United States unless there shall *be* a United States to preside over.' "

Weed should have been inclined to carry out his mission to Seymour, perhaps, for he had confidentially written from Albany, January 16, 1863, to John Bigelow at Paris: "We are in a bad way. I wish that Ben Butler had been elected president,—or that even now he was in Halleck's place."

After failing with Seymour, Weed carried to General McClellan the same proposal that had been made to Seymour. "Tell the General," said Lincoln, according to Weed, "that we have no wish to injure or humiliate him; that

we wish only for the success of our armies; that if he will come forward
and put himself at the head of a Union-Democratic party, and, through that
means, push forward the Union cause, I will gladly step aside and do all I
can to secure his election in 1864." The plan was that McClellan should
preside at a great Union-Democratic meeting in Union Square, New York,
on June 16, 1863. S. L. M. Barlow, a close friend of McClellan, took Weed's
message to the General, with written memoranda of principles to be set
forth at the big meeting.

McClellan wrote in reply to Weed that he agreed an honorable peace
was not possible at that hour, and "at whatever cost of time and treasure
and blood" the war to save the Union and the Government must go on.
Mr. Weed was kind, but "for what I cannot doubt that you would consider
good reasons, I have determined to decline the compliment of presiding
over the proposed meeting."

Talk of McClellan for President was on the increase. Regiments marching up Broadway had cheered him and his friend Fitz-John Porter as they
stood on a balcony and saluted the troops. A reception in Boston was a
perfect triumph, according to the *Transcript*. McClellan received a sword
embossed in Latin that translated "Often for the king: always for the country." He visited a shipyard where ironclads were a-building and "the workmen enthusiastically cheered the General."

Closer home to Lincoln was Secretary Chase, of whom Aaron F. Perry
noted: "He informed me that the government had no plan nor policy, that
it was time to have one, and—with a kindling face and outstretched arm—
'It would have one if I were President!' He thought we could not have one
while the President allowed so much of his time to be consumed with idle
visitors. He knew, however, that I was a friend of Mr. Lincoln, and desired
the success of his administration. I believe that what he said was sincere and
loyal to the country."

Groans, yells, catcalls, "assorted vegetables and rotten eggs," met Thaddeus Stevens, House leader of the Republicans in Congress, said press accounts, when on March 14, 1863, he spoke in his home town of Lancaster,
Pennsylvania. The disorder ran back to the day that month in the House
when Stevens drove through with little debate a bill authorizing the President to suspend the writ of habeas corpus and providing funds to reimburse
Stanton, Seward, or other officials when civil courts awarded damages for
false arrest. Also on the last day before a new Congress with new Democratic members would take their seats, a Conscription Act was passed em-
powering the Government to divide the country into districts with provost
marshals and enrollment boards authorized to raise troops by drafting all
able-bodied citizens between the ages of twenty and forty-five.

Stevens held that when the laws of war are led forth, the Constitution
retires. Cicero would guide: "In the midst of arms laws are silent." In a legal
sense the Peace Democrats were counselors at law for "rebels." "I deny,"
said Stevens, "that they have any right to plead at all. I deny that they have

any standing in court. I deny that they can be permitted to tell us that we must be loyal to the Constitution."

Over the country raged the debate on what the Constitution meant in saying "The . . . writ of *habeas corpus* shall not be suspended, unless when in cases of rebellion or invasion the public safety may require it." Had the President alone the power to suspend the writ, or did he need Congress to tell him when? This issue rose and would not down. English history and law seemed to favor Parliament as against the King and Congress as against the President. Lincoln himself had not directly ordered arrests of the sort complained of. His ministers, Stanton and Seward, had. And Lincoln had not interfered with their policy.

Seward telegrams would read, "Arrest Leonard Sturtevant and send him to Fort La Fayette," or, "Send William Pierce to Fort La Fayette." Stanton would notify a United States Marshal that John Watson was in Boston at No. 2 Oliver Place. "Watch him, look out for the clothes and letters, and seize them and arrest him when it is the right time. Don't let him see or communicate with anyone, but bring him immediately to Washington." Men arrested were charged with treason, disloyalty, inciting or participating in riot, aiding and abetting rebels, defrauding the Government, stealing government property, robbing the United States mail, blockade-running, smuggling, spying, enticing soldiers to desert, aiding and harboring deserters, defrauding recruits of bounty, horse-stealing. The charges went into the records or again they did not. General Dix once reported to Seward that he had arrested two men on testimony vouched for by the United States Marshal but found on investigation that he had in custody "two of the most consistent and active Union men in the neighborhood." Again he reported to Seward that having examined the papers in a particular case, he would suggest that the prisoner be held at least three weeks or longer "until after the fall elections—say the tenth of November."

The former Governor of Kentucky, who had been a Whig Congressman with Lincoln, Charles S. Morehead, the Peace Convention delegate whom Lincoln sent for immediately on his arrival in Washington for inauguration, had tried to keep Kentucky "neutral," had accused Seward of inconsistency, and publicly criticized cutting off trade with the South. By order of the Secretary of War, and without trial, ex-Governor Morehead was held four months in cells of Fort Lafayette and Fort Warren. Mainly through the efforts of Congressman John J. Crittenden, he was released on parole. When later discharged from parole, he fled to England and addressed public meetings, giving a recital of his interview with Lincoln just before inauguration, stressing his personal impression that Lincoln was anxious to be a war lord. These Morehead speeches published in England were reprinted in American newspapers.

Seward was widely and repeatedly quoted in the opposition press as having remarked to the British Minister in Washington: "I can touch a bell on my right hand and order the arrest of a citizen in Ohio. I can touch the bell again and order the imprisonment of a citizen of New York, and no power on earth but that of the President can release them. Can the Queen of England, in her dominions, say as much?"

Seward denied the remark, but his friends knew it sounded like a flash from Seward after several fingers of old brandy. "Arrest Charles W. Adams," he telegraphed the New York chief of police. "Secure his papers and send him to Fort Lafayette." The arrests, usually at night, had secrecy, a weird anonymous reach, and spread fear and hate among many not saying Yes to the Government.

The terror of secret and arbitrary arrests was softened somewhat by the Habeas Corpus bill of March 3, 1863. The Secretaries of State and of War were directed to furnish courts with names of all persons held as prisoners by authority of the Secretaries or the President. Congress made it clear that control over the habeas-corpus writ rested with Congress, yet it directly authorized the President to suspend the writ. This was carefully done so that no appearance was presented of any conflict of authority between the President and Congress. Senator Collamer phrased the viewpoint: "The Executive is just as much clothed with authority, and bound in duty when called on, to give construction to the Constitution in the execution of it as we are, and his decision is just as binding as ours . . . and it is not common courtesy for one department of the Government to say to another, 'We say the Constitution means so and so, and we are infallible.'" Congress should not pass any bill in which the necessary implication was that the President's decision was incorrect, urged Collamer, nor should the President be asked to approve any such bill and thus "publish to the world that he has done that which he had no legal right to do."

The act of March 3 also ordered that all persons then in prison should be discharged unless indicted by a grand jury, and that in the future no one arrested should be held longer than twenty days unless so indicted. This, of course, took many cases out of the power of the military, yet commanders and provost marshals went their way and often overrode the civil authorities, arrested and carried to unknown prisons men and women they believed or suspected to be in league with the enemy. "The greatest care was taken by the President," noted Nicolay and Hay, "to restrain the officers acting under his authority from any abuse of this tremendous power. He watched over this with increasing vigilance as the war went on."

From house to house enrollers in the spring of '63 took the names of men and boys fit for the army. Cripples, the deaf and dumb, the blind, and other defectives were exempt. So were the only son of a widowed mother, the only son of aged and infirm parents, others having dependents. In a family where two or more sons of aged and infirm parents were drafted, the father if living, or if dead the mother, must say which son would stay home and which go to war. Also anyone having $300 cash, and willing to pay it as "bounty" to a substitute, was exempt and could stay at home and laugh at the war if he felt like laughing.

"We are coming, Father Abraham, three hundred dollars more, is the tune sung by the conscripts," ran a jest of the opposition press. The *Crisis* printed a comment: "In the vast army of 300,000 which Mr. Lincoln has ordered to be raised, there will not be *one* man able to pay $300. Not one! think of that!"

The comic phase was struck by Artemus Ward in a lecture. "I have already given two cousins to the war, & I stand reddy to sacrifiss my wife's brother, ruthurn'n not see the rebellion krusht. And if wuss comes to wuss, I'll shed every drop of blood my able-bodied relations has got to prosekoot the war."

Western governors reported the secret Knights of the Golden Circle as disguising itself under various names, with signs, oaths, passwords, rituals, and rifles, organized to encourage desertion, defeat the draft, and protect its members by force and by appeals to the courts. Press items of civil war began to appear: "A party of soldiers sent to Rush County, Indiana, captured six deserters. On their way to the cars the deserters were rescued by 'Southern sympathizers' armed with rifles. Two companies of infantry were then sent from Indianapolis, and the deserters again taken into custody." In a few weeks 2,600 deserters had been arrested. Seventeen deserters fortified a log cabin and, provisioned by neighbors, defied siege. Two draft-enrollers were murdered in Indiana; women threw eggs, men rioted with clubs, guns, bricks. In a Pennsylvania county one enroller was forced to quit taking names, another was shot, the sawmill of another was burned. The Molly Maguires, an Irish miners' secret society in Pennsylvania, made resistance; coal operators refused to give the names of leaders to the Government in fear that their breakers be burned; Stanton sent troops to quell the disturbers. In Delaware, New Jersey, New Hampshire, Vermont, Connecticut, the Government met varied forms of opposition to the draft. An enrolling officer was stoned out of Richmond Township, Ohio, and 1,000 men with squirrel rifles and revolvers encamped at Napoleon prepared to battle 600 United States troops ordered there by the State provost marshal. After a few minor collisions, a committee of influential citizens arranged for the arrest of thirteen men who had used force to drive out enrolling officers and to rescue drafted men from the custody of United States officials; the troops withdrew and the insurgents dispersed from Napoleon, Ohio.

At the Vine Street Church in St. Louis, the Reverend Dr. McPheeters refused to declare himself for the Union; he baptized a baby with the name of the Confederate General Sterling Price. A provost marshal arrested McPheeters and took control of the church. President Lincoln studied the matter and wrote to General Curtis: "I tell you frankly I believe he does sympathize with the rebels, but the question remains whether such a man, of unquestioned good moral character . . . can, with safety to the government, be exiled upon the suspicion of his secret sympathies. . . . I must add that the United States Government must not . . . undertake to run the churches. When an individual in a church or out of it becomes dangerous to the public interest, he must be checked. . . . It will not do for the United States to appoint trustees . . . or other agents for the churches."

In Natchez, Mississippi, the Catholic bishop, having refused to read the prescribed prayer for the President of the United States, was expelled from the Union Army lines, the order later being rescinded. Also in Natchez an Episcopalian clergyman omitted the prayer for the President and a young officer of the Union Army led the loudly protesting rector to the door. Then, marching to the pulpit, the officer read in the hearing of Confederate worshipers a "Prayer for the President of the United States, and all in Civil Authority":

Almighty God, whose kingdom is everlasting and power infinite; Have mercy upon this whole land, and so rule the hearts of thy servants THE PRESIDENT OF THE UNITED STATES, *The Governor of this State*, and all others in authority, that they, knowing whose ministers they are, may above all things seek thy honor and glory; and that we and all the People, duly considering whose authority they bear, may faithfully and obediently honour them, according to thy blessed Word and ordinance; through Jesus Christ our Lord, who with thee and the Holy Ghost liveth and reigneth ever, one God, world without end. *Amen.*

Illinois had 2,001 deserters arrested in six months. In March of '63 desertions brought the ranks of the 128th Illinois regiment at Cairo down to 35 men. In January the wholesale desertions and fraternizing with the enemy among troops of the 109th Illinois regiment began to look so much like a mutiny that the entire regiment was arrested, disarmed, and put under guard at Holly Springs, Mississippi; these were recruits from southern Illinois, from a triangle of land wedged between the Slave States of Kentucky and Missouri. They were disgusted with Lincoln and the Emancipation Proclamation, said they had enlisted to fight for the Union, not Negro freedom. The Democratic majority in the Illinois Legislature prepared bills to restore the habeas-corpus writ, to bar Negroes from entering Illinois, and otherwise to oppose the Federal Government. Then for the first time in the history of Illinois a governor prorogued the legislature, disbanded them, ordered them to go home.

Forty thousand shouting, enthusiastic Democrats went to a mass convention at Springfield and heard United States Senator Richardson, Congressman S. S. Marshall, and others in speeches excoriating the Federal Administration. Resolutions scored President Lincoln for violation of the ancient Anglo-Saxon right of every man to his own home as a castle of defense.

Governor Morton telegraphed Lincoln that he expected the Indiana Legislature in January, 1863, to acknowledge the Southern Confederacy and to urge the Northwest to break all bonds of law with New England. Though the legislature did not go that far, it did return the Governor's message with insults and a resolution saying the policies of Governor Seymour of New York were a better model. Also this Indiana Legislature tried to take military power from the Governor, with the result that the Republican members stayed away, there was no quorum, and the legislature adjourned without appropriations of money to run the State government.

Needing $250,000, Governor Morton went to Washington and got it from a fund of $2,000,000 which had been set aside for munitions of war, to be used where rebellion existed or was threatened. Morton told Stanton that for this use of money they would be in a bad mess if the Union cause failed. "If the cause fails I do not wish to live," said Stanton to Morton.

A committee of New Yorkers, William M. Tweed, Orison Blunt, John Fox, and Smith Ely, alleging that the draft on their State was beyond their quota, had been refused access to the War Department records by Stanton. They went to Lincoln. They said New York was getting 50 volunteers daily and a postponement of the draft would enable them to enlist all the men called for, whether beyond their quota or not. Lincoln said he feared if the draft order were postponed volunteering would cease; a committee from Cincinnati had asked for a similar postponement, as they were getting 20 volunteer enlistments a day; the draft order was postponed, as they had asked; and the next day not one volunteer showed.

"That," said Lincoln, "is human nature. When you think death is after you, you run. But as soon as death stops, you stop."

Then, wrote one of the committee, "He sprang from his chair, throwing his arms about, and laughed loudly at his own dismal joke." After which the President wrote an order giving them access to the draft records.

In the War Office, as recruitment figures arrived Lincoln personally tabulated the telegraphic reports on a slip of paper, which he rolled around a short lead pencil and put in his vest pocket for comparison again the next day. Said one of the men in the office, "If the number was satisfactory he would sit for a time conversing brightly; but if otherwise, the furrows on his face would indicate his disappointment, and without a word he would depart." Thomas B. Bryan of Illinois quoted for Lincoln a verse:

> Here lies old thirty-three and a third per cent,
> The more he got the more he lent,
> The more he lent the more he craved,
> Good Lord! can such a man be saved?

"Pretty good," was the rejoinder, "but I know a better, and you can get it chiselled on the draft-dodgers' tombs:

> "Here lies old Dodge, who dodged all good,
>   And never dodged an evil;
> And after dodging all he could,
>   He could not dodge the Devil."

A committee from a little village in Illinois came to complain of draft enrollment. Perhaps they were more frightened than hurt, Lincoln suggested, and according to *Leslie's Weekly*, used an illustration: "There is a little one-horse village in Maryland whose quota was one man. When the enrolling officer went round to the farm-houses to get the names he was very solemn in his injunctions to the old woman to give the name of every male creature on the farm. One she called Billy Bray. And when drafting came around the lot fell on poor Billy Bray. In due time the provost-marshal came for his conscript, and found that Billy Bray was the farmer's donkey. 'So,' quoth

Lincoln, 'gentlemen, you may be the donkey of your town, and so escape. Don't distress yourselves by meeting trouble half-way.' "

Senator McDonald, seeking pardons for men condemned by a military commission, heard Lincoln say, "Nothing can make me believe that one hundred thousand Indiana Democrats are disloyal." Nicolay and Hay noted as to the largest of the secret disloyal organizations, "The President's attitude was one of good-humored contempt rather than anything else."

The Knights of the Golden Circle claimed 1,000,000 members. At its height it probably had hundreds of thousands on its rolls. The army secret service penetrated it, one private soldier joining and becoming Grand Secretary for the State of Kentucky. The Government kept informed, guarded against upheavals, arrested ringleaders, and convicted them whenever possible. Naturally, too, some of the spies and informers reported men they personally hated, paid off old grudges. Also some officials credentialed from Washington used their powers like fools and petty tyrants.

Two sergeants, John McFarland and Thomas Long, claiming to act for Indiana authorities, tried to kidnap one Illinois citizen and did arrest four men on charges of desertion. Judge Charles H. Constables, in circuit court of the fourth judicial circuit of Illinois, ordered discharge of the four men. One of the four, James Gamron, proved that he was a private in an Illinois regiment, was taken prisoner in Tennessee, and on parole was sick at his mother's house when arrested. Judge Constables also held that the bigoted Sergeants McFarland and Long should give bonds for $500 to appear for trial on the kidnapping charge. Bigoted military authorities then arrested Judge Constables on the charge of interfering with the capture of deserters. An examination before Judge Samuel H. Treat of the southern district of Illinois, an old acquaintance of Lincoln's, was followed by a decision that the Indiana Sergeants had no authority to take deserters in Illinois and Judge Constables had acted properly in releasing the four arrested soldiers and holding the Sergeants under bonds.

From Evansville, Indiana, came a seminary professor, D. Y. Kilgore, who informed Lincoln of passwords, grips, and other secret devices of a "circle" of the Knights of the Golden Circle into which Kilgore had sent student spies. And as Kilgore's account ran, the President seemed pleased and inquired further.

"Now Professor, you have the secrets of the Knights of the Golden Circle, the number and location of their Circles, and when they meet. This is all very good. Now what will be your next move?"

"We will make a concerted rush at one time and arrest all active members of the Knights of the Golden Circle."

"Yes. You have them all arrested. What will you do with them?"

"We will put them in jail."

"Professor, if the jails will hold the Knights of the Golden Circle, they are numerically too small to be a serious menace to the government. If the jails will not hold the Knights of the Golden Circle, what will you do with them?"

Kilgore said he had not thought as far as that and could not answer the question.

The Sons of Liberty, the Circle of Hosts, the Union Relief Society or the Order of American Knights, and other oath-bound secret societies of like aims progressed in size. They sometimes bought a storekeeper's stock entire of Colt revolvers, rifles, and ammunition. Union men horsewhipped by masked committees in lonesome woodlands at night, Union men shot down in their own homes by Southern sympathizers, had their friends and kin who banded and took oaths. Violence met violence, blood called for blood. In the oath of the Circle of Hosts each member swore and bound himself "under no less penalty than having my bowels torn out and cast to the four winds of heaven; so help me God." Furthermore, "I promise and swear that I will do all in my power against the present Yankee-abolition-disunion administration; so help me God."

The Union League, the Loyal Legion, the Order of the Stars and Stripes, also oath-bound organizations, sprang up to combat the Copperheads, which became the standard name applied to all defeatists and political opponents of the war. Their emblem was a head cut from a copper cent with the word "Liberty" engraved on it. This, fastened to a pin, was worn on the coat lapel at mass meetings.

Hundreds of lists naming alleged Copperheads went secretly to Stanton, sometimes accompanied by documents that had value. In one case Stanton stumbled into proof that a personal friend of his who sat as a judge in the court of claims also sat secretly as an official of a disloyal society. On the papers of evidence being laid before him, the guilty judge took the oath of allegiance and gave information that helped break up the order in the District of Columbia.

Personal mail of government employees at Washington was opened and read, the evidence at one time resulting in dismissal of clerks, arrest of army officers for frauds. One high civil official was sent on an errand from which he came back to find his job gone. Lincoln happened to be present when the official was being ordered away, inquired where the man was going, and was told, "Up in a balloon."

Protests of innocence came often from men plainly guilty. They reminded Lincoln of a governor who visited a state prison. The convicts one by one had the same story of innocence and of wrongs done them by conspiracy and perjury. At last, however, the governor came to one who frankly said he had committed a crime and the sentence given him was perfect justice. "I must pardon you," said the governor. "I can't have you here corrupting all these good men."

The seething of strife was not eased in the spring of '63 by Order No. 38, issued by General Burnside, commanding the Department of the Ohio, with Cincinnati headquarters. Treason, of course, was forbidden in Order No. 38. Giving aid and comfort to the enemy was forbidden. Also sympathy for the enemy was forbidden. That is, if the sympathy were spoken and it was a habit to so speak, then it was forbidden.

Order No. 38 was positive: "The habit of declaring sympathy for the enemy will not be allowed in this department."

Order No. 38 made Burnside and his officers the judges of what was sympathy and how many times sympathy had to be declared in order to become a habit. They would also decide whether treason hid and lurked in the words of any suspect, Order No. 38 admonishing, "It must be distinctly understood that treason, express or implied, will not be tolerated in this department."

The intention of the order under the conditions was perfectly proper and an ancient custom of war. The idea was to tell those who were talking treason and helping the enemy, "Shut up or we lock you up." Sergeants and corporals so interpreted. They said so when hauling suspects out of bed at 2 A.M.

But Burnside in framing Order No. 38 gave it a wrong tone, as wrong as his tone when he took command of the Army of the Potomac and told his generals he wasn't the man for command.

At both times Burnside was a sufferer from chronic diarrhoea. He was soon to write the President asking if he could resign on account of this physical disability. Neither the Fredericksburg disaster nor Order No. 38 could be appraised historically without considering the factor of Burnside's bowel trouble. It would be what historians call one of the imponderables. To the opposition element Order No. 38 was no imponderable, but a red rag of blundering, arrogant authority.

Vallandigham, now out of Congress, leaped to challenge the foes of liberty; it was in his special field of effort. From city to city he went with his cry: "If it be really the design of the administration to force this issue, then come arrest, come exile, come death itself! I am ready here to-night to meet it." At Hamilton, Ohio, he spoke of a colonel under Burnside: "He must know that two years hence, a Democratic President or Secretary of War—and who knows but I may be Secretary of War myself [Laughter and cheers.]—can strike his name from the roll without even a why or a wherefore."

On May 1 at Mount Vernon, Ohio, Vallandigham rode in a parade four miles long of wagons, buggies, carriages, horsemen, and a six-horse float holding thirty-four pretty flower girls, one for each State in the Union. The *Democratic Banner* of Mount Vernon reported it "a proud and glorious day for the faithful and unconquerable Democracy of old Knox County, and one that will long be remembered by them with high and patriotic pleasure." On the platform sat Congressmen Samuel S. Cox and George Hunt Pendleton. Their speeches followed the two-hour address of Vallandigham, "a noble and glorious effort in behalf of Liberty, Union, and the Constitution, a most able, eloquent, and truly patriotic speech" if you believed the Columbus *Crisis*.

Vallandigham had practiced for this speech. He gave again his ideas that the Government at Washington was thirsty for despotism, had no intention to restore the Union, had rejected peace offers from the South and mediation proposals from Europe, was waging war to liberate black slaves and enslave white men; no men deserving to be free would submit to its conscription. Order No. 38 was a base usurpation of arbitrary power; he despised it, spat upon it, and trampled it under his feet. The President was "King Lincoln," and he would advise the people to come together at the ballot box and hurl the tyrant from his throne. Applause came often, the going was good. Vallandigham faced acres of people, thousands beyond reach of his voice. They led him on. His defiance and scorn of the Government ran farther than in any previous hour in his career as an orator.

Three army captains from Cincinnati, in plain clothes, up close to the platform, took notes. They reported to Burnside. Three nights later a company of soldiers arrived in Dayton, Ohio, and went to Vallandigham's home at three o'clock in the morning. From an upper window Vallandigham asked them their business. A captain answered they were an escort to take him to Cincinnati. He shouted at the top of his voice up and down the street, "Asa! Asa! Asa!" A revolver shot rang from another upper window. These were signals to alarm his friends.

Fire bells tolled while soldiers with axes battered down doors, reached Vallandigham, gave him a few minutes for a toilet, then took him to the train for Cincinnati before a crowd assembled.

A crowd of some 500 gathered in riotous mood, moved to the office of the *Dayton Journal*, a Republican newspaper, hooted and yelled, broke the office windows with bricks and stones, smashed the doors, fired revolvers, put a torch to the building, gutted it, then joined the fire department in trying to put out the flames that had spread to Leobold's hat store, the Darrow shoe store, Bornsten's Segar store, the *Gospel Herald* office, and as far back as Wild's livery stable. Most of these were a total loss, as well as the *Journal* office.

Vallandigham from a jail cell in Cincinnati issued, without censorship by his captors, an address to his friends: "I am a Democrat—for the Constitution, for law, for the Union, for liberty—this is my only 'crime.' In obedience to the demand of Northern abolition disunionists and traitors, I am here in bonds today."

A military commission gave Vallandigham a trial, and sentenced him to Fort Warren, Boston Harbor, till the war was over. His lawyers petitioned for a writ of habeas corpus before Judge Humphrey H. Leavitt. The court's decision recited that the President had clothed General Burnside with necessary powers. "He is the representative and agent of the President, within the limits of his department." The powers of the President under the Constitution were not clearly specified. "Where there is no express legislative declaration, the President is guided solely by his own judgment and discretion, and is only amenable for an abuse of his authority by impeachment, prosecuted according to the requirements of the Constitution. The occasion which calls for the exercise of this power exists only from the necessity of the case; and when the necessity exists, there is a clear justification of the act. If this view of the power of the President is correct, it undoubtedly im-

plies the right to arrest persons, who, by their mischievous acts of disloyalty, impede or endanger the military operations of the Government.
And, if the necessity exists, I see no reason why the power does not attach
to the office of General in command of a military department. The only
reason why the appointment is made, is that the President cannot discharge
the duties in person."

So the court denied a habeas-corpus writ to Vallandigham, who penciled
a note, freely delivered, to Governor Seymour on "the infamous conduct
and doctrines" of Judge Leavitt: "The purpose is—believe me—to prevent
any Presidential election in 1864, or to control it by force. . . . Your voice
—the voice of New York, to the Administration, will break my bonds."

By this time there were anger, indignation, and high crying from many
newspapers and partisan Democrats. The roar of it reached Burnside, who
telegraphed the President that he would resign if so desired. The President
replied: "When I shall wish to supersede you I will let you know. All the
Cabinet regretted the necessity of arresting, for instance, Vallandigham,
some doubting there was a real necessity for it; but, being done, all were
for seeing you through with it."

The rapid action in the arrest and conviction of Vallandigham "took
the President somewhat by surprise," Nicolay and Hay noted. "If he had
been consulted before any proceedings were initiated there is reason to believe he would not have permitted them."

Lincoln's choice now seemed to lie between approval of the sentence or
annulment of it. He chose still another course. He commuted the sentence
of Vallandigham and ordered him sent beyond Union Army lines into the
hands of the Confederates.

The order was telegraphed to Burnside: "The President directs that without delay you send C. L. Vallandigham under secure guard to the headquarters of General Rosecrans, to be put by him beyond our military lines;
and in case of his return within our lines, he be arrested and kept in close
custody for the term specified in his sentence."

Vallandigham, hearing the sentence of banishment, issued, without interference or censorship by his jail-keepers, an address to the Democracy of
Ohio: "Because despotism and superior force so will it, I go within the
Confederate lines. I well understand the purpose of this order. But in vain
the malice of enemies shall thus continue to give color to the calumnies and
misrepresentations of the past two years. They little comprehend the true
character of the man with whom they have to deal."

To his wife Vallandigham wrote: "I am as calm and unmoved as ever.
Bear it all like a woman—a heroine. Take care of my dear, dear boy till I
return. All goes well for the cause. Do not worry yourself in the least. Your
time will come. Meantime, and until I return, friends will take care of
you. Many, many kisses for yourself and Charlie."

Down in Murfreesboro, Tennessee, the prisoner met General Rosecrans,
who gave him a lecture ending, "Why, sir, do you know that unless I protect you with a guard my soldiers will tear you to pieces in an instant?"

Vallandigham replied: "That, sir, is because they are just as ignorant of my character as yourself. But, General, I have a proposition to make. Draw your soldiers up in a hollow square to-morrow morning, and announce to them that Vallandigham desires to vindicate himself, and I will guarantee that when they have heard me through they will be more willing to tear Lincoln and yourself to pieces than they will Vallandigham."

General Rosecrans shook his head, talked long with the prisoner and, laying his hand on Vallandigham's shoulder, said to a staff colonel, "He don't look a bit like a traitor, now does he, Joe?" Thus Vallandigham reported to friends what happened between him and the General, while newspaper correspondents wrote that the usually pious Rosecrans pointed a terrible forefinger at the man without a country and said: "Vallandigham, don't you ever come back here. If—you—do—Vallandigham, I'll be God damned, and may God forgive me for the expression—I'll be—God damned if I don't *hang* you!" The correspondents added, "The General claims that he 'never blasphemes, but sometimes swears.'"

At a house near the farthest outlying Confederate picket line, Vallandigham was left in the early morning by Union officers who heard him say to a Confederate private sent to meet him: "I am a citizen of Ohio and of the United States. I am here within your lines and by force and against my will. I therefore surrender myself to you as a prisoner of war." The Union officers galloped away while the Confederate private hesitated about what to do; at last he rode off toward his army for further orders.

Vallandigham sat in a no man's land between the two armies. "They were hours," he wrote, "of solitude but calmly spent—the bright sun shining in the clear sky above me, and faith in God and the future burning in my heart." At noon came an ambulance and took him to Bragg's headquarters; messages arrived inviting him to the hospitality of the South. He went to Wilmington, North Carolina, reporting on parole.

Meantime on June 1 General Burnside ordered the *Chicago Times* suppressed. Soldiers from Camp Douglas left the work of guarding Confederate prisoners, marched downtown, and seized the newspaper plant. Copperheads made speeches that night to a Chicago crowd of 20,000 people on Court House Square. Mobs threatened to sack and burn the *Chicago Tribune* in retaliation. Senator Lyman Trumbull, Congressman Isaac N. Arnold, and other Republicans held a conference with leading Democrats and telegraphed resolutions to President Lincoln asking him to revoke Burnside's order.

Lincoln wrote Stanton that many dispatches had been received on June 4 "which, with former ones, induce me to believe we should revoke or suspend the order suspending the Chicago 'Times'; and if you concur in opinion, please have it done." And the order which had brought Chicago close to mob war was revoked. The *Chicago Times* again appeared as usual with its customary columns of curses on Lincoln and all his works.

Meantime also the State convention of the Democratic party of Ohio solemnly and formally nominated the exiled Clement L. Vallandigham for the next Governor of the Buckeye State, while tongues of denunciation raged at Lincoln and his Administration. Governor Seymour and the New York Democrats in a State convention at Albany added their roars of disapproval and opposition to arbitrary arrests and despotism. "For the crime of dispensing with the laws and statutes of Great Britain, our ancestors brought one monarch to the scaffold and expelled another from his throne," said the *Albany Commercial.*

"We consider Mr. Vallandigham now the most prominent candidate for the next Presidency," said the *Fort Wayne* (Indiana) *Sentinel,* "and we fully expect that in March, 1865, his shortsighted persecutors will have the gratification of seeing him change his quarters from Fort Warren to more commodious and fitting ones in the White House. Who will succeed him in his vacated cell at Fort Warren remains to be seen."

Old Sam Medary in the *Crisis* employed his ancient Anglo-Saxon right of free speech by telling his readers: "The *Ohio State Journal* charges that the raid of the Southern Army into the North, grows out of information they received from Mr. Vallandigham! If so, Mr. Lincoln should be hung as a traitor for communicating information to the South, by sending a Northern man there in violation of an act of Congress and the order of the Military Department. Lincoln is the *traitor,* not Vallandigham." Snakes had entered the bosoms of men, it was said, and *Vanity Fair* with a catechism set itself up as an authority on reptiles:

Question. Can you give me the name of any remarkably venomous reptile?
Answer. Yes; the Viper.
Question. Is there any more venomous reptile than the Viper?
Answer. Yes; the Asp.
Question. Is there any more venomous reptile than the Asp?
Answer. Yes; the Cobra de Capello.
Question. Is there any more venomous reptile than the Cobra de Capello?
Answer. Yes; the Whip-Snake.
Question. Is there any more venomous reptile than the Whip-Snake?
Answer. Yes; the Moccassin Snake.
Question. Is there any more venomous reptile than the Moccassin Snake?
Answer. Yes; the Carpet Snake.
Question. Is there any more venomous reptile than the Carpet Snake?
Answer. Yes; the Rattle-Snake.
Question. Is there any more venomous reptile than the Rattle-Snake?
Answer. Yes; the COPPER-HEAD.
Question. Is there any more venomous reptile than the COPPER-HEAD?
Answer. NARY!!!

On June 12 of '63 Lincoln gave to the country a letter addressed to "Hon. Erastus Corning and Others." They were the resolutions committee of the Albany Democratic convention, which had denounced the Administration and demanded Vallandigham's return to freedom. In his reply Lincoln covered the main points brought against him as to personal liberty, jails, gags, handcuffs. He thanked them for being resolved "to maintain our common government and country, despite the folly or wickedness, as they may conceive, of any administration." On this position as "eminently patriotic," he would congratulate the country. He and they had a common object, though differing as to means and measures for effecting the object.

The President might close his paper at such a point and let it go at that, only the matter was more than a personal one. He proceeded as to violence and despotic power during an insurrection and a civil war. His argument aimed only incidentally at Erastus Corning, the politician, railroad millionaire, banker, head of the Albany Iron Works. What was he to Corning or Corning to him? He was directing an offensive defense framed in words to be read by the educated classes, by the armies, by the people in their homes, the masses. They could judge.

The President began: "The resolutions promise to support me in every constitutional and lawful measure to suppress the rebellion; and I have not knowingly employed, nor shall knowingly employ, any other. But the meeting, by their resolutions, assert and argue that certain military arrests, and proceedings following them, for which I am ultimately responsible, are unconstitutional. I think they are not."

Guarantees and safeguards of the individual's right to a speedy and public trial by an impartial jury he would discuss: "They were secured substantially to the English people after years of protracted civil war, and were adopted into our Constitution at the close of the revolution." He inquired: "Would not the demonstration have been better if it could have been truly said that these safeguards had been adopted and applied during the civil wars and during our revolution, instead of after the one and at the close of the other? I, too, am devotedly for them after civil war, and before civil war, and at all times, 'except when, in cases of rebellion or invasion, the public safety may require' their suspension."

A personal story was inextricably bound up in the annals of a nation: "Prior to my installation here it had been inculcated that any State had a lawful right to secede from the national Union, and that it would be expedient to exercise the right whenever the devotees of the doctrine should fail to elect a president to their liking. I was elected contrary to their liking; and, accordingly, so far as it was legally possible, they had taken seven States out of the Union, had seized many of the United States forts, and had fired upon the United States flag, all before I was inaugurated, and, of course, before I had done any official act whatever. The rebellion thus begun soon ran into the present civil war." The insurgents and their friends had "a well-pondered reliance" on the Constitution and on the right of habeas corpus as a hindrance rather than a help to the President and the Government.

As a Chief Magistrate he saw a distinction between peacetime arrests and the jailing of men during a gigantic rebellion. "The former is directed at the small percentage of ordinary and continuous perpetration of crime, while the latter is directed at sudden and extensive uprisings against the government, which, at most, will succeed or fail in no great length of time. In the latter case arrests are made not so much for what has been done, as for what probably would be done. . . . In such cases the purposes of men are much more easily understood than in cases of ordinary crime. The man who stands by and says nothing when the peril of his government is discussed, cannot be misunderstood. If not hindered, he is sure to help the enemy; much more if he talks ambiguously—talks for his country with 'buts,' and 'ifs' and 'ands.' "

The accusation of the Albany Democrats that Vallandigham was seized by a military commander and tried "for no other reason than words addressed to a public meeting in criticism of the course of the administration, and in condemnation of the military orders of the general," needed reply. "If there be no mistake about this, if this assertion is the truth, and the whole truth, if there was no other reason for the arrest, then I concede that the arrest was wrong. But the arrest, as I understand, was made for a very different reason. Mr. Vallandigham avows his hostility to the war on the part of the Union; and his arrest was made because he was laboring, with some effect, to prevent the raising of troops, to encourage desertions from the army, and to leave the rebellion without an adequate military force to suppress it. He was not arrested because he was damaging the political prospects of the administration or the personal interests of the commanding general, but because he was damaging the army, upon the existence and vigor of which the life of the nation depends. . . .

"Under cover of 'liberty of speech,' 'liberty of the press,' and 'habeas corpus,' they hoped to keep on foot amongst us a most efficient corps of spies, informers, suppliers, and aiders and abettors of their cause in a thousand ways. They knew that in times such as they were inaugurating, by the Constitution itself the 'habeas corpus' might be suspended; but they also knew they had friends who would make a question as to who was to suspend it; meanwhile their spies and others might remain at large to help on their cause."

Or if the Executive should suspend the writ without ruinous waste of time, arrests of innocent persons would result in clamor or service to the insurgent cause. "Yet, thoroughly imbued with a reverence for the guaranteed rights of individuals, I was slow to adopt the strong measures which by degrees I have been forced to regard as being within the exceptions of the Constitution, and as indispensable to the public safety."

Would a search of history reveal one civil war where the prevailing government had not used individuals with violence and injustice in cases where civil rights were involved? "Nothing is better known to history than that courts of justice are utterly incompetent in such cases. Civil courts are organized for trials of individuals . . . in quiet times. . . . Even in times of peace bands of horse-thieves and robbers frequently grow too numerous and powerful for the ordinary courts of justice. But what comparison, in numbers, have such bands ever borne to the insurgent sympathizers even in many of the loyal States?

"Again, a jury too frequently has at least one member more ready to hang the panel than to hang the traitor. And yet again, he who dissuades one man from volunteering, or induces one soldier to desert, weakens the Union cause as much as he who kills a Union soldier in battle. Yet this dissuasion or inducement may be so conducted as to be no defined crime of which any civil court would take cognizance."

Pointing to the death penalty as a requisite of military organization, he inquired: "Must I shoot a simple-minded soldier boy who deserts, while I must not touch a hair of a wily agitator who induces him to desert? This is none the less injurious when effected by getting a father, or brother, or friend into a public meeting, and there working upon his feelings till he is persuaded to write the soldier boy that he is fighting in a bad cause, for a wicked administration of a contemptible government, too weak to arrest and punish him if he shall desert. I think that, in such a case, to silence the agitator and save the boy is not only constitutional, but withal a great mercy."

Again came reference to the Constitution being applied differently in cases of rebellion or invasion. "The Constitution itself makes the distinction, and I can no more be persuaded that the government can constitutionally take no strong measures in time of rebellion, because it can be shown that the same could not be lawfully taken in time of peace, than I can be persuaded that a particular drug is not good medicine for a sick man because it can be shown to not be good food for a well one.

"Nor am I able to appreciate the danger apprehended . . . that the American people will by means of military arrests during the rebellion lose the right of public discussion, the liberty of speech and the press, the law of evidence, trial by jury, and *habeas corpus* throughout the indefinite peaceful future which I trust lies before them, any more than I am able to believe a man could contract so strong an appetite for emetics during temporary illness as to persist in feeding upon them during the remainder of his healthful life."

The authors of the Albany resolutions had referred to themselves as "Democrats" rather than as "American citizens" in time of national peril. "I would have preferred to meet you upon a level one step higher than any party platform, because I am sure that from such more elevated position we could do better battle for the country we all love, than we possibly can from those lower ones where, from the force of habit, the prejudices of the past, and selfish hopes of the future, we are sure to expend much of our ingenuity and strength in finding fault with and aiming blows at each other. But since you have denied me this, I will yet be thankful for the country's sake that not all Democrats have done so."

The general who arrested and tried Vallandigham, also the judge who denied the writ of habeas corpus to Vallandigham, were both of them Democrats. "And still more, of all those Democrats who are nobly exposing their lives and shedding their blood on the battle-field, I have learned that many approve the course taken with Mr. Vallandigham, while I have not heard of a single one condemning it."

General Andrew Jackson, the President would remind the country, had abolished habeas corpus during the siege of New Orleans, Jackson *after* the siege being arrested and fined $1,000 by a judge he had arrested. Thirty years later Senator Douglas had led in passing a measure through Congress to refund principal and interest of Jackson's fine from Federal moneys.

"It may be remarked," noted Lincoln, "first, that we had the same Constitution then as now; secondly, that we then had a case of invasion, and now we have a case of rebellion; and thirdly, that the permanent right of the people to public discussion, the liberty of speech and of the press, the trial by jury, the law of evidence, and the *habeas corpus*, suffered no detriment whatever by that conduct of General Jackson, or its subsequent approval by the American Congress."

He would be frank about the Vallandigham case. "Let me say that, in my own discretion, I do not know whether I would have ordered the arrest of Mr. Vallandigham. While I cannot shift the responsibility from myself, I hold that, as a general rule, the commander in the field is the better judge of the necessity in any particular case. Of course I must practise a general directory and revisory power in the matter."

The Albany Democrats had specifically called on him to discharge Vallandigham. "I regard this as, at least, a fair appeal to me on the expediency of exercising a constitutional power which I think exists. In response to such appeal I have to say, it gave me pain when I learned that Mr. Vallandigham had been arrested (that is, I was pained that there should have seemed to be a necessity for arresting him), and that it will afford me great pleasure to discharge him so soon as I can by any means believe the public safety will not suffer by it."

The letter to Erastus Corning and others ended with the President's saying that as the confusion of opinion and action of wartimes took shape and fell into more regular channels "the necessity for strong dealing" might decrease. He so desired. "Still, I must continue to do so much as may seem to be required by the public safety."

A committee from the Ohio convention which nominated Vallandigham for the governorship called at the White House and read to Lincoln a lengthy reply to his Albany response, and asked, "not as a favor," that Vallandigham be given back his rights as a citizen. "Banishment is an unusual punishment and unknown to our laws," urged the committee. "If the President has the right to change the punishment prescribed by the court martial from imprisonment to banishment, why not from imprisonment to torture upon the rack or execution upon the gibbet?" The gist of their legalistic argument was around the question, "Has the President, at the time of invasion or insurrection, the right to engraft limitations or exceptions upon constitutional guarantees whenever, in his judgment, the public safety requires it?" If so, the President was creating a new and "an indefinable kind of constructive treason."

Lincoln too could be legalistic, and in a letter to "M. Birchard and Others" replied: "You ask, in substance, whether I really claim that I may override all the guaranteed rights of individuals, on the plea of conserving the public safety—when I may choose to say the public safety requires it.

This question, divested of the phraseology calculated to represent me as struggling for an arbitrary personal prerogative, is either simply a question who shall decide, or an affirmation that nobody shall decide, what the public safety does require in cases of rebellion or invasion. The Constitution contemplates the question as likely to occur for decision, but it does not expressly declare who is to decide it. By necessary implication, when rebellion or invasion comes, the decision is to be made, from time to time; and I think the man whom, for the time, the people have, under the Constitution, made the commander-in-chief of their army and navy, is the man who holds the power and bears the responsibility of making it. If he uses the power justly, the same people will probably justify him; if he abuses it, he is in their hands to be dealt with by all the modes they have reserved to themselves in the Constitution."

Their "earnestness" about the Constitution's being violated he saw as noteworthy and would add to his Albany response: "You claim that men may, if they choose, embarrass those whose duty it is to combat a giant rebellion, and then be dealt with in turn, only as if there were no rebellion. The Constitution itself rejects this view." He was unable to perceive an insult to Ohio in the case of Mr. Vallandigham, was unaware at the time of the arrest that Vallandigham was a candidate for nomination for governor of Ohio.

He pointed them to the state of the country, how "armed combinations" had resisted the arrests of deserters, had resisted enrollment for the draft, and "quite a number of assassinations" from the same animus had occurred. "These had to be met by military force, and this again has led to bloodshed and death. And now, under a sense of responsibility more weighty and enduring than any which is merely official, I solemnly declare my belief that this hindrance of the military, including maiming and murder, is due to the course in which Mr. Vallandigham has been engaged in a greater degree than to any other cause; and it is due to him personally in a greater degree than to any other one man. . . . When it is known that the whole burden of his speeches has been to stir up men against the prosecution of the war, and that in the midst of resistance to it he has not been known in any instance to counsel against such resistance, it is next to impossible to repel the inference that he has counseled directly in favor of it."

"With all this before their eyes, the convention you represent have nominated Mr. Vallandigham for governor of Ohio, and both they and you have declared the purpose to sustain the National Union by all constitutional means. But of course they and you in common reserve to yourselves to decide what are constitutional means; and, unlike the Albany meeting, you omit to state or intimate that in your opinion an army is a constitutional means of saving the Union against a rebellion, or even to intimate that you are conscious of an existing rebellion being in progress with the avowed object of destroying that very Union. At the same time your nominee for governor, in whose behalf you appeal, is known to you and to the world to declare against the use of an army to suppress the rebellion.

"Your own attitude, therefore, encourages desertion, resistance to the draft, and the like, because it teaches those who incline to desert and to escape the draft to believe it is your purpose to protect them, and to hope that you will become strong enough to do so. After a short personal intercourse with you, gentlemen of the committee, I cannot say I think you desire this effect to follow your attitude; but I assure you that both friends and enemies of the Union look upon it in this light."

The President asked them to sign three propositions. "Thus indorsed, I will cause them to be published, which publication shall be, within itself, a revocation of the order in relation to Mr. Vallandigham." That is, he would revoke the order of Vallandigham's banishment if they would sign the following:

"1. That there is now a rebellion in the United States, the object and tendency of which is to destroy the National Union; and that, in your opinion, an army and navy are constitutional means for suppressing that rebellion;

"2. That no one of you will do anything which, in his own judgment, will tend to hinder the increase, or favor the decrease, or lessen the efficiency of the army or navy while engaged in the effort to suppress that rebellion; and

"3. That each of you will, in his sphere, do all he can to have the officers, soldiers, and seamen of the army and navy, while engaged in the effort to suppress the rebellion, paid, fed, clad, and otherwise well provided for and supported."

These were the simplest basic conditions the President could offer them, holding his judgment as to what a large mass of loyalist people would agree on as basic. He closed his letter to "M. Birchard and Others" of Ohio in the tone of one at the head of a Government: "Still, in regard to Mr. Vallandigham and all others, I must hereafter, as heretofore, do so much as the public safety may seem to require."

The Ohio committee spurned his three propositions. Excitement rose high in the Buckeye State campaign to decide whether John Brough, the Union-party nominee for Governor, would in November win over Vallandigham, who had vanished into a shroud of silence behind the fog-gray Confederate Army lines in the Deep South.

Had the President ordered Vallandigham shot by a firing squad it would have pleased *Harper's Weekly*, which took Lincoln's Albany response as a warning to "the secret traitors who swarm in our midst." Men and newspapers in New York were saying and publishing words which could not fail "to provide lazy and discontented soldiers with an ample supply of reasons for deserting." A shrewd soldier attending the peace meeting under Fernando Wood's auspices in New York "must have almost deemed it a duty to desert."

Those who had relatives in the army read the dispatch three or four times a week in the newspapers: "Two or more deserters were shot this morning." As to that *Harper's* inquired, "Instead of wanting Vallandigham back, ought we not rather to demand of the President, in justice and mercy, that a few more examples be made of Northern traitors?"

A duplex clamor went into the President's ears, the Peace Democrats in one key and tempo, the antislavery radicals in another. Why, the latter asked, since the Emancipation Proclamation had he taken no effective steps to hurl armed Negroes at the enemy? The President sat in Washington, doubtful what he ought to do, how far he might go, said Wendell Phillips in May of '63 at a Sixteenth Ward Republican meeting in New York. "Month after month, stumbling, faithless, uncertain, he ventured now a little step, and now another, surprised that at every step the nation were before him, ready to welcome any word he chose to say, and to support any policy he chose to submit; so that matters of vexed dispute, of earnest doubt, the moment the bugle gave a certain sound, have passed into dead issues."

Phillips asked why the President did not put Frémont, Butler, Sigel, commanders who loved and understood the Negro, at the head of armies. "I would put men, whose names you know too well, among the black masses of the Carolinas and Mississippi, and fight outward, grinding the rebellion to powder. When we bring the negro into the war, we fight in his home, in the Gulf States, where he ought to fight. The heart of the rebellion is where the negro is."

As to the constitutional power in the hands of the President, Phillips was diametrically opposed to Vallandigham and Seymour. "I believe that the President may do anything to save the Union. He may take a man's houses, his lands, his bank-stock, his horses, his slaves,—anything to save the Union. . . . We need one step further,—an act of Congress abolishing slavery wherever our flag waves." They were too slow by far at Washington. "Judging by the past, whose will and wit can we trust? None of them—I am utterly impartial,—neither President nor Cabinet nor Senate."

Phillips jeered at their tardiness. "Lincoln and Halleck,—they sit in Washington, commanders-in-chief, exercising that disastrous influence which even a Bonaparte would exercise on a battle, if he tried to fight it by telegraph a hundred miles distant." If the President had any feeling for the Negro, he was too reserved about it. "It seems to me the idlest national work, childish work, for the President, in bo-peep secrecy, to hide himself in the White House and launch a proclamation at us on a first day of January. The nation should have known it sixty days before, and should have provided fit machinery for the reception of three million bondmen into the civil state." In the mighty work ahead Phillips's advice would be: "Cease to lean on the government at Washington; it is a broken reed, if not worse." The people would have to ride out of the storm without captain or pilot at the helm.

Once Phillips hacked at the roots of the peculiar "honesty" he said was alleged of Lincoln on the slave question. "The President is an honest man; that is, he is Kentucky honest, and that is necessarily a very different thing from Massachusetts or New York honesty. A man cannot get above the atmosphere in which he was born. Did you ever see the Life of Luther in four volumes of seven hundred pages each? The first volume contains an account of the mineralogy of his native country, the trees that grow there, the flowers, average length of human life, the color of the hair, how much rain falls, the range of the thermometer, etc., and in the second volume Luther is born. That was laying the foundation of Luther's character.

"Lincoln was born in Kentucky, and laid the foundation of his honesty in Kentucky. He is honest, with that allowance. He means to do his duty, and within the limit of the capacity God has given him he has struggled on, and has led the people struggling on, up to this weapon, partial emancipation, which they now hold glittering in their right hand. But we must remember the very prejudices and moral callousness which made him in 1860 an available candidate, when angry and half educated parties were struggling for victory, necessarily makes him a poor leader,—rather no leader at all,—in a crisis like this. I have no confidence in the counsels about him."

Phillips swept into a shrill realm of hate, into a gospel of nihilism and obliteration. He hoped his words would blast and wither. The army of Jefferson Davis had been brought together by hatred of the North. "Will being beaten make them love us? Is that the way to make men love you? Can you whip a man into loving you? You whip him into a bitterer hate." Where would the Southern Army go on being beaten? "Into a state of society more cruel than war,—whose characteristics are private assassination, burning, stabbing, shooting, poisoning. The consequence is, we have not only an army to conquer, which, being beaten, will not own it, but we have a state of mind to annihilate."

What would the Southern soldiers do on going back from the army to peaceful pursuits? "They don't know how to do anything. . . . You might think they would go back to their professions. They never had any. You might think they would go back to the mechanic arts. They don't know how to open a jackknife. [Great merriment.] There is nowhere for them to go, unless we send them half a million of emancipated blacks, to teach them how to plant cotton."

A proud, mad war speech Phillips was making, voicing that hard New England element which had created a tradition of contempt for Southern methods and culture, also that same element which had been first and then had never forsaken Lincoln with troops, money, and supplies. "Which shall rule this one and indivisible country?" asked the impetuous orator. "The South said, 'I load my cannon in order that I may annihilate Massachusetts.' 'I accept it,' said the Bay State, and, her cannon being the largest and the strongest, she annihilates the South instead. [Applause.] That is the argument. We should have gone to the wall had she beaten. One nation!—she goes to the wall when we beat."

Phillips pictured the Southern young man, "melted in sensuality, whose face was never lighted up by a purpose since his mother looked into his cradle," lifted by the war to a higher level. "Over those wrecks of manhood breathed the bugle-note of woman and politics, calling upon them to rally and fight for an idea,—Southern independence. It lifted them, for the moment, into something which looked like civilization . . . and war to them is a gain. They go out of it, and they sink down. . . . They go back to bar-rooms, to corner-groceries, to plantation sensuality, to chopping straw, and calling it politics. [Laughter.]"

What of the future? Phillips could see only conquest, subjugation. "When England conquered the Highlands, she held them,—held them until she could educate them; and it took a generation. That is just what we have to do with the South; annihilate the old South, and put a new one there." He referred to the former control of the Federal Government by the South, of how it had always been able to arrange compromises. It had been like a drama staged in Rome once where monkeys impersonated people. "In the midst of the performance some Roman wag flung upon the stage a handful of nuts, and immediately the actors were monkeys again. Our statesmen went to Washington monkeys in human attire, determined to compromise if possible; the South flung nuts among them for eighteen months, and they were on all fours for the temptation. [Laughter and applause.] That epoch is ended."

Phillips considered himself a participant in a world-wide struggle be-tween free and caste institutions. "Wherever caste lives, wherever class power exists, whether it be on the Thames or the Seine, whether on the Ganges or the Danube, there the South has an ally, just as the surgeon's knife gives pain when it touches the living fibre." Thus in the opening of his speech. And to close: "Never until we welcome the negro, the foreigner, all races as equals, and, melted together in a common nationality, hurl them all at despotism, will the North deserve triumph or earn it at the hands of a just God."

So baffling was the future for those who tried to read it at this time that the minds of men turned to alternatives that might end the war, Henry Adams writing to his brother: "Of all results, a restoration of the Union on a pro-slavery basis would be most unfortunate. Yet I dread almost equally a conquest that would leave us with a new and aggravated Poland on our hands. If we could only fight a peace that would give us Virginia, Tennessee and the Mississippi River, then we might easily allow slavery to gather to a head in the cotton states, and crush it out at our leisure on the first good opportunity; but such a vision is reserved for the just made perfect."

From its own aloof outlook the *Spectator* of London noted that Lincoln had not the courage "to rise above the bonds of the Constitution" in his Emancipation Proclamation. "Had he appealed to God and not to his party tenets, he might have roused a fanaticism, and possibly by giving his armies an idea, have given them also victory. Instead of this, he adheres, as he has consistently done, to his Constitutional obligations, emancipates as a war measure exclusively."

Then the *Spectator* touched on the reply proclamation of Jefferson Davis, which had declared that all slaves caught availing themselves of the Lincoln proclamation would be handed over to the respective States where they belonged and thus be put to death, and that all officers commanding them or executing the proclamation would also die. "In excellent English, possessed of a certain character of stateliness of which Mr. Lincoln is wholly devoid, Mr. Davis announces that whole classes of prisoners, shall, when captured, be massacred in cold blood. He makes no mistakes, professes no restrictions of constitutional law; wherever the man commanding black troops is found, he shall be handed over to men who will inevitably send him to the gallows. There is no weakness in his order, and no blundering; but there is a thorough contempt at once for law and for humanity. Every section of it is intended to rivet the chains of the slave.

"Mr. Lincoln's [proclamation] may, and Mr. Davis' certainly, will not succeed. . . . If a slave is to be executed because he takes arms he will not be taken prisoner; if the officer is to be hanged he will prefer a bullet. Mr. Davis has given to both classes new reasons for meeting a death which no decree can make other than an honourable one. Mr. Lincoln's proclamation, on the other hand, *may* pulverize the power of the South. . . . Reunion, if it arrives, must be a reunion among the free. . . . Separation or conquest are now the only alternatives."

In the confusion of tongues that cried across the gulf between Vallandigham and Phillips, Lincoln occasionally gave his point of view to the country through an impromptu utterance to callers at the White House. An excited delegation of clergymen, troubled about the conduct of the war, came with loud protests. The President heard them through and, as the reading public had it from newspapers, he replied: "Gentlemen, suppose all the property you were worth was in gold, and you had put it in the hands of Blondin to carry across the Niagara River on a rope, would you shake the cable, or keep shouting out to him, 'Blondin, stand up a little straighter!— Blondin, stoop a little more—go a little faster—lean a little more to the north —lean a little more to the south'? No! you would hold your breath as well as your tongue, and keep your hands off until he was safe over. The Government is carrying an immense weight. Untold treasures are in their hands. They are doing the very best they can. Don't badger them. Keep silence, and we'll get you safe across."

The incident made Lincoln "a little shy of preachers" for a time, according to Marshal Hill Lamon, who quoted the President as saying, "But the latch-string is out, and they have the right to come here and preach to me if they will go about it with some gentleness and moderation."

Lamon quoted the President as saying more than once: "In God's name! if anyone can do better in my place than I have done, or am endeavoring to do, let him try his hand at it, and no one will be better contented than myself."

Once Lamon found the door to Lincoln's office locked, went through a private room and through a side entrance into the office, finding the President on a sofa, restless over the day's outlook. He jumped up to say to Lamon, as between old companions: "You know better than any man living that from my boyhood up my ambition was to be President. I *am* President of one part of this divided country at least; but look at me! I wish I had never been born! It is a white elephant on my hands, and hard to manage. With a fire in my front and rear; having to contend with the jealousies of military commanders and not receiving that cordial co-operation and support from Congress which could reasonably be expected; with an active and formidable enemy in the field threatening the very life-blood of the government—my position is anything but a bed of roses."

Lamon surmised he was like Richelieu, "the first man in Europe but second only in his own country," which brought the response "Oh, no, very far from it. Richelieu never had a fire in his front and rear at the same time, but a united constituency." Then the President brightened and a twinkle rose in his eye. "If I can only keep my end of the animal pointed in the right direction, I will yet get him through this infernal jungle and get my end of him and his tail placed in their proper relative positions." He spoke of obstructive Congressmen, and rising to his full height exclaimed: "This state of things shall continue no longer. I will show them at the other end of the Avenue whether I am President or not!"

A *Vanity Fair* wag wrote, "Lincoln's noncommittal policy is considered so knowing by the politicians that henceforth he is to be called the *Fox populi*." Certainly an elusive sagacity was required to negotiate the issues stated and implied in the *Kittanning* (Pennsylvania) *Mentor* paragraph: "When the tax collector comes round with his warrant; when we have to go and buy a stamp to put upon a deed, note, &c; when we have to take out a license to buy or sell; when we go to the store and pay forty cents a pound for coffee instead of ten; when we look at our public debt and find it accumulating at the rate of over $2,000,000 per day; when we look at our sons and brothers dragged from their homes to fight in a war they abhor; and when we look at the vacant chair or new made graves of those who have died, let us remember that all these we owe to Mr. Abraham Lincoln and the party that supports him."

The *New York Times* took as "one of the deepest sensations of the war" the order of General Grant excluding all Jews as a class from his military department. "The order, to be sure, was promptly set aside by the President but the affront to the Jews conveyed by its issue, was not so easily effaced. A committee of Jews took it upon themselves to *thank* President Lincoln at Washington for so promptly annulling the odious order. Against the conduct of this committee the bulk of the Jews vehemently protest. They say they have no thanks for an act of simple and imperative justice—but grounds for deep and just complaint against the Government, that General Grant has not been dismissed from the service."

A letter of Lincoln to General Schofield, military head in Missouri, counseled: "If both factions, or neither, shall abuse you, you will probably be about right. Beware of being assailed by one and praised by the other."

Browning advised the President that because he had a more comprehensive and minute view of the national affairs than any other person could have, he should make up his mind calmly and deliberately, and then allow no one to bully or cajole him. "He answered," Browning noted in the diary, "that he had done so to a greater extent than was generally supposed—That when he made up his mind to send supplies to Fort Sumter he was sustained by only two members of his cabinet . . . and that when he determined to give the rebels at Charleston notice of his purpose the entire cabinet was against him, though they all now admitted that he was right."

Congressman George Julian came asking that Frémont again be given a command. Lincoln said he did not know where to place Frémont, and was reminded of the old man who advised his son to take a wife, the young man responding, "Whose wife shall I take?" Then Lincoln pointed to practical difficulties, Julian urging that Frémont's reappointment would "stir" the country.

"It would stir the country on one side," observed Lincoln, "and stir it the other way on the other. It would please Frémont's friends, and displease the conservatives, and that is all I can see in the *stirring* argument." He added, "My proclamation was to stir the country, but it has done about as much harm as good."

The conniving Fernando Wood went to the White House early in June of '63. "During the interview many droll and important sayings were uttered by the President," said the mercurial *New York Herald*. "Mr. Wood did not disavow his peace speeches, as some journals assert. On the contrary he stated the masses of New York were in favor of peace. 'So am I,' replied Mr. Lincoln, 'and so is everybody. The only point in dispute is how peace may be best secured.' After this the conversation was more confidential. . . . The President enumerated some of the trials of his position, warned Mr. Wood never to accept the office, and declared he often wished himself back in Springfield, Illinois. . . . Mr. Wood has been looking for an honest man among politicians for the past thirty years. At last, more fortunate than Diogenes, he found an honest man in the White House."

An Illinois acquaintance casually mentioned to Lincoln that So-and-So, whom they had both known as an old Whig friend in Champaign County, had talked hotly against the war and the Administration till his neighbors threatened to tar and feather him. He was found dead in bed, largely from fright—sort of scared to death. "He died, then," said Lincoln, "to save his life, it seems."

On the snarled and tangled matter of policy as to Negro recruiting Lincoln cleared the air for himself in a memorandum of points he set down for his own guidance:

To recruiting free negroes, no objection.

To recruiting slaves of disloyal owners, no objection.

To recruiting slaves of loyal owners, *with their consent*, no objection.

To recruiting slaves of loyal owners, *without* consent, objection, *unless the necessity is urgent.*

To conducting offensively, while recruiting, and to carrying away slaves not suitable for recruits, objection.

Early in '63 a bill passed the House which authorized the President "to enroll, arm, equip, and receive into the land and naval service of the United

States such number of volunteers as he may deem useful to suppress the present rebellion." The Senate returned the House bill as unnecessary because the President had such power under previous acts. In the House debate, Maynard of Tennessee declared, "We shall have not only brigadier generals but major generals of the African race, if under the powers conferred by this bill the President should choose to confer that high authority upon men of that race." By a vote of 23 to 12 the Senate rejected an amendment that "no negro, free or slave, shall be enrolled in the military or marine, or naval service of the United States," while by a vote of 18 to 7 it adopted an amendment that "no person of African descent shall be commissioned or hold an office in the army of the United States."

The Negro was still a chattel, bought and sold on slave soil not touched by the Emancipation Proclamation. The *Lexington Observer and Reporter* in Kentucky printed hundreds of advertisements during 1863 of "one yellow boy" or "two black men" or "one negro man" held in the county jail, who "unless claimed by the owner" would "be sold according to law to pay expenses." On February 4, 1863, it advertised "A Negro Girl at Public Sale." She was eighteen years old, "a likely girl," and would go to "the highest bidder, terms cash."

Lincoln mentioned, according to L. E. Chittenden, a proposed contract "to remove the whole colored race of the slave States into Texas." Chittenden named John Bradley, a Vermonter, as possibly able to undertake the scheme. Bradley came from a two-hour interview with Lincoln. Chittenden asked whether it wasn't impracticable to establish a Negro republic in the Lone Star State. "The President has not decided to favor it," said Bradley.

Thousands of Negroes had been enlisted as soldiers in the first six months of 1863, though when the President had issued the Emancipation Proclamation it had merely specified that he would receive them "into the armed service of the United States to garrison forts, positions, stations, and other places, and to man vessels of all sorts." He wrote to General John A. Dix, commanding at Fortress Monroe, that while bearing the disadvantages of the Emancipation Proclamation "we must also take some benefit from it, if practicable." He asked a well-considered opinion from Dix on whether the fort, and Yorktown near by, could not be garrisoned by colored troops, leaving the white troops for service elsewhere.

Dix, once a Buchanan Democrat, doubted whether a garrison could be raised in that part of Virginia, and reported to the President: "An officer from Massachusetts, who has taken an interest in the question, interrogated the adult males of the colored population at Camp Hamilton and Newport News, and found only five or six who were willing to take up arms. The general reply was that they were willing to work, but did not wish to fight. I deem it not improper to say further that the feeling towards the North among a considerable portion of the colored refugees is not a cordial one. They understand that we deny them in many of the free States the right of suffrage, and that, even in those where political equality is theoretically established by law, social prejudices practically neutralize it."

Other commanders, however, such as Hunter in the Department of the South, Banks at New Orleans and in Louisiana, Lane in Kansas, had found varying success in raising regiments and brigades. Also Adjutant General Lorenzo Thomas of the War Department, on a trip to the lower Mississippi region in March, reported renewed faith in the experiment of arming the blacks. He addressed 11,000 troops of the McArthur and Logan divisions, telling them: "I came from Washington clothed with the fullest power in this matter. With this power, I can act as if the President of the United States were himself present. I am directed to refer nothing to Washington, but to act promptly. . . . You know full well the rebels have sent into the field all their available fighting men, and have kept at home all their slaves for the raising of subsistence for their armies in the field. The administration has determined to take from the rebels this source of supply—to take their negroes and compel them to send back a portion of their whites to cultivate their deserted plantations. They must do this or their armies will starve.

"On the first day of January last the President issued his Proclamation declaring from that day forward all the slaves in the States then in rebellion should be free. You know that vast numbers of these slaves are inside the lines of this army. They come into your camps and you cannot but receive them. The authorities at Washington are very much pained to hear, and I fear with truth in many cases, that some of those poor unfortunates have, on different occasions, been turned away from us, and their applications for admission within our lines have been refused by our officers and soldiers. This is not the way to use freedmen."

The Adjutant General direct from Washington was delivering a message he had gone over thoroughly with Lincoln and Stanton. "All of you will some day be on picket duty," he told the assembled thousands of troops, "and I charge you all if any of this unfortunate race come within your lines, that you do not turn them away, but that you receive them kindly and cordially. They are to be encouraged to come to us. They are to be received with open arms; they are to be fed and clothed; they are to be armed. This is the policy that has been fully determined upon. I am here to say that I am authorized to raise as many regiments of blacks as I can. I am authorized to give commissions from the highest to the lowest, and I desire that those persons who are in earnest in this work take hold of it."

Word had spread of the Confederate Government's order that white officers commanding Negro troops should never be taken prisoner, but put to death. Officers and men listening to the Adjutant General well knew this. "I desire only those whose hearts are in it, and to them alone will I give commissions. I don't care who they are or what their present rank may be. I do not hesitate to say that all proper persons will receive commissions. While I am authorized thus, in the name of the Secretary of War, I have the fullest authority to dismiss from the army any man, be his rank what it may, whom I find maltreating the freedmen. This part of my duty I will most assuredly perform if any case comes before me."

The Adjutant General would like to raise twenty regiments before going back to Washington. Colored women, children, and all men unfit for military duty would be placed on captured plantations, while Negro troops familiar with roads and swamps would sweep the interior of guerrillas. "Recollect, for every regiment of blacks I raise, I raise a regiment of whites to face the foe in the field. This, fellow soldiers, is the determined policy of the administration. You all know full well when the President of the United States, though said to be slow in coming to a determination, when he once puts his foot down, it is there, and he is not going to take it up. He has put his foot down; I am here to assure you that my official influence shall be given that he shall not raise it."

Thus began a recruiting campaign. Immediately south in the Department of the Gulf, General Banks ordered eighteen regiments to be raised of 500 men each, to be called "Corps d'Afrique." The War Department in May of '63 announced a new bureau to handle Negro recruiting. A steady drift of press items on Negro fighters in Federal uniforms began appearing. Robert Gould Shaw, twenty-six years old—his grandfather a rich merchant who fought in the Revolutionary War, his father a lover of humanity who gave money freehandedly to the poor, the ignorant, the criminal, the enslaved—became colonel of the 54th Massachusetts, the first regiment of colored soldiers mustered into United States service. What would happen to this valorous young white man heading platoons of black troops, now landed on a Carolina coast, with the definite threat from Confederate officers that if taken alive he would be put to death?

From Port Hudson on the Mississippi on June 14 came word that colored troops under General Paine had led an assault, put their flag on a fort parapet amid fearful slaughter, leaving their commander wounded in front of the enemy's works as they retired. A half-mile away on a call for volunteers to go back and rescue the General's body, sixteen stepped out from the colored regiments, moved forward in squads of four. And they brought back their General, though only two of the sixteen Negroes were alive.

A new status of the Negro was slowly taking form. In August of '62 for the first time was sworn testimony taken from a Negro in a court of law in Virginia. Also Negro strikebreakers in New York were attacked by strikers, and in Chicago Negroes employed in meat-packing plants were assaulted by unemployed white men. The colored man was becoming an American citizen.

Stories arose that Confederate troops had a law to themselves: "Kill every nigger!" No distinctions would be made in battle as between free Negroes and fugitive slaves. Written petitions and spoken appeals came to Lincoln that he must retaliate: kill one Confederate white prisoner for every Negro Union soldier executed.

Negroes marching to war—with weapons—to kill—and to kill white men —it was at first a little unreal. Longfellow wrote in his diary on May 28, 1863, of a visit to Boston: "Saw the first regiment of blacks march through Beacon Street. An imposing sight, with something wild and strange about it, like a dream. At last the North consents to let the Negro fight for freedom."

In an Indiana town, controlled by Copperheads, Sojourner Truth was introduced to speak at an antislavery meeting. A local physician and leading Copperhead rose and said that word had spread over the community that the speaker of the evening was a man in woman's disguise and therefore it was the wish of many present that the speaker of the evening should show her breasts to a committee of ladies. Sojourner Truth, tall, strong, unafraid, illiterate though having a natural grace of speech and body, stood silent a few moments. Then she loosed the clothing of her bosom, showed her breasts, and said in her own simple words and her deep contralto voice that these breasts she was showing had nursed black children, yes, but more white children than black. The audience sat spellbound. A few Copperheads slowly filed out. Toward one of them who had a look of hate and doubt on his face, Sojourner Truth shook her breasts with the melancholy query, "You want to suck?" And in this tense and quiet atmosphere, the gaunt black woman, the former slave, began her plea for the freedom of her race.

Strange was the play of men's thought and imagination around the Negro and his role. Several Northern antislavery journals picked up a fable from the *Memphis Bulletin:* "A Negro went into a menagerie, in which was a large baboon in a cage. He approached the cage closely while the baboon went through several gyrations, such as nodding and shaking his head, holding out his hands to shake, etc., to the evident delight of both Negro and baboon. Finally, the baboon seemed so intelligent and knowing, the Negro addressed him some remarks, which the baboon only answered by a nod of the head. At length the Negro was still more delighted, and broke forth with the remark, 'You're right; don't open your mouth, kase if you spokes a word the white man'l have a shovel in your hand in less dan a minit.' "

Senator Pomeroy of Kansas brought to Lincoln's office an ex-slave, the foremost of fugitive slaves. Lincoln had issued authority to Governor Andrew of Massachusetts to raise two regiments of colored men for war and this ex-slave had then led in recruiting from the 200,000 free Negroes of the North the 54th and 55th Massachusetts regiments, two of his own sons in the 54th. Hundreds of black men of the 54th, and their white colonel, had been killed assaulting a fort in South Carolina, the white colonel's body resting, as South Carolinians reported, "between layers of dead niggers." And as months had passed this ex-slave saw what he believed wrongs and discriminations in the handling of colored troops and a neglect or indifference in the President.

The ex-slave published an open letter: "The piratical proclamation of Jefferson Davis, announcing slavery and assassination to colored prisoners, was before the country and the world. But men had faith in Mr. Lincoln and his advisers. He was silent, to be sure, but charity suggested that being a man of action rather than words he only waited for a case in which to act. This faith in the man enabled us to speak with warmth and effect in urging enlistments among colored men. That faith is nearly gone. No word comes that inquisition shall be made for innocent blood. No word of retaliation when a black man is slain by a rebel in cold blood."

To this the ex-slave knew his moderate friends would say, "Wait a little longer," but he wondered how long. "If the President is ever to demand justice and humanity for black soldiers, is not this the time to do it? How many 54th's must be cut to pieces, its mutilated prisoners killed, and its living sold into slavery, to be tortured to death by inches, before Mr. Lincoln shall say, 'Hold, enough!'" Some of the 54th Massachusetts men had been sold into a slavery worse than death. "Pardon me if I hesitate about assisting in raising another regiment until the President shall give the same protection to them as to white soldiers."

Now Senator Pomeroy had brought this ex-slave to Lincoln's office. Chase, Sumner, Seward, had encouraged him, saying the President would give him a civil reception. Entering the office, he saw the President in a chair amid documents and secretaries, everybody looking overworked and tired. The President rose. Senator Pomeroy introduced to the President, Frederick Douglass, and as Douglass told it: "Mr. Lincoln's face lighted up as soon as my name was mentioned. He extended his hand and bade me welcome." Douglass started telling who he was and his errand, Lincoln interrupting: "I know who you are, Mr. Douglass; Mr. Seward has told me all about you. Sit down; I am glad to see you."

Then began Lincoln's first conference on important business of state with a mulatto. Born in Maryland of a black slave mother, his father a white man, Douglass had grown up as a plantation boy living through Maryland winters without shoes or stockings, eating with his brothers and sisters from a common trough where they scooped out cornmeal mush with an oyster shell or a piece of wood. Yet he grew to a superb physical strength. He saw his kin working from daybreak till dark, more of them whipped for oversleeping than for any other fault. Sold as a boy into family service in Baltimore, Douglass wore shoes and stockings, ate with a spoon, and his new mistress had taught him four letters of the alphabet when she heard from her husband: "Learning would spoil the best nigger in the world; if you teach that nigger how to read the Bible there will be no keeping him. Next he'll want to know how to write and then run away."

On the streets of Baltimore, in shipyards as a calker, Douglass learned to spell, to read, to bring home $6 to $9 a week of his earnings, receiving food, clothes, lodging, and sometimes a quarter of a dollar a week for himself. In the red shirt and bandanna of a sailor, with papers loaned to him by a free Negro, he rode out of Baltimore one day on a railroad train. The conductor collecting fare did not bother to read the papers offered or he would have seen they were for a black and not a yellow-skinned man. A German blacksmith recognized Douglass on the train, guessed he was escaping, said nothing. To Philadelphia and then New York Douglass made his way, recognizing on Broadway another escaped slave, who told him to stay away from all Negroes, as there were informers among them who would send him back where he came from for a few dollars' reward.

Then Douglass met abolitionists who paid his way to New Bedford, where he worked at his trade of a calker, thrilled at the wages paid him being "my own! my own!" As in the Baltimore shipyards, one or more white men would hit him, he would hit back, and during the fight the other white men of the gang would cry, "Kill the nigger!" When at Baltimore he had fought four white men and they finally had him on the ground, one of the four bade farewell by kicking a boot into Douglass's left eye, which for a long time was not so good as the other eye.

Antislavery men noticed at public meetings that Douglass was a natural orator; he was sent from city to city to tell the story of his life as a slave. Though word was spread that his wife was white and he was teaching inter-marriage of whites and blacks, he actually had sent to a free black woman in Maryland, whom he had promised to marry, a message that he had escaped. She had come North and they were married and made a home in Rochester, New York.

From the South came rumors that Douglass would be arrested and under the law returned to Maryland. He took a steamer to England, was the guest of John Bright and his sisters, made fifty speeches in Ireland, was accorded a public breakfast at which Daniel O'Connell introduced him as "the Black O'Connell." The British and Foreign Anti-Slavery Society presented him with a Bible bound in gold, a fund of $2,500 was raised for propaganda under his direction in America, and £150 sterling was subscribed to buy his free-dom. The Baltimore man who so long ago had said, "If you teach that nigger to read the Bible there will be no keeping him," for some $600 now signed a document: "I, Hugh Auld . . . by these presents do hereby release from slavery, liberate, manumit, and set free, *my negro man*, named *Frederick Bailey*, otherwise called *Douglass*."

Back home again in Rochester the house of Douglass sheltered fugitive slaves making the last leg of the journey to Canada, his cellar once hiding eleven runaways. His weekly issue of *Frederick Douglass' Paper*, his speeches and policies, began to veer away from the Garrisonians, who opposed the use of either force or political action and who favored the secession of the North from the South. He leaned to John Brown, had long talks about a nucleus of white men gathering small armies of slaves in the Southern moun-tains and gradually spreading insurrections that would win freedom. His book *My Bondage and Freedom* went to large sales, a German translation selling 20,000 copies in America.

Douglass resented the color line, accepted the advice of white friends that his role was to make contacts with the white race and protest the bar of color. On a ship from New York to Boston he slept overnight on the deck, he and Wendell Phillips huddled under their overcoats. Phillips as a man of white skin could have had a cabin, and Douglass too if he would have met an officer's suggestion that he was an Indian, but he blurted, "No— I'm only a damned nigger." Alongside placards announcing his lectures would be other placards posted: "Nigger Fred Is Coming." The *New York Herald* urged Rochester people to throw the whole Douglass outfit into Lake Ontario. The opposition dramatized him, and his name grew.

John Brown being met secretly at an old stone quarry near Chambersburg, Pennsylvania, the anxious old man asked Douglass to join in a capture of the Harper's Ferry arsenal and fort, to rally Negroes of Maryland and Virginia, who would "swarm as bees to a hive." He advised Brown that the old strategy of mountain guerrilla warfare was better, and the Harper's Ferry project would bring death to all in it—as it did. Then Douglass hid out in England and Canada. A Federal dragnet was out for him. The Governor of Virginia requisitioned the Governor of Michigan for his arrest; near Chambersburg old John Brown had left behind a carpetbag of letters, some of them fixing Douglass as a conspirator.

Then the cyclone of sectional war had opened and slowly Douglass had made the interpretation that Negro freedom must come "as a consequence and not as a cause of the conflict." He read Lincoln as completely mistaken in his Negro colonization policy. "The colored race can never be respected anywhere till they are respected in America. The true policy of the colored American is to make himself, in every way open to him, an American citizen, bearing with proscription and insult till these things disappear." With a crowd of abolitionists Douglass sat, walked, talked, sat again, all day and into the night of January 1, 1863, waiting in Tremont Temple of Boston for the news of whether President Lincoln would issue the promised Emancipation Proclamation. With the girl orator Miss Anna E. Dickinson he joined his efforts to cheer the audience and hold them to believe good news would come.

Among doubters Douglass heard those who said Lincoln would be too softhearted to chance slave insurrections by an edict of freedom; others believed that Mrs. Lincoln, coming from an old slaveholding family of Kentucky, would influence him to delay. The hours passed.

At last a man hurried in with a glad face crying: "It is coming! It is on the wires!"

Then in a surge of shouting, weeping, and hosannas, the proclamation was read and a colored preacher named Rue led all voices in an anthem: "Sound the loud timbrel o'er Egypt's dark sea, Jehovah hath triumphed, his people are free." Douglass took as his text "This is the year of jubilee." At midnight the crowd adjourned to the Twelfth Baptist Church and held forth till near dawn.

The question of what should be done with 3,000,000 or 4,000,000 slaves, if and when emancipated, Douglass answered: "Do nothing with them; mind your business and let them mind theirs. If you see him ploughing, let him alone. If you see him on his way to school, spelling-book, geography, and arithmetic in hand, let him alone. Don't shut the door in his face. Don't pass laws to degrade him. If he has a ballot in his hand, let him alone. Deal justly with him. He is a human being. Give him wages for his work, and let hunger pinch him if he don't work. 'But would you turn them all loose?' Certainly. We are no better than our Creator. He has turned them loose, and why should not we?"

Thus ran backgrounds of the revolutionary ex-slave, "the Black O'Connell," with two sons in the 54th Massachusetts regiment in South Carolina, the man to whom Lincoln said: "Sit down; I am glad to see you." Then, according to Douglass's account of their interview, the President listened with patience and silence, was serious, even troubled, by what Douglass had to say and by what he had evidently thought himself on the same points. To the item that colored soldiers ought to receive the same wages as white soldiers, the President said that employment of colored soldiers at all was a great gain to the colored people; that the wisdom of making colored men soldiers was still doubted; that their enlistment was a serious offense to popular prejudice; that they had larger motives for being soldiers than white men; that they ought to be willing to enter the service upon any conditions; that the fact they were not to receive the same pay as white soldiers seemed a necessary concession to smooth the way to their employment as soldiers, but that ultimately they would receive the same pay as whites.

On the second point, that colored prisoners should receive the same protection and be exchanged as readily and on the same terms as white prisoners, and that there should be retaliation for the shooting or hanging of colored prisoners, the President said the case was more difficult. Retaliation was a terrible remedy—once begun, no telling where it would end; that if he could get hold of the Confederate soldiers who had been guilty of treating colored soldiers as felons, he could easily retaliate, but the thought of hanging men for a crime perpetrated by others was revolting to his feelings. He thought that the "rebels" themselves would stop such barbarous warfare, and less evil would be done if retaliation were not resorted to; that he had already received information that colored soldiers were being treated as prisoners of war.

"In all this," noted Douglass, "I saw the tender heart of the man rather than the stern warrior and Commander-in-Chief of the American army and navy, and while I could not agree with him, I could but respect his humane spirit."

On the third point, that colored soldiers who performed great and uncommon service on the battlefield should be rewarded by distinction and promotion precisely as were white soldiers, the President had less difficulty, though he did not absolutely commit himself, simply saying he would sign any commissions to colored soldiers whom his Secretary of War should commend to him. "Though I was not entirely satisfied with his views," noted Douglass, "I was so well satisfied with the man and with the educating tendency of the conflict, I determined to go on with the recruiting." Of the close of the interview Douglass recorded:

"We discussed means to induce slaves in the rebel States to come within the Federal lines. The increasing opposition to the war in the North, and the mad cry against it because it was being made an abolition war, alarmed Mr. Lincoln, and made him apprehensive that a peace might be forced upon him which would leave still in slavery all who had not come within our lines. What he wanted was to make his proclamation as effective as possible in the event of such peace. He said, in a regretful tone, 'The slaves are not coming into our lines as rapidly and numerously as I had hoped.' I replied that the slaveholders knew how to keep such things from their slaves, and probably very few knew of his proclamation. 'Well,' he said, 'I want you to set about devising some means of making them acquainted with it, and for bringing them into our lines.'

"What he said showed a deeper moral conviction against slavery than I had ever seen before in anything spoken or written by him. I listened with the deepest interest and profoundest satisfaction, and at his suggestion, agreed to undertake the organizing of a band of scouts, composed of colored men, whose business should be, somewhat after the original plan of John Brown, to go into the rebel States beyond the lines of our armies, carry the news of emancipation, and urge the slaves to come within our boundaries."

In an interlude of their talk Lincoln asked, "Who is this Phillips who has been pitching into me?" adding later: "Well, tell him to go on. Let him make the people willing to go in for emancipation; and I'll go with them."

Others heard jokes and saw humor or levity in the President. Douglass wrote, "I seemed never to have the faculty of calling them to the surface."

From the President's room Douglass went to the War Office, heard from Stanton what he regarded as "the best defense" he had yet heard of the Government's treatment of colored soldiers. "On assuring Mr. Stanton of my willingness to take a commission, he said he would make me assistant adjutant to General Lorenzo Thomas, then recruiting in the Mississippi valley." Returning to Rochester, Douglass waited; no commission arrived; he wrote to the War Department about the commission and was asked to report to General Thomas. This he had not expected.

Douglass wrote to Stanton that he would report to Thomas on receipt of his commission: "It did not come and I did not go to the Mississippi valley as I had fondly hoped. I have no doubt that Mr. Stanton in the moment of our meeting meant all he said, but thinking the matter over he felt that the time had not then come for a step so radical and aggressive."

From Memphis early in '63 Charles A. Dana reported to the War Department "a mania for sudden fortunes made in cotton, raging in a vast population of Jews and Yankees." Under Federal permits they bought cotton low from Southern planters and sold high to New England textile works. Dana himself had put in $10,000, with a like amount from Congressman Roscoe Conkling, and gone into partnership with a cotton expert, was in line to make a fortune, yet wrote to Stanton, "I should be false to my duty did I . . . fail to implore you to put an end to an evil so enormous, so insidious."

Grant agreed with Stanton; the cotton trade was corrupting in and out of the army; the profits of it should go to the Government. Dana arrived at Washington, had many conversations with Lincoln and Stanton. The President in March issued a proclamation outlawing all commercial intercourse with insurrectionary States except under Treasury Department regulations. One public sale by an army quartermaster of 500 bales of cotton confiscated by Grant at Oxford and Holly Springs, Mississippi, brought over $1,500,000 cash, nearly paying the cost of Grant's supplies and stores burned by the enemy at Oxford.

Lawrence Weldon, an old Illinois associate in law and politics, came to Lincoln saying he spoke for a number of gentlemen then in Washington. They had permits from civil authorities to trade in cotton, had bought cotton but could not bring it out; the military authorities obstructed. Weldon requested from Lincoln a word as to who might win in this dispute.

Lincoln smiled, then queried as to what had become of Robert Lewis, circuit-court clerk, storyteller, and wit of De Witt County, Illinois. Lewis was still at the old home, said Weldon, and Lincoln asked if Weldon remembered Bob Lewis's going to Missouri to look up some Mormon lands that belonged to his father. Weldon had forgotten. So Lincoln told of Bob Lewis finding among his father's papers a number of warrants and patents for lands in northeast Missouri, and of how Bob took saddlebags and rode a horse for days till he located what seemed to be his piece of land. On it was a cabin where a lean, leathery-looking man was making bullets for a hunting trip. He listened while Bob Lewis showed his title papers and finished with saying, "Now, that is my title, what is yours?"

The pioneer pointed a long finger at a rifle hanging from buck horns over the fire: "Young man, do you see that gun?" The young man admitted he did. "Well," came the spitfire words, "that is my title, and if you don't get out of here pretty damned quick you will feel the force of it." Bob Lewis got on his horse and galloped away, the rifle snapping at him twice before he rounded a corner of safety.

"Now," said Lincoln to Weldon, as a message for Weldon's clients, "the military authorities have the same title against the civil authorities that closed out Bob's Mormon title in Missouri. You may judge what may be the result in this case."

"Cincinnati furnishes more contraband goods than Charleston, and has done more to prolong the war than the State of South Carolina," wrote General Sherman from Memphis. "Not a merchant there but would sell salt, bacon, powder and lead, if they can make money by it. I have partially stopped this and hear their complaints."

A war prosperity was on, gold rising in price, paper money getting cheaper. Amos A. Lawrence, humanitarian millionaire merchant of Boston, wrote to Sumner: "Cheap money makes speculation, rising prices and rapid fortunes, but it will not make patriots. Volunteers will not be found for the army when paper fortunes are so quickly made at home; and drafting will be resisted." Lawrence could not see the rebellion put down till there had been "hard times," factories closed, men's thoughts turned from money. "We must have Sunday all over the land, instead of feasting and gambling."

One embalmer had profited $30,000 in a year. The firm of Brown & Alexander sought through act of Congress to get exclusive embalming rights, with an authorized corps of embalmers for each army division. "The charges," said a Leslie's Weekly correspondent, "are $50 for an officer, $25 for a private, and I must say the bodies look as life-like as if they were asleep."

Copperhead newspapers waxed satirical with an editorial item: "An Abolitionist made a speech from the steps of a banking institution the other night. We understand he has contracts to furnish the Government with horses, mules, shoes, beef, pork, coffee, sugar, rice, onions, saddles, harness, powder, shot, lead, revolvers, Sharpe's rifles, Armstrong guns, percussion caps, Enfield rifles, Springfield rifles, Parrott guns, caissons, ambulances, sanitary stores, monitors, surgeons, chaplains, nurses, and other articles too tedious to mention, as the auctioneer says. In short, he devotes himself entirely to seeing others go to war while he stays at home, saves his bacon and makes money. This is right, and just what a patriot should do."

A *New York World* writer saw a new moneyed class attaining domination of American society, culture, and art of living. "The lavish profusion in which the old southern cotton aristocracy used to indulge is completely eclipsed by the dash, parade, and magnificence of the new northern shoddy aristocracy of this period. Ideas of cheapness and economy are thrown to the winds. The individual who makes the most money—no matter how—and spends the most money—no matter for what—is considered the greatest man. To be extravagant is to be fashionable. These facts sufficiently account for the immense and brilliant audiences at the opera and the theatres; and until the final crash comes such audiences undoubtedly will continue. The world has seen its iron age, its silver age, its golden age, and its brazen age. This is the age of shoddy.

"The new brown-stone palaces on Fifth Avenue, the new equipages at the Park, the new diamonds which dazzle unaccustomed eyes, the new silks and satins which rustle overloudly, as if to demand attention, the new people who live in the palaces, and ride in the carriages, and wear the diamonds and silks—all are shoddy. From devil's dust they sprang, and unto devil's dust they shall return.

"They set or follow the shoddy fashions, and fondly imagine themselves à la mode de Paris, when they are only à la mode de shoddy. They are shoddy brokers in Wall Street, or shoddy manufacturers of shoddy goods, or shoddy contractors for shoddy articles for a shoddy government. Six days in the week they are shoddy business men. On the seventh day they are shoddy Christians." A lamentation was this over traders and gamblers suddenly tumbled into streams of ready money, a new class of upstarts in wealth, social interlopers so naïve in throwing cash at the birds that they had none of the dignity and awareness of the older and approved aristocracy. This new class almost seemed to portend that a future lay ahead where money would count for more, and blood and breeding less, in social distinction.

Food prices had slowly gone up. Clothes, house rent, coal, gas, cost the users more. This pressure on workingmen brought an agitation in New York that resulted in new trade-unions. The *New York World* reported a mass meeting in Cooper Union with the building crammed to capacity and hundreds waiting outside. Nearly all trades were represented, and resolutions were adopted unanimously pointing to wage rates inadequate to the cost of living and urging all trades to organize and send delegates to a central body. Delegate Buckland on behalf of the hatters referred to the intelligence of the crowd before him and said he believed it would compare favorably with that of an equal crowd from any class in the community. "He believed it was only for the laboring class to will to do anything they pleased. Mr. Baldwin was very radical in his opinions on our present social system and on the means of remedying the faults of it. He exclaimed, it was a base press we have in the land, and in appealing to the audience whether that was not true a few hissed but the majority applauded."

Banking combinations and brokers were shaving their profits here, there, and the final shave comes off the laboring man. "The machinery is forging fetters to bind you in perpetual bondage. It gives you a distracted country with men crying out loud and strong for Union. Union with them means no more nor less than that they want the war prolonged that they may get the whole of the capital of the country into their breeches pocket and let it out at a percentage that will rivet the chain about your neck."

Delegate Buckland would cut loose from the politicians and by labor organization alone win better conditions. "The working class want education, but many of them cannot spare even the time to let the children get the common school. The children have to work to live. Every day the rich are growing richer—the poor poorer." And, noted the *World*, "The speaker made some concluding remarks strongly tainted with communism, which did not meet with general approval."

Delegate Harding for the painters said the Government of the country was an organization, that the Chamber of Commerce unified the merchants and manufacturers, and workingmen should likewise gather into trade-unions. "The hours of labor must be shortened so there will be more time for education." Difficulties between capital and labor could be arbitrated by a court appointed by the State legislature.

Delegate Crowe for the tailors said the achievements of man's ingenuity in mechanical industry were marvelous, "but the welfare of the industrious workmen who suffer from the tyranny of capital is of far more consequence. [Applause.]" The speaker alluded bitterly to a firm of large wholesale clothiers, "parading the whole force of their establishment at the great Union mass meeting of April, 1861, and of their going a few days afterward to intrigue for the contracts which had resulted, as everyone knew, in 'shoddy.'" Over a hundred firms had consented to the union wage rates. "There were honest men among the employers as well as Shylocks."

Delegate Keady for the printers said the workingman was the first to feel the evil of currency inflation, cheaper money. "It interfered with the hard savings of years; it deranged the commonest business transactions; it deprived the private soldier of half his pay. To find protection each trade must organize by itself and then come into a grand central organization. They would meet with difficulties. The worst would be the interference of politicians. That overcome, they would go on to greater strength each day until they became the strongest body of workingmen on the face of the globe. [Great cheering.]"

In spite of corruption and chicanery, an economic system of new factors was getting deep rootholds. The A. T. Stewart department store in New York was completing a new one-block structure, which with John Wanamaker's growing establishment in Philadelphia was undertaking mass merchandising on a new scale. Colt's firearms factory at Hartford, Connecticut, declared a 30 per cent dividend for the year 1862. Aspinwall, Vanderbilt, Drew, Gould, and others foresaw, once the war ended, an era of moneymaking, speculations and developments, individual fortunes to surpass by far any reckonings of finance in the former generation. Exports of petroleum were in '63 nearly tripling those of the previous year. In coal it was becoming known that the United States had such areas that it would take its place as a principal producer among World Powers. Likewise in steel, iron, and copper. Emigration was bringing to American shores a supply of workers that would result in a labor market more than requisite to the needs of capitalist industry. The Union Pacific Railway to span the continent was more a definite project than a dream; it was mentioned when in February of '63 the press said, "The President's Message was published in Honolulu, Sandwich Islands, in 12 days and 20 hours after its delivery in Washington."

The future was to be written in big numbers, bulking billions rather than merely millions. Editor Joseph Medill of the *Chicago Tribune* wrote to his brother William, who died of battle wounds a few weeks later, in the summer of '63: "There is a great, grand, and glorious future to our country when the slaveholders' hellish revolt is crushed out; there will never be another rebellion. Emigration from Europe is already pouring into New York at the rate of 1,000 a day, which will fill up the gap made by the war in our labor population." He could see 500,000 emigrants a year entering Northern ports after the war with the South. Then two other wars loomed, "one to clear the British out of Canada and the other to clear the French out of Mexico."

Medill was decisive. "This continent belongs to the Free American race and they are bound to have it—every inch of it, including the West Indian Islands. We have got a taste of blood and learned the art of war and our own tremendous strength and exhaustless resources. Our navy will domineer the seas and our army the continent. The insults received from England must be wiped out, and the only reparation she can give us is to vacate North America. Peaceably if she will—forcibly if we must. As to France, we claim the right to turn her up on Uncle Sam's knee and spank her bottom for not behaving herself. Old Abe says, 'Bring on your niggers. I want 200,000 of them to save my white boys as soon as I can get them.' Our people are learning sense. The war has pounded new ideas into their heads and old prejudices out. It is a great teacher, and great progress is never made by a people except through war. The tree of Liberty must be watered by blood of patriots at least once in every three generations."

Thus Medill wrote in May of '63, though two months earlier he was less hopeful, writing to a friend that "an awful responsibility" rested on the Republican party. "If it fails, all is lost. Hence we sustain Chase and his National Bank scheme, Stanton and his impulsiveness, Welles and his senility, Lincoln and his slowness. Let us first get the ship out of the breakers; then court-martial the officers if they deserved it." Thus men veered between hope and gloom.

The National Bank Act, passed in February of '63, was presented as a device to get money to run the war, and a method to achieve stability in currency and finance through co-operation with the bankers, bondholders, and business interests having cash and resources. Therefore it stipulated gold payment of interest on bonds. Therefore bankers and bondholders were given such attractions of safe investment and assured profits in the National Bank system that it was understood that they were satisfied, Thaddeus Stevens saying the act favored "the unfortunate money lenders who were clamorous lest the debtor should the more easily pay his debt." He demurred that the propertied and creditor groups of the country would through finance unduly control the Government.

Five or more persons, under the National Bank Act, could associate and form a bank having capital of $50,000 or more. On depositing in the United States Treasury interest-bearing bonds to the amount of one-third of the paid-in capital of the bank, the Government would engrave money for them, National Bank certificates, to the amount of 90 per cent of the par value of the bonds deposited. The banks would use these new certificates for carrying on a regular banking business, receiving the full profit as though they were the bank's own notes. Also the banks would receive, from the Government, interest payment in gold on the bonds deposited in the Treasury.

Thus the double profit of banker's interest on government guaranteed and supervised money issues, and the gold-paid interest on bonds, was the inducement by which Chase, with Lincoln's complete endorsement, proposed to rally cash resources to the war for the Union.

Also the aim was to bring order out of chaos in currency. Across the country there were in circulation more than 8,300 sorts of paper money of solvent banks, according to one financial writer, while the issues of fraudulent, broken, and worthless banks brought the total up to more than 13,000. Also 6,000 counterfeits were circulating.

"Shinplasters" was the nickname for much of this mongrel money; once a soldier had used them as plasters for a wounded shinbone.

Retail storekeepers kept publications, the *Monitor*, the *Detector*, which they consulted as to whether the paper money offered by a customer was counterfeit or genuine and if genuine, whether issued by a solvent bank. Except for the issues of Federal greenbacks or gold and silver, there was no money of the Union. Bills of the banks of one State found no circulation in another. A traveler passing through several States must change his money several times, pay heavy discounts and sometimes commissions.

One hundred and seventy dollars of government greenbacks was buying

$100 of gold money, perhaps moving toward the time Secretary Chase had in mind when he had said earlier, "The war must go on until the rebellion is put down, if we have to put out paper until it takes a thousand dollars to buy a breakfast."

At that time, in 1862, Lincoln had come one late afternoon into the room of the Register of the Treasury, L. E. Chittenden. As that official told it, Lincoln "dropped wearily into a seat" and after a short silence asked about the recent paper moneys put out by the Governor: "What have you to say about this legal-tender act? Here is a committee of great financiers from the great cities who say that, by approving this act, I have wrecked the country. They know all about it—or they are mistaken."

The Government by its declaration that its greenbacks would be full payment, legal tender, for all debts, had made trouble for the bankers, bond-holders, the creditor class. Their money was becoming cheapened by the issue of $100,000,000 of greenbacks. Chittenden replied to Lincoln: "The time for argument has passed. Legal tender is inevitable. The gentlemen you mention have made it a necessity. The people would take our notes without the legal tender clause. The banks and the copperheads will not. We cannot risk the country in their hands. You have followed your own good judgment in signing the act. The people will sustain you and Secretary Chase and Congress."

"I do not see that I am exclusively responsible," Lincoln went on. "I say to these gentlemen, 'Go to Secretary Chase; he is managing the finances.' They persist, and have argued me almost blind. I am worse off than St. Paul. He was in a strait betwixt two. I am in a strait betwixt twenty, and they are bankers and financiers."

"You are right in signing the act. That point has passed debate."

"Now that is just where my mind is troubled. We owe a lot of money which we cannot pay; we have got to run in debt still deeper. Our creditors think we are honest, and will pay in the future. They will take our notes, but they want small notes which they can use among themselves. So far I see no objection, but I do not like to say to a creditor you shall accept in payment of your debt something that was not money when it was contracted. That doesn't seem honest, and I do not believe the Constitution sanctions dishonesty."

Chittenden agreed that the Constitution was vague as to legal tender: "I have read no speech in which that right is broadly asserted. I believe it safer to defend our position on the ground of necessity."

"I understand that is Chase's ground," said Lincoln, "though he does not put it so strongly. We shall see. We will wait to hear from the country districts, from the people."

Chase had urged the National Bank Act as "a firm anchorage to the Union of States," which would "reconcile as far as practicable the interests of existing institutions with those of the whole people." Lincoln in his December, 1862, message to Congress advocated its passage. He noted fluctuations of currency values as "always injurious" and that wise legislation would always reduce such shifting values to the lowest possible point: "It is extremely doubtful whether a circulation of United States notes, payable in coin, and sufficiently large for the wants of the people, can be permanently, usefully, and safely maintained."

What then? Was there any other mode of providing for the public wants with a safe and uniform currency? The President reasoned: "I know of none which promises so certain results, and is at the same time so unobjectionable, as the organization of banking associations under a general act of Congress well guarded in its provisions. To such associations the government might furnish circulating notes, on the security of United States bonds deposited in the treasury. These notes, prepared under the supervision of proper officers, being uniform in appearance and security, and convertible always into coin, would at once protect labor against the evils of a vicious currency, and facilitate commerce by cheap and safe exchanges. A moderate reservation from the interest on the bonds would compensate the United States for the preparation and distribution of the notes and a general supervision of the system, and would lighten the burden of that part of the public debt employed as securities. The public credit, moreover, would be greatly improved and the negotiation of new loans greatly facilitated by the steady market demand for government bonds which the adoption of the proposed system would create."

This, in brief, was Lincoln's argument for the National Bank Act, which he was pleased to sign. A Republican element, holding the view of Thaddeus Stevens that it was a moneylender's measure, unjust to the debtor class, had little to say by way of criticism, waited to see if it would bring in the war funds promised while also, as Lincoln hoped, operating to "protect labor against the evils of a vicious currency." From opposition Democrats, few in number and influence, an outcry arose that the new national banking system would create a more insidious centralization of money power than the old Bank of the United States which Andrew Jackson had destroyed, that the purse and the sword of the nation were now put into the same hand, a combination dangerous to liberty.

In these financial matters, Nicolay and Hay noted, "Mr. Chase had the constant support of the President," who sometimes made suggestions but did not insist on their being adopted. When the Secretary needed his help with Congress, the President gave it ungrudgingly. In conferences at the White House with committee members of House and Senate, the President urged the Chase proposals. It was, however, the one department of the Government where he was least expert: "Mr. Lincoln exercised less control and a less constant supervision over the work of the Treasury than over some other departments; but he rated at their true value the industry and the ability of the Secretary and the immense responsibility devolved upon his department."

About the time of the *Merrimac-Monitor* battle, a committee of New Yorkers were announced as waiting to see the President at the White House. They wanted a gunboat to protect their city. Lincoln was puzzled and said to the man arranging the interview, "I have no gun-boats or ships of war that can be spared from active service; but as they have come to see me, I shall have to see them and get along as best I can." The committee were introduced as "gentlemen representing $100,000,000 in their own right." Their chairman made an earnest speech requesting protection and stressed the fact that the committee represented the wealth of the city, "one hundred millions in their own right."

Lincoln heard them through, and made a speech, which Lawrence Weldon wrote out as follows: "Gentlemen, I am, by the Constitution, commander-in-chief of the army and navy of the United States, and, as a matter of law, I can order anything done that is practicable to be done; but, as a matter of fact, I am not in command of the gun-boats or ships of war—as a matter of fact, I do not know exactly where they are, but presume they are actively engaged. It is impossible for me, in the condition of things, to furnish you a gun-boat. The credit of the Government is at a very low ebb. Greenbacks are not worth more than 40 or 50 cents on the dollar, and in this condition of things, if I was worth half as much as you gentlemen are represented to be, and as badly frightened as you seem to be, I would build a gun-boat and give it to the Government."

Weldon quoted one who listened as saying he "never saw one hundred millions sink to such insignificant proportions as it did when that committee recrossed the threshold of the White House, sadder but wiser men; they had learned that money was a factor of war."

Riding among cheering troops at Chancellorsville, Lincoln had heard a grinning volunteer call out, "Send along more greenbacks." Tad heard it too, asked his father about it, and learned that for months the soldiers had not been paid. The boy thought a moment and chirped, "Why doesn't Governor Chase print some more greenbacks?"

The press told of a reception at which a Western paymaster, in full major's uniform, was introduced to the President. "Being here, Mr. Lincoln, I thought I'd call and pay my respects." "From the complaints of the soldiers," came the reply, "I guess that's about all any of you do pay." Once at a Cabinet meeting when it was proposed to engrave "In God We Trust" on greenbacks, as on silver coins, Lincoln said, "If you are going to put a legend on the greenbacks, I would suggest that of Peter and John: 'Silver and gold have I none, but such as I have I give thee.'"

The spring and early summer of '63 saw Lincoln's rating among large groups of respectable people of influence sink lower than at any time since he had become President. Richard H. Dana, author of the notable sea story *Two Years before the Mast*, also an able attorney who had managed government cases in prize courts, wrote in March to Charles Francis Adams at London: "As to the politics of Washington, the most striking thing is the absence of personal loyalty to the President. It does not exist. He has no admirers, no enthusiastic supporters, none to bet on his head. If a Republican convention were to be held to-morrow, he would not get the vote of a State. He does not act, or talk, or feel like the ruler of a great empire in a great crisis. This is felt by all, and has got down through all the layers of society. It has a disastrous effect on all departments and classes of officials, as well as on the public.

"He likes rather to talk and tell stories with all sorts of persons who come to him than to give his mind to the noble and manly duties of his great post. It is not difficult to detect that this is the feeling of his cabinet. He has a kind of shrewdness and common sense, mother-wit, and slipshod, low-levelled honesty, that made him a good Western jury lawyer. But he is an unutterable calamity to us where he is. Only the army can save us. Congress has passed some good laws to enable the President to do the work, but the nation does not look up to it for counsel or lead."

"We are going to the Devil as fast as we can, and ought to be very grateful that we have got a Devil to go to," wrote George Ticknor, founder of the Boston Public Library, Harvard professor, and author of a history of Spanish literature. He quoted a friend: "Many people are glad that the President is substantially made an irresponsible Dictator, though they have no confidence in him or his advisors." Congressman George Julian quoted a colleague: "The country is going to hell, and the scenes witnessed in the French Revolution are nothing in comparison with what we shall see here."

Greeley's unrest and worry set him searching in the spring of '63 for a presidential candidate to replace Lincoln the next year, according to a detailed account by Gilmore. "How does Horace feel now?" Lincoln had asked Gilmore, who answered, "Somewhat downhearted." And when Gilmore said to Greeley, "Why not see Lincoln?" the answer was that Lincoln could not be trusted, had not kept his agreement to give the *Tribune* early information, had been slow in letting Greeley know of the Emancipation Proclamation, and had answered the "Prayer of Twenty Millions" with an open letter "adroitly using me to feel the public pulse, and making me appear an officious meddler."

Greeley huffed: "No . . . I can't trust your 'honest old Abe.' He is too smart for me. He thinks me a damned fool; but I am never fooled twice by the same individual." Lincoln had imbibed an idea that God was managing the war and he thought himself the vice-regent, Greeley went on. During the next two years of war, the country, saddled with Lincoln, would be ravaged so that it would hardly be worth saving. But the Republican leaders had their backs up; he had talked with them; they would fight till Doomsday rather than consent to disunion. Every prominent Republican he had conversed with thought the only hope lay in defeating a re-election of Lincoln. Some suitable candidate should be at once decided upon, and during the succeeding eighteen months be "written up" by the entire loyal press so that he might be sure to carry the country. Greeley's own first choice would be Robert J. Walker. He looked at Gilmore, as if inquiring, and Gilmore said, promptly: "He would not be a candidate. He shares Henry Wilson's opinion that God's hand is in the war, and he believes that Lincoln is his selected leader."

Next to Walker, those Greeley had consulted inclined to General Rosecrans as the best and most available candidate to beat Lincoln. Rosecrans had been uniformly successful in the war, had the air of a "coming man," and though some might object to him as a Roman Catholic, Greeley deemed that an advantage, as it would command the solid Irish vote. Only one doubt remained as to Rosecrans: "Is he sound on the goose?" That is, would he refuse to listen to any peace that did not provide for the total extinction of slavery? Greeley and his friends desired an answer to that question, and if Gilmore would go to Rosecrans' headquarters and get an answer to the question, also taking Rosecrans' measure from head to foot, Greeley would equip Gilmore with letters and credentials that would carry him through a stone wall.

"I replied," wrote Gilmore, "that I did not relish the idea of thus going deliberately to work to undermine Mr. Lincoln,—that I had a strong personal liking for him." Greeley answered there would be no undermining of Mr. Lincoln—no harsh criticism. The aim would be to build a strong man up, not to pull a weak man down. Left to himself, Lincoln would fall of his own weight. This was not a time for anyone to consult his personal likes or dislikes. He had himself a liking for Lincoln personally, but he would sacrifice his best friend, cut off his right arm, if it would serve the country in its great extremity. He had always thought Gilmore would do the same.

Gilmore said he was too frank and open, that Rosecrans would detect his purpose in a day. Greeley insisted, "You are just the man for the business." Gilmore said he would go, but he must not be expected to take sides against Lincoln either then or after his return. The fault was not with Lincoln but with his commanders. All, interrupted Greeley, except Rosecrans, who had always won.

Greeley "then gave me the names of his principal associates in this movement," wrote Gilmore. "The list included Thaddeus Stevens, Senator Wade, Henry Winter Davis, David Dudley Field, Governor Andrew of Massachusetts, and . . . about all the more prominent Republican leaders, except Roscoe Conkling, Charles Sumner, and Henry Wilson. . . . It was to me a fearful revelation. What chance of success had Mr. Lincoln, thus forsaken by his friends, and forced to fight, with incompetent generals, some of the ablest soldiers of the time? From sheer pity my feeling grew warmer towards him."

Then in a few days had come the news of Chancellorsville, and Gilmore saw Greeley clutching a telegram as, pale-faced and trembling, he cried, "My God! it is horrible—horrible; and to think of it, 130,000 magnificent soldiers cut to pieces by less than 60,000 half-starved ragamuffins!" Greeley sank into a chair, finished reading the telegram, and with tremulous lips said to Gilmore: "I have your letters all ready,—can't you go at once? I will give you my word that if you find Rosecrans the man that is needed, I will go personally to Lincoln and force him to resign. Hamlin will give Rosecrans command of the armies, and there'll be a chance of saving the country." The letters, said Gilmore, included more than a dozen from Republican leaders, all commending him strongly to the courtesy and confidence of Rosecrans.

After the long roundabout journey to Murfreesboro, Tennessee, Gilmore spent two weeks with Rosecrans and his staff. On all points he became satisfied that the General would be a suitable candidate for the Presidency. He waited days for the chance to lay his message before the General. Near midnight of a long day, with the last visitor gone from the private apartment of the General, Rosecrans heard Gilmore through "with evident surprise and gratification" and then said: "The good opinion of those gentlemen is exceedingly gratifying to me, and so is yours, and I assure you that I have not had the remotest suspicion that you were here for any such purpose. I have supposed that you were merely gathering literary material; but, my good friend, it cannot be. My place is here. The country gave me my education, and so has a right to my military services; and it educated me for precisely this emergency. So this, and not the presidency, is my post of duty, and I cannot, without violating my conscience, leave it. But let me tell you, and I wish you would tell your friends who are moving in this matter, that you are mistaken about Mr. Lincoln. He is in his right place. I am in a position to know, and if you live you will see that I am right about him." Thus Gilmore took pen and made note of the words half an hour after they had been spoken.

As though inklings of the movement to replace Lincoln had reached it, the *New York Herald* shrewdly noted that this same month "the most important subject of our time" was whether it was expedient and necessary to give another four-year term to Lincoln as President. "For all the signs of the times, we can not shake off the conviction of the Republicans, whom we love as Satan loves holy water, that they have no other alternative for 1864 except President Lincoln or a reign of terror."

One of the three Republican Congressmen—three and no more—who defended Lincoln on the floor of the House was Albert G. Riddle of Ohio. For weeks the denunciations of the President by his own party men had flowed on and on, mixed with clamor and sniping criticism, Riddle interposing that "the just limit of manly debate" had been "brutally outraged." The press had "caught up and reëchoed" the clamor. If the masses of people should believe what they were hearing, "no power on earth can save us from destruction, for they would shiver the only arm that must bring us safety." Riddle was tired of "such masters—generals"—on the art of war who for a year and a half had poured a "causeless tide of criticism" on the military operations of the Administration.

Worse than what these critics were saying in Congress was their whisperings, complainings, gloomy predictions, sulkings, "so freely and feebly indulged in." Riddle cried for fair play: "If any man here distrusts the President, let him speak forth here, like these bad leaders, openly, and no longer offend the streets and nauseate places of common resort with their unworthy clamor about him. He may not have in excess that ecstatic fire which makes poets and prophets and madmen; he may not possess much of what we call

heroic blood, that drives men to stake priceless destinies on desperate ven-
tures, and lose them; he may not in an eminent degree possess that indefinable something that school-boys call genius, that enables its possessor
through new and unheard-of combinations to grasp at wonderful results,
and that usually ends in failure; or, if he possesses any or all of these qualities,
they are abashed and subdued in the presence of a danger that dwarfs giants,
and teaches prudence to temerity."

So Riddle gave his own impression: The President "is an unimpassioned,
cool, shrewd, sagacious, far-seeing man, with a capacity to form his own
judgments, and a will to execute them; and he possesses an integrity pure
and simple as the white rays of light that play about the throne. It is this
that has so tied the hearts and love of the people to him, that will not un-
loose in the breath of all the demagogues in the land." Why make comparisons with Washington or Jackson? "Like all extraordinary men, he is an
original, and must stand in his own niche. . . . He commits errors. Who
would have committed fewer?" Carrying a crushing load of responsibilities,
"Is it not a marvel, a most living wonder, that he sustains them so well?"

Finally Riddle would have them remember: "The war is greater than
the President; greater than the two Houses of Congress . . . greater than
all together; and it controls them all, and dictates its own policy; and woe
to the men or party that will not heed its dictation."

Amid the snarling chaos of the winter of 1862-63 there were indications
of a secret movement to impeach President Lincoln and get him out of the
White House. Stubbornly had he followed his own middle course, earning
in both parties enemies who for different reasons wanted him out of the
way. There were radical Republicans who wanted a man obedient to their
wishes. There were reactionaries in both parties who hoped that the confusion of an impeachment would slow down the war, bring back habeas
corpus and other civil rights. The radical Republicans who took part in the
secret movement, their names, could only be guessed. They felt their way
carefully toward throwing Lincoln out of the White House. They knew
that in any final vote to impeach they could count on a large block of Ayes
from the political opposition. The New York Democratic-party leader,
Horatio Seymour, heard of the movement but was not invited to share in it
as was Simon Cameron of Pennsylvania. Long after this embryo conspiracy
had failed of its aim, Cameron said to an interviewer, Howard Carroll, in
guarded statements that would implicate neither dead nor living Republicans:

"Late in 1862 or early in 1863 there can be no doubt that a secret effort
was made to bring about the ejectment of President Lincoln from the White
House. Some time after I returned from the Russian mission, and while I
was resting at my home in Pennsylvania, I received from a number of the
most prominent gentlemen an invitation to visit Washington and attend a
meeting which, according to my information, was to be held in regard to
national affairs. I afterward discovered that this invitation was extended to
me because it was believed that my somewhat unpleasant exit from the War

Department had rendered me hostile to Mr. Lincoln and his Administration. Knowing nothing of this at the time, I went to the capital, and found there assembled a number of prominent men who had come together ostensibly for the purpose of advising with each other regarding the condition of the country. This, I say, was their ostensible purpose, but I soon discovered that their real object was to find means by which the President could be impeached and turned out of office. The complaint against Mr. Lincoln was, that he lacked ability and energy, and that he was not pushing the war with sufficient vigor. These reasons, and the plan of attack, if I may use the expression, were all made known to me, and I was asked for my advice. I gave it, stating, with as much earnestness as I could command, that the movement proposed would be a disastrous one, and strongly urging that it would be little short of madness to interfere with the Administration."

Report and gossip finally shaped specific accusations that Mrs. Lincoln was connected with Union disasters, that there was a Southern spy in the White House who was the wife of the President. Newspaper dispatches had reported the killing in battle of two of her brothers, Confederate officers, and a third wounded. They were sons of her father's first wife. A full brother of Mrs. Lincoln, George R. C. Todd, was a surgeon in the Confederate Army. Then there was Benjamin Hardin Helm, husband of Mary Todd Lincoln's half-sister Emilie; a West Point graduate, he had visited his sister-in-law at the White House before war had opened and had gone forth and talked with several West Point friends, including Robert E. Lee, who had said with a sad wag of the head, "I have just resigned my commission in the United States Army." Helm had asked Colonel Lee, "Did you know that Mr. Lincoln is my brother-in-law?" "No, I did not," replied Lee, "but now let me say one word. I have no doubt of his [Lincoln's] good intentions, but he cannot control the elements. There must be a great war. I cannot strike at my own people, so I wrote out my resignation. My mind is too much disturbed to give you any advice. Do what your conscience and honor bid." In the finish Benjamin Hardin Helm put on a gray uniform and was now commanding a brigade with Bragg's army. Confederate Major General John C. Breckinridge was a kinsman of Mrs. Lincoln's stepmother and his name was linked with the President's wife. That General Helm had married into the Todd family fifteen years after Mrs. Lincoln left her Kentucky home, that her brother, Dr. George R. C. Todd, had been estranged from the family for years previous to 1861, with similar matters of fact, did not get into the common report and gossip. Also that she had as much of kith and kin in the Union army did not enter into current conversation. Two of her cousins, Porter by name, were listed as officers in the Army of the Potomac; a son-in-law of her sister, Mrs. Wallace, was in a blue uniform. Other Todd relatives were in the Northern ranks.

Yet the talk of a Southern woman spy in the White House arrived at the point where Senate members of the Committee on the Conduct of the War had set a secret morning session for attention to reports that Mrs. Lincoln was a disloyalist. So the story goes, though vaguely authenticated.

One member of the committee told of what happened. "We had just been called to order by the Chairman, when the officer stationed at the committee room door came in with a half-frightened expression on his face. Before he had opportunity to make explanation, we understood the reason for his excitement, and were ourselves almost overwhelmed with astonishment. For at the foot of the Committee table, standing solitary, his hat in his hand, his form towering, Abraham Lincoln stood. Had he come by some incantation, thus of a sudden appearing before us unannounced, we could not have been more astounded." There was an "almost unhuman sadness" in the eyes, and "above all an indescribable sense of his complete isolation" which the committee member felt had to do with fundamental senses of the apparition. "No one spoke, for no one knew what to say. The President had not been asked to come before the Committee, nor was it suspected that he had information that we were to investigate reports, which, if true, fastened treason upon his family in the White House."

At last the morning caller spoke slowly, with control, though a depth of sorrow in the tone of voice: "I, Abraham Lincoln, President of the United States, appear of my own volition before this Committee of the Senate to say that I, of my own knowledge, know that it is untrue that any of my family hold treasonable communication with the enemy."

Having attested this, he went away as silent and solitary as he had come. "We sat for some moments speechless. Then by tacit agreement, no word being spoken, the Committee dropped all consideration of the rumors that the wife of the President was betraying the Union. We were so greatly affected that the Committee adjourned for the day."

A party of Bostonians called at the White House one Sunday evening a few weeks after the Emancipation Proclamation was issued. They included Senator Henry Wilson, Wendell Phillips, Francis W. Bird, Elizur Wright, J. H. Stephenson, George L. Stearns, Congressman Oakes Ames, and the Reverend Moncure D. Conway. The remarkable interview that took place was scrupulously and luminously recorded by Conway: "The President met us, laughing like a boy, saying that in the morning one of his children had come to inform him that the cat had kittens, and now another had just announced that the dog had puppies, and the White House was in a decidedly sensational state. Some of our party looked a little glum at this hilarity; but it was pathetic to see the change in the President's face when he presently resumed his burden of care.

"We were introduced by Senator Wilson, who began to speak of us severally, when Mr. Lincoln said he knew perfectly who we were, and requested us to be seated. Nothing could be more gracious than his manner, or more simple.

"The conversation was introduced by Wendell Phillips, who, with all his courtesy, expressed our gratitude and joy at the Proclamation of Emancipation, and asked how it seemed to be working. The President said that he had not expected much from it at first, and consequently had not been disappointed; he had hoped, and still hoped, that something would come of it after awhile.

"Phillips then alluded to the deadly hostility which the proclamation had naturally excited in pro-slavery quarters, and gently hinted that the Northern people, now generally anti-slavery, were not satisfied that it was being honestly carried out by all of the nation's agents and Generals in the South.

" 'My own impression, Mr. Phillips,' said the President, 'is that the masses of the country generally are dissatisfied chiefly at our lack of military successes. Defeat and failure in the field make everything seem wrong.' His face was now clouded, and his next words were somewhat bitter. 'Most of us here present,' he said, 'have been nearly all our lives working in minorities, and many have got into a habit of being dissatisfied.'

"Several of those present having deprecated this, the President said, 'At any rate, it has been very rare that an opportunity of "running" this administration has been lost.' To this Mr. Phillips answered, in his sweetest voice: 'If we see this administration earnestly working to free the country from slavery and its rebellion, we will show you how we can "run" it into another four years of power.'

"The President's good humor was restored by this, and he said: 'Oh, Mr. Phillips, I have ceased to have any personal feeling or expectation in that matter—I do not say I never had any—so abused and borne upon as I have been.'

"On taking our leave we expressed to the President our thanks for his kindly reception, and for his attention to statements of which some were naturally not welcome. The President bowed graciously at this, and, after saying he was happy to have met gentlemen known to him by distinguished services, if not personally, and glad to listen to their views, added: 'I must bear this load which the country has intrusted to me as well as I can, and do the best I can with it.' "

The author of *Uncle Tom's Cabin* came to the White House, and Lincoln, as she related it, strode toward her with two outreached hands and greeted her, "So you're the little woman who wrote the book that made this great war," and as they seated themselves at the fireplace, "I do love an open fire; I always had one to home."

They talked of the years of plowshares beaten into swords, days that vivified for Mrs. Stowe the Old Testament verse: "The sun and the moon shall be darkened, and the stars shall withdraw their shining."

She felt about him "a dry, weary, patient pain, that many mistook for insensibility." He said of the war, "Whichever way it ends, I have the impression I shan't last long after it's over."

William Bender Wilson, military telegrapher, brought a boy "raised in a pro-slavery though patriotic atmosphere." Lincoln put a hand on the lad's head: "What a fine boy, where did he come from?" Wilson said he was a nephew from Pennsylvania. "This is President Lincoln," he told the boy, who shook hands, looked up into the President's eyes, and spoke out his innocent query: "And this is Abraham Lincoln, the *abolitionist* President of these United States?" Lincoln had to smile, turned to Seward with a pathos of voice. "Governor, the children even do not understand me."

"Rest?" he said to Noah Brooks after a horseback ride. "I don't know about 'the rest' as you call it. I suppose it is good for the body. But the tired part of me is *inside* and out of reach." Calling on House business, one morning, said Speaker Colfax, he noticed the President more pale and careworn than usual and asked about it. Bad news had come from the front late at night, must yet be given to the press; he had not closed his eyes through the night nor yet had breakfast, Colfax heard, and: "How willingly would I exchange places today with the soldier who sleeps on the ground in the Army of the Potomac!"

Again, and to Mary Livermore, he said he envied "the soldier sleeping in his blanket on the Potomac." In an hour of talk with him, she noted a haggard face and a flow of comment on the slow headway of the armies, the unrest of the people: "All wore hues of midnight." She called with other women the next day on her work of organizing for the Sanitary Commission a Northwestern Soldiers' Fair to raise money for comforts and necessaries for the sick and wounded, and to rouse back home a deeper loyalty to the boys at the front.

Speaking for herself and her companions, she said: "Mr. President, we find ourselves greatly depressed by the talk of last evening; you do not consider our national affairs hopeless, do you? Our country is not lost?"

"Oh, no!" came the answer. "Our affairs are by no means hopeless, for we have the right on our side. We did not want this war, and we tried to avoid it. We were forced into it; our cause is a just one, and now it has become the cause of freedom. [The Emancipation Proclamation had just been issued.] And let us also hope it is the cause of God, and then we may be sure it will ultimately triumph. But between that time and now there is an amount of suffering and trial for the people that they do not look for, and are not prepared for." Of several interviews afterward Mrs. Livermore noted, "Each time I was impressed anew with the look of pain and weariness stereotyped on his face."

Some of the deeper roots of Lincoln's guiding philosophy in the encircling gloom of the first half of '63 were made clear to Senator Browning one night that winter. He wrote in his diary of December 29, 1862, that after the treason and dismissal of Major John James Key had been discussed: "The President took up a pamphlet on the war by Stille and saying that was the best thing he had seen on the subject added he would read some of it to me. He commenced and read the entire pamphlet."

The title was *How a Free People Conduct a Long War;* it was published in both America and England. The author, Charles Janeway Stille of Philadelphia, later appointed by Lincoln to be a member of the executive committee of the Sanitary Commission, was a Yale graduate, an attorney, later filling the chair of history in the University of Pennsylvania. His pamphlet, so interesting and timely that Lincoln took an hour or more to read it aloud

to Browning, ran a series of parallels between the American sectional war
and a number of wars in which England had slogged and muddled through
without being destroyed.

"War is always entered upon amidst a vast deal of popular enthusiasm,
which is utterly unreasoning," read Lincoln. "It is the universal voice of
history, that such enthusiasm is wholly unreliable in supporting the prolonged and manifold burdens inseparable from every war waged on an extensive scale, and for a long period. The popular idea of war is a speedy
and decisive victory and an immediate occupation of the enemy's capital,

An envelope cartoon represents Lincoln as a comet—up among the stars

followed by a treaty of peace. Nothing is revealed to the excited passions
of the multitude but dazzling visions of national glory, purchased by small
privations, and the early and complete subjugation of their enemies."

At the first reverses they yield to depression, blame the government and
the armies; the unreasoning abuse then matches the original enthusiasm:
"Experience has taught the English people that the progress of a war never
fulfils the popular expectations . . . during the continuance of a long war,
there can be no well-founded hope of a uniform and constant series of brilliant triumphs in the field, illustrating the profound wisdom of the policy of
the Cabinet; that, on the contrary, all war, even that which is most successful in the end, consists rather in checkered fortunes, of alternations of victory and disaster . . . blunders so glaring in the policy adopted by the Government, or in the strategy of its generals, that the wonder is success was
achieved at all."

The English had been taught that "not hopefulness or impatience of
immediate results" was the true necessity, but rather "a stern endurance—
that King-quality of heroic constancy which, rooted deep in a profound

conviction of the justice of the cause, supports a lofty public spirit equally well in the midst of temporary disaster, and in the hour of assured triumph."

Lincoln found it interesting that in the Napoleonic and the Peninsular wars, humanity had performed in England much the same as in America in the 1860's. During the war with Spain "that hideous moral leprosy, which seems to be the sad but invariable attendant upon all political discussions in a free government, corrupting the very sources of public life, breeding only the base spirit of faction, had taken complete possession of the opposition, and in its sordid calculations, the dishonor of the country, or the danger of the army, was as nothing provided the office, the power and the patronage of the Government were secured in their hands. It was of little concern to them, provided they could drive the Ministry from office, whether its downfall was brought about by blunders in Spain, or by the King's obstinacy about Catholic Emancipation, or by an obscure quarrel about the influence of the Lords of the bed-chamber."

The noisy clamor weakened the Government, prolonged the strife, alarmed the timid, discouraged the loyal, and encouraged Napoleon to think he would find the English easy to conquer. Bankruptcy and ruin fell on the trading classes, and absolute exhaustion of the resources of the country seemed almost reached. Yet the English Government raised during the Napoleonic Wars such funds that the national debt rose above £1,000,000,000 sterling. "Discontent and violence among the laboring classes became universal." Announcement of the greatest of English victories came to a population groaning under taxes on the necessaries of life, prevented from securing a livelihood by the strictest industry, "and thus pauperism had been generated throughout the land, a pauperism aggravated by a spirit of pillage, which required a strong military force to repress."

And what did history say as to whether the South could be subjugated and turned into conquered provinces? "To say nothing of instances in ancient history, Poland, Hungary, and Lombardy, in our day, were just as determined to be free as the South is, and quite as full of martial ardor." In still other modern instances armies had marched into enemy countries, broken their governments, and settled the fate of the inhabitants for a long future. "What is an army but only another argument, the *ultima ratio?*" The question was simply of how long it takes to wear down a population till they are tired of fighting and just naturally quit. Said the Duke of Wellington in the high tide of Waterloo, "Hard pounding, this, gentlemen, but we'll see who can pound the longest."

Lincoln's counsel earlier in the war, that the contest must not "degenerate into remorseless revolutionary warfare," was in its edging of despair in perfect kinship to the mood of a letter of Sir James Mackintosh during the Napoleonic Wars to a friend in Vienna: "I believe, like you, in a resurrection, because I believe in the immortality of civilization, but when, and by whom, and in what form, are questions which I have not the sagacity to answer. A dark and stormy night, a black series of ages may be prepared for our posterity, before the dawn that opens the more perfect day. Who can tell how long that fearful night may be before the dawn of a brighter morrow? The race of man may reach the promised land; but there is no assurance that the present generation will not perish in the wilderness."

Thus ran portents and guesses in the Stille pamphlet that Lincoln read aloud to his friend Browning as though they might mean much.

Not so long before this evening of reading to Browning, Lincoln had been daily riding the three miles between the White House and the Soldiers' Home, where the family lived through the hot-weather months. Lamon had been urging that the President have a military escort, the President each time laughing it off. One morning as Lincoln came riding up to the White House steps he met Lamon with a merry twinkle of eye foretelling to Lamon "fun of some kind." While still on the horse Lincoln said, "I have something to tell you," and they went to the President's office, locked the doors, sat down, and began a talk.

Executive Mansion
June 5 1861.
The bearer of this, W. H. La-
mon, is entirely reliable, and
trust-worthy.—
A. Lincoln.

The bearer of this, W. H. Lamon, is
Marshal of D.C.,— my particular
friend,
L.

In the extraordinary relationship of trust and fellowship between Lamon and Lincoln, the President termed him "my particular friend" and "entirely reliable, and trustworthy." Original from Dorothy Lamon Teillard.

As Lamon later wrote down the talk of Lincoln, he said he would not be sure of the exact words but was giving them to the best of his recollection. The tone of the moment was that of the old Illinois Eighth Circuit lawyers in zero weather gathered around a hot stove. Lincoln began: "You know I have always told you I thought you an *idiot* that ought to be put in a strait jacket for your apprehensions of my personal danger from assassination. You also know that the way we skulked into this city, in the first place, has been a source of shame and regret to me, for it did look so cowardly!" Lamon: "Yes, go on."

"Well," said Lincoln, "I don't now propose to make you my father-confessor and acknowledge a change of heart, yet I am free to admit that just now I don't know what to think: I am staggered. Understand me, I do not want to oppose my pride of opinion against light and reason, but I am in such a state of 'betweenity' in my conclusions that I can't say that the judgment of *this court* is prepared to proclaim a reliable 'decision upon the facts presented.' "

He paused. Lamon: "Go on, go on."

"Last night, about 11 o'clock, I went out to the Soldiers' Home alone, riding *Old Abe*, as you call him [a horse he delighted in riding], and when I arrived at the foot of the hill on the road leading to the entrance of the Home grounds, I was jogging along at a slow gait, immersed in deep thought, contemplating what was next to happen in the unsettled state of affairs, when suddenly I was aroused—I may say the arousement lifted me out of my saddle as well as out of my wits—by the report of a rifle, and seemingly the gunner was not fifty yards from where my contemplations ended and my accelerated transit began. My erratic namesake, with little warning, gave proof of decided dissatisfaction at the racket, and with one reckless bound he unceremoniously separated me from my eight-dollar plug-hat, with which I parted company without any assent, expressed or implied, upon my part. At a break-neck speed we soon arrived in a haven of safety. Meanwhile I was left in doubt whether death was more desirable from being thrown from a runaway federal horse, or as the tragic result of a rifle-ball fired by a disloyal bushwhacker in the middle of the night."

This was all told in what Lamon termed "a spirit of levity," as though the little affair might be exaggerated in importance. Lincoln seemed to want to believe it a joke. "Now," he went on, "in the face of this testimony in favor of your theory of danger to me, personally, I can't bring myself to believe that anyone has shot or will deliberately shoot at me with the purpose of killing me; although I must acknowledge that I heard this fellow's bullet whistle at an uncomfortably short distance from these headquarters of mine. I have about concluded that the shot was the result of accident. It may be that someone on his return from a day's hunt, regardless of the course of his discharge, fired off his gun as a precautionary measure of safety to his family after reaching his house." This was said with much seriousness.

He then playfully proceeded: "I tell you there is no time on record equal to that made by the two Old Abes on that occasion. The historic ride of John Gilpin, and Henry Wilson's memorable display of bareback equestrianship on the stray army mule from the scenes of the battle of Bull Run, a year ago, are nothing in comparison to mine, either in point of time made or in ludicrous pageantry. My only advantage over these worthies was in having no observers. I can truthfully say that one of the Abes was frightened on this occasion, but modesty forbids my mentioning which of us is entitled to that distinguished honor. This whole thing seems farcical. No good can result at this time from giving it publicity. It does seem to me that I am in more danger from the augmentation of imaginary peril than from a judicious silence, be the danger ever so great; and, moreover, I do not want it understood that I share your apprehensions. I never have."

Lamon sat studying a companion who to him had always seemed prepared for the inevitable, for fate, always careless about his personal safety, and at this time not yet recovered from sorrow over the death of his son Willie. Lincoln went on:

"I am determined to borrow no trouble. I believe in *the right*, and that it will ultimately prevail; and I believe it is the inalienable right of man, unimpaired even by this dreadful distraction of our country, to be *happy* or *miserable* at his own election, and I for one make choice of the former alternative."

Lamon protested that such a choice was no protection against a shotgun in time of war: "Unless you are more careful and discreet . . . in less than a week you'll have neither inalienable nor any other rights. . . . The time . . . may not be far distant when this republic will be minus a pretty respectable President."

Death was in the air. So was birth. What was dying men did not know. What was being born none could say.

CHAPTER 40

THE MAN IN THE WHITE HOUSE

I have heard the veery thrush in the trees near the White House; and one rainy April morning, about six o'clock, he came and blew his soft, mellow flute in a pear-tree in my garden. The tones had all the sweetness and wildness they have when heard in June in our deep northern forests.

—JOHN BURROUGHS, Washington, 1863

ALONG Pennsylvania Avenue when Congress was in session the crowds tended toward the Capitol till midafternoon, after which the human traffic was away from the Capitol. The sunny side of the street had the taller buildings and the finer stores and shops. The races and breeds on promenade ranged, noted one observer, "from fairest blond to sootiest black, a panorama of nationalities—blue-eyed, light-haired Saxons; swarthy, dreamy-eyed Creoles; vivacious, fine-featured sons of France and Italy; olive-tinted quadroons, and every shade of mulatto, ebony-black 'contrabands,' an occasional John Chinaman, and here and there a 'lone' Indian making the customary visit to the Great Father."

Horsecars passed every few minutes on the double-track six-mile line from the navy yard to Georgetown. Mounted police at busy street corners sat with drawn swords, sometimes riding their horses straight at violators of speed regulations. They watched horses and buggies, mule-drivers with government wagons, ambulances, private carriages with liveried coachmen and footmen—and the hacks. More than any other vehicle, the hack filled the streets. Those in a hurry, who could afford it, called a hack, usually driven by a colored man. On the street corners the bootblacks, with boxes slung over their shoulders, were colored boys. The newsboys were mostly white. A street competition went on for the nickels and dimes of passers-by— peddlers with patent soap they swore would take out grease spots in a jiffy —men with artificial bright bugs tied to the end of an elastic cord—Italians roasting their chestnuts—telescope men asking you to look at Venus in broad daylight—lung-testers who would let you blow "to see what kind of a chest you've got"—organ-grinders, some with monkeys, occasionally one with a bear—candy men with stands piled with tall rocks of taffy which they hit with hammers to chip off the customer's purchase, with no extra charge for the avenue dust that might have blown on it. At times under the grinding of traffic the cobblestoned pavements wore out and Pennsylvania Avenue was dusty in dry weather and muddy after rain.

Across from the White House, on the north side of Pennsylvania Avenue, was the one-square city block called Lafayette Square, occasionally termed President's Square. The walks had nicely figured curves. The trees and garden plots had many specimens from foreign countries. Its central showpiece was a statue by Clark Mills of Andrew Jackson on a horse. Around this people would gather to wonder or to laugh. The horse, reared on its hind legs, stood pawing the air with its front feet. And while the frisky animal poised snorting and threatening in a way to throw an ordinary rider out of balance, what was Andrew Jackson doing? Quietly and easily holding the saddle and lifting the cocked hat from his head in a grand salutation of respect for the great American people. The sculptor meant well and got a result better than he intended—and different. The effect was Yankee Doodle extravaganza, and people liked it for that. Lincoln saw it many times, often enough to have had some opinion of it. Possibly because his view of it could have been mistaken for a merely humorous view of Andrew Jackson it was as well to say nothing about it.

Facing Lafayette Square stood elegant and spacious homes. The former home of Banker Corcoran was occupied by the French Minister, M. Mercier, and next to it was the mansion of Secretary Welles. A corner house where Dolly Madison gave her charming and garrulous parties now was used by Admiral Wilkes. Seward had his home in the middle of the block, a few doors from the oldest Episcopal church building in the city, St. John's, old-fashioned and ivy-covered. In cold weather the square was deserted, but on warm and pleasant days children romped on the grass, ladies in crinoline walked around the flower plots and pointed their parasols at exotics new to them. On benches sat rows of soldiers who had limped in and sat with their crutches and empty sleeves—bronzed veterans belonging in "C"—the Condemned or unfit for service. They talked of the war, some of them. Others said nothing and listened to the birds.

The White House gave a feeling of Time. The statue of Thomas Jefferson in front of the main portico facing Pennsylvania Avenue had this feeling. In one hand the bronze Jefferson held the Constitution. He stood with green mold covering him, the rusty testimony of verdigris on him and the Constitution—the work of weather and years.

The White House grounds during Lincoln's first year of residence had a smooth outward serenity that was not all it seemed to an ordinary gazer. Hidden in shrubbery encircling the Executive Mansion were armed men. In a basement room were reserve troops with muskets and bayonets. Two riflemen in bushes stood ready to cover the movements of any person walking from the main gate to the building entry.

News of Lincoln's death would be welcome, would bring hope, to the Southern cause. This was the rather direct implication in the *Charleston Mercury* reprint, October 14, 1862, of a *New York Herald* item from its Washington correspondent: "The President's life is considered unsafe by many persons here. As in all great political and social crises, there are now monomaniacs whose peculiar insanity points toward the assassination of the person who wields the power of the government. Mutterings have been heard in reference to the President by persons who have this form of insanity in Washington, and the personal safety of the commander-in-chief ought to be looked after with the utmost diligence."

With glee the *Mercury* picked up from Paris correspondence of the *New York Times* a paragraph it headed "Lincoln's Phiz in Europe." Export of Lincoln portraits, such as were coming to France, should be stopped: "The person represented in these pictures, looks so much like a man condemned to the gallows, that large numbers of them have been imposed upon the people here by the shopkeepers as Dumollard, the famous murderer of servant girls, lately guillotined near Lyons. Such a face is enough to ruin the best of causes; and people read the name inscribed under it with astonishment, or rather bewilderment, for the thing appears more like a hoax than a reality."

The *Pittsburgh* (Pennsylvania) *Gazette*, the *Lansing* (Michigan) *State Republican*, and other newspapers reported a witness before a Federal commission testifying that one secret disloyalist society had in its ritual for induction of new members the lines:

"Are you in favor of the abduction of Abraham Lincoln?"

"By force, if necessary."

Under orders from General in Chief Scott, Colonel Charles P. Stone took precautions to guard the President, with care to attract no public attention, saying, "Mr. Lincoln was not consulted in the matter," and justifying the secrecy: "It was not considered advisable that it should appear that the

President of the United States was, for his personal safety, obliged to surround himself with armed guards." One guard officer saw in the President "an almost morbid dislike" of an escort or a guard. When his eyes first lighted on cavalry troopers detailed by the War Department to sit with boots and saddles, carbine and saber, at the White House gates, he protested, worried, urged, "It would never do for a President to have guards with drawn sabers at his door, as if he fancied he were, or were trying to be, an emperor."

Danger being mentioned, the President answered that the only effective way to avoid all risk was to shut himself up in an iron box, where he could not possibly perform the duties of President: "Why put up the bars when the fence is down all around? If they kill me, the next man will be just as bad for them; and in a country like this, where our habits are simple, and must be, assassination is always possible, and will come if they are determined upon it." His mind had dwelt on the chance of a violent end and he said he felt the force of the expression "to take one's life in his hand," but that he would not like to face sudden death. He said he believed himself a good deal of a coward physically, would probably make a poor soldier and unless there was something exceptional in the excitement of battle he would drop his gun and run. He spoke thus according to Major Charles G. Halpine ("Miles O'Reilly"), a humorist and versifier, and made it plain he would not like to go so far as to call himself a brave man. He would say, however, "Moral cowardice is something which I think I never had."

He walked alone often in the streets near the White House, across the way to Lafayette Square, sometimes picking up conversation with strangers there. Often with but one unarmed companion, such as Noah Brooks or John Hay, he went on errands to the home of McClellan or Seward or some other official. Though accepting a War Department cavalry guard for the three-mile ride between the White House and the Soldiers' Home on summer mornings and evenings, several times when he returned to town for work after dark he rode alone in an open carriage without guards, or on horseback alone.

Stanton insisted the Adjutant General be detailed to attend him, and Lincoln said that he had no objection to the personal presence of the Adjutant General but "it would be an uncompensating encumbrance both to him and to me." That officer would do better in public service and not personal attendance. "When it shall occur to me to go anywhere, I wish to be free to go at once, and not to have to notify the Adjutant-General and wait till he can get ready." The decision was made at last that he *must* accept the cavalry guard on the daily drive in and out of town, and he acquiesced. "Why, Mrs. Lincoln and I cannot hear ourselves talk for the clatter of their sabers and spurs; and some of them appear to be new hands and very awkward, so that I am more afraid of being shot by the accidental discharge of a carbine or revolver, than of any attempt upon my life by a roving squad of Jeb Stuart's cavalry."

One of the guards suggested that they were needed more at the front. Lincoln half-assented. "You boys remind me of a farmer friend of mine in Illinois who said he could never understand why the Lord put the curl in a pig's tail. It never seemed to him to be either useful or ornamental, but he reckoned the Almighty knew what he was doing when he put it there. I don't think I need guards, but the Secretary of War thinks I do, and as it is in his Department, if you go to the front he will insist upon others coming from the front to take your place. And boys—I reckon it is pleasanter and safer here than there."

The captain of the cavalry guard at the Soldiers' Home knocked at Lincoln's door at half-past six or seven in the morning, and they went to breakfast together. Usually, he said, he would find the President reading or busy dressing, though one morning the President was sewing on a button and made the greeting, "All right; just wait a moment while I repair damages." The captain also noted that he did at times refer to the "rebels" as "those Southern gentlemen."

One windy winter night at the west corner of the White House, Lincoln, returning from the telegraph office, said to a sentry, "Young man, you've got a cold job tonight; step inside and stand guard there." The sentry said his orders kept him there. "Yes, but your duty can be performed just as well inside as out there, and you'll oblige me by going in." Again the soldier refused; he was under orders, began pacing his beat. "Hold on there!" snapped Lincoln. "It occurs to me that I am Commander-in-Chief, and I order you to go inside."

Company K of the 150th Pennsylvania Volunteers went on guard duty the first week in September on their arrival as rather raw recruits in Washington. When later an attempt was made to transfer Company K, Lincoln wrote a little note which in time was memorized by members of the company so they could repeat word for word:

Executive Mansion, Washington
November 1, 1862

To Whom it May Concern: Captain Derrickson, with his company, has been for some time keeping guard at my residence, now at the Soldiers' Retreat. He and his company are very agreeable to me, and while it is deemed proper for any guard to remain, none would be more satisfactory than Captain Derrickson [sic] and his company.
A. Lincoln

In a way Company K became part of the White House family, taking care of Tad's goats and doing other chores. "He always called me Joe," said one private. The President asked about their sick, sometimes personally looked after their passes and furloughs. Captain C. M. Derickson of Mercer, Pennsylvania, told of camp fun—the Kepler boys rigged out with army blankets would perform like a trained baby elephant, would kneel, stand on one leg, and do other tricks. "The President strolled into camp, amused at the elephant, and a few evenings after brought a friend with him and asked the captain to have the elephant brought out."

Guards, ushers, doormen, and secret-service officers held a festive and gossipy meeting in a little anteroom late one evening, against orders. The door opened, and there stood the President, his boots in one hand. The crowd scattered in a hurry, except one named Pendel, known as trustworthy and kind to the Lincoln children. And as Pendel told it, the President shook a finger at him with an assumed ferocity. "Pendel, you people remind me of the boy who set a hen on forty-three eggs." "How was that, Mr. President?" "The youngster put forty-three eggs under a hen, and then rushed in and told his mother, who said, 'But a hen can't set on forty-three eggs!' 'No,' said the boy, 'I guess she can't, but I just wanted to see her spread herself.'" And Lincoln, leaving: "That's just what I wanted to see you boys do when I came in."

Mrs. Keckley noted that letters threatening assassination troubled Mrs. Lincoln, who would say to him as he was putting on overshoes and shawl, "Where are you going now, father?" "To the War Department, mother, to try and learn some news." "But, father, you should not go out alone. You know you are surrounded with danger." "All imagination. What does anyone want to harm me for? Don't worry about me, mother, as if I were a little child, for no one is going to molest me."

On the winding, dark staircase of the War Department building, a young officer carrying reports to Stanton rushed along one evening taking three steps at a time, butted his head with full force into the President's body at about the point of the lower vest pocket. Seeing what he had hit, he groaned, "Ten thousand pardons." Lincoln: "One's enough, I wish the whole army could charge like that."

Once, according to Robert Lamon, Deputy Marshal of the District of Columbia and a brother of Marshal Ward Hill Lamon, these two brothers drove rapidly to the Soldiers' Home in a search for the President. Near the entrance to the grounds they met a carriage and behind it could see a man on horseback. The younger Lamon ordered the party to halt. "Who are you?" he demanded. A voice from the carriage: "Why do you ask?" Then they recognized each other. In the carriage was Stanton; the horseman was his orderly. Stanton queried: "Where is Mr. Lincoln? I have been to Soldiers' Home and he is not there. I am exceedingly uneasy about him. He is not at the White House." "No," returned Robert Lamon, "he is not there. I have looked for him everywhere."

They hurried back to Washington. Arriving at the White House before Stanton, the Lamons found Lincoln walking across the lawn, Robert Lamon's narrative of the affair ending: "My brother went with Mr. Lincoln to the War Department, and from there took him to his (Lamon's) house, where Mr. Lincoln slept that night and the three or four nights following, Mrs. Lincoln being at that time in New York."

Marshal Lamon had received "a report of an alarming character" from one of his detectives. Of "threatening news" received at the War Department Stanton said he had "never had so great a scare." Each at the Soldiers' Home entrance had suspected the other as an assassin. "The incident," wrote

The White House from Lafayette Square,
and the Jackson statue, '61

From a stereograph in the author's collection

A thinker, deep in abstraction—Lincoln in
late '63

Photograph by Brady, from the Meserve collection

The War Office daily and usually nightly visited by Lincoln

From the U. S. Army Signal Corps

Relief map (1861) of Washington, the Potomac, and Virginia

From the Library of Congress

Willard's Hotel, "the conversational capitol of the United States"

Photograph from the L. C. Handy studios

Marshal Lamon, "provoked much merriment among the parties concerned, no one enjoying the serio-comic part of it more than Mr. Lincoln himself."

Of the many callers and hangers-on at the White House, it seemed that only one was named by Lincoln as a possible assassin. "From this man Gurowski, and from him alone, Mr. Lincoln really apprehended danger by a violent assault," wrote Lamon. Gurowski's slanderous talk and published slurs on Seward had resulted in his dismissal as a translator from the State Department, where, as he told Robert Carter, his work was "to read the German newspapers and keep Seward from making a fool of himself." Nearing sixty years of age, side-whiskered, gray and bald as a buzzard, large of head, with a noticeable paunch, wearing a red flannel vest, a broad-brimmed hat, a flowing blue cape from the shoulders, Gurowski would come into the President's office and give advice in a sharp peremptory tone, his voice nervously tense.

As a European republican revolutionary and as a scholar and author of political volumes, Gurowski assumed that the American Republic needed his counsel and experience, and he rushed and raged, flung his arms in all directions as he poured out torrents of words, Sumner once saying that Gurowski reminded him of the whale in Barnum's museum, which circled its narrow tank, heaving and blowing preposterously whenever it came to the surface. Behind large green goggles one good eye glared and blazed, while a sightless one stayed mute and pitiful, as he would snort to people that Lincoln was "the great shifter, the great political shuffler," lacked energy and executive ability, was even "a beast," or "Chase is a thousand times more fit for a President than Lincoln or Seward." This or that public man was "a humbug or an ass," blurted Gurowski, who punctuated many sentences with "Bah!" reveled in argument, received friends at his room with no clothes on, argued as he dressed, and would send the word to a friend who owed him a letter, "Tell Carter he is an ass."

Crossing Pennsylvania Avenue one day and threading a path amid rearing horses of a cavalry troop, Gurowski roared to Carter above the tumult his opinion that Horace Greeley was "an ass, a traitor and a coward." He had held a job under Greeley and been let out, even though he was the author of two books, *Russia as It Is*, and *America and Europe*. At the White House, with his high-keyed, staccato talk on men and issues, Lincoln kept an eye on him. Lamon wrote that he heard Lincoln more than once remark: "So far as my personal safety is concerned, Gurowski is the only man who has given me a serious thought of a personal nature. From the known disposition of the man, he is dangerous wherever he may be. I have sometimes thought that he might try to take my life. It would be just like him to do such a thing." An estimate went into Welles's diary on June 8, 1863:

"Count Adam Gurowski, who is splenetic and querulous, a strange mixture of good and evil, always growling and discontented, who loves to say harsh things and speak good of but few, seldom makes right estimates and correct discrimination of character, but means to be truthful if not just, tells me my selection for the Cabinet was acquiesced in by the radical circle to which he belongs because they felt confident my influence with the President would be good, and that I would be a safeguard against the scheming and plotting of Weed and Seward, whose intrigues they understood and watched. When I came here, just preceding the inauguration in 1861, I first met this Polish exile, and was amused and interested in him, though I could not be intimate with one of his rough, coarse, ardent, and violent partisan temperament. His associates were then Greeley, D. D. Field, Opdyke, and men of that phase of party.

"I have no doubt that what he says is true of his associates, colored to some extent by his intense prejudices. He was for a year or two in the State Department as a clerk under Seward, and does not conceal that he was really a spy upon him, or, as he says, watched him. He says that when Seward became aware that the radicals relied upon me as a friend to check the loose notions and ultraism of the State Department, he (S.) went to work with the President to destroy my influence; that by persisting he so far succeeded as to induce the President to go against me on some important measures, where his opinion leaned to mine; that in this way, Seward had intrenched himself. There is doubtless some truth—probably some error—in the Count's story. I give the outlines."

The few times Lincoln had been close to death no news of it reached the public. Press wires carried the information one day that when he visited the French frigate *Gassendi*, it was the first time that a President of the United States had set foot aboard a foreign man-of-war. "He was received with the honors paid to crowned heads, the same as usually shown the French Emperor," wrote Frederick Seward. "The yards were manned by the crew who shouted, '*Vive le Président*.' The *Gassendi* was gay with bunting in honor of her distinguished guest. Drums rolled and bugles sounded, while the Stars and Stripes were unfurled at the top of the mainmast. The French Minister was on board to receive the President and the Secretary of State. Champagne and a brief conversation in the cabin preceded an inspection of her armament and equipment. Mr. Lincoln chatted affably with some of the officers who spoke English."

The visit over, an accident happened that the newspapermen missed. Climbing down the side ladder and seating himself in the barge to go ashore, the President suggested: "Suppose we row around her bows. I should like to look at her build and rig from that direction." Captain Dahlgren shifted the helm—and as the little boatload of men reached her bow and looked up they saw the deck officer of the *Gassendi* pacing the bridge, watch in hand, heard him counting off seconds, "*Un, deux, trois*"—"One, two, three" —then came a flash, the booming roar of one cannon, another and another.

Lincoln could hardly make out Dahlgren standing up in the smoke yelling: "Pull like the devil, boys! Pull like hell!" The French were firing a salute of honor, believing the presidential party was at stern and not bow. As the sailor boys rowed the party out of danger, Dahlgren took his seat, calmed down, and Fred Seward said to him, in a low voice, "Of course those guns were not shotted, and we were below their range?"

Dahlgren, between gritted teeth: "Yes, but to think of exposing the President to the danger of having his head taken off by a wad." And Dahlgren explained that wadding fragments commence dropping soon after leaving the cannon and sometimes have power enough to take off a human head; it had been done.

In no one of the thirty-one rooms of the White House was Lincoln at home, except in fugitive moments. In occasional family hours, in lighted

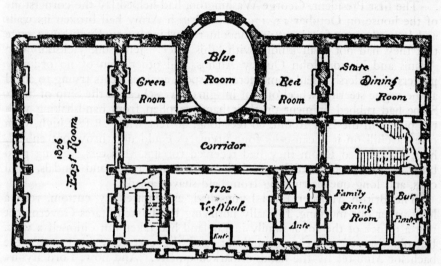

First or main floor of the White House

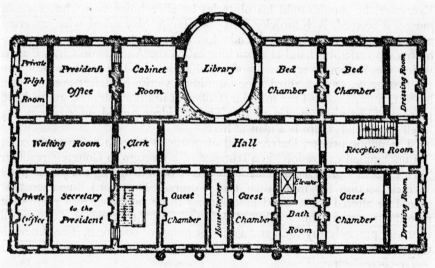

Second floor of the White House

moments that came, through sudden events or by work or wit, he forgot himself. Among the Ionic columns of the covered carriageway at the north front of the Executive Mansion had set foot delegates, dignitaries, and ambassadors from all the States of the Union, from all countries and continents of the globe. Through the massive main entrance they had walked, some pausing to gaze in the main hall at the portraits hung on the walls of all the past Presidents of the United States.

The first President, George Washington, had helped lay the cornerstone of the house on October 13, 1792. The British Army had broken its walls and burned part of it in 1814, Lincoln remarking to an Englishman once that they had not dealt kindly with "this place." Jefferson, Jackson, John Adams and his son John Quincy Adams, and other men of no ordinary powers of leadership had come here and spent anxious years trying to stand at the vague steering wheel of that imaginary vessel called the Ship of State. Some had rubbed liniment on their hands swollen from handshaking with the public in the East Room, 86 feet long, 40 feet wide, 28 feet high, with often a chill on it because its four fireplaces could not throw out enough heat. In the Red Room they had received foreign Ministers wearing gold braid, long plumes, medals and insignia, wearing robes and sandals, skull caps, and long queues running from bald shaven heads.

The British Minister Lord Lyons had, as required by custom, read a long paper one morning, formally notifying the United States Government that a prince of the royal family in England had taken unto himself a wife. Lincoln listened gravely throughout, and the ceremony over, took the bachelor Minister by the hand, remarked quietly, "And now, Lord Lyons, go thou and do likewise."

The human touch, a living face and voice, should be in this house of the Executive; he should amid his obstacles be alive howsoever; thus Lincoln mused, it seemed. A Kentucky man one gloomy day asked what cheering news he might take home to friends. Lincoln told of a chess-player seldom beaten who tried his hand at a machine called the Automaton Chess Player, which was baffling everyone who played against it. The machine beat him the first game, second, third. The astonished victim of defeat got up from his seat, walked around the machine, looked at it a few minutes, stopped and pointed: "There is a man in there." The President paused, added his point: "Tell my friends there is a man in here!"

The public printer, Defrees, told of going to Lincoln to protest against "an undignified expression" in a sentence of a message to Congress reading: "With rebellion thus *sugar-coated*, they have been drugging the public mind of their section for more than thirty years." The word "sugar-coated" should be altered for a word more fitting to be published as a permanent record for government archives. "Defrees," said the President, "that word expresses precisely my idea, and I am not going to change it. The time will never come in this country when the people won't know exactly what *'sugar-coated'* means!"

The main executive office and workroom on the second floor, 25 by 40 feet, had a large white marble fireplace, with brass andirons and a high brass fender. A few chairs, two hair-covered sofas, and a large oak table for Cabinet meetings were part of the furniture. Gas jets in glass globes, or in an emergency kerosene lamps, gave the illumination. Tall windows opened on a sweep of lawn to the south, on the unfinished Washington Monument, the Smithsonian Institution, the Potomac River, Alexandria, and slopes alive with the white tents, beef cattle, wagons, men of the army. Between the windows was a large armchair in which the President usually sat at a table for his writing. A pull at a bell cord would bring one of the secretaries, Nicolay or Hay, from the next room. A tall desk with many pigeonholes stood near by at the south wall. Among books present were the *United States Statutes*, the Bible, and Shakespeare's plays. At times the table had been littered with treatises on the art and science of war. Two or three frames held maps on which blue and red pins told where the armies were moving, fighting, standing still.

"Sitting at the window with a spyglass in his hand," wrote Henry C. Whitney, "the President would talk in a free-and-easy manner, with whomsoever came—write a note on a card on his knee with a lead pencil, look through the spyglasses at the distant Virginia hills and down the vista of the Potomac. I recollect seeing a vessel as far down as we could see to Alexandria, with its masts leaning toward the Virginia shore. Lincoln was puzzled about it; he looked long and earnestly at it. 'I wonder what that *can* mean,' he said half a dozen times. He liked to go from one thing to another in his office; he would sit and sign commissions for a while—then take a document out of his drawer or off the table and read it—possibly sign it—reflect on it a while, and then put it back for further consideration. Then he would gaze out of the window, then a thought would strike him, and he would go to his table or desk, and write vigorously for a while, then lapse into thought. Sometimes he would sit and write for an hour at a time, and of course when people came in he would attend to them in a purely informal way."

Once when visitors called to pay respects, a secretary placed papers on a table for signature. The President excused himself: "Just wait now until I sign some papers, that this government may go on." At the finish of an afternoon's work with the secretaries he would say: "Boys, I reckon that'll do. We'll shut up shop for the rest of the day." They were his young comrades, those two loyal secretaries, Nicolay and Hay. "I believe I feel trouble in the air before it comes," he said to them one day as he entered their room with news of another lost battle.

An undersized Irishman in tight-fitting black clothes, Edward McManus, rather keen at reading faces, was the official doorkeeper in the main hall below Lincoln's second-floor office. McManus had served through several administrations, said he could "tell from a look" the business and hopes of a caller. Sent upstairs one day for a new umbrella, McManus couldn't find it and brought down another. This reminded Lincoln of Vice-President Fillmore's becoming President when Zachary Taylor died and of how Fillmore once had taken McManus along to look at a carriage for sale. "How do you think," asked Fillmore, "it will do for the President of the United States to ride in a second-hand carriage?" "Sure, your excellency," rippled McManus, "you're only a second-hand President, you know."

Belowstairs the President more than once heard a crying child in the arms of a woman and sent word asking what the woman wanted. Or again he might hear a bawling bass voice, "I want to see Old Abe," or a seeker of a munitions contract orating: "The President must be made to understand, sir, that the eyes of the people are on him, sir! They are watching him, sir! This way of doing things can't go on, sir! He must meet the requirements of the age, sir! Or he must take the consequences, sir!" Thus Stoddard, the clerk, wrote of these interruptions. A gentle little woman in widow's weeds, with a wide lace collar fastened by the pin of a large miniature, refused to send up a card to the President. "I will see him! He must give me my rights! I want my rights! They have robbed me of my right! He can give it back to me!" Her low-toned voice rises in pitch and gets more emphatic. McManus tells her in his own low-toned way: "I do not think the President can see you today, ma'am. He is very busy about the war." This reminds the little woman. "So he is. Busy about the war. I forgot that. But I want my right. Yes, sir, if I can't see him now I'll come some other time. He is President. I will have my right," and she walked away with a sorry face and didn't call again.

Another woman, who got past McManus, demanded a colonel's commission for her son, not as a favor but as a right. "Sir, my grandfather fought at Lexington, my father fought at New Orleans, and my husband was killed at Monterey." She left the office and went down the stairs with a dismissal in her ears: "I guess, Madam, your family has done enough for the country. It is time to give someone else a chance."

A tale later disproved said a country girl and a farm hand sent up word that they were at the White House to be married. Lincoln came down. "So you children want to be married? Come right in and we'll get at the marrying." The President stood up while they were pronounced man and wife, Mr. and Mrs. Henry Chandler, the bride saying later: "I don't remember so much about Mr. Lincoln, except that I wished Henry's coat was long like his. And I remember thinking Henry was a lot handsomer." According to the bride, Lincoln had asked her, "If I help you to be married, will you be willing to give your husband to fight for his country?" She had answered Yes and her man later went into Company A, 1st New Jersey Cavalry.

The President was at his duties often before seven o'clock in the morning, after "sleep light and capricious," noted Hay. His White House bed, nine feet long, nearly nine feet high at the head end, had bunches of grapes and flying birds carved in its black walnut. Near by was a marble-topped table with four legs, each shaped as a stork; near the floor under its center was a bird's nest of black walnut filled with little wooden bird eggs. The wood-carvers were in vogue. On the Schomacker piano in a room belowstairs stood forth a large froglike dragon. Another family piece was the Comprehensive Bible, printed in London for J. B. Lippincott & Company of

Philadelphia in 1847. The entries in Lincoln's writing were: "Abraham Lincoln and Mary Todd, married November 4, 1842," then the names of four sons, dates of birth, and the death of Eddie in 1850. The record of Willie's death in 1862 was in Robert Lincoln's handwriting.

In the earlier days of the Administration a digest of the day's news was ready for the President before breakfast at nine o'clock. Then he would usually go over to the War Office, read telegrams, discuss "the situation" with Halleck or Stanton; back at the White House, take up the morning

Editor "Star":

Please Publish the within notice and oblige.

Yours truly

Jno. G. Nicolay

Priv Sec.

John G. Nicolay, "Priv Sec.," sends the *Washington Star* a "notice" the President wishes published. From Crosby Noyes Boyd.

mail with his secretaries. Tuesday and Friday were usually for Cabinet meetings. On other days a stack of cards from callers would be sifted for old acquaintances and persons on business requiring immediate attention.

"On other days [than Tuesday and Friday]," wrote Hay, "it was the President's custom at about that hour [noon], to order the doors to be opened and all who were waiting to be admitted. The crowd would rush in, thronging the narrow room, and one by one would make their wants known."

Some came merely to shake hands, to wish God-speed, others for help or mercy, wailing their woe. Still others lingered, stood at the walls, hanging back in hope of having a private interview. These were often met by a hearty and loud greeting, "Well, friend, what can I do for you?" which forced them to speak or to wait another time for a private hearing.

At lunchtime the President threaded his way through crowds that lined the corridors between his office and the rooms at the west end of the house, where the family lived. "The afternoon wore away in much the same manner as the morning," wrote Hay; "late in the day he usually drove out for an hour's airing; at six o'clock he dined. He was one of the most abstemious of men; the pleasures of the table had few attractions for him. His breakfast was an egg and a cup of coffee; at luncheon he rarely took more than a biscuit and a glass of milk, a plate of fruit in its season; at dinner he ate sparingly of one or two courses. He drank little or no wine; not that he remained always on principle a total abstainer . . . but he never cared for wine or liquors of any sort, and never used tobacco.

"He pretended to begin business at ten o'clock in the morning, but in reality the ante-rooms and halls were full long before that hour—people anxious to get the first axe ground. He was extremely unmethodical; it was a struggle on Nicolay's part and mine to get him to adopt some systematic rules. He would break through every regulation as fast as it was made.

Closing part of a letter Hay wrote for the President. From the Barrett collection.

Anything that kept the people away from him he disapproved. He wrote very few letters and did not read one in fifty that he received. At first we tried to bring them to his notice, but at last he gave the whole thing over to me, and signed, without reading them, the letters I wrote in his name. He wrote, perhaps half a dozen a week himself—not more.

"Nicolay received Members of Congress and other visitors who had business with the Executive Office, communicated to the Senate and House the messages of the President, and exercised a general supervision over the business. I opened and read letters, answered them, looked over the newspapers, supervised the clerks who kept the records, and in Nicolay's absence did his work also. When the President had any rather delicate matter to manage at a distance from Washington, he rarely wrote but sent Nicolay or me. The house remained full of people nearly all day. Sometimes, though rarely, he would shut himself up and see no one. He scarcely ever looked into a newspaper unless I called his attention to an article on some special subject. He frequently said, 'I know more about it than any of them.'"

Early in the Administration Seward wrote his wife, "The President proposes to do all his work." That did not last long. He learned to detail routine and to assign pieces of work to others. "At first," wrote Fred Seward, "when I would take up to the President a paper for his signature, he would spread it out and carefully read the whole of it. But this usage was speedily abandoned, and he would hastily say, 'Your father says this is all right, does he? Well, I guess he knows. Where do I put my name?'" The procedure got him into several mixed affairs. More and more, however, as the months passed the letters and documents were sifted for his attention and signature.

Most evenings Lincoln spent in his office, wrote Hay. "Occasionally he remained in the drawing-room after dinner, conversing with visitors or listening to music, for which he had an especial liking, though he was not versed in the science, and preferred simple ballads to more elaborate compositions. In his office he was not often suffered to be alone; he frequently passed the evening there with a few friends in frank and free conversation. If the company was all of one sort he was at his best . . . but if a stranger came in he put on in an instant his whole armor of dignity and reserve. . . . Where only one or two were present he was fond of reading aloud."

Of the daily program one friendly newspaperman wrote: "Those who know the habits of President Lincoln are not surprised to hear of his personal visit to some general, nor would any such be astonished to know that he was in New York at any time. If he wanted to see anything or anybody, he would be as likely to go as to send. He has an orbit of his own; and no one can tell where he will be, or what he will do, from anything done yesterday. If he wants a newspaper, he is quite as likely to go out and get it as he is to send after it. If he wants to see the Secretary of State, he generally goes out, and makes a call. At night, from ten to twelve, he usually makes a tour all around—now at Seward's, and then at Halleck's. Those who know his habits and want to see him late at night, follow him around from place to place; and the last search generally brings him up at General Halleck's, as he can get the latest army intelligence there. Whoever else is asleep or indolent, the President is wide awake and around."

The *Chicago Tribune* correspondent, Horace White, wrote of one day, "I dropped in upon Mr. Lincoln on Monday last, and found him busily engaged in counting greenbacks." As he fingered dollar bills, the President explained: "This, sir, is something out of my usual line; but a President of the United States has a multiplicity of duties not specified in the Constitution or acts of Congress; this is one of them. This money belongs to a poor negro, porter in the treasury department, at present very sick with the small-pox. He is now in the hospital, and could not draw his pay because he could not sign his name. I have been at considerable trouble to overcome the difficulty, and get it for him, and have at length succeeded in cutting red tape, as you newspaper men say. I am now dividing the money, and putting by a portion labelled in an envelope with my own hands, according to his wish."

Occasionally the President disappeared into some such corner as the office of L. E. Chittenden in the Treasury building. That official quoted him: "When the old monks had tired themselves out in fighting the devil, did they not have places to which they retired for rest, which were called retreats? I think of making this office one of my retreats. It is so quiet and restful here."

C. Van Santvoord, a college chum of the Reverend Phineas D. Gurley, in whose church the Lincolns rented a pew, stood in a corner of Lincoln's office and took note of what went on for an hour. The President sat at his desk in a big armchair, wearing a black broadcloth suit, on his feet neat cloth slippers. The doors had been thrown open for the general public. A dapper, boyish fellow got the President's eye and ear, and encouraged by a nod and a smiling "Well, what can I do for you?" stepped forward and spoke in an undertone. The answer: "Well, I will consider the matter and see what can be done," indicated that nothing further need be said. The young fellow kept on with earnest whispers until the President's dismissal: "Yes, yes, I know all about it, and will give it proper attention."

Next came an older man, in lieutenant's shoulder straps, asking to be appointed colonel of a regiment of colored troops. Negro recruiting had hardly begun, was in an experimental stage. The President: "The whole thing amounts only to a colonelcy for the applicant, as, should a regiment be raised, in six months there would be a colonel without a negro left in the command." The lieutenant protested, "My purpose is not that; it is to serve the cause, not myself," and left dissatisfied with the response, "That may be your purpose but the certain *effect* none the less will be what I have described."

A white-haired gentleman with his pretty daughter, "shy, bashful and even frightened," met warm courtesy. They had no business, would not trespass on the President's time; before traveling to their distant home the father wished to have the honor of presenting his daughter to the Chief Magistrate. Lincoln rose, shook hands with both of them, Van Santvoord noting: "With the frank, bland, and familiar manner which made strangers feel unconstrained and at ease in his presence, he chatted pleasantly, even playfully, with them for some minutes, to the evident delight of both visitors. When they were about to go away, he politely escorted them to a door different from that through which the visitors entered, and dismissed them with charming courtesy."

Returning to his desk, he found a man of Scotch brogue with letters from Scotland and from people there who had congratulations and greetings on

Washington, Aug. 9. 1862.

His Excellency,

Abraham Lincoln.

President of the U. States: —

Dear Sir:

I take pleasure in commending to your kindness & confidence, my excellent neighbor and friend, the Rev. J. B. Meek of the Methodist Episcopal church. Mr Meek is a man of unblemished moral character and true Christian consistency. I believe he is truly devoted to the cause of the Saviour and well qualified to give sound and faithful religious instruction to those who need it. He has a zeal for Christ and for the salvation of men which seems to me to be the gift of the Holy Spirit. I should, therefore, rejoice to see him appointed to a Hospital chaplaincy—a position for which his gifts and graces peculiarly qualify him. Can you not, Mr President, give him an appointment for the new hospitals on Arsenal Square or somewhere else in the District? yours truly, P. D. Gurley.

The Lincoln family pastor writes a recommendation. From the Barrett collection.

the Emancipation Proclamation. The act met the warmest sympathy of his countrymen; all trusted and prayed that the President would stand firm on it. "Well," said the President, "I am inclined to remain firm, but do not say I will, certainly, though all others should fail, as Peter once said and repeated with so much confidence and only saw his folly and weakness as the cock crew—yet, God helping me, I trust to prove true to a principle which I feel to be right, of which the public sentiment approves, and which the country is prepared to support and maintain. Tell this to your friends at home with my acknowledgments for their sympathy and good wishes." The Scotchman said farewell.

A tall, broad-shouldered hulk of a man, of a somewhat breezy Western look, sidled up awkwardly alongside the President, hesitated and half stuttered, then said that before leaving Washington he wanted the honor of shaking hands with the President. After passing a few remarks, Lincoln ran his eye curiously up and down the stranger and with a touch of fun said, "I rather think you have a little the advantage of me in height; you are a taller man than I am." The visitor, more than puzzled, and almost as though he might be guilty of treason, mumbled, "I guess not, Mr. President, the advantage cannot be on my side." "Yes, it is," insisted Lincoln. "I have a pretty good eye for distances, and I think I can't be mistaken in the fact of the advantage being slightly with you. I measure six feet, three and a half inches, in my stockings, and you go, I think, a little beyond that." The visitor held back, respectful, bashful.

"It is very easily tested," said the President, taking a book from the table, holding it edgewise against the wall, calling, "Come under." The stranger now turned red in the face, half scared, half smiling. The President's voice rang: "Come under, I say. Now straighten yourself up, and move your head in this way"—showing how with his own head—"and now you hold the book and be sure not to let it slip down a hair-breadth, and I will try."

Then Lincoln stepped under the book, stretched to his tallest, pivoted his head, fell a trifle short of the mark, and said: "There, it is as I told you. I knew I could not be mistaken. I rarely fail in taking a man's true altitude by the eye."

By now the other visitors in the room were having a laugh and the tall one found tongue to say, "Yes, but Mr. President, you have slippers on and I boots, and that makes a difference."

"Not enough to amount to anything in *this* reckoning," finally insisted Lincoln. "You ought at least to be satisfied, my honest friend, with the proof given you that you actually *stand higher* today than your President."

Washington and the East were so different from the West, an Illinois man remarked. Lincoln agreed and fell into a reminiscence of his first speech in Congress, when, as always if he got up to talk, he was embarrassed. He had felt like the boy whose teacher asked him why he did not spell better, the boy saying, "Cause I hain't just got the hang of the school-house, but I'll get on better later."

T. B. Bancroft stood for an hour within three feet of Lincoln's desk, waiting to ask for a pass through Army of Potomac lines to visit the son of a friend in the 3d Pennsylvania Cavalry. Bancroft had waited half an hour with about fifty others in the Blue Room belowstairs until the announcement from a colored servant that the President was ready to receive them, when the crowd rushed pell-mell upstairs into the office.

"I studied his face and listened to the conversations between him and the petitioners who came to offer their cases for his decision," wrote Bancroft. "The railing at which I stood ran almost across the room, with a gate at one end, through which the applicants were admitted one at a time. Mr. Lincoln sat at the back end of the enclosure, and his secretary at the end nearest the gate. Between them stood a chair in which the applicant sat. Except for the guard at the front door, I had seen no evidence of any special care being taken for the President's protection. He had just come from a Cabinet meeting and looked worn and wearied.

"His hair stood up all over his head as though he had been running his hands through it, and in this respect he looked not unlike the pictures of Andrew Jackson that we often see. His appearance almost justified the gibes and jeers with which his enemies were accustomed to describe him—all but his eyes, calm, piercing, searching; not to be deceived, yet practicing no guile. He sat in his chair loungingly, giving no evidence of his unusual height; a pair of short-shanked gold spectacles sat low down upon his nose, and he could easily look over them."

A young man asked a pardon for his brother who had been taken prisoner by the enemy, had managed to escape, and then instead of reporting to the nearest officer for duty, had gone to his home in the North, was arrested by the provost marshal, tried for desertion, and sentenced to death. The President took the mass of papers on the case, read slowly the statements of many officers, endorsements of pardon, from corps commander down to captain. The last one he read aloud, saying slowly: "Hm—hm—hm— 'Approved and respectfully forwarded with the suggestion that if the said J. L. will re-enlist for three years or during the war, a pardon be granted.—Signed, Gen'l A——, John Doe, Adjutant.' . . . I don't know but what I agree with General A——, and if the young man will re-enlist for three years or during the war, I will pardon him."

The brother said in a hurry this would be satisfactory. The President reached to a pigeonhole in the desk before him, took out a card, wrote on it, and gave it to the brother: "Take that to the War Department, and I guess it will be all right." With his brother's pardon assured him, the young man, smiling all over, left the room.

An Irishman of perhaps sixty years was the next to seat himself as Lincoln said, "My friend, what can I do for you?"

"Well, your Excellency, I am a night watchman at Mr. Gardner's in the city, and I do be sick all the time, and I think 'tis the night work that doesn't agree with me, and I was thinking if your Excellency could give me a job in the Treasury—"

"Stop! stop!" cried the President. "Have you any brief to show me?"

"Fwat's that?"

"Give me something to read. Have you nothing in writing to show me?"

"Sir, I have two letters from me byes in the army," and he thrust two worn and torn thick envelopes into the hands of the President, who looked at them, tempted, then forced them back on Michael with a "Tut, tut, I haven't time to read a book." Michael began a rapid and fluent plea filled with many "your Excellency's." Then, from want of breath or arguments, Michael paused.

"My friend, I don't know you, nor do I know that I ever saw you. I cannot put you in the Treasury without some reference. Suppose that I should put you there and you should prove to be a thief and should steal the money—"

"Sir"—with indignation—"I'm an honest man."

"I believe you are but I know nothing about you. Do you not know someone in the city that I also know and who can speak for you?"

"Well, your Excellency, I know Mr. Graham beyont on C. Street, and Mr. Brown and Mr. Jones and Mr. Robinson and Mr. Swayne, the sculptor, and—"

"Stop! I know Mr. Swayne, and if you will bring me a letter from him, stating what he knows about you, I will see what can be done for you."

Exit Michael, cramming his boys' letters back into a pocket. A boy in army blue took the chair, handing his papers to the President, who read them and said, "And you want to be a captain?"

"Yes, sir."

"And what do you want to be captain of? Have you got a company?"

"No, sir, but my officers told me that I could get a captain's commission if I were to present my case to you."

"My boy—excuse my calling you a boy—how old are you?"

"Sixteen."

"Yes, you are a boy, and from what your officers say of you, a worthy boy and a good soldier, but commissions as captains are generally given by the governors of the States."

"My officers said *you* could give me a commission."

"And so I could, but to be a captain you should have a company or something to be captain of. You know a man is not a husband until he gets a wife—neither is a woman a wife until she gets a husband. I might give you a commission as captain and send you back to the Army of the Potomac, where you would have nothing to be captain of, and you would be like a loose horse down there with nothing to do and no one having any use for you."

The boy began breaking, tears in his eyes. The President put a hand on the boy's shoulder, patting while he spoke: "My son, go back to the army, continue to do your duty as you find it to do, and with the zeal you have hitherto shown, you will not have to ask for promotion, it will seek *you*. I may say that had we more like you in the army, my hopes of the successful outcome of this war would be far stronger than they are at present. Shake hands with me, and go back the little man and brave soldier that you came." The boy stepped away as if he had been home to see a wise and kindly father.

Bancroft, after an hour of seeing and listening three feet from Lincoln's desk, now came forward and presented a provost marshal's certificate, which

Lincoln read, handed back: "And what can I do for you?" Bancroft asked for a pass through army lines; the War Department had refused him. "Well, I must refuse you for the same reason that the War Department did. If we were to allow all to go through that wish to do so, we would not have boats enough to carry them. They would get down there and be in the way, and"—scrutinizing the well-dressed Bancroft—"I judge by your appearance you know what it means to have people in the way."

Tales came to be told in divers versions, one of an old farmer and his wife who came to the capital to see their soldier boy in hospital. At a White House reception they shrank against a wall, unaccustomed to chandeliers, diplomats, uniforms, the international motley that buzzed in the room. A young English nobleman had been formally presented to the President. Lincoln's glance happened to sweep over and beyond those nearest him till his eye caught the old couple, and he blurted, "Excuse me, my lord, there's an old friend of mine." Making way toward them, he took the old farmer's hand: "Why, John, I'm glad to see you! I haven't seen you since you and I made rails for old Mrs. So-and-So in Sangamon County."

The old man turned to his wife with quivering lips. "Mother, he's just the same old Abe!" Then turning again: "Mr. Lincoln, you know we had three boys, all in the same company. John was killed in the Seven Days' fight, Sam was taken prisoner and starved to death, and Henry is in the hospital. We had a little money and I said, 'Mother, we'll go to Washington an' see Henry.' And while we were here I said, 'We'll go up and see the President.'" Lincoln, with dim eyes: "John, we all hope this miserable war will soon be over. I must see all these folks here for an hour or so and I want to talk with you."

A Washington resident came with the personal complaint that a man with a hand organ disturbed him day and night by grinding out music in front of his residence. Lincoln: "I'll tell you what to do. Speak to Stanton about it, and tell him to send Baker [secret-service head] after the man. Baker will steal the organ and throw its owner into the Old Capitol [Prison], and you'll never be troubled with his noise again."

From Illinois came a young lieutenant who had served his time and had promised his mother he wouldn't re-enlist in the army. But he wanted more of the war and was willing to take a place in the navy, if Noah Brooks would mention it at the White House. Brooks quoted the President's answer: "I think that young man ought to have a chance to fight if he wants it, even at the risk of evading his promise. Go over to the Navy Department, tell Captain Fox I sent you, and if between you two you can mouse out something in the fresh-water navy for this young man, come back and let me know, and the thing is done." And soon the young Illinoisan was with the Mississippi River gunboats, commissioned an acting master.

A delegation of Indians with grave faces, in blankets and moccasins, entered the President's room and seated themselves around a large globe of the earth. The President, according to Edward Malet, after introductions and formalities, stepped to the globe. "This," he said, putting his hand on it and giving it a little whirl, "is a representation in small of this great earth on which we live," and then, catching himself, with a twinkle in the eye as though he must be careful and not mislead them, "Not the legs, they don't form part of the shape of the earth, only the globe," and he made it swiftly revolve. Then he suddenly stopped it, put his finger on Great Britain and said: "We white people all come from this little spot. It is small but we have spread amazingly since we began to wander."

A kindhearted gentleman pleaded for a private locked up because he had knocked down his captain. "I tell you what I'll do," said Lincoln. "You go up to the Capitol and get Congress to make it legal for a private to knock down his captain, and I'll pardon your man with pleasure." A farmer from a border county in Virginia claimed that Union soldiers had taken a horse and a lot of hay from his farm and he would now like the President to send him to the proper department to have his claims paid. The President referred him to a claim department, and was reminded of a steamboat running at full speed on a Western river one day when a boy tugged at the captain's coat sleeve and cried for the boat to stop: "I've lost my apple overboard."

A stranger shaking hands remarked casually that he had been elected to Congress as Lincoln was leaving it some years back. "Yes," said the President, naming the man's State. "I remember reading of your election in a newspaper one morning on a steamboat going down to Mount Vernon." Often a committee or a friendly citizen would present a cane, and to one who had an interesting walking-stick he philosophized: "When a boy my favorite was a knotted beech stick and I carved the head myself. There's a mighty amount of character in sticks. Dogwood clubs were favorite ones with the boys. I suppose they use them yet. Hickory is too heavy, unless you get it from a young sapling. Have you ever noticed how a stick in one's hand will change his appearance? Old women and witches wouldn't look so without sticks."

A well-dressed man murmured, "I presume, Mr. President, you have forgotten me?" The quick reply was, "No, your name is Flood. I saw you last twelve years ago," naming the place and occasion, and cheerily proceeding, "I am glad to see that the *Flood* flows on." To another, a banker, he pointed out that the Union vote had fallen off in his home district. The banker protested that the Union majority had increased there. The President: "You fell off about six hundred votes." And going to records in a bookcase, he showed the banker that his figure was correct. Patiently he heard a long paper read by Robert Dale Owen. Three months Owen had worked on it, a digest of historical precedents aimed to help Lincoln write a proclamation of amnesty. As Owen got going Lincoln brightened, and the reading over, he thanked Owen for the paper. "I have not the time necessary for such an examination of authorities—and if I had the time I could not have done the work as well as you have done it."

The errands they came on were many. Hay wrote in his diary one day: "Blair and the Prest continue to be on very good terms in spite of the publication of Blair's letter to Frémont. Blair came to explain it to the Prest but he told him he was too busy to quarrel with him. If he, B., didn't show him the letter he would probably never see it." Lank mountaineers from East Tennessee came to say they were for the Union and Lincoln greeted them "like younger brothers," wrote Hay. "He is one of them really. I never saw him more at ease than he is with these first-rate patriots of the border."

Once as Lincoln stood chatting with two or three other men, a casual caller rambled in and took the one chair reserved for the President. When the President was again ready for his chair, he spoke to the seated intruder

Sec. of Interior, please see, hear, & oblige if you can my friend T. J. Carter'

Oct. 3. 1863   A. Lincoln

Card of introduction. From the Barrett collection.

while holding out his hand far enough away so that the uninvited fellow had to rise for the handshake. Then Lincoln took his seat.

Information as to the naval and military expedition which captured Port Royal was requested by a man itching with curiosity. "Will you keep it entirely secret?" the President asked. The fellow sure would. "Well," said the President, "I will tell you," and pulling the man toward him, and waiting during a moment of suspense, he said in a stage whisper heard by the others in the room: "The Expedition has gone to sea!"

A young chiropodist, Isachar Zacharie, an English Jew, was introduced, with the result later that Lincoln wrote a testimonial: "Dr. Zacharie has operated on my feet with great success, and considerable addition to my comfort." The New York Herald said: "Dr. Zacharie trimmed the feet of President Lincoln and all his Cabinet. He is a wit, gourmet and eccentric, with a splendid Roman nose, fashionable whiskers and an eloquent tongue, a dazzling diamond breast-pin, great skill in his profession and an ingratiating address." A corps of trained chiropodists should accompany each army; Zacharie urged the scheme on Lincoln and Stanton. Each regiment had a chaplain—why not a chiropodist? Thus souls and soles of each foot soldier would be cared for. Punsters could not miss the opportunity. Meanwhile the satirists had their day, the New York Herald saying: "Dr. Zacharie has made his début on the national stage to cut the Presidential corns. When

Dr. Zacharie called at the White House, Secretary Stanton mistook him for some visionary Greeley or Jewett, refused to listen to him. But Zacharie passed on into the President's private reception room and as soon as Mr. Lincoln saw him he held out his foot and complained of his corns."

"I voted for you, Mr. Lincoln," chirped a short, fat man with a pleasant face. "I—I'm glad I did. I—I'd do it again. I—I'm putting in an application for paymaster. I—I—" The President laughed. "Want to be a paymaster, eh? Well, some people would rather take money than pay it out. It would about kill some men I know to make paymasters of 'em."

Later came a full-bosomed woman of rare face and gleam. "I have three sons in the army, Mr. Lincoln."

"You may well be proud of that, madam."

"There were four, but my eldest boy—" and that was all she could say as she passed on with his low-spoken "God bless you, madam" in her ear.

A committee from Philadelphia resented the appointment of a Universalist clergyman of their city as a chaplain. "Oh, yes, gentlemen," said Lincoln, "I have sent his name to the Senate and he will no doubt be confirmed at an early date." A young man spoke up. The committee was *against* and not for

Dr. Zacharie has operated on my feet with great success, and considerable addition to my comfort.

A. Lincoln

Sep. 22. 1862.

Lincoln adds his recommendations to those of William Cullen Bryant and others whose feet were benefited by the chiropodist Zacharie. Original in the Barrett collection.

the appointment. "Ah! that alters the case," said Lincoln, as he heard further a statement that the newly appointed chaplain "does not believe in endless punishment; not only so, sir, but he believes that even the rebels themselves will be finally saved." The President called the roll of the committee, asking, "Is that so?" getting from each the answer "Yes," and closed the interview: "Well, gentlemen, if that be so, and there is any way under Heaven whereby the rebels can be saved, then, for God's sake and their sakes, let the man be appointed."

A fleshy and dignified man, stern and homely of face, entered the President's office one day in swallow-tail coat, ruffled shirt, white cravat, orange gloves. His watch chain had a topaz seal, his cane a gold head. He looked "ominous," said Lamon, and gave the President the impression, "I'm in for it now." The conversation began and ran on in a chilly way. The visitor, keeping a frozen face, shocked the President with his closing remarks as he was about to leave: "Mr. President, I have no business with you, none whatever. I was at the Chicago convention as a friend of Mr. Seward. I have watched you narrowly ever since your inauguration, and I called merely to pay my respects. What I want to say is this: I think you are doing everything for the good of the country that is in the power of man to do. You are on the right track. As one of your constituents I now say to you, do in the future as you damn please, and I will support you!" Lincoln almost collapsed with glee. He took the visitor's hand: "I thought you came here to tell me how to take Richmond." They looked into each other's faces. "Sit down, my friend," said the President. "Sit down, I am delighted to see you. Lunch with us today. I have not seen enough of you yet."

A fair, plump woman from Dubuque, Iowa, buttonholed Secretary Welles at the entrance to the Cabinet room. He took her message to Lincoln—she wished merely to have a look at the President, had come from Baltimore just for that, and so told him when she was admitted for a handshake and greeting. "Well, in the matter of looks, I have altogether the advantage."

An Illinois Congressman entered to protest the dismissal of a Western doctor, a major, for immoral practices. The War Department officers had tried him, had cut off his army buttons, and refused to show the papers in the case to the Congressman. Lincoln sent for the papers, examined them, and laughed grimly to a regular-army major: "So you ordered the doctor's buttons cut off? I am sorry I cannot approve this sentence," as though a light and easy punishment had been handed to the doctor.

Two Wisconsin privates got in with a request that the President frank their letters home. The President referred them to their Congressman. "I am very busy." The boys said the folks at home would like to see his name on the envelopes. With a smile he wrote: "Let this go. A. Lincoln"—told them the Congressman would fix the rest of it, and "I want you to be brave soldiers."

An army man entering on an appointed matter, they shook hands. "Now, Lieutenant Morse, I want you to sit down and wait till I finish this letter, then I want to talk with you. I have to finish anything when I begin it, if I didn't I never would get through anything in the day."

In an interlude of business he got acquainted with a new orderly, asking name, age, what place he called home, and questions: "Is your mother living? Do you send her money regularly?" and meditative talk that it means much for a mother to have a good son and the mother lives a hard life with a son not trustworthy and loving. That orderly only a few days before had been offered $100 for dispatches he carried from the President. He held off till $200 was paid him, then whipped out a revolver and took the briber prisoner, later finding out that the briber was a secret-service operative and he as an orderly was being tested.

The manner in which Lincoln might receive a well-accredited stranger, his customary method in many a brief interview, was presented by the editor of the *Free Press* of London, Canada, who entered a White House waiting-room where he saw other persons walking to and fro, also waiting, as he handed his credentials to a doorman for delivery to the President.

With scarcely a moment's delay, I was ushered into his presence, when he arose and stepped forward in a stooping position, extended his hand and shook mine kindly, but rather loosely, as if he was afraid of hurting it, remarking, at the same time,

"I am glad to see you, Sir; be seated."

"I am a stranger in the capital," I replied, "and have sought an interview with you, Mr. President, and have been much pleased with the easy means of access."

"Yes," said the President, "this ready means of access is, I may say, under our form of government, the only link or cord which connects the people with the governing power; and, however unprofitable much of it is, it must be kept up; as, for instance, a mother in a distant part, who has a son in the army who is regularly enlisted, has not served out his time, but has been away as long as she thinks he ought to stay, will collect together all the little means she can to bring her here to entreat me to grant him his discharge. Of course, I cannot interfere, and can only see her and speak kindly to her. How far is your place from Detroit, Sir?"

"About one hundred miles east from Detroit; we have no water communications, but have a very nice inland city. I intend remaining in Washington for a few days; all seems stir and commotion here."

"Yes, there never was anything in history to equal this."

"Your position must indeed be responsible and trying, Mr. President."

"Yes, to think of it, it is very strange that I, a boy brought up in the woods, and seeing, as it were, but little of the world, should be drifted to the very apex of this great event."

"I read your proclamation of this morning, calling for more men; it will, no doubt, be filled up."

"Yes, Sir, it will be filled up."

"I thank you, Mr. President, for your kindness and courtesy," I said, as I rose. The President shook hands again, and said, "I am most happy to have made your acquaintance."

A committee of temperance advocates urged their cause, and as Hay heard it, they said "the reason we did not win was because our army drank so much whiskey as to bring the curse of the Lord upon them." Lincoln replied it was "rather unfair on the part of the curse, as the other side drank more and worse whiskey than ours did."

Though a teetotaler himself, Lincoln avoided committals that would ally him politically with any group on the liquor question. As Chief Magistrate he was as reserved as when he answered an inquiry whether he had in 1860 personally served a pitcher of cold water instead of the customary wine or whisky to the committee notifying him of his nomination as President. The reply: "I think it would be improper for me to write or say anything to, or for, the public, upon the subject of which you inquire. I therefore wish the

letter I do write to be held as strictly confidential. Having kept house sixteen years, and having never held the 'cup' to the lips of my friends then, my
judgment was that I should not, in my new position, change my habit in this
respect. What actually occurred upon the occasion of the committee visiting me, I think it would be better for the others to say."

Something of this reserve was in his replies to committees and individuals
who pressed for his support of temperance. Noah Brooks recorded: "Wine
was never on the table at the White House, except when visitors, other than
familiar friends, were present. The President's glass was always filled, and
he usually touched it to his lips. Sometimes he drank a few swallows, but
never a whole glass, probably."

Several fires broke out in Washington in the fall of '61 and offers of fire
engines were brought to the President. The day after the Washington In-
firmary burned down, a Philadelphia committee arrived and the President
listened to a flow of oratory regarding a fully equipped fire brigade for
Washington. In the midst of much earnest language he seemed to rouse himself as though just awakened to the true import of their visit, saying gravely,
"Ah, yes, gentlemen, but it is a mistake to suppose that I am at the head of
the fire department of Washington—I am simply the President of the United
States." Then it dawned on the committee their business was elsewhere.

A soft-voiced fellow wished the President to approve his claim for damages against the Government, and heard a hard voice: "You know you can't
prove what is in this paper by all the people in the United States, and you
want me to prove it for you by writing my name on the back of it; yes, in
plain words you wish me to lie for you that you may get your money; I
shall not do it."

Halpine saw the President bowing out an elderly woman slow to go:
"I am really very sorry, madam, very sorry. But your own good sense must
tell you that I am not here to collect small debts. You must appeal to the
courts in regular order." She left, and Lincoln sat down, crossed his legs,
locked his hands over his knees, and laughed to Halpine: "What odd kinds of
people come in to see me, and what odd ideas they must have about my
office! Would you believe, Major, that the old lady who has just left, came
in here to get from me an order for stopping the pay of a Treasury clerk
who owes her a board bill of seventy dollars!" The President rocked to and
fro. "She may have come in here a loyal woman but I'll be bound she has
gone away believing that the worst pictures of me in the Richmond press
only lack truth in not being half black and bad enough."

Congressman A. W. Clark of Watertown, New York, pleaded for a constituent who had one boy killed in battle, another dying in prison, and a
third son sick at Harper's Ferry—the mother at home having gone insane.
The father sat by and wept while the Congressman begged that he could take
the sick boy home, as it might help bring back the wandering reason of the
mother. Lincoln listened, asked no questions, took the papers in the case and
wrote "Discharge this man." This matter of official business closed, Lincoln
wiped a tear from his cheek, turned to a doorman and said, "Bring in that

man"—as if bothered—and the departing Congressman asked why. "He replied that it was a writing-master who had spent a long time in copying his Emancipation Proclamation, and had ornamented it with flourishes which made him think of an Irishman who said it took him an hour to catch his old horse and when caught he wasn't worth a darn!"

A Massachusetts woman wrote home of seeing the President refuse a pass to a Negro, saying the Negro must have a certain officer vouch that he belonged where he wanted to go. "But it is all the way to the Capitol," remonstrated the Negro. "And it is so cold today, I can tell you myself that I am all right." So the President took time to examine the Negro, and after a series of questions about the locality involved, the Negro got his presidential pass. Then in came an Irish boy. The President: "Well, did you get the place?"

"No, sir. I want another recommend."

"Where is the one I gave you?"

"I lost it."

"Careless! I have a great mind not to give you another."

The father of the nation was "dealing with his children," wrote the Massachusetts woman, "generally patient, but sometimes fretted." She saw two women meet refusal of their request. The younger one "used very saucy language to the President," who beckoned a doorman to usher the women out, and it was done without further ado.

"Yesterday a piteous appeal was made to me by an old lady of genteel appearance," he wrote to the Secretary of War on New Year's Day of '63. She had opened up a boardinghouse in the old Duff Green building on what she thought sufficient assurance she would not be disturbed by the Government, had some boarders already and more promised, including members of Congress. "Now she is ordered to be out of it by Saturday, the 3d instant," wrote the President. "Independently of the ruin it brings on her, by her lost outlay, she neither has nor can find another shelter for her own head. I know nothing about it myself, but promised to bring it to your notice."

Official stationery not being conveniently at hand, the President wrote at the top of a sheet of notepaper, "Executive Mansion," and penned a note: "My dear Madam: Gen. McDowell did me the honor yesterday to enquire when you could see Mrs L. If you please she will see you to-day at 2. o'clock."

A Quaker farmer and wife had left their farm in Clinton County, Ohio, and traveled to see the President in his office. They had heard of him as a kind man who would surely listen to a plan, yes, a plan that had pressed on the mind of the Quaker farmer and kept him awake night after night for many hours. The local council of Quakers had endorsed the plan. The President bowed and shook hands and gazed deep into their faces, and they told him everything about the plan and they were struck deep that he already had thought about the plan and favored it and prayed for its success and told them so. The war could end instantly and slavery too end instantly by this plan. It would only be needed that the Federal Government should offer to pay $300 each for slaves, and all slaveowners accept the offer, whereupon the Government would free the slaves—and the armies go home from their bloody work.

To the Quaker farmer from Clinton County, Ohio, the plan was so simple and reasonable that he could not stay at home with it nor trust it to

Executive Mansion
March 21, 1862.

My dear Madam

Gen. McDowell did me the honor yesterday to enquire when you could see Mrs. L. If you please she will see you to-day at 2. o, oclock.

Yours truly

A. Lincoln

The President serves as social secretary to his wife. From the Barrett collection.

a letter. He must take it personally to the President. And the answer from the President was that the plan was wise, humane, and the cheapest way to end the war. In his next message to Congress the President would use his every power of persuasion to get Congress to see the plan exactly as the Quaker farmer and his wife saw it. A half-hour glided by while the President talked with the two Friends. He stood up. They arose. He put his hands in theirs. "I thank you for this visit. May God bless you." The Quaker man asked if he would object to writing just a line or two, "certifying that I have fulfilled my mission, so that I can show it to the council at home." The President sat to his table and wrote:

I take pleasure in asserting that I have had profitable intercourse with friend Isaac Harvey and his good wife, Sarah Harvey. May the Lord comfort them as they have sustained me.

Sept. 19, 1862   Abraham Lincoln

A petition for pardon was brought by Congressman John B. Alley of Lynn, Massachusetts, in behalf of a slave-trader who had served his five-year sentence in prison but was held in Newburyport jail for nonpayment of a $1,000 fine. In a letter to Alley, the man in jail acknowledged his guilt, the justice of the sentence and fine, and begged for freedom. Lincoln said he was touched by its pathetic appeal to the feelings, that he had a weakness for being too easily moved by prayers for mercy. And as Alley heard him, he went on: "If this man were guilty of the foulest murder that the arm of man could perpetrate, I might forgive him on such an appeal; but the man who could go to Africa, and rob her of her children, and sell them into interminable bondage, with no other motive than that which is furnished by dollars and cents, is so much worse than the most depraved murderer, that he can never receive pardon at my hands. No! he may rot in jail before he shall have liberty by an act of mine."

Thus ran a few specimens and instances of the stream of thousands who wore the thresholds of the White House, nicked its banisters, smoothed the doorknobs, and spoke their wants and errands.

Why should the President wear himself down meeting this incessant daily procession, this never-ending scramble, this series of faces, so many asking trifles that could be attended to elsewhere? Halpine asked that. In Halleck's office they had system, said Halpine. Nine cases out of ten were turned away from the General in Chief to bureaus and departments. Usually when it was explained that the General in Chief could do nothing for them they went away satisfied.

"Ah, yes!" said Lincoln to Halpine, gravely, almost dreamily, as though he had thought it over many a time. "Ah, yes! such things do very well for you military people, with your arbitrary rule, and in your camps. But the office of President is essentially a civil one, and the affair is different. For myself, I feel, though the tax on my time is heavy, that no hours of my day are better employed than those which bring me again within the direct contact and atmosphere of the average of our whole people. Men moving only in an official circle are apt to become merely official—not to say arbitrary—in their ideas, and are apter with each passing day, to forget that they only hold power in a representative capacity. Now this is all wrong. I go into these promiscuous receptions of all who claim to have business with me, twice each week, and every applicant for audience has to take his turn, as if waiting to be shaved in a barber shop. Many of the matters brought to my notice are utterly frivolous, but others are of more or less importance, and all serve to renew in me a clearer and more vivid image of that great popular assemblage out of which I sprang, and to which at the end of two years I must return.

"I tell you, Major"—he had been talking with half-shut eyes as if in soliloquy, but Halpine knew now it was more than a monologue—"I tell you that I call these receptions my *public opinion baths*—for I have little time to read the papers and gather public opinion that way; and though they may not be pleasant in all particulars, the effect, as a whole, is renovating and invigorating."

A woman from Alexandria requested an order from the President to quit the use of a church there as a hospital for wounded soldiers so that the church could again be used for worship. Lincoln asked what she would be willing to subscribe toward building a hospital there. "You may be aware, Mr. Lincoln, that our property has been very much embarrassed by the war, and I could not afford to give much for such a purpose." Lincoln suggested that the war wasn't over; soon again fighting might render the church more useful for the care and nursing of soldiers. "It is my candid opinion that God wants that church for our wounded fellows. So, madam, you will excuse me. I can do nothing for you." Later he told Lamon he was reminded of a well-to-do father and mother whose only son, feeling that the old folks had outlived their usefulness, "took and killed" his parents. Convicted of murder, the court in passing judgment called on the young man to give any reason he might have why sentence of death should not be passed on him. The glib reply came from the young murderer that he "hoped the court would take pity and be lenient on him because he was a poor orphan!"

In a day's clamor and confusion, Carpenter noted the President saying: "I do the very best I know how—the very best I can; and I mean to keep doing so until the end. If the end brings me out all right, what is said against me won't amount to anything. If the end brings me out wrong, ten angels swearing I was right would make no difference."

Harriet Beecher Stowe told of a man who pressed his own particular viewpoint on the President till the reply came, "Perhaps you'd like to run the machine yourself."

An old Springfield friend after an evening in the White House drawled: "How does it feel to be President of the United States?"

"You have heard about the man tarred and feathered and ridden out of town on a rail? A man in the crowd asked him how he liked it, and his reply was that if it wasn't for the honor of the thing, he would much rather walk."

Lamon wrote of the President listening through an officer's story of a street fight, a free-for-all fracas near the National Theatre about eleven o'clock one night. And the officer had with his bare fist nearly killed a secession sympathizer who had led in the fighting. Surgeons were saying the man would die of concussion of the brain, and the officer had come at two o'clock in the morning, waked up the President, and poured out grief over what had happened. The President asked a few questions and said: "I am sorry you had to kill the man, but these are times of war, and a great many men deserve killing. This one, according to your story, is one of them; so give yourself no uneasiness about the matter. I will stand by you." The officer protested he hadn't come for approval of what he had done. "I felt great grief over the affair, and I wanted to talk to you about it."

Lincoln put a hand on the officer's shoulder. "You go home now and get some sleep; but let me give you this piece of advice—hereafter, when you have occasion to strike a man, don't hit him with your fist; strike him with a club, a crowbar, or with something that won't kill him." The officer went home, but not to sleep, for his conscience hurt him during the fourteen months that the invalid lingered alive. Lamon said that the officer cherished with consecration Lincoln's fidelity to friendship as shown on that occasion, Lamon saying it in a way to indicate that he himself might be the officer concerned.

A Senator went to Lincoln and delivered a message, a sort of mandate, it was said, from a conference of the governors of the Northern States, and Lincoln listened in silence to a long recital of advice, saying eventually: "What comes from those who sent you here is authoritative. The Governors of the Northern States are the North. What they decide must be carried out. Still, in justice to yourself, you must remember that Abraham Lincoln is President of the United States. Anything that the President of the United States does, right or wrong, will be the acts of Abraham Lincoln, and Abraham Lincoln will by the people be held responsible for the President's actions. But I have a proposition to make to you. Go home and think the matter over. Come to me to-morrow morning at nine o'clock and I will promise to do anything that you have then determined upon as right and proper. Good night."

The Senator went away pleased with himself, pleased that the President had put such a responsibility on him. He did considerable thinking during the night, took up one problem and suggestion after another, but when morning broke his mind wasn't clear as to what policies he would have the President put into action. He did not go to the White House that morning nor the next nor the next.

Three weeks later the long arm of the President shot out and dragged him from a crowd at a reception. "I had an appointment with you for one morning about three weeks ago." The Senator recalled it was so. "Where have you been all these weeks?" He had been in Washington, but, "To tell the truth, Mr. President, I have decided never to keep that appointment." Lincoln: "I thought you would not when I made it for you."

He saw Sumner, as chairman of the Foreign Relations Committee of the Senate, continuously at outs with Seward over affairs foreign and domestic. Once when Seward was informed of the President quoting an opinion of Sumner and favoring it as against Seward, Seward said, "There are too many secretaries of State in Washington."

"Who has been abusing me in the Senate today?" he asked Senator Morrill in his office one day. The Senator hoped none of them were abusing him knowingly and willfully. "Oh, well," said Lincoln, "I don't mean that. Personally you are all very kind—but I know we do not all agree as to what this administration should do and how it ought to be done. . . . I do not know but that God has created some one man great enough to comprehend the whole of this stupendous crisis from beginning to end, and endowed him with sufficient wisdom to manage and direct it. I confess I do not fully understand and foresee it all. But I am placed where I am obliged to the best of my poor ability to deal with it. And that being the case, I can only go just as fast as I can see how to go."

In quite another humor, at a time when Congress had been trying to clip his powers and drive him into policies he wasn't ready for, the President said to Lamon, "I have great sympathy for these men, because of their temper and their weakness; but I am thankful that the good Lord has given to the vicious ox short horns, for if their physical courage were equal to their vicious dispositions, some of us in this neck of the woods would get hurt."

Entrusting a piece of confidential political work to John W. Forney and Alexander K. McClure, the President opened the conversation with them by saying, "You know that I was never much of a conniver; I don't know the methods of political management, and I can only trust to the wisdom of leaders to accomplish what is needed."

Seward mentioned to his son that he had known people to arrive early and sleep for hours in the hall of the White House waiting to interview the President. The *Intelligencer* said on June 15, 1863, "It is one of the tribulations which must greatly add to the fatigue of office at this juncture, that our amiable President has to give so much of his time and attention to persons who apparently having no business of their own, expend a large degree of their surplus energy in benevolently minding the business of the President."

Sometimes the decisions were too rapid, with regrets afterward. Early in the cool of one summer morning the President went to a man and gave an apology that was quoted: "I treated you brutally last night, I ask your pardon. I was utterly tired out, badgered to death. I generally become about as savage as a wildcat by Saturday night, drained dry of the milk of human kindness. I must have seemed to you the very gorilla the rebels paint me. I was sorry for it when you were gone." Writhing under the grind once, he told General Schenck, "If to be the head of Hell is as hard as what I have to undergo here, I could find it in my heart to pity Satan himself."

After a formal evening reception or levee in the Red Room, the country would be told of it by the newspapers. "The foreign Ministers and attachés in full court dress, and afterwards the Army and Navy officers in uniform formally paid their respects to the President at noon of New Year's day. The outside gates were thrown open to the public. The large mass of impatient human beings rushed in. There was music in the vestibule of the White House, and all was jollity."

One reporter strove to render the atmosphere. "To an old campaigner in Washington, it is a new thing under the sun—a strange invasion, terribly suggestive of a great revolution in politics, parties, principles, and marking the beginning of a new epoch. Among these strange faces may be detected something of all the isms and kinks and crotchets of our Northern reformers—spiritualism, free speech, free soil, free men, free love, free farms, free rents, free offices, free negroes, woman's rights, bran bread and patent medicines. The intellectual calibre of this office-seeking crowd, a hostile and bigoted party man would say, is not above the average of the village post-master. Indeed it is apparent that the rural districts are largely in the ascend-ant here, and that for every post-office in the Northwest, there are one, two, or half a dozen or more candidates in this happy family around us. But here we are in the presence.

"After an hour's crushing and pushing and suffocation in this energetic mob, fresh and strong from the body of the people, we are rewarded with a propulsive movement in the rear, which nearly precipitates our whole party of five into Abraham's bosom. Our ladies blush with shame and indig-nation, but promptly recovering their self-possession, they are introduced to 'Old Abe,' who shakes their hands cordially, smiles graciously, addresses them familiarly, and we pass on to Mrs. Lincoln, who nearer the centre of the room, maintains her position with the steadiness of one of the Imperial Guard.

"She is dressed on this occasion in what the ladies call a Magenta watered silk, with a lace cape and with her abundant light brown hair tastefully re-lieved by a half dozen red and white japonicas in a wreath behind the ears. Her sister, Mrs. Edwards, Mrs. Edwards' daughters, and Mrs. Baker formed an agreeable body-guard to our amiable and social hostess. Mrs. Lincoln was pronounced satisfactory by the ladies competent to decide; and by the unanimous voice of the rougher sex she was declared *comme il faut* in per-son, dress, and deportment. Her round and pleasant face, without affecta-tion, expressed a generous welcome to her visitors, and a charming degree of confidence that their judgment would be in her favor.

"Our President, like Saul among the sons of Israel, stands a head and shoulders above the crowd. He has a most amiable expression of counte-nance. He is fond of fun and can crack a joke with anybody, but he does not look like General Jackson, a man with a will of his own. He seems rather to be a man who would like to please everybody, and who is himself so much pleased with his position as to forget its great responsibilities."

Or again the notation of the reporter might be: "Although the President looked careworn, he was exceedingly pleasant and talkative." Or again there might be a compliment to the First Lady. "The most exquisite carpet ever on the East Room floor was one chosen by Mrs. Lincoln. Its ground was of pale green and in effect looked as if ocean in gleaming and transparent waves were tossing roses at your feet." One news item told of English, French, Spanish, Italian, and Swedish Ministers present, also the only man with whom Lincoln ever made arrangements to fight a duel: "General James Shields made his appearance at the levee, and being originally from Illinois, and an acquaintance of the President and his family, was the special object of attention by Mr. and Mrs. Lincoln."

The military telegraph office at the War Department was for Lincoln both a refuge and a news source. He said to A. B. Chandler, one operator in whose room he spent many hours: "I come here to escape my persecutors.

Many people call and say they want to see me for only a minute. That means, if I can hear their story and grant their request in a minute, it will be enough."

At a large flat-topped desk Lincoln sat opposite the operator and went through yellow tissue copies of telegrams received. Chandler often would see him sloped to the edge of a chair, with his right knee dragged down to the floor. When he got to the bottom of the new telegrams, and began again reading important ones he had sifted out for second and more careful reading, he often said, "Well, I guess I have got down to the raisins." Chandler asked what this meant, which brought a story of a little girl who often overate of raisins, and one day followed the raisins with many other sweet goodies. It made her sick; she began vomiting, and after a time the raisins began to come up. She gasped and looked at her mother. "Well, I will be better now, I guess, for I have got down to the raisins."

In this telegraph room Lincoln had first heard of the killing of Ellsworth, of the first and second Bull Run routs, of the Seven Days' battles and McClellan's cry for help at Harrison's Landing, of the *Monitor* crippling the *Merrimac*, of the Antietam shaded victory, of Burnside and Hooker failing at Fredericksburg and Chancellorsville, of blood up to the bridles of horses, of Lee moving his army far up in Pennsylvania toward Gettysburg.

Here Lincoln received a telegram about a skirmish in Virginia where "opposing troops fought the enemy to a standstill," which he said reminded him of two dogs barking through a fence, continuing their barking until they came to a gate, when both ran off in opposite directions. Here he quoted from Petroleum V. Nasby: "Oil's well that ends well"; and after one of McClellan's Peninsular defeats, from Orpheus C. Kerr: "Victory has once again perched upon the banners of the conquerors." Here when news of blunders and treachery had arrived, he referred to an old nonsense book that illustrated his idea of allaying anger by adopting a conciliatory attitude. Under a picture of a maiden seated on a stile smiling at an angry cow were the lines:

> I will sit on this stile
> And continue to smile,
> Which may soften the heart of that cow.

He became acquainted with the cipher code, and in dispatches at the words "Hosanna and Husband" or "Hunter and Happy" would say "Jeffy D" or "Bobby Lee" and sometimes make running comments.

The cipher operator, Charles A. Tinker, told of Lincoln at a street crossing turning out into the mud for a colored woman to pass, and being asked if it had happened so. "Yes, it has been a rule of my life that if people would not turn out for me, I would turn out for them. Then you avoid collisions."

An official letter on one desk had the signature of John Wintrup, operator at Wilmington, written with extraordinary and sweeping flourishes; Lincoln's eye caught it. "That reminds me of a short-legged man in a big overcoat, the tail of which was so long that it wiped out his footprints in the snow."

One day, hand in hand with Tad, he came in chuckling over what he had found in a storybook of Tad's. A mother hen lost several of her chicks and spoke about it to a sly old fox who had eaten them and yet pretended he was perfectly honest. The mother hen had a serious talk with the fox about his wickedness.

"Well, what was the result?" asked an operator when Lincoln did not go on with the story.

"The fox reformed, and became a highly respected paymaster in the army, and now I am wondering which one he is."

The bonds were close between Lincoln and David Homer Bates, manager of the war telegraph office, and the chief of staff, Thomas T. Eckert. Once Stanton ordered Eckert's resignation, blaming him for carelessness that resulted in leaks of information. And Eckert was in Stanton's office answering heated questions from the Secretary of War. The accused man stood giving answers that he had been on duty constantly, had been at the office night-long many times, seldom slept in his bed at his hotel, and for weeks in one period had hardly taken his clothes off—he would insist on his resignation's being accepted.

Just then Eckert felt an arm placed around his shoulder and was surprised on turning to find that it was the President, who had quietly entered and now said: "Mr. Secretary, I think you must be mistaken about this young man neglecting his duties. I have been a daily caller, and I have always found Eckert at his post." Lincoln went far in certifying to loyal performance of duty, was joined by others—and Stanton tore to pieces Eckert's resignation, also tore up a formal dismissal from the army which had been prepared, threw the pieces on the floor, spoke an apology for himself in not having investigated more thoroughly, and announced that he would promote Eckert from captain to major.

On duty in Lincoln's office one morning, Eckert heard Lincoln: "Who is that woman crying out in the hall? What is the matter with her?" Eckert said she had traveled a long distance expecting to go down to the army to see her husband—but an army order had gone out a short time before to allow no women in the army except in special cases. Lincoln sat moodily a moment, suddenly looked up. "Let's send her down. You write the order, Major." Eckert hesitated and asked if it wouldn't be better for a War Office man to write the order. Lincoln said Yes; Eckert went out and came back suggesting, "Mr. President, would it not be better in this case to let the woman's husband come to Washington?" The President's face lighted up. "Yes, yes, that's the best way; bring him up." And it was so ordered.

Seeing George Low, a junior operator, at work cleaning a blue vitriol battery, the President's greeting was, "Well, sonny, mixing the juices, eh?" Another day the pleasantries were:

"Good morning, what's the news?"

"Good news because there is none."

"Ah, my young friend, that rule does not always hold good, for a fisherman does not consider it good luck when he can't get a bite."

Eckert bantered the War Department clerk who supplied the office with soft-iron pokers for use at the open fireplaces that heated the building. Lincoln happened to be there when Eckert took one of the pokers in his right hand, struck it a smart blow across the tensed muscles of his left forearm, bending the poker "so you could notice it." Lincoln told the War Department clerk, "You will have to buy a better quality of iron in future if you expect your pokers to stand the test of this young man's arm."

The President was more at ease, had a looser dignity, among the telegraph operators than amid the general run of politicians and office-seekers. Leaving the big special chair set apart for him one day, he took a vacant one at a table and began writing. The telegraph instrument in front of him started dash-dot-dashing a call; the operator hurrying to answer it leaned far over Lincoln's shoulder. Lincoln apologized. "My young friend, have I hunkered you out of your chair?" From then on a man elbowed out of his rightful place in that office was "hunkered" out of it.

A dispatch from General Schenck reported a skirmish in Virginia and 30 prisoners taken, all armed with Colt's revolvers. Lincoln read it and with a twinkle of eye said to the operator that with customary newspaper exaggeration of army news they might be sure in the next day's prints that "all the little Colt's revolvers would have grown into horse-pistols."

A reckless Irish artilleryman, according to Tinker, got isolated below Edward's Ferry from the Army of the Potomac, believed himself with one gun of the battery to be facing Lee's entire army. Somehow he managed to send a telegram through to the President, who read: "I have the whole rebel army in my front. Send me another gun, and I assure your honor they shall not come over." Lincoln enjoyed it, sent an encouraging reply, suggested to the lone trooper that he get in touch with his commanding officer.

A message from a part of McClellan's command once reported that Union pickets still held Ball's Cross Roads and "no firing had been heard *since* sunset." The President asked if any firing had been heard *before* sunset, and the answer being that none was reported, he laughed about the man who spoke of a supposed freak of nature, "The child was *black* from his hips *down*," and on being asked the color from the hips *up*, replied, "Why, *black*, of course."

A cipher operator heard from the President Artemus Ward's yarn of the *Polly Ann* on the Erie Canal chased by pirates, how the vessel "huv to" and a sailor went ashore and scattered oats along the towpath. Mules of the pursuing pirate craft came to the oats, stopped to eat; no coaxing or beating would move them, and by the time they had eaten all the oats the *Polly Ann* had escaped. The President was interrupted at this point on business of state, but a few moments later added the clincher of the yarn: "Now that was true strategy because the enemy was diverted from his real purpose."

David Homer Bates told other operators of Lincoln rising from an old haircloth lounge, where he sometimes rested while telegrams were being deciphered, to brush from his coat lapel a small insect known to scientists as a *cimex lectularius*, or a bedbug, saying, "Boys, I have been very fond of that old lounge, but as it has become a little buggy I fear I must stop using it." His triflings went to the extent of reading to the boys from a California humorist who described a hair restorative, one bottle of which fell and broke over his leather trunk, so that the next day a fine growth of hair showed up.

William Bender Wilson, an operator, spoke of going to Pennsylvania for a few days one October week. "All right, my young friend," smiled the President, "but before you go, tell me if you ain't going over to Pennsylvania to vote." Wilson said he was and it would be his first vote in his native State. Lincoln questioned further and it came out that Wilson was going home to vote the Democratic ticket. Lincoln's good-by: "Be sure you vote for the right kind of Democrats."

Wilson one day noticed the President and Seward coming into the office as though they had just escaped from bothersome persons, Lincoln sinking into an armchair with "By jings! Governor, we are here!" Seward chafed. "Mr. President, where did you learn that inelegant expression?" The President turned to the operators: "Young gentlemen, excuse me for swearing before you. 'By jings' is swearing, for my good old mother taught me that anything that had a 'by' before it was swearing."

One morning of a day he had officially designated for a national fast, Lincoln sat up to a table, adjusted his spectacles, fussed a little with the short spring ends to clasp the sides of the head just back of his eyes, and then became aware that all the operators were busy. As operator Wilson noted it, he drawled: "Gentlemen, this is *fast* day, and I am pleased to observe that you are working as *fast* as you can; the proclamation was mine, and that is my interpretation of its bearing on you. Now we will have a little talk with Governor Morton at Indianapolis. I want to give him a lesson in geography. Bowling Green affair I set him all right upon; now I will tell him something about Muldraugh Hill. Morton is a good fellow, but at times he is the skeeredest man I know of."

"Oftentimes," noted Bates, "he would lean back in his chair, with his feet upon a near-by table, and relapse into a serious mood, idly gazing out of the window upon Pennsylvania Avenue, over which he had seen so many brave soldiers march to the front never to return. In these intervals Lincoln's face was a study, the sadness evident to us youngsters. Soon he would come out of the clouds, his face light up." Sober transactions came off. A few weeks before Burnside waded into the slaughter at Fredericksburg, Lincoln wrote this telegram to be sent to the head of the Army of the Potomac:

If I should be in boat off Aquia Creek at dark to-morrow (Wednesday) evening, could you, without inconvenience, meet me and pass an hour or two with me?

A. Lincoln

Suspecting that a Confederate operator had the wire to Burnside tapped, Bates and his operators sent Lincoln's message in what they called a home-made cipher, depending on Burnside's operators to work it out by themselves, as it was not in any code. The text ran:

John George Nicolay

John Hay

The White House; front portico and roadway

A section of the East Room in the White House

From the Meserve collection

The President's cousin Dennis Hanks

The newlywed "General" and Mrs. Tom Thumb

The eminent tragedian John McCullough

The ex-slave Sojourner Truth

WHITE HOUSE CALLERS

From the Barrett collection

Can Inn Ale me withe 2 oar our Ann pas Ann me flesh ends N. Y. Corn Inn out with U cud Inn heaven day nest Wed roe Moore Tom darkey hat Greek Why Hawk of Abbott Inn B chewed if.

Bates

Thus Lincoln's signature "Can Inn Ale" was the beginning of the message; Burnside's operator read it hind end to, and the meeting, with its risks, was arranged.

Amid the clicking wires Lincoln wrote part of the first Emancipation Proclamation. "He would look out of the window a while," noted Eckert, "and then put his pen to paper, but he did not write much at once. He would study between times and when he had made up his mind he would put down a line or two, and then sit quiet for a few minutes. After a time he would resume his writing, only to stop again at intervals to make some remark to me or to one of the cipher-operators as a fresh despatch from the front was handed to him." His eye in a pause of writing caught a large spiderweb stretched from a lintel of the portico to the side of an outer window sill. The spiders there performing had been nicknamed by the operators "Major Eckert's lieutenants," and when Lincoln commented on the web Eckert said that the lieutenants would soon be reporting and paying their respects to the President. "Not long after," as Eckert saw it, "a big spider appeared at the cross-roads and tapped several times on the strands, whereupon five or six others came out from different directions. Then what seemed a great confab took place, after which they separated, each on a different strand of the web."

Thus amid the silent antics of insects and the incessant dot-dot-dot-dash-dot of telegraph keys, the Edict of Freedom proceeded. On several days Lincoln left with Eckert the sheets he had written. "I should be glad to know that no one will see it, although there is no objection to your looking at it, but please keep it locked up until I call for it to-morrow." On the New Year's Day of the final Emancipation Proclamation, after hours of hand-shaking, Lincoln came in the evening to the telegraph office, settled himself in his chair at Eckert's desk, put his feet on a table and rested while telegrams trickled in from the bloody huggermugger at Murfreesboro.

The operator, Charles A. Tinker, heard Lincoln telling of an occurrence in Pekin, Illinois, before his election as President. And as seldom happened, Lincoln could not recall a Pekin name, ran his fingers through his disheveled hair but could not fish it up. Tinker in a mild, apologetic way put in, "Mr. President, permit me to ask if it is not Judge Puterbaugh?" Lincoln fairly shouted: "Why, yes, that's the name. Did you know him?" Whereupon Tinker: "Yes, sir, down in Pekin, where I once had the honor of explaining to the future President of the United States the workings of the Morse telegraph in the office of the Tazewell House." Lincoln was pleased. "Isn't it funny that Mr. Tinker and I should have met way out in Illinois before the war and now here again in the War Department telegraph office?" And he went on with the details of how, when the telegraph was new, he was initiated into the workings of wires, batteries, and the Morse code.

Among these men of the key, who could solve weird cipher combinations, Lincoln was at home; they were partners in war as a modern enterprise, a drama they often visualized as an immense unity. "The rail connects city with city," said an *Atlantic Monthly* writer. "The wire hangs between camp and camp, and reaches from army to army. Steam is hurling his legions from one point to another; electricity brings him intelligence, and carries his orders; the aëronaut in the sky is his field glass searching the horizon. It is practically but one great battle that is raging beneath him, on the Potomac, in the mountains of Virginia, down the valley of the Mississippi, in the interiors of Kentucky and Tennessee, along the seaboard and on the Gulf Coast. The combatants are hidden from each other, but under the chieftain's eyes the dozen armies are only the squadrons of a single host, their battles only the separate conflicts of a single field, the movements of the whole campaign only the evolutions of a prolonged engagement."

From the telegraph office, with its smooth concentration on direct results, to the White House, with its own peculiar endless turmoils and shifting anxieties, was a step to another scene for Lincoln. Charles A. Dana, the new Assistant Secretary of War, had arrived at the White House while still managing editor of the *New York Tribune* with a delegation of New Yorkers interested in the State patronage. "Mr. Lincoln received us in the large room upstairs in the east wing where he had a working office," wrote Dana. "The President stood up while General Wadsworth, our principal spokesman, and Mr. Opdyke stated what was desired. After the interview had begun, a big Indianian, who was a messenger in attendance at the White House, came into the room and said to the President: 'She wants you.'

" 'Yes, yes,' said Mr. Lincoln, without stirring.

"Soon afterwards the messenger returned again, exclaiming, 'I say, she wants you!' The President was evidently annoyed, but instead of going out after the messenger he remarked to us: 'One side shall not gobble up every thing. Make out a list of places and men you want, and I will endeavor to apply the rule of give and take.' "

Senator Fessenden wrote to his family, "If the President had his wife's will and would use it rightly, our affairs would look much better." The impression of the historian George Bancroft was given in a letter to Mrs. Bancroft: "I made my way to the President's mansion, where Hiram Barney [Collector of the Port of New York] was in waiting to introduce me. Mrs. Lincoln just dismissing a visitor or two, and Barney left to go upstairs, I was left to a tête-à-tête with Madame. She tells me she is a conservative; repudiates the idea that her secessionist brothers can have the slightest influence on her, spoke of the *Herald* as a paper friendly to Mr. Lincoln, and seemed resolved to adhere to that opinion in spite of a gentle hint from me that it was all persiflage and insincere, discoursed eloquently on a review the other day, as if parading 70,000 men had been a sort of great event in the war. She told what orders she had given for renewing the White House; her elegant fitting up of Mr. Lincoln's room; her conservatory and love of flowers; and ended with giving me a most gracious invitation to repeat my visit, and saying she should send me a bouquet. . . . As you are great upon autographs I send you that of the first American lady. Madame wished a rogue who had cheated the government made a lieutenant; the cabinet thrice put the subject aside. One morning in came Lincoln sad and sorrowful: 'Ah!' said he, 'today we must settle the case of Lieutenant ——. Mrs. Lincoln has for three nights slept in a separate apartment.' Things do not look very promising. It is well I am near the end of the page, or I might become lugubrious."

Thus a sedate historian recorded his mood, what he saw and heard. The sober and meticulous Bancroft would also have written his wife, had he stayed longer and talked with Cabinet members, that there was no known instance of the President in his intercourse with Cabinet members making any slighting reference to Mrs. Lincoln or saying anything that touched the dignity of her position. Of marital relations and household mishaps he had yarns and philosophy in an endless stream, but the wives of men, including his own, did not enter by name or implication into his talk in the Cabinet room.

Mrs. Lincoln had, inevitably, become a topic. "I went to the reception at Mrs. Eames'," wrote Charles Francis Adams, Jr., in a letter. "If the President caught it at dinner, his wife caught it at the reception. All manner of stories about her were flying around; she wanted to do the right thing, but not knowing how, was too weak and proud to ask; she was going to put the White House on an economical basis, and, to that end, was about to dismiss 'the help' as she called the servants; some of whom, it was asserted, had already left because 'they must live with gentlefolks'; she had got hold of newspaper reporters and railroad conductors, as the best persons to go to for advice and direction. Numberless stories of this sort were current; and, while Mrs. Lincoln was in a stew, it was obvious that her friends in Illinois were in a rumpus. Much fun is brewing in Washington."

Her hand was in squabbles over who of her kith and kin should have small post offices and West Point cadetships. While the President was steering a delicate course trying to hold his Cabinet together, she wrote on October 4, 1862, to James Gordon Bennett, whose editorials were clamoring for a Cabinet shake-up, a letter saying: "From all parties the cry for a 'change of cabinet' comes. I hold a letter, just received from Governor Sprague [of Rhode Island], in my hand, who is quite as earnest as you have been on the subject. Doubtless if my good patient husband were here instead of being with the Army of the Potomac, both of these missives would be placed before him, accompanied by my womanly suggestions, proceeding from a heart so deeply interested for our distracted country. I have a great terror of strong-minded ladies, yet if a word fitly spoken and in due season can be urged in a time like this, we should not withhold it. As you suggest, the cabinet was formed in a more peaceful time, yet some two or three men who compose it would have distracted it. Our country requires no ambitious fanatics to guide the helm and were it not that their counsels have very little

Being a Native of Kentucky, it would be a great pride to me, to Know that this selec- tion had been made. I ask this as an especial favor. Lieut Scotts, is going to Baltimore this evening, and it would give me great pleasure, if he could hand the order to Major Belger— In the battle for the Union, it would gratify me, to see the horses used, from my native state." Hoping I will receive a favorable answer, I remain Yours very sincerely,

Mary Lincoln.

Mrs. Lincoln uses her influence in behalf of Kentucky horses for the army. Original in the Barrett collection.

control over the President, when his mind is made up as to what is right there might be some cause for fear." These lines had the flow of her normal conversation.

She had been pleased rather than troubled that the *New York Herald* printed two and three columns a day about her arrival at the New Jersey

Long Branch beach resort, her baggage, accommodations, companions, visits, amusements, toilets, gowns, seclusions, places and events where she was invited yet absent. "Mrs. Lincoln, looking like a queen in her long train and magnificent coronet of flowers, stood near the centre of the room, surrounded by a brilliant suite, bowing as the ladies were presented to her. Around her stood the ladies who accompanied her to the Branch, and whose dresses have already been described. Before her, forming a sort of semicircle, were a number of gentlemen, dressed *en règle*, in all the glory of fine black suits and heavy white neckties. Beside her were Mrs. Lester Wallack, dressed in white silk, ruffled, and with an overdress of white tarleton, and Mrs. Hoey, in an elegant blue moiré antique, a flounce and shawl of honiton lace."

The *Herald* writer was out to make people gape and buzz, and had a verbal debauch "amidst this glare of lights, this blaze of jewels, this soft rustling of silks, this cloud of rich and elegant laces." America, he alleged, was coming of age with her settings like those of European royalty. "The scene suggested a court. We are destined to be aristocratic in spite of the fates. The involuntary groupings of the company at the ball certainly showed a proclivity that way." Editorially the *Herald* took the blame off Mrs. Lincoln in saying that she, like Queen Victoria and other personages, must meet the fate of being gaped at. "Like a sensible, unpretending woman as she is, she kept to her apartments for some days, thinking that, the first impulse of curiosity past, the crowd of fashionable idlers assembled there would cease to occupy themselves with her movements. Vain expectations!"

Of course, that the *Herald* had done much to incite this curiosity and rouse these expectations was not acknowledged. The *Herald* wanted readers, and so its man wore out many pencils on gay, garrulous, and sometimes piquant persiflage. "Volumes might be written upon the proverbial slowness of Jersey people; but even Jersey people read the *Herald*, and ought to know about Mrs. Lincoln. Yet, when her carriage drove up to the Post Office at the village yesterday, there was not the slightest excitement. One Jerseyman, a-straddle an empty box, sung out to the storekeeper and Postmaster— for the Post Office is part of the store fixings—'Here's Mrs. Lincoln's wagon, I guess.' 'Is it?' replied the interior colloquialist. 'Well, what of it?' and nobody stirred. Now this may be either ignorance or that politeness which would not trouble a lady by any demonstration. No one gives a Jerseyman credit for politeness, and so Jersey ignorance and dullness have had another exemplification and illustration." Even *Vanity Fair*, with its deep goodwill and kindliness for Lincoln, was led by the Long Branch show-off to publish a cover-page cartoon of Mrs. Lincoln postured as a funny sort of Queen.

Bonnet gossip by a correspondent who signed merely "Burleigh" ran in several newspapers. "A number of cities are contending for the honor of furnishing a hat for the head that reclines on Abraham's bosom. . . . In New York from Canal to Fourteenth, from Philadelphia to Bangor, can be seen on exhibition a 'Bonnet for Mrs. President Lincoln.' These establishments send on and notify Mrs. Lincoln that they have a love of a bonnet, which they are desirous to present to her as a testimonial of their loyalty and great regard for her personally. The amiable and kind-hearted lady of the White House (for such she is) condescends to accept the gift, and at once 'Mrs. Lincoln's Hat' is on exhibition and crowds flock to see it. And such a hat! a condensed milliner's stock in trade, arched high enough to admit a canal boat under it, scalloped, fluted and plaited, loaded with bugles, birds of Paradise, French lace and gewgaws known by name only to the trade, black and white crape, with a mingling of ribbons of all hues, and as many contradictions as there are in a glass of punch. A fit capstone to the cranium of a 'Madge Wildfire.' Mrs. Lincoln may wear all these bonnets, but judging from the specimen I saw, 'uneasy lies the head that wears'—such a bonnet."

"The Prince of Wales, in the exuberance of his bridal joys, did not forget his American cousins, but sent to the amiable wife of President Lincoln the conventional slice of bride cake," wrote Brooks for the *Sacramento Union*. "Of course it had to go through the usual diplomatic channel, and was transmitted, at the request of the happy bridegroom of Wales, by his Chamberlain to the British Minister for Foreign Affairs. He duly forwarded it to Lord Lyons, British Minister Resident at Washington, which functionary passed it over to our Secretary of State, as it is not *en règle* for a foreign minister to recognize any channel of communication with the President but that of the Department of State. So, in due season, but rather dry, the wedding cake reached the White House from the State Department, the Secretary, it is slanderously asserted, whipping off a good bite as his share. Mrs. Lincoln cut the somewhat meager modicum of cake into a large number of small bits and sent the precious relics to her friends. She selected All Fools' Day as the most appropriate time to perform such a kind action for her friends, some of whom were at a loss to know if they were really the happy owners of a simon-pure piece of cake crumbs from the Prince's table, or whether they had been sold at a low price. But Red Tape says that the thing was genuine."

By what means the *New York Herald* gave publication to parts of a message of the President to Congress—before it reached Congress—was a scandal that a congressional committee investigated. Henry (nicknamed "Chevalier") Wikoff admitted to the committee that it was he who had filed the stolen paragraphs at the telegraph office, but he was "under an obligation of strict secrecy" not to tell how he got them. The House ordered Wikoff held in close custody and he was locked up with special accommodations while the inquiry went on. "It was generally believed that Mrs. Lincoln had permitted Wikoff to copy those portions of the message that he had published," wrote Ben Perley Poore, "and this opinion was confirmed when General Sickles appeared as his counsel. The General vibrated between Wikoff's place of imprisonment, the White House, and the residence of Mrs. Lincoln's gardener, named Watt. The Committee finally summoned the General before them and put some questions to him. He replied sharply and for some minutes a war of words raged. He narrowly escaped Wikoff's fate,

(Continued from page 210.)

THE PRESIDENTIAL PARTY.

But to return to the Presidential party. Early in the evening the windows of the White House were brilliant with lights, and by half-past nine the entrance was thronged with guests from a long line of carriages reaching to the avenue. The cards of invitation were received at the door, and the guests passed to the second story of the mansion, which had been fitted up expressly for the occasion. Between the grand entrance, and were driven into the Blue Room, whence they passed to the grand saloon, or East Room, where they were received by Mr. and Mrs. Lincoln, with a gracious welcome and a kind word. Meanwhile the marine band discoursed sweet music from a side saloon.... contemplated and designed by Mrs. Lincoln, of a large, select and elegant private party, with its animated conver-

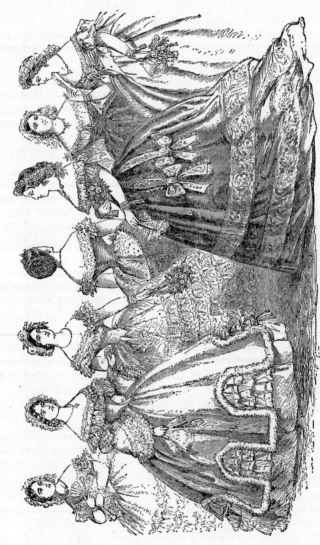

Mrs. Tillotso. Mrs. L. G. Squier. Mrs. Cunningham. Mrs. O'Sullivan. Mrs. Senator Weller. Mrs. Senator Avra. Mrs. Griffin.

SOME OF THE PRINCIPAL COSTUMES WORN AT THE GRAND PRESIDENTIAL PARTY AT THE WHITE HOUSE, WEDNESDAY EVENING, FEBRUARY 5.

Leslie's Weekly sketches White House guests in crinoline

but finally, after consulting numerous books of evidence, the Committee concluded not to go to extremities. While the examination was pending, the Sergeant-at-Arms appeared with Watt. He testified that he saw the message in the library, and, being of a literary turn of mind, perused it; that, however, he did not make a copy, but, having a tenacious memory, carried portions of it in his mind, and the next day repeated them word for word to Wikoff. Meanwhile, Mr. Lincoln had visited the Capitol and urged the Republicans on the Committee to spare him disgrace, so Watt's improbable story was received and Wikoff was liberated."

Henry Villard, who had earlier written such friendly and persuasive *New York Herald* news paragraphs about the Lincolns that there was mild surprise over their publication, wrote later that Mrs. Lincoln was a sorry player of her White House role. "She allowed herself to be approached and continuously surrounded by a common set of men and women whose barefaced flattery easily gained controlling influence over her. 'Chevalier' Wikoff, who made pretensions to the role of a sort of cosmopolitan knight-errant, and had the entree of society, was, in fact, only a salaried social spy or informer of the *New York Herald*. Wikoff was of middle age, an accomplished man of the world, a fine linguist with graceful presence, elegant manners, and a conscious, condescending way—altogether, just such a man as would be looked upon as a superior being by a woman accustomed only to Western society.

"Wikoff showed the utmost assurance in his appeals to the vanity of the mistress of the White House. I myself heard him compliment her upon her looks and dress in so fulsome a way that she ought to have blushed and banished the impertinent fellow from her presence. She accepted Wikoff as a majordomo in general and in special, as guide in matters of social etiquette, domestic arrangements, and personal requirements, including her toilette, and as always welcome company for visitors in her salon and on her drives."

William Howard Russell of the London *Times* recorded in his diary the reports from many sources. "The lady is surrounded by flatterers and intriguers, seeking for influence or such places as she can give. As Selden says, 'Those who wish to set a house on fire begin with the thatch.'" Russell gave the stage setting. "The impression of homeliness produced by Mrs. Lincoln on first sight, is not diminished by closer acquaintance. Few women not to the manner born there are, whose heads would not be disordered, and circulation disturbed, by a rapid transition, almost instantaneous, from a condition of obscurity in a country town to be mistress of the White House. Her smiles and her frowns become a matter of consequence to the whole American world.

"As the wife of the country lawyer, or even the Congressman, her movements were of no consequence. Now if she but drive down Pennsylvania Avenue, the electric wire thrills the news to every hamlet in the Union which has a newspaper; and fortunate is the correspondent who, in a special despatch, can give authentic particulars of her destination and of her dress. Her features are plain, her nose and mouth of an ordinary type, and her

manners and appearance homely, stiffened, however, by the consciousness
that her position requires her to be something more than plain Mrs. Lincoln,
the wife of the Illinois lawyer. . . . On returning to the hotel, I found a
magnificent bouquet of flowers, with Mrs. Lincoln's compliments, and a card
announcing that she had a 'reception' at 3 o'clock."

Russell's impression ran the same as that in many American circles. "Her
manner was too animated, her laugh too frequent," wrote a woman. Congressman Washburne, entirely friendly to Lincoln, wrote to his wife, "Mrs.
Lincoln came last night; I shall not express my opinion of her until I see
you." John Lothrop Motley, historian and Minister to Vienna, wrote to
Mrs. Motley that he found her "youngish, with very round white arms, well
dressed, chatty enough, and if she would not, like all the South and West,
say 'Sir' to you every instant, as if you were a royal personage, she would
be quite agreeable." Welles wrote in his diary: "Mrs. Lincoln has the credit
of excluding Judd of Chicago from the Cabinet."

On New Year's Day, 1863, Browning rode in her carriage once more.
"Mrs. Lincoln told me she had been, the night before, with Old Isaac Newton, out to Georgetown, to see a Mrs. Laury, a spiritualist and she had made
wonderful revelations to her about her little son Willy who died last winter,
and also about things on the earth. Among other things she revealed that the
cabinet were all enemies of the President, working for themselves, and that
they would have to be dismissed, and others called to his aid before he had
success."

Her conversation and letters had much to do with executive details, as in
writing Cousin Lizzie, "Notwithstanding Dr. Wallace has received his portion of life from the Administration, yet Frances always remains quiet." Or:
"Nicolay told me, that Caleb Smith said to him, a few days since that he had
just received a letter from Kellogg, of Cincinnati that he did not know why
he had received his appointment as consul. Is not the idea preposterous?"
To Murat Halstead, the Cincinnati editor who in private letters frequently
referred to her as silly and vain, she sent information: "I write you in great
haste to say that after all the excitement General Banks is to be returned to
his command at New Orleans, and the great Nation will be comforted with
the idea that he *is* not to be in the Cabinet."

A reputation for busyness in appointments often brought her name into
affairs where she may or may not have been busy. To Herndon she said at
a later time that her husband placed great reliance on her judgment of
human nature, "often telling me, when about to make some important appointment that he had no knowledge of men and their motives." He was
kind, indulgent, she told Herndon, "saying to me always when I asked for
anything, 'You know what you want, go and get it.'" She could hold a
peremptory air and one man wrote home after a levee, "I saw Mrs. Lincoln—
she looks as if she made the excellent Abe stand around." She consulted her
personal wishes as against those of many outdoor-music-lovers in Washington, Welles writing in his diary on June 8, 1863:

"Spoke to the President regarding weekly performances the Marine

Band. It has been customary for them to play in the public grounds south of the Mansion once a week in summer, for many years. Last year it was intermitted, because Mrs. Lincoln objected in consequence of the death of her son. There was grumbling and discontent, and there will be more this year if the public are denied the privilege for private reasons. The public will not sympathize in sorrows which are obtrusive and assigned as a reason for depriving them of enjoyments to which they have been accustomed, and it is a mistake to persist in it. When I introduced the subject to-day, the President said Mrs. L. would not consent, certainly not until after the 4th of July. I stated the case pretty frankly, although the subject is delicate, and suggested that the band could play in Lafayette Square. Seward and Usher, who were present, advised that course. The President told me to do what I thought best." Five days later Welles wrote, "We had music from the Marine Band today in Lafayette Square [opposite the White House]. The people are greatly pleased."

Mrs. Lincoln and her cousin, Lizzie Todd Grimsley, said they should be credited with the appointment of the Reverend James Smith, their old Springfield Presbyterian pastor, to the consulate at Dundee, Scotland. Dr. Smith's son, consul under Buchanan, had died, and the father, having retired from the ministry, replaced the son. He was a Democrat, and Republicans seeking the post were not pleased. Mrs. Lincoln and her cousin insisted that the good old parson deserved it and he got it. Appointment of Cousin Lizzie's son, John Todd Grimsley, to the United States Naval Academy at Annapolis did not come so smoothly from Lincoln. During the mother's six months' residence at the White House the appointment did not arrive, though the President had promised it. His chance to give her what she asked was at hand one day when the Secretary of the Navy notified the President that a cadet had been found guilty and expelled for neglect of duty, insubordination, and possession of an obscene book. Instead of seizing this opening to throw out one boy and put another in, the President wrote on the back of Secretary Welles's letter an endorsement that the President was under obligation to give his first appointment to John T. Grimsley of Illinois, and no one else should have precedence: "After saying this much, I add that I would be glad for the boy within named [the expelled one], to have another chance if at all consistent with the service." Four days later he wrote to "My Dear Cousin Lizzie" at Springfield explaining the classes of appointments and as to the unrestricted class and Johnny, "I have intended for months and still intend, to appoint him to the very first vacancy I can get." Ten days passed and he telegraphed Mrs. Elizabeth J. Grimsley, "I mail the papers to you today appointing Johnny to the Naval school."

Early in her residence at the White House Mrs. Grimsley had written in a letter of how the mansion was filled with office-seekers: "Halls, corridors, offices and even private apartments were invaded. This throng continued and increased for weeks, intercepting the President on his way to meals. The ladies of the family were not exempt from marked attention and flattery; but they soon had their eyes open to the fact that almost every stranger that approached us 'hoped that we would use our influence with the President in his behalf.' And it was a hard matter to persuade them that they would stand a better chance without interference."

Jenkins also was in the White House, Jenkins being slang for the peeper and tattler seeking reports and gossip, then writing luridly for newspapers such as the *New York Herald*. He would sleep in a guest bed, eat with the President's family, and send to his newspaper as much as he dared that would not reveal his identity. Male and female Jenkinses had made use of dining-room hints and kitchen gossip. When the stay of one or another came to a sudden end because a leak had been traced, the White House could not give to the public the meaner details of the story. In the cases of "Chevalier" Wikoff and the gardener actually conniving to steal a presidential message before it went to Congress, the leading facts were hushed up.

One night of the first year of the Lincoln family in the White House, the parents and children were taken suddenly sick; physicians were called; poisoning was suspected; but it turned out that they had eaten too freely on first acquaintance with "Potomac shad."

When reports ran that battles near Washington were Union defeats and the Confederate Army would soon be swarming into the city, the White House family naturally worried. General Scott and others had on occasions urged Mrs. Lincoln to take the children and go to Philadelphia for perfect safety. She refused, saying she would stay with her husband to the last. Lincoln guarded against one indiscretion, when Mrs. Grimsley planned to go with a party of friends to visit Mount Vernon. On hearing her announce it, noted Mrs. Grimsley: "Mr. Lincoln rose from his chair, looked at me silently an instant, then said gently, 'Cousin Lizzie, have you taken leave of your senses? Can you compute the amount of trouble if a member of my family should be captured? And the enemy would be only too glad to get you in their clutches, particularly your cousin, David Todd, now in charge of the rebel prison at Richmond.'" One night a rumor had it the President was to be assassinated or captured by a large squad of picked Confederate dare-devils. The President's wife was nervous. John Hay wrote in his diary, "I had to do some very dexterous lying to calm the awakened fears of Mrs. Lincoln in regard to the assassination suspicion."

One White House breakfast had in the guest chairs David Davis, Hill Lamon, Major William S. Wallace, and other associates of law-practice days in Springfield. Mrs. Grimsley noted a story told at this breakfast by one of the lawyers—of how John T. Stuart and Lincoln were at a hotel in Tazewell County where a familiar landlady burst out: "Mr. Stuart, how fine and pert you do look! But Mr. Lincoln, whatever have you been doing? You do look powerful weak," Lincoln replying mournfully: "Nothing out of the common, ma'am, but did you ever see Stuart's wife, or did you ever see mine? Whoever marries into the Todd family gets the worst of it." Merry talk followed, according to Mrs. Grimsley, herself a Todd, and the anecdote was enjoyed by Major Wallace, who married a Todd, and by Mr. and Mrs. Lincoln. Between old acquaintances there were such moments of familiarity without embarrassment.

In a little speech which newspapers reported but which started no discussions at all, Lincoln gave out a plain little rule or principle as to men and women. An old friend of his had lost a wife who was a great help. "He thought he was ruined," said Lincoln, "that he could never find another to fill her place. At length, however, he married another, who he found did quite as well as the first, and that his opinion now was that any woman would do well who was well done by." A point was added: "So I think of the whole people of this nation—they will ever do well if well done by."

Harsh criticism from Greeley in the *New York Tribune* was eased off: "It reminds me of the big fellow whose little wife beat him over the head without resistance. The man said to others, 'Let her alone. It don't hurt me and it does her a power of good.' "

Thomas Wentworth Higginson wrote to his mother, "Mrs. Lincoln at the levee was well and quite expensively dressed; that is, her laces were fine, worth two thousand dollars, and she told a lady she hardly felt it right to wear them in these times, although they were a present." An item went the rounds of many newspapers, Republican and Democratic: "A Love of a Shawl—At the last levee at the White House, Mrs. Lincoln wore a lace shawl, presented to her by A. T. Stewart, of New York, which cost $2,500." When she took her small boys to Niagara Falls and returned, when she stopped at the Metropolitan Hotel in New York and shopped at the big stores, it was chronicled from day to day. *Leslie's Weekly* gave brief items: "Mrs. Lincoln held a brilliant levee at the White House on Saturday evening. She was superbly dressed." Once *Leslie's* had the one-sentence item: "The reports that Mrs. Lincoln was in an interesting condition are untrue."

Harper's Weekly published a drawing of her at a White House reception in conversation with Colonel John Jacob Astor, the nation's foremost multi-millionaire. The *New York Express* correspondent protested, "How unbecoming does it seem for Mrs. President Lincoln to be daily dashing through the lines of soldiers upon the avenue, with her driver and postillion in livery, in a glaringly labelled carriage to denote who is a passer!" Persiflage ran in the *Crisis* in the summer of '63: "The 'Government's' wife in a new bonnet, and the 'Government's' son Bob, in plain clothes, have reached the White Mountains, and are supposed to be 'enjoying theirselves.' The 'Government' has not yet fixed the time when he will join them." The *Dayton Empire* had its say: "The Lincoln-Chase contest has extended into the women's department. Mrs. Lincoln has got a new French rig with all the posies, costing $4,000, Miss Chase sees her and goes one better, by ordering a nice little $6,000 arrangement, including a $3,000 love of a shawl. Go it, greenbacks, while it is yet today."

The run of press items about Southern relatives was steady. One day: "New Orleans papers state that D. H. Todd, brother-in-law of Mr. Lincoln, has been appointed a lieutenant in the Confederate army." Another day: "The Rebel officer who called the roll of our prisoners at Houston is Lieu-

Mrs. McClellan.   Mrs. Lincoln.   Mrs. Senator Crittenden.

SOME OF THE PRINCIPAL COSTUMES WORN AT THE GRAND PRESIDENTIAL PARTY AT THE WHITE HOUSE, WEDNESDAY EVENING, FEBRUARY 5.

tenant Todd, a brother of the wife of President Lincoln. He is tall, fat, and savage against the 'Yankees.'" Or again: "Eleven second cousins of Mrs. Lincoln are members of the Carolina Light Dragoons of the Confederate forces." Or: "There has been some intestinal trouble in the White House. Mr. Lincoln desired Mrs. Lincoln to return to Springfield with the family, at least for a short time, but Mrs. Lincoln positively refuses to secede and there the matter rests." Or: "A gentleman was asked, on arrival from Washington, what was the politics of Mrs. Lincoln, replying that she was 'one-

The President & Mrs Lincoln request the honor of Mrs. Goddard's company at dinner on Thursday February 4th at 7 o'clock

An early answer is requested.

Card of invitation to dinner at the White House. From the Barrett collection.

half pro-slavery and the other half secessionist.'" A paragraph from London *Punch* had reprint:

"The American Correspondent of the *Standard* states, we know not how truly, that her Majesty Mrs. Lincoln is doing much to make King Abraham unpopular. Her conduct is described as that of an uneducated female without good sense, who has been unluckily elevated into a sphere for which she cannot fit herself. This may or may not be, but when the writer in question, in designing to clench the nail, adds, 'In fact, Mrs. Lincoln is making a Judy of herself,' we beg to scrunch that Correspondent under the heel of our thickest cricketing shoe, and he is hereby scrunched accordingly. Making a Judy of herself, indeed! What nobler aspiration, what more beautiful ambition could fill the bosom of created woman? The Correspondent of the *Standard* has unwittingly bestowed on Mrs. L. the highest praise which pen can set down, and if it be true that a lady of such a nature is the Queen-regnant in the Union, the North is indeed to be congratulated. We hope to hear more of her Judyising proclivities."

A letter "to Mrs. Abraham Lincoln," over the initials H.S.D. in the *New York Express,* was much reprinted. "We are tempted to ask from you abandonment for the time of the frivolous, childish chatter that falls upon all earnest people," ran what was partly rebuke, partly partisan rancor. "Shall the inanities of a ball room and theater be now the order of your life, when there is scarcely a family in our midst but immediately or remotely is suffering the cruel pangs of mortal bereavement? When anxiety for the beloved imperilled by war is dimming the eyes of the worthiest of our land, shall you be cheating time and thought by the laugh of the festal group? When the quiet dignity of a Martha Washington graced the Presidential mansion, we know how freely the superfluities of dress, equipage, table, and parade, were relinquished to the needy and suffering soldier. Would she so have sought self-aggrandizement and the éclat of fashionable watering places? Are there no duties pressing upon you which should cover you with the mantle of humiliation?" More to her liking were such newspaper notices as: "Mrs. Lincoln, Mrs. Banks, General Dix and a distinguished party visited the Russian frigate lying off the Battery, New York. They were received with the usual courtesy of that diplomatic people, and as all the officers spoke English very well, the cold collation went off admirably, our republican queen winning all hearts by her matronly dignity and unaffected kindness."

A foreign visitor of distinction, dining at the White House, wished to say nice words to the President about the self-possession of Mrs. Lincoln, her indifference to the many vexations of her position. "Your Excellency's lady makes it very indifferent!" was his first attempt, and seeing the President's eye twinkle, he tried to correct his language—"Your Excellency's lady has a very indifferent face."

One summer day in '63 Mrs. Lincoln's carriage horses ran away. "She threw herself out of her carriage," reported a newspaper. "Fortunately no bones were broken, and after some restoratives she was taken to her residence." The husband and father telegraphed Robert at Harvard: "Don't be uneasy. Your mother very slightly hurt by fall."

Mrs. Keckley fitted a dress on Mrs. Lincoln one day shortly after the Chancellorsville disaster. Lincoln came into the room with slow and heavy step, threw himself on a sofa, shaded his eyes with his hands. Mrs. Lincoln asked, "Where have you been, father?" "To the War Department." "Any news?" "Yes, plenty of news, but no good news. It is dark, dark everywhere." He took a Bible from a stand near by, read for a quarter-hour, seemed easier as Mrs. Keckley in occasional glances studied his face.

Mrs. Lincoln spoke to her dressmaker one day in early '62 about the high cost of a series of state dinners every winter. "I want to avoid this expense; and my idea is that if I give three large receptions, the state dinners can be scratched, from the programme. If I can make Mr. Lincoln take the same view of the case, I shall not fail to put the idea into practice." Later the President came in, she spoke to him, and he considered. "Mother, I am afraid your plan will not work." "But it *will* work, if you will only determine that it *shall* work." "It is breaking in on the regular custom." "But you forget, father, these are war times, and old customs can be done away with for once." "Yes, mother, but we must think of something besides economy."

"I do think of something else. Public receptions are more democratic than stupid state dinners—are more in keeping with the spirit of the institutions of our country, as you would say if called upon to make a stump speech. There are a great many strangers in the city, foreigners and others, whom we can entertain at our receptions, but whom we cannot invite to our dinners." "I believe you are right, mother. You argue the point well. I think that we shall have to decide on the receptions." Thus Mrs. Keckley recorded it.

Mrs. Lincoln visited hospitals, gave time and care to sick and wounded. She interceded with General McClellan, won pardon for a soldier ordered shot. McClellan in letters referred to her as "Mrs. President." From several dressmakers who applied she chose the comely mulatto woman, Mrs. Elizabeth Keckley, who once had been dressmaker to the wife of Jefferson Davis. Mrs. Lincoln explained to Elizabeth Keckley that the Lincolns had just come from a small town in the West, were still poor, could not afford high prices, and that White House patronage would bring distinction and good business. Mrs. Keckley arrived late with the inaugural reception gown; Mrs. Lincoln scolded over the delay, said she would not go to the reception, but was persuaded. The first spring and summer fifteen new dresses were made, and as time passed Mrs. Lincoln felt a rare loyalty and spirit of service in Elizabeth Keckley, giving her trust and confidence not offered to others.

Sister Emilie, widowed by war, received a pass in which her brother-in-law used the word "Confederate," which he so rarely wrote or spoke, writing:

Whom it may concern: It is my wish that Mrs. Emilie T. Helm (widow of the late General B. H. Helm, who fell in the Confederate services), now returning to Kentucky, may have protection of person and property, except as to slaves, of which I say nothing.

A. Lincoln

However, when Emilie refused to take the oath of allegiance to the United States, feeling that it would be treason to her dead husband, her pass would not let her into Kentucky. Lincoln telegraphed the puzzled Federal officer who had her in custody, "Send her to me." So Emilie Todd Helm returned to the White House to live, to write sometimes in a diary: "Sister Mary's tenderness for me is very touching. She and brother Lincoln pet me as if I were a child, and without words, try to comfort me. Sister Mary was sitting in a drooping, despondent attitude as I came across the room to kiss her good morning. The newspaper she had been reading dropped to the floor as she held her arms out to me and said, 'Kiss me, Emilie, and tell me that you love me! I seem to be the scapegoat for both North and South.' Then suddenly she held up her head and smiled, as brother Lincoln's voice came to us, 'I hope you two are planning some mischief.'"

Later in the day he said to Emilie: "Little Sister, I hope you can come up and spend the summer with us at the Soldiers' Home. You and Mary love each other. It is good for her to have you with her. The strain she has been under has been too much for her mental as well as her physical health. What do you think?" Emilie: "She seems nervous and excitable and once or twice when I have come into the room suddenly the frightened look in her eyes has appalled me. I believe if anything should happen to you or Robert or Tad, it would kill her."

Out of repeated visits to spiritualist séances Mrs. Lincoln, for a time, believed in communication with forms of the invisible world and seeing apparitions of the dead. With eyes smiling through tears she came to the room of Emilie one night, spoke of her mother's heart and of Willie: "He lives, Emilie! He comes to me every night and stands at the foot of my bed, with the same sweet, adorable smile he always had."

Away on frequent shopping trips to New York or Philadelphia, she had telegrams from her husband: "Do not come on the night train. It is too cold. Come in the morning." Or: "Your three despatches received. I am very well, and am glad to hear that you and Tad are so." Or the domestic news that he was "tolerably well" and "have not rode out much yet, but have at last got new tires on the carriage wheels, and perhaps shall ride out soon now." Gossip once had it that when they first entered a White House carriage he had grinned. "Well, mother, this is just about the slickest glass hack in town, isn't it?"

Both the country and the White House could be much better managed, according to a letter of Elizabeth Cady Stanton whose tongue on occasion had free rein and no check on it. She wrote from New York City on May 6 of '63 to her cousin Gerrit Smith: "I returned from Washington last evening . . . Henry [her husband] and I had a long talk with Abraham, he told us some good stories, he impressed me as a stronger & better man than I had from his official acts supposed him to be, but I am not in favor of his reëlection. They say Abraham's shrivelled appearance & poor health is owing to being underfed. Madame is an economist & the supplies at the White House are limited. In front of the Mansion she has fenced off a place where she pastures her cow, thus she sacrifices taste to thrift. But the cow is happy, more so probably than any personage connected with this Administration for it is not all peace in Abraham's bosom."

In diary and letters John Hay used the nicknames "Tycoon" and "The Ancient" for Lincoln. Mrs. Lincoln was "Madame," and occasionally the "Hellcat" who could become more "Hell-cattical day by day." The secretaries disbursed some $20,000 a year appropriated to White House uses. They could not always agree with her opinion that wages specified for an unfilled position might be handed to her directly. She questioned whether the Government or the secretaries should pay for the grain of the secretaries' horses in the White House stables. On whether the Marine Band could give a concert on the White House lawn the next day, Mrs. Lincoln penciled a note to Hay: "It is our *especial* desire that the Band does not play in these grounds this Summer. We expect our wishes to be complied with." The two secretaries eventually were to find it more comfortable to move from the White House and lodge at Willard's Hotel.

The boy Tad meant more to Lincoln than anyone else. They were chums. "Often I sat by Tad's father reporting to him about some important matter that I had been ordered to inquire into," wrote Charles A. Dana, "and he would have this boy on his knee; and, while he would perfectly understand the report, the striking thing about him was his affection for the child." Tad usually slept with him, wrote John Hay. Often late at night this boy came to the President's office: "He would lie around until he fell asleep, and Lincoln would shoulder him and take him off to bed."

"Tad" was short for Tadpole, a wriggler, nervous, active, with a defective palate. His occasional "papa dear" sounded more like "pappy day." He could burst into the President's office and call out what he wanted. Or again Tad would give three sharp raps and two slow thumps on the door, three dots and two dashes he had learned over in the war telegraph office. "I've

Executive Mansion
April 2. 1862

My Dear Sir

Allow me to thank you in behalf of my little son for your present of White Rabbits. He is very much pleased with them.

Yours truly

Abraham Lincoln

Michail. Crock Esq
860 N Fourth St. Philada.

Mr. Lincoln thanks Mr. Crock of "Philada" (Philadelphia) for white rabbits presented to Tad. A secretary wrote the note for Lincoln to sign. In any minor matter it was very unusual for him to spell out the name of Abraham. From the Barrett collection.

got to let him in," Lincoln would say, "because I promised never to go back on the code." Once at the telegraph office Tad dipped his fingers into an inkwell, smeared long fingerprints over a marble-topped table. An operator, Buell, took the boy by the collar, marched him at arm's length into the cipher room to face his father; Buell, somewhat embarrassed, pointed through the open door to the smutted table top. Lincoln saw what had been going on, lifted his boy into his arms, walked out of the office saying in a pleasant and even tone, "Come, Tad, Buell is abusing you." Once, carrying Tad, he referred to him as "this colt."

Boston ladies, a party of them, one day admired the velvet carpet, plush upholstery, mahogany furniture, and pompous chandeliers of the East Room. The air was quiet, dignified, as befitted the government Executive Mansion. There was a slam-bang racket, a shrill voice, "Look out there!"—and young Tad came through flourishing a long whip, driving two goats hitched tandem to a kitchen chair. These goats figured in telegrams to Mrs. Lincoln, away with Tad on a visit: "Tell Tad the goats and father are very well, especially the goats." And again in a letter: "Tell dear Tad poor 'Nanny Goat' is lost, and [the housekeeper] and I are in distress about it. The day you left, Nanny was found resting herself and chewing her little cud in the middle of Tad's bed; but now she's gone! The gardener kept complaining that she destroyed the flowers, till it was concluded to bring her down to the White House. This was done, and the second day she had disappeared, and has not been heard of since. This is the last we know of poor 'Nanny.'" Stanton appointed Tad a lieutenant and he swaggered in uniform with sword and belt, signed his name "Col. Tad L." Once the father bribed sick Tad to take medicine, writing a check:

No. 79   Washington, D. C. March 10, 1862
        Pay to "Tad" (when he is well enough to present)
                        or bearer
    Five .... Dollars
    $5.00   A. Lincoln

On a steamer trip Tad broke into the conversation too freely. The father promised the boy a dollar to keep still until Fortress Monroe was reached. "Be a good boy and don't disturb me any more." But the boy forgot, soon was noisy again, and forgetting how noisy he had been, at Fortress Monroe chirped, "Father, I want my dollar." The father asked if the dollar had been earned; the boy was sure it had. A dollar bill passed into Tad's hand with a half-reproachful, "Well, my son, at any rate, I will keep my part of the bargain." Spring blossoms dotted the riverbank, and the President asked Porter, as if a special favor: "Commodore, Tad is very fond of flowers— won't you let a couple of your men take a boat and go with him an hour or two along shore, and gather a few? It will be a great gratification to him."

The boy did things with a rush. "I was once sitting with the President in the library," wrote Brooks, "when Tad tore into the room in search of something, and having found it, he threw himself on his father like a small thunderbolt, gave him one wild, fierce hug, and without a word, fled from the room before his father could put out a hand to detain him." Tutors came and went, Brooks noted. "None stayed long enough to learn much about the boy; but he knew them before they had been one day in the house." Of this the father would say: "Let him run. There's time enough yet for him to learn his letters and get poky." A national fast day had been proclaimed by his father, and Tad made inquiries and got the idea it would be a day when nobody would eat. So he hid food from the dining-room table and from the kitchen, out under the seat of a coach in the carriage house. There a servant cleaning the carriage came on the provisions. Tad looked on, fussed and fumed. The President told of it to Brooks: "If he grows to be a man, Tad will be what the women all dote on—a good provider." Photographed together, Tad stood by his father's side, scanning the pages of a large book. Of this picture, published in many journals, Brooks noted: "Lincoln explained to me that he was afraid that this picture was a species of false pretense. Most people, he thought, would suppose the book a large clasped Bible, whereas it was a big photograph album which the photographer, posing the father and son, had hit upon as a good device to use in this way to bring the two sitters together. Lincoln's anxiety lest somebody should

Let Master Tad have
a Navy sword.
A Lincoln

The President wishes "Master Tad" might have a "Navy sword." From the Barrett collection.

think he was 'making believe read the Bible to Tad,' was illustrative of his scrupulous honesty."

Visiting the navy yard hand in hand with his father, Tad got interested in miniature models. Next day the father wrote: "Captain Dahlgren may let Tad have . . . the little gun that he cannot hurt himself with."

A delegation arrived from Kentucky. For political reasons Lincoln did not want to see them and had held them off. They were half-cursing among themselves about not getting to see "Old Abe." Tad laughed to them, "Do you want to see Old Abe?" They laughed "Yes," and the boy scooted in to his father. "Papa, may I introduce some friends to you?" "Yes, son." And Tad brought in the men whom the President had carefully avoided for a week, introduced them with formality—and the President reached for the boy, took him on his lap, kissed him and told him it was all right and that he had gone through the introductions like a little gentleman. Afterward, as Julia Taft told it, he asked Tad why he called those gentlemen his "friends."

TAD. Well, I had seen them so often, and they looked so good and sorry, and said they were from Kentucky, that I thought they must be our friends.

LINCOLN. That's right, my son, I would have the whole human race your friends and mine, if it were possible.

Managing to get muskets and equipment for the menservants of the White House, Tad drilled them without his father's knowing it. One night he put them all on guard duty, relieving the regular sentries, who accepted orders from the boy lieutenant to go to their quarters. The father laughed when he heard of it, waited till Tad was asleep, and then as Commander in Chief of the Army restored the old order of things.

A paymaster, Samuel Grisson, wrote his wife a brief impression: "The President's son Thaddeus is out pretty often. He is twelve years old and acts rather silly and childish. His governor or gentleman in attending is always with him. One day the boy stood close by me cramming his mouth constantly with handfuls of popped corn."

Of Tad's playmates, Julia Taft and her brother Bud, Julia was small and slight for her sixteen years, wore long curls, flew from one room to another in a ruffled white frock and blue sash. Lincoln called her "Jew-ly," told her she was a "flibbertigibbet," once held a handful of small photographs over her head. "Do you want my picture, Jewly?" She danced on her tiptoes, saying, "Please," and heard, "Give me a kiss and you can have it." The shy girl reached up, he leaned over, and she gave him a peck on the cheek. Into his arms he swept her with, "Now we will pick out a good one." Sometimes he put his hand on top of Julia's head, twisted his fingers and sent her long curls standing out in all directions. As she sat on the family staircase reading, he stooped, kissed her head, and told her to go to the sitting-room to read. She climbed too far out on a window ledge one day to see a regimental band go past. He lifted her inside. "Do you want to break your neck, honey?"

Another girl playing with Lincoln's big heavy watch asked him if it could be broken. "Of course it can't. Why, little girl, you hit it as hard as you can with a bunch of wool and even that won't break it." He asked a little boy some questions the lad enjoyed answering, patted the fellow on the shoulder, and sent him away with the pleasant but puzzling remark in his ears, "Well, you'll be a man before your mother yet."

Charles A. Dana brought his own nine-year-old to a New Year's reception. From a nice corner the girl watched the envoys plenipotentiary in splendorous costumes, army and navy heads in gold and blue and brass, wives and daughters in crinolines curved like Chinese pagoda bells. After this show Dana spoke to Lincoln of his little girl, who wanted to shake hands. Lincoln walked over, took up the girl, kissed her, and talked to her. Dana considered it worth mentioning. Important men of high office usually lacked a natural and easy grace in handling a child. With Lincoln, Dana noticed, the child felt easy, as if in the arms of Santa Claus or at home as with some friendly, shaggy big animal dependable in danger. He played games with Tad's gang on the White House lawn, ran with flying coattails. Boys came to tell him of a cat having kittens, of a new litter of pups and how funny the pups acted and what names should be given them.

Congressman W. D. Kelley brought in a thirteen-year-old powder monkey who had served a year in the gunboat *Ottawa*. The boy's coolness in two sea battles had won him promotion to captain's messenger. Short for his age, wearing sailor-blue pants and shirt, the lad came forward. Lincoln laid down his spectacles, stood up. "Bless me! is that the boy who did so gallantly in those two great battles? Why, I feel I should bow to him and not he to me." The boy made a bow, the President signed papers for him later to go to naval school, then put his hand on the lad's head, told him to go home and "have good fun!" in the coming months, "for they are about the last holiday you will get." Congressman Kelley noted that "the little fellow bowed himself out, feeling that the President of the United States, though a very great man, was one that he would nevertheless like to have a game of romps with."

Robert T. Lincoln, his press nickname "The Prince of Rails," away at Harvard, never saw his father, even during vacations, for more than ten minutes of talk at a time, so he said. Stepping up to his father at one reception and bowing with severe formality, "Good evening, Mr. Lincoln," his father handed Robert a gentle openhanded slap across the face. The two of them in a carriage one day were halted at a street corner by marching troops. "Father was always eager to know which state they came from. And in his eagerness to know from where they hailed, father opened the door and stepping half way out, shouted to a group of workmen standing close

Robert T. Lincoln writes a telegram, his father adding "Charge to me." From the Barrett collection.

by, 'What is that, boys?' meaning where did they come from. One short, little red-haired man fixed him with a withering glance and retorted, 'It's a regiment, you damned old fool.' In a fit of laughter father closed the door, and when his mirth had somewhat subsided, turned to me and said, 'Bob, it does a man good sometimes to hear the truth.' A bit later, somewhat sadly he added, 'And sometimes I think that's just what I am, a damned old fool.'"
A young friend of Bob's failed to pass the entrance examinations at Harvard, and Bob's father took it to heart, wrote a letter:

"I have scarcely felt greater pain in my life than learning yesterday from Bob's letter, that you had failed to enter Harvard College. And yet there is very little in it, if you will allow no feeling of *discouragement* to seize, and prey upon you. It is a *certain* truth, that you *can* enter, and graduate in, Harvard College; and having made the attempt, you *must* succeed in it. *Must* is the word. I know not how to aid you, save in the assurance of one of mature age, and much severe experience, that you *can* not fail, if you resolutely determine that you *will* not. . . . Always bear in mind that your resolution to succeed is more important than any other thing." Another cub was Cadet Quintin Campbell at West Point, whose mother, Mrs. Ann Campbell, was a cousin of Mrs. Lincoln, and a daughter of former Chief Justice Todd of Missouri. To Quintin in June of '62 after the collapse of the bloody Peninsular campaign, the President wrote:

"Your good mother tells me you are feeling very badly in your new situation. Allow me to assure you it is a perfect certainty that you will very soon feel better—quite happy—if you only stick to the resolution you have taken to procure a military education. I am older than you, have felt badly myself, and *know* what I tell you is true. Adhere to your purpose and you will soon feel as well as you ever did. On the contrary, if you falter, and give up, you will lose the power to keep any resolution, and will regret it all your life. Take the advice of a friend who, though he never saw you, deeply sympathizes with you, and stick to your purpose."

Mrs. Lincoln's afternoon receptions and the President's public levees were held regularly during the winters. Usually twice a week, on Tuesday evenings at so-called dress receptions and on Saturday evenings at a less formal function, the President met all who came. "A majority of the visitors went in full dress," wrote Noah Brooks, "the ladies in laces, feathers, silks, and satins, without bonnets; and the gentlemen in evening dress. But sprinkled through the gaily attired crowds were hundreds of officers and private soldiers, the light blue army coat being conspicuous. Here and there a day-laborer, looking as though he had just left his work-bench, or a hard-working clerk with ink-stained linen, added to the popular character of the assembly. Usually the President stood in the famous Blue Room, or at the head of the East Room; and those who wished to shake hands made their entrance, one by one, and were introduced by a functionary.

"So vast were the crowds, and so affectionate their greetings, that Mr. Lincoln's right hand was often so swollen that he would be unable to use it readily for hours afterward. The white kid glove of his right hand, when the operation of handshaking was over, always looked as if it had been dragged through a dust-bin."

Much of the time the President went through the handshaking absent-mindedly: "His thoughts were apt to be far from the crowds of strangers that passed before him. On one occasion, bringing up a friend, I greeted the President as usual and presented my friend. The President shook hands with me in a perfunctory way, his eyes fixed on space, and I passed on, knowing that he had never seen me nor heard the name of my friend; but after I had reached a point seven or eight persons beyond, the President suddenly seemed to see me, and, continuing the handshaking of strangers while he spoke, shouted out, 'Oh, Brooks! Charley Maltby is in town, and I want you to come and see me to-morrow.' " Maltby of California was up for a Federal appointment; the President wished a little talk with Brooks about some phase of it, and in conveying the wish astonished all within earshot. The informal-ity of the President, his amusement at formality, were given to the country in a paragraph much reprinted from the *New York Evening Post*:

A man from New York telling of an interview he had with the President: "How are you?" said the President. "I saw your card but did not see you. I was glad, how-ever, you carded me and I was reminded of an anecdote of Mr. Whittlesey. When one young man first came to work here, Mr. Whittlesey said to him, 'Sir, have you carded the Senators?' 'No, sir, I thought I would curry favor first and then comb them.' 'It's no joking matter,' said Whittlesey seriously. 'It is your duty to card the Senators and it is customary to card the Cabinet also and you ought to do it, sir. But,' he added after a moment's thought, 'I think I am wrong. The Cabinet may card you.' "

A letter was put into Lincoln's hand as he came out on the White House portico one day. While he stood reading it, near by a plain farmer with wife and two little boys stood frozen to their foot tracks a few moments, the farmer saying, "Sh-h—there is the President!" Leaving his family, the farmer walked a half-circle around Lincoln, keeping a fixed eye on the President. Finally, he came up to shake hands, asked if his wife and boys could shake hands too. The bashful boys shrank toward their mother as Lincoln reached down toward them. "The Lord is with you," the farmer solemnly intoned, adding with emphasis, "and the people too, sir, the people too!"

"Great men have various estimates," thought Lincoln—and told of Daniel Webster visiting Springfield amid pomp and processions and a small boy saying to another, "The biggest man in the world is coming." The two lads met later. "Did you see him?" "Ye-es, but laws—he ain't half as big as old G——," meaning the biggest fat man in town.

In some weeks of the summer of '63 the President's health brought worry. "The cares and responsibilities of his office are adversely telling upon the health of the President," wrote the *New York Evening Post* correspond-ent. "He looks thin and feeble, and his eyes have lost their humorous expres-sion. His friends entertain much solicitude about his health and have endeav-ored to persuade him to leave Washington to recuperate, but, so far, the pilot sticks to his helm, and does not seem disposed to leave it so long as he has strength to hold it." The siege of Vicksburg, and what the fleet might yet do at Charleston, were troubling him when he met Admiral Dahlgren one day. He wondered how "any sensible man" could favor taking Vicksburg by canal-digging. As to Charleston, they were asking for one ironclad after another and he leveled a couple of jokes at them. "He feared the favorable state of public expectation would pass away before anything could be done," wrote Dahlgren. "Poor gentleman! How thin and wasted he is!"

The query came, Why not take a vacation and rest? "I sincerely wish war was a pleasanter and easier business than it is, but it does not admit of holidays." At his desk one day his casual word on the hour was, "I wish George Washington or some of the old patriots were here in my place so that I could have a little rest."

Outside the White House a tall volunteer held out a brawny hand with, "I'm from Indianny!"

Lincoln, shaking hands: "So am I. I almost wish I was back there again."

"That's jest what I was a-wishin' myself, but instid of that I've got to go back to camp. Ain't they a-workin' of ye pretty hard, Mr. Lincoln?"

"I reckon they are."

"Well, now, some of us boys was a-sayin' so. You'd better take right smart good keer of yerself. There isn't anybody else, lyin' round loose, that'd fit into your boots jest now."

Noah Brooks, somewhat scholar and dreamer, a failure as merchant in Illinois and farmer in Kansas, correspondent of the *Sacramento Union*, writing under the pen name of "Castine" news letters widely reprinted on the West Coast, often had close touch with Lincoln, and wrote of one phase: "He was cordial and affable, and his simple-hearted manners made a strong impression upon those who saw him for the first time. I have known impressionable women, touched by his sad face and his gentle bearing, to go away in tears. Once I found him sitting in his chair so collapsed and weary that he did not look up or speak when I addressed him. He put out his hand, mechanically, as if to shake hands, when I told him I had come at his bidding. It was several minutes before he was roused enough to say that he 'had had a hard day.'"

In one news letter the third year of the war Noah Brooks wrote, "The President is affable and kind, but his immediate subordinates are snobby and unpopular." What Nicolay and Hay had done to him, and why he disliked them, Brooks didn't say beyond writing, "These secretaries are young men, and the least said of them the better, perhaps."

The affection of the President for Noah Brooks steadily grew. Their friendship wore well. Brooks wrote a genuine personal adoration in one news letter. "No man living has a kinder heart or a more honest purpose than Abraham Lincoln, and all who meet him go away thoroughly impressed with the preponderance of those two lovable and noble traits of his character. . . . Is it not wonderful that so little that is open to criticism is done by him, rather than that we have anything to find fault with? . . . While the most enthusiastic admirer of Lincoln would reluct to claim for him a combination of all the endowments and acquirements of his predecessors in office, it does appear to me that it is impossible to designate any man in public life whose character and antecedents would warrant us in the belief that we have anyone now living whose talents and abilities would fit him to administer this Government better than it has been conducted through the past stormy years by the honesty, patriotism, and far-sighted sagacity of Abraham Lincoln. That is merely an opinion, to be sure, but it is not an unintelligent one, and the writer hereof shares it in common with a great

The Soldiers' Home

cloud of candid witnesses." This was, in part, Brooks's way of saying that he was tired of the mudslinging.

Of Mrs. Lincoln, Brooks wrote that he could not refrain "from saying a word in strict justice to this distinguished and accomplished woman." Scandalous stories, slanders innumerable, he had heard of her and the President's family, from "loyal people, more shame to them, not knowing the truth of what they repeat. . . . Shame upon these he-gossips and envious retailers of small slanders. Mrs. Lincoln, I am glad to be able to say from personal knowledge, is a true American woman." Brooks dealt with no specific instances, filed his protest and rebuke of the cruel male gossips: "They would resent as an insult to their wives, sisters or mothers that which they so glibly repeat concerning the first lady in the land."

Out at the Soldiers' Home, three miles from the White House, were trees and cool shade, long sweeps of grassy land. In its five hundred acres were drives that overlooked the city, the Potomac, and wide landscapes. Here were catbirds, blackbirds, wrens, the whistling fox sparrow, the orchard starling in the forenoon, and thrushes at all hours of the day. The black-throated bunting poured out its musical notes, which John Burroughs

recorded as sounding like *fscp fscp, fee fee fee*. Burroughs found too hepat-
ica, anemone, arbutus, bloodroot, water cress, buttercups, and on a hill slope
the bird's-foot violet.

In the birds and the flowers Lincoln had only a passing interest. But
there were trees—oak, chestnut, and beech—maple and cypress and cedar—
and they gave rest and companionship. He was still a kinsman of these
growths that struggled out of the ground and sprawled and spread against
the sky and kept their rootholds till storm, disaster, or time and age brought
them down. (A major bowed good morning to him amid trees on the White
House grounds: "I was just looking for a few horse chestnuts." "Horse
chestnuts!" hooted Lincoln. "Do you expect to find horse chestnuts under
a sycamore tree?") He strolled of an evening over to the camp of the guard
company, saluting sentries, calling men Joe, Dick, and Tom, once sitting on
a campstool and eating a plate of beans, another time calling, "That coffee
smells good, boys, give me a cup." Browning noted of June 30, 1862:

"In the evening went out to Soldiers Home with Mr & Mrs Dorman
of Florida. The President got home soon after we reached there. He asked

The President's Cottage at the Soldiers' Home

me to sit down with him on the stone steps of the portico—then took from
his pocket a map of Virginia and pointed out to me the situation of army
before Richmond, and gave me all the news he had from there He then
took from his pocket a copy of Hallack's [sic] poems, and read to me
about a dozen stanzas concluding the poem of Fanny. The song at the end
of the poem he read with great pathos, pausing to comment upon them, and
then laughed immoderately at the ludicrous conclusion"

On the way to the Soldiers' Home the Lincoln carriage passed through a city where one traveler had commented that everything worth looking at seemed unfinished. New York was still the capital to many New Yorkers, likewise Boston to the Yankees, New Orleans to the Southwesterners, Chicago to the Midwestern men. The War between the States might decide whether Washington was truly to be a great national capital. Forts bristled from encircling hilltops. In March of '63 the public grounds around the unfinished Washington Monument held droves of cattle, 10,000 beeves on the hoof. Soldiers in field garb were at gateways and doors. Shed hospitals covered acres in the outlying suburbs; one of the better they named the Lincoln Hospital.

Into churches, museums, art galleries, public offices, and private mansions had been carried the wounded and dying of the Union armies. Mrs. John A. Logan wrote: "The noisy rumblings of the army wagon disturbed every hour of the day and night. The rattle of the anguish-laden ambulance, the piercing cries of the sufferers it carried, made morning, noon and night, too dreadful to portray. The streets were filled with marching troops, with new regiments, their hearts strong and eager, their virgin banners all untarnished as they marched up Pennsylvania Avenue, playing 'The Girl I Left Behind Me' as if they came to holiday glory—and to easy victory. Every moment had its drumbeat, every hour was alive with the tramp of troops going, coming."

And the passing months saw more and more of wooden-legged men, of men with empty sleeves, of men on crutches or men wearing slings and bandages, of footsore and sunburnt men who slouched or languished; some of them had fought hard and long under torn and shot banners.

From a population of 60,000 the city had gone above 200,000. Among the newcomers were contractors, freed Negroes, blockade-runners, traders, sutlers, office-seekers, elocutionists, gamblers, keepers of concert saloons with waiter girls, liquor dealers, card-writers who put names into Spencerian script, candy-criers, umbrella-menders, circus men and women, organ-grinders and monkeys, vagabonds with performing bears, thimbleriggers who offered to bet as to which of three thimbles a manipulated pea was under, embalmers, undertakers, manufacturers of artificial limbs, patent-medicine peddlers, receivers of stolen goods, pickpockets, burglars, sneak thieves. Of the new arrivals of footloose women it was noted they ranged "from dashing courtesans who entertained in brownstone fronts to drunken creatures summarily ejected from army camps." With the influx of population had come a large trade in nameless brands of whisky; many locked up by the police for minor infractions of law, disorderly conduct, or assault and battery, said the Washington whisky made them crazy.

"Houses of ill fame are scattered all through the city," wrote one observer. "With rare exceptions, however, they have not yet ventured to intrude into respectable neighborhoods. A few of these houses are superbly furnished, and are conducted in the most magnificent style. The women are either young, or in the prime of life, and are frequently beautiful and accomplished. They come from all parts of the country, and they rarely

return more than two seasons in succession, for their life soon breaks down
their beauty. The majority of the 'patrons' of the better class houses are men
of nominal respectability, men high in public life, officers of the army and
navy, Governors of States, lawyers, doctors, and the very best class of the
city population. Some come under the influence of liquor, others in cool
blood. They come openly, too, and exchange greetings with each other,
and go away and talk eloquently about morality and virtue. A proprietress
of one of these houses boasts that 'it would be impossible to carry on the
Government without her aid.' Besides the better class houses there are a
number of a character ranging from a bagnio to a dance-house."

Beer, whisky, performances of nude or scantily dressed women, brought
many a farm boy with his payday greenbacks into saloon concert halls where
he was drugged to awake on the streets with empty pockets. Into his drinks
someone had slipped "knockout drops." At intervals the lower grade of
houses were raided by police or provost marshals in the interest of having
more men and officers present at regimental roll calls. One of the larger
raids had netted sixty officers and men, who were locked up in the guard-
house.

Yet it wasn't bad, cheap whisky at the source of the matter, for the
Washington correspondent of the New York *Independent* wrote one day in
'63: "In broad daylight a few days ago, in front of the Presidential mansion,
was a sight. A woman clad in the richest and most fashionable garments,
with diamonds flashing from her slender fingers, sat upon the stone balus-
trade, unable to proceed on her homeward walk without betraying herself.
At last she rose and started on, swaying to and fro, and soon rested again,
unable to proceed. The carriage of a foreign minister passed, stopped, took
in the lady, and carried her to her luxurious home. For the lady is wealthy,
occupies a high social position, but she was drunk in the streets of Washington. Drunkenness is a vice that, above all others, cripples the army. The
poor soldier drinks, gets drunk, and is punished for it. The officer does the
same and is not even reprimanded. The War Department is making every
effort to prevent intoxicating liquors from the common soldiers, but why
does it not prohibit drinking among the officers? One half of the Brigadier-
Generals now on pay know far better how to swallow prodigious quantities
of whiskey, than to manage a brigade of troops upon a field of battle."

The high-class gambling-houses, located mostly on Pennsylvania Avenue,
were carpeted, gilded, frescoed, garnished with paintings and statuary. Faro
and poker were the principal games. At the four leading establishments introductions were necessary, and in these rooms could be found governors,
members of Congress, department officials, clerks, contractors, paymasters.
In one place was the tradition of a Congressman who broke the bank in a
single night's play, winning over $100,000. From these upper-class haunts
the gambling-places shaded off into all styles, ending at the bottom, where
smooth-spoken women plied the young infantrymen with drink and played
them out of their last payday greenbacks. Colonel La Fayette C. Baker

reported to Stanton in the summer of '63 that 163 gaming-houses in full blast required attention.

Of the gawdy and bawdy features of Washington, John Hay wrote in a letter, "This miserable sprawling village imagines itself a city because it is wicked, as a boy thinks he is a man when he smokes and swears." One diary entry of Hay in the summer of '63 gave a picture: "I rode out to Soldiers' Home with the Tycoon tonight. . . . . Had a talk on philology for which the T. has a little indulged inclination. Rode home in the dark amid a party of drunken gamblers & harlots returning in the twilight from [erased]."

Willard's Hotel could more justly be called the center of Washington and the Union than either the Capitol, the White House, or the State Department, according to Nathaniel Hawthorne, the novelist. "Everybody may be seen there," he wrote, finding men of business and all manner of loafers. "You exchange nods with governors of sovereign States; you elbow illustrious men, and tread on the toes of generals; you hear statesmen and orators speaking in their familiar tones. You are mixed up with office-seekers, wire pullers, inventors, artists, poets, editors, army correspondents, attachés of foreign journals, long-winded talkers, clerks, diplomatists, mail contractors, railway directors, until your own identity is lost among them. You adopt the universal habit of the place, and call for a mint-julep, a whiskey-skin, a gin-cocktail, a brandy-smash, or a glass of pure Old Rye; at any hour all these drinks are in request."

As the author of *The Scarlet Letter, The House of Seven Gables,* and *The Marble Faun* drank and scanned the crowd at Willard's he estimated two-thirds of the guests and idlers wore military garb. "Many of them, no doubt, were self-commissioned officers, and had put on the buttons and the shoulder-straps, merely because captain is a good traveling name. The majority, however, had been duly appointed by the President, but might be none the better warriors for that." On how many had treasonable sympathies and wishes he mused: "Traitors there were among them, no doubt of that, civil servants of the public, who yet deserved to dangle from a cord; or men who buttoned military coats over their breasts, hiding perilous secrets there, which might bring the gallant officer to stand pale-faced before a file of musketeers, with his open grave behind him."

One idea kept coming back to Hawthorne. Even with the war ended and the army melted back into its homes, he could see military men running the nation for fifty years after. "Every country neighborhood will have its general or two, its three or four colonels, half a dozen majors, and captains without end—besides non-commissioned officers and privates, more than the recruiting offices ever knew of. Military merit, or rather military notoriety, will be the measure of all claims to civil distinction. One bullet-headed general will succeed another in the Presidential chair; and veterans will hold the offices at home and abroad, and sit in Congress and the State legislatures, and fill all the avenues of public life." He did not say this deprecatingly. "Very likely, it may substitute something more real and genuine, instead of the many shams on which men have heretofore founded their claims to public regard; but it behooves civilians to consider their wretched prospects in the future, and assume the military button before it is too late."

In his carriage on the way to the Soldiers' Home or in the incessant stream of callers at the White House, Lincoln saw these pieces and pawns of the human motley. Hawthorne had called to see the President and was interested rather than impressed. Not so with the loafer, the lazy, dreaming Walt Whitman, author of *Leaves of Grass,* prophet of the Average Man, crier of America as the greatest country in the world—in the making. He wrote in a diary: "Called at the President's house on John Hay. Saw Mr. Lincoln standing, talking with a gentleman, apparently a dear friend. His face and manner have an expression inexpressibly sweet—one hand on his friend's shoulder, the other holding his hand. I love the President personally."

In a letter to Mrs. Abby Price, Whitman wrote, "I believe fully in Lincoln—few know the rocks and quicksands he has to steer through." Yet Whitman never tried to break in and get to the President for an interview, easy as it would have been through his knowing John Hay, who knew him and his poetry, though not rating the poetry high. And John Hay once arranged transportation for Whitman so that the poet could go to his home in New York and vote the Union ticket at a time when ballots counted, Hay's diary saying: "I went down to Willard's today & got from Palmer . . . a free ticket to New York and back for Walt. Whitman, the poet, who is going to New York to electioneer and vote for the Union ticket."

Lincoln's attraction for Whitman stood forth in a letter on Washington in the Hot Season which he wrote to the *New York Times* in the summer of '63: "I see the President almost every day, as I happen to live where he passes to or from his lodgings out of town, three miles north. I saw him this morning about 8½ coming in to business, riding on Vermont-avenue, near L street. He always has a company of twenty-five or thirty cavalry, with sabres drawn, and held upright over their shoulders. The party makes no great show in uniforms or horses. Mr. Lincoln generally rides a good-sized easy-going gray horse, is dress'd in plain black, somewhat rusty and dusty; wears a black stiff hat, and looks about as ordinary in attire, &c., as the commonest man. A lieutenant, with yellow straps, rides at his left, and following behind, two by two, come the cavalrymen in their yellow-striped jackets. They are generally going at a slow trot, as that is the pace set them by the dignitary they wait upon. The sabres and accoutrements clank, and the entirely unornamental *cortège* trots slowly toward Lafayette-square. It arouses no sensation, only some curious stranger stops and gazes.

"I saw very plainly the President's dark brown face, with the deep cut lines, the eyes, &c., always to me with a deep latent sadness in the expression. Sometimes the President comes and goes in an open barouche. The cavalry always accompany him, with drawn sabres. Often I notice as he goes out evenings, and sometimes in the morning, when he returns early, he turns off and halts at the large and handsome residence of the Secretary of War, on K-Street, and holds conference there. If in his barouche, I can see from my window he does not alight, but sits in the vehicle, and Mr. Stanton comes out to attend him. Sometimes one of his sons, a boy of ten or twelve, accompanies him, riding at his right on a pony.

"Earlier in the summer you might have seen the President and his wife, toward the latter part of the afternoon, out in a barouche, on a pleasure ride through the city. Mrs. Lincoln was dressed in complete black, with a long crape veil. The equipage is of the plainest kind, only two horses, and they nothing extra. They pass'd me once very close, and I saw the President in the face fully, as they were moving slow, and his look, though abstracted, happen'd to be directed steadily in my eye. I noticed well the expression I have alluded to. None of the artists have caught the deep, though subtle and indirect expression of this man's face. They have only caught the surface. There is something else there. One of the great portrait painters of two or three centuries ago is needed."

Thus the poet wrote his most sober impressions of Lincoln while giving the *New York Times* readers a variety of other jottings, including one: "I regret to say that I doubt very much whether there is *any* good lager in Washington."

Undersized, with graying whiskers, Quaker-blooded, softhearted, sentimental, a little crazy, this Walt Whitman sang to the war years, "Rise O days, from your fathomless deeps," proclaimed to Manhattan that once he had chanted peace but now "War, red war is my song through your streets, O city!" His dithyrambic recruiting-piece in *Harper's Weekly* opened:

> Beat! beat! drums!—blow! bugles! blow!
> Through the windows—through doors—burst like a ruthless force,
> Into the solemn church and scatter the congregation,
> Into the school where the scholar is studying;
> Leave not the bridegroom quiet—no happiness must he have now with his bride;
> Nor the peaceful farmer any peace, ploughing his field or gathering his grain,
> So fierce you whirr and pound you drums—so shrill you bugles blow.

This poet had gone to the Fredericksburg scene after the battle, with small funds raised among kindhearted people, carrying tobacco, oranges, apples, reading matter, for the sick and wounded. He saw the mutilated and languishing on blankets laid on the bare frozen ground, lucky if layers of pine or dry leaves were between the blanket and the hard clay. "No cots; seldom a mattress," he wrote. "I go around from one case to another. I do not see that I do much good to these wounded and dying; but I can not leave them. Once in a while some youngster holds on to me convulsively, and I do what I can for him . . . sit near him for hours if he wishes it."

Hearing the screams of men lifted into ambulances, among the cases of diarrhea, pneumonia, fever, typhoid, amid the cripples, among "the agonized and damned," he said they had met terrible human tests, and noted: "Here I see, not at intervals, but quite always, how certain man, our American man—how he holds himself cool and unquestioned master above all pains and bloody mutilations. What frightened us all so long? Why! it is

Willie and Tad Lincoln with Major Lockwood Todd

William ("Willie") Wallace Lincoln

From the Meserve collection

Julia ("Julie") Taft Bayne at sixteen

Halsey Cook ("Holly") Taft, at eight
Horatio Nelson ("Bud") Taft, Jr., at eleven

WHITE HOUSE PLAYMATES

From *Tad Lincoln's Father* by Julia Taft Bayne (Little, Brown and Company)

The earliest known photograph

The boy has grown

From the Barrett collection

The War Department gave him a sword, a uniform, and a colonel's commission

From the U. S. Army Signal Corps

From the Barrett collection

THOMAS TODD ("TAD") LINCOLN, CHUM, PLAYMATE, AND MOST
BELOVED COMPANION OF HIS FATHER

put to flight with ignominy—a mere stuffed scarecrow of the fields. Oh death where is thy sting?"

In soft weather one moonlit February night Whitman sauntered over Washington: "Tonight took a long look at the President's house. The white portico—the palace-like, tall, round, columns, spotless as snow—the tender and soft moonlight, flooding the pale marble—everywhere a hazy, thin, blue moonlace, hanging in the air—the White House of future poems, and of dreams and dramas, there in the soft and copious moon—the gorgeous front, in the trees under the lustrous flooding moon, full of reality, full of illusion, —the White House of the land, of beauty and night—sentries at the gates, by the portico, silent, pacing there in blue overcoats." Another evening he went to the foot of Sixth Street and saw two boatloads of wounded from Chancellorsville put off during a heavy downpour, to lie in torchlight with the rain on their faces and blankets till ambulances should arrive in an hour or two hours at the wharves. "The men make little or no ado, whatever their sufferings."

Whitman with the passing months felt a deepening faith in the gifts and the face of Lincoln. A letter for two boys in New York went from him in March of '63, noting that Congress had "much gab, plenty of low business talent, but no masterful man," which was probably best so, he believed. And "I think well of the President. He has a face like a Hoosier Michael Angelo, so awful ugly it becomes beautiful, with its strange mouth, its deep cut, criss-cross lines, and its doughnut complexion. My notion is, too, that underneath his outside smutched manner, and stories from third-class county bar rooms (it is his humor), Mr. Lincoln keeps a fountain of first class practical telling wisdom. I do not dwell on the supposed failures of his government; he has shown I sometimes think an almost supernatural tact in keeping the ship afloat at all, with head steady, not only not going down and now certain not to, but with proud and resolute spirit, and flag flying in sight of the world, menacing and high as ever. I say never yet Captain, never ruler, had such a perplexing dangerous task as his the past two years. I more and more rely upon his idiomatic western genius careless of court dress or court decorum."

Lincoln's health was up and down, often depending on the state of the country and the war. On one of the darkest days, however, Donn Piatt heard him say to General Schenck, "I enjoy my rations and sleep the sleep of the just." Piatt saw a tough physical fiber back of "the hard, angular, coarse face" of Lincoln, and put his decisive viewpoint: "A man of delicate mould and sympathetic nature, such as Chase or Seward, would have broken down, not from overwork, although that was terrible, but from the over-anxiety that kills; Lincoln had none of this."

Occasionally word came to Lincoln of persons saying that as to looks he was "hard-favored." James B. Fry, provost marshal general, sketched the President physically: "His feet, hanging loosely to his ankles, were prominent objects; but his hands were more conspicuous even than his feet—due perhaps to the fact that ceremony at times compelled him to clothe them in white kid gloves which always fitted loosely. Both in the height of conversation and in the depth of reflection his hand now and then ran over or supported his head, giving his hair habitually a disordered aspect. I never saw him when he appeared to me otherwise than a great man and a very ugly one. His expression in repose was sad and dull; but his ever recurring humor, at short intervals, flashed forth with brilliancy."

Of the same drift was Congressman George Ashmun's remark in a public address: "You may not say he is the handsomest man in the world, but we did not nominate him for ball-room purposes." General Viele, who had profound admiration for Lincoln, summarized his personal impressions from living several days on the revenue cutter *Miami* with Lincoln, and seeing him at many other times: "Physically, as everyone knows, Mr. Lincoln was not a prepossessing man, with scarcely a redeeming feature, save his benignant eye, which was the very symbol of human kindness." One Englishman wrote of his meeting "two bright dreamy eyes that seem to gaze through you without looking at you." Hay said of Lincoln's gaze at one suspicious character, "He looked through him to the buttons on the back of his coat."

The conventional, educated Englishman sketched the Lincoln exterior when Russell, the London *Times* correspondent, wrote: "There entered, with a shambling, loose, irregular, almost unsteady gait, a tall, lank, lean man, considerably over six feet in height, with stooping shoulders, long pendulous arms, terminating in hands of extraordinary dimensions, which, however, were far exceeded in proportion by his feet." Russell had no doubt his picture was correct, though the sculptor Thomas D. Jones saw Lincoln as a panther-sinewed wrestler, "an athlete of the first order . . . spare, bony, lean, muscular." To some who saw him stand or walk Lincoln seemed in a degree clumsy, at a disadvantage with his arms and legs getting in his way or his lengthy bodily frame being an instrument he could not manage with ease and grace. A Philadelphian found him unlike most very tall men, "lithe and agile, quick in all his movements and gestures," yet this same friendly observer commented: "Unfortunately for his personal appearance his great height makes his lankness appear to be excessive; he has by no means been studious of the graces; his bearing is not attractive." Nicolay registered his point that this was not on account of any disproportion in figure but "the general western habit of an easy-going, loose-jointed manner of walking—a manner necessarily acquired by the pioneers in their forest life, where their paths over logs and stones made impossible the stiff, upright carriage of men on the unobstructed pavements of cities."

No child shrank from his presence, it was noticed, and the little ones enjoyed him as they might a trusted horse. His face lighted when a little girl walked away after he had bent and kissed her, calling out, "Why, he is only a man after all!" And he knew what was in the heart of another he took on his lap in his office; as he chatted with her she called to her father, "Oh, Pa! he isn't ugly at all; he's just beautiful!" And he gathered the intent of the old woman who came with Thaddeus Stevens seeking pardon for her boy court-martialed and sentenced to be shot at sunrise. Her story told, Lincoln turned to hear Stevens say, "I should have no hesitation in granting a pardon." Leaving with the precious paper she had prayed for, she broke out in a loud voice, "I knew it was a Copperhead lie." Stevens asked to what she was referring. "Why, they told me he was an ugly-looking man. He is the handsomest man I ever saw in my life."

A Congressman on urgent business entered a room to see Lincoln lathered for a shave and had the greeting, "I hope I don't scare you; I look frightful enough by nature without the addition of this lather." John Lothrop Motley, historian and Minister to Austria, wrote to his wife: "We went to the White House, in order to fall upon Abraham's bosom. I found the President better- and younger-looking than his pictures. He is very dark and swarthy, and gives me the idea of a very honest, confiding, unsophisticated man, whose sincerity of purpose cannot be doubted. . . . Went with Seward in the evening to see the President. He looks less haggard than the pictures. His conversation was commonplace enough, except when he observed 'Scott will not let us outsiders know anything of his plans.'"

One sketch of Lincoln by Russell ran: "He was dressed in an ill-fitting, wrinkled suit of black, which put one in mind of an undertaker's uniform at a funeral; round his neck a rope of black silk was knotted in a large bulb, with flying ends projecting beyond the collar of his coat; his turned-down shirt-collar disclosed a sinewy muscular yellow neck, and above that, nestling in a great black mass of hair, bristling and compact like a ruff of mourning pine, rose the strange quaint face and head, covered with its thatch of wild republican hair, of President Lincoln. The impression produced by the size of his extremities, and by his flapping and wide projecting ears, may be removed by the appearance of kindliness, sagacity, and the awkward bonhommie of his face; the mouth is absolutely prodigious; the lips, straggling and extending almost from one line of black beard to the other, are only kept in order by two deep furrows from the nostril to the chin; the nose itself— a prominent organ—stands out from the face, with an inquiring, anxious air, as though it were sniffing for some good thing in the wind; the eyes dark, full, and deeply set, are penetrating, but full of an expression which almost amounts to tenderness; and above them projects the shaggy brow, running into the small hard frontal space, the development of which can scarcely be estimated accurately, owing to the irregular flocks of thick hair carelessly brushed across it."

Thus one English journalist. Still another Londoner, who wrote pieces for *Once a Week*, achieved a different portrait: "Abraham Lincoln is a gaunt giant more than six feet high, strong and long-limbed. He walks slow, and, like many thoughtful men (Wordsworth and Napoleon, for example), keeps his head inclined forward and downward. His hair is wiry black, his eyes dark gray; his smile is frank, sincere and winning. Like most American gentlemen, he is loose and careless in dress, turns down his flapping white collars, and wears habitually what we call evening dress. His head is massive, his brow full and wide, his nose large and fleshy, his mouth coarse and full; his eyes are sunken, his bronzed face is thin, and drawn down into strong corded lines, that disclose the machinery that moves the broad jaw. This is the great leader of the Republican party—Abolitionist—terror of the Democrats—an honest old lawyer, with face half Roman, half Indian, wasted by climate, scarred by a life's struggle."

Round the world to the readers of that molder and register of British upper-class opinion, the London *Times*, had gone Russell's plain-spoken account: "A person who met Mr. Lincoln in the street would not take him to be what—according to the usages of European society—is called a 'gentleman'; and, indeed, since I came to the United States, I have heard more disparaging allusions made by Americans to him on that account than I could have expected among simple republicans, where all should be equals; but, at the same time, it would not be possible for the most indifferent observer to pass him in the street without notice." Russell would read character by a mouth. "One would say that, although the mouth was made to enjoy a joke, it could also utter the severest sentence which the head could dictate, but that Mr. Lincoln would be ever more willing to temper justice with mercy, and to enjoy what he considers the amenities of life, than to take a harsh view of men's nature and of the world, and to estimate things in an ascetic or puritan spirit."

Still another Englishman, Edward Dicey, author of *Cavour: A Memoir*, and *Rome in 1860*, a special correspondent for *Macmillan's Magazine* and the *Spectator*, set forth his personal impression of the physical and vocal Lincoln, confessing to begin with, "His aspect, once seen, cannot easily be forgotten," admitting withal: "If you take the stock English caricature of the typical Yankee, you have the likeness of the President." Then came Dicey's sketch published in English periodicals, printed in '63 in a two-volume work titled *Six Months in the Federal States*, and reprinted in a number of American newspapers. It read:

"To say that he is ugly is nothing; to add that his figure is grotesque is to convey no adequate impression. Fancy a man six-foot high, and then *out of* proportion, with long bony arms and legs, which, somehow, seem to be always in the way, with large rugged hands, which grasp you like a vice when shaking yours, with a long scraggy neck, and a chest too narrow for the great arms by its side; add to this figure a head cocoa-nut shaped and somewhat too small for such a stature, covered with rough, uncombed and uncombable lank dark hair, that stands out in every direction at once; a face furrowed, wrinkled, and indented, as though it had been scarred by vitriol; a high narrow forehead; and, sunk deep beneath bushy eyebrows, two bright, somewhat dreamy eyes that seem to gaze through you without looking at you; a few irregular blotches of black bristly hair in the place where beard and whiskers ought to grow; a close-set, thin-lipped, stern mouth, with two rows of large white teeth, and a nose and ears, which have been taken by mistake from a head of twice the size.

"Clothe this figure, then, in a long, tight, badly-fitting suit of black, creased, soiled and puckered up at every salient point of the figure—and every point of this figure is salient—put on large, ill-fitting boots, gloves too long for the long bony fingers, and a fluffy hat, covered to the top with dusty, puffy crape; and then add to all this an air of strength, physical as well as moral, and a strange look of dignity coupled with all this grotesqueness, and you will have the impression left upon me by Abraham Lincoln."

Before and after gathering this impression from a personal meeting with Lincoln, Dicey had heard much talk. He found that in America the tongues of men ran freely and merrily in matters that in England were held in a discreet reserve. "I was many times in the company of men holding high official positions in Washington, when strangers, not only to myself, but to most of the gentlemen in whose company I was, happened to be present, and yet the conversation was as unguarded as if we had all been friends. . . . Gossip is an institution of the country. Before you have been a week in Washington, you may learn the private history, friendships, and antipathies of every public man in the place, if you choose to listen to the talk you hear around you. With regard to the President himself, everybody spoke with an almost brutal frankness.

"Politically, at that time [latter '62] Abraham Lincoln was regarded as a failure. Why he, individually, was elected, or rather, selected, nobody, to this day, seems to know. One thing is certain, amidst many uncertainties, that the North had no belief that his election would lead to the secession movement. Had this belief been entertained, a very different man would have been chosen for the post. Whether, under such circumstances, a Republican candidate would have been chosen at all is doubtful, but there is no doubt that Lincoln would not have been the man."

Dicey in these widely published views gave conclusions arrived at from talks with hundreds of persons in nearly all of the Northern and Border States, on a trip which took him west of the Mississippi and from Canada to Tennessee. "The North desired to make a protest, and the name of Lincoln was as good a one to protest in as any other. It was for his negative, not his positive qualities that he was chosen, and the wonder is, that his positive merits have turned out as decided as they have done. A shrewd, hard-headed, self-educated man, with sense enough to perceive his own deficiencies, but without the instinctive genius which supplies the place of learning, he is influenced by men whom he sees through, but yet cannot detect. 'An honest man' may be 'the noblest work of God,' but he is not the noblest product of humanity, and when you have called the President 'honest Abe Lincoln,' according to the favourite phrase of the American press, you have said a great deal, doubtless, but you have also said *all* that can be said in his favour. He works hard, and does little; and unites a painful sense of responsibility to a still more painful sense, perhaps, that his work is too great for him to grapple with."

Dicey in his six months' travel in America seemed to have met few, or none at all, who took Lincoln for a great man. In presenting the longest sketch and appraisal of Lincoln written by any European visitor to America, he could not recall any testimony worth his recording which would point to Lincoln as an outstanding figure of either courage,. sagacity, dogged power, or the possession of a common touch that went far among the masses. Dicey was under the disadvantage of being alien to American ways, employing the tone of the arrogant sections of the English upper classes; he came with prejudices; his sources of opinion were chiefly those Americans who aped the English and were bothered by the twangs and devices of the President.

Had Dicey read Greeley in the *New York Tribune* or Storey in the *Chicago Times* or such journals as the *New York Express* or the *Crisis*, he could not have written of his six months in '62:

"For very obvious reasons the public press of the North was, at this period, almost unanimously, in favour of Mr. Lincoln. The Republican papers could not criticize their own nominee—the champion of their first triumph—without damaging their own party. The Democrat journals were afraid of driving the President into the arms of the Republicans, and therefore outvied their rivals in the ardour of their encomiums. From these causes, to judge from the language of the press, you might have supposed that the whole hope and confidence of the country was reposed in 'Abe Lincoln.' But the truth is, that the talk then current of proposing him for re-election was not a genuine one, and that when the President leaves the White House, he will be no more regretted, though more respected, than Mr. Buchanan. When Wendell Phillips described him as 'a first-rate second-rate man,' he uttered one of those epigrammatic sarcasms which stick to their victim for ever."

Thus Dicey prophesied what the future held for the name and repute of Lincoln. At recording what he saw and heard in the immediate present, when not speaking as a clairvoyant and crystal-gazer, Dicey was more dependable. He was interested in "the almost incredible manner in which stories are coined about Mr. Lincoln" and had traveled one day in the West with "a gentleman who professed to be an intimate personal acquaintance of the President" and told anecdotes to illustrate the free and easy manners of the President: "He told me that he had once been present in a Western law court, where Mr. Lincoln was engaged to defend a prisoner for murder. Mr. Lincoln came late, apologized to the judge for his detention, owing to his having over-slept himself, and then stated that he was never comfortable until he had smoked his morning cigar, and proposed, with the judge's permission, that they should have cigars all around. The permission being granted, he proceeded, with a cigar in his mouth, to defend his client.

"Now, unless I had had personal reason for knowing that Mr. Lincoln was not a smoker, I should certainly have recorded this with a variety of other similar anecdotes, as gospel truth, coming as they did on such apparently indubitable evidence. From all that I saw and heard myself, I have no doubt that Mr. Lincoln would say hosts of things which seem to us [English] utterly undignified, but he is the last man to say anything which would seem undignified to himself. Unlike most Western politicians, he was noted for not being 'hail fellow well met' with every bar-room lounger that he came across. He is a humourist, not a buffoon."

The question whether Lincoln was a gentleman entered Dicey's account too: "You would never say he was a gentleman: you would still less say he was not one. There are some women about whom one never thinks in connexion with beauty, one way or the other—and there are men to whom the epithet of 'gentlemanlike' or 'ungentlemanlike' appears utterly incongruous, and of such the President is one. Still there is about him a complete absence of pretension, and an evident desire to be courteous to everybody, which is the essence, if not the outward form, of high-breeding. There is a softness, too, about his smile, and a sparkle of dry humour about his eye which redeem the expression of his face, and remind me more of the late Dr. Arnold, as a child's recollection recalls him to me, than any other face I can call to memory." In a series of paragraphic impressions Dicey took his readers on a personal visit to Lincoln:

"On the occasion when I had the honour of passing some hours in company with the President, the gathering was a very small one, and consisted of persons with all of whom, except myself, he was personally acquainted. I have no doubt, therefore, that he was as much at his ease as usual, and yet the prevailing impression left upon my mind was that he felt uncomfortable. There was a look of depression about his face, which, I am told by those who see him daily, was habitual to him, even before the then recent death of his child, whose loss he felt acutely. You cannot look upon his worn, bilious, anxious countenance, and believe it to be that of a happy man. In private life, his disposition, unless report and physiognomy both err, is a sombre one; but, coupled with this, he has a rich fund of dry, Yankee humour, not inconsistent, as in the case of the nation itself, with a sort of habitual melancholy.

"It was strange to me to witness the terms of perfect equality on which he appeared to be with everybody. Occasionally some of his interlocutors called him 'Mr. President,' but the habit was to address him simply as 'Sir.' There was nothing in his own manner, or in that of his guests, to have shown a stranger that the President of the United States was one of the company. He spoke but little, and seemed to prefer others talking to him to talking himself. But when he did speak, his remarks were always shrewd and sensible. The conversation, like that of all American official men I have ever met with, was unrestrained in the presence of strangers to a degree perfectly astonishing. It is a regard for English, rather than for American rules of etiquette, which induces me to abstain from reporting the conversation that I overheard. Every American public man, indeed, appears not only to live in a glass-house, but in a reverberating gallery, and to be absolutely indifferent as to who sees or hears him. . . .

"The President asked me several questions about the state of public feeling in England, and obviously, like almost all Americans, was unable to comprehend the causes which have alienated the sympathies of the mother-country. At the same time, it struck me that the tone in which he spoke of England was, for an American, unusually fair and candid. . . .

"Some of the party began smoking, and Mr. Seward, who was present, remarked laughingly, 'I have always wondered how any man could ever get to be President of the United States with so few vices. The President, you know, I regret to say, neither drinks nor smokes.' 'That,' answered the President, 'is a doubtful compliment. I recollect once being outside a stage in Illinois, and a man sitting by me offered me a cigar. I told him I had no vices. He said nothing, smoked for some time, and then grunted out, "It's my experience in life that folks who have got no vices have plaguey few virtues."' . . .

"A gentleman present happened to tell how a friend of his had been expelled from New Orleans as a Unionist, and how, on his expulsion, when he asked to see the writ by which he was expelled, the deputation, which brought him the notice to quit, told him that the Confederate Government had made up their minds to do nothing unconstitutional, and so they had issued no illegal writ, but simply meant to *make* him go of his own free will. 'Well,' said Mr. Lincoln, 'that reminds me of an hotel-keeper down at St. Louis, in the cholera time, who boasted that he had never had a death in his hotel. And no more he had, for, whenever a guest was dying in his house, he carried him out in his bed and put him in the street to die.' . . .

"The conversation turned upon . . . the Missouri Compromise, and elicited the following quaint remark from the President:—'It used to amuse me some (sic) to find that the slaveholders wanted more territory because they had not room enough for their slaves, and yet they complained of not having the slave-trade because they wanted more slaves for their room.' . . .

"Of these [newspaper] Lincoln anecdotes, let me mention a few which I have reason to believe authentic. Shortly after Mr. Cameron's resignation, an old acquaintance called upon the President, and, after American fashion, asked him point-blank why, when he turned out the Secretary of War, he did not get rid of the whole Cabinet. 'Well, you know,' was the answer, 'there was a farmer, far West, whose fields were infested with skunks, so he set a trap and caught nine; he killed the first, but that made such an infernal stench that he thought he had better let the rest go.'

"Again, at the first council of war, after the President assumed the supreme command-in-chief of the army, in place of McClellan, the General did not attend, and excused himself next day by saying he had forgotten the appointment. 'Ah, now,' remarked Mr. Lincoln, 'I recollect once being engaged in a case for rape, and the counsel for the defence asked the woman why, if, as she said, the rape was committed on a Sunday, she did not tell her husband till the following Wednesday? and when the woman answered, she did not happen to recollect it—the case was dismissed at once.'

"The wit, indeed, of many of these anecdotes is too Aristophanic to be quoted here, but there is one other which will bear repeating. When the rebel armies were closely beleaguering Washington, two gentlemen insisted, late one night, on seeing the President, in order to inform him of a plot they had discovered on the part of some government officials for communicating with the enemy by means of signals. The President listened attentively to their story, which was clearly of the *gobemouche* order, and on inquiring what remedy his informants proposed, was told, after some hesitation, that the best plan would be to replace the traitorous officials by loyal men like themselves. 'Gentlemen, gentlemen,' was the President's comment, 'I see it is the same old, old coon. Why could you not tell me at once that you wanted an office, and save your own time as well as mine?'

"Stories such as these read dull enough in print. Unless you could give also the dry chuckle with which they are accompanied, and the gleam in the speaker's eye, as, with the action habitual to him, he rubs his hand down the side of his long leg, you must fail in conveying a true impression of their quaint humour. This sort of Socratic illustration is his usual form of conversation amongst strangers, but I believe in private life he is a man of few words, and those simple ones. . . .

"One remark he made of a more reflective character, and which, though perhaps not of great value in itself, is curious as coming from a man who has achieved distinction. Speaking of the fluency of American orators, he said, 'It is very common in this country to find great facility of expression, and common, though not so common, to find great lucidity of thought. The combination of the two faculties in one person is uncommon indeed; but whenever you do find it, you have a great man.'"

Thus one English temperament adjusted itself to a personality and its emanations. The significance of the Dicey appraisal lay in its having a quite general concurrence with the judgments of Americans as diverse as Charles Francis Adams, Sr., and Wendell Phillips and Wilbur F. Storey and Horatio Seymour, Clement Vallandigham and Robert Toombs and Jefferson Davis. A certain aristocratic temperament was not at home with Lincoln, personally, could not find ease or basis of fellowship in his presence. On the other hand were men of democratic type and saturation, such as Tom Corwin or Owen Lovejoy, who were joined to him by some common touch that ran back to a feeling about masses of people, the many against the few, the ruled-over as against the rulers. For all their deadly enmity in politics, Stephen A. Douglas, for instance, never made an unkind personal reference to Lincoln.

Dicey's philosophy colored his reporting, and he felt free to write: "The man who has his living to earn is better off, in almost every respect, in America than he is in England. The very circumstances that render the United States unattractive as a residence for the man of wealth and refinement, are a positive boon to those who possess neither of these attributes."

About the same time that Dicey saw Lincoln, James R. Gilmore noted: "A smile positively transfigured his whole face, making his plain features actually good-looking, so that I could agree with Caroline M. Kirkland, who not long before had told me that he was the handsomest man she had ever seen." A living characteristic of Lincoln was this facial mobility. When it was not there he was "gaunt, woe-begone," as Sergeant Stradling had noticed. "A puzzled shadow settled on his features and his eyes had an inexpressible sadness in them, with a far-away look," said the painter Thomas Hicks. There was "a lack of apparent force" as Henry Adams saw him handshaking at a reception.

The faraway look was in the impression set down by Charles Francis Adams, Jr.: "The only remark Lincoln made to me was—'A son of Charles Francis Adams? I am glad to see you, sir'; but at the same time I saw a look of interest. Lincoln's face is a good one, and he has proved his skill as a debater; but, if I could judge from a passing glance at a moment when the man was obviously embarrassed, I should say that his eye never belongs to a man great in action; it is neither the quick sharp eye of a man of sudden and penetrating nature, nor the slow firm eye of one of decided will; but it is a mild, dreamy, meditative eye which one would scarcely expect to see in a successful chief magistrate in these days of the republic. *Mais nous verrons.*"

At times the President near the White House, or at some of the government departments, when spoken to had passed on with abstracted face, not speaking in return, and they knew his mind was far away. The mobility of face might come quickly. One spoke of "his summer lightning smile," another of his face as "an ever-varying mirror." Nicolay wrote that this swift changefulness was the despair of artists who came to paint him. A dozen had set up their easels and gone away baffled, said Nicolay. They made measurements so as to be exact. They took one expression and petrified it: "Before these paintings were finished they were unsatisfactory to the artists themselves, and much more so to the intimate friends of the man; this was not he who smiled, spoke, laughed, charmed. The picture was as the dead to the living."

At one portrait of himself Lincoln shuddered and said it was "horridly like." Nicolay held there were many pictures of Lincoln; no portrait: "Graphic art was powerless before a face that moved through a thousand delicate gradations of line and contour, light and shade, sparkle of the eye and curve of the lip, in the long gamut of expression from grave to gay, and back again from the rollicking jollity of laughter to that far-away look."

Gustave Koerner, practical Illinois politician, wrote, "Something about the man, the face, is unfathomable." Congressman Henry Laurens Dawes of Massachusetts said early in the Administration: "There is something in his face which I cannot understand. He is great. We can safely trust the Union to him," and later: "I could never quite fathom his thoughts but it grew upon me that he was wiser than the men around him. He never altogether lost to me the look with which he met the curious and, for the moment, not very kind gaze of the House of Representatives on that first morning after what they deemed a pusillanimous creep into Washington. It was a weary look of one struggling to be cheerful under a burden of trouble." To Dawes and others the face indexed a cyclopedia of anxieties.

Grace Greenwood (pen name of Sara J. C. Lippincott) lingered at receptions while Lincoln was handshaking, studied his face, finding "always the same impression . . . melancholy unfathomable." He talked with her one day after the public had gone, "favored me," she said, "with a few of his stories . . . most amused by one wherein the joke was against himself." An honest old farmer, the story ran, visiting the capital for the first time, was taken by his Congressman to a gathering where he expected to see the President, who did not arrive that evening, and so the Congressman pointed out a large red-faced member from Minnesota as the President. The honest old farmer burst forth: "Is that Old Abe? Well, I do declare! He's a better-lookin' man than I expected to see; but it does seem as if his troubles had driven him to drink." Thomas Hicks, while painting Lincoln, heard from his subject, "It interests me to see how, by adding a touch here and a touch there, you make it look more like me."

HICKS. That is the reason why painting is called one of the fine arts.

LINCOLN. I once read a book which gave an account of some Italian painters and their work in the fifteenth century, and, taking the author's statement for it, they must have had a great talent for the work they had to do.

Visitors interposed and broke off one of the few fine-art commentaries on which Lincoln had ever ventured. To Seward and Hay he observed that one sculptor might have done better had he known more about woodchopping. Hay's diary had the note: "Rode today with the President and the Secretary of State to the Capitol. Saw the statuary of the East Pediment. The Prest objected to Power[s]'s statue of the Woodchopper, as he did not make a sufficiently clean cut."

In dress Lincoln let tailor, hatter, and bootmaker dictate his apparel. John H. Littlefield, once a law student with Lincoln & Herndon, said, "I used to wonder why he did not appear to be 'dressed up' . . . his angularity and individuality were so pronounced that the clothes seemed to lose their character." Those who caught him in the White House wearing a faded dressing-gown and slippers down at the heel "thrust themselves upon him at unseasonable and unexpected hours," according to Nicolay, who reasoned that with office hours from seven in the morning till midnight, the President could not always be considering his attire. In the scrutiny of a ceremonial or a private audience, said the loyal secretary, "Lincoln outranked any mortal who ever questioned him eye to eye." When too easy familiarities were attempted with him, he had his ways.

An Illinois politician from Freeport, Jared Patterson, once started a comparison of himself and Lincoln—their resemblance in height, their eyes, their high cheekbones. "Yes," interrupted Lincoln, "but you have more cheek, Mr. Patterson, more cheek." Thus the girl Jane Addams, living near Freeport, had the incident from her father.

One Peter Harvey, of chubby elephant proportions, came to the White House, and on account of his long-time acquaintance with Daniel Webster, began telling Lincoln how Webster would run the Government. And Harvey came out feeling less consequential and reported in his chubby manner what had happened. "I told Mr. Lincoln that I had talked so much with Daniel

Webster on the affairs of the country that I felt personally competent to tell him what Mr. Webster would advise in the present crisis, and thereupon, I explained just what he should do and not do, and would you believe it, sir, when I got all through, all that Mr. Lincoln said was, as he clapped his hand on my leg, 'Mr. Harvey, what tremendous calves you have got!' "

A beaming and officious visitor slid into the office one day as Lincoln sat writing and chirruped, "Oh, why should the spirit of mortal be proud?" The President turned a noncommittal face. "My dear sir, I see no reason whatever," and went on writing.

The Buffalo Congressman, John Ganson, entered a conference on military affairs, and told Lincoln that he and other Congressmen must have more information as to army movements. Ganson's smooth face and bald head grew red as he half threatened, "Mr. President, I am entitled to your confidence and I demand to know what is the present situation and prospects of our several campaigns and armies." Lincoln gave him a slow quizzical scrutiny and drawled, "Ganson, how close you shave!" Ganson retreated for the door, and when he was gone a general asked, "Mr. President, is that the way you manage the politicians?" "Well," said Lincoln, "you mustn't suppose you have all the strategy in the army."

Watching the tryout of a new gun at the navy yard one afternoon, Lincoln happened to see an ax hanging outside a ship cabin. He took the ax and said, "Gentlemen, you may talk about your Raphael repeaters and your eleven-inch Dahlgrens, but here is an institution which I guess I understand better than any of you." With that he held out the ax by the helve at arm's length. Not another man there could do the same. A guard officer at the War Department, Henry W. Knight, on duty up the first flight of stairs, would rise to salute when Lincoln walked in, often at eleven or twelve o'clock at night. "We were all sure of one thing," said Knight. "The harder it rained or the fiercer the winds blew, the more certainly he would come, for he seemed to love to go out in the elements." One night Lincoln asked about a pair of axes hanging crossed on the wall of the stairs landing, to be used in case of fire. He took one down, held it at arm's length several seconds. "I thought I could do it," he said to Knight. "You try it." Knight couldn't. Lincoln laughed as he passed on. "Thirty years ago in Illinois, I could lift two axes that way; I believe I could do it now, and I will try it some other time."

Lincoln seemed to believe this ax exercise good for him; he performed it on a number of occasions. General Egbert L. Viele, who commanded at the taking of Norfolk, wrote of a trip on the revenue cutter *Miami:* "Few were aware of the physical strength of Mr. Lincoln. In muscular power he was one in a thousand. One morning while we were sitting on deck, he saw an ax in a socket on the bulwarks, and taking it up, held it at arm's length at the extremity of the helve with his thumb and forefinger, continuing to hold it there for a number of minutes. The most powerful sailors on board tried in vain to imitate him. Mr. Lincoln said he could do this when he was eighteen years of age, and had never seen a day since that time when he could not."

Arriving in Washington for the inauguration, he gave his soft felt hat to Lamon and bantered: "Hill, this hat of mine won't do. . . . Give me that plug of yours, until you can go out in the city and buy one either for yourself or for me. I think your hat is about the style. I may have to do some trotting around soon, and if I can't feel natural with a different hat, I may at least look respectable in it."

The wearing of gloves for ceremony he regarded as "cruelty to animals," said Lamon, who witnessed Lincoln at a levee trying to give an extra hearty handshake to an old Illinois friend—when his white kids burst with a rip and a snort. The procession of guests waited and heard: "Well, my old friend, this is a general bustification. You and I were never intended to wear these things. . . . They are a failure to shake hands with between old friends like us." And he went on handshaking without gloves. With Mrs. Lincoln he drove to a hotel to get a man and wife, old friends from the West, to take them for a drive. As the guest got into the carriage seat alongside Lincoln he was fixed out with brand-new gloves, his wife's doing. So Lincoln began pulling on his gloves—just as the other fellow shed his with the cry, "No! no! no! put up your gloves, Mr. Lincoln," and they rode along and had a good old-time visit. "He disliked gloves," said Brooks, "and once I saw him extract seven or eight pairs of gloves from an overcoat pocket where they had accumulated after having been furnished to him by Mrs. Lincoln."

Important Republican-party men stood around while he received an old neighbor woman, a farmer's wife, who handed him a pair of blue woolen socks, saying, "I spun the yarn and knit them socks myself." He thanked her, asked about the folks at home, escorted her to the door with all courtesies. Then, returning, he picked up the socks by the toes, one in each hand, and remarked to the party men, "The old lady got my latitude and longtitude about right, didn't she?" He probably had his clothes rumpled from riding a horse when on the Rappahannock he was introduced to Septima Levy Collis, wife of a captain of a Philadelphia company. She wrote home: "It puzzles me very much to tell whether his shirt collar was made to stand up or turn down—it was doing a little of both."

A religious journal, the *Watchman and Reflector*, recorded how a deputation of clergymen presented an address to Lincoln in which they styled him "a *pillar* of the church." Though the matter at hand was serious, the editor noted, "he gently and perhaps truthfully remarked that they 'would have done much better to call him a *steeple*.'" Talking with Humphrey W. Carr of Jersey City, his eyes ranged up and down till he finally asked, "Mr. Carr, how tall are you?" Carr was six feet two and a half. "When I get the kinks all out I am six feet four inches," said Lincoln. Meeting a soldier six feet seven inches high, Lincoln surveyed him and asked, "Say, friend, does your head know when your feet get cold?" To another high boy just out of hospital and typhoid he grinned. "Fever is worse than a bullet but it must have taken a heap of fever to go all over you."

A strapping cornhusker easily three inches taller than the President had the greeting, "Really, I must look up to you; if you ever get into a deep place you ought to be able to wade out." He shook hands with a new Senator, "And so you are John Sherman," and stepping back, "Well, I am taller than you are, anyway." They put backs and Lincoln was two inches the taller. A Pennsylvania trooper said he saw Lincoln at a corps review shortly after Antietam and felt sorry so small a horse was under him that the President's feet nearly dragged the ground. A redheaded Irishman of the 4th United States Artillery put his face out of a tent that day, saw the equestrian head of the Government wearing a high silk hat, feet almost scraping the ground as he rode by, and the artilleryman snorted "two words unfit to print," and dropped back into the tent.

At Aquia Creek landing, going to see Burnside, workmen hurried to move boards and planks so the President would not have to step over them. "Never mind, boys," he smiled, "my legs are pretty long, have brought me thus far through life and I think they will take me over this difficulty."

"Bub! bub!" called the President to a line-up of 93d Pennsylvania Volunteers, pointing to a member of Company B of Reading. The "bub" thus addressed was Mahlon Shaaber. He strode forth to shake hands with the President. "Excuse my manners. It was jealousy made me call you out to size you up. How tall are you?" Shaaber was six feet six and one-half inches, seventeen years old, weight 140 pounds. Lincoln wrote a memorandum and, according to Shaaber, the jottings finished, showed to Shaaber the aggregate length of the tall men present at the review that day. It read:

> Abraham Lincoln, 6 feet 4 inches.
> Vice-President Hamlin, 6 feet 2½ inches.
> General Cameron, 6 feet 1 inch.
> Governor Curtin, 6 feet 2 inches.
> Mahlon Shaaber, 6 feet 6½ inches.
> Total 31 feet 4 inches.

Said Shaaber: "The President remarked jokingly that it was rarely so many tall men met at one time and it would probably never occur again. He told me I should eat no pies or pastry in any form, and advised against the use of intoxicating liquors. He introduced us to the guests of the day, invited us to dine at the White House. I declined saying I would enjoy my bean soup and hardtack better than the reception dinner. The President took both my hands in his. 'Good-by, my son! God bless you! Come back soon!'" And Shaaber, a long bag of bones, had gone forth to Seven Pines, where a piece of shell went into his right leg and a minié ball into his left, so that he had hospital days before he again walked.

A tall infantryman, with extra big feet, called on a street bootblack for a shine, so Lincoln told it, and as the gamin kneeled before the leather gunboats and was getting his brushes and blacking ready, he called to a brother across the street, "Come over and help, Jimmy, I've got an army contract."

When the most famous midget on earth presented himself at the White House with a newly taken midget wife, the President enjoyed the occasion.

The showman P. T. Barnum had arranged that Tom Thumb, having been the guest of English and French royalty and nobility, should as an American citizen loyal to the Union be received at the Executive Mansion in Washington. Barnum had shortly before let the newspapers know that "General" Tom Thumb, twenty-four years old, weighing twenty-one pounds, had "popped the question" to Miss Lavinia Warren, twenty years old, weighing twenty-nine pounds, each about 32 inches high. Miss Warren answered the General that she loved him but must have her mother's consent and "you know that mother objects to your mustache." He replied, "I will cut that off and my ears also if that will induce her to give an affirmative to my question." Grace Church swarmed with "the social élite" of New York for the wedding in February of '63. The Army of the Potomac was represented by Major General Ambrose E. Burnside. Another midget couple as best man and bridesmaid escorted the bride and groom. Up a specially erected stairway of six petite steps the four midgets mounted to a platform before the chancel, where three clergymen officiated in the ceremonies.

"The benediction was pronounced by the Rev. Dr. Taylor, Rector of Grace Church," said one newspaper, "whereupon the General saluted his wife with an honest kiss, the last of nearly three millions pressed in public upon the lips of his lady admirers." Through crowded streets the bride and groom were driven to the Metropolitan Hotel, where two thousand boxes of wedding cake were distributed to reception guests, who were also permitted to view the gifts. The press listed among gifts a gorgeous set of Chinese fire screens, "richly inlaid with gold, silver, and pearl," as coming from Mrs. Abraham Lincoln. The Vanderbilts, Belmonts, Bennetts, were represented with jewelry, plate, charms, "very chaste souvenirs." Barnum gave a tortoise-shell casket which at a finger touch on a spring would release a mechanical bird in natural feathers to rise and burble. A midget billiard table, a midget sewing machine, and other gifts in miniature were sent by manufacturers. The groom's tokens for his bride were a necklace, brooch, bracelets, earrings, hairpins, of eighteen-carat gold set with diamonds. Also on display was an international gown for Mrs. Thumb, ordered by Barnum, newspapers related, "without regard to style or cost, designed and made by Madame Demorest, No. 473 Broadway." On a thin silk changing from pale amber to a silvery white, its breadths connected at each seam by marabou feathers and lace, the skirt had national emblems traced in folds of white satin, "in front Growing Corn for America, on the right a Rose for England, on the left a Laurel for France, on other breadths an Acorn in oak leaves for Germany, a Shamrock for Ireland, the Thistle for Scotland, and a Vine with Cluster of Grapes for Italy." In this dress it was planned Mrs. Thumb with her husband was to meet royalty and nobility of Europe.

After spectacular receptions in Philadelphia and Baltimore the honeymooning midgets arrived in Washington. They entered the Executive Mansion one evening at eight o'clock and stood with composure and dignity in the doorway of a reception room filled with guests that included five Cabinet members, several Senators and generals, still more Congressmen, many bringing their families unto the smallest children. All eyes turned toward the doorway framing the man and woman whose physical growth had ended before they were ten years old. The couple were announced in loud tones and the bridegroom in an elegant wedding suit, taking the arm of the bride in white satin, point lace, orange blossoms, and pearls, with a two-yard train of white satin sweeping in her trail, advanced in what Grace Greenwood saw as "pigeon-like stateliness," almost to the feet of the President: "With profound respect they looked up, up, to his kindly face. It was pleasant to see their tall host bend, and bend, to take their little hands in his great palm, holding Madame's with special chariness, as though it were a robin's egg, and he were afraid of breaking it. He made them feel from the first as though he regarded them as real folks, presented them very courteously and soberly to Mrs. Lincoln."

Refreshments came and Lincoln watched Tad personally serve General and Mrs. Tom Thumb, placing wine and ices on a chair within comfortable reach. "Later," said Miss Greenwood, "while the bride and groom were taking a quiet promenade by themselves up and down the big drawing-room, I noticed the President gazing after them with a smile of quaint humor; but, in his sorrow-shadowed eyes, there was something more than amusement—a gentle sympathy in the apparent happiness and good-fellow-ship of this curious wedded pair—come to him out of fairyland."

The *Washington Star* reporter heard of the President in the course of the evening remarking to General Thumb: "You are now the great center of attraction. You have thrown me completely in the shade."

Leslie's Weekly ran an item: "A Delaware paper says that when General Tom Thumb was introduced to the President the other night, Mr. Lincoln said, 'Well, General, what is your opinion of the war, as a military man?' The General replied, 'My opinion is that my friend Barnum would settle the whole affair in a month!'"

Miss Greenwood mused over the reception: "I suppose that Mr. Barnum, a good loyal Republican, had solicited an audience for his then most famous, comely and *comme il faut* human curiosities, and that the President and Mrs. Lincoln, with an amiable desire to share a novel little entertainment with their friends, had sent out a limited number of invitations. Rather to my surprise, the high-toned and austere Secretary of the Treasury, Mr. Chase, was one of the guests, coming in early, as though in boyish haste to see the show. He was then but little past his prime, and a superb looking man. With him was his darling daughter Kate, 'the prettiest Kate in Christendom,' tall, graceful, her small Greek head borne royally, her lovely, piquant face un-touched by care or sorrow, her exquisite dark eyes, with their heavily fringed lids, full of a certain entangling charm."

Miss Greenwood noted the President, dressed in somber black, had white kid gloves giving "a rather ghastly effect on his large, bony hands." Talking with him, she found him easier to look at. "Before I heard his sweet-toned voice and saw his singularly sympathetic smile, Mr. Lincoln was cer-tainly an awesome personage to me." She read his face as "furrowed and harrowed by infinite perplexities, while over all was a simple dignity more than sacerdotal—a peculiar, set-apart look, which I have never seen in any other man." For contrast she found Mrs. Lincoln in a low-necked gown of rich pink silk, with flounces climbing high up over a hoop-skirt trellis, and pink roses in her hair.

One sultry summer morning the presidential carriage came on a regiment marching to Washington, and the President spoke to a straggler plodding along under musket and knapsack. "My lad, what *is* that?" "It's a regiment." "Yes, I see that but I want to know what regiment." "Steenth Pennsylvania," was the grunted reply as the man plodded on, looking neither right nor left. The carriage passed and Lincoln turned to the captain of the guard. "It is very evident that chap smells no blood of 'royalty' in this establishment."

Grim with a border of laughter at fate was a moment in the Patent Office Hospital when the President, Mrs. Lincoln, Mrs. Abner Doubleday, and Noah Brooks visited the patients. Lincoln and Brooks lingered at the cot of a wounded soldier who held with a weak white hand a tract given him by a well-dressed lady performing good works that morning. The soldier read the title of the tract and began laughing. Lincoln noticed that the lady of good works was still near by, told the soldier undoubtedly the lady meant well. "It is hardly fair for you to laugh at her gift."

The soldier gave Lincoln something to remember: "Mr. President, how can I help laughing a little? She has given me a tract on the 'Sin of Dancing' and both of my legs are shot off."

With the passing months during the war Lincoln's interest was unabated in seeking better rifles, cannon, powder, ships, mechanisms. Early he wrote Captain Dahlgren as to a new gun model: "What think you of it? Would the Government do well to purchase some of them? Should they be of the size of the one exhibited, or of different sizes?" Dahlgren's diary told of Lincoln's trip to the navy yard to see a new 150-pounder fired, of questions on naval ordnance, calls at the Bureau of Ordnance, "to see about some new powder," of examining "guns, iron plates, etc." He sent for Dahlgren: "Captain, here's a letter about some new powder," said he had burned a sample of the powder but there was too much residuum. "Now I'll show you." And Dahlgren noted: "He got a small sheet of paper, placed on it some of the powder, ran to the fire, and with the tongs picked up a coal, which he blew, specs still on his nose. It occurred to me how peaceful was his mind, so easily diverted from the great convulsion going on. The President clapped the coal to the powder, and away it went, he remarking, 'There is too much left there.' He handed me a small parcel of the powder to try."

Another diary entry of Dahlgren: "The President sent for me. Some man in trouble about arms. President holding a breech-loader in his hands. He asked me about the ironclads and Charleston." The two of them interviewed an inventor's agent, and on his leaving, the President began on army matters, and alluding to a great battle soon to come: "Now I am to have a sweat of five or six days."

One day came Joshua C. Stoddard, inventor of the steam calliope, an automatic elevator, hay rakes, to demonstrate an aerial torpedo. As he told it: "I struck a match and lit the model I had, whereupon Mr. Lincoln, fearful of an explosion, got down behind a desk, and I said, 'Mr. Lincoln, you make a better President, I guess, than you would a soldier.' But after seeing how it worked Mr. Lincoln was much pleased with it and told me I could go and practice on the rebels all I wanted to." An inventor of a composition supposed to burn its way through the enemy and all their works set up wooden boards near the White House grounds, threw his stuff on the wooden boards and destroyed them. Lincoln stalked down to where the stuff still smoldered, pulled up a handful of grass, came back, and said to the inventor: "That's very curious, indeed—very interesting. Now, can't you invent something to burn bricks, mortar, earth-works, or even green grass? Up to this date, our armies find no difficulty in burning wood."

The inventor Christopher M. Spencer presented Lincoln with one of his new repeating rifles in the summer of '63. "He examined it carefully and handled it like one familiar with firearms," said Spencer. "He requested me to take it apart and show 'the inwardness of the thing,' asked me to come over about 2 o'clock the next day, when, he said, 'we will go out and see the thing shoot.'" The next afternoon, with Robert T. Lincoln and a War Department rifle expert, they started for a target near the Washington Monument. On the way the President sent Robert to ask Stanton to come see the shooting. "While waiting Mr. Lincoln told us some good stories, and, noticing that one of the pockets of his black alpaca coat was torn, he took a pin from his waistcoat, and proceeded to mend it, saying, 'It seems to me that this does not look quite right for the chief magistrate of this mighty republic.' Robert reported Mr. Stanton was too busy to accompany us. 'Well,' said the President, 'they do pretty much as they have a mind to over there.' The target was a board about six inches wide and three feet long, with a black spot painted at each end. The rifle contained six 50-caliber, rim-fire, copper cartridges. Mr. Lincoln's first shot was to the left and five inches low, but the next shot hit the bull's eye and the other five were placed close around it. 'Now,' said Mr. Lincoln, 'we will see the inventor try it.' The board was reversed and I did somewhat better than the President. 'You are younger than I am,' he said, 'and have a better eye and steadier nerve.'"

Hay was along and wrote that the new gun was a wonder, firing seven balls, readily and deliberately, in less than half a minute. "The President made some pretty good shots. Spencer, the inventor, a quiet little Yankee who sold himself in relentless slavery to his idea for six weary years before it was perfect, did some splendid shooting." One bystander came up to the President and "seeing the gun recoil slightly, said it wouldn't do; too much powder; a good piece of audience [ordnance] should not rekyle; if it did at all, it should rekyle a little forrid." Hay and the President would thereafter in other affairs refer to how there had been "rekyle a little forrid."

A Navy Department clerk working overtime one night heard someone in a hallway muttering, "I do wonder if they have gone already and left the building alone." He looked out to meet the President's "Good-evening, I was just looking for that man who goes shooting with me sometimes." The man had gone for the day, so the clerk went along to the south lawn of the White House, where Lincoln fixed up a target cut from a sheet of official notepaper. "Then," said the clerk, "pacing off a distance of about eighty or a hundred feet, he took quick aim, drove the round of seven shots in quick succession, the bullets shooting all around the target and one striking near the center." Then Lincoln said, "I believe I can make this gun shoot better," and he took from his vest pocket a small wooden sight he had whittled from a pine stick, and adjusted it over the sight of the carbine. "He then shot two rounds," said the clerk, "and of the fourteen bullets nearly a dozen hit the paper." William O. Stoddard in the White House noted: "He took an especial interest in the new idea of breech-loaders and repeaters, but the Bureau offices are against him. He studies every new pattern that comes."

Receiving a committee having a new repeating gun that had the peculiar merit of preventing the escape of gas, he made an inspection and said: "I believe this really does what it is represented to do. Now, have any of you heard of any machine or invention for preventing the escape of gas from newspaper establishments?"

The inventor streak in Lincoln had play in the case of a man who proposed to do away with bridges by giving each soldier a pair of little watertight canoes, one for each foot—and another who had a scheme for moving artillery by the use of ironclad balloons. An old soldier brought in a polished steel coat of mail, claimed to be bulletproof. Stoddard noted, "Mr. Lincoln says if that's the case he approves of it, but there must be a thorough test; the inventor can put it on, and sharpshooters practice at it; the test seems to be postponed." On his desk was a model of a cast-iron bomb serving as a paperweight. "It is thoroughly infernal," wrote Stoddard, "a horrible thing for close combat, but of no practical use in these days of long-range rifles."

In Halleck's office one evening in the summer of '63 Lincoln discussed plans for a joint naval and land attack on Charleston, illustrating gradual approaches of artillery and infantry with three or four lead pencils and pen handles which he arranged in parallels and shifted according to his notions of the strategy. Gustavus Vasa Fox came in, agreed with Lincoln, but Halleck could not see it, and as Lincoln walked home that evening he spoke to Brooks of his discouragement with what he termed "General Halleck's habitual attitude of demur."

Steaming down the Potomac early one morning, Lincoln noticed a vessel sailing into the long shadow cast by a headland. He told Brooks that a poet would probably find a fine figure in that ship sailing out of the sunshine into the shadow. Brooks agreed, and then made the correction that the vessel was not a ship but a three-masted schooner. Lincoln laughed, carefully fixed in his mind the points that gave that type of vessel its name: "I shall certainly know a three-masted schooner from a ship the next time I ever see either. When I came to this place, I was deplorably ignorant of all marine matters, being only a prairie lawyer. But I do think that I knew the difference between the bow of a ship and her stern, and I don't believe Secretary Welles did."

Inquiries as to the physical law or mechanical principle that underlay a phenomenon or operation came frequently from Lincoln. "Unless very much preoccupied," wrote Brooks, "he never heard any reference to anything that he did not understand without asking for further information." He would ask, "What do you suppose makes that tree grow that way?" and was not satisfied until he had found out. Or he would take one of his boy's toys to pieces, find out how it was made, and put it together again. Tad had occasion more than once, said Brooks, to bewail his father's curiosity. One day Lincoln showed Brooks a photograph of himself in a sitting position with legs crossed, calling attention to the foot of the leg crossed above the other. "Now I can understand why that foot should be so enormous. It's a big foot, anyway, and it is near the focus of the instrument. But why is the outline of it so indistinct and blurred? I am confident I did not move it." Brooks studied for a moment and surmised that it was the throbbing of the large arteries inside of the bend of the knee that caused an almost imperceptible motion. Lincoln was interested, took the position he had held while being photographed, and watching his foot, exclaimed: "That's it! that's it! Now that's very curious, isn't it?" From this and similar incidents Brooks made the notation: "Lincoln's shrewdness was well-known; sometimes it almost seemed like cunning. But with all of this, was a certain element of simplicity in his character which was child-like."

The politician, the Executive, the quixotic human being, were inextricable. On board the steamer *Daylight*, which had performed bravely down the Potomac, Lincoln stood where a half-dozen members of the crew brought a tarpaulin to protect him from a rain while he insisted on shaking hands with the crew. A fireman in shirt sleeves was the last up, his face and hands sooty and smoked, saying, "My hand isn't fit to give you, sir, but there's not a man aboard loves you more than I do." "Put that hand in mine," cried the President. "It has been blackened by making fires for the Union." Or again on the B. & O. Railroad when a conductor asked him, "Why do you always bother shaking hands with the engineer and fireman, whose hands are always covered with soot and grease?" the answer came, "That will all wash off, but I always want to see and know the men I am riding behind."

When he could not grant a favor, he would, generally, make an appearance of so doing. A committee requested him to take action in certain claim cases—and he did not want to act. However, it looked like action, and partially satisfied the committee, when he wrote a formal order on Secretary Welles to send him the evidence in the cases. He told Welles later that there was no other way to get rid of the callers. An old acquaintance in Illinois, having organized a bank under the new National Bank Act, wrote offering some of the stock to Lincoln, who replied with thanks, saying he recognized that stock in a good national bank would be a good thing to hold, but he did not feel that he, as President, ought to profit from a law which had been passed under his Administration. "He seemed to wish to avoid even the appearance of evil," said the banker.

"They are a swindle," said John Hay of a delegation waiting audience. "Let them in," said the President. "They will not swindle me." He could not be rushed into a decision. "He will not be bullied even by his friends," wrote Nicolay. One memorandum to the Adjutant General ended, "Let there be no further question about it." He sent for Sumner to come to the White House as soon as convenient after breakfast to scrutinize a message to Congress. Sumner's secretary noted: "At the interview the President read the draft of the message. Sumner gave his own opinion against gradualism [graduated emancipation of slaves], and also designated a certain passage which was subject to a mischievous construction. The President, as Sumner was proceeding to put it in a different shape, volunteered to strike it out; and as Sumner continued to study the paper, at length interrupted in a pleasant way, saying: 'Enough; you must go, or the boys [the private secretaries] won't have time to copy it.'"

With one leg over the arm of a chair Lincoln slouched at ease talking with John Eaton, in charge of a bureau for relieving needs of freed Negroes. Suddenly the doorman was letting somebody in. The end of a cane, with a handle at right angles to the stick itself, was entering first. "There was not the faintest doubt as to who was behind that stick," wrote Eaton of this little affair in manners. Both Lincoln and Eaton knew it was one Senator who had free approach at all times and without ceremony. And, wrote Eaton, "As quick as thought Mr. Lincoln had untangled himself and was upon his feet, returning with the utmost dignity the courteous bow with which Mr. Sumner greeted him."

Eaton retired to the other end of the room while President and Senator exchanged news and Lincoln pointed to maps on his table and indicated army movements. Presently Sumner said, "I have thought over the matter of that consulate, and have come to say I think [giving the name] is the man for the place." Lincoln thanked Sumner for the attention and they parted with pleasant good-bys. The door closed and Lincoln, again at ease with one leg over the arm of a chair, called loudly and cheerily: "Come up, Eaton. When with the Romans, we must do as the Romans do!"

Eaton was a man of thiry-five who had been superintendent of schools in Toledo, Ohio, had become a Presbyterian minister and as chaplain of the 27th Ohio Volunteers had seen active service in Missouri, twice being taken prisoner and more than once preaching to Confederate soldiers on request of their commanders. At Shiloh and Corinth Eaton had been under fire, and when the slaves flocked by thousands into the Union Army lines in Tennessee had begun his work of organizing for relief of the homeless fugitives. Early in the Missouri turmoil he had written in a newspaper letter, "A pro-slavery fanatic in Missouri is twin brother to an anti-slavery fanatic in Ohio."

Something about Eaton won Lincoln's trust. It may have taken root when in their first interview Lincoln questioned him about what he had seen of Grant, of the Vicksburg campaign, of the Negroes: "How far did they understand the changes that were coming to them, and what were they able to do for themselves?" The President had plied his questions rapidly and mercilessly, almost as though it were a cross-examination in a court of law, and suddenly stopped, "quickly turned the conversation one side, as if he realized the severity of his catechism."

The next morning in a discussion of deportation and colonization of Negroes, Eaton was astonished to hear the President bring up the matter of Negroes in the Cow Island settlement on the coast of Hayti suffering intensely from a pest of "jiggers." His distress was "as keen as it was sincere," noted Eaton. "The President of the United States, conducting the affairs of the nation in the midst of civil war, and genuinely affected by the discomfort occasioned a little group of negroes by an insect no bigger than a pinhead, was a spectacle that stayed by me."

"The freedom with which he discussed public affairs with me often filled me with amazement," wrote Eaton. The President spoke one day "quite fully" of the opposition, expressing surprise that there should be so much antagonism to his policy in the ranks of the great abolitionists. The criticism of such men as Greeley and Wendell Phillips was "a great grief and trial" to Lincoln, Eaton believed.

"Of a well-known abolitionist and orator," wrote Eaton, "the President once exclaimed in one of his rare moments of impatience, 'He's a thistle! I don't see why God lets him live!'"

In a day's work, as an incident, the President rejected a final appeal resulting in an order by the Secretary of War reading as follows: "Surgeon David S. Hays, 110th regiment Pennsylvania Volunteers, having been ordered to conduct to this city a large detachment of sick and wounded men, and having shamefully neglected them after their arrival, the President directs that for this gross dereliction of duty he be dismissed from the service, and he is hereby accordingly dismissed."

Finishing inspection of General O. O. Howard's corps at Fredericksburg, the President asked about a large part of the command, off duty, on hillsides watching the review. They were quartermaster's men, orderlies, cooks, and other essential details, General Howard explained. And as Howard told it, Lincoln smiled and said gently, "That review yonder is about as big as ours!" Howard got the point, admitted it was wholesome criticism to a young corps commander, confessed later "those altogether too large 'details' were always a source of great weakness to us in time of battle." It made a difference with Howard that officers high in command had asked Lincoln to remove him and the reply was: "He is a good man. Let him alone; in time he will bring things straight."

Congressman John B. Alley said he had often seen Lincoln provoked and tried, but only once saw him in a burst of temper, on a day when bad news came from the army. "A couple of office-seekers who knew him well intercepted him, on his way from the White House to the War Department, and teased him for an office which he told them he could not give. They persisted. The President, evidently worn by care, turned upon them, and such an angry and terrific tirade against those two incorrigible bores, I never before heard from the lips of mortal man."

A messenger boy for the American Telegraph Company, Charles Frederick, meeting Lincoln near the outer gate of the White House, handed him a telegram one night. Lincoln while opening the telegram "smiled pleasantly enough," thought the boy. Then came the demand, "Have you the other telegrams?" The boy said he had only one, though he had been told that day there were one or two others from General McClellan. "That is what he says," blurted the President, "and what annoys me is that I haven't received them." Then, turning to the sentry at the gate, swift and short-spoken: "Send up to the door for the officer in charge and tell him that when telegrams come here addressed to me they should and must be delivered to me. Tell him also that if he sends any more of my telegrams over to Mr. Stanton's house I'll drive him away from here. Mr. Stanton has enough telegrams of his own, and should not have mine."

The President had been "mad clear through," the messenger boy felt, and it was still in the voice that spoke to him: "Boy, tell your folks that I must have my telegrams, and if those soldiers about the door interfere any more, I'll drive every one of them away. I don't want them and never did want them about the place."

A Union general telegraphed for copies of correspondence that had passed between the President and a Border State governor. "The Tycoon," wrote Hay, "came into his room with the despatch in his hands, clad in an overcoat pure & simple reaching to his knees, & sleepily fumbled for the papers in his desk till he found them & travelled back to bed. I took the letters to the telegraph office & sent them off about midnight."

Though an Executive amid modern devices, he drew parallels from primitive rural sources. On a Vermont man proposed for a responsible post he commented: "As they say in the hayfield he requires a good man to 'rake after him.' If such men were in command there would be a movement at the front. I can find men enough who can rake after, but the men with long arms and broad shoulders, who swing a scythe in long sweeps, cutting a swath ten feet wide, are much more difficult to find." Dispatches lay before the President one morning from a Northern governor who wanted his own way and in one telegram after another was sending threats and warnings that orders from Washington could not be carried out. Lincoln was amused rather than disturbed, and in a cheerful tone made a few guesses that worked out as he foretold:

"Never mind, never mind; those despatches don't mean anything. Just go right ahead. The Governor is like a boy I saw once at a launching. When everything was ready they picked out a boy and sent him under the ship to knock away the trigger and let her go. At the critical moment every-thing depended on the boy. He had to do the job well by a direct, vigour-ous blow, and then lie flat and keep still while the ship slid over him.

"The boy did everything right, but he yelled as if he were being mur-dered from the time he got under the keel until he got out. I thought the hide was all scraped off his back; but he wasn't hurt at all. The master of the yard told me that this boy was always chosen for that job, that he did his work well, that he never had been hurt, but that he always squealed in that way.

"That's just the way with Governor Blank. Make up your minds that he is not hurt, and that he is doing his work right, and pay no attention to his squealing. He only wants to make you understand how hard his task is, and that he is on hand performing it."

"There is but one vote in the Cabinet, and that is cast by the President," wrote Seward to his wife in the spring of '61. It was told and published that an officious patriot got to the President and said, "Sir, you must get rid of Mr. Seward—throw him overboard." "Mr. Seward," said the Presi-dent, "is Secretary of State. He conducts the diplomacy of the country. Have you read his diplomatic correspondence?" "Yes, sir." "Have you any fault to find with it?" "No, sir." "Well, sir, he is my clerk; I got him for that purpose." "Well—but you should throw Blair overboard." "Sir, Mr. Blair is Postmaster General. Do you get all your papers and letters regu-larly?" "Yes, sir." "Well, sir, he is my clerk for that purpose; and I am President of the United States."

When necessary the President could tell a man of bright mind some-thing the man wished to know without being guilty of directly revealing a state secret, Nicolay noted. Senator Sumner called with Hamilton Fish of New York one day, and asked questions about General Burnside's expedi-tion against Roanoke Island. "Well," said the President, "I am not a mili-tary man, and of course I cannot tell about these matters—and indeed if I did know, the interests of the public service require that I should not di-vulge them. But," and he rose and swept a long hand over a map of the North Carolina coast which hung in a corner, "now see here. Here are a large number of inlets, and I should think a fleet might perhaps get in there somewhere. And if they were to get in there, don't you think our boys would be likely to cut up some flip-flaps? I think they would." Fish then turned the talk in another direction, but on leaving the White House was surprised to hear Sumner impatient because the President had not answered his first question. "Why," said Fish, "he told you where Burnside was going! He wanted to satisfy your curiosity, but of course he could not make an official declaration. I think you ought to be well pleased that he was so frank."

A big cavalry raid had filled the newspapers and raised noisy enthusiasm, but failed to cut the enemy's communications. Lincoln remarked to Whit-ney, "That was good circus riding; it will do to fill a column in the news-papers, but I don't see that it has brought anything else to pass."

Lamon wrote that in '62 Senator Sherman had ready a speech to prove Lincoln a failure, and that unless Congress acted the war would be a failure. Someone told Lincoln of the Sherman speech—yet to be delivered—and Lincoln said: "Sherman is a patriot and a statesman and is thoroughly for the Union; perhaps his opinion of me may be just. . . . I would not have him change a word." These remarks, according to Lamon, were passed on to Sherman "and they made such an impression on him that he omitted from his speech the criticism on Lincoln."

He would often get the pitch and key of a situation or personality and address himself to it as a sharpshooter. His method or instinct varied with Sumner, Sherman, Governor Morton of Indiana—or the King of Siam, Somdetch Phra Paramender Maha Mongkut, whose letter saluted the President as "Respected and Distinguished Sir" and affirmed at its close that it was "given at our royal audience hall, Anant Samagome, in grand palace of Ratue Kosinder Mahindra aqudia, at Bangkok, Siam, on Thursday, fifth night of waxing moon, in the lunar month of Phagun, the fourth month from the commencement of cold season, in the year of Monkey, second decade Siamese astronomical era 1222, corresponding to the solar date of 14th February, anno Christi 1861, which is the eleventh year and this date is the 3564th day of our reign." It was the most polite and exceedingly embossed document ever laid in Lincoln's hands. Never before had he seen human language, as translated, spread around with such informational munificence.

The Oriental potentate to begin with set forth that he ruled "by the blessing of the highest superagency of the whole universe, the King of Siam, the sovereign of all interior tributary countries adjacent and around in every direction," and his letter was addressed to none other than "his most respected excellent presidency, the President of the United States of America, who, having been chosen by the citizens of the United States as most distinguished, was made President and Chief Magistrate in the affairs of the nation for an appointed time of office."

Buried far down in a long paragraph was the statement that on the 10th night of waxing moon in the lunar month of Visakh, the 6th month recurring from the commencement of the cold season in the year of Goat, 1st decade of the Siamese astronomical era 1221, a package of 192 volumes, United States Government publications, had arrived as a present from the Buchanan Administration.

And in what spirit and by what manifestation was this gift of 192 government publications from Washington celebrated in Siam? "It was received by us in full assembly of the royal princes and nobles of the highest rank, all in full court dress, with their insignia of office, in like manner as though they were receiving a visit in person from the President of the United States." And whereas between countries at least half civilized "a friendly intercourse has sprung up, to communicate one another with letters and complimentary presents from time to time," the King was embracing the opportunity to send by separate envelope "a sword, with a photographic likeness of ourselves," two elephant tusks, and an offer of elephants for breeding and use in the United States.

"If the President of the United States and Congress, who conjointly with him rule the country, see fit to approve, let them provide a large vessel loaded with hay and other food suitable for elephants on the voyage, with tanks holding a sufficiency of fresh water, and arranged with stalls so that the elephant can both stand and lie down in the ship. We, on our part, will procure young male and female elephants, and forward them, one or two pairs at a time. When the elephants are on board the ship, let a steamer take it in tow, that it may reach America as rapidly as possible, before they become wasted and diseased by the voyage. When they arrive in America, do not let them be taken to a cold climate out of the regions of the sun's declinations or torrid zone, but let them, with all haste, be turned out to run wild in some jungle suitable for them, not confining them any length of time. If these means can be done, we trust that the elephants will propagate their species hereafter in the continent of America. It is desirable that the President of the United States and Congress give us their views in reference to this matter at as early a date as possible."

In suave sentences having both pomp and pomposity, mingling delicate jest with the kindliest of sentiment, Lincoln (perhaps jointly with Seward) wrote the notable document of state dated February 3, 1862, titled "The President of the United States to the King of Siam," and transmitted to Congress for consideration. It read:

"*Great and good friend:* I have received your Majesty's two letters of the date of February 14, 1861. I have received in good condition the royal gift which accompanied those letters, namely, a sword of costly materials and exquisite workmanship, a photographic likeness of your Majesty and of your Majesty's beloved daughter, and also two elephant's tusks of length and magnitude, such as indicate that they could have belonged only to an animal which was a native of Siam.

"Your Majesty's letters show an understanding that our laws forbid the President from receiving these rich presents as personal treasures. They are therefore accepted in accordance with your Majesty's desire as tokens of your good will and friendship for the American people. Congress being now in session at this capital, I have had great pleasure in making known to them this manifestation of your Majesty's munificence and kind consideration.

"Under their direction the gifts will be placed among the archives of the government where they will remain perpetually as tokens of mutual esteem and pacific dispositions more honorable to both nations than any trophies of conquest could be.

"I appreciate most highly your Majesty's tender of good offices in forwarding to this government a stock from which a supply of elephants might be raised on our own soil. This government would not hesitate to avail itself of so generous an offer if the object were one which could be made practically useful in the present condition of the United States. Our political jurisdiction, however, does not reach a latitude so low as to favor the multiplication of the elephant, and steam on land, as well as on water, has been our best and most efficient agent of transportation in internal commerce.

"I shall have occasion at no distant day to transmit to your Majesty some token of indication of the high sense which this government entertains of your Majesty's friendship.

"Meantime, wishing for your Majesty a long and happy life, and for the generous and emulous people of Siam the highest possible prosperity, I commend both to the blessing of Almighty God."

He subscribed himself as "Your good friend" and signed the full name of "Abraham Lincoln."

Vastly different in tone and approach was a letter to General David Hunter beginning, "Yours of the 23d is received, and I am constrained to say it is difficult to answer so ugly a letter in good temper. . . . I aver that with as tender a regard for your honor and your sensibilities as I had for my own, it never occurred to me that you were being 'humiliated, insulted and disgraced'; nor have I, up to this day, heard an intimation that you were being wronged, coming from anyone but yourself." The General's transfer to a Western post was for responsible and honorable duty, and complaint against having a command of only 3,000 men was mere impatience: "Have you not known all the while that you are to command four or five times that many?" He gave assurance and warning: "I have been, and am sincerely your friend; and if, as such, I dare to make a suggestion, I would say you are adopting the best possible way to ruin yourself. 'Act well your part, there all the honor lies.' He who does *something* at the head of one regiment, will eclipse him who does *nothing* at the head of a hundred."

On the outside of the envelope in which General Hunter received this letter, the General wrote a memo: "The President's reply to my 'ugly letter.' This lay on his table a month after it was written, and when finally sent was by a special conveyance, with the direction that it was only to be given to me when I was in a good humor."

The London *Times*, annoyed by the loose and familiar style of Lincoln's papers, commented on one of his open letters intended for the public and aimed straight at the masses of people: "How any man in his sober senses could have sat down to compose such a rhapsody as this, or having composed it, could have read it over with gravity and ordered it to be printed, passes our comprehension." It mused on Lincoln in 1863: "Among the many marvels and paradoxes of the American Revolution there is none greater than the part played by the President himself. That such a man should have been called upon to guide the destinies of a mighty nation during a grand historical crisis is surely strange enough, but that he should have blundered and vacillated as he has, without for a single moment losing confidence in himself, or altogether forfeiting that of his countrymen, is stranger still. His language on the great questions at issue has varied so much at different

times as to show that he never can have had anything worthy of being
called a policy, unless it can be that which he describes in the wisest of
all his homely sayings as a resolution to 'keep pegging away.' "

The London *Herald* agreed with the *Times*. The American President's
"awkwardness of style and form" was disappointing: "The age of cultivated
American statesmanship has long passed away. The refined intellect of the
United States now shuns political life. It would have been absurd to expect
from a man who has passed the best part of his life in the backwoods and
the wooden capital of a new state the elegance and lucidity which distinguish the state papers of the first fifty years of the Union."

To Thomas L. James of Utica, New York, the President said, "I do not
lead; I only follow." When the Prince de Joinville asked what was his
policy, he replied: "I have none. I pass my life preventing the storm from
blowing down the tent, and I drive in the pegs as fast as they are pulled
up." In an evening of discussion with the Reverend Robert Livingston
Stanton, a Connecticut Yankee whose twelve years' pastoral service in
Woodville, Mississippi, had taught him complexities of the slavery question,
Lincoln referred to States' Rights, acknowledged that some things he had
done, decisions made, were possibly beyond his constitutional right, yet he
knew the necessity, did what he felt to be right, explaining, "I am like the
Irishman, I have to do some things 'unbeknownst to myself.' "

In a later call at the White House in company with Judge Jesse L.
Williams of Indiana, the Reverend Mr. Stanton discussed Lincoln's letter
to General Curtis about the Reverend Dr. McPheeters in St. Louis, charged
with disloyalty. Did the President recall this letter? Judge Williams inquired. "Yes, I remember that letter." "Well," said the Judge, "on the trial
of Dr. McPheeters by the general assembly of the Presbyterian Church,
your letter to General Curtis was read. But the curious part of the affair
was this: One party read a portion of your letter and claimed the President
was on their side, and the other party read another portion of the same
letter and claimed the President was on their side. So it seems, Mr. President,
that it is not so easy to tell where you stand."

Lincoln joined in the laughter and was reminded of an Illinois farmer
and his son out in the woods hunting a sow. After a long search they came
to a creek branch, where they found hog tracks, and signs of a snout
rooting, for some distance on both sides of the branch. The old man said
to his boy, "Now, John, you take up on this side of the branch and I'll go
up t'other, for I believe the old critter is on both sides."

A sense of speech values in Lincoln registered in such degree that he
could say of another, "He can compress the most words into the smallest
ideas of any man I ever met." Nicolay heard him tell of a Southwestern
orator who "mounted the rostrum, threw back his head, shined his eyes, and
left the consequences to God."

At Brown University, however, rumor held that a youth it had sent
forth with a sheepskin, John Hay, was writing the messages of the President.
J. C. Welling wrote to Sumner of one presidential message: "Its style is

exceedingly *plain*, not to say *hard-favored*. Of course, the concluding sentence was written by you or by Seward. I intend no disrespect to the President's English when I say he would have done better if he had submitted the whole document to the revision of your scholarly taste." Another, G. E. Sewall, felt that the Emancipation Proclamation would measure up with the Declaration of Independence as a historic document, and wrote to Sumner, "I wish the President would direct you to write it for him."

Storey and his *Chicago Times* deprecated Lincoln's style, alleged he wrote too much and was careless: "Who does not remember the epistolary old gentleman in the play who had such an extensive correspondence with Grenoble, Adrianople, Constantinople, and all the other noples; with Haddam, Potsdam, Suydam, Amsterdam, and all the other dams. Even such a garrulous old joker with his pen is our President." The *Times* satirically listed various letters of Lincoln as confiding, social, piquant, exalting, crushing, condescending, clear, concise, conciliatory, cunning, curious, immediate, interpretative: "A very 'phunny' man is our President; fond of correspondence."

A woman who had asked the President to use his authority in her behalf at the War Department quoted him: "It's of no use, madam, for me to go. They do things in their own way over there, and I don't amount to pig tracks in the War Department."

One newspaper assembled Lincoln idioms in advising, "If the President hopes ever to amount to more than 'pig tracks' in any of the departments, he must let his secretaries know that when he 'puts his foot down' he intends that his directions shall be something else than 'a Pope's bull against a comet.' "

A writer in *Blackwood's Magazine*, published in England, took note of Americans' forcing new words into English language dictionaries; he feared that America might make a language of its own; he mentioned "words knocking loudly at our gates for admittance, and certain to be admitted sooner or later on their merits," such as "bogus," "skedaddle," and "deadhead." These new words of the American language streamed across the Lincoln addresses, letters, daily speech. The *Boston Transcript* noted his use of "the plain homespun language of a man of the people, who was accustomed to talk with the 'folks' " and "the language of a man of vital common sense, whose words exactly fitted his facts and thoughts." That ex-President John Tyler should protest Lincoln's grammar was natural. W. O. Stoddard wrote that the President knew how some of his plainer phrasings would sound in the ears of millions over the country and did not "care a cornhusk for the literary critics."

Brooks acquainted Lincoln with the derivation of a word, and he said, "Now that is very queer, and I shall never say *capricious* again without thinking of the skipping of a goat." He coined a few words for his own uses. Brooks noted his saying "du-pen'ance" to indicate the quality of being easily duped. He picked words for his own use; a man who had been overtaken by a just retribution "had got his come-up-ence." Mary Boykin

Chesnut of South Carolina wrote in her diary on July 7, 1861: "We are always picking up some good thing of the rough Illinoisan's saying. Lincoln objects to some man—'Oh, he is too *interruptious*'; that is a horrid style of man or woman, the interruptious. I know the thing, but had no name for it before."

He was afraid of long speeches and had a fear of sentiment when fact and reasoning had not laid the way for it. His effort at a flag-raising speech before the south front of the Treasury building was one sentence only:

"The part assigned to me is to raise the flag, which, if there be no fault in the machinery, I will do, and when up, it will be for the people to keep it up."

Suppose the war ran on three years, four, and seemed at no end, what then? An anxious White House visitor asked that. "Oh, there is no alternative but to keep pegging away."

He feared, and said so, "explanations explanatory of things explained." He referred several times to men who were loyal with "buts" and "ifs" and "ands." The Mississippi Valley was "this Egypt of the West." What was past was past; "broken eggs cannot be mended." To Illinois sponsors of a proposed major general he wrote that "major-generalships are not as plenty as blackberries." The Republican party should not become "a mere sucked egg, all shell and no meat, the principle all sucked out." As to a current issue, he said to Chittenden: "We shall see. We will wait to hear from the country districts, from the people." He had told Robert Dale Owen, it was said, when Owen had read to him a long paper on an abstruse subject akin to spiritualism, "Well, for those who like that sort of thing, I should think it is just about the sort of thing they would like." He may have said this to Owen or it may have been attributed to him with slight changes out of a certificate of endorsement which Artemus Ward fabricated and published as follows:

Dear Sir—

I have never heard any of your lectures, but from what I can learn I should say that for people who like the kind of lectures you deliver, they are just the kind of lectures such people like.

Yours respectfully,

O. Abe

The famous open letter to Greeley, declaring that the paramount object of the Administration was to save the Union with or without slavery, went for initial publication into the hands of the editors of the *National Intelligencer*. These editors pressed Lincoln till he ran his pen through and crossed out one sentence reading "Broken eggs can never be mended, and the longer the breaking proceeds the more will be broken."

James C. Welling, who once wrote Sumner that he wished Sumner could be writing the President's messages, was one of the editors who urged the omission of the sentence, saying later, "The omitted passage was erased, with some reluctance, by the President, on the representation, made to him by the editors, that it seemed somewhat exceptionable, on rhetorical grounds, in a paper of such dignity." Welling believed the expunged sentence had a "homely similitude" that was too homely.

Welling edits Lincoln

A foreign diplomat demurred at Lincoln's condemning a certain Greek history as tedious: "The author of that history, Mr. President, is one of the profoundest scholars of the age. Indeed, it may be doubted whether any man of our generation has plunged more deeply in the sacred fount of learning."

"Yes," said Lincoln, "or come up dryer."

He had one style for the effulgent King of Siam and another for Mrs. Susannah Weathers of Rossville, Indiana, and formerly of Kentucky, who sent him a letter and a pair of socks she had knitted: "I take great pleasure in acknowledging the receipt of your letter and in thanking you for the present by which it was accompanied. A pair of socks so fine, and soft, and warm, could hardly have been manufactured in any other way than the old Kentucky fashion." In a girl's autograph album: "With pleasure I write my name in your album. Ere long some younger man will be more happy to confer his name upon you. Don't allow it, Mary, until fully assured that he is worthy of the happiness." To Bill Herndon, still his law partner, he wrote a letter perhaps once a year in the manner of one in February of '62:

Dear William: Yours of January 30th just received. Do just as you say about the money matter. As you well know, I have not time to write a letter of respectable length. God bless you, says

                                        Your friend   A. Lincoln

Lincoln disliked dictation of letters and orders, according to William A. Croffut of the *New York Tribune* staff, who heard him say, "I can never think except with my fingers." And Croffut noted, "He did the wise thing—saying conversationally what he wanted to reply to a letter, and trusting Nicolay or Hay to put it in shape."

Congressman James F. Wilson of Ohio noted Lincoln inquiring, "I suppose you have read some of my official papers?" Wilson had read all that had been made public.

LINCOLN. That is more than I should have expected of anyone. . . . Tell me frankly which one you regard most favorably.

WILSON. Your letter of the 13th of June, [1863] in reply to the one signed by Erastus Corning and others . . . relative to the arrest of Mr. Vallandigham is, in my judgment, your best paper.

LINCOLN. I am glad you think so, and I agree with you. I put that paper together in less time than any other of like importance ever prepared by me. [*Turning toward the desk at which he was sitting and pulling a drawer partly out.*] When it became necessary for me to write that letter, I had it nearly all in there [*Pointing to the drawer.*] but it was in disconnected thoughts, which I had jotted down from time to time on separate scraps of paper. I had been worried a good deal by what had been said in the newspapers and Congress about my suspension of the writ of *habeas corpus*, and the so-called arbitrary arrests. I did not doubt my power to suspend the writ, nor the necessity which demanded its exercise.

But I was criticised harshly, and sometimes by men from whom I expected more generous treatment, and who ought to have known more and better than the character of their expressions indicated. This caused me to examine and re-examine the subject. I gave it a great deal of thought, studied it from every side; it was seemingly present with me continually. Often an idea about it would occur to me which seemed to have force and make perfect answer to some of the things that were said and written about my actions. I never let one of those ideas escape me, but wrote it on a scrap of paper and put it in that drawer. In that way I saved my best thoughts on the subject. . . . Many persons have expressed to me the opinion you have of that paper, and I am pleased to know that the present judgment of thoughtful men about it is so generally in accord with what I believe the future will, without serious division, pronounce concerning it.

"I asked the President if he would speak to the Secretary of War in my behalf," wrote the Reverend Robert Livingston Stanton, D.D. "Certainly I

Lincoln

Photograph by Gardner in early '63, from the Mc-Lellan Lincoln collection, Brown University

Lincoln

Photograph by Brady, probably late '63, from the Meserve collection

Robert Todd Lincoln, Harvard student

Mary Todd Lincoln, in mourning garb after the death of Willie in '62

From the Barrett collection

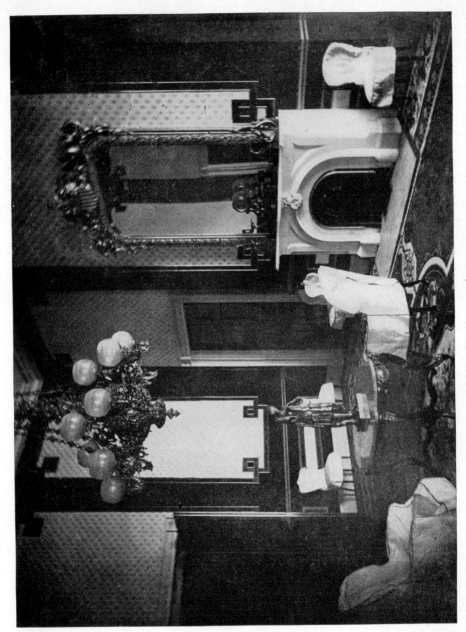

The President's reception room

From the L. C. Handy studios

will," was the answer, and then, pausing: "Or what is better, I will write him a note. Sit down and I will write it now." At his desk scribbling away he suddenly looked over his spectacles at the Reverend Dr. Stanton and said: "O-b-s-t-a-c-l-e: is that the way you spell obstacle?"

The Reverend Dr. Stanton was upset, "disconcerted," saw that Lincoln had turned to face him, recovered himself to say, "I believe that is right, Mr. President." Lincoln eased along slowly: "When I write an official letter, I want to be sure it is correct, and I find I am sometimes puzzled to know how to spell the most common word." For twenty years, he enlightened his visitor, he had difficulty about whether there were two r's in "very," sometimes getting it v-e-r-r-y. Also he would misspell "opportunity" as op-per-tunity. "He finished his letter to the Secretary of War, and handed it to me with a warm expression of hope that my mission might be successful," wrote the Reverend Dr. Stanton. "It was." Another visitor found him amused over having just learned that the word "main-tain-ance," when spelled correctly, is "main'te-nance."

Punctuation, Lincoln said to Noah Brooks, was with him a matter of feeling rather than education. The semicolon he found to be "a very useful little chap." He joined with Seward in laughter at Hay's reading aloud from a little guidebook titled *English as She Is Spoke.* Important letters were sometimes read aloud to friends, corrections and changes adopted occasionally. In an office cabinet divided into pigeonholes were compartments for correspondence and memoranda. Greeley had a pigeonhole. So did each of several letter-writing generals. And one labeled "W. & W." Brooks was curious about, Lincoln laughing: "That's Weed and Wood—Thurlow and Fernandy—that's a pair of 'em."

An unofficial adviser drew from Lincoln the remark that he had a great reverence for learning. "This is not because I am not an educated man. I feel the need of reading. It is a loss to a man not to have grown up among books." The spry visitor was hearkening and rejoined: "Men of force can get on pretty well without books. They do their own thinking instead of adopting what other men think."

"Yes," said Lincoln in a tone that shortened the interview, "but books serve to show a man that those original thoughts of his aren't very new, after all."

Among books drawn out of the Library of Congress by the President and his household during '61 were four volumes of the works of Thomas Jefferson and eight volumes on the United States Constitution. General Halleck's *Elements of Military Art and Science,* Emerson's *Representative Men,* Plutarch's *Lives, The Sparrowgrass Papers* by Frederick Swartwout Cozzens, *Key to Uncle Tom's Cabin* by Harriet Beecher Stowe, *History of Minnesota* by Edward Duffield Neill, *The Song of Hiawatha* by Henry Wadsworth Longfellow, *Dramatic Works* by William Shakespeare, *The Wagoner of the Alleghenies; a Poem of the Days of Seventy-Six* by Thomas Buchanan Read, were titles of books in which Lincoln was interested though he could not have had time to read them. His fascination with Stille's little book drawing a parallel of the American civil war with that of English turmoils may have led to the withdrawal in '63 from the Library of Congress of five volumes, one or two at a time, as though he might wish to scan the series, of a *History of England from the Invasion of Julius Caesar to the Revolution of 1688* by David Hume. Also his interest in firearms would account for his wanting to see *Burk on the Rifle* and for *The Shot-Gun and Sporting Rifle* by John Henry Walsh.

On the night of April 25, 1862, Browning visited Lincoln at the White House and wrote of it in his diary: "At night I went to the Presidents. He was alone and complaining of head ache. Our conversation turned upon poetry, and each of us quoted a few lines from Hood. He asked me if I remembered the Haunted House. I replied that I had never read it. He rang his bell—sent for Hood's poems and read the whole of it to me, pausing occasionally to comment on passages which struck him as particularly felicitous His reading was admirable and his criticisms evinced a high and just appreciation of the true spirit of poetry. He then sent for another volume of the same work, and read me the 'lost heir,' and then the Spoilt Child, the humour of both of which he greatly enjoyed. I remained with him about an hour & a half, and left high [him] in high spirits, and a very genial mood; but as he said a crowd was buzzing about the door like bees, ready to pounce upon him as soon as I should take my departure, and bring him back to a realization of the annoyances and harrassments [sic] of his position."

The reading aloud of Lincoln to Browning that night, with comments, took an hour and a half or two hours, for he read long poems. In the two pieces of Hood ran something of Lincoln's own range of melancholy and laughter, verses from a poet of folk touch, widely read, often in newspaper reprints. Hood's life had run from the year 1799 to 1845, and he sang in his way a spirit of the time. With Charles Lamb, his dearest friend, Hood made puns and contrived fun, yet the two of them also wrought in melodrama and shuddering shadow shapes. Out amid the vast audience to which Lincoln sent his messages and addresses were millions who had read Hood's "Song of the Shirt," dignifying and protesting the piecework sewing woman of the slums, "in unwomanly rags, in poverty, hunger and dirt," weaving a shirt for a customer and a shroud for herself on starvation wages. The same millions had read of the suicide streetwalker dropping from "The Bridge of Sighs" to friendly waters:

> One more Unfortunate,
> Weary of breath,
> Rashly importunate,
> Gone to her death!

The first piece Lincoln read aloud to Browning told of an empty house, rusty with time, splintered by gales, overgrown with weeds and thistles, the two opening verses:

Some dreams we have are nothing else but dreams,
Unnatural, and full of contradictions;
Yet others of our most romantic schemes
Are something more than fictions.

It might be only on enchanted ground;
It might be merely by a thought's expansion;
But, in the spirit or the flesh, I found
An old deserted Mansion.

In the ninety-four following verses that Lincoln read aloud came shapes of fear, rats, spiders, the wood louse, moths, maggots, midges, tattered flags, ancestral things shivered to mold and dust, gloomy stairs, toads, bones and relics, mildew, a deathwatch ticking, the verses ending:

One lonely ray that glanced upon a Bed,
As if with awful aim direct and certain,
To show the BLOODY HAND in burning red
Embroider'd on the curtain. . . .

What human creature in the dead of night
Had coursed like hunted hare that cruel distance?
Had sought the door, the window in his flight,
Striving for dear existence?

What shrieking Spirit in that bloody room
Its mortal frame had violently quitted?—
Across the sunbeam, with a sudden gloom,
A ghostly Shadow flitted. . . .

O'er all there hung the shadow of a fear,
A sense of mystery the spirit daunted,
And said as plain as whisper in the ear,
The place is Haunted!

The rhymed sketch of "The Lost Heir" which Lincoln next read to Browning was a rattling hilarious monologue beginning in a dirty London alley, where:

I saw a crazy woman sally,
Bedaub'd with grease and mud.
She turned her East, she turned her West,
Staring like Pythoness possest,
With streaming hair and heaving breast,
As one stark mad with grief,
This way and that she wildly ran,
Jostling with woman and with man—
Her right hand held a frying pan,
The left a lump of beef.

She was hunting the streets for her "crying lost-looking child," her little Billy, whom she describes as to clothes, nose, eyes, hair, and she's scared he may have been run over:

Or may be he's stole by some chimbly sweeping wretch, to stick fast in narrow flues
and what not,

And be poked up behind with a picked pointed pole, when the soot has ketch'd, and
the chimbly's red hot.

Oh I'd give the whole wide world, if the world was mine, to clap my two longin' eyes
on his face,

For he's my darlin' of darlin's, and if he don't soon come back, you'll see me drop
stone dead on the place.

I only wish I'd got him safe in these two Motherly arms, and wouldn't I hug and
kiss him!

Lauk! I never knew what a precious he was—but a child don't not feel like a child
till you miss him.

Why, there he is! Punch and Judy hunting, the young wretch, it's that Billy as sartin
as sin!

But let me get him home, with a good grip of his hair, and I'm blest if he shall have
a whole bone in his skin!

Thus ran lines with which Lincoln passed the time reading aloud while,
as he said to Browning, a crowd was "buzzing about the door like bees."
In verse that appealed to him was a resource. From newspaper columns,
said Nicolay, "he rescued many a choice bit of verse, which he carried with
him till he was quite familiar with it; it was noticeable that they were almost
always referable to his tender sympathy with humanity, its hopes and its
sorrows. I recall one of these extracts, which he took out of his pocket one
afternoon as we were riding to the Soldiers' Home. It began:

> A weaver sat at his loom
> Weaving his shuttle fast,
> And a thread that should wear till the hour of doom
> Was added at every cast.

"The idea was that men weave in their own lives the garment which they
must wear in the world to come. The opening lines were fixed in my mind
by their frequent repetition by the President who seemed to be strongly
impressed by them. During the evening he murmured them to himself once
or twice as if in soliloquy."

On board the revenue cutter *Miami* down the Potomac General Viele
noted of one of these newspaper clippings, just cut out by the President:
"This little scrap amused him exceedingly. It was a very absurd idea, absurdly expressed, but there was something about it that pleased his fancy,
and he was not satisfied until he had read it to each one of the party, appearing to enjoy it the more the oftener he read it." A rhyme in *Harper's
Weekly* with such lines as "They sat side by side, and she sighed and he
sighed, Then they both sighed, side by side," interested Lincoln so that he
spread the paper on the deck, sprawled himself over it, and, "Viele, lend
me your penknife." As he clipped he looked up and said, "Not a very dignified position for the President of the United States, but eminently convenient for the purpose." Early in the war a newspaper clipping of a speech

delivered in New York came to Lincoln's hands, and at its close his eye
caught stanzas from Longfellow's "The Building of the Ship" beginning:

> Thou, too, sail on, O Ship of State!
> Sail on, O Union, strong and great!

Nicolay was surprised at the way these lines hit the President. He seemed to
be reading them for the first time. And as Brooks had memorized the piece
at school he recited it for Lincoln to the last lines:

> Our hearts, our hopes, our prayers, our tears,
> Our faith triumphant o'er our fears.

They stirred something deep in Lincoln. "His eyes filled with tears, and
his cheeks were wet," wrote Brooks. "He did not speak for some minutes,
but finally said with simplicity: 'It is a wonderful gift to be able to stir
men like that.'"

On board a steamer for a visit with the Army of the Potomac, Lincoln
read aloud to Stanton and Dahlgren from a volume of Fitz-Greene Halleck's
verses the piece "Marco Bozzaris" beginning:

> At midnight, in his guarded tent,
>   The Turk was dreaming of the hour
> When Greece, her knee in suppliance bent,
>   Should tremble at his power.

The piece ran on in a turgid narrative that closed with the lines:

> For thou art Freedom's now, and Fame's,
> One of the few, the immortal names,
> That were not born to die.

The Burns Club of Washington held an annual meeting and Lincoln on
request penciled a toast to be presented after the dinner: "I cannot frame a
toast to Burns; I can say nothing worthy of his generous heart and tran-
scending genius; thinking of what he has said I cannot say anything which
seems worth saying."

In the White House, as at Springfield, he occasionally recited "O Why
Should the Spirit of Mortal Be Proud" by William Knox. When Chittenden
quoted to him from what Father Prout sang of "The Groves of Blarney"—

> There gravel walks are
> For recreation
> And conversation
> In sweet solitude—

he called cheerily: "Tell me more of that ballad. I like its jingle. What
an Irish conceit that is—'conversation *in sweet solitude*.'" Chittenden promised to bring a book with the rest of the ballad (which actually reads
"meditation in sweet solitude"). "I must have that book to-night," said Lincoln. "A good Irish bull is medicine for the blues." He left the office, said

Chittenden, "actually to the sound of his own musical laugh." And he sent for the book, a copy of Crofton Croker's *Popular Songs of Ireland*.

Nicolay, Noah Brooks, and others who saw him at close range said he had a remarkable and retentive memory. "He once recited to me," said Nicolay, "a long and doleful ballad, something like Vilikins and His Dinah, the production of a Kentucky rural bard, and when he had finished, he added with a laugh, 'I don't believe I have thought of that before for forty years.'" One of Brooks's cousins, John Holmes Goodenow of Alfred, Maine, was appointed Minister to Turkey, and on presentation to Lincoln at the White House, Lincoln learned that Goodenow was a grandson of John Holmes, one of the first Senators from Maine, and began reciting a poem of more than a hundred verses. The stanzas ran on and on. The new Minister to Turkey was a little shocked. Brooks surmised that "the suspicion crossed his mind that Lincoln had suddenly taken leave of his wits." The recitation over, the President made the matter clear: "There! that poem was quoted by your grandfather Holmes in a speech he made in the United States Senate in"—and he named the day and occasion. He told Brooks it was no sign that he especially liked a thing because he could repeat it. He would recite a passage from some oration or address, recent or remote, and remark that he "couldn't help remembering" it.

As he drove with Brooks to the Soldiers' Home one November day when the trees were bare, he slowly recited Oliver Wendell Holmes's "The Last Leaf." He had never seen a volume of Holmes's verses, so Brooks left at the White House a little blue-and-gold volume of Holmes and a week later chatted about the work with the President, who read and recited pieces that pleased him. He had been surprised to find verses that had drifted around in newspapers unsigned; it was an unsigned printing of "The Last Leaf" in a newspaper that had first given him that poem. He liked "Lexington" as well as any piece in the book, he told Brooks, and began to read, coming to the lines

> Green be the graves where her martyrs are lying!
> Shroudless and tombless they sunk to their rest,

when, said Brooks, "his voice faltered, and he gave me the book with the whispered request, 'You read it; I can't.'" He learned, however, to go through with the poem, for at a later time he recited it from memory, without missing a word, to a company of ladies calling on Mrs. Lincoln, and again for Governor John Andrew of Massachusetts.

On a Fortress Monroe trip, not long after the boy Willie had died, he took up a volume of Shakespeare and read aloud to General Wool's aide several passages from *Hamlet* and *Macbeth;* then after reading from the third act of *King John*, he closed the book and repeated from memory the lament of Constance for her boy—

> And, father cardinal, I have heard you say
> That we shall see and know our friends in heaven.
> If that be true, I shall see my boy again.

His reading aloud was most often Shakespeare. Hay noted of a summer evening in '63: "Last night we went to the Observatory with Mrs. Long. They were very kind and attentive. The Pres't took a look at the moon and Arcturus. I went with him to the Soldiers' Home, and he read Shakespeare to me, the end of Henry VI and the beginning of Richard III, till my heavy eyelids caught his considerate notice & he sent me to bed. This morning we ate an egg, and came in very early. He went to the library to write a letter . . . & I went to pack my trunk for the North." In the war telegraph office, Bates noted that Lincoln carried in his pocket at one time a well-worn copy in small compass of *Macbeth* and *The Merry Wives of Windsor*, from which he read aloud. "On one occasion," said Bates, "I was his only auditor and he recited several passages to me with as much interest apparently as if there had been a full house." Occasionally he questioned the omission of certain passages of a Shakespeare play as acted.

Leslie's Weekly of April 11, 1863, chronicled: "President Lincoln visited Grover's Theatre, Washington, on Thursday night, to see 'Hamlet.' It was his first visit since he has been President." The Shakespearean drama flourished. Opinions of its characters, quotations of lines, sprinkled polite conversation of the day. Junius Brutus Booth, Sr., an English tragedian, had played in Richmond in 1821, had become an American citizen, had played Shakespeare for thirty years, had won the critics of New York and Boston, had given *Richard III* and *King Lear* in hundreds of smaller cities. Lincoln had received at his home in Springfield, and at the White House, a dramatic reader, James E. Murdoch, who had played with Junius Brutus Booth, Sr., and could tell of the ferocity and abandon which that tragedian threw into a Shakespearean role, sometimes so terrifying to other actors that they forgot their lines.

Murdoch in the White House recited Shakespeare for Lincoln and Browning, and Browning felt the delivery noisy and fulsome. Murdoch was impressed with Lincoln as at once a serious thinker and a joker of Shakespearean values, quoting: "He hath a right ready wit and a queasy mode of raillery that to querulous questioners may not sit so nicely as might be on shoulders somewhat bowed with dignities and honors. But yet, beshrew me, his mirth has meaning in it, and I would rather quarrel with than miss it. Ah, he's a merry man, ay, a merry and a proper. There can be no better gossip to counsel, or crack a nut or joke withal, than our good keeper of the seals and parchments." A patriotic poem, meant to stir the blood of men for war, written by Thomas Buchanan Read and published early in '63, was read by Murdoch. It was titled "The Oath," but when Lincoln, on occasion, requested its recitation by Murdoch, he asked for "The Swear." Four oath-taking lines closed each verse. The first of the verses read:

> Ye freemen, how long will ye stifle
> The vengeance that justice inspires?
> With treason, how long will ye trifle,
> And shame the proud name of your sires?

Out, out with the sword and the rifle
In defence of your homes and your fires.
The flag of the old Revolution,
Swear firmly to serve and uphold,
That no treasonous breath of pollution
Shall tarnish one star on its fold,
Swear!
And, hark, the deep voices replying
From graves where your fathers are lying:
"Swear, oh, Swear!"

The comedian James H. Hackett, playing Falstaff, pleased Lincoln. In the tragic parts of *Hamlet* and *King Lear* Hackett had failed, but his Falstaff had for years been rated as the best on the English-speaking stage. Hackett, having seen the President in his audience, sent to the White House a copy of his book *Notes and Comments on Shakespeare*. The President replied:

"Months ago I should have acknowledged the receipt of your book and accompanying kind note; and now I have to beg your pardon for not having done so. For one of my age I have seen very little of the drama. The first presentation of *Falstaff* I ever saw was yours here, last winter or spring. Perhaps the best compliment I can pay is to say, as I truly can, I am very anxious to see it again.

"Some of Shakespeare's plays I have never read; while others I have gone over perhaps as frequently as any unprofessional reader. Among the latter are 'Lear,' 'Richard III,' 'Henry VIII,' 'Hamlet,' and especially 'Macbeth.' I think nothing equals 'Macbeth.' It is wonderful.

"Unlike you gentlemen of the profession, I think the soliloquy in 'Hamlet' commencing 'Oh, my offense is rank,' surpasses that commencing 'To be or not to be.' But pardon this small attempt at criticism. I should like to hear you pronounce the opening speech of Richard III. Will you not soon visit Washington again? If you do, please call and let me make your personal acquaintance."

This letter Hackett could not refrain from making public. So the newspapers had lively accounts of the President in a fresh role. "He is turning skollard and what a skollard!" snorted one Copperhead critic, while a *New York Herald* writer skilled in gossip and persiflage, touched with a humor lacking malice, leaped to the incident:

"Mr. Lincoln is wonderfully versatile. No department of human knowledge seems to be unexplored by him. He is equally at home whether discussing divinity with political preachers, debating plans of campaign with military heroes, illustrating the Pope's bull against the comet to a pleasure party from Chicago, arguing questions of Constitutional law with Vallandigham sympathizers, regulating political parties in Missouri, defending his policy before party conventions or inditing letters to the philosopher in chief of the *Tribune* academy. In countless questions he has displayed a variety of attainments, a depth of knowledge, a fund of anecdote, a power of analysis and correct judgment that stamp him as the most remarkable man of the age. It remained for him to cap the climax of popular astonishment and admiration by showing himself to be a dramatic critic of the first order and a profound commentator on Shakespeare. The Falstaff of our age has been honored with an autograph letter from the American autocrat just as Shakespeare himself was honored with an amicable letter from King James the First and which we are told that 'most learned prince and great patron of learning was pleased with his own hands to write.' "

More often, however, the comment was that the President had better conduct the war and let drama alone. A letter from Hackett promised a visit at the White House and expressed regret over the publicity and comments on Lincoln and Shakespeare which had ensued. Lincoln replied to the actor that he should give himself no uneasiness on the subject:

"My note to you I certainly did not expect to see in print; yet I have not been much shocked by the newspaper comments upon it. Those comments constitute a fair specimen of what has occurred to me through life. I have endured a great deal of ridicule without much malice; and have received a great deal of kindness, not quite free from ridicule. I am used to it."

Hackett paid his visit to the White House, a comedian of sixty-three years of age, his stage career near an end. And he asked the President for an office. Something like an English consulate would please him. Noah Brooks noted of this visit and a second one: "Going to the President's on a summons from him very late at night, I noticed this prominent comedian waiting alone in the corridor outside the President's door. Lincoln asked me if anyone was waiting without, and when I told him that I had seen the actor sitting there, he made a gesture of impatience and regret, and said that the little courtesies which had passed between them had resulted in the comedian applying to him for an office. Lincoln almost groaned as he said that it seemed impossible for him to have any close relations with people in Washington without finding that the acquaintance thus formed generally ended with an application for office."

In formal dress, including white kid gloves, the President went with Mrs. Lincoln to Ford's Theatre to hear a concert, entered a box late, and bowed to the audience, which rose and cheered. He had just seated himself when a harsh voice came from the middle aisle: "He hasn't any business here! That's all he cares for his poor soldiers!" After a second of silence came yells, "Put him out! put him out!" followed by a voice with dialect calling: "De President has a right to hees music! He ees goot to come! He shall haf hees music! Dot is vot I shay! He shall haf hees music!" And by then a few soldiers had located the croaker, who was hoisted and carried out. "The President seemingly paid no attention to the incident," wrote Stoddard. "The orchestra took a hint from somebody and struck up a storm of patriotic music, out walked the prima donna and Mr. Lincoln and all the volunteers present had their music."

Hay wrote to Nicolay of one evening: "I went last night to a sacred concert of profane music at Ford's. Young Kretchmar and old Kretchpar were running it. Hs. and H. both sang; and they kin if anybody kin. The Tycoon and I occupied a private box, and both of us carried on a hefty flirtation with M. girls in the flies." The concert-going of the President was chronicled in the newspapers, and the *New York Herald* in April of '63 had its say again:

"Mr. Lincoln, it is said, has become a devotee of the Italian opera. After attending one or two of the representations of Grau's troupe at Washington, he thinks like Oliver, he would take a little more. No wonder. From the troubles of the war it is natural that he should seek occasional relaxation. His happy faculty as a joker has doubtless done him a world of good but the wear and tear of the mind from the cares of the state demand more substantial diversions. No wonder, therefore, that Honest Old Abe has become a lover of music and the opera."

The impresario Maretzek was to open "another operatic campaign," said the *Herald*, and it would be a good time for the President to hear music and Mrs. Lincoln to do some shopping in New York:

"How grateful will be the change between Washington and New York! It will be a translation and transformation as by the magic lamp of Aladdin. From the hospitals of sick and wounded soldiers, camps of contrabands, corrals of army horses and hordes of hungry politicians, to the shops of Broadway, the concerts of the Park and fascinations of Opera! We expect a series of victories over the rebels in the meantime so that our great father, or great grandfather as some of the Indians call him, may pack up and pack off from Washington for a few days with a light heart and an easy conscience. We want President Lincoln as well as Mrs. Lincoln to come during this May campaign of Maretzek. We want the President to compare for himself the strategy of Maretzek with the strategy of the War Office; the harmony of the Italians with the discords of the politicians; the music of Mazzoleni with the jargon of the Cabinet; the delicious strains of Guerrabella with the tedious orders of General Halleck."

Because of the unwanted publicity and the interruptions of politicians and office-seekers, Lincoln arranged with managers of two theatres that he could go in privately by the stage door and slip into a stage box without being seen from the audience. "Concealed by the friendly screen of the drapery, he saw many plays without public observation," said Brooks. He saw the notable Edwin Forrest in *King Lear*, and when John McCullough played Edgar, Lincoln asked Brooks the simple question, "Do you suppose he would come to the box if we sent for him?" Brooks said the actor would undoubtedly be gratified. And McCullough came, in stage rags and straw, and received discriminating praise and thanks for an evening of pleasure given the President.

After a production of John Brougham's *Pocahontas*, Brooks accompanied the President to the White House, listening to cheery talk about the play. At the door of the White House was an intimate friend who had not stayed through the play, but on hearing that the President had been there without guards, made a protest against the President's thus exposing himself. Lincoln was a little nettled, didn't like the subject brought up, didn't like to discuss the matter of his own physical courage, and ended with saying good-naturedly: "Nevertheless, the fact is I am a great coward. I have moral courage enough, I think, but I am such a coward, physically, that if I were to shoulder a gun and go into action, I am dead sure that I should turn and run at the first fire—I know I should."

The playhouse gave him ease; at Ford's Theatre he "made many comical remarks," wrote Brooks. Edwin Booth was playing in *The Merchant of Venice* and two or three of the supernumeraries in scarlet hose constantly getting between Lincoln's line of sight and the main actors, he said: "I wonder if those red-legged, pigeon-toed chaps don't think they are playing this play? They are dreadful numerous." Just before the act drop went up each time, he consulted his program and said, "This is Act two eyes" or "Act three eyes" or "Act eye V." Going home, he said: "It was a good performance, but I had a thousand times rather read it at home, if it were not for Booth's playing. A farce or a comedy is best played; a tragedy is best read at home."

On December 19, 1863, Hay noted that the President took him, Nicolay, and Swett to Ford's to see *Henry IV* with Hackett as Falstaff. "Hackett was most admirable. The President criticized H.'s reading of a passage where Hackett said, 'Mainly *thrust* at me,' the President thinking it should read 'Mainly thrust at *me*.' I told the Pres^t I tho't he was wrong, that 'mainly' merely meant 'strongly,' 'fiercely.' The Pres^t thinks the dying speech of Hotspur an unnatural and unworthy thing—as who does not?"

Into the White House one day a Congressman brought Jean Louis Rodolphe Agassiz, a Doctor of Laws at the universities of Edinburgh and Dublin before he was thirty years of age, protégé of Cuvier and Humboldt, the world's foremost ichthyologist, authority on fishes, fossils, animal life, glaciers, professor of geology and zoology at Harvard—sometimes referred to as the greatest man of learning in the United States. "Agassiz!" blurted Lincoln to Brooks. "I never met him yet." Brooks started to leave. "Don't go, don't go. Sit down and let us see what we can pick up that's new from this great man."

Agassiz and Lincoln talked. The conversation did not seem very learned to Brooks: "The President and the savant seemed like two boys who wanted to ask questions which appeared commonplace, but were not quite sure of each other. Each man was simplicity itself. Lincoln asked for the correct pronunciation and derivation of Agassiz's name, and both men prattled on about curious proper names in various languages." Agassiz asked Lincoln if he had ever lectured any, Lincoln having offered some of his speculations on man's discoveries and inventions: "I think I can show, at least in a fanciful way, that all the modern inventions were known centuries ago." Agassiz urged him to finish the lecture. Perhaps sometime he would, Lincoln guessed. The two men shook hands warmly, Agassiz left, and Lincoln smiled quizzically at Brooks: "Well, I wasn't so badly scared after all, were you?" Brooks said it seemed as though Lincoln had expected to be weighed down by the great man's learning. Lincoln admitted to Brooks that he had cross-examined Agassiz on "things not in the books."

With Professor Joseph Henry, discoverer of electrodynamic principles that linked him with Benjamin Franklin in that field, physicist, meteorologist, director of the Smithsonian Institution, Lincoln was more at home than with Agassiz, though Henry and Agassiz were perfectly alike in refusing salaries twice what they were getting, and agreeing with each other, "I can not afford to waste my time in making money." Visiting Chittenden's office one day, Professor Henry said he was coming to know the President better: "I have lately met him five or six times. He is producing a powerful impression on me. It increases with every interview. I think it my duty to take philosophic views of men and things, but the President upsets me. If I did not resist the inclination, I might even fall in love with him." Chittenden said Yes, he was inclined to agree.

Professor Henry went on to the effect that he had not yet arranged his thoughts in a form to warrant expression but he could say: "President Lincoln impresses me as a man whose honesty of purpose is transparent, who has no mental reservations, who may be said to wear his heart upon his sleeve. He has been called coarse. In my interviews with him he converses with apparent freedom, and without a trace of coarseness. He has been called ignorant. He has shown a comprehensive grasp of every subject on which he has conversed with me. His views of the present situation are somewhat novel, but seem to me unanswerable. He has read many books and remembers their contents better than I do. He is associated with men who I know are great. He impresses me as their equal, if not their superior. I desired to induce him to understand, and look favorably upon, a change which I wish to make in the policy of the Light-House Board in a matter requiring some scientific knowledge. He professed his ignorance, or rather, he ridiculed his knowledge of it, and yet he discussed it as intelligently—"

At that point a messenger announced "The President!"—and Lincoln walked in. Professor Henry blushed as Chittenden said to Lincoln, "You have interrupted an interesting commentary," and out of kindness to Henry changed the subject. The President and Henry then went into a long talk, starting on the Confederate destruction of all lights, buoys, and signal stations along their coasts, and how Union vessels could best navigate under such conditions. They discussed illuminants and the Professor's experiments with lard oil. Professor Henry took his leave, apologizing for using so much time. Chittenden and Lincoln talked about Henry, Chittenden hearing: "I had an impression that the Smithsonian was printing a great amount of useless information. Professor Henry has convinced me of my error. It must be a grand school if it produces such thinkers as he is. He is so unassuming, simple, and sincere. I wish we had a few thousand more such men!"

A man with a black mustache, a well-modeled head surmounted by wavy dark hair and a slouch hat, wearing a cape like an artist who had been to Italy and Spain, was at the White House one day in the spring of '62 for a look at the President. He was rather a sad man, one of those who took the human procession as tragic rather than comic, grotesque rather than gay, and he was shy and did not care to talk with the President—though he wanted a look. An interview could easily have been arranged, for the man was Nathaniel Hawthorne, then recognized as America's leading novelist, a human spirit beautifully unafraid, darkly independent as to where his personal thought and dream might carry him. An aloof, brooding spectator of life, joined painfully to it by imagination and insight, by solemn Puritan inheritances of blood, by grim meditations on fate, free will, foreordination, the guilt of the human individual in subtle and cruel phases, Hawthorne had written, "I approve the war as much as any man, but I don't quite see what we are fighting for." He hovered in a neutral twilight between his publisher, James T. Fields, who was strongly for the Union, and his benefactor, the antiwar and anti-Lincoln Franklin Pierce. As President, Pierce had given Hawthorne the best-paying consulate in Europe for four years in partial appreciation of Hawthorne having written the least readable of all his books, a campaign biography of Pierce. Still later his viewpoint had verged till he stood alongside Pierce on the point that the war could have been avoided, and the best settlement would be a separation of North and South "giving us the west bank of the Mississippi and a boundary line affording as much Southern soil as we can hope to digest into freedom in another century."

Though Franklin Pierce could only see Lincoln as one of God's mistakes, Mrs. Hawthorne, known in their circle as one of the better and rarer wives of the time, thought otherwise, once writing in a letter: "I suspect the President is a jewel. I like him very well."

Hawthorne had found one man at the Capitol "satisfactorily adequate to the business which brought him thither." That was Emanuel Leutze, the German painter, executing mural frescoes "emphatically original and American, embracing characteristics that neither art nor literature have yet dealt with, and producing new forms of artistic beauty from the natural features of the Rocky Mountain region, which Leutze seems to have studied broadly and minutely." Instead of symbolic and imagined ancient figures, Leutze was employing frontiersmen: "The garb of the hunters and wanderers of those deserts, under his free and natural management, is shown as the most picturesque of costumes." Coming away from Leutze, however, Hawthorne saw big cracks in the freestone walls of the central edifice; the iron dome above was threatening to come thundering down, "an appropriate catastrophe enough, if it should occur on the day when we drop the Southern stars out of our flag."

As to seeing Lincoln, he wrote in an article published in the *Atlantic Monthly*, July, 1862: "Of course, there was one other personage, in the class of statesmen, whom I should have been truly mortified to leave Washington without seeing; since (temporarily, at least, and by force of circumstances) he was the man of men. But a private grief [the death of Willie Lincoln] had built up a barrier about him, impeding the customary free intercourse of Americans with their chief magistrate; so that I might have come away without a glimpse of his very remarkable physiognomy, save for a semi-official opportunity of which I was glad to take advantage. The fact is, we were invited to annex ourselves, as supernumeraries, to a deputation that was about to wait upon the President, from a Massachusetts whip-factory, with a present of a splendid whip.

"Our immediate party," continued Hawthorne, "consisted only of four or five (including Major Ben Perley Poore, with his note-book and pencil), but we were joined by several other persons, who seemed to have been lounging about the precincts of the White House, under the spacious porch, or within the hall, and who swarmed in with us to take the chances of a presentation. Nine o'clock had been appointed as the time for receiving the deputation, and we were punctual to the moment; but not so the President, who sent us word that he was eating his breakfast, and would come as soon as he could. His appetite, we were glad to think, must have been a pretty fair one; for we waited about half an hour in one of the antechambers, and then were ushered into a reception-room, in one corner of which sat the Secretaries of War and of the Treasury, expecting, like ourselves, the termination of the Presidential breakfast. During this interval there were several new additions to our group, one or two of whom were in a working-garb, so that we formed a very miscellaneous collection of people, mostly unknown to each other, and without any common sponsor, but all with an equal right to look our head-servant in the face."

At this point the editor of the *Atlantic*, and a good friend of Hawthorne, insisted that Hawthorne omit a personal sketch of Lincoln which followed: "Considered as the portrait of a living man, it would not be wise or tasteful to print." Hawthorne himself then wrote a footnote to asterisks that indicated deleted paragraphs. This footnote read:

"We are compelled to omit two or three pages, in which the author describes the interview, and gives his idea of the personal appearance and deportment of the President. The sketch appears to have been written in a benign spirit, and perhaps conveys a not inaccurate impression of its august subject; but it lacks *reverence*, and it pains us to see a gentleman of ripe age, and who has spent years under the corrective influence of foreign institutions, falling into the characteristic and most ominous fault of Young America."

The deleted paragraphs which failed to reach the eyes of the readers of the *Atlantic* read as follows:

"By and by there was a little stir on the staircase and in the passageway, and in lounged a tall, loose-jointed figure, of an exaggerated Yankee port and demeanor, whom (as being about the homeliest man I ever saw, yet by no means repulsive or disagreeable) it was impossible not to recognize as Uncle Abe.

"Unquestionably, Western man though he be, and Kentuckian by birth, President Lincoln is the essential representative of all Yankees, and the veritable specimen, physically, of what the world seems determined to regard as our characteristic qualities. It is the strangest and yet the fittest thing in the jumble of human vicissitudes, that he, out of so many millions, unlooked for, unselected by any intelligible process that could be based upon his genuine qualities, unknown to those who chose him, and unsuspected of what endowments may adapt him for his tremendous responsibility, should have found the way open for him to fling his lank personality into the chair of state,—where, I presume, it was his first impulse to throw his legs on the council-table, and tell the Cabinet Ministers a story.

"There is no describing his lengthy awkwardness, nor the uncouthness of his movement; and yet it seemed as if I had been in the habit of seeing him daily, and had shaken hands with him a thousand times in some village street; so true was he to the aspect of the pattern American, though with a certain extravagance which, possibly, I exaggerated still further by the delighted eagerness with which I took it in. If put to guess his calling and livelihood, I should have taken him for a country school-master as soon as anything else.

"He was dressed in a rusty black frock coat and pantaloons, unbrushed, and worn so faithfully that the suit had adapted itself to the curves and angularities of his figure, and had grown to be an outer skin of the man. He had shabby slippers on his feet. His hair was black, still unmixed with gray, stiff, somewhat bushy, and had apparently been acquainted with neither brush nor comb that morning, after the disarrangement of the pillow; and as to a nightcap, Uncle Abe probably knows nothing of such effeminacies. His complexion is dark and sallow, betokening, I fear, an insalubrious atmosphere around the White House; he has thick black eyebrows and an impending brow; his nose is large, and the lines about his mouth are very strongly defined.

"The whole physiognomy is as coarse a one as you would meet anywhere in the length and breadth of the States; but, withal, it is redeemed, illuminated, softened, and brightened by a kindly though serious look out of his eyes, and an expression of homely sagacity, that seems weighted with rich results of village experience.

"A great deal of native sense; no bookish cultivation, no refinement; honest at heart, and thoroughly so, and yet, in some sort, sly,—at least, endowed with a sort of tact and wisdom that are akin to craft, and would impel him, I think, to take an antagonist in flank, rather than to make a bull-run at him right in front. But, on the whole, I like this sallow, queer, sagacious visage, with the homely human sympathies that warmed it; and, for my small share in the matter, would as lief have Uncle Abe for a ruler as any man whom it would have been practicable to put in his place.

"Immediately on his entrance," continued Hawthorne's deleted and unpublished paragraphs that would have amused Lincoln with their half-audible laughter, "the President accosted our member of Congress, who had us in charge, and, with a comical twist of his face, made some jocular remark about the length of his breakfast. He then greeted us all round, not waiting for an introduction, but shaking and squeezing everybody's hand with the utmost cordiality, whether the individual's name was announced to him or not.

"His manner towards us was wholly without pretense, but yet had a kind of natural dignity, quite sufficient to keep the forwardest of us from clapping him on the shoulder and asking him for a story. A mutual acquaintance being established, our leader took the whip out of its case, and began to read the address of presentation. The whip was an exceedingly long one, its handle wrought in ivory (by some artist in the Massachusetts State Prison, I believe), and ornamented with a medallion of the President, and other equally beautiful devices; and along its whole length there was a succession of golden bands and ferrules. The address was shorter than the whip, but equally well made, consisting chiefly of an explanatory description of these artistic designs, and closing with a hint that the gift was a suggestive and emblematic one, and that the President would recognize the use to which such an instrument should be put.

"This suggestion gave Uncle Abe rather a delicate task in his reply, because, slight as the matter seemed, it apparently called for some declaration, or intimation, or faint foreshadowing of policy in reference to the conduct of the war, and the final treatment of the Rebels. But the President's Yankee aptness and not-to-be-caughtness stood him in good stead, and he jerked or wiggled himself out of the dilemma with an uncouth dexterity that was entirely in character; although, without his gesticulation of eye and mouth, —and especially the flourish of the whip, with which he imagined himself touching up a pair of fat horses,—I doubt whether his words would be worth recording, even if I could remember them.

"The gist of the reply was, that he accepted the whip as an emblem of peace, not punishment; and, this great affair over, we retired out of the presence in high good humor, only regretting that we could not have seen the President sit down and fold up his legs (which is said to be a most extraordinary spectacle), or have heard him tell one of those delectable stories for which he is so celebrated. A good many of them are afloat upon the common talk of Washington, and are certainly the aptest, pithiest, and funniest little things imaginable; though, to be sure, they smack of the frontier freedom, and would not always bear repetition in a drawing-room, or on the immaculate page of the *Atlantic*."

The closing Hawthorne-on-Lincoln paragraphs, which were published, circulated, and read, held an estimate written in "unfeigned respect and measurable confidence." The artist beholder was not unkind to his maelstrom subject and wrote:

"Good Heavens! what liberties have I been taking with one of the potentates of the earth, and the man on whose conduct more important consequences depend than on that of any other historical personage of the century! But with whom is an American citizen entitled to take a liberty, if not with his own chief magistrate? However, lest the above allusions to President Lincoln's little peculiarities (already well known to the country and to the world) should be misinterpreted, I deem it proper to say a word or two, in regard to him, of unfeigned respect and measurable confidence. He is evidently a man of keen faculties, and, what is still more to the purpose, of powerful character. As to his integrity, the people have that intuition of it which is never deceived.

"Before he actually entered upon his great office, and for a considerable time afterwards, there is no reason to suppose that he adequately estimated the gigantic task about to be imposed on him, or, at least, had any distinct idea how it was to be managed; and I presume there may have been more than one veteran politician who proposed to himself to take the power out of President Lincoln's hands into his own, leaving our honest friend only the public responsibility for the good or ill success of the career. The extremely imperfect development of his statesmanly qualities, at that period, may have justified such designs. But the President is teachable by events, and has now spent a year in a very arduous course of education; he has a flexible mind, capable of much expansion, and convertible towards far loftier studies and activities than those of his early life; and if he came to Washington a backwoods humorist, he has already transformed himself into as good a statesman (to speak moderately) as his prime-minister."

George William Curtis read what his good friend Hawthorne had written about Lincoln, and was fascinated. Curtis laughed, and wondered over it, seeing it as "pure intellect, without emotion, without sympathy, with principle . . . as unhuman and passionless as a disembodied intelligence."

Lincoln's speech acknowledging the whip presented by the factory committee was adroit with quick thinking, connected the main political issues of the day with a new buggy whip, and closed with proper appreciation of buggy-riding as one of the foremost of American recreations: "I thank you . . . for your kindness in presenting me with this truly elegant and highly creditable specimen of the handiwork of the mechanics of your State of Massachusetts, and I beg of you to express my hearty thanks to the donors. It displays a perfection of workmanship which I really wish I had time to acknowledge in more fitting words, and I might then follow your idea that it is suggestive, for it is evidently expected that a good deal of whipping is to be done. But as we meet here socially let us not think only of whipping rebels, or of those who seem to think only of whipping negroes, but of those pleasant days, which it is to be hoped are in store for us, when seated behind a good pair of horses we can crack our whips and drive through a peaceful, happy, and prosperous land. With this idea, gentlemen, I must leave you for my business duties."

Senator Sumner brought Ralph Waldo Emerson, "the Yankee Buddha," to Lincoln in February of '62. "The President impressed me more favourably than I had hoped," wrote Emerson in his journal. "A frank, sincere, well-meaning man, with a lawyer's habit of mind, good, clear statement of his fact; correct enough, not vulgar, as described, but with a sort of boyish cheerfulness, or that kind of sincerity and jolly good meaning that our class meetings on Commencement Days show, in telling our old stories over. When he has made his remark, he looks up at you with great satisfaction, and shows all his white teeth, and laughs."

The English author and historian Goldwin Smith, professor of modern history at Oxford University, secretary of one commission to recommend changes in university education and secretary of another commission on popular education, attended a reception and dinner in the White House. Congressman William D. Kelley happened to hear a scrap of conversation between his next neighbor and Goldwin Smith, which he noted:

"Professor, can you give me the impression President Lincoln has made upon you?"

"Yes, it was a very agreeable one. Such a person is quite unknown in our official circles or to those of the Continental nations. Indeed, I think his place in history will be unique. He has not been trained to diplomacy or administrative affairs, and is in all respects one of the people. But how wonderfully he is endowed and equipped for the performance of the duties of the chief executive officer of the United States at this time! The precision and minuteness of his information on all questions to which we referred was a succession of surprises to me."

For more than two years now Lincoln had been acting as President, while an immense audience sat in judgment on his performance. Many appraisals had been made, portraits, estimates, absolute pronouncements as well as frank and apologetic surmises that he was this, that, the other. The least assailed and assailable feature seemed to be on the point of personal integrity. One Al Woolford of Alton, Illinois, a plain Kentucky-born citizen, touched this point in writing to a friend, as between two Kentuckians, in May of '61: "I told Charlie in my letter to him some time ago that if Uncle Abe said the Horse was 16 feet high he would stand to it. I have known him for 23 years and he means what he says. He will do or die. You may rest assured he will never give up until he is left by the country to his own resources and has no aid nor backing. He will take Sumter if money and men can be found to do it or I am mistaken in the man."

The President's character appeared "to have been defiled by no vices," and he was "undoubtedly patriotic, sincerely so, by instinct, habit and sentiment," in the view of George Lunt, lawyer, politician, a Whig who had gone Democrat when the Whig party died, and a coeditor of the *Boston Courier*. But for all the honesty and integrity, he found "Lincoln's thoughts ran in narrow channels"; he was "infirm of purpose, so far as to be liable to be led by sharper minds and more resolute wills; though, like persons of that character, not unfrequently insisting upon minor points of consideration, whether right or wrong," and it was "no wonder that he seldom understood what the situation demanded, and seldom failed to commit mistakes when he acted for himself." Mr. Lincoln was "of that class of men, who, under color of good intentions, often fail of bringing any good purpose to pass." Mr. Lincoln had "a certain shrewdness, but was inoffensive in disposition; and in most inferior stations could scarcely have failed to win good-will." Mr. Lincoln was "as far from being a tyrant, as he was from being a statesman."

Another equally cool judgment, that of George William Curtis in *Harper's Weekly*, November 22, 1862, read: "The President is a man of convictions. He has certain profound persuasions and a very clear purpose.

He knows what the war sprang from, and upon what ground a permanent peace can be reared. He is cautious, cool, judicial. But he knows that great revolutions do not go backward; while he is aware that when certain great steps in their prosecution are once taken, there will be loud outcries and apprehension. But the ninth wave touches the point to which the whole sea will presently rise, although the next wave and the next should seem to show a falling off."

In the two and a half years that he had been President it seemed as though Lincoln had slowly won favorable consideration for himself in quarters where there was suspicion or hostility at the beginning. This moderated and less peremptory opinion of him rose partly out of a closer approach to understanding his personality and partly out of the clearer sensing that a Jackson or a Napoleon would probably not have managed this particular kind of a civil war and won thus far the advantages held by Lincoln. In June of '62 Motley wrote to his mother: "I think Mr. Lincoln embodies singularly well the healthy American mind. He revolts at extreme measures, and moves in a steady way to the necessary end. He reads the signs of the times, and will never go faster than the people at his back. So his slowness seems sometimes like hesitation; but I have not a doubt that when the people wills it, he will declare that will."

Did the President vacillate? Was he managed by others? Men and journals shifted in view. The *New York Herald* in May of '63 approved Lincoln's reversal of a court-martial order for the hanging as traitors of citizens of loyal States captured wearing uniforms of Confederate officers. Lincoln had declared them to be merely prisoners of war. The *Herald* commented: "The barbarity of such a proceeding, leading to bloody retaliation, would cause a greater loss to the North, besides being slaughter in cold blood. We always said the President was humane. His decision in this proves he is and that he is above the malignant passions of those who seek to influence him in the Cabinet or the camp." A vivid editorial printed in the *New York World* in the first week of July, 1863, and reprinted in the *Chicago Times* and other newspapers, breathed a spirit of democracy not alien to that of Lincoln. Being published in organs ruthlessly opposed to the Lincoln Administration, it was of peculiar significance in the time color of the opening paragraphs and its evaluation of Lincoln in its closing comment. The editorial read:

"This Northern section of the land has become a great variety-shop, of which the Atlantic cities are the long-extended counter. We have grown rich for what? To put gilt bands on coachmen's hats? To sweep the foul sidewalks with the heaviest silks that the toiling artisans of France can send us? To look through plate-glass windows, and pity the brown soldiers,— or sneer at the black ones?—to reduce the speed of trotting horses a second or two below its old maximum? To color meerschaums? To flaunt in laces, and sparkle in diamonds? To dredge our maidens' hair with gold-dust?— to float through life the passive shuttlecocks of fashion, from the avenues to the beaches, and back again from the beaches to the avenues? Was it for this that the broad domain of the Western hemisphere was kept so long unvisited by civilization?—for this, that Time, the father of empires, unbound the virgin zone of this youngest of his daughters and gave her, beautiful in the long veil of her forests, to the rude embrace of the adventurous Colonists? All this is what we see around us, now—now, while we are actually fighting this great battle, and supporting this great load of indebtedness. Wait till the diamonds go back to the Jews of Amsterdam; till the plate-glass window bears the fatal announcement 'For Sale,' or 'To Let,' till the voice of our Miriam is obeyed, as she sings:

'Weave no more silks, ye Lyons looms!'

Till the gold-dust is combed from the goldenlocks, and hoarded to buy bread; till the fast-driving youth smokes his clay-pipe on the platform of the horse-car; till the music-grinders cease because none will pay them; till there are no peaches in the windows at twenty-four dollars a dozen, and no heaps of bananas and pine-apples selling at the street corners; till the ten-flounced dress has but three flounces, and it is felony to drink champagne; wait till these changes show themselves, the signs of deeper want, the preludes of exhaustion and bankruptcy; then let us talk of the Maelstrom; but till then, let us not be cowards with our purses, while brave men are emptying their hearts upon the earth for us; let us not whine over our imaginary ruin, while the reversed current of circling events is carrying us farther and farther, every hour, beyond the influence of the great failing which was born of our wealth and of the deadly sin which was our fatal inheritance!

"There are those who profess to fear that our Government is becoming a mere irresponsible tyranny. If there are any who really believe that our present Chief Magistrate means to found a dynasty for himself and family, —that a *coup d'état* is in preparation by which he is to become Abraham the First, Dei Gratia,—they cannot have duly pondered his letter of June 12th, in which he unbosoms himself with the simplicity of a rustic lover called upon by an anxious parent to explain his intentions. The force of his argument is not at all injured by the homeliness of his illustrations. The American people are not much afraid that their liberties will be usurped. An army of legislators is not very likely to throw away its political privileges, and the idea of a despotism resting on an open ballot-box, is like that of Bunker Hill Monument built on the waves of Boston Harbor. We know pretty nearly how much sincerity there is in the fears so clamorously expressed, and how far they are found in company with uncompromising hostility to the armed enemies of the nation. We have learned to put a true value on the services of the watch-dog who bays the moon but does not bite the thief."

In North and South were atrocities in rhyme, the "Song of the Southern Woman" beginning:

O Abraham Lincoln! we call thee to hark,
Thou Comet of Satan! thou Boast of the Dark!

In the North, George W. Bungay wished popularity for a marching song having the stanza:

God bless our gallant President, and grant him length of days;
Let all the people crown him with fame's unfading lays,
And generations yet unborn perpetuate his praise—
Our men are marching on.

More of perplexity and of heart-searching rested in the diary entries of Mrs. Chesnut, to whom gossip and information were not merely report and fact. She wrote on July 12, 1862: "At McMahan's our small colonel, Paul Hayne's son, came into my room. To amuse the child I gave him a photograph album to look over. 'You have Lincoln in your book!' said he. 'I am astonished at you. I hate him!' and he placed the book on the floor and struck Old Abe in the face with his fist. An Englishman told me Lincoln has said that had he known such a war would follow his election he never would have set foot in Washington, nor have been inaugurated. He had never dreamed of this awful fratricidal bloodshed. That does not seem like the true John Brown spirit. I was very glad to hear it—to hear something from the President of the United States which was not merely a vulgar joke, and usually a joke so vulgar that you were ashamed to laugh, funny though it was."

In Howells's '60 biography, an overassured story of the rise of Lincoln from log cabin to White House, was inscribed in the hand of Robert T. Lincoln "The champion liar of history."

An anonymous sonnet-writer sent one of his pieces to the *Trenton* (New Jersey) *Monitor*. The praise of Lincoln was phrased in an acrostic with the capital letters alleging "Lincoln is an ass"; Western Democratic newspapers reprinted it, one saying, "For a Republican paper this rap at Father Abraham is rather severe." It read:

ABRAHAM LINCOLN

Lincoln! be firm, and fear not; bigot men
In vain assail thee with their senseless word;
Not in the future shall their voice be heard
Conveying censure. The historian's pen—
Oh! wand magic!—shall destroy the sneers,
Laughter, and carping of the world; be wise,
Nor heed the slaves of party, and their lies,
In making up its judgment on these years,
Second to few patriots in esteem,
And sorer tried than many hast thou been;
Now few the stars that thro' the darkness gleam,
And not as yet are signs of daylight seen;
Soon stars shall come, and when these pass away,
Shall gleam the light that marks thy coming glorious day.

A bombinating twang of politics was in the *Illinois State Journal* of January 6, 1863, urging "re-election of our present honored Chief Magistrate," and continuing: "In the language of a distinguished member of Congress from Illinois, we say, 'Let Abraham Lincoln finish the great work he has begun.' This great man, whom it is not extravagant to say is God-like in his moral attributes, child-like in the simplicity and purity of his character, yet manly and self-relying in his high and patriotic purpose—this man who takes no step backward—let him consummate the grandest achievement ever allotted to man, the destruction of American slavery."

Across the sea one Edmund Ollier had a sonnet published in the London *Morning Star,* reprinted in the *Living Age* in Boston:

TO PRESIDENT LINCOLN

January 1, 1863

Lincoln, that with thy steadfast truth the sand
  Of men and time and circumstance dost sway!
  The slave-cloud dwindles on this golden day,
And over all the pestilent southern land,
Breathless, the dark expectant millions stand
  To watch the northern sun rise on its way,
  Cleaving the stormy distance—every ray
Sword-bright, sword-sharp, in God's invisible hand.

Better, with this great end, partial defeat,
  And jibings of the ignorant worldly-wise,
  Than laud and triumph won with shameful blows.
The dead Past lies in its dead winding-sheet;
  The living Present droops with tearful eyes;
  But far beyond the awaiting Future glows.

As literature or belles-lettres this was second- or third-rate. As a sign and symptom, as an attempt at expressing the awe of men at history they knew was in the making, it indicated human force that demanded unlocking.

In English liberal journals estimates of Lincoln occasionally mingled drab facts with shimmering hazard; the writers had decided the American President might develop into a spokesman of deep world trends. "The second Message of Mr. Lincoln shows him to be still what he has always been," said the London *Spectator* in December of '62, "a shrewd, second-rate lawyer, very ignorant of foreign affairs and very well acquainted with those of his own country, with a few immovable convictions, and many floating and somewhat dreamy ideas, having a tolerably clear view of the end to which he aspires, and but a faint perception of the mode in which that end is ultimately to be attained. To men who can only judge by the outside, who are critics in grammar and careful for the dignity of officials, the document may seem weak or even contemptible, but to those who remember that Cromwell could not speak, or Bentham write intelligibly, and who will therefore take the trouble to search for instead of merely receiving ideas, it will, we think, become sufficiently suggestive."

Lincoln had dignity in his mild-toned refusal of mediation by European nations, in silence as to the Trent Affair. The *Spectator* continued: "He is not malignant against foreign countries; on the contrary, thinks they have behaved rather better than he expected. No power in Europe can take offense at the wording of the Message, nor can anyone say that the Republic bends to dictation, or craves in any undignified way for foreign forbearance. The words might have been more elegant, but the astutest diplomatist could have accomplished no more, and might, perhaps, have shown a reticence less complete."

The gist of the message was epitomized: "Mr. Lincoln has from the first explained that he is the exponent of the national will. He has not merely recognized it. Amidst a cloud of words and phrases, which, often clever, are always too numerous, a careful observer may detect two clear and definite thoughts. 1. The President will assent to no peace upon any terms which imply a dissolution of the Union. 2. He holds that the best reconstruction will be that which is accompanied by measures for the final extinction of slavery."

In the President's discussions of peace, said the *Spectator*, "He expresses ideas, which, however quaint, have nevertheless a kind of dreamy vastness not without its attraction. The thoughts of the man are too big for his mouth." He was saying that a nation can be divided but "the earth abideth forever," that a generation could be crushed but geography dictated that the Union could not be sundered. As to the rivers and mountains, "all are better than one or either, and all of right belong to this people and their successors forever." No possible severing of the land but would multiply and not mitigate the evils among the American States.

"It is an oddly worded argument," said the *Spectator*, "the earth being treated as if it were a living creature, an Estate of the Republic with an equal vote on its destiny." In the proposals for gradual emancipated compensation there was magnitude: "Mr. Lincoln has still the credit of having been first among American statesmen to rise to the situation, to strive that reconstruction shall not mean a new lease for human bondage." The President's paragraph was quoted having the lines: "Fellow-citizens, we cannot escape history. The fiery trial through which we pass will light us down in honor or dishonor to the latest generation," as though this had the attractive "dreamy vastness" that brought from the English commentator the abrupt sentence "The thoughts of the man are too big for his mouth."

Greeley and others could not resist the impact of some judgments pronounced on Lincoln abroad. Greeley did not accept these judgments. He questioned them sharply. He saw, however, that they had significance and they were of historic quality. Under the heading "Mr. Lincoln in Europe" the *New York Tribune* of January 10, 1863, reprinted from the Edinburgh *Mercury*:

"In Mr. Lincoln's Message, we appreciate the calm thoughtfulness so different from the rowdyism we have been accustomed to receive from Washington. He is strong in the justice of his cause and the power of his people. He speaks without acerbity even of the Rebels who have brought so much calamity upon the country, but we believe that if the miscreants of the Confederacy were brought to him today, Mr. Lincoln would bid them depart and try to be better and braver men in the future. When we recollect the raucous hate in this country toward the Indian rebels, we feel humiliated that this 'rail splitter' from Illinois should show himself so superior to the mass of monarchical statesmen.

"Mr. Lincoln's brotherly kindness, truly father of his country, kind, merciful, lenient even to a fault, is made the sport and butt of all the idle literary buffoons of England. The day will come when the character and career of Abraham Lincoln will get justice in this country and his assailants will show their shame for the share they took in lampooning so brave and noble a man, who in a fearful crisis possessed his soul in patience, trusting in God. 'Truly,' Mr. Lincoln speaks, 'the fiery trial through which we pass will light us down in honor or dishonor to the latest generation.' There is little doubt what the verdict of future generations will be of Abraham Lincoln.

"Before two years of his administration has been completed, he has reversed the whole constitutional attitude of America on the subject of Slavery; he has saved the territories from the unhallowed grasp of the slave power; he has purged the accursed institution from the Congressional District; he has hung a slave trader in New York, the nest of slave pirates; he has held out the right hand of fellowship to the negro Republicans of Liberia and Hayti; he has joined Great Britain in endeavoring to sweep the slave trade from the coast of Africa! There can be no doubt of the verdict of posterity on such acts as these. Within the light of the 'fiery trial' of which Mr. Lincoln speaks, another light shines clear and refulgent—the torch of freedom—to which millions of poor slaves now look with eager hope."

At home and abroad judgments came oftener that America had at last a President who was All-American. He embodied his country in that he had no precedents to guide his footsteps; he was not one more individual of a continuing tradition, with the dominant lines of the mold already cast for him by Chief Magistrates who had gone before. Webster, Calhoun, and Clay conformed to a classicism of the school of the English gentleman, as did perhaps all the Presidents between Washington and Lincoln, save only Andrew Jackson.

The inventive Yankee, the Western frontiersman and pioneer, the Kentuckian of laughter and dreams, had found blend in one man who was the national head. In the "dreamy vastness" noted by the London *Spectator*, in the pith of the folk words "The thoughts of the man are too big for his mouth," was the feel of something vague that ran deep in American hearts, that hovered close to a vision for which men would fight, struggle, and die, a grand though blurred chance that Lincoln might be leading them toward something greater than they could have believed might come true.

Also around Lincoln gathered some of the hope that a democracy can choose a man, set him up high with power and honor, and the very act does something to the man himself, raises up new gifts, modulations, controls, outlooks, wisdoms, inside the man, so that he is something else again than he was before they sifted him out and anointed him to take an oath and solemnly sign himself for the hard and terrible, eye-filling and center-staged, role of Head of the Nation.

To be alive for the work he must carry in his breast Cape Cod, the Shenandoah, the Mississippi, the Gulf, the Rocky Mountains, the Sacramento, the Great Plains, the Great Lakes, their dialects and shibboleths. He must be instinct with the regions of corn, textile mills, cotton, tobacco, gold, coal, zinc, iron.

He would be written as a Father of his People if his record ran well, one whose heart beat with understanding of the many who came to the Executive Mansion, wore its thresholds, nicked the banisters, smoothed the doorknobs, and made vocal their wants and offerings.

In no one of the thirty-one rooms of the White House was Lincoln at home.

Back and forth in this house strode phantoms—red platoons of boys vanished into the war—thin white-spoken ghosts of women who would never again hold those boys in their arms—they made a soft moaning the imagination could hear in the dark night and the gray dawn.

To think incessantly of blood and steel, steel and blood, the argument without end by the mouths of brass cannon, of a mystic cause carried aloft and sung on dripping and crimson bayonet points—to think so and thus across nights and months folding up into years, was a wearing and a grinding that brought questions. What is this teaching and who learns from it and where does it lead? "If we could first know where we are and whither we are tending, we could better judge what to do and how to do it."

Beyond the black smoke lay what salvations and jubilees? Death was in the air. So was birth. What was dying no man was knowing. What was being born no man could say.

The dew came on the White House lawn and the moonlight spread lace of white films in the night and the syringa and the bridal wreath blossomed and the birds fluttered in the bushes and nested in the sycamore and the veery thrush fluted with never a weariness. The war drums rolled and the telegraph clicked off mortality lists, now a thousand, now ten thousand in a day. Yet there were moments when the processes of men seemed to be only an evil dream and justice lay in deeper transitions than those wrought by men dedicated to kill or be killed.

CHAPTER 41

GETTYSBURG—VICKSBURG—
DEEP TIDES '63

THE *Cincinnati Gazette* correspondent with the Army of the Potomac
chanced to hear Lincoln say shortly before appointing George Gordon
Meade to command of the Army of the Potomac, "I tell you I think a great
deal of that fine fellow Meade." The grandfather of Meade was a Philadelphia merchant, an original member of the Hibernian Society, an orig-
inator of the Society of the Friendly Sons of St. Patrick, an organizer of
the first Catholic Sunday schools in Philadelphia. Meade's father was a merchant, shipowner, United States naval agent in Cadiz, Spain; and because of
misunderstandings involved in certain debt collections, the father was serving a two-year period in jail when the boy was born in Cadiz in 1815.
Graduating from West Point, the son took a hand in fighting Seminole
Indians, resigned from the army, worked on War Department surveys, was
brevetted first lieutenant for gallantry in the Mexican War, and for five
years was a lighthouse-builder among Florida reefs. He married Margaretta,
daughter of John Sergeant, a noted Philadelphia lawyer, in 1840, and often
when away on duty wrote her a letter every day, sharing with her his ideas
and impressions, writing to her fluently of all that interested him; his words
ran on as though the two of them had good talks together when there was
time to talk; day by day the letters went to her as though she were the best
listener in the world.

From Monterey during the Mexican War Meade wrote her of the Mexican War as "brought on by our injustice to a neighbor," of how Mexican
stupidity and folly had given "our rulers plausible excuses for their conduct," and now once in the war he desired to see it carried on with energy
well directed. "But such has not been the case, nor will it ever be so, as
long as generals are made in the counting-house and soldiers on farms."
The young women of Mexico would "not pass for beauties" up North.
"But I have been struck with one remarkable fact with regard to the
women, and that is the grace and ease of manner they all possess . . . the
way they wear their clothes, always nicely made, clean and gracefully worn.
A really pretty girl, with a *reboso* thrown over her shoulder to conceal her
dress, with her pretty patterned French calico or printed muslin, well made
and fitting perfectly, will hand you a cup of water in a graceful way that
would put to blush many of our finely dressed ladies of the upper ten
thousand."

A quiet religious tone, pious but not canting, ran through parts of nearly every letter, references to "Our Saviour," to "the will of God and the uncertainty of human plans and projects," and his own "innumerable sins," which he prayed would be forgiven. While in charge of topographical surveys of the Great Lakes, with headquarters at Detroit, Meade's scientific turn of mind had attracted Professor Henry of the Smithsonian Institution, who urged on Meade a career in research and scientific discovery. He inclined toward this, was not a soldier by instinct, writing his wife, "I like fighting as little as any man." The war came. He went to Washington in June, 1861, offered himself as a West Pointer of Mexican War experience; in the confusion and red tape they withheld a commission; he returned to Detroit.

Then came Meade's appointment as brigadier general of volunteers on August 31, 1861, and he had seen active and often front-line service in every battle of the Army of the Potomac—except for a short interval of recovery from a gunshot wound at New Market Road on the Peninsula. The bullet pierced his forearm, entered the side, and came out two inches from the spine. Hearing a doctor after hurried examination then say he had been hit in the back, he moaned to the surgeon often through the night, "Just think, doctor, of my being shot in the back!" After forty-two days off duty, and against physician's advice, he left his family and comfortable home in Philadelphia for action in the second Bull Run battle.

In camp at Fredericksburg he had told President Lincoln that he believed the army was gratified with the President's revocation of General Hunter's emancipation proclamation, writing to his wife that the President said, "I am trying to do my duty, but no one can imagine what influences are brought to bear upon me."

From camp at Falmouth he wrote her of "a very handsome and pleasant dinner" with the President and Mrs. Lincoln, of how the report of the Committee on the Conduct of the War had been too severe on General Franklin, whom Burnside blamed for the Fredericksburg failure. "I took occasion when I had a chance to say a good word for Franklin to the President, who seemed very ready to hear anything in his behalf, and said promptly that he always liked Franklin and believed him to be a true man. The President looks careworn and exhausted. It is said he has been brought here for relaxation and amusement, and that his health is seriously threatened. He expresses himself greatly pleased with what he has seen, and his friends say he has improved already." Meade had dwelt on human behavior as to Franklin and Burnside. "I endeavored to convince the President that the whole affair turned on a misapprehension, Burnside thinking he was saying and ordering one thing, and Franklin understanding another."

Also Meade quietly confessed to his wife, by letter, that he was using the President's visit to improve any chance he might have for promotion. "Since our review, I have attended the other reviews and have been making myself (or at least trying to do so) very agreeable to Mrs. Lincoln, who seems an amiable sort or personage. In view also of the vacant brigadier-ship in the regular army, I have ventured to tell the President one or two stories, and I think I have made decided progress in his affections."

A few days later Meade wrote his wife that he had been astonished at receiving a large bouquet of beautiful flowers with a card and the compliments of Mrs. Lincoln. "At first I was very much tickled, and my vanity insinuated that my *fine appearance* had taken Mrs. L's eye and that my fortune was made. This delusion was speedily dissolved by the orderly who brought the bouquet. All the principal generals had been similarly honored."

Less than ten weeks later, however, there came crashing down on Meade, against his wish, in the form of an order that as a soldier he could not disobey, the President's appointment of him to the command of the Army of the Potomac, promotion so swiftly and vastly upward that he wrote his wife half-groaning under his new responsibility: "Love, blessings and kisses to all. Pray for me and beseech our heavenly Father to permit me to be an instrument to save my country."

Now it was well Meade had been a modest man, holding aloof from cliques and intrigues, serving loyally under McClellan, Pope, McClellan again, Burnside, Hooker, his unlucky predecessors and comrades. Now it was well Duty meant more to him than Glory. Where McClellan most often wrote to his wife that any lack of success on his part must be laid on others, Meade more often was moderate and apologetic, writing to his wife, "Sometimes I have a little sinking at the heart, when reflecting that perhaps I may fail at the grand scratch; but I try to console myself with the belief that I shall probably do as well as most of my neighbors, and that your firm faith must be founded on some reasonable groundwork."

The President on June 15 of '63 issued a call for 100,000 troops, from Pennsylvania (50,000), Maryland (10,000), West Virginia (10,000), Ohio (30,000), to serve for six months unless sooner discharged against "armed insurrectionary combinations threatening to make inroads" into the States named. Nothing like the number called for sprang forward to enlist.

The Pennsylvania Governor urged that with the enemy six miles from Chambersburg, and advancing to threaten the State capital, men should not quibble; the President had fixed the term of service at six months, but it was not intended they should serve longer than the immediate emergency. The Governor of Maryland issued an appeal to loyal men, trying to overcome their fears that once sworn into the United States service they would be sent out of the State. The Governor of New Jersey hurried two regiments of militia to Harrisburg, but when they learned they must take an oath and be mustered into the Federal Army they went back to New Jersey. The Secretary of War called for help from the governors of thirteen States. Thirty regiments of Pennsylvania militia, besides artillery and cavalry, and nineteen regiments from New York, were mobilized at Harrisburg under General Couch from the Army of the Potomac. Governor Seymour's pledge telegraphed to Stanton, "I will spare no effort to send you troops at once," and his setting in motion nineteen regiments at once, resulted in Stanton's replying on June 18, "The President directs me to re-

Philadelphia Post Office, June 16th, 1863.

I have just received the following dispatch from the Governor of this State, with a request that it be conspicuously posted in the City.

C. A. WALBORN, P. M.

Harrisburg, June 16th, 1863.

THE ENEMY

is

APPROACHING!

I RELY UPON THE PEOPLE FOR THE

DEFENCE OF THE STATE!

AND HAVE

CALLED THE MILITIA

FOR THAT PURPOSE.

The term of service will only be while the danger to the State is imminent.

Send forward Companies

AS SOON AS POSSIBLE

Signed,

ANDREW G. CURTIN.

Handbill sounding the alarm as Lee "invaded" the North. From the Barrett collection.

turn his thanks to His Excellency Governor Seymour and his staff for their energetic and prompt action."

From day to day through latter June the news overshadowing all else in the public prints was that of Lee's army. Far behind Lee now was Richmond and its small defensive force. When he had requisitioned for rations, it was said the Confederate Commissary General replied, "If General Lee wishes rations let him seek them in Pennsylvania." When Lee had been asked about a Union army taking Richmond while he was away, he smiled, it was said. "In that case we shall swap queens." He and his chief, Davis, had decided that "valuable results" might follow the taking of Harrisburg, Philadelphia, Baltimore, Washington. In that case, besides immense amounts of supplies, provisions, munitions, there would be European recognition.

As his troops steadily plodded up the Cumberland Valley Lee's orders were strict against plundering and straggling. The army would seize needed supplies and pay for them in Confederate money, a currency that would be good and valid if they should capture Harrisburg, Philadelphia, Baltimore, Washington. On June 15 Lee's vanguard drove Union troops out of Hagerstown, Maryland, ordered all stores kept open, telegraph wires cut and poles pulled down, cattle seized, payments in Confederate paper money. Into McConnellsburg, Chambersburg, York, Greencastle, Gettysburg, the long lines of gray- and butternut-clad soldiers moved, living on fat rations they had not tasted the like of in many months. Many who had marched barefoot out of Virginia again wore socks and shoes, taken from storekeepers' stocks and paid for with Confederate money.

Men well informed believed that Lee had nearly 100,000 men and 250 cannon, so Simon Cameron at Harrisburg sent word to Lincoln. Retreating Union forces burned a bridge a mile and a half long. The Mayor of York went out several miles from town to meet the enemy, arranging for peace and immunity; he surrendered his borough, and the Confederates left it with tribute of $28,000 in United States Treasury notes, 40,000 pounds of fresh beef, 30,000 bushels of corn, 1,000 pairs of shoes, besides sundries.

Lee's men were in a high and handsome stride, off on a great adventure. In two contests within seven months they had routed, sent reeling, threatened to crush, the Army of the Potomac. Soon again they would meet that old rival, this time overwhelm it, they were sure. They had the officers of genius and the rank and file of proved endurance and courage to perform on a grand scale.

"There were never such men in an army before," said Lee. "They will go anywhere and do anything if properly led." They believed this themselves, and had reasons. The English Lieutenant Colonel Fremantle, traveling from day to day with the invading army, noted, as did other observers, that the universal feeling in the army was "one of profound contempt for an enemy whom they have beaten so constantly, and under so many disadvantages." The fear that smote deep among classes and masses in the North was that recorded by Welles on June 15, of Lee "putting forth his whole energy in one great and desperate struggle which shall be decisive; he means to strike a blow of serious consequences, and thus bring the War to a close."

Unnoticed in the public prints was the mood of the women of the invaded Pennsylvania region. Transferred to soldiers repelling invaders of home soil, it might be reckoned on. Fremantle wrote of Hood's ragged Jacks from Texas, Alabama, Arkansas, marching through Chambersburg with cheers and laughter at the taunts of scowling, well-dressed women: "One female had seen fit to adorn her ample bosom with a huge Yankee flag, and she stood at the door of her house, her countenance expressing the greatest. contempt for the barefooted Rebs; several companies passed her without taking any notice; but at length a Texan gravely remarked, 'Take care, madam, for Hood's boys are great at storming breastworks when the Yankee colors is on them.' . . . The patriotic lady beat a precipitate retreat." No repartee was flung at a gaunt woman with a face of doom who cried from a window at the passing troops: "Look at Pharaoh's army going to the Red Sea." To a woman who sang "The Star-spangled Banner" at him, General R. E. Lee lifted his hat and rode on. From another window a woman gazed at the cool and impressive Lee riding by and murmured, "Oh, I wish he was ours!"

Like a foretokening a girl in Greencastle, "sweet sixteen and never yet kissed," came running out of a house at Pickett's Virginians, her face flushed and her eyes blazing. For an apron she wore the Union flag. And she hurled a défi: "Come and take it, the man that dares!" Pickett bowed, sweeping his hat. His soldiers gave the girl a long cheer and a gale of bright laughter.

The *Springfield Republican* urged Lincoln himself to take the field; he was as good a strategist as the Northern generals had proved, and his personal presence would arouse enthusiasm. As days passed in latter June Welles wrote that "great apprehension" prevailed in Washington, though Meade's taking command on June 28 was well received. From Lincoln, Stanton, and others Welles tried to pry loose information. "Where is the army?" he asked those who came from Pennsylvania. On June 28 he heard of "rebel" scouts seen near Georgetown, a Washington suburb. "Just at sunset, the Blairs rode past my house to their city residence, not caring to remain at Silver Spring [their country home near Washington] until the crisis is past."

David Homer Bates at the telegraph office noticed the President's anxiety increased as communication with the army was interrupted: "All the news we received dribbled over a single line of wire via Hagerstown; and when Meade's headquarters were pushed beyond that place through the necessity of following Lee's advance, we lost telegraphic connection altogether, only regaining it by the Hanover Junction route a day later. From that point to Hanover there was a railroad wire. Thence to Gettysburg the line was on the turnpike, and the service was poor and desultory. Lincoln was in the telegraph office hour after hour days and nights until the morning of July 4."

When Lee's army had vanished into the Shenandoah Valley to reappear in Pennsylvania, Lincoln's instructions to Meade ran that not Richmond but Lee's army must be the objective. Meade followed Lee with orders from Lincoln "to find and fight" the enemy. From day to day neither

Meade nor Lee had been certain where the other was. Lee would rather have taken Harrisburg, its stores and supplies, and then battled Meade on the way to Philadelphia. In that case Lee would have had ammunition enough to keep his artillery firing with no letup, no orders during an infantry charge that ammunition was running low and must be saved.

Lee rode his horse along roads winding through bright summer landscapes to find himself suddenly looking at the smoke of a battle he had not ordered nor planned. Some of his own marching divisions had become entangled with enemy columns, traded shots, and a battle had begun that Lee could draw away from or carry on. He decided to carry on. He said Yes. His troops in their last two battles and on general form looked unbeatable. Against him was an untried commander with a jealous staff that had never worked as smoothly as his own. If he could repeat his performances with his men at Fredericksburg and Chancellorsville, he could then march to Harrisburg, use the State capitol for barracks, replenish his needs, march on to Philadelphia, Baltimore, and Washington, lay hold of money, supplies, munitions, win European recognition and end the war.

The stakes were immense, the chances fair. The new enemy commander had never planned a battle nor handled a big army in the wild upsets of frontal combat on a wide line. Also fifty-eight regiments of Northern veterans who had fought at Antietam, Fredericksburg, Chancellorsville, had gone home, their time up, their places filled by militia and raw recruits.

One factor was against Lee: he would have to tell his cannoneers to go slow and count their shells, while Meade's artillery could fire on and on from an endless supply. Another factor too was against Lee: he was away from his Virginia, where he knew the ground and the people, while Meade's men were fighting for their homes, women, barns, cattle, and fields against invaders and strangers, as Meade saw and felt it.

To Lee's words, "If the enemy is there, we must attack him," Longstreet, who now replaced Stonewall Jackson, spoke sharply, "If he is there, it will be because he is anxious that we should attack him—a good reason, in my judgment, for not doing so." This vague and involved feeling Longstreet nursed in his breast; attack was unwise, and his advice rejected. It resulted in hours of delay and wasted time that might have counted.

Lee hammered at the Union left wing the first day, the right wing the second day, Meade on that day sending word to Lincoln that the enemy was "repulsed at all points." On the third day, July 3 of '63, Lee smashed at Meade's center. Under Longstreet's command, General George Edward Pickett, a tall arrow of a man, with mustache and goatee, with long ringlets of auburn hair flying as he galloped his horse, sent his 15,000 men, who had nearly a mile to go up a slow slope of land to reach the Union center. Pickett might have had thoughts in his blanket under the stars some night that week of how long ago it was, twenty-one years, since he, a Virginia boy schooled in Richmond, had been studying law in his uncle's office in Quincy, Illinois, seeing men daily who tried cases with the young attorney Abraham Lincoln. And the Pickett boy had gone on to West Point, graduated at the bottom of his class, the last of all, though later he had been first to go over the parapets at Chapultepec in 1847, and still later, in 1859, had taken possession of San Juan Island at Puget Sound on the delicate mission of accommodating officials of the Buchanan Administration in bringing on a war with Great Britain, with the hope of saving his country from a threatened civil war by welding its divided sections. British diplomacy achieved joint occupation of the island by troops of two nations and thus averted war. On the Peninsula, Pickett's men had earned the nickname of "The Game Cock Brigade," and he considered love of woman second only to the passion for war.

Before starting his men on their charge to the Union center, Pickett handed Longstreet a letter to a girl in Richmond he was to marry if he lived. Longstreet had ordered Pickett to go forward and Pickett had penciled on the back of the envelope, "If Old Peter's [Longstreet's] nod means death, good-bye, and God bless you, little one!" An officer held out a flask of whisky to Pickett: "Take a drink with me; in an hour you'll be in hell or glory." And Pickett said No; he had promised "the little girl" he wouldn't.

Across the long rise of open ground, with the blue flag of Virginia floating ahead, over field and meadow Pickett's 15,000 marched steadily and smoothly, almost as if on a drill ground. Solid shot, grape and canister, from the Union artillery plowed through them, and later a wild rain of rifle bullets. Seven-eighths of a mile they marched in the open sunlight, every man a target for the Union marksmen behind stone fences and breastworks. They obeyed orders; Uncle Robert had said they would go anywhere and do anything.

As men fell their places were filled, the ranks closed up. As officers tumbled off horses it was taken as expected in battle.

Perhaps half who started reached the Union lines surmounting Cemetery Ridge.

Then came cold steel, the bayonet, the clubbed musket. The strongest and last line of the enemy was reached. "The Confederate battle flag waved over his defences," said a Confederate major, "and the fighting over the wall became hand to hand, but more than half having already fallen, our line was too weak to rout the enemy."

Meade rode up white-faced to hear it was a repulse and cried, "Thank God!" Lee commented: "They deserved success as far as it can be deserved by human valor and fortitude. More may have been required of them than they were able to perform." To one of his colonels Lee said, "This has been a sad day for us, a sad day, but we cannot expect always to gain victories."

As a heavy rainfall came on the night of July 4 Lee ordered a retreat toward the Potomac.

Meade was seen that day sitting in the open on a stone, his head held in his hand, willing it should rain, thankful that his army had, as he phrased it, driven "the invaders from our soil." For three days and nights Meade wasn't out of his clothes, took only snatches of sleep, while he had spoken the controlling decisions to his corps commanders in the bloodiest battle of modern warfare up till that time. Tabulations ran that the Union Army lost 23,000 killed, wounded and missing, the Confederate Army 28,000. Pickett came out of it alive to write his Virginia girl, "Your soldier lives and mourns and but for you, he would rather, a million times rather, be back there with his dead to sleep for all time in an unknown grave."

One tree in line of fire had 250 bullets in it, another tree 110 lead messengers that missed human targets. Farmer Rummel's cow lane was piled with thirty dead horses. Farmer Rummel found two cavalrymen who had fought afoot, killed each other and fallen with their feet touching, each with a bloody saber in his hand. A Virginian and a 3d Pennsylvania man had fought on horseback, hacking each other head and shoulders with sabers; they clinched and their horses ran out from under them; they were found with stiff and bloody fingers fastened in each other. The pegleg Confederate General Ewell, struck by a bullet, had chirped merrily to General John B. Gordon, "It don't hurt a bit to be shot in a wooden leg."

Military experts studied 27,000 muzzle-loading muskets picked up on the battlefield; 24,000 were loaded, one half had two loads, many had ten loads; and the experts deduced that in the bloody work and the crying out loud that day many soldiers lost their heads, loaded, forgot to fire, and then forgot their muskets were loaded. Also they figured it out that each soldier in battle fired away about his own weight in lead before he killed one of the opposition.

Where cannon and muskets had roared with sheets of flame on Cemetery Ridge was a tall graveyard gate with a sign forbidding the use of firearms out of respect to the dead and decently buried on the premises. The dead on the battlefield lay where they had fallen during three days' fighting, and on July 3 Fremantle noticed an "offensive" odor of decomposing bodies. "Through the branches of the trees and among the gravestones in the cemetery a shower of destruction crashed ceaselessly," wrote the New York World correspondent. He noted with one storm of shell from the Confederate guns that soldiers and officers leaping from rest on the grass died "some with cigars in their teeth, some with pieces of food in their fingers, and one, a pale young German, with a miniature of his sister in his hands."

The brave and able General John F. Reynolds, who had once peremptorily refused Lincoln's offer of command of the Army of the Potomac, felt a bullet sink into his neck, called to his men, "Forward! for God's sake, forward!" and fell into the arms of a captain with the words, "Good God, Wilcox, I am killed."

Companies of students from the Lutheran Theological Seminary and from the Pennsylvania College of Gettysburg took a hand in the action. A seventy-year-old farmer, John L. Burns, in a swallowtail coat with brass buttons, joined up with the Iron Brigade, went under fire, amazed the youngsters with his coolness, took three wounds and was carried to the rear. When a Wisconsin sergeant asked Burns whatever made him step out into the war without being enlisted, the old man said "the rebels had either driven away or milked his cows and he was going to be even with them." A son of Harriet Beecher Stowe was sent to the rear with bad wounds. Joseph Revere, a grandson of the famous Paul Revere of Boston, was killed.

Confederate bayonets had taken Union cannon and Union bayonets had retaken the cannon. Round Top, Little Round Top, Culp's Hill, rang with the yells of men shooting and men shot. Meadows of white daisies were pockmarked with horse hoofs. Dead and wounded lay scattered in rows, in little sudden piles, in singles and doubles, the spindrift of a storm wave.

The names of Plum Run, Peach Orchard, Devil's Den, Ziegler's Grove, Trostle's Barnyard, became sacred and terrible to those who had touched a mystery of human struggle and suffering in those ordinarily peaceful landscape corners where spiders could ordinarily weave their webs and linger in the sunshine without interruption. The *Richmond Enquirer* man wrote when the firing ceased: "One by one the stars came out in the quiet sky, and over that field of carnage hung the sweet influences of the Pleiades."

The first battle of the war fought outside a Slave State was over. Lee could have managed it better. So could Meade. The arguments began. Longstreet said Lee was "off his balance" in major decisions. Sickles, a Union general, said Meade did him wrong. The *New York World* correspondent wrote the day after the battle, from the cemetery where the sign was posted forbidding the shooting of firearms: "I, who sit this evening on a camp-stool, beside the ruins of the monument against which I leaned listening to the robin yesterday, find it impossible to recall with distinctness the details of the unparalleled battle just closed." Smoke got in his eyes, confusion in his ears: "With a vision deceived, perhaps, in many instances, by the mere tumult of the conflict, and with ears filled by divers reports and estimates of officers and surgeons, I cannot, I dare not attempt to give you an account or opinion of our losses; they are great."

Meade issued an order thanking the Army of the Potomac for glorious results: "An enemy superior in numbers and flushed with the pride of a successful invasion, attempted to overcome and destroy this Army. Utterly baffled and defeated, he has now withdrawn from the contest. . . . The Commanding General looks to the Army for greater efforts to drive from our soil every vestige of the presence of the invader."

On the wall map in his office, Lincoln had watched the colored pins as they changed to indicate military positions. Zach Chandler came in, spoke of painful anxiety because the fate of the nation seemed to hang in the balance, noted "the restless solicitude of Mr. Lincoln, as he paced up and down the room, reading despatches, soliloquizing, and often stopping to trace positions on the map."

The President announced to the country on July 4 that news had arrived up to 10 P.M. of July 3 such as to cover with honor the Army of the Potomac, to promise great success to the cause of the Union, and to claim condolence for the many gallant fallen. "For this he especially desires that on this day He whose will, not ours, should ever be done be everywhere remembered and reverenced with profoundest gratitude."

Fry of the Adjutant General's office had noticed Lincoln clinging to the War Office and devouring every scrap of news as it came over the wires. "I saw him read General Meade's congratulatory order to the Army of the Potomac. When he came to the sentence about 'driving the invaders from our soil,' an expression of disappointment settled upon his face, his hands dropped upon his knees, and in tones of anguish he exclaimed, ' "Drive the *invaders* from our soil." My God! Is that all?' "

On July 6 Lincoln and Halleck talked with Brigadier General Hermann Haupt, direct from Gettysburg, where he had been in charge of transportation, roads, bridges, telegraph lines. Haupt had commandeered a railroad locomotive for his ride to Washington in a hurry to report his three-hour conversation of the previous day with Generals Meade and Pleasanton. "General Meade was much surprised to learn that the bridges and telegraph lines had nearly been reconstructed, and that in a few hours he could begin to send his wounded to the hospitals. After many incidents connected with the battle had been related, General Pleasanton made the remark that if Longstreet had concentrated his fire more and had kept it up a little longer, we would have lost the day; to which Meade made no reply, and appeared to acquiesce in this opinion. After other matters had been disposed of, I remarked to General Meade that I supposed he would at once follow up his advantage and capture the remains of Lee's army before he could cross the Potomac. The reply was, 'Lee's pontoon-trains have been destroyed, and the river is not fordable. My army requires a few days' rest, and cannot move at present.' "

Haupt had argued with Meade that his construction corps could put an army across the Potomac in less than forty-eight hours "if they had no material except such as could be procured from barns, houses, trees, and it is not safe to assume that the enemy cannot do what we can." Haupt could not convince Meade, and feeling sure that Lee would escape across the river, had walked out of the three-hour conversation and taken an engine to Washington to report what he considered a sorry situation.

The next day at seven in the evening Lincoln sent from the Soldiers' Home a telegram to Halleck saying that he had left the telegraph office "a good deal dissatisfied." He quoted from Meade's address to the army at Gettysburg about driving "the invaders from our soil," saying, "You know I did not like the phrase." Since then had come word that the enemy was crossing his wounded over the Potomac, while the news of troop movements seemed to connect with a purpose to cover Baltimore and Washington "and to get the enemy across the river again without a further collision, and they do not appear connected with a purpose to prevent his crossing and to destroy him." Lincoln feared the latter purpose had been rejected, and instructed Halleck: "If you are satisfied the latter purpose is entertained, and is judiciously pursued, I am content. If you are not so satisfied, please look to it."

While the battle of Gettysburg was being fought the President had wondered a good deal what was happening to Grant down at Vicksburg, Mississippi. One evening in June when the Associated Press correspondent L. A. Gobright had asked about Vicksburg news, Lincoln said, "I have nothing new; I can't sleep tonight without hearing something; go with me to the War Department." They walked over, and according to Gobright: "We had no sooner ascended to the second story, than a messenger of the telegraph-office in that building handed him a despatch, reading as follows, dated somewhere in the Southwest: 'A report has reached here that our troops at Vicksburg have been defeated, and our army dispersed.' Mr. Lincoln read the telegram under the disadvantage of imperfect light. He was extremely nervous; his hands and legs shook violently; his face, upon which the gas shone, was ghastly. He again read the telegram. 'Bad news, bad news,' he added. 'Don't say anything about this—don't mention it.' 'Mr. President, allow me to say one word.' 'Well, sir.' 'The despatch you have received mentions that the communication of disaster is founded on mere report. More than one half of war rumors are false. So it may be in this case.' The President, somewhat relieved, repeated, 'But don't say anything about this.'"

Undoubtedly Lincoln was a troubled man that night. For months he had been haunted by the colossal Vicksburg affair. Grant was trying to starve out one Confederate army in Vicksburg while he held off other Confederate armies from reaching Vicksburg. Against many representations and pleadings Lincoln had kept Grant in command and was hoping for great results. But the months passed. Probably Lincoln that night shook his head and said to Gobright in a low trembling voice, "Bad news, bad news," admonishing the newspaperman, "Don't say anything about this." But the state of nervous collapse indicated by Gobright—"his hands and legs shook violently"—had not been noted by other, and at least equally acute, observers who were seeing the President oftener.

Daily came the routine, the accidents, affairs, requiring guidance, decisions from the President, even though they might be small matters alongside of the fury preparing or already raging at Gettysburg or Vicksburg. He must write a memorandum as though to record some gnawing of conscience: "Mr. Israel D. Andrews appeals to me, saying he is suffering injury by something I have said of him. I really know very little of Mr. Andrews. As well as I can remember, I was called on by one or two persons asking me to give him or aid him in getting some public employment; and as a reason for declining I stated that I had a very unfavorable opinion of him, chiefly because I had been informed that, in connection with some former service of his to the government, he had presented an enormous and unjustifiable claim, which I understood he was still pressing the government to pay. I certainly did not pretend to know anything of the matter personally, and I say now, I do not personally know anything which should detract from Mr. Andrews's character." To this the President signed his name, filed it among his personal papers as a gesture by which he dismissed it from his mind and was more free to think about Gettysburg and Vicksburg. He recommended a French officer, Colonel Duffié, to Stanton as "well spoken of" because Duffié when surrounded by Jeb Stuart's cavalry near Millersburg had "cut his way out with proportionately heavy loss to his then small command."

When Lee's van was a day's march from Harrisburg, Lincoln had issued a long letter to an Ohio Democratic committee regarding habeas corpus and the Constitution; sent General R. H. Milroy a sharp letter for losing a division of troops and blaming it on the West Pointers who were his superiors; written a note of comfort to General David Hunter that he must not grumble so much, for he was still held in respect and esteem. On the third day's fighting he pardoned a deserter sentenced to be shot, and sent the telegram to Robert Lincoln at Harvard: "Don't be uneasy. Your mother very slightly hurt by her fall." Welles wrote in his diary:

July 7, Tuesday. The President said this morning, with a countenance indicating sadness and despondency, that Meade still lingered at Gettysburg, when he should have been at Hagerstown or near the Potomac, to cut off the retreating army of Lee. While unwilling to complain and willing and anxious to give all praise to the general and army for the great battle and victory, he feared the old idea of driving the Rebels out of Pennsylvania and Maryland, instead of capturing them, was still prevalent among the officers. He hoped this was not so, said he had spoken to Halleck and urged that the right tone and spirit should be infused into officers and men, and that General Meade especially should be reminded of his (the President's) wishes and expectations. But General Halleck gave him a short and curt reply, showing that he did not participate and sympathize in this feeling, and, said the President, "I drop the subject."

From this Cabinet meeting Welles went to his office to wait on Vice-President Hamlin, two Maine Senators, and a Massachusetts Senator, on a matter of coast defense and protection of fishermen turned over to him by the President. And Welles was just saying good afternoon to this distinguished delegation when a dispatch was handed to him. It was from Admiral Porter at Vicksburg, with news that the city, its defenses, and Pemberton's army of some 30,000 troops had surrendered, fallen into the hands of Grant and the Union army.

Welles excused himself to the delegation and headed for the Executive Mansion as fast as his short legs would take him. He went in to find the President with Chase and others, pointing on a map to details of Grant's movements.

Welles gave the news of the Porter telegram, Vicksburg fallen, Pemberton's army of 30,000 bagged. The President put down the map, rose at once, said they would not discuss Vicksburg and the map any more, and, "I myself will telegraph this news to General Meade." He took his hat as if to go, suddenly stopped and looked down with a shining face at Welles, took him by the hand, put an arm around him, and broke forth: "What can we do for the Secretary of the Navy for this glorious intelligence? He is always giving us good news. I cannot, in words, tell you my joy over this result. It is great, Mr. Welles, it is great!"

The two of them walked out across the White House lawn. "This," said the President, "will relieve Banks. It will inspire me." Welles thought the opportunity a good one to request the President to insist upon his own views, to enforce them, not only on Meade but on Halleck.

Lincoln directed Halleck to send word at once to Meade that Vicksburg had surrendered to Grant on July 4, and furthermore: "Now, if General Meade can complete his work so gloriously prosecuted thus far, by the literal or substantial destruction of Lee's army, the rebellion will be over."

Over the country as the news spread were mass meetings and speeches, rejoicing, firing of guns, ringing of bells. In hundreds of cities large and small were celebrations with torchlight processions, songs, jubilation, refreshments. "The price of gold . . . fell ten or fifteen cents and the whole country is joyous," wrote Welles. A brass band and a big crowd serenaded the President, who, after sending his telegram to Meade via Halleck from the Soldiers' Home at seven o'clock, had driven in to the White House. He spoke to the crowd. "I am very glad indeed to see you to-night, and yet I will not say I thank you for this call; but I do most sincerely thank Almighty God for the occasion on which you have called." He mentioned three Presidents who had died on the Fourth of July.

An offhand speech it was, as though he had been so pressed by other affairs that he had given little or no time to what he might say to a crowd. "Now on this last Fourth of July just passed, when we have a gigantic rebellion, at the bottom of which is an effort to overthrow the principle that all men are created equal, we have the surrender of a most powerful position and army on that very day. And not only so, but in the succession of battles in Pennsylvania, near to us, through three days, so rapidly fought that they might be called one great battle, on the first, second, and third of the month of July; and on the fourth the cohorts of those who opposed the Declaration that all men are created equal 'turned tail' and run. Gentlemen, this is a glorious theme, and the occasion for a speech, but I am not prepared to make one worthy of the occasion." He would praise those who had fought so bravely. "I dislike to mention the name of one single officer, lest I might do wrong to those I might forget." It had been a long day of hard work and high excitement for Lincoln, and he talked to the crowd mostly as though they were friends who had dropped into his office.

The colloquial phrase "turned tail" was as old to him as his boyhood and had the graphic edge he wished to convey. But it wasn't correct English, and he would hear about such language, not merely from the opposition but from Sumner and others who believed this was carrying homespun simplicity too far. He closed this serenade speech with a breezy and careless sentence that would do him no good among the purists of diction. "Having said this much, I will now take the music."

And not merely on points of style would this little address be criticized but also as to hidden motives. The *New York World* commented: "President Lincoln's omission to mention General Meade in his congratulatory speech has caused a great deal of remark. It is notorious that he is on the track for the next presidency." This and similar comments in hostile news-papers had reference to Lincoln's saying: "I dislike to mention the name of one single officer, lest I might do wrong to those I might forget. Recent events bring up glorious names, and particularly prominent ones; but these I will not mention."

The smoke of Gettysburg still lingered when the President took under consideration and turned over to Welles for adjustment a minor matter of rival claims from Maine. Welles recorded the facts along with his own pique and prejudice on July 8:

"The President sends me a strange letter from Hamlin, asking as a *personal* favor that prizes may be sent to Portland for adjudication,—says *he* has not had many favors, asks this on *personal* grounds. Mr. Hamlin spoke on this subject to me,—said the President referred it to me;—and both he and Mr. Fessenden made a strong local appeal in behalf of Portland. I informed them that such a matter was not to be disposed of on personal grounds or local favoritism; that Portsmouth, Providence, New Haven, and other places had equal claims, if there were any claims, but that public consideration must govern, and not personal favoritism; that additional courts would involve great additional expense; that we had no navy yard or station at Portland, with officers to whom the captors could report, no prison to confine prisoners, no naval constructors or engineers to examine captured vessels, etc., etc. These facts, while they somewhat staggered the gentlemen, quieted Fessenden, but did not cause Hamlin, who is rapacious as a wolf, to abate his demand for government favors. He wanted these paraphernalia, these extra persons, extra boards, and extra expenditures at Portland, and solicited them of the President, as special to himself personally."

An odd number was Grant, a thousand miles from home, bagging an entire army, winning the greatest Union victory of the war thus far, clearing the Mississippi River of the last Confederate hold on it, yet failing to send word to Washington about his grand performance unless he let it go at telling Admiral Porter that the navy should be first to wire the big news to the Government at Washington. This was more of Grant's careless ways. Welles wrote, "The Secretary of War and General Halleck are much dissatisfied that Admiral Porter should have sent me information of the capture of Vicksburg in advance of any word from General Grant, and also with me for spreading it at once over the country without verification from the War Office."

Welles wrote a letter of congratulation to Porter, called on the President and advised that Porter should be made a rear admiral: "He assented very cheerfully, though his estimate of Porter is not so high as mine. Stanton denies him any merit; speaks of him as a gas-bag, who makes a great fuss and claims credit that belongs to others. Chase, Seward, and Blair agree with me that Porter has done good service. I am aware of his infirmities. He is selfish, presuming, and wasteful, but is brave and energetic."

The detailed facts arrived at Washington of Grant receiving 31,600 prisoners, 172 cannon, 60,000 muskets of improved pattern that had most of them run the blockade, and of the uniform caliber needed in many of the Northern commands. Port Hudson, a little farther south on the Mississippi, had fallen to General Banks with 6,000 prisoners, 51 cannon, 5,000 muskets. The starved Confederates filed out of Vicksburg in silence, the Union soldiers obeying Grant's instructions "to be orderly and quiet as these prisoners pass, and to make no offensive remarks." They were paroled, Grant explaining they were largely from the Southwest. "I knew many of them were tired of the war and would get home just as soon as they could. A large number of them had voluntarily come into our lines during the siege, and requested to be sent North where they could get employment until the war was over." The prisoners included Lieutenant General John C. Pemberton, a favorite of President Davis, four major generals, fifteen brigadiers, eighty staff officers.

The City of a Hundred Hills, termed by Davis "The Gibraltar of the West," was a Confederate ruin, where flour had risen to $400 a barrel, payment in gold, where for days lead and steel had poured as in a rain, where a diarist wrote on July 4: "One man had his head shot off while in the act of picking up his child. One man had a shell to explode close by him and lift him some distance in the air. One shell exploded between two officers riding on the street and lifted both horses and riders into the air without hurting man or beast. A little girl, the daughter of a Mr. Jones, was sitting at the entrance of a cave, when a Parrott shell entered the portal and took her head off."

Lincoln's mental picture of events around Vicksburg, his eager anxiety about a military drama enacted along river bends where he had navigated flatboats, was told in a tender handshake letter of July 13, 1863, that went to Grant, a letter he gave shortly to press and public:

"My dear General: I do not remember that you and I ever met personally. I write this now as a grateful acknowledgment for the almost inestimable service you have done the country. I wish to say a word further. When you first reached the vicinity of Vicksburg, I thought you should do what you finally did—march the troops across the neck, run the batteries with the transports, and thus go below; and I never had any faith, except a general hope that you knew better than I, that the Yazoo Pass expedition and the like could succeed. When you got below and took Port Gibson, Grand Gulf, and vicinity, I thought you should go down the river and join General Banks, and when you turned northward, east of the Big Black, I feared it was a mistake. I now wish to make the personal acknowledgment that you were right and I was wrong."

Four days after Lee had moved his army from Gettysburg toward the Potomac Halleck wired Meade to watch the "divided forces" of the enemy. "The President is urgent and anxious that your army should move against him by forced marches." Lincoln wrote to General Lorenzo Thomas at Harrisburg that Lee was moving faster than Union troops far behind in pursuit, and the pursuers "will in my unprofessional opinion be quite as likely to capture the 'man in the moon' as any part of Lee's army."

Meade on that same day had received two letters from his wife, and replied to her: "I am truly rejoiced that you are treated with such distinction on account of my humble services. I see also that the papers are making a great deal too much fuss over me. I claim no extraordinary merit for this last battle, and would prefer waiting a little while to see what my career is to be before making any pretensions. Knowing that battles are often decided by accidents, and that no man of sense will say in advance what their result will be, I wish to be careful in not bragging before the right time."

On this same day of July 8 the *Richmond Enquirer* reported in headlines and text "Glorious Victory at Gettysburg. Forty Thousand Prisoners Captured," while the *Savannah Republican* down in Georgia gave its readers "The Best News of the War" and chronicled "overwhelming defeat of the Yankees at Gettysburg," with an embarrassingly large number of prisoners to be sent South.

Lee was writing to Davis on July 11 that rainstorms had swollen the Potomac beyond fording, that his army was in good condition and he would accept battle if the enemy offered it. On the next day he wrote to Davis that "but for the power the enemy possesses of accumulating troops" he would await attack; his supplies were running low, the river was going down and he might cross the next day on a bridge that was being built. Meade was writing to Halleck on July 8, "I think the decisive battle of the war will be fought in a few days," receiving from Halleck two days later the advice, "I think it will be best for you to postpone a general battle till you can concentrate all your forces and get up your reserves and reinforcements."

"The President seemed in a specially good humor today," ran John Hay's diary for July 11, "as he had pretty good evidence that the enemy were still on the north side of the Potomac, and Meade had announced his intention of attacking them in the morning. The Prest seemed very happy at the prospect of a brilliant success. He had been rather impatient with General Meade's slow movements since Gettysburg, but concluded today that Meade would yet show sufficient activity to inflict the *coup de grace* upon the flying rebels." The next day it rained. Hay wrote, "Have not yet heard of Meade's expected attack."

On July 12 Meade reported to Halleck that he would attack the next day "unless something intervenes to prevent it," recognizing that delay would strengthen the enemy and would not increase his own force. The war-telegraph office operator Albert B. Chandler said that when this dispatch arrived from Meade, Lincoln paced the room wringing his hands and saying, "They will be ready to fight a magnificent battle when there is no enemy there to fight."

The next day a telegram went from Halleck to Meade in words surely Lincoln rather than Halleck: "You are strong enough to attack and defeat the enemy before he can effect a crossing. Act upon your own judgment and make your generals execute your orders. Call no council of war. It is proverbial that councils of war never fight. Reinforcements are being pushed on as rapidly as possible. Do not let the enemy escape."

The night before, however, Meade had already called a council of war, finding that only two of his corps commanders wanted to fight. Meade himself was for immediate combat, but when the discussion was over decided to wait. Lincoln sent a telegram to Simon Cameron, then at Meade's headquarters, saying he would give much to be relieved of the impression that since Gettysburg Meade and his generals had striven only to get the enemy over the river without another fight. "Please tell me, if you know, who was the one corps commander who was for fighting in the council of war on Sunday night."

On the Monday following Meade's council of war, July 13, Hay's diary noted "the President begins to grow anxious and impatient about Meade's silence." On the morning of the fourteenth "the President seemed depressed by Meade's despatches of last night. They were so cautiously & almost timidly worded—talking about reconnoitering to find the enemy's weak place, and other such." The President said he feared Meade would do nothing. About noon came a dispatch. The enemy had got away unhurt. The President was deeply grieved.

"We had them within our grasp," he said to Hay. "We had only to stretch forth our hands & they were ours. And nothing I could say or do could make the Army move." It seemed to Hay that one of the President's dispatches to Meade of a few days before "must have cut like a scourge, but Meade returned so reasonable and earnest a reply" that the President concluded that Meade knew best what he was doing, and was reconciled to the apparent inaction, which the President hoped was merely apparent: "Every day he [the President] has watched the progress of the Army with agonizing impatience, hope struggling with fear."

Still uneasy about Meade's phrase as to driving the invader from our soil, Lincoln said to Hay: "This is a dreadful reminiscence of McClellan. The same spirit that moved McC. to claim a great victory because Pa. & Md. were safe. The hearts of 10 million people sunk within them when McClellan raised that shout last fall. Will our generals never get that idea out of their heads? The whole country is our soil."

Welles recorded of this same mournful Tuesday, the fourteenth of July, that Cabinet members were gathering to meet the President when Stanton came in a hurry and took the President aside for three minutes alone in the library. "When they returned, the President's countenance indicated trouble and distress; Stanton was disturbed, disconcerted. Usher asked Stanton if he had bad news. He said, 'No.' Something was said of the report that Lee had crossed the river. Stanton said abruptly and curtly he knew nothing of Lee's crossing. 'I do,' said the President emphatically, with a look of painful rebuke to Stanton. 'If he has not got all of his men across, he soon will.'"

The President said he did not believe they could take up anything in the Cabinet for that day. Welles believed the Cabinet members were hardly in the right frame of mind for deliberation; certainly the President was not. The President wanted to see Halleck at once. Stanton left abruptly. Welles walked out slowly. The President hurried and overtook Welles. They walked across the White House lawn to the departments and stopped to talk a few moments at the gate. The President said he had dreaded and expected what had come; that there seemed to him for a full week a determination that Lee, "though we had him in our hands," should escape with his force and plunder.

Welles believed he could never forget the voice and face of the President as he spoke. "And that, my God, is the last of this Army of the Potomac! There is bad faith somewhere. Meade has been pressed and urged, but only one of his generals was for an immediate attack, was ready to pounce on Lee; the rest held back. What does it mean, Mr. Welles? Great God! what does it mean?"

Welles asked the President what orders had gone from him while the army had been quiet with a defeated and broken enemy in front, short of ammunition, and an impassable river to cross. The President could not say that anything positive had been done, but both Stanton and Halleck professed to agree with him and he thought Stanton did; Halleck was waiting all the time to hear from Meade. Welles pointed out that Halleck was only four hours' travel from Meade, could have gone personally to advise and encourage Meade. Welles blamed "the inertness, if not incapacity" of Halleck, said he had hoped that the President, who had better and more correct views, would issue peremptory orders. The President took a softer tone and said, as Welles noted it: "Halleck knows better than I what to do. He is a military man, has had a military education. I brought him here to give me military advice. His views and mine are widely different. It is better that I, who am not a military man, should defer to him, rather than he to me." Welles replied that on some things the President could more correctly, certainly more energetically, direct military movements than Halleck, who could originate nothing.

"I can see," wrote Welles in his diary, "that the shadows which have crossed my mind have clouded the President's also. On only one or two occasions have I ever seen the President so troubled, so dejected and discouraged." Later on the day of this talk Welles went to the War Department on Stanton's suggestion that reports from Vicksburg were worth reading: "The President lay upon a sofa in Stanton's room, completely absorbed, overwhelmed, with the news. He was, however, though subdued and sad, calm and resolute." At Vicksburg 31,200 prisoners had been paroled. "Had Meade attacked and captured the army above us, as I verily believe he might have done, the Rebellion would have been ended."

A telegram from Halleck to Meade that day told Meade that Lee's escape had "created great dissatisfaction in the mind of the President." Meade's immediate reply was that having performed his duty conscientiously and to the best of his ability, "the censure of the President conveyed in your dispatch of 1 P.M. this day, is, in my judgment, so undeserved that I feel compelled most respectfully to ask to be immediately relieved from the command of the army." Halleck notified Meade the same day that Lee's escape was "not deemed a sufficient cause" for Meade being relieved of command. "My telegram stating the disappointment of the President was not intended as a censure, but as a stimulus to an active pursuit."

To his wife that day Meade wrote that he had found Lee entrenched in a very strong position, that his own corps commanders voted against attack, that his cavalry had captured 2,000 prisoners as Lee's army was nearly across the river, that a telegram from Halleck expressing the President's dissatisfaction had brought his request to be immediately relieved of command, that Halleck had replied no censure was intended and there was not sufficient cause for relieving him of command. As Meade penned this letter to his wife he seemed to have no blame to put on others, no bitterness, no sarcasm nor irony nor pettiness. He wrote gently in the detached spirit of science which Professor Henry had detected in him. "This is exactly what I expected; unless I did impracticable things, fault would be found with me. I have ignored the senseless adulation of the public and the press, and I am now just as indifferent to the censure bestowed without just cause. I start tomorrow to run another race with Lee."

Lincoln, still on this same day of July 14, wrote a long letter to Meade, at a later time scribbling on the envelope: "To General Meade, never sent or signed." It began: "I have just seen your despatch to General Halleck, asking to be relieved because of a supposed censure of mine. I am very, very grateful to you for the magnificent success you gave the cause of the country at Gettysburg; and I am sorry now to be the author of the slightest pain to you. But I was in such deep distress myself that I could not restrain some expression of it." He mentioned evidences that Meade and two of his generals were not seeking a collision with the enemy but were trying to get him across the river without another battle. "What these evidences were, if you please, I hope to tell you at some time when we shall both feel better." Then Lincoln told shortly and bluntly what the failures were that had given him distress, perhaps feeling later that the entire setup was too complicated to be put in so few sentences. "The case, summarily stated, is this: You fought and beat the enemy at Gettysburg, and, of course, to say the least, his loss was as great as yours. He retreated, and you did not, as it seemed to me, pressingly pursue him; but a flood in the river detained him till, by slow degrees, you were again upon him.

"You had at least twenty thousand veteran troops directly with you, and as many more raw ones within supporting distance, all in addition to those who fought with you at Gettysburg, while it was not possible that he had received a single recruit, and yet you stood and let the flood run down, bridges be built, and the enemy move away at his leisure without attacking him. And Couch and Smith! The latter left Carlisle in time, upon all ordinary calculations, to have aided you in the last battle of Gettysburg, but he did not arrive. At the end of more than ten days, I believe twelve, under constant urging, he reached Hagerstown from Carlisle, which is not an inch over fifty-five miles, if so much, and Couch's movement was very little different."

Now the war would be prolonged indefinitely. "My dear general, I do not believe you appreciate the magnitude of the misfortune involved in Lee's escape. He was within your easy grasp, and to have closed upon him would, in connection with our other late successes, have ended the war. . . . Your golden opportunity is gone, and I am immeasurably distressed because of it. I beg you will not consider this a prosecution or persecution of yourself. As you had learned that I was dissatisfied, I have thought it best to kindly tell you why."

This letter was neither signed nor sent by Lincoln nor received and read by Meade. It lacked the tone of Lincoln's remark to Simon Cameron in a later reference to Meade: "Why should we censure a man who has done so much for his country because he did not do a little more?"

The unsent letter was too much in the mood of the President's remark to Robert Lincoln, who said he went into his father's room to find him "in tears, with head bowed upon his arms resting on the table at which he sat." To the call, "Why, what is the matter, father?" the answer came slowly, "My boy, I have just learned that at a council of war, of Meade and his Generals, it had been determined not to pursue Lee, and now the opportune chance of ending this bitter struggle is lost." Hay noted in his diary of July 15: "R[obert] T. L[incoln] says the Tycoon is grieved silently but deeply about the escape of Lee. He said, 'If I had gone up there, I could have whipped them myself.'" Hay added, "I know he had that idea."

Welles and others were blaming General in Chief Halleck, Welles's animadversion being caught in his notation: "Halleck sits, and smokes, and swears, and scratches his arm . . . but exhibits little military capacity or intelligence; is obfuscated, muddy, uncertain, stupid as to what is doing or to be done." Yet Hay noted on July 15: "The President says however you may doubt or disagree from Halleck, he is very apt to be right in the end."

General Wadsworth arrived fresh from Meade's council of war and answered the question, "Why did Lee escape?" with a gruff four words: "Because nobody stopped him."

Wadsworth told Hay of the council of war. On the question of fight or no fight, the weight of authority was against fighting. Four generals strenuously opposed a fight. Meade favored attack. "So did Warren, who did most of the talking on that side, & Pleasanton was very eager for it, as was also Wadsworth himself: The non-fighters thought, or seemed to think, that if we did not attack, the enemy would, & even Meade, though he was in for action, had no idea that the enemy intended to get away at once. Meade was in favor of attacking in three columns of 20,000 men each."

Hay then noted that Wadsworth delivered earnestly to General Hunter, who sat beside him, a remark that flashed deep into the significant and controlling factors: "General, there are a good many officers of the regular Army who have not yet entirely lost the West Point [idea] of Southern superiority. That sometimes accounts for an otherwise unaccountable slowness of attack."

Six days after Lee had slipped away from Meade, Hay noted "the Tycoon was in very good humor" as they talked of what was just past. The President said, "Our Army held the war in the hollow of their hand, & they would not close it." And again, "We had gone through all the labor of tilling & planting an enormous crop, and when it was ripe we did not harvest it. . . . 'Still,' he added, 'I am very grateful to Meade for the great service he did at Gettysburg.'"

Two days more and Lincoln was writing to General Howard, a corps commander with Meade, that he had believed "General Meade and his noble army had expended all the skill, and toil, and blood, up to the ripe harvest, and then let the crop go to waste." Perhaps his mortification was heightened by a notion that the main rebel army going north of the Potomac could never return. And perhaps he had been too greatly flattered in this belief by the operations at Gettysburg. "A few days having passed, I am now profoundly grateful for what was done, without criticism for what was not done. General Meade has my confidence, as a brave and skilful officer and a true man." A few days having passed, he could see that it was well he had not sent Meade the letter he meant to be kindly which was not kindly. Having met in Meade a rare humility and sincerity throughout their many difficult interchanges, Lincoln sent through Howard the salutation that Meade was more than a brave and skillful officer, was "a true man." Howard gave the letter to Meade and Meade mailed it to his wife.

Also there came a letter from Halleck to Meade saying: "You should not have been surprised or vexed at the President's disappointment at the escape of Lee's army. He had examined into all the details of sending you reinforcements to satisfy himself that every man who could possibly be spared from other places had been sent to your army. He thought that Lee's defeat was so certain that he felt no little impatience at his unexpected escape. I have no doubt, General, that you felt the disappointment as keenly as anyone else."

At a Cabinet meeting on July 17 came remarks on the great error of Meade at the Potomac, which led the President to say he would not yet give up that officer. Welles noted Seward as commenting, "Excepting the escape of Lee, Meade has shown ability," and Lincoln as declaring, "He has committed a terrible mistake, but we will try him farther." As the days passed Welles continued to blame chiefly General in Chief Halleck: "In this whole summer's campaign I have been unable to see, hear, or obtain evidence of power, or will, or talent, or originality on the part of General Halleck. He has suggested nothing, decided nothing, done nothing but scold and smoke and scratch his elbows. Is it possible the energies of the nation should be wasted by the incapacity of such a man?"

Between Lee and Davis passed two masterly letters, Lee proposing a new commander younger and abler than himself. "I cannot even accomplish what I myself desire. How can I fulfill the expectations of others?" Davis replied that "letter writers" had not diminished his confidence in Lee. "Suppose, my dear friend, that I were to admit, with all their implications, the points which you present, where am I to find that new commander?"

On the last day of the battle of Gettysburg Alexander H. Stephens, Vice-President of the Confederate States, had with one companion started down the James River from Richmond in the small steamer *Torpedo,* aiming to reach Washington as Commissioners of the Confederate Government and hold a conference with the President of the United States. The little ninety-pound sage and humanitarian from Georgia had left his home in that State two weeks before on receiving a telegram from President Davis requesting him to come to Richmond. There he had urged on Davis that Lee's army invading the North would excite the war party and that President Lincoln would refuse to see him. Davis argued that the very presence of Lee's victorious regiments in Pennsylvania would increase the probability of a conference being granted. Davis's Cabinet agreed with him.

So Stephens started, in company with a Confederate agent for the exchange of prisoners, Robert Ould. While they were still on their way Lee began his rainstorm retreat to the Potomac. While they were detained by a blockade squadron Vicksburg surrendered. Their dispatch of July 4 requesting permission to pass through the blockade and as representatives of Jefferson Davis, Commanding General of the Confederate Army, to meet and confer with Abraham Lincoln, President and Commanding General of the Army and Navy of the United States, was forwarded by naval officers to Secretary Welles. Welles showed the dispatch to Blair, who said nothing; to Stanton, who swore and growled; to Seward, who was emphatic against any conference. The President was at the Soldiers' Home for supper and not expected for an hour or two. Late in the evening when Welles saw the President, he noticed that the President had already been warned by Stanton and others to hold no conference: "The President treats the subject as not very serious nor very important, and proposes to take it up tomorrow."

At the Sunday morning Cabinet meeting at eleven o'clock the next day the President read the communications, said he was at first disposed to put the matter aside without many words, or much thought, but a night's reflection and some remarks yesterday had modified his views, and as Welles noted: "While he was opposed to having Stephens and his vessel come here, he thought it would be well to send someone—perhaps go himself—to Fortress Monroe. Both Seward and Stanton were startled when this remark was made. Seward did not think it advisable the President should go, nor anyone else; he considered Stephens a dangerous man, who would make mischief anywhere." Stanton and Chase were against any intercourse. Blair favored receiving any communications, while not permitting Stephens to come personally. Welles wrote a note to the effect that "indefinite information" concerning the object of Mr. Stephens's communication made it inexpedient to let him pass the blockade, this note to go to the admiral commanding the squadron. Welles noted:

"None of the gentlemen adopted or assented to this, nor did they approximate unity or anything definite on any point. After half an hour's discussion and disagreement, I read what I had pencilled to the President, who sat by me on the sofa. Under the impression that I took the same view as Chase and Stanton, he did not adopt it. Seward . . . thought with Stanton it would be best to have nothing to do with the mission in any way. The President was apprehensive my letter had that tendency. Mr. Blair thought my suggestion the most practical of anything submitted. Chase said he should be satisfied with it. Stanton the same. . . . The President said my letter did not dispose of the communication which Stephens bore. I told him the dispatch did not exclude it. . . . Everything was purposely left open, so that Stephens could, if he chose, state or intimate his object. . . . I had not the least objection, and should for myself prefer to add, 'I am directed by the President to say that any communication which Mr. Stephens may have can be forwarded.' This addendum did not, as I knew it would not, meet the views entertained by some of the gentlemen.

"The President prefers that a special messenger should be sent to meet Stephens, to which I see no serious objection, but which no one favors. I do not anticipate anything frank, manly, or practical in this mission, though I do not think Stephens so dangerous a man as Mr. Seward represents him. It is a scheme without doubt—possibly for good, perhaps for evil,—but I would meet it in a manner not offensive, nor by a rude refusal would I give the Rebels and their sympathizers an opportunity to make friends at our expense or to our injury. This, I think, is the President's purpose. Mr. Blair would perhaps go farther. . . . We must not put ourselves in the wrong by refusing to communicate with these people. On the other hand, there is difficulty in meeting and treating with men who have violated their duty, disregarded their obligations, and who lack sincerity. . . . The President thought it best to send no word until we gave a conclusive answer tomorrow."

The next day's decision was that Stephens's request to come to Washington was "inadmissible," but any military communication should be made through the prescribed military channel. The President directed Seward to go to the telegraph office and see that dispatches to this effect were correctly transmitted to the proper army and navy officials.

Stephens returned to Richmond, to Georgia, saying he had warned President Davis that nothing else was to be expected. The telegram sent by Lincoln to the blockading admiral read: "The request of A. H. Stephens is inadmissible. The customary agents and channels are adequate for all needful communication and conference between the United States forces and the insurgents." Thus curtly and with no direct message to Stephens did Lincoln dismiss his old-time colleague in antiwar efforts in Congress in 1848, his little Whig-party friend who had brought tears to his eyes by a moving speech advocating justice to Mexico or any weaker neighbor of the United States. Lincoln had written a much longer telegram with a message for the blockading admiral to transmit to Stephens, closing: "Anything will be received, and carefully considered by him [the President of the United

States], when offered by any influential person or persons in terms not assuming the independence of the so-called Confederate States." This was not sent.

Why should Stanton and Seward have been startled, as Welles noted, at Lincoln's saying perhaps he himself should go to Fortress Monroe and confer with Stephens? Why did Lincoln toward the end of the long discussion say that he preferred a special messenger should be sent to meet Stephens? Was Lincoln testing their sentiment, and would he have gone to meet the Vice-President of the Confederacy or sent a special messenger if more of his Cabinet had quickly agreed and had they wished the affair luck? Did he finally override his personal inclinations toward a good talk with Little Aleck by a decision that it was more important he should give his time to the expected battle between Meade and Lee north of the Potomac?

What Stephens hoped for out of a conference was outlined by him later; he wrote, "The idea was not so much to act upon Mr. Lincoln and the then ruling authorities at Washington, as *through* them, when the mass of correspondence should be published, upon the great mass of the people in the Northern States, who were becoming sensitively alive to the great danger of their own liberties." Also Stephens believed "the conference suggested would most probably have been agreed to" if Southern cavalry were not at the time raiding Ohio and "if General Lee had remained quietly on the defensive south of the Rappahannock."

An officer from Grant's army arrived at the White House from Vicksburg, Lincoln drawing chairs close together and saying, "Now I want to hear all about Vicksburg." He put questions on the siege, losses, morale, sanitary conditions, hospital service, Grant, and said: "I guess I was right in standing by Grant, although there was great pressure made after Pittsburg Landing to have him removed. I thought I saw enough in Grant to convince me that he was one on whom the country could depend. That 'unconditional surrender' message to Buckner at Donelson suited me. It indicated the spirit of the man." Lincoln with others was beginning to see clearly that Grant could transmit to his own officers, who might be lacking it, his own carelessness on the point of what General Wadsworth termed "the West Point [idea] of Southern superiority," which to Wadsworth in the Army of the Potomac "accounted for an otherwise unaccountable slowness of attack."

Three days after Lee's escape and eleven days after the repulse of Lee at Gettysburg and the surrender of Pemberton's army to Grant at Vicksburg, there was issued from the White House a document titled "Proclamation for Thanksgiving, July 15, 1863, by the President of the United States of America." In the flowing text and the undeniably mystic spirit that ran through this document, in the announcements that marched in diapasons of Old Testament prose, in the attitude of piety in which the name of Almighty God in various appellations was invoked, Lincoln set forth the Chief Magistrate of the Republic as a man of faith. Some could read a belief in fate and foreordination, or gambler's luck, or a superstitious individual's obedience to hoodoos and mascots, in this proclamation, but these were isolated philosophers.

"It has pleased Almighty God to hearken to the supplications and prayers of an afflicted people," ran the opening chords, "and to vouchsafe to the army and navy of the United States victories on land and on the sea so signal and so effective as to furnish reasonable grounds for augmented confidence that the union of these States will be maintained, their Constitution preserved, and their peace and prosperity permanently restored." Those who had bought these winnings should be mentioned. "These victories have been accorded not without sacrifices of life, limb, health, and liberty, incurred by brave, loyal, and patriotic citizens. Domestic affliction in every part of the country follows in the train of these fearful bereavements."

Then came the direct recognition of a mystic power beyond mortal hand interposing its decisions amid the projects of men. "It is meet and right to recognize and confess the presence of the Almighty Father, and the power of his hand equally in these triumphs and in these sorrows."

Then came a long paragraph composed entirely of one sentence, the longest in either a private letter or a state paper having the signature of Abraham Lincoln. In it was noticeable some of the tone and style of the churchman Seward, and the proclamation may have been a joint product as in the closing paragraph of the first inaugural address. It employed three different appellations for the Deity, and was a formidable effort at delivering the impression that the Union of States and its Chief Magistrate were in possession of dignity, security, and high calm purpose in the midst of tumult, red-handed violence, and the smoke of desolate destruction. The sentence read:

"Now, therefore, be it known that I do set apart Thursday, the 6th day of August next, to be observed as a day for national thanksgiving, praise, and prayer, and I invite the people of the United States to assemble on that occasion in their customary places of worship, and, in the forms approved by their own consciences, render the homage due to the Divine Majesty for the wonderful things he has done in the nation's behalf, and invoke the influences of his Holy Spirit to subdue the anger which has produced and so long sustained a needless and cruel rebellion, to change the hearts of the insurgents, to guide the counsels of the government with wisdom adequate to so great a national emergency, and to visit with tender care and consolation throughout the length and breadth of our land all those who, through the vicissitudes of marches, voyages, battles, and sieges have been brought to suffer in mind, body, or estate, and finally to lead the whole nation through the paths of repentance and submission to the Divine Will back to the perfect enjoyment of union and fraternal peace."

On the date given to this proclamation the dignity and majesty of the United States Government was challenged, upset, smeared with insult, and threatened with the disorders and violence of revolution, in the largest city in the United States.

Never before in an American metropolis had the police, merchants, bankers, and forces of law and order had their power wrenched loose by mobs so skillfully led, with so direct a strategy of seizing armories, guns, munitions, supplies, with announced aims of getting possession of the United States Treasury vaults and the surplus funds of banks, along with forts, communications, and approaches to the city.

So definite were the slogans and purposes of some of the mobs that they would be more correctly termed crowds, or units of mass action, operating an insurrection. Underlying the violence which overrode Federal, State, and municipal government for three days were ideas, opinions, and organizations to an extent that made correct the designation in an official State proclamation that the safety, peace, lives, and property of the City of New York were endangered by "manifest combinations for forcible resistance to the laws."

During the three days of July 13, 14, 15, mobs or crowds that met by prearrangement, with a specific design as to what points they would attack and carry, drove out the United States provost marshal from his office at Forty-third Street and Third Avenue, wrecked the wheel or revolving drum from which the names of drafted men were drawn, tore to pieces the books and papers, broke up the furniture, poured turpentine on the floor, set the building on fire, fought off police and firemen, burned the draft office and six adjoining buildings. They wrecked and burned the United States draft office on Broadway two doors from Twenty-ninth Street, looted stores near by, and burned twelve buildings; they smashed windows and doors and sacked the home of the Republican Mayor Opdyke and burned at midnight the home of the United States Postmaster Abram Wakeman, first stripping the premises of furniture and clothing; they burned a ferry house, hotels, drugstores, clothing stores, factories, saloons where they were refused free liquor, police stations, a Methodist church, a Protestant mission, the Colored Orphan Asylum at Forty-third Street and Lexington Avenue. They drove out forty policemen and fifteen armed workmen from the State arsenal at Twenty-first Street and Second Avenue, trampling over five of their dead, seizing muskets and cartridges, setting the building on fire; they hanged a Negro from a tree on Clarkson Street and burned the body with loud howling; they hanged three a day of Negroes; they hanged to a lamppost a captain of the 11th regiment of the State guard; they hanged, shot, or beat and trampled to death at least thirty Negroes and so terrorized the colored population that it disappeared upstate and across to New Jersey. They erected for protection and refuge barricades on First Avenue from Eleventh to Fourteenth streets, on Ninth Avenue from Thirty-second to Forty-third streets, with smaller barricades across intersecting thoroughfares. They sang "We'll hang old Greeley to a sour apple tree, And send him straight to hell!"; they yelled "To hell with the draft and the war!"; they yelled "Tell Old Abe to come to New York!" They destroyed shipyards, railroad and streetcar lines, and cut telegraph wires connecting with Albany. They killed, crippled, or bruised policemen till at the end of the third day nearly .

the whole force was ineffective; among their first victims was Superintendent of Police John Kennedy, who received seventy-two gashes, wounds, and bruises and managed to live through; among the later victims was Colonel H. T. O'Brien of the 11th regiment of the State guard, who was stoned and kicked to death and received in a gutter the ministrations of a passing Catholic priest. They destroyed property estimated at $5,000,000 in value; of rioters, police, and bystanders, upward of 400 were killed and wounded, including a little Negro girl in the Colored Orphan Asylum who hid under a bed and was pulled out and beaten to death; the mutilated and bruised numbered thousands; banks, groceries, jewelry shops, and practically all business establishments closed their doors—except the 5,000 saloons, grogshops, beer tunnels, weinstubes, and sample rooms.

The mobs were not driven in their work by mere blind wrath. Somebody had done some thinking, somebody had chosen a time when all the State guards the Governor could scrape together had gone to Gettysburg. The only organized force ready against the first riots was a police department of 1,500 members. With club and revolver they had fought night and day, and their dead lay in scores, their wounded and gashed by the hundreds.

The mobs of the first day's riots aimed straight at a thing they hated: the Draft. It was a Monday, and on the previous Saturday 1,200 names had been picked by a blindfolded man out of the wheel, the revolving drum that shook and mixed the pieces of paper each folded and bound with a rubber band. These 1,200 names had been published, and unless something happened to make the Government change its mind most of the men answering to those 1,200 names would be put into uniforms and sent to fight, march, go hungry, and be lousy under fatigue duty, serve under generals whom newspapers called ignorant and incompetent, and perhaps die of bullet, fever, or homesickness or prison fare. As soldiers what would they be fighting for?

If they believed such newspapers as the *World*, the *Journal of Commerce*, the *Express*, the *Daily News*, the *Day Book*, the *Mercury*, they were to be the willing cannon fodder of a tyrannical and oppressive Government which was daily violating the Constitution and the fundamental law of the land. The war had become "the total of evil-minded men to accomplish their ends," had been criminally prolonged, was unjustifiable and sinful, according to the *Journal of Commerce*. Weak and reckless men had thrust into the statute books by force, and by an unnecessary stretch of governmental control over individual liberty, a Conscription Act "profoundly repugnant to the American mind," according to the *World*. Said the *Daily News:* "The people are notified that one out of about two and a half of our citizens are to be brought off into Messrs. Lincoln & Company's charnelhouse. God forbid! We hope that instant measures will be taken to prevent the outrage."

In the matter of ideas, opinions, intellectual guidance, the crowds who gathered in the streets, and from whom the rioting mobs were formed, had plenty of authority to go on. The newspapers had printed the Fourth of

July speech at a great Democratic mass meeting at Concord, New Hampshire, of Franklin Pierce, former President of the United States, friend of Jefferson Davis. He hurled contempt at the Washington Government and spoke words in such close sympathy with the Richmond Government that any listener accepting Pierce's argument would have been justified in joining the Confederate Army.

"Here in these free States," said Pierce, "it is made criminal for that noble martyr of free speech, Mr. Vallandigham, to discuss public affairs in Ohio—ay, even here, in time of war the mere arbitrary will of the President takes the place of the Constitution, and the President himself announces to us that it is treasonable to speak or to write otherwise than as he may prescribe; nay, that it is treasonable even to be silent, though we may be struck dumb by the shock of the calamities with which evil counsels, incompetency and corruption, have overwhelmed our country." In the same tone and belief Governor Seymour of New York, with nineteen of his State guard regiments at Gettysburg, told a Fourth of July audience in the New York Academy of Music that the country was on "the very verge of destruction" because of government coercion, "seizing our persons, infringing upon our rights, insulting our homes, depriving us of those cherished principles for which our fathers fought."

The tremendous and continued applause which came when Governor Seymour referred to liberty as suspended, "men deprived of the right of trial by jury, men torn from their homes by midnight intruders," meant that the audience believed he was in favor of opposition to the draft and that the "outrages" and "usurpations" of the Government should be resisted. Naturally he said afterward that he did not mean they should resist by riot and burning, by stealing and mayhem, by gun and torch and stone and brickbat. And he was a rather gentle man, who probably did not know what hell would break loose nine days after he told the Academy of Music audience, "If you would save your country, begin right; begin at the hearthstones; begin in your family circle; declare that your privileges shall be held sacred; and, having once proclaimed your own rights, take care that you do not invade those of your neighbor." Thus they should resist the draft in their own homes, but not on the streets. So it seemed. The fight for liberty should be at the hearth with hearthstones and not on the streets with brickbats.

By the time the subtle arguments of the newspapers and of Pierce and Seymour had been simplified into plain words for the 400,000 foreign-born citizens of New York, of whom 203,740 were Irish, they had lost their fine philosophic distinctions. And far beyond any discussion was the terribly simple and outstanding fact that any man having $300 could buy his freedom from the draft. It was "a rich man's war and a poor man's fight," ran the talk in five thousand saloons and twenty times as many homes.

Drafted men, their relatives and friends, reinforced by thousands of sympathizers who favored some kind of direct action, gathered early in the morning of July 13 on vacant lots with clubs, staves, cart rungs, pieces of iron, and moved as if by agreement to a lot near Central Park where they organized, began patrolling the city, and put the first sign of their wrath and vengeance on the draft offices wrecked and burned. That is, the first acts of the three days' tornado had some semblance of an uprising of the people against a Government discriminating in its conscription between the rich and the poor. The second and third of the three days, however, saw the events come under the sway of criminal and gang elements, who then numbered between 50,000 to 70,000 in the city, and who swarmed out for loot and the diabolical joy of seeing the police defied and overrun.

"We have *awful* good news from New York," wrote J. B. Jones, War Department clerk at Richmond in his diary. "An *insurrection*, the loss of many lives, extensive pillage and burning, with a suspension of the conscription!"

"I am your friend," said Governor Seymour, as he stood between the Tammany leaders William M. Tweed and A. Oakey Hall and spoke to a noisy crowd in front of the City Hall on the second day of the uprising. "I implore you to take care that no man's property or person is injured. I rely on you, and if you refrain from further riotous acts, I will see to it that your rights shall be protected. On Saturday last I sent the Adjutant-General of the State to Washington to urge postponement of the draft. The question of the legality of the Conscription Act will go before the Courts. If the Act be declared legal I pledge myself, the State and the city authorities to see that there shall be no inequality between the rich and poor." One Judge McCunn had held the previous week that the Conscription Act was unconstitutional, and the only forces the President could use for the war, besides the regular army, were volunteers and militia contributed by States.

Governor Seymour was in a peculiar position, and he probably set forth a sincere viewpoint in a proclamation that day calling for enforcement of law and order and declaring, to "the People" of the City of New York: "A riotous demonstration in your city, originating in opposition to the conscription of soldiers for the military service of the United States, has swelled into vast proportions, directing its fury against the property and lives of peaceful citizens."

There was hardly any mistaking Seymour's underlying idea. He meant to say he might have favored a few small riots which would show a healthy Democratic opposition to the draft, but when the mobs ran wild and made war against the rich who could buy their escape from the draft, and furthermore turned the demonstration into a race conflict with a cry for death to all Negroes, it was time to place the emphasis on property, safety, strict law enforcement, rather than on personal liberty and the class discrimination of the Conscription Act.

From the steps of the City Hall in New York the Governor told an immense crowd (which included hundreds of rioters) that the city could furnish its quota by volunteering. "I have received a dispatch that the draft is suspended. There is no doubt the conscription is postponed. I learn this from a number of sources. If I get any information of a change of policy at Washington I will let you know."

Besides the many mobs which had carried banners inscribed "No Draft" and "No $300 Arrangements with Us," there had been many other mobs with varied and mixed motives. Class war was the cry behind the big placards of one division: "The Poor Man's Blood for the Rich Man's Money." Eagerness for loot, money, keepsakes, articles of use, lay back of the stripping of houses of jewelry, plate, furniture, rugs, mirrors, clothes. Primitive race antagonism, set aflame by political malevolence, underlay the hanging and beating of black men by white men. In thousands of boys the savage was unleashed; they robbed houses and set them on fire; they beat to death with fists and clubs the young Negro cripple Abraham Franklin; they tore off the clothes of Jeremiah Robinson, who was trying to escape to a ferryboat wearing his wife's dress and hood, threw him to the pavement, kicked him in the face and ribs, killed him and threw the body into the river. One gang seized Neil Stanton, son of Elizabeth Cady Stanton, with the cry, "Here's one of those $300 fellows," but when he led them into a saloon, bought drinks for all, joined them in three cheers for Jefferson Davis, they let him go.

The draft, however, and the arrangement that any man having $300 could buy his release from military service, were the focal points of the mass drive of the mobs. Robert Nugent, assistant provost marshal in charge of conscription, received on the second day of the riots a telegram from his Washington chief, James B. Fry, directing him to suspend the draft. Governor Seymour and Mayor Opdyke clamored that he should publish this order. Nugent said he had no authority to, but he finally consented to sign his name to a notice: "The draft has been suspended in New York City and Brooklyn," which was published in newspapers. This had a marked quieting effect.

The storm in the streets began to slow down as though winds had changed. And of course there was added quieting effect as infantry, cavalry, artillery, from the Army of the Potomac commenced arriving.

On July 14, the second of the three-day riots and mob control of New York City, a telegram dated at the War Department, Washington, and signed "A. Lincoln" went addressed to Robert T. Lincoln, Fifth Avenue Hotel, New York, with the query, "Why do I hear no more of you?"

After 150 regular-army soldiers with ball cartridges had faced a crowd of 2,000, fired in the air, and received a volley of stones in reply, and had then shot into the swarming and defiant mass, killing 12 and wounding more, the hullabaloo began to die down. "The left wing of Lee's army," as some had called the New York mobs, could not stand against the arriving regiments from the Southern battle fronts.

On the fourth day, as the incipient revolution was fading out, John Hughes, Roman Catholic Archbishop of New York, placarded the city with an announcement "To the men of New York, who are now called in many of the papers rioters: Men! I am not able, owing to the rheumatism in my

✝ JOHN

By the Grace of God, and the authority of the Holy See,

BISHOP OF BUFFALO.

To the Dearly Beloved Faithful Laity of the Diocese, Health and Benediction.

DEARLY BELOVED!---In the name of the God of Charity, and through that charity which He, who called us to be your Bishop, has given us for you; through that charity of Christ, in us, however unworthy, through which we would cheerfully give our life, if necessary, for each and every one of you; we beg of you, for Christ's sake, and for the sake of all that you love in heaven and on earth, to abstain from all resistance to law, from all riot, from all tumultuous gatherings, from all violence

In New York, many misguided men, yet very few we believe, of practical Catholics, have shed blood in the late riot; "and the voice of their brother's blood *cried to the Lord* from the earth." Some of the rioters have fallen, many more will, we fear, suffer much, many will, perhaps, be ruined; *all* will feel the painful sting of a guilty conscience, during the rest of life, and on their death-bed, (if indeed rioters who aid in murder could die otherwise than as it is written; "He that shall kill by the sword, must be killed by the sword." Apoc. XIII, 10;) they will either through God's mercy, sincerely repent for their participation in the riot; or be lost forever! Dearly beloved listen to the advice of a father who dearly loves you; submit to law and God will protect you. Should there be a draft, fewer will be drafted, than would, probably, be killed in an unholy struggle against law. And if any of you be drafted, we will try to protect and aid; friends will protect and aid; God will protect, aid, and bless, in more ways than we know or dare name.

Withdraw yourselves, then, we beg and exhort, from all who would excite to associations against the law of the land, or to violence, and mob-law. For God's sake; for the sake of your dear families; for the sake of your fathers and mothers, whether still pilgrims on earth, or mingling with the "blessed crowd of witnesses," who, from heaven, watch over your conduct on earth; we exhort you to *trust in God*, and not to lend yourselves to any exciter to mob or violence, which leads so often to murder. If you follow this advice of your Father in Christ, we confidently assure you that "Whosoever shall follow this rule, *peace will be unto him, and mercy;* and upon the Israel of God.---Gal. VI.

We require that this letter be read in every church on the Sunday after its reception.

Given at St. Joseph's Cathedral, Buffalo, on the Feast of Our Lady of Mount Carmel, A. D., MDCCCLXIII.

✝ JOHN, Bishop of Buffalo.

The Roman Catholic Bishop of Buffalo beseeches his flock to keep the peace during the draft. Reduced three-fourths from the size of the original poster in the Barrett collection.

limbs, to visit you; but that is not a reason why you should not pay me a visit in your whole strength. Come, then, to-morrow (Friday) at two o'clock, to my residence, northwest corner of Madison Avenue and Thirty-sixth Street. I shall have a speech prepared for you."

A crowd of between 3,000 and 5,000 greeted Archbishop Hughes as he stepped out on a balcony, clad in purple robes and other insignia of office, surrounded by priests and influential citizens of the Roman Catholic Church. After tremendous applause he spoke in a familiar and kindly way, saying a man should defend his house or shanty only for a just cause. "I have been hurt by the reports that you are rioters. You cannot imagine that I could hear those things without being pained grievously. Is there not some way by which you can stop these proceedings, and support the laws, of which none have been enacted against you as Irishmen and Catholics? You have suffered enough already. . . . Would it not be better for you to retire quietly; not to give up your principles or convictions, but to keep out of the crowd where immortal souls are launched into eternity, and, at all events, get into no trouble till you are at home? Would it not be better? There is one thing in which I would ask your advice.

"When these so-called riots are over, and the blame is justly laid on Irish Catholics, I wish you to tell me in what country I could claim to be born? [Voices, "Ireland."] Yes, but what shall I say if these stories be true? Ireland that never committed a single act of cruelty until she was oppressed. Ireland, that has been the mother of heroes and poets, but never the mother of cowards. I thank you for your kindness, and I hope nothing will occur till you return home, and if, by chance, as you go thither, you should meet a police officer or a military man, why, just—look at him."

The extent of Irish participation in the riots became a topic. Lincoln in an idle moment at the war telegraph office repeated for the operator, A. B. Chandler, a pun he had heard after the New York riots. "It is said that General *Kilpatrick* is going to New York to quell the riot, but his name has nothing to do with it." *Harper's Weekly* urged, "Turbulence is no ex-clusive attribute of the Irish character; it is common to all mobs in all countries," citing riots more atrocious in Paris, Madrid, Naples, Rome, Berlin, Vienna. *Harper's* admonished:

It happens in this city that, in our working classes, the Irish element largely pre-ponderates over all others, and if the populace acts as a populace Irishmen are naturally prominent therein. It happens, also, that, from the limited opportunities which the Irish enjoy for education in their own country, they are more easily misled by knaves, and made the tools of politicians, when they come here, than Germans, or men of other races. The impulsiveness of the Celt, likewise, prompts him to be foremost in every outburst, whether for a good or for an evil purpose.

But it must be remembered, in palliation of the disgrace which, as Archbishop Hughes says, the riots of last week have heaped upon the Irish name, that in many wards of the city the Irish were during the late riot stanch friends of law and order; that Irishmen helped to rescue the colored orphans in the asylum from the hands of the rioters; that a large proportion of the police, who behaved throughout the riot with the most exemplary gallantry, are Irishmen; that the Roman Catholic priesthood to a man used their influence on the side of the law; and that perhaps the most scathing rebuke administered to the riot was written by an Irishman—James T. Brady. It is important that this riot should teach us something more useful than a revival of Know-Nothing prejudices.

Whatever the number of Irish fighting under the Union flag, it was sufficient to cause War Secretary Benjamin of the Confederate Government to send first an army lieutenant and then a Roman Catholic priest to Ireland to agitate against Irish workingmen emigrating to America, to advise them they would be promised jobs as railroad-builders but the real object of the Lincoln Government was to lure them into the army. The Confederate Lieutenant Capston circulated among priests a poster with headlines "Persecution of Catholics in America," "The Tabernacle Overthrown!" "The Blessed Host Scattered on the Ground!" "Benediction Veil Made a Horse Cover Of!" "All the Sacred Vessels Carried Off!" Father John Bannon, following Capston, circulated an "Address to the Catholic Clergy and People of Ireland" covering a six-column newspaper sheet, alleging that Catholic churches had been burned by Union soldiers, that Catholics had been shot

Titled " 'Rowdy' Notions of Emancipation," *Punch's* cartoon holds Lincoln's proclamation the incitement to white men beating and hanging Negroes in the New York riots

down ruthlessly in the streets of many American cities, and that while the men of the North were Roundheads or Cromwellians, those of the South were chiefly descendants of Spanish and French Catholics.

During and after the riots Lincoln received reports from Sidney Howard Gay, managing editor of the *New York Tribune*, relaying information from a prominent Democratic politician. According to James R. Gilmore, "daily, as the politician made these disclosures, Mr. Gay communicated them to me, and I wrote them out and forwarded them to the President through Samuel Wilkinson [sic], then the Washington editor of the *Tribune*, to be by him personally handed to Mr. Lincoln."

As the days passed Gay and Gilmore decided that a searching judicial investigation would show the public that leading Copperheads had secretly instigated and directed the riots. After puzzling over who among jurists had the courage and intelligence for such an investigation they chose Judge John W. Edmonds, father-in-law of Gilmore. Gay and Gilmore then addressed a joint letter to President Lincoln recommending that Edmonds be appointed a special commissioner to investigate the origin of the riots and urging their belief that good results would follow. Gilmore then took a train to Lake George to tell Judge Edmonds what had been done. The Judge said if he undertook the work his life would not be worth a bad half-dollar, that he would be shot on sight, but he was getting along in years and might do worse by his country. "You can tell Mr. Lincoln that I will accept the appointment."

Meantime Gay at the *Tribune* office had no word from Lincoln. He telegraphed his Washington man to see the President and ask for a reply. In about an hour came the reply that Lincoln said in substance: "I have no answer to make. I never before had anything asked of me that I could not say yes or no to; but to this I can't make any reply."

Soon afterward Gilmore called on Lincoln at the White House and asked why the President could not say Yes or No to the recommendation for a special commissioner to expose the instigators of the New York riots. Lincoln hesitated and in a peculiar half-bantering manner, according to Gilmore, replied: "Well, you see if I had said no, I should have admitted that I dare not enforce the laws, and consequently have no business to be President of the United States. If I had said yes, and had appointed the judge, I should—as he would have done his duty—have simply touched a match to a barrel of gunpowder. You have heard of sitting on a volcano. We are sitting upon two; one is blazing away already, and the other will blaze away the moment we scrape a little loose dirt from the top of the crater. Better let the dirt alone,—at least for the present. One rebellion at a time is about as much as we can conveniently handle."

At Boston, Massachusetts, at Portsmouth, New Hampshire, in Holmes County, Ohio, and at still other points disorders and minor riots had taken place in protest against the draft.

Of the three days in which mobs ruled New York Welles wrote, "In all this time no Cabinet-meeting takes place." They had assembled on the second day, but "The President said he did not believe we could take up anything . . . to-day."

A week after the riots were over Senator Morgan and Samuel J. Tilden, leading New Yorkers, called on government officials in Washington and, as Welles wrote, "The gentlemen seemed to believe a draft cannot be enforced in New York." Still other Senators and Congressmen went to the President and asked him to declare martial law in New York City, sending General Butler or General Wadsworth to enforce it, but the President declined,

The Government transports one drafted man. From the Barrett collection.

the *New York World* commenting, "It is satisfying to know the President has more sense than some of his advisers."

Governor Seymour wrote to the President asking for suspension of the draft, the President replying that he could not consent. "Time is too important." Due credit in the quota would be made for volunteers, Lincoln stipulated; he also said he would be willing to facilitate a decision from the United States Supreme Court on whether the draft law was constitutional. "But I cannot consent to lose the time while it is being obtained. We are contending with an enemy, who, as I understand, drives every able-bodied man he can reach into his ranks, very much as a butcher drives bullocks into a slaughter-pen. . . . This produces an army . . . with a rapidity not to be matched on our side, if we first waste time to reëxperiment with the volunteer system."

Lincoln closed this letter of August 7 with saying his purpose was in his action to be "just and constitutional, and yet practical." He was yielding nothing to the astute and persistent Governor of New York, who had at various times so often given words of hope to New York City that the draft would be got rid of. On August 11 Lincoln wrote to Seymour that Seymour's communication dated August 8 was received on August 11. "Asking you to remember that I consider time as being very important, both to the general cause of the country and to the soldiers already in the field, I beg to remind you that I waited, at your request, from the 1st till the 6th instant, to receive your communication dated the 3d." He repeated for Seymour that the draft would proceed, "at the same time employing infallible means to avoid any great wrongs," meaning plainly that all possible danger would be evaded of New York's being required to furnish more troops than her quota.

In closing he noted for Seymour's eye, "No part of my former letter is repudiated by reason of not being restated in this, or for any other cause." He was yielding no points to Seymour. Copperhead newspapers in printing his letter said he spoke in the tone of a despot.

It seemed Lincoln believed the hour was one for a strong hand, for an attitude that carried the quiet assertion, "This is not the time for argument; we shall see who is the stronger; what have you?" For he did during those hectic summer weeks prepare an address to the country giving the facts and logic which dictated his actions in the draft. He finished about the middle of August this paper which would answer the questions: "Why do you, Abraham Lincoln, believe the draft should be enforced? By what right does the Government of the United States select men for military service and by force thrust them into the army unless they hire substitutes or each pay the Government $300?"

Having written this argument, Lincoln did not give it to the country. He filed it away in a pigeonhole of personal papers and it was not heard of till long afterward. He began it by saying: "It is at all times proper that misunderstanding between the public and the public servant should be avoided; and this is far more important now than in times of peace and tranquillity. I therefore address you without searching for a precedent upon which to do so."

On the mind of each man physically fit to be a soldier were pressing motives that effected his decision to volunteer for military service or not. "Among these motives would be patriotism, political bias, ambition, personal courage, love of adventure, want of employment, and convenience, or the opposites of some of these." Now through "this voluntary weighing of motives" the Government had obtained substantially all the men to be thus had for service.

"And yet we must somehow obtain more, or relinquish the original object of the contest, together with all the blood and treasure already expended in the effort to secure it. To meet this necessity the law for the draft has been enacted. You who do not wish to be soldiers do not like this law. This is natural; nor does it imply want of patriotism. Nothing can be so just and necessary as to make us like it if it is disagreeable to us. We are prone, too, to find false arguments with which to excuse ourselves for opposing such disagreeable things. In this case, those who desire to see the rebellion succeed, and others who seek reward in a different way, are very active in accommodating us with this class of arguments."

As to their point that the draft was unconstitutional, he would quote from the Constitution, "The Congress shall have power . . . to raise and support armies; but no appropriation of money to that use shall be for a

THE NAUGHTY BOY GOTHAM, WHO WOULD NOT TAKE THE DRAFT.

MAMMY LINCOLN—"*There now, you bad boy, acting that way, when your little sister Penn takes hers like a lady!*"

Leslie's cartoons "Mammy Lincoln," the good girl "Philadelphia," and the "Naughty Boy Gotham" kicking loose "the draft"—overly facile treatment of **a** violently complicated subject

longer term than two years." The whole scope of the Conscription Act was "to raise and support armies." He went into a long paragraph of legal argument that the law was made in "literal pursuance" of the part of the Constitution quoted, and cited another part of the Constitution declaring that "this Constitution, and the laws made in pursuance thereof . . . shall be the supreme law of the land, and the judges in every State shall be bound thereby, anything in the constitution or laws of any State to the contrary notwithstanding."

The question might be raised that Congress had not exercised the power given it in a constitutional mode, had not done the thing in a right way. "Who is to judge of this? The Constitution gives Congress the power, but it does not prescribe the mode, or expressly declare who shall prescribe it. In such case Congress must prescribe the mode, or relinquish the power. There is no alternative. Congress could not exercise the power to do the thing if it had not the power of providing a way to do it, when no way is provided by the Constitution for doing it. In fact, Congress would not have the power to raise and support armies, if even by the Constitution it were left to the option of any other or others to give or withhold the only mode of doing it. If the Constitution had prescribed a mode, Congress could and must follow that mode; but, as it is, the mode necessarily goes to Congress, with the power expressly given. The power is given fully, completely, unconditionally. It is not a power to raise armies if State authorities consent; nor if the men to compose the armies are entirely willing; but it is a power to raise and support armies given to Congress by the Constitution, without an 'if.' " It was also clear that this was not a law "to raise armies when no armies were needed."

Now for the maintenance of republican institutions and territorial integrity the country required further raising and supporting of armies. "There can be no army without men. Men can be had only voluntarily or involuntarily. We have ceased to obtain them voluntarily, and to obtain them involuntarily is the draft—the conscription. If you dispute the fact, and declare that men can still be had voluntarily in sufficient numbers, prove the assertion by yourselves volunteering in such numbers, and I shall gladly give up the draft. Or, if not a sufficient number, but any one of you will volunteer, he for his single self will escape all the horrors of the draft, and will thereby do only what each one of at least a million of his manly brethren have already done. Their toil and blood have been given as much for you as themselves. Shall it all be lost rather than that you, too, will bear your part?"

He would be explicit. "I do not say that all who would avoid serving in the war are unpatriotic; but I do think every patriot should willingly take his chance under a law made with great care, in order to secure entire fairness." Congress had at great length and with much labor considered, discussed, modified, and amended the law and finally passed it almost unanimously. Any one man, either out of Congress or in it, might have made the

George Gordon Meade

Oliver Otis Howard

From the author's collection

William Starke Rosecrans

From the author's collection

John Adams Dix

From the Meserve collection

Archbishop John Hughes

From the author's collection

Bishop Matthew Simpson

From the Meserve collection

Henry Ward Beecher

From the author's collection

The bullet-pierced, lifesaving pocket New Testament of Carter E. Prince, 4th Maine Volunteers

In the Barrett collection

law differently. It was a joint work, and like the Constitution, better than any one of its framers.

Now he came to the one bitter sore spot that had raised up violence and devices of evasion, the $300 clause by which the men having that amount of money could escape military service. On this Lincoln reasoned:

"Much complaint is made of that provision of the conscription law which allows a drafted man to substitute three hundred dollars for himself; while, as I believe, none is made of that provision which allows him to substitute another man for himself. Nor is the three hundred dollar provision objected to for unconstitutionality; but for inequality, for favoring the rich against the poor. The substitution of men is the provision, if any, which favors the rich to the exclusion of the poor. But this, being a provision in accordance with an old and well-known practice in the raising of armies, is not objected to. There would have been great objection if that provision had been omitted. And yet, being in, the money provision really modifies the inequality which the other introduces. It allows men to escape the service who are too poor to escape but for it.

"Without the money provision, competition among the more wealthy might, and probably would, raise the price of substitutes above three hundred dollars, thus leaving the man who could raise only three hundred dollars no escape from personal service. True, by the law as it is, the man who cannot raise so much as three hundred dollars, nor obtain a personal substitute for less, cannot escape; but he can come quite as near escaping as he could if the money provision were not in the law.

"To put it another way: is an unobjectionable law which allows only the man to escape who can pay a thousand dollars made objectionable by adding a provision that anyone may escape who can pay the smaller sum of three hundred dollars? This is the exact difference at this point between the present law and all former draft laws. It is true that by this law a somewhat larger number will escape than could under a law allowing personal substitutes only; but each additional man thus escaping will be a poorer man than could have escaped by the law in the other form.

"The money provision enlarges the class of exempts from actual service simply by admitting poorer men into it. How then can the money provision be a wrong to the poor man? The inequality complained of pertains in greater degree to the substitution of men, and is really modified and lessened by the money provision.

"The inequality could only be perfectly cured by sweeping both provisions away. This, being a great innovation, would probably leave the law more distasteful than it now is.

"The principle of the draft, which simply is involuntary or enforced service, is not new. It has been practised in all ages of the world. It was well-known to the framers of our Constitution as one of the modes of raising armies, at the time they placed in that instrument the provision that 'the Congress shall have power to raise and support armies.' It had been used just before in establishing our independence, and it was also used under the

Constitution in 1812. Wherein is the peculiar hardship now? Shall we shrink from the necessary means to maintain our free government, which our grandfathers employed to establish it, and our own fathers have already employed once to maintain it? Are we degenerate? Has the manhood of our race run out?"

He then pointed out how a law may be constitutional and expedient and yet work out in an unjust and unfair way. No laws to distribute burdens or

PENNSYLVANIA BEEF CONTRACTOR. "Want Beefsteak? Good Gracious, what is the World coming to? Why, my Good Fellow, if you get Beefsteak, how on earth are Contractors to live? Tell me. that."

Harper's Weekly contrasts contractor and soldier

benefits equally had ever been practically administered "with that exactness which can be conceived of in the mind." Tax laws always worked out an unequal proportion. And it was merely theory that in the United States House of Representatives each member is sent by the same number of people that each other is sent by. The districts cannot be made precisely equal in population at first, and if they could, they would become unequal in a single day, and much more so in the ten years the districts, once made, are to continue. They cannot be remodeled every day nor every year.

The same sort of difficulty applied to the draft law, was in fact greater. The congressional district was based on entire population, while the draft was based only on those fit for soldiers. Furthermore, credit must be given for the soldiers who had already gone from the several districts. In administering the law the Government was bound to "good faith and fidelity," and any great departures should be corrected and any agent shown to have caused such departures intentionally should be dismissed.

The closing part of this paper, in a somewhat different form, went into an open letter to Governor Seymour; the argument for constitutionality had been stated in the published letter to Erastus Corning. But the elaborate defense of the $300 clause was not made public. It seemed as though Lincoln wrote out all the reasons that came to his mind which could be urged in favor of the upper and middle classes buying exemption by payment of $300 to the Government or by hiring substitutes. As he reasoned about it his mind told him there was an "inequality," which was the word he used, and possibly his mind also told him that this inequality was violently in conflict with the pretenses and claims of republican institutions, for he wrote: "The inequality complained of pertains in greater degree to the substitution of men, and is really modified and lessened by the money provision. The inequality could only be perfectly cured by sweeping both provisions away. This, being a great innovation, would probably leave the law more distasteful than it is now."

His mind had dwelt, evidently, on a conscription law which would enforce universal selective service, the Government taking all men physically fit, no man escaping by purchase or substitution. Such an enforced service of conscription for military service or training was operating in several European monarchies and republics, but as Lincoln looked out across the American scene in 1863 he seemed to believe it could not then be put to work in the United States, even if he could find Congressmen to advocate it. Perhaps when he told Gilmore that he was sitting on a volcano he had considered that the orators and editors of the opposition had more than a demagogue's idle phrase in the cry "The rich man's money against the poor man's blood."

His elaborately prepared address, said Nicolay and Hay, was intended more especially for the honest and patriotic Democrats of the North, "but after he had finished it, doubts arose in his mind as to the propriety or the expediency of addressing the public directly in that manner," and "with reserve and abnegation, after writing it, he resolved to suppress so admirable a paper." He was an opportunist and a practical politician, besides an old jury lawyer who knew that on some issues of a case it was best to say little or nothing. Having made out the best case he could for the $300 clause, he

A FAIR ARRANGEMENT.

ALDERMAN (*just elected*).—"Now, Sonny, you go and do the fighting, and me and the Judge will look after the Government and the Contracts."

Harper's Weekly cartoons the inequity of which Lincoln wrote in a memorandum not made public

decided, probably with a laugh at himself, that it stood rather poorly in its class discriminations; too many of the opposition would leap to meet his argument. He would not be maneuvering politically in key with his old-time saying to T. W. S. Kidd in Springfield, that the most valuable special ability for a winning politician was "to be able to raise a cause which shall produce an effect, and then to fight the effect."

Also the man in him, with early roots among people to whom $300 was a young fortune that would tide over a year or two of crop failures, could find no lights of high philosophy or grand conduct about it.

To inquire as he did in the same paper: "Are we degenerate? Has the manhood of our race run out?" while entering into open defense of patriots who parted with cash to evade showing the valor of their manhood, would have been a faultier argument than Lincoln had ever made in a public appeal.

He laid his paper aside as a meditation that had exercised his mind and sharpened his humility and perhaps deepened his patience. He would enforce the law but not become dialectical about it. "The inequality could only be perfectly cured by sweeping both provisions away." Meanwhile, though volunteering was practically at an end, he would do his best not to relinquish what had been gained by the toil and blood of something like 1,000,000 volunteers.

From his explorations in merciless logic the President turned to Artemus Ward's circular on who should be exempted: "Any gentleman living in Ireland, who was never in this country, is not liable to the draft, nor are our forefathers." Enrolling officers should not use names from cemetery tombstones. "The term of enlistment is for three years, but any man who may have been drafted in two places has a right to go for six years. The only sons of a poor widow, whose husband is in California, are not exempt, but a man who owns stock in the Vermont Central Railroad is. So also are incessant lunatics, habitual lecturers, persons born with wooden legs or false teeth, blind men, and people who deliberately voted for John Tyler."

New York City saw amid her streets on August 19 of '63 no less than 10,000 foot troops from the Army of the Potomac and three batteries of artillery, "picked troops including the regulars," assisted by the 1st Division of the New York State Guards. Governor Seymour proclaimed that citizens should obey the law of Congress as to conscription. New draft offices in place of those burned down, and new rotating wheels for the choosing of names, went into operation. Cavalry patrols rode up and down the streets.

The draft proceeded. But how? Now it met covert instead of open resistance. Tammany, Tweed, A. Oakey Hall, Fernando Wood and his brother Ben, J. P. Morgan, the *World*, the *Express*, the *Day Book*, the *Mercury*, many scurrying politicians, examining physicians, and fixers, lawyers, did their work. Upward of $5,000,000 was appropriated by the municipality of New York for draft-evasion purposes. According to the "infallible" record which Lincoln had mentioned to Seymour, of 292,441 men whose names were drawn from the wheels 39,877 failed to report for examination. Of the remaining 252,564, for good or bad reasons 164,394 were exempted. This left 88,170 available for duty, of whom 52,288 bought exemption at $300 apiece, which yielded the Government $15,666,400. The original 292,441 names were thus cut down to 35,882 men, of whom 26,002 hired substitutes to go to war for them. This left 9,880 who lacked political pull or seemed to want to join the army and fight.

It was thirty months since Fernando Wood, then Mayor of New York, had declared that New York should secede from the Union, establish herself as a Free City, Lincoln privately commenting then that it was not yet time for the Front Door to set up housekeeping for itself. Thus far neither

ABUNDANT DISQUALIFICATION.

"Ugh! How d'you make out that *you* are exempt, eh?"
"I'm over age, I am a Negro, a Minister, a Cripple, a
British Subject, and an Habitual Drunkard."

Harper's Weekly puts a current joke into a cartoon

Wood nor Lincoln had won the contest decisively, though on points scored
Lincoln was gaining.

As if the American political scene required one more seriocomic element, there now arose at Niagara Falls, Canada, the form and voice of
Clement L. Vallandigham, Democratic candidate for the governorship of
Ohio, crying that on British soil he was a freeman but if he crossed over
into the U.S.A. he was a felon and would be clapped into jail. Discussion
of habeas corpus and the right of free speech flared higher. The *New York
World* declared that the crime of arresting Vallandigham was a Lincoln
blunder and inquired why the President had not arrested Fernando Wood

for remarks at New York mass meetings as treasonable as those of Vallandigham in Ohio. The French had created a state offense which they punished under the title of "Attempts to bring the government into ridicule and contempt," said the *World*, and "Of this offense Mr. Lincoln has clearly been guilty. It is not possible to respect an executive who pettifogs grave questions of constitutional law."

Vallandigham said the same in his own grandiose style in an address to the Democracy of Ohio, dated July 15. "Six weeks ago, when just going into banishment, because an audacious but most cowardly despotism compelled it, I addressed you as a fellow-citizen. Today and from the very place then selected by me, but after wearisome and most perilous journeyings for more than four thousand miles by land and upon the sea—still in exile, though almost in sight of my native State—I greet you as your representative."

Vallandigham then repeated the points familiar to all who had followed his speeches, with the added information that he had traveled a thousand miles through half the Confederacy and "I met not one man, woman or child who was not resolved to perish rather than yield to the pressure of arms." Nor did he meet anyone not ready to discuss reunion if the war could be ended and the armies withdrawn. He did not say that he met with rather a cold reception throughout the South, that the *Charleston Mercury* repudiated him, that nothing came of his interview with President Davis, that the Confederates were glad to put him on a boat for Bermuda, where he had taken passage to Halifax.

Mrs. Vallandigham left her home in Dayton, Ohio, to join her husband at Windsor, Canada, opposite Detroit, to help him campaign from there for the governorship of Ohio. It was reported she told her friends that she never expected to return from Canada until she did so as the wife of the Governor of Ohio. This reminded Lincoln of a man out in Illinois running for supervisor on the county board. On leaving home election morning he said, "Wife, tonight you shall sleep with the supervisor from this township." News came in the evening that her husband was beaten in the election, and she was all dressed up for going out when she met her defeated man at the door. "Wife, where are you going all dressed up this time of night?" he exclaimed. "Going?" she countered. "Why, you told me this morning that I should sleep tonight with the supervisor of this town and as the other man was elected instead of you, I was going to his house." Whereupon the husband, as newspapers quoted Lincoln, "acknowledged the corn, she didn't go out, and he bought a new Brussels carpet for the parlor."

During those six weeks since Vallandigham had been thrust as an exile beyond Union Army lines, to reappear on British soil proclaiming across the border the same defiance as before, Lee had gone up into Pennsylvania and the most brilliantly performing of Confederate armies had been repulsed at Gettysburg and returned to Southern soil; Grant had taken Vicksburg and Confederate power on the Mississippi River was gone from St. Louis to the Gulf; a violent three-day uprising in the largest city in the North, and minor revolts at other points, had been smoothed out until it seemed that the Washington Government had a decent measure of power and dignity.

Lincoln was pleased at the outlook in general. He decided to write a letter telling the country so, and incidentally smiting the opposition hip and thigh with simple arguments. Stanton had muttered to Welles one day that the President was writing too many letters. But Lincoln took himself as a spokesman. Therefore when an invitation came for him to attend a mass meeting of unconditional Union men to be held in Springfield, Illinois, September 3, he seriously considered journeying West to speak, but when a friend called to ask if he was going to Springfield he replied, "No, I shall send them a letter instead; and it will be a rather good letter." It was addressed to James C. Conkling, to be read at the meeting, expressing regrets that he could not be there in person.

And Conkling read at the mass meeting Lincoln's message: "My old political friends will thank me for tendering, as I do, the nation's gratitude to those . . . whom no partizan malice or partizan hope can make false to the nation's life." He became very personal. "There are those who are dissatisfied with me. To such I would say: You desire peace, and you blame me that we do not have it. But how can we obtain it? There are but three conceivable ways: First, to suppress the rebellion by force of arms. This I am trying to do. Are you for it? If you are, so far we are agreed. If you are not for it, a second way is to give up the Union. I am against this. Are you for it? If you are, you should say so plainly. If you are not for force, nor yet for dissolution, there only remains some imaginable compromise."

The strength of the rebellion lay in its army. Any offer of peace terms must come from men having power to enforce a compromise. "In what way can . . . compromise be used to keep Lee's army out of Pennsylvania? Meade's army can keep Lee's army out of Pennsylvania, and, I think, can ultimately drive it out of existence. But no paper compromise to which the controllers of Lee's army are not agreed can at all affect that army. In an effort at such compromise we would waste time which the enemy would improve to our disadvantage; and that would be all."

He promised that if any peace proposition came from those who controlled the Confederate Army, or from people liberated from domination of that army by the success of the Union armies, he would let the country know of it. "It shall not be rejected and kept a secret from you."

There was another issue. "But to be plain: You are dissatisfied with me about the negro. Quite likely there is a difference of opinion between you and myself upon that subject. I certainly wish that all men could be free, while I suppose you do not. Yet, I have neither adopted nor proposed any measure which is not consistent with even your view, provided you are for the Union. I suggested compensated emancipation, to which you replied you wished not to be taxed to buy negroes. But I had not asked you to be taxed to buy negroes, except in such way as to save you from greater taxation to save the Union exclusively by other means."

There were those who said the Emancipation Proclamation was unconstitutional. "I think differently. I think the Constitution invests its commander-in-chief with the law of war in time of war." Slaves were property and in time of war the property both of enemies and friends might be taken when needed. Furthermore, the war had gone on a year and a half before the proclamation was issued, the last hundred days passing under explicit notice that it was coming, unless averted by those in revolt. The war had progressed as favorably since as before the proclamation was issued. He could name commanders of armies in the field who believed the emancipation policy and the use of colored troops constituted the heaviest blows yet dealt to the rebellion.

"You say you will not fight to free negroes. Some of them seem willing to fight for you; but no matter. Fight you, then, exclusively, to save the Union. I issued the proclamation on purpose to aid you in saving the Union. Whenever you shall have conquered all resistance to the Union, if I shall urge you to continue fighting, it will be an apt time then for you to declare you will not fight to free negroes. I thought that in your struggle for the Union, to whatever extent the negroes should cease helping the enemy, to that extent it weakened the enemy in his resistance to you. Do you think differently? I thought that whatever negroes can be got to do as soldiers, leaves just so much less for white soldiers to do in saving the Union. Does it appear otherwise to you? But negroes, like other people, act upon motives. Why should they do anything for us if we will do nothing for them? If they stake their lives for us they must be prompted by the strongest motive, even the promise of freedom. And the promise, being made, must be kept."

Then Lincoln launched into the finish of what was really a paper aimed at the masses of people in America and Europe, knowing too that it would be curiously scrutinized by European governments, achieving in a way a triumphant cry of the American Eagle emblematic of the Washington Government. Hay referred to it as a stump speech. It closed:

"The signs look better. The Father of Waters again goes unvexed to the sea. Thanks to the great Northwest for it. Nor yet wholly to them. Three hundred miles up they met New England, Empire, Keystone, and Jersey, hewing their way right and left. The sunny South, too, in more colors than one, also lent a hand. On the spot, their part of the history was jotted down in black and white. The job was a great national one, and let none be slighted who bore an honorable part in it.

"And while those who have cleared the great river may well be proud, even that is not all. It is hard to say that anything has been more bravely and well done than at Antietam, Murfreesboro', Gettysburg, and on many fields of less note. Nor must Uncle Sam's web-feet be forgotten. At all the watery margins they have been present. Not only on the deep sea, the broad bay, and the rapid river, but also up the narrow, muddy bayou, and wherever the ground was a little damp, they have been and made their tracks. Thanks to all: for the great republic—for the principle it lives by and keeps alive—for man's vast future—thanks to all.

"Peace does not appear so distant as it did. I hope it will come soon, and come to stay; and so come as to be worth the keeping in all future time. It will then have been proved that among free men there can be no successful appeal from the ballot to the bullet, and that they who take such appeal are sure to lose their case and pay the cost.

"And then there will be some black men who can remember that with silent tongue, and clenched teeth, and steady eye, and well-poised bayonet, they have helped mankind on to this great consummation, while I fear there will be some white ones unable to forget that with malignant heart and deceitful speech they strove to hinder it.

"Still, let us not be over-sanguine of a speedy final triumph. Let us be quite sober. Let us diligently apply the means, never doubting that a just God, in his own good time, will give us the rightful result."

No previous letter nor address nor state paper of Lincoln received such warmhearted comment as this one to the Union mass meeting in his home town in Illinois. While the opposition tried to tear it to pieces, many newspapers joined with the *New York Times* in noting it as having hard sense, sharp outlines, a temper defying malice. "Even the Copperhead gnaws upon it as vainly as a viper upon a file. The most consummate rhetorician never used language more pat to the purpose and still there is not a word not familiar to the plainest plowman. He 'hits the nail upon the head.' In spite of all the hard trials and the hard words to which he has been exposed, Abraham Lincoln is today the most popular man in the Republic. All the denunciation and all the arts of the demagogue are perfectly powerless to wean the people from their faith in him." He was, with his clear head, peculiarly adapted to the needs of the hour, said the *Times*, "dispassionate, discreet, steadfast, honest Abraham Lincoln."

By reading this latest letter one would know why the people of Illinois had conferred on Mr. Lincoln the familiar nickname of "Honest," said the *New York Evening Post*. "Thorough honesty, a sincere desire to do right, a conscientious intention to preserve faithfully the oath of office and to do his duty as an American and a lover of the liberty upon which our government is founded, these are the traits which mark every sentence of the letter. To these must be added a quaint yet shrewd and pointed way of putting his argument which is characteristic of a man who is of the 'plain people' and has not mixed much with those great managers of the world's affairs who are accustomed to use language to conceal their thoughts."

At such praise for Lincoln many Democratic newspapers revolted. The *New York World* said his traducing of the motives of his opponents was unbecoming a Chief Magistrate, and went into a long review of Lincoln's acts of administration. "The war is managed not in the interest of the Union but in the interest of the Republican party and its greedy retinue of contractors." The President was vacillating in his Cabinet appointments; he had hung in doubt about reinforcing Fort Sumter; he had constantly halted in half-decisions regarding McClellan, not daring to face the radicals of Congress; his feebleness of character was even more strikingly exhibited with the Emancipation Proclamation, when "Mr. Lincoln was tossed upon his doubts like a chip upon the waves"; his mind never master of itself, he had been badgered by the radicals until "after the usual fashion of weak minds" he finally did the thing by halves. "Perhaps there never was another man called to act a conspicuous part in great conjunctures who possessed so little of indispensable robustness of purpose as Mr. Lincoln." In the Trent Affair he had been frightened out of a proper and dignified course. On what ground could an Administration journal say, "In general cast of mind and heart Mr. Lincoln more resembles Washington than any of his predecessors"?

Pusillanimity, vacillation, and feebleness of purpose had marked Mr. Lincoln's whole public course, and to mention Washington in the same breath was a profanation of the illustrious and venerated dead, continued the *New York World*, leading organ of the Democratic party. "Nature has not endowed Mr. Lincoln with a single great or commanding quality. He has indeed a certain homely untutored shrewdness and vulgar honesty which are common enough in every plain community but no such consciousness of resources superior to an ordinary station has ever led him to exact from others a higher degree of consideration than belongs to a village lawyer. Nor is he endowed with any of that confident self-reliance and steady vigor of will which are the natural accompaniment of strong faculties. Indeed a hesitating infirmity of purpose which can with difficulty rescue itself from the suspense of conflicting motives and make a decision feeble when at last a decision is reached, is the key to Mr. Lincoln's character. His resolutions not only on all great occasions but on all occasions whatsoever where there are opposing reasons to be balanced, struggle into being like the animals in Milton's description of creation: 'Now half appeared the tawny lion, pawing to get free his hinder parts.' "

The London *Times* was annoyed, more than on any occasion before, by Lincoln's style as well as content. His latest utterance was "something between a prophecy and an oracular response, with a dash of Yankee slang and terms of expression which remind us alternately of Ossian, of the incoherent utterances of the Maori chiefs, and of school-boy translations of corrupt choruses in Greek tragedies." Cromwell never spoke and Carlyle never wrote anything so hopelessly obscure as Lincoln's latest letter, said this leading English conservative journal, "and the persons, if there be any such, to whom such jargon can appear impressive or even intelligible, must have faculties and tastes of which we can form no idea. One is really tempted to think that Mr. Lincoln cannot have been himself when he penned so grotesque a production. Herodotus tells us that the ancient Persian deliberated drunk as well as sober on important affairs of state; but we may be sure that the conclusion of a debate was conducted in the latter condition. It is difficult to believe that the American President can have observed this precaution, though he winds up with the timely injunction, 'Let us be quite sober.' "

The English Tory organ could not see Lincoln as counseling patience

and restraint in a stubby little sentence that might have been picked out of
the King James translation of St. Paul or out of John Milton or John Bun-
yan or the best of very early English writings. In his "ambitious paragraphs" the *Times* found "a lawyer-like smartness, that secures to Mr. Lincoln, in spite of his arbitrary weakness, a certain popularity among a people
who enjoy a joke, even at the expense of themselves." Following which
the *Times* proceeded to argue that the war was a tragic joke that Lincoln
was playing on his country.

Lincoln's reference to "Uncle Sam's web-feet," where they had "been
and made their tracks," was ridiculed by the opposition. How could the
American Eagle have the foot of a water bird? The *Peoria Morning Mail*
went versifying:

> We have no eagle—change is there—
> Abe swapped our bird away;
> We have no eagle any more,
> Bald-headed, black or gray.
> Abe swapped away our glorious bird—
> Got cheated like the deuce!
> The talons for the web-foot went—
> The eagle for the goose!

The *Illinois State Journal* reprinted, with credit to the London *Star*, an
English liberal journal, a rounded panegyric pronounced on the Sangamon
County man who had moved to the White House. "The text of President
Lincoln's letter to the Springfield convention confirms our faith in the man
who has the conduct of the war. It is a master-piece of cogent argument,
sublime in the dignified simplicity of its eloquences. No nobler state paper
was ever penned. It is the manifesto of a truly great man in an exigency
of almost unequalled moment. It is worthy of a Cromwell or a Washington.
It breathes the calm heroism of a Christian patriot—trust in the blessing of
God upon dauntless exertions in a just cause. It is such as Garibaldi or
Mazzini might have written from Rome if events had placed them at the
head of an Italian commonwealth threatened by a formidable combination
of enemies of its freedom and integrity. It is the utterance of a statesman
who has nothing to conceal—of a ruler guiltless of oppression—of the genius
that consists in transparent honesty and unflinching resolution. Addressed
to friends and neighbors, supporters and opponents, it is open to all the
world to read. It really challenges the judgment of contemporary civilization, though it contains scarce a hint of any country but the United States."

John Hay in a letter to Nicolay gave a close-up estimate as between
intimates and confidants. "His last letter is a great thing. Some hideously
bad rhetoric—some indecorums that are infamous—yet the whole letter takes
its solid place in history, as a great utterance of a great man. The whole
Cabinet could not have tinkered up a letter which could have been compared with it. He can rake a sophism out of its hole, better than all the
trained logicians of all schools. I do not know whether the nation is worthy
of him for another term. I know the people want him. There is no mistak-

ing that fact. But politicians are strong yet & he is not their 'kind of a cat.'
. . . Next winter will be the most exciting and laborious of all our lives."

In the same letter from Washington Hay gave his view of Lincoln at
the center of operations. "You may talk as you please of the Abolition Cabal
directing affairs from Washington; some well-meaning newspapers advise
the President to keep his fingers out of the military pie; and all that sort
of thing. The truth is, if he did, the pie would be a sorry mess. The old
man sits here and wields like a backwoods Jupiter the bolts of war and the
machinery of government with a hand equally steady & equally firm."

Living in the same house, seeing the chief in many moods, Hay felt that
Lincoln was steadily widening his grasp. "The Tycoon is in fine whack. I
have rarely seen him more serene & busy. He is managing this war, the
draft, foreign relations, and planning a reconstruction of the Union, all at
once. I never knew with what tyrannous authority he rules the Cabinet,
till now. The most important things he decides & there is no cavil. I am
growing more and more firmly convinced that the good of the country
absolutely demands that he should be kept where he is till this thing is over.
There is no man in the country, so wise, so gentle and so firm. I believe
the hand of God placed him where he is."

One of the so-called Abolition Cabal had spoken at the Springfield mass
meeting where Lincoln's letter was read, Senator Zach Chandler saying:
"Mr. Lincoln entered resolutely and manfully upon his duties, and for what
has been accomplished I feel grateful to Almighty God and Abraham Lincoln. [Cheers.] . . . At the end of eighteen months we found ourselves
not quite as well off as at the beginning. Some of us found fault and
thought President Lincoln had been making mistakes. But we all knew that
he was honest and patriotic. [Cheers.] He does not act as quickly as some
men, but when he puts his foot down, he is there." Another of the so-called
Abolition Cabal, Senator Sumner, immediately wrote to Lincoln: "Thanks
for your true and noble letter. It is a historical document. The case is admirably stated, so that all but the wicked must confess its force. It cannot
be answered." Senator Henry Wilson wrote: "God Almighty bless you for
your noble, patriotic and Christian letter. It will be on the lips and in the
hearts of hundreds of thousands this day."

From the veteran moderate antislavery Josiah Quincy, ninety-one years
of age, came words of gratitude for the letter to the Springfield meeting.
"It was due to truth and to your own character, shamefully assailed as it
has been. The development is an imperishable monument of wisdom and
virtue." The old man believed compromise between the North and South
impossible. "Peace on any other basis [than emancipation] would be the
establishment of two nations, each hating the other, both military, both necessarily warlike, their territories interlocked with a tendency of never-
ceasing hostility. Can we leave to posterity a more cruel inheritance or one
more hopeless of happiness and prosperity?" In replying Lincoln addressed
Josiah Quincy as "Dear and honored Sir," thanked him cordially for "wise
and earnest words of counsel," and before signing gave an unusual salute of

grave courtesy to the extraordinary and venerable Massachusetts sage: "Believe me, my dear sir, to be very respectfully and sincerely your friend and servant."

In September of '63 the Boston publisher Benjamin B. Russell issued a collection of *The Letters of President Lincoln on Questions of National Policy*, with a preface, as though the letters were literature and unique reading matter. "We have believed that very many would be glad to have these letters—which, though peculiar in style, are marked by a very high ability and statesmanship—in a collected form." The sheaf included letters to McClellan, Greeley, Fernando Wood, Erastus Corning, and the Albany Committee, Governor Seymour, and the Springfield meeting, filled twenty-two pages, and sold at 8 cents a copy, two copies 15 cents.

In a letter to Richard Cobden, the English liberal, on the unfriendly course of Great Britain, Professor Mahan of West Point drew the contrast which he saw between Lincoln and Jefferson Davis. The letter as published in newspapers in September of '63 noted: "Mr. Lincoln's great defect is that his heart too often controls his head. Jefferson Davis has many excellent individual characteristics, but his heart, in all public matters, never disturbs his brain. They are both representative men; the one kindly and genial, even in official station, never troubling himself with etiquette or dignification; speaking and writing often without deliberation, and without a care as to how grammarians may dissent what he utters, or what the *salons* may pass upon his taste. Napoleon I. was, we know, very sensitive as to what was said of him in the *salons* of the Faubourg St. Germain.

"Abraham Lincoln has no such anxieties. He has no dynasty to found; no unstable seat that totters at a *mot pour rire*, or a sarcasm. He has no prestige of an old nobility to fear. Those who claim the F.F.V.'s and S's are all on the other side. Bullets and bayonets are the weapons of warfare between him and them. He has read history to little purpose who has not learned from it how futile the prittle-prattle of the *salons* is in the face of grand events; how hushed it becomes in the tumult of the people, roused by some great principle, which penetrates into the inner hearts of humanity, and sends its life blood rushing through millions of channels to fire the masses.

"Abraham Lincoln, one of the people, instinctively feels this. Sprung from the people, and not one of a class, he feels that his words, however quaint or even uncouth to polite ears, will reach the popular heart. Jefferson Davis suffers no thought or word to escape him, which is not duly weighed; suffers no man to trench on his official dignity; is respected, admired, extolled by his class; but except by some few friends, not loved. Nature formed him for an imperial despot. He must be that or nothing. What one of his generals loves him? Not one. Not one. And yet he has warm friends, perhaps in the North the most so, as they have never been brought into collision with him. Does Lee love him, does Beauregard, does Bragg, does even Joe Johnston? Not one; and more than one of these it is said, hate him bitterly."

This contrast between the two opposed spokesmen was being drawn more often. The skill of each in plain argument and in appeal to what Mahew called "the popular heart" was a factor difficult to weigh, an imponderable of the war, yet as definitely important as men, armies, guns, money. A German military expert, Clausewitz, had written a heavy book on the value in modern warfare of the opinion and feeling of the civil populations not directly engaged in fighting. "War is the continuation of politics —by other means." Whether or not Lincoln had read Clausewitz, he was applying rather strictly some of the principles laid down by that philosopher on the technique of kindling mass sentiment to keep a war going.

By the carefully wrought appeal in simple words aimed to reach millions of readers and by the face-to-face contact with thousands who came to the White House, Lincoln was holding to the single purpose of adding momentum to the popular will for war. As the months passed there was registered in many letters such an impression as closed one paragraph of a letter John Burroughs wrote to his wife in the autumn of '63: "From my window in the Treasury Building I used to see Lincoln stepping over the piles of lumber with his long, lank legs. When he wanted to see Seward he took that way to avoid the crowd. I saw him often, but never spoke to him but once, and then briefly—at a reception at the White House. I passed along in line with hundreds of others. When my turn came I lingered a little, but was pulled along—I can yet feel the pull of his great hand as he drew me along past him to make room for those coming after." Lincoln, of course, was not aware that he was hustling along the one man who knew more than anybody else about the birds and wild life of the District of Columbia, and possibly even more than Lincoln about trees.

The late summer and early fall of '63 seemed to mark a deepening of loyalties to Lincoln and his vision of where to go and how. His maneuvers and shifts on ways and policies began to take on a color of reason and a light of faith for men such as "The Lounger," writing in *Harper's Weekly* toward the end of the summer: "The practical sagacity of the President is daily justified. His impulses are wiser than the wary plans of more cunning men." In his public letters "both the resolution to write and the time of writing were most happy illustrations of his shrewdness." Since his inauguration his ability no less than his honesty had overcome the desperate effort to make him seem a partisan. "He has aimed only at the maintenance of the Government; and to secure that end he has no more hesitated to adopt a policy which his own party approved than he has to take measures which the party opposed to him applauded. He has filled the chief posts of command with men of all political views.

"Yet he has been most sharply denounced from the beginning of the war no less by his old party friends than enemies. The consequence is, that, at this moment, he stands a little outside of all parties even among loyal men. The rebels, and their tools the Copperheads, of course, hate him. The War Democrats doubt some points of his policy. The Conservative Republicans think him too much in the hands of the radicals; while the Radical Republicans think him too slow, yielding, and half-hearted. And yet, without doubt, the more thoughtful and patriotic men of all parties can not but see how time confirms his wisdom, and were a President to be named tomorrow they would declare for Mr. Lincoln."

The Lounger reviewed the slow and gradual steps that led up to the Emancipation Proclamation, seeing it as the result of a calm temperament and a policy never wavering. "The loyal men who sustain it today are of all the late political parties and of all shades of opinion in regard to slavery. The order was not issued by the Commander-in-Chief nor is it supported by the loyal country because slavery is wrong but because it [slavery] helps the enemy. Doubtless the conviction that it is the root of the war has made many assent with more alacrity to the act of emancipation; but the President adopted it as a military and not as a moral measure. The way in which it was done, and the time, are both indications of the practical wisdom of the Chief Magistrate."

The Lounger finished off his meditations almost as though he might be saying that in the future, in case of doubt, and even when the President might seem to be wrong, he would be worth following. "History will vindicate the President, even if our impatience should be unjust to him. It will show that succeeding to the executive head of the Government at a moment of most complicated military and political peril, and when national salvation seemed almost impossible, he displayed such simplicity, earnestness, honesty, patience and sagacity—neither overwhelmed by disaster, nor confounded by treachery, nor disquieted by the distrust of friends—that he may be truly called a Providential man."

A delegation whose views somewhat agreed with those of The Lounger presented Lincoln with a cane made of live oak from the old battleship *Constitution*, with a head of polished iron from a bolt out of the *Monitor* where she was broken by the first shot from the *Merrimac*. The two ships' names and the dates "1812" and "1862" formed a circle on the iron head, while the center was engraved with an anchor, emblematic—they told the President—of hope.

The President needed anchors, needed hope. A million volunteers, as he had said, had answered his call and given toil and blood for the causes of which he was the mouthpiece. Soon in this coming autumn of '63 he was to order a draft to be enforced for 300,000 more conscripts. He had told Mary Livermore there was little realization of the agony and cost that yet lay ahead. The reports of Grant and Sherman far down in the intestinal center of the Confederacy told him their belief that the war had only truly begun, as it could only be ended by complete and bloody conquest. So furiously had it raged thus far that both sides had often been left no time to bury their dead.

At this summer's end the correspondent of the *Philadelphia Press* wrote from New Brandy Station, Virginia, one day: "Last night I slept on historic ground. The white bones of those who had been slain before gave forth a ghastly gleam when the soft moonlight shimmered down upon them through the heavy foliage. But a short distance from here can be seen the perfect skeleton of a large sized man. The bare skull, with its great, hollow, eyeless sockets, was there; the long finger bones and each particular rib was in its place. All was bare and white and ghastly. No; I forgot to mention that a well-preserved pair of boots still encase what were the soldier's feet, but in whose friendly cover now rattled the shin bones of the deceased. The wayward winds played through the cavity of the chest, and sighed through the empty skull, which gave forth a long, melancholy wail —the only dirge that has there been played, save the requiem which the song birds twitter from the neighboring trees. The bones of the horse bleached close by the side of the master."

CHAPTER 42

LINCOLN AT STORM CENTER

EARLY in that August of 1863 John Hay went one Sunday with the President to Gardner's photographic studio. "He was in very good spirits," wrote Hay. "He thinks that the rebel power is at last beginning to disintegrate, that they will break to pieces if we only stand firm now. Referring to the controversy between two factions at Richmond, one of whom believes still in foreign intervention, Northern treason & other chimeras, and the other, the Administration party, trusts to nothing but the army, he said, 'Davis is right. His army is his only hope, not only against us, but against his own people. If that were crushed the people would be ready to swing back to their old bearings.' "

Down in the Gulf States General Tecumseh Sherman had decided opinions on these same points of which Lincoln spoke to Hay. And Sherman wrote them out for Lincoln. From Halleck, Sherman had heard that the President needed "cool and discreet opinions" and would rather have "the advice of our Generals" in the deep South than "gassy politicians in Congress." Sherman sent on a 2,700-word letter. Lincoln wanted to print the whole of it and scatter it across the country. But Sherman answered in effect that he was not in politics. "If I covet any public reputation it is as a silent actor. I dislike to see my name in print."

Sherman advised against trying to run civil governments in conquered States until the war was over. Restoration of peace and order would not come from the plantation-owners, the ruling class; they still hoped for a Southern Confederacy. "I know we can manage this class, but only by action. Argument is exhausted, and words have lost their usual meaning. Nothing but the logic of events touches their understanding; but of late this has worked a wonderful change." The smaller farmers, mechanics, merchants, laborers, probably three-quarters of the population of the South, in all things followed blindly the lead of the planters. "The Southern politicians understand this class, use them as the French do their masses . . . consult their prejudices, while they make their orders and enforce them. We should do the same." For the Union men of the South, Sherman had "little respect," had found them of no service. "Their sons, horses, arms, and everything useful, are in the army against us, and they stay at home, claiming exemptions of peaceful citizens. I account them as nothing in this great game of war." (This opinion ran counter to that of General Grenville M. Dodge of Grant's staff, who continuously found the information service of Southern Union men to be trustworthy, though given at great risk.)

Sherman then described for Lincoln a class of whom he noted: "These men must all be killed or employed by us before we can hope for peace . . . the young bloods of the South: sons of planters, lawyers about town, good billiard-players and sportsmen, men who never did work and never will. War suits them, and the rascals are brave, fine riders, bold to rashness. . . . They care not a sou for niggers, land or any thing. They hate Yankees *per se*, and don't bother their brains about the past, present, or future. As long as they have good horses, plenty of forage and an open country, they are happy. This is a larger class than most men suppose, and they are the most dangerous set of men that this war has turned loose upon the world. . . . They have no property or future, and therefore cannot be influenced by anything, except personal consideration. I have two brigades of these fellows in my front. I have frequent interviews with their officers, a good understanding with them, and am inclined to think, when the resources of their country are exhausted, we must employ them."

On the Big Black River in Mississippi, not far from the Louisiana State Military Academy where he had been headmaster when the war broke out, Sherman was writing: "No other choice is left us but degradation. The South must be ruled by us, or she will rule us. We must conquer them, or ourselves be conquered. They ask, and will have, nothing else, and talk of compromise is bosh; for we know they would even scorn the offer. . . . I would not coax them, or even meet them half-way, but make them so sick of war that generations would pass away before they would again appeal to it. . . . The people of this country in after-years will be better citizens from the dear-bought experience of the present crisis. Let them learn it now, and learn it well, that good citizens must obey as well as command.

Obedience to law, absolute—yes, even abject—is the lesson that this war, under Providence, will teach the free and enlightened American citizen."

A tough insolence would Vallandigham, Seymour, the organization Democrats, have found in this treatise if Sherman had let Lincoln publish it. "I know what I say when I repeat that the insurgents of the South sneer at all overtures looking to their interests. They scorn the alliance with the Copperheads; they tell me to my face that they respect Grant, McPherson, and our brave associates who fight manfully and well for a principle, but despise the Copperheads and sneaks at the North, who profess friendship for the South and opposition to the war, as mere covers for their knavery and poltroonery."

As though a final determination slowly wrought by Sherman out of meditations over many campfires of the Army of the Tennessee, he invoked his doctrine of the terror to be spread for the sake of ending the war: "Our officers, marshals, and courts, must penetrate into the innermost recesses of their land, before we have the natural right to demand their submission . . . we will do it in our own time and in our own way; that it makes no difference whether it be in one year, or two, or ten, or twenty; that we will remove and destroy every obstacle, if need be, take every life, every acre of land, every particle of property, every thing that to us seems proper; that we will not cease till the end is attained; that all who do not aid us are enemies, and that we will not account to them for our acts. If the people of the South oppose, they do so at their peril; and if they stand by, mere lookers-on in this domestic tragedy, they have no right to immunity, protection, or share in the final results."

In the North Sherman would enforce a stricter regime. The man caught dodging his share of taxes or of military duty "should be deprived of all voice in the future elections of the country," or banished, or "reduced to the condition of a mere denizen." The time had come to draw a line between citizens and denizens.

"The President has read your letter," Halleck telegraphed Sherman, "and desires to publish it, but without using your name. Can I give him your permission?" The answer seemed to be that Sherman still preferred "to be a silent actor," still disliked to see his name in print, and believed the name of the author of the letter would become known and revive the discussion of whether or not he was crazy.

Meantime Lincoln stood ready to work with anyone inside the Confederate structure who might help the Union cause. When the vaguely furtive and definitely garrulous James R. Gilmore of the *New York Tribune* came again with a scheme, Lincoln listened. It was doubtful whether Lincoln gave Gilmore a glad hand and took him to his bosom in the easy and familiar way that Gilmore wrote about it. Yet it seemed rather definite that Gilmore and others in the summer of '63 interested Lincoln, at least mildly and tentatively, in plans to sound out Zebulon B. Vance, the thirty-three-year-old Governor of North Carolina, on how far Vance might be willing to go toward bringing his State back into the Union.

The break between Vance and the Davis Government at Richmond ran deep, the feeling bitter. The planter aristocracy, the slaveholders, the original secessionists, had no such hold in North Carolina as in the Cotton States. Her mountaineers, farmers, seacoast population, were "different." Vance spoke for his people when he served notice on the Richmond Government that his State troops would go into action against Confederate authorities who should try to override the right of any citizen to the writ of habeas corpus. Vance wrote to Davis, quoted a Confederate lieutenant colonel at Wilmington who threatened to shoot anyone trying to get off the steamer Vance was on, the officer snorting that he "did not care for Governor Vance nor Governor Jesus Christ." Vance protested to Richmond against Confederate War Department officers "engaging in speculations of private account" in North Carolina. Vance warned Secretary Seddon as to the Richmond War Department's distilling spirits in North Carolina, "that no person can under the authority of the Confederate Government violate State laws with impunity." Vance telegraphed and wrote Davis that a Georgia regiment, its men and officers, started a riot on the night of September 9, burned and destroyed the *Raleigh Standard*, and in retaliation a mob of citizens the next morning burned and destroyed the *Raleigh State Journal*. "I feel very sad in the contemplation of these outrages," Vance told Davis. "The distance is quite short to either anarchy or despotism, when armed soldiers, led by their officers, can with impunity outrage the laws of a State. A few more such exhibitions will bring the North Carolina troops home to the defense of their own State." To Secretary Seddon, Vance protested against "depredations . . . by detached bands of troops, chiefly cavalry," and asked that a few men be shot as examples. "If God Almighty had yet in store another plague—worse than all others which he intended to have let loose on the Egyptians in case Pharaoh still hardened his heart, I am sure it must have been a regiment or so of half armed, half disciplined Confederate cavalry! . . . Unless something can be done, I shall be compelled in some sections to call out my militia and levy actual war against them."

The Georgia regiment that had wrecked and burned the *Raleigh Standard* newspaper plant hated its peace tone, hated a four-column address published on July 31, 1863. Governor Vance had helped, it was said, to write the address with its cry "The great demand of the people of this part of the State is *peace; peace* upon any terms that will not enslave and degrade us."

Vance would welcome reunion of the States and "any peace compatible with honor," according to the information Gilmore brought Lincoln. And where did Gilmore get this information? He had it, he said, from Edward Kidder, a merchant of Wilmington, North Carolina. And why was Kidder so interested? It seemed that Kidder was born in New Hampshire, had gone to Wilmington in 1826 when he was twenty-one years old, had lived there ever since, "accumulating a vast fortune, and having larger business transactions than any other man in the State." And now Gilmore, as an old cotton-trader who had operated in Wilmington, wished to vouch for Kidder as a "stanch" Union man. In line with this, Gilmore laid before Lincoln a letter that Edward Kidder had sent—in a bag of peanuts—to a brother in Boston.

Lincoln read Kidder's confidential report of a talk with Governor Vance of North Carolina. Slavery was dead, the report ran, the Confederacy hopeless, and Vance favored a return to the Union on terms of honor and equity. Therefore Kidder hoped that Gilmore would run the blockade into Wilmington, interview Governor Vance at Kidder's home, bringing to Vance Lincoln's peace terms. Also, Kidder believed "Ten thousand Union troops in possession of Wilmington would be a powerful argument with Vance and the Legislature." Enclosed with Kidder's letter was a map of Wilmington Harbor and its fortifications.

After some discussion of this, according to Gilmore, Lincoln dictated a letter to go to Governor Vance, Gilmore to sign the letter, Lincoln endorsing it as read by him and having "my entire approval." In the months that followed, with further errands and with the plans changing, nothing much directly came of the scheme. Whether Lincoln reached across the State lines and convinced Governor Vance that peace efforts would be worth while was not clear. It was clear as daylight, however, that a few months after Gilmore and Kidder had laid their plans before Lincoln, Governor Vance was going nearly as far as Lincoln could wish in blunt suggestions and arguments sent to Jefferson Davis.

A letter of Vance to Davis in December of '63 was a straight and open plea for "some effort at negotiation with the enemy." In his own State Vance saw public hope of the Northern mind's looking towards peace, and "if fair terms are rejected it will . . . strengthen and intensify the war feeling, and will rally all classes to a more cordial support of the government." The "effort," not the method, of seeking peace was the principal matter. "Though statesmen might regard this as useless, the people will not."

There was a Union sentiment in North Carolina, as in several areas of the South—as in one county in Alabama having no slaves and sending no troops to the Confederate armies. Lincoln was responsive to all such Union areas. What he did in some cases might never be known. In many affairs he was careful to keep no record.

Once in this year of '63 Thurlow Weed (so Weed told it) was summoned from New York to Washington by Seward, who said, "The President will tell you why." In Lincoln's office Weed heard that the Administration was "in a tight place" for money, lacking $15,000 for certain legitimate purposes. "I did not know how to raise it, so I sent for you." Weed said, "Give me two lines to that effect." Lincoln wrote and handed Weed a slip of paper. "Will that do?" Weed said the money would be on hand the next morning, took a train for New York, and before five o'clock that afternoon had fifteen leading New York businessmen, the names including A. T. Stewart, W. H. Aspinwall, Cornelius Vanderbilt, signed for $1,000 each on Lincoln's signed slip, which read:

Mr. Weed,—The matters I spoke to you about are important. I hope you will not neglect them.

A. Lincoln

Duff Green, sixty-four-year-old Virginia politician and editor, once a member of Andrew Jackson's Kitchen Cabinet, who had in his time done international errands and negotiations for Presidents Jackson, Tyler, Taylor, and had been a messenger from Buchanan to Lincoln, wrote from Richmond to President Lincoln asking a permit to visit Washington. He was sure that a talk between him and the President would pave the way for peace. He was tall and stately, with flowing white hair and beard, a clear-cut face, and would have strode through the White House portals like a Bible engraving of the prophet Ezekiel. But Lincoln would not invite him. He represented merely Duff Green.

Day and night, more often night, came the palavering Fernando Wood to the White House, to the State and Treasury departments, trying to hold confidential relations with government heads, writing once to the President congratulating him on "executive power and will," ability to govern. "No rebuffs daunted him," noted Nicolay and Hay. "He used every occasion to ingratiate himself with the President." Notwithstanding that Congressman Wood had done his best as Mayor of New York to secede that city from the Union along with the Cotton States, Wood still intimated that he should be one of several peace commissioners to negotiate with the Richmond Government, as he had no particular sympathies with secession. That he and his brother Ben had run a lottery incorporated in Louisiana was not to be taken as having any bearing. He would see to it, he assured the President, that in case Vallandigham were permitted to return to Ohio, there would be two Democratic presidential candidates in the field at the next election.

"The President declined his proposition, but he would not take no for an answer," said Nicolay and Hay. Wood called again and the President sent word there was nothing further to say. Later that day Wood offered a resolution, which the House of Representatives tabled, requesting the President to appoint peace commissioners to negotiate with Richmond.

Seward came with reports for Lincoln on Mexico, of the French armies sent by Napoleon III having occupied during 1863 most of that country from Mexico City to San Luis Potosí on the north and Guadalajara on the west, and on the east all territory between Vera Cruz and the capital. This included some of the richest soil and most thickly peopled provinces of Mexico.

Lincoln in writing to Grant, after Vicksburg was taken, suggested for whatever bearing it might have on Grant's plans, "I am greatly impressed with the importance of reëstablishing the national authority in Western Texas as soon as possible." He suggested to General Banks, then also operating in the Southwest: "Recent events in Mexico, I think, render early action in Texas more important than ever. I expect, however, the general-in-chief will advise you more fully." And not many weeks later Banks did take Brownsville, Texas, and command the coast between it and Galveston, for which operations Lincoln wrote him thanks. When the gunboat *Mononga-hela* landed the 14th and 15th Maine regiments on Mustang Island, not far from Corpus Christi and Aransas Pass, Texas, those troops were a long way from home.

A note of Seward to the French Government intimated that Lincoln believed Napoleon III was scattering seed for bitter fruit. Of rumors that the Emperor was allied in various schemes with the insurgent cabal at Richmond, Seward wrote: "The President apprehends none of these things. He does not allow himself to be disturbed by suspicions so unjust to France and so unjustifiable in themselves; but he knows, also, that such suspicions will be entertained more or less extensively by this country, and magnified in other countries equally unfriendly to France and to America; and he knows also that it is out of such suspicions that the fatal web of national animosity is most frequently woven." Seward's note warned, "In no case are we likely to neglect such provision for our own safety as every sovereign state must always be prepared to fall back upon when nations with which they have lived in friendship cease to respect their moral and treaty obligations."

The French Government advised the American Minister in Paris that the sooner the American Government showed a willingness to recognize the Government of Archduke Maximilian, set up in Mexico by French armies, the sooner would those armies be ready to leave Mexico. Seward replied that the determination of President Lincoln was to err on the side of neutrality, if he erred at all, as between France and Mexico. "The French Government has not been left uninformed that, in the opinion of the United States, the permanent establishment of a foreign and monarchical government in Mexico will be found neither easy nor desirable."

The note made clear in gentle though firm language that the United States was not recognizing any government just at that time in Mexico, as it was still "the theatre of a war not yet ended," and the United States still remained friendly to the republican government that had long existed there.

This outlook brought sharp criticism, demands for stern assertion of the old Monroe Doctrine that the United States must take as a threat any attempt of European powers to get footholds in the Western world. Lincoln continued to consider it more immediately important to re-establish national authority north of the Rio Grande in Texas before taking on France for a war. Yet he must watch the Mexican mess. It held threats.

In the American language, and in plainer words than the covert phrasings of diplomacy, Lincoln had answered General John M. Thayer's query, "Mr. President, how about the French army in Mexico?" He shrugged his shoulders and wrinkled his eyebrows. "I'm not exactly 'skeered,' but I don't like the looks of the thing. Napoleon has taken advantage of our weakness in our time of trouble, and has attempted to found a monarchy on the soil of Mexico in utter disregard of the Monroe doctrine. My policy is, attend to only one trouble at a time. If we get well out of our present difficulties and restore the Union, I propose to notify Louis Napoleon that it is about time to take his army out of Mexico. When that army is gone, the Mexicans will take care of Maximilian."

As far north of the Rio Grande as the State of Missouri, the "national authority" was on ragged edges and worse off for wear, having a hard time keeping itself smoothly established. Its dignity was hooted and kicked around just north of the Ozarks.

At the head of the Military Department of Missouri was General John M. Schofield, thirty-two years old, a cool, sober, blond West Pointer who had been professor of natural philosophy at the national military academy, and had served a year as professor of physics at Washington University, St. Louis. As chief of staff for General Lyon, in the fighting at Wilson's Creek and in other field actions, Schofield had a bright record. Now he was the main buffer of the Washington Government in a Slave State seething with civil war. To the President, he reported the return of thousands of soldiers from defeated Confederate armies at Vicksburg and elsewhere. At first organized secretly as gangs, they joined up into regiments and small armies; they had raided, foraged supplies from Unionists, stolen money and horses, burned houses and railroad bridges, looted villages and towns, shot and hanged Union men. Toward keeping order Schofield organized ten regiments of Federal troops into an Enrolled Militia supplied by the United States and looking to the State government for their pay. At railroad bridges Schofield had guards posted and blockhouses erected. Schofield defined guerrillas as "robbers and assassins" to be caught and "shot down upon the spot." He ordered "rebels and rebel sympathizers" held responsible in property, and if necessary in person, for damages committed by "the lawless bands which they have brought into existence, subsisted, encouraged and sustained." These bands he found living by "the aid of influential and wealthy sympathizers, many of whom have taken the oath of allegiance to the United States." From this class, announced Schofield, in the vicinity of places where unlawful acts were committed $5,000 would be assessed and collected for every soldier or Union citizen killed, from $1,000 to $5,000 for every one wounded, and the full value of all property destroyed by guerrillas.

Schofield estimated the armed and banded guerrillas at one time to number 5,000. His cavalry chased one mounted band twelve days, clashing in nine sharp engagements on a 500-mile trip, ending at Kirksville, where of the guerrillas 180 were killed and about 500 wounded. Another guerrilla army took the town of Independence, fought off the first detachments sent to gather them in, but were finally driven down into Arkansas. In one six-month period, reported Schofield, "our troops met the enemy in more than one hundred engagements, great and small, in which our numbers varied from forty or fifty to 1000 or 1200 and those of the enemy from a few men to 4,000 or 5,000."

Complaints came this year to Lincoln that arrests, banishments, and assessments in Missouri were made more for private malice, revenge, and "pecuniary interest" than for the public good. So Lincoln wrote Schofield in January: "This morning I was told by a gentleman who I have no doubt believes what he says, that in one case of assessments for $10,000, the different persons who paid compared receipts, and found they had paid $30,000. If this be true, the inference is that the collecting agents pocketed the odd $20,000. And true or not in the instance, nothing but the sternest necessity can justify a system liable to such abuses."

The military department run by Schofield often got tangled with the State of Missouri civil government run by sixty-five-year-old Hamilton Rowan Gamble. Born in Virginia of Irish emigrants, a jurist with a gift for politics, Gamble had been member of the legislature in Missouri, secretary of state, presiding judge of the State supreme court, prosperous practicing attorney in St. Louis. His marriage to Caroline J. Coalter of Columbia, South Carolina, had its bearing on his secession sympathies. Gamble had pronounced Lincoln's call for troops in April of '61 to be unconstitutional and had leaned then toward those who wished to make Missouri independent of both North and South, repelling invaders whether in blue or in gray. As chairman of the committee on Federal relations in the State constitutional convention of '61, Gamble hoped for "amicable adjustment" without civil war. That same convention appointed him provisional Governor of the State, replacing Claiborne F. Jackson, the fugitive rebel Governor.

Lincoln had written General Samuel R. Curtis, the earlier Federal military commander in Missouri, of those complaining that "Governor Gamble's unionism, at most, is not better than a secondary spring of action; that hunkerism and a wish for political influence stand before unionism with him." However, that was merely the complaint. "My belief," wrote Lincoln, "is that Governor Gamble is an honest and true man, not less so than yourself." Lincoln had with this urged General Curtis to co-operate with Governor Gamble.

But Curtis could not so co-operate.

And when Lincoln put in Schofield to replace Curtis, he told Schofield it was not because Curtis had done wrong. "I did it because of a conviction in my mind that the Union men of Missouri, constituting, when united, a vast majority of the whole people, have entered into a pestilential quarrel among themselves—General Curtis, perhaps not of choice, being the head of one faction and Governor Gamble that of the other. After months of labor to reconcile the difficulty, it seemed to grow worse and worse, until I felt it my duty to break it up somehow; and as I could not remove Governor Gamble, I had to remove General Curtis." The months had passed, however, and Schofield did not get along with Gamble any better than Curtis, Lincoln writing to Gamble in July:

My private secretary has just brought me a letter, saying it is a very "cross" one from you, about mine to General Schofield, recently published in the "Democrat." As I am trying to preserve my own temper by avoiding irritants so far as practicable, I decline to read the cross letter. I think fit to say, however, that when I wrote the letter to General Schofield, I was totally unconscious of any malice or disrespect toward you, or of using any expression which should offend you if seen by you.

Three months later Gamble wrote to Lincoln that the radicals were "openly and loudly" threatening to overthrow the State provisional government by violence. Lincoln replied that Schofield would take care of the violence, that it was not a party but individual radicals making the threats. Lincoln was sticking solidly by Gamble. "I have seen no occasion to make a distinction against the provisional government because of its not having been chosen and inaugurated in the usual way. Nor have I seen any cause to suspect it of unfaithfulness to the Union."

Yet Lincoln knew that the face of Gamble was toward the past, that the emancipation ordinance passed by the conservative convention in the summer of '63 was evasive, odorous of politics, setting the year 1870 for slavery to "cease" in Missouri, but to "cease" under the peculiar conditions that all slaves over forty years of age would still be slaves till they died, while all slaves under twelve years of age would be slaves until they were twenty-three, and those of all other ages until the Fourth of July, 1876. In the atmosphere of the convention that passed this ordinance Governor Gamble felt called on to offer his resignation, but it was refused by a vote of 51 to 29.

Schofield had telegraphed Lincoln asking whether the Federal Government would protect slaveowners in their property during the time gradual emancipation was working out. Lincoln replied on June 22, 1863: "Desirous as I am that emancipation shall be adopted by Missouri, and believing as I do that gradual can be made better than immediate for both black and white, except when military necessity changes the case, my impulse is to say that such protection would be given. . . . I do not wish to pledge the General Government to the affirmative support of even temporary slavery beyond what can be fairly claimed under the Constitution. . . . I have very earnestly urged the slave States to adopt emancipation; and it ought to be, and is, an object with me not to overthrow or thwart what any of them may in good faith do to that end."

From time to time conservatives and radicals from Missouri interviewed Lincoln and harassed him. One conservative, ex-Governor Austin Augustus King, in a speech at Lexington, Missouri, May 23, 1863, told of his talk with Lincoln:

The President said he could sum it all up in a few words, which was "That Governor Gamble was a conservative man." The President then related an anecdote about killing a snake. He said that if he met a rattlesnake in his path, and he had a stick in his hand, his first impression would be to kill it; but if he found one in the bed between his children he would pursue a different course, for by killing the snake he may injure the children; therefore he would take a more gentle way to get the snake out before he killed it. The same with slavery; he was satisfied that immediate emancipation would be detrimental to the interest of the State.

A delegation of German radicals from Missouri called at the White House and later published their report that the President had refused their demands for dismissal of Seward, Blair, and Halleck, had declined their requests that he restore Frémont, Sigel, and Butler to important commands. A delegate from St. Louis, James Taussig, told of the interview:

The President said that the dissensions between Union men in Missouri are due solely to a factious spirit which is exceedingly reprehensible. The two parties "ought to have their heads knocked together." "Either would rather see the defeat of their adversary than that of Jefferson Davis." The Union men in Missouri in favor of gradual emancipation represented his views rather than those in favor of immediate emancipation. . . . In his speeches he had frequently used as an illustration the case of a man who had an excrescence on the back of his neck, the removal of which, in one operation, would result in the death of the patient, while "tinkering it off by degrees" would preserve life. Although sorely tempted, I did not reply with the illustration of the dog whose tail was amputated by inches, but confined myself to arguments. The President announced clearly that, as far as he was at present advised, the radicals in Missouri had no right to consider themselves the exponents of his views on the subject of emancipation in that State.

Wendell Phillips chimed in with a Cooper Union speech demanding that the President dismiss Seward, Halleck, and Blair. "Death to the slave system and death to the master" Phillips announced as his motto.

Sumner came to Lincoln with a plan for raising in the North colored regiments to be commanded by Frémont. Lincoln wrote to Sumner that he would favor 10,000 such troops to be sent to the field, Frémont assigned command of a department, with white troops possibly added. This Lincoln letter Sumner gave to the delegation of German radicals from Missouri who had called on Lincoln. They took it to Frémont in New York and Frémont sent it back to Sumner with an icy note: "I beg you will say to the President that this movement does not in the remotest way originate with me. On the contrary when the Committee called upon me I declined positively to enter into it, or to consent to have my name mentioned to the President in connection with it. I beg you to say to the President that I have no design to embarrass him with creating a department for me."

John Jay, an old antislavery wheel horse, wrote to Sumner that month, "Do for heaven's sake inspire the President with the courage he requires to toss his mal-advisers overboard." Governor Yates told the Illinois Methodist Church conference at Springfield that he wanted slavery "eternally and everlastingly damned," winning "Amen!" and "God grant it!" from his audience, after which he remarked casually that Old Abe's backbone "tapered too much towards the lower end."

To the old friends of Frémont, Lincoln was a Mr. Facing-Both-Ways. Missouri radicals who had trained in politics under the Blairs, with the passage of the extremely "gradual" emancipation ordinance in June of '63 arose, snorted, swore, and prepared to send men of their own stripe to the Senate and House at Washington. They included Benjamin Gratz Brown, Kentucky-born, a lawyer who had helped organize the Free Soil party in

Missouri, who owned with Frank Blair, Jr., an interest in the *Missouri Democrat*, a radical Republican newspaper which Brown edited. To Gratz Brown, Lincoln had telegraphed once that year, "The administration takes no part between its friends in Missouri, of whom I, at least, consider you one."

Playing along with the Missouri radicals was the human cyclone, General James Henry Lane of Kansas, thirty-eight years old, restless firebrand of the frontier, an Indiana boy who rose to brigadier in the Mexican War, became lieutenant governor of Indiana, took one term in Congress from Indiana, then moved to Kansas, where he was a major general in the repulse of "border ruffians" from Missouri who aimed to make Kansas a Slave State. When he was elected to the United States Senate in 1856, that body refused to seat him. Soon indicted for high treason in Douglas County, Kansas, Jim Lane fled the territory. Returning to Kansas, he was chosen president of the Kansas constitutional convention and appointed major general of State troops. He shot and killed one of his neighbors, was tried and acquitted. He turned up with his menacing eyes and underslung jaw at the White House in April of '61, heading a squad of Jayhawkers ready to defend the Executive Mansion or march to Richmond or Baltimore.

Hay had one day noted Jim Lane growling, "Let me tell you we have got to whip these scoundrels like hell, Carl Schurz." Schurz: "I heard you preached a sermon to yr. men yesterday." Jim Lane: "No sir, this is no time for preaching. When I went to Mexico there were four preachers in my rigiment. In less than a week I issued orders for them all to stop preaching and go to playing cards. In a month or so they was the biggest devils & best fighters I had."

Then Lincoln appointed Jim Lane brigadier general of two regiments of volunteers he was to raise, Lincoln writing the Secretary of War, "Tell him, when he starts, to put it through—not to be writing or telegraphing back here, but put it through." The Senate passed a resolution of inquiry as to whether the Honorable James H. Lane of Kansas had really been made a brigadier, and Lincoln wrote to the Secretary of War asking for all records in the case. A few months later Halleck, at St. Louis, wrote Lincoln that the operations of Lane and others on the Kansas border had "so enraged the people of Missouri" that the region had become enemy country. Twice Lincoln had to write General Hunter that Hunter was senior officer over Lane and Lane must so understand. And it seemed that one of the few letters that Lincoln ever wrote to Lane had to do with the dismissal of a colored regimental officer, was written on the request of Governor Carney of Kansas, and had at the bottom of it Lincoln's memo: "Not sent because Governor Carney thought it best not be."

Jim Lane was at home in Lawrence, Kansas, forty miles from the Missouri line, on August 21 of '63, when Quantrell came—Quantrell the Guerrilla, under oath to neither Union nor Confederate Government, with 300 picked riding men, including the wild boys Frank and Jesse James. These reckless night riders had zigzagged and circled by an "eccentric route" through all of Schofield's wide-flung patrols. At sunrise they crashed into the town of Lawrence, spread over it to make it a ruin, to yell, swear, rob, burn, shoot, kill, leaving as they rode away 182 buildings in ashes, 205 men dead and many more wounded and mangled, 85 widows, 240 orphans. The bloody work was over in two hours.

Jim Lane headed a pursuit, killed thirty or forty, but lost the trail where Quantrell's riders reached timberland full of friendly farmers. One of the friendly farmers had fixed supper for twenty of Quantrell's desperadoes; the pursuers came up, killed nine, including the friendly farmer, and burned the farmhouse.

The lavender-and-rose military critic of the *Richmond Examiner*, Edward Pollard, wrote of the Quantrell outfit that "like poor houseless birds of passage, the gallant three hundred broke up their rendezvous and left for the plains of Texas." Which they did not. They put on Union Army uniforms, hovered on the Kansas southern border, and 300 strong ambushed 100 men escorting General Blunt, who had been so quick to hang all guerrillas falling into his hands. Having shot to death seventy-eight of Blunt's men, Quantrell's guerrillas rode off.

General Ewing, in command of western Missouri and Kansas under Schofield, took a possibly necessary action, and two days after the Lawrence massacre issued General Order No. 11 that all persons in Jackson, Cass, and Bates counties, Missouri, not able to "prove their loyalty" to the nearest commanding officer, should be driven out, their hay and grain crops confiscated or destroyed, by September 9. General Ewing pictured an exodus, a depopulation, many houses with nobody home. A frenzied mass meeting in Leavenworth set September 8 for "a general rising" of Kansans to enter Missouri and recover their stolen property. A mass meeting at Paola, Kansas, resolved that "milk and water for traitors is poison to patriots," the only good guerrilla one plugged with lead. Massacres in Missouri, to pay off the one in Kansas, were planned in detail.

Then Schofield with cool determination notified the Governor of Kansas, "You cannot expect me to permit anything of this sort," giving assurance he would make every effort to punish the Lawrence murderers and make the future secure.

In Missouri excitement flared high as the radical Union Emancipation Convention met. Delegates came from four-fifths of the counties of the State. The high cry in Jefferson City on September 1 was that Governor Gamble's "pro-slavery" provisional government was paralyzing Federal power. One resolution of the convention aimed to set up a vigilante government through appointment of a Committee of Public Safety, one member from each congressional district to be appointed by the president of the convention.

Also a Committee of Seventy, one from each county in the State, was appointed to call on President Lincoln and lay their cause before him. At train stops on the way to Washington this Committee of Seventy was hailed by brass bands, antislavery delegations and orators who bade them

Godspeed. At Washington they were joined by a Committee of Eighteen from Kansas on the same errand. Senator Jim Lane referred to the joint body as "my little army." The next Missouri election would go to the radicals, they gave it out, and the President could decide "whether he will ride in our wagon or not."

Lincoln told Hay that if they could show that Schofield had done anything wrong, their case was made, that he believed they were against Schofield because Schofield would not take sides with them. "I think I understand this matter perfectly and I cannot do anything contrary to my convictions, to please these men, earnest and powerful as they may be." Meanwhile the Missouri-Kansas committees dominated the Washington scene, took in a big reception to themselves at the Union League Hall, where the Gamble government of Missouri was denounced and immediate emancipation demanded by eminent orators.

The Missouri-Kansas delegation took two days to prepare an address to the President. The wrongs their people had borne were heavy. They listed the crimes and outrages. They alleged and enumerated these for Lincoln's eye. They were exasperated men whose voices rose out of mixed motives of war and politics; public service and private revenge; the hangover of greed and corruption among Frémont's associates, of connivance and trickery by the Blairs in their animosities toward Frémont and others, of anger that Schofield had loaned detachments of Enrolled Militia to Grant for the Vicksburg operation, of wrath that Lincoln and members of Congress were trying to emancipate the slaves of Missouri by gradual purchase instead of direct bestowal of freedom by proclamation, of indignation at Schofield's Order No. 92, which prohibited Kansans from pursuing guerrillas over the State line, of disgruntlement on the part of some with the apportionment of Federal offices and favors, of suspicion on the part of others that Lincoln's policy was Kentuckian and his leanings were proslavery.

Their prepared address to the President voiced three demands. First, General Schofield must be relieved, and General Butler be appointed to command the Military Department of Missouri. Second, the system of Enrolled Militia in Missouri must be broken up and national forces be substituted. Third, at elections persons must not be allowed to vote who were not entitled by law to do so.

Lincoln sent for the committee's secretary, Dr. Emil Preetorius, a leading German radical from St. Louis. Senator Jim Lane walked into the President's office with Preetorius but soon excused himself and left Lincoln alone with Preetorius. Of their interview Preetorius noted:

"I had a long talk with him, explaining the situation in Missouri, as we Radicals viewed it, and stating just why we had come to Washington. We Germans had not felt so kindly toward Mr. Lincoln since he had set aside Frémont's proclamation of emancipation. We thought he had missed a great opportunity and had thereby displayed a lack of statesmanship. We believed him to be under the influence of the Blair family.

"Now that he himself had issued an emancipation proclamation we felt wronged because it applied only to the States in rebellion, and not to our own State. 'Thus,' I said to the President, 'you are really punishing us for our courage and patriotism.' We felt, as Gratz Brown expressed it, that we had to fight three administrations—Lincoln's, Jeff Davis's, and our own Governor Gamble's. We felt that we had a right to complain because Lincoln sent out to Missouri generals that were not in sympathy with us.

"Our talk was of the very frankest kind. Lincoln said he knew I was a German revolutionist and expected me to take extreme views. I recollect distinctly his statement that he would rather be a follower than a leader of public opinion. He had reference to public opinion in the Border States. 'We need the Border States,' said he. 'Public opinion in them has not matured. We must patiently educate them up to the right opinion.' The situation at that time was less favorable in the other Border States than in Missouri. Their Union men had not the strong fighters that Missouri had. As things were then going, the attitude of the Border States was of the very highest importance. I could realize that the more fully as Lincoln argued the case."

At nine o'clock in the morning of September 30, the eighty-eight delegates walked through the great front doors and into the White House. Then the great front doors were locked and stayed locked till the conference was over. At the committee's own request, all reporters and spectators were barred. Up in the East Room Senator Jim Lane ranged his "little army" along three sides.

Lincoln looked along panels of faces. His eyes roved over stubborn men, in the main sincere, some with a genius of courage and sacrifice. As he told John Hay later: "They are nearer to me than the other side, in thought and sentiment, though bitterly hostile personally. They are utterly lawless—the unhandiest devils in the world to deal with—but after all, their faces are set Zionwards."

The prepared address was read to the President by the chairman, Charles Daniel Drake, a St. Louis lawyer fifty-two years old, educated as a midshipman in the United States Navy, author of notable law treatises, member of the Missouri Legislature, an early leader against secession. His voice carried what Enos Clarke, another St. Louis delegate, described as "a deep, impressive, stentorian tone."

And Enos Clarke took note that while Chairman Drake read, the President listened with patient attention, and when the reading was over rose slowly, and with a deliberation born of what they knew not, began a lengthy reply. Said Clarke: "I shall never forget the intense chagrin and disappointment we all felt at the treatment of the matter in the beginning of his reply. He seemed to belittle and minimize the importance of our grievances and to give magnitude to minor or unimportant matters. He gave us the impression of a pettifogger speaking before a justice of the peace jury. But as he talked on and made searching inquiries of members of the delegation and invited debate, it became manifest that his manner at the beginning was really the foil of a master, to develop the weakness of the presentation. Before the conclusion of the conference, he addressed himself to the whole matter in an elevated, dignified, exhaustive, and impressive manner."

No official report was made of the conference, but Enos Clarke recalled Lincoln as saying: "You gentlemen must bear in mind that in performing the duties of the office I hold I must represent no one section, but I must act for all sections of the Union in trying to maintain the supremacy of the Government." This from Lincoln could have been predicted. He had used it over and again privately, publicly, in letters and speeches.

The ears of Enos Clarke, however, caught another expression that could not have been anticipated, but when it came that day it befitted Lincoln as though it dovetailed and mortised with his past known record. "I desire to so conduct the affairs of this administration that if, at the end, when I come to lay down the reins of power, I have lost every other friend on earth, I shall at least have one friend left, and that friend shall be down inside of me."

Two hours ran on, some of it in speechmaking, some in random talk. Hay noted the President saying he could not give a hasty answer. "I will take your address, carefully consider it, and respond at my earliest convenience. I shall consider it without partiality for, or prejudice against any man or party. No painful memories of the past and no hopes for the future, personal to myself, shall hamper my judgment."

They did not relish his reference to the Missouri turmoil as a "pestilent factional quarrel," the President told them, but Governor Gamble liked it less yet. He referred to Gamble as the choice for governor by their own State convention, the Union people of the State seeming to give universal consent. As President, he had uniformly refused to give the Governor exclusive control of the Missouri State Militia, while on the other hand the Enrolled Militia existed solely under State laws with which he had no right to interfere, either in Missouri or elsewhere; if that organization were inconsistent with their State laws, he, as President, had no power over it.

As to Schofield, Lincoln was sorry they had not made specific complaints. "I cannot act on vague impressions." He went into details as to Schofield's record. "I know nothing to his disadvantage. I am not personally acquainted with him. I have with him no personal relations. If you will allege a definite wrong-doing, and, having clearly made your point, prove it, I shall remove him." The suspension of habeas corpus by Schofield in Missouri was in obedience to the President's official decree. "You object to its being used in Missouri. In other words, that which is right when employed against opponents is wrong when employed against yourselves. Still, I will consider that."

They objected to Schofield's muzzling the press. "As to that," continued Lincoln, "I think when an officer in any department finds that a newspaper is pursuing a course calculated to embarrass his operations and stir up sedition and tumult, he has the right to lay hands upon it and suppress it, but in no other case. I approved the order in question after the 'Missouri Democrat' had also approved it."

John McAllister Schofield

From the Meserve collection

Lincoln, February 9, '64

Photograph by Brady, from the U. S. Signal Corps

Ben Butler at his headquarters

David Hunter

From the Chicago Historical Society

George William Curtis

Bayard Taylor

James Russell Lowell

John Bright, M.P.

From the author's collection

DELEGATE. We thought it was to be used against the other side.

LINCOLN. Certainly you did. Your ideas of justice seem to depend on the application of it.

He went into finely shaded questions on what he might be owing them. "You have spoken of the consideration which you think I should pay to my friends as contra-distinguished from my enemies. I suppose, of course, that you mean by that those who agree or disagree with me in my views of public policy. I recognize no such thing as a political friendship personal to myself." Repeating familiar points as to the expediency and legality of the Emancipation Proclamation, Lincoln spoke of how many a good man "very far north" opposed it and yet was spending time, money, and influence in favor of the Union. "I think it ungenerous, unjust, and impolite to make his views on abstract political questions a test of his loyalty. I will not be a party to this application of a pocket inquisition."

Hay noted that as an inquisition the morning did not work out, Lincoln meeting each point, issue, grievance, "with a quick counter-statement so brief and clinching that the several volunteer spokesmen who came forward to support the main address retired, one by one, disconcerted and overwhelmed." Hay noted too: "The President knew that a certain unreasoning radicalism which pervaded the whole North might, and probably would, range itself behind this unreasonable radicalism of these Missourians, and the whole thing together might prevent his renomination or reelection . . . while he had a sincere respect for, and faith in, their undying political convictions."

The formal session drew to a close with Lincoln saying he appreciated perfectly the difference between the ultimate value of conservatives and radicals in the long controversy, that his radical friends would see that he understood their position. "Still you appear to come before me as my friends, if I agree with you, and not otherwise. I do not here speak of mere personal friendship. When I speak of my friends I mean those who are friendly to my measures, to the policy of the Government." He was well aware that some of the delegates before him ("I shall not name them") had charged him with a disposition to make his own will supreme. "I do not intend to be a tyrant. At all events I shall take care that in my own eyes I do not become one. I have no right to act the tyrant to mere political opponents."

And they knew the President was referring to loyal Union men who might even be proslavery in viewpoint when he said: "If a man votes for supplies of men and money, encourages enlistments, discourages desertions, does all in his power to carry the war on to a successful issue, I have no right to question him for his abstract political opinions. I must make a dividing line somewhere between those who are opponents of the Government, and those who only approve peculiar features of my Administration while they sustain the Government."

One of the men from Missouri felt that Lincoln was not so quick in his answers, not so much at ease as John Hay believed. "The President in the course of his reply hesitated a great deal," said this man, "and was manifestly, as he said, very much troubled over affairs in Missouri. He said they were a source of more anxiety to him than we could imagine. He regretted that some of the men who had founded the Republican party should now be arrayed apparently against his administration."

Twice before, the Missourian had met Lincoln, and had not seen such a perplexed look on Lincoln's face. "When he said he was *bothered* about this thing he showed it. He spoke kindly, yet now and then there was a little rasping tone in his voice that seemed to say, 'You men ought to fix this thing up without *tormenting* me.' But he never lost his temper."

When all points had been covered, and there seemed nothing more to say, Chairman Drake stepped forward. "Mr. President, the time has now come when we can no longer trespass upon your attention but must take leave of you." Then came the most impressive moment of the two hours, Drake saying the men who stood before the President now would return, many of them to homes surrounded by "rebel" sentiment. "Many of them, sir, in returning there do so at the risk of their lives, and if any of those lives are sacrificed by reason of the military administration of this government, let me tell you, sir, that their blood will be upon your garments and not upon ours."

This was terribly, though only partly, true and near to ghastly prophecy. Enos Clarke noted that during this address "the President stood before the delegation with tears streaming down his cheeks, seeming deeply agitated."

One by one then the delegates shook hands with the President and took leave. To Enos Clarke it was memorable. He shook hands, walked off with others, and at the door turned for a final look. "Mr. Lincoln had met some personal acquaintances with whom he was exchanging pleasantries, and instead of the tears of a few moments before, he was indulging in hearty laughter. This rapid and wonderful transition from one extreme to the other impressed me greatly."

The night of the next day Secretary Chase opened his home and gave the delegation a reception, told them he was heartily in sympathy with their mission, hoped their military department would be entrusted to a gentleman whose motto was "Freedom for All." On to New York then went the delegates to a rousing public meeting in Cooper Union, where William Cullen Bryant spoke for them, where conservatives were rhetorically torn to shreds, and President Lincoln threatened with revolutionary action if he did not yield to their demands.

As in the cases of Seward, Grant, and others, Lincoln had listened. As before, he now stood by his men. In a long letter of October 5 he began with telling "Honorable Charles D. Drake and Others, Committee" that he had carefully considered their original address of September 30, besides four supplementary ones on October 3. Enough of suffering and wrong was stated. "Yet the whole case, as presented, fails to convince me that General Schofield or the enrolled militia is responsible for that suffering and wrong. The whole can be explained on a more charitable and, as I think, a more

rational hypothesis." Then he plunged into paragraphs of anatomical por-
traiture, current historical analysis, of what underlay the human seething
and clashing in Missouri:

"We are in a civil war. In such cases there always is a main question;
but in this case that question is a perplexing compound—Union and slavery.
It thus becomes a question not of two sides merely, but of at least four
sides, even among those who are for the Union, saying nothing of those who
are against it. Thus, those who are for the Union with, but not without,
slavery—those for it without, but not with—those for it with or without,
but prefer it with—and those for it with or without, but prefer it without.

"Among these again is a subdivision of those who are for gradual, but
not for immediate, and those who are for immediate, but not for gradual,
extinction of slavery.

"It is easy to conceive that all these shades of opinion, and even more,
may be sincerely entertained by honest and truthful men. Yet, all being
for the Union, by reason of these differences each will prefer a different
way of sustaining the Union. At once sincerity is questioned, and motives
are assailed. Actual war coming, blood grows hot and blood is spilled.
Thought is forced from old channels into confusion. Deception breeds and
thrives. Confidence dies and universal suspicion reigns. Each man feels an
impulse to kill his neighbor, lest he be first killed by him. Revenge and retaliation follow. And all this, as before said, may be among honest men
only; but this is not all. Every foul bird comes abroad and every dirty reptile rises up. These add crime to confusion.

"Strong measures deemed indispensable, but harsh at best, such men
make worse by maladministration. Murders for old grudges, and murders
for pelf, proceed under any cloak that will best cover for the occasion."

These causes would account for what was happening in Missouri without blaming it on the weakness or wickedness of any general. Under four
generals preceding Schofield were the same evils. For the control of spies
and illegal trading, a system of searches, seizures, permits, and passes had
begun under Frémont, had continued under Halleck and Curtis.

"That there was a necessity for something of the sort was clear," ran
Lincoln's analysis, "but that it could only be justified by stern necessity,
and that it was liable to great abuse in administration, was equally clear.
Agents to execute it, contrary to the great prayer, were led into temptation. Some might, while others would not, resist that temptation. It was not
possible to hold any to a very strict accountability, and those yielding to
the temptation would sell permits and passes to those who would pay most
and most readily for them; and would seize property and collect levies in
the aptest way to fill their own pockets. Money being the object, the man
having money, whether loyal or disloyal, would be a victim. This practice
doubtless existed to some extent, and it was a real additional evil that it
could be and was plausibly charged to exist in greater extent than it did.

"When General Curtis took command of the department, Mr. Dick,
against whom I never knew anything to allege, had general charge of this

system. A controversy in regard to it rapidly grew into almost unmanageable proportions. One side ignored the necessity and magnified the evils of the system, while the other ignored the evils and magnified the necessity, and each bitterly assailed the motive of the other. I could not fail to see that the controversy enlarged in the same proportion as the professed Union men there distinctly took sides in two opposing political parties. I exhausted my wits, and very nearly my patience also, in efforts to convince both that the evils they charged on each other were inherent in the case, and could not be cured by giving either party a victory over the other."

Schofield had been put in to modify this "irritating" system, if he could, if any man could. The President's instructions were that Schofield should be independent of both parties. "Neither anything you have presented me nor anything I have otherwise learned has convinced me that he has been unfaithful to this charge." The late massacre at Lawrence, Kansas, was pressed as evidence of the "imbecility" of Schofield. Yet that massacre was only an example of what other raiding parties might repeatedly have done had they chosen to take the risk and had they possessed the fiendish hearts to do it. As to Schofield stopping the pursuit of the Lawrence murderers into Missouri, and admitting that no punishment could be too sudden or too severe for those murderers, "I am well satisfied that the preventing of the threatened remedial raid into Missouri was the only safe way to avoid an indiscriminate massacre there, including probably more innocent than guilty. Instead of condemning I therefore approve what I understand General Schofield did in that respect."

Also while the President would not arraign the veracity of gentlemen as to Schofield taking sides between loyal and disloyal men, he would question judgments as to the purposes of Schofield. Also in declining to remove Schofield he was deciding nothing against General Butler. Also he would not close out the Enrolled Militia of Missouri. "Few things have been so grateful to my anxious feelings as when, in June last, the local force in Missouri aided General Schofield to so promptly send a large general force to the relief of General Grant, then investing Vicksburg, and menaced from without by General Johnston." Finally, he had directed General Schofield that the request of the committee regarding elections was proper. The third demand of the Committee of Seventy was granted.

Then he closed with personal philosophy having direct bearing on the relation of a Chief Magistrate to human strife and civil war in Missouri— or elsewhere: "I do not feel justified to enter upon the broad field you present in regard to the political differences between Radicals and Conservatives. From time to time I have done and said what appeared to me proper to do and say. The public knows it all. It obliges nobody to follow me, and I trust it obliges me to follow nobody. The Radicals and Conservatives each agree with me in some things and disagree in others. I could wish both to agree with me in all things, for then they would agree with each other and would be too strong for any foe from any quarter. They, however, choose to do otherwise; and I do not question their right. I too shall do what seems to be my duty. I hold whoever commands in Missouri or elsewhere responsible to me and not to either Radicals or Conservatives. It is my duty to hear all, but at last I must, within my sphere, judge what to do and what to forbear."

Then for the Missouri-Kansas committees, Lincoln subscribed himself "Your obedient servant," whatever that might mean to them.

A week after publication of this letter Jim Lane made a Union speech in Turnverein Hall, St. Louis, Schofield writing in his diary: "Lane informed me . . . through Major Vaughan, that he had stopped the war on me. . . . Said the President told him that whoever made war on General Schofield, under the present state of affairs, made war on him—the President. Said he never had made war on General S., 'except incidentally.'" That was Lane. He took on some wars essentially, others incidentally. The *New York Herald* tried to be cool about Jim Lane, though news of his death, either sudden or lingering, would be welcome. Lane was not forgotten in the *Herald's* October advice to the President. With sarcasm that newspaper said Ben Butler seemed to be just the "peg" for the "vacant hole" in Missouri, if the President removed Schofield.

"Or, if Butler's appointment be inexpedient," continued the *Herald*, "let the President ask Robert Dale Owen to summon the ghost of Robespierre, and then send that energetic Frenchman to Missouri. Robespierre would give the border ruffians blood enough, and would handle the political guillotine admirably. Or, if Robespierre will not consent to revisit the glimpses of the moon, or is not considered sufficiently strong for the position, let President Lincoln appoint either Jim Lane or the Devil—it matters little which—to the post of Military Governor of that unhappy State. These are all the available candidates, and Mr. Lincoln must take his choice among them. For ourselves, we are rather in favor of Jim Lane or the Devil. Both of these personages work with about the same means, and appear determined to accomplish about the same results. Besides this fact, we would especially recommend to President Lincoln's attention one consideration which has great weight with us, and will doubtless prove equally potential with him. That consideration is, that if Jim Lane or the Devil cannot wipe out the Missouri border ruffians, then the border ruffians will certainly wipe out Jim Lane or the Devil. In either case, therefore, the President and the country will be saved a great deal of annoyance. We hope that Mr. Lincoln will follow this advice, and we assure him that it is the best and most popular thing he can do under the circumstances."

In his own serious advice to Schofield, Lincoln made it plain he had no immediate hope of peace for that region. With moderation and firmness, however, the atrocities, plots and counterplots, jealousies and bickerings, might be diminished till later events would restore affairs to normal. In the young, blond, whiskered Schofield had been found an administrator who understood Lincoln once writing to him: "If both factions, or neither, shall abuse you, you will probably be about right. Beware of being assailed by one and praised by the other."

To O. D. Filley in St. Louis, Lincoln wrote that he had received a petition and letters from three dozen citizens, the whole relating to the Rev. Dr. McPheeters, pastor of the Vine Street Church. "The petition prays, in the name of justice and mercy, that I will restore Dr. McPheeters to all his ecclesiastical rights." A letter from a Mr. Coalter was inquiring, "Is it not a strange illustration of the condition of things, that the question of who shall be allowed to preach in a church in St. Louis shall be decided by the President of the United States?" Lincoln informed Filley that nearly a year before he had touched on the case of Dr. McPheeters in a letter to General Curtis saying: "The United States Government must not . . . undertake to run the churches. . . . It will not do for the United States to appoint trustees, supervisors, or other agents for the churches." No complaint had been received from Dr. McPheeters and his friends for nearly a year, and Lincoln implied that Dr. McPheeters might possibly be in trouble with his own congregation. "If, after all, what is now sought is to have me put Dr. McPheeters back over the heads of a majority of his own congregation, that, too, will be declined. I will not have control of any church on any side."

The President's letter to Schofield of October 1 suggested advancing the efficiency of the military establishment "and to so use it as far as practicable to compel the excited people there to leave one another alone." Schofield would have a discretion to exercise with great caution, calmness, and forbearance. "You will only arrest individuals and suppress assemblies or newspapers when they may be working palpable injury to the military in your charge, and in no other case will you interfere with the expression of opinion in any form or allow it to be interfered with violently by others. . . . With the matters of removing the inhabitants of certain counties *en masse,* and of removing certain individuals from time to time who are supposed to be mischievous, I am not now interfering, but am leaving to your own discretion. Nor am I interfering with what may still seem to you to be necessary restrictions upon trade and intercourse." At elections only those should be allowed to vote who were so entitled by the laws of Missouri. As a sort of general rule for the guidance of a perplexed commander in a disorderly area, the President noted: "So far as practicable, you will, by means of your military force, expel guerrillas, marauders, and murderers, and all who are known to harbor, aid, or abet them. But in like manner you will repress assumptions of unauthorized individuals to perform the same service because, under pretense of doing this, they become marauders and murderers themselves."

What to do about the Negro and slavery in this Slave State was covered in three sentences: "Allow no part of the military under your command to be engaged in either returning fugitive slaves or in forcing or enticing slaves from their homes, and, so far as practicable, enforce the same forbearance upon the people. . . . Allow no one to enlist colored troops except upon orders from you, or from here, through you. Allow no one to assume the functions of confiscating property under the law of Congress, or otherwise, except upon orders from here."

Into the Slave State of Maryland in October of '63 went Postmaster General Montgomery Blair. In a speech he made he seemed to be some sort of mouthpiece for the President. A few months earlier Blair had done this same thing at Concord, New Hampshire. He was now publicly saying that the President's plan of reconstruction, after the overthrow of the "rebel" government, contemplated the restoration to power of the loyal Union men in the Slave States. In this Blair was not misrepresenting the President. He had heard the President say that the Government, when the war ended, must be friendly to loyal Unionists of the South, even if those Unionists were slaveholders. But this was no time for Blair, without the President's permission, to step out and talk as though he talked for the President. What was Blair's motive? In part he was trying to spread the idea, by inference, "The President is not with you radicals—he is with us moderate antislavery men."

In doing this Blair was rather cheaply cunning. He was not frank enough to tell his audiences that he was speaking for Blair and Blair only, that he spoke with no authority at all from the President. *Harper's Weekly* and other pro-Lincoln journals at once felt called on to say that Blair implied "that the President recoils from his anti-slavery policy," that Blair was making too many "foolish speeches," that it was too bad Blair could not keep his mouth shut.

"Mr. Wendell Phillips suggested that the Postmaster-General was a traveling political agent of the Cabinet," said *Harper's*. "Possibly of someone in the Cabinet he may be. But we happen to know that the President knew nothing of his Postmaster's Concord speech until long after it was delivered, and it is only fair to conclude that Mr. Blair in Maryland spoke for himself alone. Indeed, if there is one thing proved, it is that the President needs nobody to talk or to write for him. There is no man in our political history who has equaled him in the tact, timeliness, pertinence, and plainness of his speeches and letters. The last, by-the-by, have been published in a pamphlet by H. H. Lloyd & Co., and there is no better or more timely reading."

A friend called one day to find Lincoln studying a newspaper clipping of Blair's speech; Lincoln admitted he would like to know precisely what Blair had said. It had been printed, the friend said, and he would supply the President with a copy. Noah Brooks took it to the President, and noticed him "greatly amused, as well as astonished, by the ingeniously worded title-page of the queer document," where Blair paraded the fact he was "A Member of Lincoln's Cabinet." The inference was that the President stood with Blair in Blair's criticism of other Cabinet members, of Senators, of Congressmen.

Later that month the Pennsylvanians William D. Kelley and Colonel John W. Forney called on the President, with congratulations on winning the elections in that State. Forney added, in Blair's hearing, that Governor

Curtin wished the President to know that if the Blair speech had been made thirty days earlier it would have cost the Union ticket 20,000 votes.

Turning to Blair, Forney said he was astonished that a Cabinet member should have come out with such talk just before an election. Blair replied that he had spoken only his honest sentiments. "Then," cried Forney, "why don't you leave the Cabinet, and not load down with your individual and peculiar sentiments the administration to which you belong?" The President sat by, said nothing.

Thus Noah Brooks and other newspapermen had it from Forney and thus it was published. The *New York Herald*, on the authority of Blair, denied that Forney had used such language to Blair. Brooks, however, went to the President with the story as it was generally printed, "and having looked through the clipping, he said that he 'guessed it was about correct.'" Brooks gave it as a good instance of the difficulty Lincoln had with his own friends, and of the bitterness that divided some of them from each other.

The peculiar sentiment with which Blair was playing ran through an incident which the *Chicago Times* stressed in its own way. A Maryland planter named Sothoron shot and killed a Negro recruiting officer who came to take three slaves. "The slave property of this gentleman," said the *Chicago Times*, "was as exclusively his own, and as sacredly guaranteed to him, as the sum of $3,000 in gold. He saw men rob him of this property in the face of day. He could see no difference between the man who robbed him of one species of property and the man who would rob him of the other, and therefore he shot the man. . . . The blood of that man rests upon the head of Abraham Lincoln, for he has solemnly promised the people of Maryland that they should be exempt from the emancipation proclamation, secured in the possession of their slaves; and a word from him would have stopped such practices."

The *Chicago Times* then departed to quote Lincoln, "I don't amount to pig tracks at the War Department," and added: "History will record of him, though not in the same classic language, that he did not amount to pig-tracks at anything else, except at relating vulgar stories. In that line he is unapproachable."

In this same month of October, '63, Swett had called and urged Lincoln in his next annual message to Congress to recommend a Constitutional Amendment to abolish slavery. Swett as an old friend, and as no radical at all, was listened to when he said that unless Lincoln took this position first his rivals would. Lincoln turned suddenly to Swett. "Is not the question of emancipation doing well enough now?" Swett said it was. "Well, I have never done an official act with a view to personal aggrandizement, and I don't like to begin now. I can see that emancipation is coming; whoever can wait for it will see it; whoever stands in its way will be run over by it."

Incessantly the *Chicago Times* and other Democratic party organs ran stories and squibs intended to stir up hatred against the Negro. The *Times* reprinted from the *Carthage* (Illinois) *Republican* a story headed "Nigger," beginning, "Going to Galesburg the other night on the cars we saw a big, black, stinking buck negro"; after telling of their failure to throw the Negro off the train, the writer continued:

Arriving at Galesburg we found another big, black, stinking buck negro, handing about handbills for a negro meeting to be held that night, and the caption of the negro's handbill was as follows—verbatim:

"Mass Meeting! Liberty, Equality, Citizenship! TO ARMS! TO ARMS! The colored citizens of Galesburg and vicinity are requested to attend a meeting," etc., etc.

And yet a few mornings before, in that moral old pest-hell of Galesburg, a person was literally hustled out of the Chicago, Burlington and Quincy Railroad works because he was suspected of being a Democrat!

From the Deep South, Sherman wrote Lincoln, "Slavery is already gone, and to cultivate the land, negro or other labor must be hired." In August, Hay noted the President's telling Seward of an interview Frank Blair had with Poindexter at Vicksburg. Poindexter said, "We are gone up, there is no further use of talking!" "How about your institution?" asked Blair. The reply: "Gone to the devil!"

The sign of a deepening trend was seen in the *Cincinnati Telegraph and Advocate*, published under the auspices of the Roman Catholic Archbishop of Cincinnati, in July advising its readers that Negro slavery was virtually abolished; it would oppose on moral and religious grounds all efforts to restore or re-establish it. The editor said his opposition to slavery had lost him readers. "Many have left us for fear they would lose the footstools on which they sat in meekness at the ward meeting or the county convention, but for these we have received the names of *men* in whose patronage and friendship we rejoice, because they have shaken off a load of bias, and dare to use their intellect in judging of great questions."

The chief argument this Catholic editor found he had to overcome was that the North would be overrun by colored people taking jobs away from white laborers. This, to the editor, seemed fear rather than reason. "There is no danger that an undue prevalence of the negro race will ever distract the busy marts of the white man." That was merely the social aspect. "The man who has the salvation of his neighbor at heart will have ample subject for meditation when he considers slavery in a religious view. The widespread ruin of souls uncared for and untaught, the violation of natural rights, the merciless division of families, the horrible degradation—all these appeal to the Catholic; and dark indeed must be his spirit if they make no impression on his conscience."

The deepening trend was also seen at the yearly meeting of the American Anti-Slavery Society in Philadelphia in December of '63. William Lloyd Garrison said he heard complaints now that his remarks were too tame. Others had quizzical comment on how respectable a sect they were becoming, no longer requiring police escorts at halls and hotels. Most insistent in criticism of Lincoln was Stephen S. Foster, a fifty-four-year-old veteran agitator who had quit the ministry because pewholders refused to let him discuss abolition in the pulpit, and who had repeatedly been thrown out of churches for rising in a pew and disturbing worship by what he had to say of slavery, slaveholders, and the United States Government. It was twenty years since Foster had issued his pamphlet titled *The Brotherhood of Thieves: A True Picture of the American Church and Clergy*. His wife, Abby Kelley Foster, was a woman suffragist and joined her husband in refusal to pay taxes to a Government that refused her the ballot. Twice their home had been sold for taxes and twice bought in by friends.

Now Foster rose in the yearly meeting of the Anti-Slavery Society to inquire why Abraham Lincoln, holding the military and naval power of the land, was shaking that power at the slaves and telling them that if they rose and struck for freedom they would be crushed with an iron hand. Voices: "He isn't doing it." "Not doing it?" proceeded Foster. "Has he not sworn, according to his own idea, to maintain slavery in the loyal States?" Charles C. Burleigh rose: "Let me, in justice to the man, remind you that if he went against the Radicals in Missouri, he went in favor of the Radicals in Maryland. [Applause.] We have a man at the head of the Government who is not altogether to my taste, or in accordance with my feeling or policy; but let us do him justice all the more assiduously, because we do not like his position." The Reverend Samuel May, Jr., was a speaker, and a colloquy ensued:

MR. MAY. Although I have no apologies to offer for what has been wrong, timid, slow, doubting, in Mr. Lincoln's position or policy, yet, with Mr. Burleigh, I say, let us do justice; and when Mr. Foster said that the President had issued his great Proclamation with an entire disregard and indifference for the rights of the slave or the colored man, and only for the benefit of the white man, it seems to me that he did the President great injustice. [Applause.] Did not Mr. Lincoln expressly say that he "sincerely believed" that great measure "to be an act of justice"; and did he not, upon this very ground, "invoke" for it "the considerate judgment of mankind and the gracious favor of Almighty God"? Does not all that is best in the land respond to it as such, and is it not upon that basis that we all feel it most secure?

MR. FOSTER. Did not the President declare to the civilized world that he would prefer to put down this rebellion without disturbing the power of slavery?

MR. MAY. I think there was nothing about "preference," but that he was determined to put down the rebellion; and, as President of the United States, he was bound so to act.

HENRY C. WRIGHT. Has the President of the United States, as President, any right to free a single slave, purely as a matter of justice, or for his good? His only power, as President of the United States, is to free the slave as a military necessity. [Applause.]

John Joliffe, a Cincinnati lawyer who had often donated his services in behalf of fugitive slaves, said he had no faith in politicians. They were merely the exponents of the public will. "This little band of twenty or thirty men have done this mighty work. Abraham Lincoln's proclamation was not one that came, as I believe, from his heart. It was one that he was impelled to issue by the force of public opinion behind him. And if we want other proclamations of freedom, or other great enterprises successively, we must labor with renewed diligence, and they will be accomplished. If so much has been done by thirty or forty people in Massachusetts, and scattered in different parts of the United States, how much more can be done when we have a hundred thousand Abolitionists to aid in the work?"

After resolutions had been passed to petition Congress "so to amend the Constitution that slavery shall be forever prohibited within the limits of the United States," the Reverend Samuel J. May, Jr., again took the floor. "Of course, I have not been satisfied with all our good President has decreed or proposed; but I consider what he was at the commencement of his administration, and perceive that he has made great progress. His interpretation of the Constitution has trammelled him. But I believe he has always been honest. At first, he was on a very low plane—almost as low as the slaveholder's. But he has risen—recently, has risen faster than the people. I believe he is ready, willing, eager to rise as far as righteousness shall demand; yes, to the summit of the requirements of impartial justice. Has he not said something to this effect?—'I am the servant of the people. If the people want emancipation, why do they not demand it?' Who for a moment believes that our President, notwithstanding the incubus that hangs upon him in the persons of some of his Cabinet, will not do all he may think that he ought to favor the progress of liberty? He must, he will, in all good conscience, do only what at the time shall seem to himself to be right and proper. I have watched his course; and though I have been impatient with him, yet have I never seen any thing that has impaired my confidence in his good intentions. I am persuaded that he desires and intends to do right. Let us, then, persevere in the work we commenced thirty years ago,—educating the people, and the officials of the people,—the President himself, if he needs instruction,—until they and he shall be brought to see, in its original brightness, the truth, the glorious truth, that was radiated upon our nation at its birth, and which our fathers declared to be self-evident."

Senator Henry Wilson of Massachusetts quoted General Grant: "I have never been an anti-slavery man, but I try to judge justly of what I see. I made up my mind, when this war commenced, that the North and South could only live together in peace as one nation, and they could only be one nation by being a free nation. [Applause.] Slavery, the corner-stone of the so-called Confederacy, is knocked out, and it will take more men to keep black men slaves, than to put down the rebellion. Much as I desire peace, I am opposed to any peace until this question of slavery is forever settled."

Frederick Douglass, born of a black mother and a white father, an escaped slave, a natural orator, was seen on the platform, and in response to calls from all over the hall came forward and spoke. The tone of the convention, he noticed, had been one of reminiscence, as though the work of the society were drawing to a close with the emancipation of the slave.

Besides that object, however, Douglass believed the society had another: the elevation of the colored people. Not yet could they peacefully ride the streetcars in Philadelphia. "Will you mock those bondsmen by breaking their chains with one hand, and with the other giving their rebel masters the elective franchise and robbing them of theirs?"

The orator threw back his pompadoured head and with dramatic voice flung his defiance at those who would refuse the ballot to the Negro. "I will hear nothing of degradation or of ignorance against the black man. If he knows enough to be hanged, he knows enough to vote. If he knows an honest man from a thief, he knows more than some of our white voters. If he knows as much when sober as an Irishman knows when drunk, he knows enough to vote. If he knows enough to take up arms in defence of this Government, and bare his breast to the storm of rebel artillery, he knows enough to vote. [Great applause.]" In former years it was not safe for Frederick Douglass to go down into Maryland or to the nation's capital.

I can go down there now. I have been down there to see the President; and as you were not there, perhaps you may like to know how the President of the United States received a black man at the White House.

I will tell you how he received me—just as you have seen one gentleman receive another [Great applause.]; with a hand and a voice well-balanced between a kind cordiality and a respectful reserve. I tell you I felt big there! [Laughter.]

Let me tell you how I got to him; because every body can't get to him. He has to be a little guarded in admitting spectators. The manner of getting to him gave me an idea that the cause was rolling on. The stairway was crowded with applicants. Some of them looked eager; and I have no doubt some of them had a purpose in being there, and wanted to see the President for the good of the country!

They were white; and as I was the only dark spot among them, I expected to have to wait at least half a day; I had heard of men waiting a week; but in two minutes after I sent in my card, the messenger came out, and respectfully invited "Mr. Douglass" in.

I could hear, in the eager multitude outside, as they saw me pressing and elbowing my way through, the remark, "Yes, damn it, I knew they would let the nigger through," in a kind of despairing voice—a Peace Democrat, I suppose. [Laughter.]

When I went in, the President was sitting in his usual position, I was told, with his feet in different parts of the room, taking it easy. [Laughter.] Don't put this down, Mr. Reporter, I pray you; for I am going down there again to-morrow! [Laughter.]

As I came in and approached him, the President began to rise, [Laughter.] and he continued rising until he stood over me [Laughter.]; and, reaching out his hand, he said, "Mr. Douglass, I know you; I have read about you, and Mr. Seward has told me about you"; putting me quite at ease at once.

Now, you will want to know how I was impressed by him. I will tell you that, too. He impressed me as being just what every one of you have been in the habit of calling him—an honest man. [Applause.] I never met with a man, who, on the first blush, impressed me more entirely with his sincerity, with his devotion to his country, and with his determination to save it at all hazards. [Applause.]

He told me (I think he did me more honor than I deserve) that I had made a little speech, somewhere in New York, and it had got into the papers, and among the things I had said was this: That if I were called upon to state what I regarded as the most sad and most disheartening feature in our present political and military situation, it would not be the various disasters experienced by our armies and our navies, on flood and field, but it would be the tardy, hesitating, vacillating policy of the President of the United States; and the President said to me, "Mr. Douglass, I have been charged with being tardy, and the like"; and he went on, and partly admitted that he might seem slow; but he said, "I am charged with vacillating; but, Mr. Douglass, I do not think that charge can be sustained; I think it cannot be shown that when I have once taken a position, I have ever retreated from it." [Applause.]

That I regarded as the most significant point in what he said during our interview. I told him that he had been somewhat slow in proclaiming equal protection to our colored soldiers and prisoners; and he said that the country needed talking up to that point. He hesitated in regard to it, when he felt that the country was not ready for it. He knew that the colored man throughout this country was a despised man, a hated man, and that if he at first came out with such a proclamation, all the hatred which is poured on the head of the Negro race would be visited on his administration.

He said that there was preparatory work needed, and that that preparatory work had now been done. And he said, "Remember this, Mr. Douglass; remember that Milliken's Bend, Port Hudson and Fort Wagner are recent events; and that these were necessary to prepare the way for this very proclamation of mine."

I thought it was reasonable, but came to the conclusion that while Abraham Lincoln will not go down to posterity as Abraham the Great, or as Abraham the Wise, or as Abraham the Eloquent, although he is all three, wise, great and eloquent, he will go down to posterity, if the country is saved, as Honest Abraham [Applause.]; and going down thus, his name may be written anywhere in this wide world of ours side by side with that of Washington, without disparaging the latter. [Renewed applause.]

But we are not to be saved by the captain, at this time, but by the crew. We are not to be saved by Abraham Lincoln, but by that power behind the throne, greater than the throne itself. You and I and all of us have this matter in hand.

Opposition to enlistment of Negro troops was fading. As a policy it took the Confederacy in the flank. Lincoln's order that "for every soldier of the United States killed in violation of the laws of war, a rebel soldier shall be executed," was his reply to a resolution of the Confederate Congress in May that every white commissioned officer commanding Negroes against Confederate troops should be deemed as inciting servile insurrection, "and shall if captured be put to death or otherwise punished at the discretion of the Court."

Grant wrote to Lincoln in late August that arming the blacks weakened the enemy in the proportion that it strengthened the Northern forces. "I am therefore most decidedly in favor of pushing this policy." A sentiment impossible at the start of the war had gained ground in the Confederacy, and the *Richmond Whig* found it necessary to rebuke "a Southern paper's suggestion that the Confederacy should arm six hundred thousand negroes and precipitate them upon the Yankees." The new Governor of Kentucky, Thomas E. Bramlette, in his September inaugural address raised his voice against the arming of Negro regiments and asked what could be done with such soldiers at the end of the war; he was speaking for those of his Slave State who knew that such soldiers would bring embarrassments.

A sudden vision was coming to many that somehow amid the confusions of emancipation proclamations, enforced conscription, habeas corpus, there belonged in the picture many regiments of black men fighting for whatever the war was about. "I want to see 200,000 black soldiers in the field," Charles Francis Adams, Jr.—no radical—wrote to his father, "and then I shall think it time to have peace. The African question might yet take a step backward in the face of a final success won by white soldiers, but it never will after that success to which 200,000 armed blacks have contributed."

Harper's Weekly undertook to rebuke those "intelligent persons" whose hatred of the Negro helped bring on the violence of the New York riots. "Their incessant sneering and depreciation of the colored people," their argument against the blacks' being "elevated above their sphere," was in effect a plea that Negro freedom would mean social equality, whereas personal liberty of the Negro was the real issue. "God has made the black race subservient to the white in the same way that he has made Jews subservient to Christians, and the Irish to the English, and in no other. It used to please Christians to call the Jews 'dogs' and murder them. It used to please the English to consider the Irish unclean beasts, and to treat them accordingly." The editorial called for personal liberty as the natural right of every innocent human being. "How utterly undeserved this mad hatred of the colored race is, every sober man in this country knows."

From the South now, since Gettysburg and Vicksburg, came less emphasis on the right of secession and the establishment of a Confederacy. The cry was more often that the South was in a defensive war, in the key of General Magruder in Louisiana warning Confederate troops against demagogues who had told them it was a rich man's war and a poor man's fight. "The man who says so is a scoundrel. I use the term understandingly and in its broadest signification. He is a scoundrel and your worst enemy. You are fighting for yourselves, to preserve yourselves from slavery the most hateful to be conceived. The object of the Yankees is to enslave this people and put the white man beneath the Negro in the social scale."

Newspapers published a prayer that autumn of '63. It was spoken by a Negro preacher at the funeral of a child in a camp in Virginia where homeless contrabands from devastated plantations were gathered. "Like de people of de old time, de Jews, we weep by de side ob de ribber, wid de strings ob de harp all broke. But we sing de song ob de broken heart as dem people could do. You knows, King Jesus, Honey, we jes got froo de Red Sea an wander in de dark wilderness, a poor feeble broken portion ob de children ob Adam. We'se got no homes, Masser, but de shelter ob de oak tree in de daytime an de cotton tent in de night. Help us for our own good an for de help of God's own blessed Union people. Our children is dyin' fast in de camp, and we bury dem in de col' ground, Jesus, to go in sperrit to de God ob all de people, where de soul hab no spot, no color. Great doctor ob doctors, king ob kings, and God ob battles, help us to be well. Help us to be able to fight wid de Union sojers de battle for de Union, for our own free children and our children's children. Fetch out, God ob battles, de big guns, wid de big balls, and de big bustin' shells, and gib dem God-forsaken secesh, dat would carry to shame our wives and darters, O mighty Jesus if you please, a right smart double shot ob grape and canister. Make 'em glad to stop de war and come back to shoes and de fatted calf—no more murdering brudders—no more ragged and barefoot—no more slave-whippers and slave-sellers—no more fadders ob yellow skins—no more meaner as meanest niggers."

Habits of stealing and lying changed for the better when Negroes were let out of slavery into the freedom of the contraband camps. So alleged the American Freedmen's Inquiry Commission, headed by Robert Dale Owen, in their report to the Secretary of War published in June of '63. In Alexandria, Virginia, Newbern, North Carolina, and other places, "one of the first acts of the Negroes, when they found themselves free, was to establish schools at their own expense." The former crime of learning to read, being no longer a crime, some were glad about that. They were starting churches. Also now that they could be married and have a family life if they chose, some were taking that course. "The Negro is found quite ready to copy whatever he believes are the rights and obligations of what he looks up to as the superior race."

The pathos of mixed bloods, and the fact of a mulatto woman being in more peril from a Northern white soldier than from a black freedman, was recited by the commission. "Many colored women think it more disgraceful to be black than to be illegitimate; for it is especially in regard to white men that their ideas and habits as to this matter are perverted. A case came to the knowledge of the Commission, in which a mulatto girl deemed it beneath her to associate with her half sister, a black, and the daughter of her mother's husband, her own father being a white man. Such ideas, and the habits thereby engendered, render it highly important that freedmen's villages, particularly when they are chiefly inhabited by women and children, should be at a distance from any military encampment, and should be strictly guarded. And as there are no sentinels so strict as the Negroes themselves, the Commission believe, for this and other reasons, that colored guards will be found the most suitable and efficient for such service; and they recommend that, in every case, they be substituted for whites."

The report alluded to Southern rumors that the Emancipation Proclamation was a political trick and would be taken back when the proper time came; the Negroes were sensitive on this point and wanted more assurance. "We cannot expect this untutored race to understand the abstract proposition, that a great nation, after having solemnly declared, through its Chief Magistrate, that three millions of its inhabitants shall be forever free, cannot, without utter degradation in the eyes of the civilized world, repudiate that declaration and reconsign these millions to slavery." Commanders were quoted who had found the Negro valuable as a military laborer and valiant as a soldier, with the added point that in transforming a slave society into a free one, the freedman should play a role. "The history of the world furnishes no example of an enslaved race which won its freedom without exertion of its own." The Negroes were looking to Lincoln as a spokesman. From afar off they viewed the man in the White House at Washington with awe and superstition. The commission inserted in its report four sentences over which Lincoln, possibly, both laughed and cried as he read it:

No difficulty is anticipated in procuring colored men to enlist, provided those now in the field shall be regularly paid, and provided the determination of the government to protect them in all the rights of the white soldier shall be clearly made known to them; especially if this latter determination shall be signified to them by the President in his own name.

Our Chief Magistrate would probably be surprised to learn with what reverence, bordering on superstition, he is regarded by these poor people. Recently, at Beaufort, a gang of colored men, in the service of the Quartermaster, at work on the wharf, were discussing the qualifications of the President—his wonderful power, how he had dispersed their masters, and what he would undoubtedly do hereafter for the colored race—when an aged, white-headed Negro—a "praise-man" (as the phrase is) amongst them—with all the solemnity and earnestness of an old prophet, broke forth:

"*What do you know 'bout Massa Linkum? Massa Linkum be ebrywhere. He walk de earth like de Lord.*"

CHAPTER 43

CHICKAMAUGA AND ELECTIONS WON '63

HAVING fought a drawn battle at Murfreesboro in the first week of January, 1863, General Rosecrans kept the Army of the Cumberland at that same place in Tennessee for six months, fortifying, drilling, setting no troops into motion to stop Confederate armies from hitting Grant at Vicksburg, letting three brigades of Confederate cavalry get away to raid and terrorize southern Indiana and Ohio.

Stanton and Halleck kept sending letters and telegrams to Rosecrans, trying to get the Army of the Cumberland into action. Rosecrans kept asking for supplies, revolving rifles, cavalry. Late in June of '63 Rosecrans marched his forces through rough and broken country, and by September 9 had, without a battle, maneuvered the Confederate army under Bragg out of Chattanooga and put his own troops into that strategic center. While on this operation Rosecrans wrote to Lincoln early in August reciting conditions: bad roads, bad weather, cavalry weakness, long hauls for bridge material.

"I think," Lincoln replied, "you must have inferred more than General Halleck has intended, as to any dissatisfaction of mine with you. I am sure you, as a reasonable man, would not have been wounded could you have heard all my words and seen all my thoughts in regard to you. I have not abated in my kind feeling for and confidence in you. I have seen most of your despatches to General Halleck—probably all of them."

The President then told of the anxiety he had been through while Rosecrans stayed inactive as Grant was threatened at Vicksburg by Johnston's army, which might any day have been joined by Bragg's army. Soon after, "despatches from Grant abated my anxiety for him, and in proportion abated my anxiety about any movement of yours."

Then still later Lincoln had seen a Rosecrans dispatch arguing that the right time to attack Bragg would be after the fall of Vicksburg. "It impressed me very strangely, and I think I so stated to the Secretary of War and General Halleck. It seemed no other than the proposition that you could better fight Bragg when Johnston should be at liberty to return and assist him than you could before he could so return to his assistance." And now that Johnston's army was relieved from watching Grant at Vicksburg "it has seemed to me that your chance for a stroke has been considerably diminished, and I have not been pressing you directly or indirectly."

The President then gently asked Rosecrans about supplies and horses, as though preparations were costing as much as real action, and closed the letter: "And now be assured once more that I think of you in all kindness and confidence, and that I am not watching you with an evil eye."

In the matter of supplies, road and weather conditions, campaign requisites, what he thought he had to have before he could start fighting, Rosecrans seemed to be as muddled and querulous as McClellan the year before. The complaints of Rosecrans, however, did not insinuate that jealous plotters and malicious geese at Washington were trying to snare and frustrate him. Lincoln met this personal quality, and never in his letters and telegrams to Rosecrans took on the peremptory manner, the ironic tone, he had latterly used with McClellan.

On one slight affair the President telegraphed Rosecrans: "In no case have I intended to censure you or to question your ability. . . . I frequently make mistakes myself in the many things I am compelled to do hastily." It may have come to Lincoln that into Rosecrans' ear had been poured an offer, by Gilmore, that Horace Greeley and others wanted to run him for President in place of Lincoln; others besides Greeley had allied themselves with that movement. And Rosecrans had wrecked it by saying No. Though McClellan had conducted war as a gentleman and according to chivalry, in the view of the Southern press generally, Rosecrans was to the *Charleston Mercury* "Rosecrans the Ruffian," quite "the most ingrained and consummate Brute amongst military men in modern days." Though McClellan had listened to Fernando Wood, Aspinwall, and others mentioning the Presidency to him—and though McClellan had undertaken to instruct Lincoln on government policies—Rosecrans had steadily kept himself out of partisan politics, saying, "My place is in the army."

According to Bates of the telegraph office, an officer at Rosecrans' headquarters noted this incident: "A delegation of prominent Ohio Democrats called on General Rosecrans at Murfreesboro' in the spring of 1863 and made a tremendous onslaught on him to secure his consent to become a candidate for Governor of Ohio, with the expectation that . . . he might go a step higher later on. The delegation was very secretive at first with Rosecrans, and he finally broke out in his impulsive way and demanded their plans. When they were uncovered, he gave them a most vigorous tirade and in language stronger than polite, suggested their leaving the camp and returning to a more congenial clime."

So it happened that when Rosecrans wrote a long argumentative letter replying to Lincoln's long one early in August, the President sent to "Old Rosy" about as kindly wishes as he could put on paper, with a cordial presentation of delicate relationships, and assurances that Rosecrans had laid him under obligations that he could not forget so long as he could remember anything. The letter read:

Executive Mansion, Washington
August 31, 1863

My Dear General Rosecrans:

Yours of the 22d was received yesterday. When I wrote you before, I did [not] intend, nor do I now, to engage in an argument with you on military questions. You had informed me you were impressed through General Halleck that I was dissatisfied with you; and I could not bluntly deny that I was without unjustly implicating him. I therefore concluded to tell you the plain truth, being satisfied the matter would thus appear much smaller than it would if seen by mere glimpses. I repeat that my appreciation of you has not abated. I can never forget whilst I remember anything that about the end of last year and beginning of this, you gave us a hard-earned victory, which, had there been a defeat instead, the nation could scarcely have lived over.

Neither can I forget the check you so opportunely gave to a dangerous sentiment which was spreading in the North.

Yours as ever,

A. Lincoln

The major general receiving these compliments was forty-four years old, born in Kingston, Ohio, graduating fifth in the class of 1842 at West Point, serving four years as professor of natural philosophy and of engineering at the national academy. He had organized a kerosene manufacturing company just before the war began, quit coal oil and money-making, served with credit under McClellan in West Virginia; he came through hard fighting at Corinth and Murfreesboro, rated as an able commanding officer, not lacking piety.

"By the favor of God you have expelled the insurgents from middle Tennessee," ran one line of a Rosecrans order to the Army of the Cumberland in August, while an order on February 22 of '63 had the diapason note: "Companions-in-arms! Today is both the weekly commemoration of the resurrection of Our Lord and the birthday of Washington." To the Indiana Legislature resolution of thanks for his victory at Murfreesboro, Rosecrans wrote a long letter holding that the men of his army, termed "Lincoln hirelings" by the Copperheads, were fighting for equal rights under the Constitution; as to the Confederacy, "We must destroy it or it will destroy our nation." A letter from Rosecrans to several governors of Northern States urged that deserters should be stripped of the right to vote, and desertion treated as "an infamous crime." Long John Wentworth liked the letter, in his *Chicago Journal* quoted the *Chicago Times*, "William S. Rosecrans, Major-General, has written himself down as an ass," and replied, "Merely because he has spoken the plain truth and written you down a traitor." To his brother Bishop Rosecrans, the General wrote a letter published in the *Catholic Telegraph* at Cincinnati excoriating Northern "rebel leaders" who foment guerrilla warfare, "who decoy and murder pickets, fire on hospital boats, murder Union men and strip their families of their property, and boast of chivalry." These Northern "rebel" leaders, he urged, "can never be trusted in any other way than as you would trust wild beasts, when you have them secure, caged or chained! . . . Shall men who are getting rich off the Government patronage, who sleep quietly and peacefully in their beds because we watch her in the cold and wet, stab us in the back and denounce us? *Speravi in Domino; non confundar in aeternum* [In the Lord have I trusted; let me never be confounded.]"

High praise of Rosecrans as a strategist rang in many quarters after the long marches and maneuverings by which he had arrived at Chattanooga while Bragg lay to the south. At first Rosecrans felt good, elated, over his position. Then reports came indicating that Bragg had received reinforcements and more were coming, that Bragg had his army well concentrated while Rosecrans' forces were scattered over a fifty-mile line. Rosecrans did not know that Bragg, as one of Davis's most trusted commanders, was getting all the large and small armies that the Richmond War Department could order to his help, that General Lee had been to Richmond and arranged with Davis for Longstreet with 20,000 troops from the Army of Northern Virginia to be sent by railroad down across the Carolinas and up into far northern Georgia to the help of Bragg. This gave Bragg 70,000 troops as against Rosecrans' 57,000.

The two armies grappled at Chickamauga Creek near Crawfish Spring on September 19 of '63. Lincoln that day at the war telegraph office read dispatches from Charles A. Dana, Stanton's assistant and observer. At 10:30 A.M.: "As I write enemy are making diversions on our right. . . . An orderly of Bragg's just captured says there are reports in rebel army of Longstreet's arrival, but he does not know that they are true. Rosecrans has everything ready to grind up Bragg's flank." At 1 P.M.: "There is fighting." At 2:30 P.M.: "Enemy repulsed on left has suddenly fallen on right of our line of battle . . . musketry there fierce and obstinate . . . decisive victory seems assured to us." At 3:20 P.M.: "Thomas reports that he is driving rebels and will force them into the Chickamauga tonight. . . . The battle is fought in thick forest, and is invisible to outsiders. Line is two miles long." At 4 P.M.: "Everything is prosperous." At 4:30 P.M.: "I do not dare to say our victory is complete, but it seems certain. Enemy silenced on nearly whole line. Longstreet is here." At 5:20 P.M.: "Firing has ceased. . . . Enemy holds his ground in many places. . . . Now appears to be undecided contest." At 7:30 P.M.: "Enemy defeated in attempt to turn our left flank and regain possession of Chattanooga. . . . His repulse was bloody and maintained to the end. If he does not retreat, Rosecrans will renew the fight at daylight."

To the President personally, Rosecrans wired that night he had captured ten pieces of artillery. "Took prisoners from thirty different regiments, and with the blessing of God will do more tomorrow." Other telegrams from Rosecrans to the President were large with hope for the next day. Hay noted:

"Sunday morning, the 20th of September, the President showed me Rosecrans' despatches of the day before, detailing the first day's fighting, and promising a complete victory the next day. The President was a little uneasy over the promise, and very uneasy that Burnside was not within supporting distance."

Late that Sunday afternoon came a telegram from Dana at Chattanooga: "My report to-day is of deplorable importance. Chickamauga is as fatal a name in our history as Bull Run." At noon that day Dana was twelve miles from Chattanooga and, worn for sleep, lay down on the grass near where Rosecrans was directing troop movements.

"I was awakened," wrote Dana later, "by the most infernal noise I ever heard. Never in any battle I had witnessed was there such a discharge of cannon and musketry. I sat up on the grass, and the first thing I saw was General Rosecrans crossing himself—he was a very devout Catholic. 'Hello!' I said to myself, 'if the general is crossing himself, we are in a desperate situation.' I was on my horse in a moment. . . . I saw our lines break and melt away like leaves before the wind. The headquarters around me disappeared. . . . The whole right of the army had apparently been routed. . . . Bull Run had nothing more terrible than the rout and flight of these veteran soldiers. The enemy came upon them in columns six lines deep. . . . I do not think our lines would have been broken but for a gap in them caused by taking Wood's division from the centre to reinforce the left. Through that gap the rebels came in. . . . I never saw anything so crushing to the mind as that scene. I was swept away with part of Rosecrans' staff, and lost in the rabble. . . . I rode twelve miles to Chattanooga, galloping my horse all the way, to send despatches to Washington, and found the road filled all the distance with baggage-wagons, artillery, ambulances, Negroes on horseback, field and company officers, wounded men limping along, Union refugees from the country around leading their wives and children, mules running along loose, every element that could confuse the rout of a great army, not excepting a major-general commanding an army corps."

The right and the center were shattered. The left wing, under the Union Virginian General George H. Thomas, held. Till sunset, till darkness and night, his 25,000 men held solid on a horseshoe of a rocky hillock against twice their number. One brigade ran out of ammunition and met

Longstreet's veterans with the bayonet. The next day Thomas began moving in good order to Chattanooga, Bragg failing to make another attack.

A heavy day's work had been done that Sunday, with Union killed, wounded, and missing reckoned at 16,000, Confederate at 18,000, a larger affair in blood loss than Antietam.

Enough news of the battle reached Lincoln that Sunday night so he could not sleep. Welles noted on Monday: "The President came to me this afternoon with the latest news. He was feeling badly. Tells me a dispatch was sent to him at the Soldiers' Home shortly after he got asleep, and so disturbed him that he had no more rest, but arose and came to the city and passed the remainder of the night awake and watchful."

Hay's diary: "The next morning (September 21) he [the President] came into my bedroom before I was up, & sitting down on my bed said, 'Well, Rosecrans has been whipped, as I feared. I have feared it for several days. I believe I feel trouble in the air before it comes. Rosecrans says we have met with serious disaster—extent not ascertained. Burnside, instead of obeying orders which were given on the 14th & going to Rosecrans, has gone up on a foolish affair to Jonesboro to capture a party of guerillas who are there."

To Rosecrans that day Lincoln sent a telegram: "Be of good cheer. We have unabated confidence in you, and in your soldiers and officers. In the main you must be the judge as to what is to be done. If I were to suggest, I would say, save your army by taking strong positions until Burnside joins you. . . . We shall do our utmost to assist you." In a Richmond paper that came into Lincoln's hands was a dispatch from Bragg to the Richmond War Department reporting so gloomily on the Chickamauga battle that Lincoln relayed it to Rosecrans on September 23 with the comforting comment: "You see he does not claim so many prisoners or captured guns as you were inclined to concede. He also confesses to heavy loss." On the same day Rosecrans, having rested, and having won back his personal control, wired from Chattanooga to Washington, "We can hold this point, and I cannot be dislodged unless by very superior numbers and after a great battle."

For long Lincoln had wished to see the Federal force thrust down as deep as Chattanooga. Now he read despairing words telegraphed by Rosecrans, and instructed Halleck that it was important for Rosecrans to hold his position at or about Chattanooga; it kept Tennessee clear of the enemy and broke important railroad lines of the enemy. "If you concur, I think he [Rosecrans] would better be informed that we are not pushing him beyond this position; and that, in fact, our judgment is rather against his going beyond it. If he can only maintain this position, without more, this rebellion can only eke out a short and feeble existence, as an animal sometimes may with a thorn in its vitals."

Also on September 23 Lincoln again heard from one Robert A. Maxwell, a crank who sent him odd telegrams. To one in the previous July, Lincoln had replied, "Your despatch of today is received, but I do not understand it." Now came Maxwell's telegraphic query: "Will Buell's testamentary executor George Thomas ever let Rosecrans succeed? Is Bragg dumb enough?" Lincoln held this telegram through the afternoon, and in the evening handed the operator Tinker a reply to Maxwell in New York: "I hasten to say that in the state of information we have here, nothing could be more ungracious than to indulge any suspicion towards Gen. Thomas. It is doubtful whether his heroism and skill exhibited last Sunday afternoon, has ever been surpassed in the world."

This message had been in Tinker's hands a few minutes when Lincoln came over and said: "I guess I will not send this. I can't afford to answer every crazy question asked me." From then on in the telegraph office, officious crank dispatches were referred to as "crazygrams." Tinker laid away the President's unsent telegram and long afterward went out of his way to put it into the hands of "Old Pap" Thomas.

Also on the evening of September 23 John Hay rode out by moonlight to wake up the President and bring him in to Washington for a night council of war that Stanton considered necessary because of dark news from Chattanooga. Stanton was shaken by one of his frenzies of excitement. Hay had noticed the Secretary in a group trying to decipher an intricate message from Rosecrans giving reasons for the failure of the battle. Stanton snorted: "I know the reasons well enough. Rosecrans ran away from his fighting men and did not stop for thirteen miles. . . . No, they need not shuffle it off on McCook. He is not much of a soldier. I never was in favor of him for a Major-Gen¹. But he is not accountable for this business. He & Crittenden made pretty good time away from the fight to Chattanooga, but Rosecrans beat them both."

Hay's moonlight ride brought him to the Soldiers' Home, where he found the President abed. "I delivered my message to him as he robed himself & he was considerably disturbed. I assured him as far as I could that it meant nothing serious, but he thought otherwise, as it was the first time Stanton had ever sent for him."

Of the same moonlit night Chase wrote in his diary: "Was called up from my bed about midnight by a messenger from the War Department who said I was wanted there immediately. The summons really alarmed me. I felt sure that disaster had befallen us." From Stanton, Chase learned, however, that the news was not as bad as he expected, and he was handed a telegram from General Garfield at Chattanooga urging reinforcements. At the War Office Chase met Halleck, saw the President and Seward come in. Stanton opened the conference by asking what troops Burnside could add to Rosecrans and in what time.

HALLECK. Twenty thousand men in ten days, if uninterrupted.

THE PRESIDENT. Before ten days Burnside will put in enough to hold the place [Chattanooga].

STANTON (to Halleck). How many in eight days?

HALLECK. Twelve thousand.

THE PRESIDENT. After Burnside begins to arrive the pinch will be over.

STANTON. Unless the enemy anticipating reinforcements, attacks promptly. (*To Halleck*.) When will Sherman's reach Rosecrans?

HALLECK. In about ten days, if already moved from Vicksburg. His route will be to Memphis, thence to Corinth and Decatur, and a march of 100 or 150 miles on the north side of the Tennessee River. Boats have already gone down from Cairo and every available man ordered forward, say from 20,000 to 25,000.

STANTON. Are any more available elsewhere?

HALLECK. A few in Kentucky; I don't know how many; all were ordered to Burnside.

STANTON. I propose to send 30,000 from the Army of the Potomac. There is no reason to expect that General Meade will attack Lee, although greatly superior in force, and his great numbers where they are, useless. In five days 30,000 could be put with Rosecrans.

THE PRESIDENT. I will bet that if the order is given tonight the troops could not be got to Washington in five days.

STANTON. On such a subject I don't feel inclined to bet, but the matter has been carefully investigated, and it is certain that 30,000 bales of cotton could be sent in that time, and by taking possession of the railroads and excluding all other business I do not see why 30,000 men can not be sent as well. But if 30,000 can't be sent let 20,000 go.

According to Chase's memorandum, much conversation followed, the President and Halleck disinclined to weaken Meade. Seward and Chase were decisive for reinforcing Rosecrans.

At 2:30 A.M. on September 24, Meade was ordered by telegraph to prepare two army corps, under General Hooker, ready for transport, with five days' cooked provisions, with baggage, artillery, ammunition, horses, to follow. Meantime, according to the telegraph chief, Bates, further appeals for help, long ones, had come over the wires from Rosecrans and Dana; unless relief came soon the enemy might cut off their communications and supplies. Eckert brought in these later dispatches and, as an old railroader, was asked by Stanton what he knew about rail routes and schedules to Chattanooga. Eckert said it was a sixty-day trip, "and perhaps forty." Stanton told him to go work out a schedule and be quick. At 8 A.M. Eckert came with a report it could be done in fifteen days. Stanton jumped for joy and asked about details. Eckert had considered such matters as a pontoon bridge of coal barges at Louisville, cooks and waiters every fifty miles or so along the route to supply hot coffee, bread, soup, to soldiers on the train, these cooks and waiters working back on regular trains to their starting-point and resuming their food service on a moving train.

"The plan was so well laid and withal so sensible," said Bates, "that Lincoln and Stanton both indorsed it, subject to the approval of the railroad authorities and military officials." Superintendent Thomas A. Scott of the Pennsylvania Railroad was called in, said Eckert's fifteen days might possibly be bettered. Officers of the Baltimore & Ohio, and of other railroads, were called to Washington, and arrangements completed. Scott went to

Louisville, a sort of midway point, kept the wires hot with brief messages. From Bealeton, Virginia, to Chattanooga, Tennessee (1,233 miles), 23,000 men were transported in eleven and a half days. Lincoln was interested enough to inquire of Scott on October 1 by telegraph, "Tell me how things have advanced, as far as you know," while Stanton at the finish sent to Scott a message unusual for the Secretary: "Your work is most brilliant. A thousand thanks."

Before going West, three major generals had called on Lincoln. "The result of the visit, a request by the President to General Rosecrans urging him to take Slocum from Hooker's force and give Hooker some corresponding force," wrote Hay. "Hooker does not speak unkindly of Slocum while he [Slocum] never mentions Hooker but to attack him. . . . I hope they will give Hooker a fair show. Slocum's hostility is very regrettable. Hooker is a fine fellow. The President says, 'Whenever trouble arises I can always rely upon Hooker's magnanimity.' The President asked Hooker to write to him. I told him if he did not wish to write to the Tycoon, he might write to me."

To Mrs. Lincoln at the Fifth Avenue Hotel in New York, the President sent a telegram September 22 to "use your own pleasure" on whether to stay in New York or come to Washington. "I did not say it is sickly [here] and that you should on no account come. So far as I see or know, it was never healthier, and I really wish to see you." Two days later he telegraphed Mrs. Lincoln as to Chickamauga that the Union army was worsted mainly in yielding ground. "According to the rebel accounts . . . they lost six killed and eight wounded: of the killed one major-general and five brigadiers including your brother-in-law, Helm." When Helm had in the first days of the war been at the White House with his wife, Mrs. Lincoln's sister, Lincoln had offered him an appointment as paymaster in the Union army but he had gone away saying his heart lay with the Southern cause. Now Lincoln took pen in hand and wrote a pass for his wife's stepmother at Lexington, Kentucky, to proceed on a sorrowful errand: "Allow Mrs. Robert S. Todd, widow, to go south and bring her daughter, Mrs. General B. Hardin Helm, with her children, north to Kentucky."

Of one Southern area Lincoln had told a brigadier general: "What we really need is a military railroad from Louisville, Kentucky, through Cumberland Gap to Knoxville, Tennessee. Whenever we reach that point we will be between the enemy and his hog and hominy, and under such circumstances he will have to give up the contest."

Every day while Rosecrans had operated around Chattanooga that month the President had been keeping an anxious watch on East Tennessee, a region of mountaineers and hill people who owned no slaves and whose hearts, many of them, Lincoln knew were with the Union cause. In that region his grandfather had lived and died, and it held kinfolk of his. Month after month since early in the war he had urged the importance of taking and holding East Tennessee. (Frémont was to have led one expedition toward that end but didn't get started.) The sufferings of the Union people of

Missouri or Kansas were slight in comparison. The East Tennessee people had voted more than two to one against secession. They had lost horses, cattle, and grain to the Confederate armies. They had by thousands journeyed in stealth over the steep Cumberland Mountains, through brush and timber, to Union enlistment camps. Hundreds staying at home had been thrown into prison, hanged on suspicion of burning bridges, picked off by sharpshooters who regarded them as Yankees and traitors.

"The tale of these sufferings came constantly to Mr. Lincoln, and there was nothing in the war which caused him sharper pain or excited in him a more ardent desire for redress," his secretaries noted. "The President, striving with all his energies to relieve them, found for two years his efforts so unavailing that the sight of an East Tennessean at last came to give him the keenest distress."

While Rosecrans marched toward Chattanooga, and Lincoln was urging Burnside with the Army of the Ohio to take Knoxville and occupy East Tennessee, once more a delegation from that region called at the White House to lay their wrongs before the President. And the President did not have the heart to face them and talk with them. He wrote them a groaning and bitter letter, saying he knew well what they had been waiting for when on successive days they sent cards and notes asking an interview which he refused. "I knew it was the same true and painful story which Governor Johnson, Mr. Maynard, Dr. Clements, and others have been telling me for more than two years. I also knew that meeting you could do no good, because I have all the while done, and shall continue to do, the best for you that I could and can. I do as much for East Tennessee as I would or could if my own home and family were in Knoxville." He mentioned the difficulties of getting an army into the region and keeping it there. No one could fail to see those difficulties "unless it may be those who are driven mad and blind by their sufferings." He reminded them he had tried to get Congress to have a railroad built on purpose for their relief. "I know you are too much distressed to be argued with, and therefore I do not attempt it at length." He spoke of hopes that the War Department, Burnside, Rosecrans, present efforts, might win their relief.

Then in three weeks, early in September, Burnside and the Army of the Ohio had crossed the Tennessee line, entered Kingston, and marched into Knoxville to be met by cheering crowds. Flags long hidden were flashed out into sunlight, officers and soldiers welcomed into homes.

"I look upon East Tennessee as one of the most loyal sections of the United States," Burnside wrote to Lincoln, saying also, "The rebellion now seems to be pretty well checked." He reminded Lincoln, "You will remember that I sometime ago told you that I wished to retire to private life," and he, Burnside, would now ask to be allowed to resign if the President thought the good of the service would so permit. Lincoln replied with "a thousand thanks" for late successes, and "We cannot allow you to resign until things shall be a little more settled in East Tennessee."

Though repeatedly ordered to join Rosecrans, Burnside delayed, and on

September 25 Lincoln wrote him a letter: "Yours of the 23d is just received, and it makes me doubt whether I am awake or dreaming. I have been struggling for ten days, first through General Halleck, and then directly, to get you to go to assist General Rosecrans in an extremity, and you have repeatedly declared you would do it, and yet you steadily move the contrary way. On the 19th you telegraph once from Knoxville, and twice from Greenville, acknowledging receipt of order, and saying you will hurry support to Rosecrans. On the 20th you telegraph again from Knoxville, saying you will do all you can, and are hurrying troops to Rosecrans. On the 21st you telegraph from Morristown, saying you will hurry support to Rosecrans, and now your despatch of the 23d comes in from Carter's Station, still farther away from Rosecrans, still saying you will assist him, but giving no account of any progress made toward assisting him."

The letter was a patient and weary framing of the query to Burnside "How can you be so dumb?" Having written it, Lincoln delayed sending it. Then he decided not to send it at all. Instead he sent Burnside two telegrams suggesting that troops be rushed to Rosecrans at Chattanooga.

Meantime came charges that three major generals, McCook, Crittenden, Negley, had, during the Chickamauga battle, sought personal safety or had mismanaged their forces. Lincoln as Commander in Chief issued orders for a court of inquiry. The court met, heard evidence, cleared the generals of conduct unbecoming to officers; an assistant adjutant general wrote, "The President of the United States is of opinion that no further action is required," and the generals were restored to command. The arrival at this opinion required several months. One week after the Chickamauga battle Seward suggested that Rosecrans should be removed along with Crittenden and McCook. The White House anxiety about generals in the field was noted by Welles on September 28:

"The President read to Seward and myself a detailed confidential dispatch from Chattanooga very derogatory to Crittenden and McCook, who wilted when every energy and resource should have been put forth, disappeared from the battle-field, returned to Chattanooga, and—went to sleep. The officers who did their duty are dissatisfied. We had their statements last week, which this confidential dispatch confirms. It makes some, but not a very satisfactory, excuse for Rosecrans, in whom the President has clearly lost confidence. He said he was urged to change all the officers, but thought he should limit his acts to Crittenden and McCook; said it would not do to send one of our generals from the East."

To Congressman Isaac N. Arnold, Lincoln sent a letter marked "Private and confidential," telling this steadfast friend why he could not dismiss General in Chief Halleck. "If the public believe, as you say, that he has driven Fremont, Butler, and Sigel from the service, they believe what I know to be false; so that if I was to yield to it, it would only be to be instantly beset by some other demand based on another falsehood equally gross." Patiently the President explained that Frémont was relieved at his own request before Halleck came into office, and that Sigel had pressed for six months to be relieved. Now Sigel's corps had another commander. "Can I instantly thrust that other one [out] to put him in again?" Then, referring to Grant's Vicksburg campaign as "one of the most brilliant in the world," and naming Grant and his seven corps commanders, Lincoln noted: "You can scarcely name one of them that has not been constantly denounced even opposed by the same men who are now so anxious to get Halleck out, and Fremont & Butler & Sigel in. I believe no one of them went through the Senate easily, and certainly one failed to get through at all. I am compelled to take a more impartial and unprejudiced view of things." Over and again to friends like Arnold, seeking shifts among the major generals, Lincoln gave the insistent assurance: "Without claiming to be your superior, which I do not, my position enables me to understand my duty in all these matters better than you possibly can, and I hope you do not yet doubt my integrity."

From Cairo, Illinois, came a telegram to Lincoln one August day: "I have been relieved for an omission of my adjutant. Hear me." The signer was John A. McClernand, who had commanded only a corps at Vicksburg when he had fully expected to be at the head of the entire joint forces. McClernand had made the mistake of publishing over his name in the *Missouri Democrat*, St. Louis, a letter praising the bravery of his troops, exalting his own generalship, and implying blame for Grant, Sherman, and McPherson in failure to reinforce him and win a victory. Technically McClernand was guilty of insubordination in publishing a report of military action without permission from his superior officer. When his adjutant brought him Grant's order relieving him, McClernand read it and said to the adjutant: "I am relieved. By God, sir, we are both relieved." When he telegraphed Lincoln that he was relieved because of an omission of his adjutant, McClernand meant to say that the adjutant forgot to submit to Grant the letter to be published in the *Missouri Democrat*. Lincoln's answer to McClernand was written after William G. Greene, Lincoln's friend of New Salem days, had presented a letter favoring McClernand signed by Yates, Hatch, Dubois, and other Illinoisans.

The President wrote to McClernand, "I doubt whether your present position is more painful to you than to myself." He was grateful to McClernand for a patriotic stand taken early. He had done whatever appeared practicable to advance McClernand and the public interest together. No charges had been brought by anyone. The case rested on a statement from General Grant. "And even this I have not seen or sought to see; because it is a case, as appears to me, in which I could do nothing without doing harm. General Grant and yourself have been conspicuous in our most important successes; and for me to interfere and thus magnify a breach between you could not but be of evil effect. Better leave it where the law of the case has placed it. For me to force you back on General Grant would be forcing him to resign. I cannot give you a new command, because we have no forces except such as already have commanders."

The President cited for McClernand, as if for comfort, that the case was like that of Frémont, McClellan, Butler, Sigel, Curtis, Hunter, where pressure was brought "by those who scold before they think, or without thinking at all" when he had no commands to give them. "This is now your case; which, as I have said, pains me not less than it does you. My belief is that the permanent estimate of what a general does in the field is fixed by the 'cloud of witnesses' who have been with him in the field, and that, relying on these, he who has the right needs not to fear."

A peculiar and an implicative letter for McClernand to carry around with him as he trudged the streets of Springfield, Illinois, taking a few law cases, talking politics, drawing his pay as a major general off duty, giving to the old cronies of Steve Douglas his reminiscences of Donelson, Shiloh, Vicksburg, blaming Grant, Sherman, and others for his downfall, and with no hard words for Lincoln. McClernand was one more of the stars dropped in tumult. If necessary he could pull from his pocket a letter from Lincoln saying, "General Grant and yourself have been conspicuous in our most important successes," also, "your case . . . pains me not less than it does you."

Not long before Lincoln sent his letter to McClernand, Grant's chief of staff, John A. Rawlins, had arrived in Washington, and, wrote Welles: "His interview with the President and Cabinet was of nearly two hours' duration, and all . . . were entertained by him. . . . The unpolished and unrefined deportment, of this earnest and sincere man, patriot and soldier pleased me more than that of almost any officer whom I have met. He was never at West Point, and has had few educational advantages, yet he is a soldier. . . . He is a sincere friend of Grant, who evidently sent him for a purpose." Further along in his diary Welles arrived at Rawlins's purpose. "Rawlins now comes from Vicksburg with statements in regard to McClernand which show him an impracticable and unfit man . . . an embarrassment, an obstruction to, army . . . operations. In Rawlins's statements there is undoubtedly prejudice, but with such appearance of candor, and earnest and intelligent conviction, that there can be hardly a doubt McClernand is in fault, and Rawlins has been sent here by Grant in order to enlist the President rather than bring dispatches. In this, I think, he has succeeded, though the President feels kindly towards McClernand."

Meantime just after the Chickamauga battle, the one Western general most occupying Lincoln's thought was Rosecrans, who on October 3 wired Lincoln the suggestion that it might be well, if the elections in the States went favorably, to offer a general amnesty to all officers and soldiers in the "rebellion." "It would give us moral strength and weaken them very much." Lincoln replied:

"If we can hold Chattanooga and East Tennessee, I think the rebellion must dwindle and die. I think you and Burnside can do this, and hence doing so is your main object. Of course to greatly damage or destroy the enemy in your front would be a greater object, because it would include the former and more, but it is not so certainly within your power. I under stand the main body of the enemy is very near you, so near that you could 'board at home,' so to speak, and menace or attack him any day. Would not the doing of this be your best mode of counteracting his holds on your communications? But this is not an order. I intend doing something like what you suggest [as to amnesty] whenever the case shall appear ripe enough to have it accepted in the true understanding rather than as a confession of weakness and fear."

While trying to advise Rosecrans competently, the President received telegrams from major generals who had been transferred from East to West. Slocum wired that he found himself put under command of Hooker, and inasmuch as he had no confidence in Hooker he would beg to resign. Hooker wired that he hoped Slocum could be put under some other command. They seemed to understand each other. Hooker, however, added gloomy opinions of his chief, Rosecrans, as "swayed entirely by passion," and "It seems that he aspired to the command of the Army of the Potomac, and that mortal offense was given in not naming him first."

Rosecrans under strain was cracking, putting into telegrams to Lincoln many complaints of poor communications and subsistence, and such generalties as "Our future is not bright." In a telegram of October 12 Lincoln tried heartening Rosecrans: "You and Burnside now have him [the enemy] by the throat; and he must break your hold or perish. . . . Sherman is coming to you." But Rosecrans merely answered that while his army was in peril of starvation the enemy's side of the valley was full of corn, closing the telegram: "We must put our trust in God, who never fails those who truly trust."

The weird touches in Rosecrans' dispatches tallied with the report of Charles A. Dana, whom Lincoln had styled "the eyes of the Government at the front," to Stanton and Lincoln on October 12. Dana feared starvation or the Confederates would soon drive Rosecrans' army out of Chattanooga. Rosecrans, wrote Dana, was sometimes as obstinate and inaccessible to reason as at others he was irresolute and vacillating. "I have never seen a public man possessing talent with less administrative power, less clearness and steadiness in difficulty, and greater practical incapacity. . . . His mind scattered; there was no system in the use of his busy days and restless nights . . . and, with great love of command, he was a feeble commander. He was conscientious and honest, just as he was imperious and disputatious. . . . I consider this army to be very unsafe in his hands."

The Confederates had a hold on the Tennessee River by which they blocked water transport of food and supplies for Rosecrans' army; and the long rough wagon route that met rail connections with Nashville was threatened. The Dana reports ran more gloomy that second week in October. Rosecrans was "dawdling" while catastrophe hung close, starvation or disorderly retreat. "The incapacity of the commander is astonishing, and it often seems difficult to believe him of sound mind. His imbecility appears to be contagious." Thus on October 16.

On the same day Halleck wrote to Grant at Cairo, Illinois, a letter beginning: "You will receive herewith the orders of the President of the United States placing you in command of the Departments of the Ohio, Cumberland and Tennessee."

Thus Lincoln put Grant at the head of all military operations west of the Alleghenies. "It is left optional with you to supersede General G. H. Thomas or not."

After a personal conference at Indianapolis with Stanton, Grant, by a rail route and a final horseback trip of fifty-five miles, arrived at Chattanooga on October 23.

Rosecrans had left on October 20 to report at Cincinnati for further orders. While still at Chattanooga, however, Rosecrans had telegraphed Lincoln an inquiry as to a report of another battle at Bull Run, Virginia, to which Lincoln replied there had been no battle but an "affair" a few miles beyond Manassas Station, the enemy attack repulsed with losses from 400 to 700. To John Hay on October 24 the President said that ever since Chickamauga Rosecrans had been "confused and stunned like a duck hit on the head." While Rosecrans awaited further orders at Cincinnati he spoke as a loyalist to a crowd at the Burnet House one November evening: "I hope there is no disposition among you to question the Government. I do not say to you to stifle your feelings but to await further light. To prevent any misunderstanding, I will state here that since the battle of Chickamauga the President has written me personally to express his satisfaction at what was done." At Cleveland, Ohio, Rosecrans vouched for the fighting stuff of the rank and file, told of the enemy just after Chickamauga shelling a detachment of Union troops. The commanding officer took to his heels. A private leveled his gun at the fleeing officer and brought him to a stop, saying, "I'll be damned if I'll be deserted by my officers."

On the day Lincoln gave Halleck the order to relieve Rosecrans of command, a man arrived at the White House from Chattanooga. A telegram from the President had requested this man to come to Washington and General Thomas had instructed him to start at once. He was a Democrat, a politician who had played the game with loyalty to Douglas for many years, this James B. Steedman, an 1849 California gold-hunter, promoted from colonel to brigadier and now in line for further promotion because of quick thinking and valor at Chickamauga, where he brought reinforcements that helped Thomas save the Union army. Steedman wrote of how he got a warm greeting from Lincoln and then the abrupt question, "General Steedman, what is your opinion of General Rosecrans?"

STEEDMAN (*hesitating*). Mr. President, I would rather not express my opinion of my superior officer.

LINCOLN. It is the man who does not want to express an opinion whose opinion I want. I am besieged on all sides with advice. Every day I get letters from army officers asking me to allow them to come to Washington to impart some valuable knowledge in their possession.

STEEDMAN. Well, Mr. President, you are the Commander-in-Chief of the Army, and if you order me to speak I will do so.

LINCOLN. Then I will order an opinion.

STEEDMAN. Since you command me, Mr. President, I will say General Rosecrans is a splendid man to command a victorious army.

LINCOLN. But what kind of a man is he to command a defeated army?

STEEDMAN. I think there are two or three men in that army who would make a better commander.

LINCOLN. Who besides yourself, General Steedman, is there in that army who would make a better commander?

STEEDMAN. General George H. Thomas.

LINCOLN. I am glad to hear you say so. That is my own opinion exactly. But Mr. Stanton is against him, and it was only yesterday that a powerful New York delegation was here to protest against his appointment because he is from a rebel State and can not be trusted.

STEEDMAN. A man who will leave his own State, his friends, all his associations, to follow the flag of his country, can be trusted in any position to which he may be called.

Thomas was a peculiar instance. Appointed a colonel in April of '61, and with others required to renew his oath of allegiance to the United States Government, Thomas replied to an associate who spoke of the procedure as peculiar, "I don't care; I would just as soon take the oath before each meal during my life if the department saw fit to order it." Thomas was now forty-seven years old, a West Pointer of service in Indian wars and in the Mexican War, an artillery instructor at West Point, a cavalry major in a pet regiment of the then Secretary of War Jefferson Davis. His regiment had included Robert E. Lee, Fitzhugh Lee, Albert Sidney Johnston, Kirby Smith, William J. Hardee, John B. Hood, and others later to go into the top ranks of the Confederate army. A quiet man, deliberate in motion, taking his time in preparations, something cool and massive about him. Prejudice and chicanery had kept him from any quickly given and deserved promotions. A good case was made out by his friends that no promotion had come to him until it could no longer be decently withheld.

At Mill Springs Thomas had shown a flash, at Murfreesboro fire and flint, at Chickamauga granite steadiness and volcanic resistance. It was the flighty Donn Piatt who recorded what was partly true in his notation that Lincoln heard Stanton in behalf of Thomas and Chase in advocacy of Rosecrans, the President saying, "Let the Virginian wait; we will try Rosecrans." Piatt added: "The writer happened to be in the office of the War Secretary when Mr. Stanton returned from the Executive Mansion, bilious with wrath at Secretary Chase's interference and Rosecrans' success. His first words were, 'Well, you have your choice of idiots; now look out for frightful disaster.'"

Slowly in the trampling and grinding of events the men of genius for war were being sifted out, and in this process George Henry Thomas was arriving at his own. That he was a Virginian had been cited against him by those bringing pressure for appointments to the limited list of major commands. Lincoln may or may not have been correctly quoted as having said, "Let the Virginian wait," when the matter arose of appointing Thomas or another to higher rank. It was an idle remark, the like of it not to be found elsewhere in the recorded talk or letters of Lincoln. In the cases of General Winfield Scott and Admiral David Farragut Lincoln was free from prejudice that they were Virginians. Himself Kentucky-born, Lincoln would as soon have put a shading of mistrust into the mention of a Kentuckian as a Virginian; either was from a Border Slave State.

In one letter early in his Kentucky service, Thomas wrote to Halleck, "I went to my duties without a murmur, as I am neither ambitious nor have any political aspirations," which held a clue to much of his shy conduct. A laconic streak underlay the sluggish outside of him. In a council of generals at Murfreesboro, when asked by Rosecrans to protect a proposed retreat, he woke from a nap to say, "This army can't retreat." In a like council at Chickamauga he dozed, and only came out of the doze to mutter repeatedly, "Strengthen the left," almost as though he read in a crystal ball the terrible necessity of the next day, when everything crumbled except himself and the left wing. This brevity functioned again when after a battle he was asked whether the dead should be buried in the order of the States they came from. "No, no," said Old Pap Thomas. "Mix them up. I am tired of State rights."

Now Thomas was joined with Sherman and other tried commanders, with Grant as chief of the West, with forces massed at Chattanooga near the Alabama and Georgia State lines, wedging toward the Deep South as if hoping to cut it in two. Jefferson Davis had come personally from Richmond to confer with his friend Bragg, in command. On the coming grapple at Chattanooga hung the decision whether the Confederates would retake Tennessee and Kentucky, perhaps Vicksburg, and control of the Mississippi. Thus far the Northern wedge had always split deeper into the South, the map of areas occupied by the Union armies month by month showing a wider spread.

In Virginia Meade and Lee came to no grapple. According to William A. Croffut of the *New York Tribune*, when Lincoln and Meade met after the battle of Gettysburg Lincoln said with a quizzical smile, "Do you know, General, what your attitude toward Lee after the Battle of Gettysburg reminded me of?"

"No, Mr. President, what was it?"

"I'll be hanged if I could think of anything but an old woman trying to shoo her geese across the creek."

Since then some 20,000 troops from Meade had been sent to Chattanooga, besides more for a land attack on Charleston; 30,000 from Lee's army had been sent to the Chattanooga scene. And Meade and Lee had maneuvered and countermarched and clashed with minor detachments, the result a standoff. In mid-September the President wrote to Halleck an opinion that Meade, having rested his army, should move on Lee. From Meade came word: "I can get a battle out of Lee under very disadvan-

Left-hand column: James Longstreet, John Singleton Mosby, Joseph Emerson Brown, John Cabell Breckinridge. Center column: Pierre Gustave Toutant Beauregard, Braxton Bragg, Nathan Bedford Forrest, Colonel and Mrs. John Hunt Morgan. Right-hand column: James Ewell Brown ("Jeb") Stuart, Ambrose Powell Hill, Daniel Harvey Hill, James Alexander Seddon

A GALLERY OF CONFEDERATE LEADERS

From the Meserve collection

Lincoln, two of the five photographs made by Gardner November 15, '63
From the Meserve collection

Lincoln, two of the four photographs made by Brady in sittings in early '64
From the U. S. Army Signal Corps

tageous circumstances, which may render his inferior force my superior, and which is not likely to result in any very decided advantage, even in case I should be victorious. In this view I am reluctant to run the risks without the positive sanction of the Government."

Stanton sent this dispatch to the President "for reflection overnight." The President did reflect, wrote to Halleck a letter comparing the forces of Meade and Lee. "For a battle, then, General Meade has three men to General Lee's two. Yet, it having been determined that choosing ground and standing on the defensive gives so great advantage that the three cannot safely attack the two, the three are left simply standing on the defensive also. If the enemy's 60,000 are sufficient to keep our 90,000 away from Richmond, why, by the same rule, may not 40,000 of ours keep their 60,000 away from Washington, leaving us 50,000 to put to some other use?" Welles talked with the President, asked what Meade was doing with his immense army against "Lee's skeleton and depleted show in front," noting that Lincoln replied that he could not learn that Meade was doing anything or wanted to do anything. "It is," he said, "the same old story of this Army of the Potomac. Imbecility, inefficiency—don't want to *do*—is defending the Capital." He gave Welles the figures showing that 50,000 men could be detached from the Army of the Potomac for duty elsewhere, leaving 40,000 to defend the capital, and groaned, "Oh, it is terrible, terrible, this weakness, this indifference of our Potomac generals, with such armies of good and brave men."

Welles said Meade was faithful but could not originate—why not get rid of him? The President: "What can I do with such generals as we have? Who among them is any better than Meade? To sweep away the whole of them from chief command and substitute a new man would cause a shock, and be likely to lead to combinations and troubles greater than we now have. I see all the difficulties as you do. They oppress me." Welles then noted their talk of generals and admirals in a paragraph:

"Alluding to the failures of the generals, particularly those who commanded the armies of the Potomac, he thought the selections, if unfortunate, were not imputable entirely to him. The Generals-in-Chief and the Secretary of War should, he said, know the men better than he. The Navy Department had given him no trouble in this respect; perhaps naval training was more uniform and equal than the military. I thought not; said we had our troubles, but they were less conspicuous. In the selection of Farragut and Porter, I thought we had been particularly fortunate; and Du Pont had merit also. He thought there had not been, take it all in all, so good an appointment in either branch of the service as Farragut, whom he did not know or recollect when I gave him command. Du Pont he classed, and has often, with McClellan, but Porter he considers a busy schemer, bold but not of high qualities as a chief. For some reason he has not so high an appreciation of Porter as I think he deserves, but no man surpasses Farragut in his estimation."

Meade on September 24 was writing his wife: "I was summoned to

Washington and informed that the President considered my army too large for a merely defensive one, and proposed to take a portion of it away. I objected and reasoned against this, and left Washington with the belief that the President was satisfied. I had just arranged the programme for a movement, and was about issuing the orders, when orders came from Washington, taking troops away. Of this I do not complain. The President is the best judge of where the armies can be best employed, and if he chooses to place this army strictly on the defensive, I have no right to object or murmur. I was in Washington from 11 P.M. Tuesday till 1 P.M. Wednesday; saw no one but the President, Mr. Stanton and General Halleck; was treated very courteously by all. I told the President and General Halleck that if they thought I was too slow or prudent, to put someone else in my place. Halleck smiled very significantly, and said he had no doubt I would be rejoiced to be relieved, but there was no such good luck for me. . . . There still existed a feverish anxiety that I should try and do something."

Thus Meade was keeping patience and holding his temper under conditions much like those under which McClellan had let himself become a grumbler. The days went by with little action. Lee once moved against Meade with a plan for a surprise attack in the rear. Meade guessed the plan, and when Lee came up was ready and waiting where Lee would have to cross the Rappahannock and fight man for man. To staff men Meade said, "If Bob Lee will go into those fields there and fight me, man for man, I will do it."

One staff man wrote that though the newspapers were mentioning "the fine autumn weather" for fighting, Meade was not going to risk another Fredericksburg. Lincoln, however, was willing to take that risk, and on October 16 wrote to Halleck his guess that Lee, overestimating the number of soldiers stripped from Meade for Western duty, might fight in the open. The President made a proposal for Meade to consider, an offer at no time previously made to a general in the field. It read:

"If General Meade can now attack him [Lee] on a field no worse than equal for us, and will do so with all the skill and courage which he, his officers, and men possess, the honor will be his if he succeeds, and the blame may be mine if he fails."

Welles noted on the day this letter was written: "The President . . . read a confidential dispatch to General Meade, urging him not to lose the opportunity to bring on a battle, assuring him that all the honors of a victory should be exclusively his (Meade's), while in case of a defeat he (the President) would take the entire responsibility. This is taking Meade beyond his ability. If the President could tell him how and when to fight, his orders would be faithfully carried out, but the President is overtasking Meade's capability and powers."

The offer of Lincoln to Meade reached the press and was published. Lincoln evidently wished it made known to the public that, as the newspapers said, he had ordered Meade "to pursue after Lee's army, to find the

Major General Halleck

I do not believe Lee can have
'over' sixty thousand effective men. Longstreets corps
would not be sent away, to bring an equal force back
upon the same road; and there is no other
direction for them to have come from. Doubtless, in making this present movement Lee gathered in all
available scraps, and added them to Hills &
Ewells corps; but that is all. And he made
the movement in the belief that _four_ corps
had left Gen. Meade; and Gen. Meades
apparently avoiding a collision with him has
confirmed him in that belief. If Gen. Meade
can now attack. him on a field no more
than equal for us, and will do so with all
the skill and courage, which he, his officers
and men possess; the honor will be his if he
succeeds, and the blame may be mine if he
fails.   Yours truly, A. Lincoln

Lincoln writes to Halleck, for relay to Meade: "I do not believe Lee can have over
sixty thousand effective men. Longstreet's corps would not be sent away [to Tennessee],
to bring an equal force back upon the same road; and there is no other direction for
them to have come from. Doubtless, in making the present movement Lee gathered in
all available scraps, and added them to Hill's and Ewell's corps; but that is all. And he
made the movement in the belief that _four_ corps had left Gen. Meade; and Gen.
Meade's apparently avoiding a collision with him has confirmed him in the belief.
If Gen. Meade can now attack him on a field no more than equal for us, and will do
so with all the skill and courage, which he, his officers and men possess, the honor will
be his if he succeeds, and the blame may be mine if he fails." From the Barrett collection.

enemy, and to fight him wherever found; and that he [the President] would be responsible for Meade's defeat, if he should be defeated." It seemed as though the President took this step so there could be no possible mistake in the public mind on the point that he wanted fighting, had ordered fighting, and would blame no commander if there was fighting that brought more useless slaughter.

A hostile and defeatist press poured its scorn on "this silly and most unmilitary order," as the *Chicago Times* termed it in an article headed "Exposure of Lincoln's Folly." An armchair strategist at Washington wrote in the *Times* that "Old Abe's orders were peremptory" to Meade and therefore "our army has fallen into the trap that General Lee set for it." General Meade had pursued, as ordered, had found the enemy, and "The only question now is, will he obey the remainder of Old Abe's order, and 'fight the enemy,' or will he not?" With no proof, as mere assertion, as an invention serving his own ends, this writer gave his readers the false information, "Lee's army is at least 20,000 stronger than ours." And with that as a beginning, it was reasoned: "The defeat of our army will place Washington within General Lee's power. If Meade does not fight, he will disobey Old Abe's positive order—he will retreat to Washington; but, if he gets here before General Lee's army, he will have saved both his army and the capital. But he can only save either his army or the capital by downright disobedience to Lincoln's order. Well may the people blush with shame at having such a President."

Thus the *Chicago Times* used its freedom to print the news and the facts by publishing false statements meant to work harm. It must have particularly enjoyed one Lincoln anecdote, giving its readers repeated versions: "The President said to a gentleman who had asked for the interposition of his influence with the War Department, 'Can't do it, sir; can't do it. I don't amount to pig tracks in the War Department.' "

Following the extraordinary order to Meade, from various quarters came unexpected approval of the President. The antislavery New York *Independent*, for instance, often flung the harpoon of rebuke at Lincoln. Now its Washington correspondent saw him opposing "his advisers who are willing to see all our great armies go at once into winter quarters," the President being "a clearer-headed man than his enemies will admit." In pressing his generals to seek immediate battles and victories, in his cool management of military affairs when his chosen generals had lost their control, the President had "what they call in the West 'horse sense.' " The volunteers the President had called for would come sooner to join winning armies.

Victory was also needed, wrote the *Independent* man at Washington, to punish the gold speculators and "send gold from 154 back to 130." The early trust of the President in professional soldiers, advisers trained for war, was natural. The President had a right to shrink from telling them how to conduct campaigns and when to fight battles. Now he was not so shrinking. He had learned much. "That many movements, which resulted in disaster to the Union cause, were really disapproved by his judgment, is now undeniable. At the same time, it is equally undeniable that some of the most brilliant successes which have marked the history of the war, are the results of movements traceable directly to his clear and earnest mind, or which have been greatly aided by his supervising hand." When mistaken in judgment of a military plan, as with Grant at Vicksburg, he publicly admitted his error. "But even the success of a different plan does not condemn that which he had devised." For such reasons, considered the *Independent* writer, "President Lincoln seems to have been raised up especially for the present emergency in our national affairs. Despising the arts of the professional politician and demagogue, he seeks to attain important national ends with an honesty and directness of purpose which confounds the diplomatists and hangers-on upon courts of the Old World."

This appraisal of Lincoln's military ability or genius had enough keen and timely importance to be worth reprinting, so several editors decided. The *State Journal* of Springfield, Illinois, gave its readers these cool judgments that the Sangamon County youth who had gone forth to the Black Hawk War as a high private in the rear rank now was taking stature among the world's greatest commanders. Definitely in this period toward the close of '63, many an impartial observer dropped former hesitations and fully conceded that there was more plan and less muddling, more of sharp design and less of aimless blundering, than they had at first believed in Lincoln's direction of military events on a stupendous scale. His one head, it was now more often granted, held more of the basic essential details of the war, shaped more of the major and minor objectives, than any other head. That he had the stuff of a truly great commander of men—this was now less often denied. His patient and delicate course in dealing with General Meade in the fall months of '63 was based on many past lessons in reality. His curious offer to Meade was followed by an effort toward fighting, Meade writing to his wife of what happened, in probably about the same words as he later personally reported it to the President. From Centerville, Virginia, on October 17 he wrote to her: "Lee made a desperate effort to get in my rear, but I succeeded in out-manoeuvring him, and got into position at this place, Centreville, with my back to Washington, and ready for his attack if he had chosen to make it. This is the third day we have been here and he has not come forward; I am trying to find out where he now is. If he is near me I shall attack him, but I fear that, failing in his manoeuvre, he is either going back, or going up into the Valley of the Shenandoah, where I shall have to follow him."

But Lee had again outguessed Meade, as Meade so humbly and frankly confessed to his wife in a note from Warrenton, Virginia, four days later: "Lee has retired across the Rappahannock, after completely destroying the railroad on which I depend for my supplies. His object is to prevent my advance, and in the meantime send more troops to Bragg. This was a deep game, and I am free to admit that in the playing of it he has got the advantage of me."

When Lincoln groaned to Hay or Welles, or to himself alone, over the inaction of the Army of the Potomac, it was not because of any trickery, evasion, or politics of that army's commander. For Meade had not asked command. It had been thrust on him. And always with the gravest courtesy he made it plain to Lincoln, Halleck, and Stanton that if they believed he was "too slow or prudent," as he phrased it, he would willingly fight under someone else. On October 23 he wrote to Mrs. Meade: "Yesterday I received an order to repair to Washington, to see the President. I arrived in Washington at 2 P.M., and expected to leave at 6 P.M., but was detained so late that I remained there all night, and left this morning, early. The President was, as he always is, very considerate and kind. He found no fault with my operations, although it was very evident he was disappointed that I had not got a battle out of Lee. He coincided with me that there was not much to be gained by any farther advance; but General Halleck was very urgent that something should be done, but what that something was he did not define."

A week later the General was writing to Mrs. Meade that in her letter to him she seemed to be very puzzled about what she "misnamed" his retreat. He explained for her, as he later did to the President, that it was "not a retreat, but a withdrawal of the army—manoeuvring to get into a proper position to offer battle, and made to prevent Lee from compelling me to fight at a disadvantage." Lincoln heard such explanations, or excuses, from Meade, and could not fail to be aware of the clear, crystal candor of this honest commander giving the best that was in him and reporting of it:

"Had I been able to ascertain his movements, I would have given him battle the day Warren was attacked; but I was misled by information which induced me to believe he was farther ahead. As it afterwards turned out, I was ahead of him; which was the object I was trying to attain before fighting. It was greatly to my interest to fight, and I was most anxious to do so, but I would not do so with all the advantages on his side, and the certainty that if the battle went against me I could not extricate the army from its perilous position. I don't suppose I shall ever get credit for my motives, except with the army. The soldiers realize the necessity of not letting the enemy have the game in their hands entirely; hence they cheerfully submitted to all the hardships, such as night and forced marches, that I was compelled to impose on them."

Four days later the General tells his wife he understands why there is disappointment about his failure to hit Lee. Halleck had telegraphed him he had "better fight instead of running away," and again gravely and courteously Meade reasoned, "as he did not explain how I could fight to advantage, I paid no attention to the very rough manner in which he expressed his views, except to inform him that, if my judgment was not approved, I ought to be and deserved to be relieved; to which I received no reply beyond a disclaiming of any intention to give offence."

A gentleman and a scholar, Meade was more than a soldier; sometimes he referred to his biographers' neglecting the importance of his work before the war in lighthouse-building and map surveying. It pleased him to hear from a *New York Tribune* man that when a member of Congress was belittling him to Thaddeus Stevens, sneering that Meade was an aristocrat, "Mr. Stevens laughed and said he knew all about my family, and he wished the country had more such aristocrats."

From the Southern side and among his own people, General Robert E. Lee was receiving the same sort of criticism as that heaped on Meade in the North. Like Meade, he was too slow and too prudent, ran many an editorial.

They were both Christian gentlemen, Meade and Lee, reverent and pious, each strict in the observance of Episcopal forms, praying regularly to the same God while they led their hosts seeking to mangle and eviscerate each other. Lincoln thought about this and meditated whether he might some day make note of one phase of it in a state paper.

From the Army of the Potomac, troops had been sent by sea to take Charleston, South Carolina. From month to month the President interfered in no way with naval and land forces trying to capture "the hell-hole of secession," the city more hated by the North than any in the South. In letting out Admiral Du Pont to leave the naval service forever, and in promoting Admiral Dahlgren, Lincoln gave his approval to aggressive tactics at Charleston, whatever the increased cost. During six days in August a fleet of monitors and gunboats bombarded Charleston; an army of 18,000 troops waited while twelve batteries of heavy rifled cannon opened fire at a two-mile distance; in one forty-minute period they dropped 120,000 pounds of projectiles into the defending forts. A storming column of Negro soldiers led by the white Colonel Robert Gould Shaw, of an old and distinguished Boston family, captured Fort Wagner. Shaw, "the blue-eyed child of fortune," crying, "Onward, boys!" fell dead from bullets, and became an enshrined memory and a symbol to the antislavery forces of the North.

Lincoln read the news telegraphed by the commanding general, on August 24: "Fort Sumter is today a shapeless and harmless mass of ruins." Five days later he telegraphed Mrs. Lincoln, summering at Manchester, up in Vermont: "Fort Sumter is *certainly* battered down and utterly useless to the enemy, and it is *believed* here but not entirely certain, that both Sumter and Fort Wagner are occupied by our forces. It is also certain that General Gil[l]more has thrown some shot into the city of Charleston." As later news trickled in it turned out that the much-hated city still serenely held her own. And though Fort Sumter seemed to be a ruin, it kept a garrison. Thirty rowboats of Union troops landed for a surprise attack on the night of September 8, were met and repulsed with a loss of 200 men, four boats, and three flags. In October, however, Gillmore's cannon pounded Fort Sumter into such shape that it was useless to the enemy. From time to time Gillmore tried to shoot away the defenses of the city so that the waiting fleet could enter. After weeks of this he decided he was wasting ammunition, ceased firing. For many months Charleston was let alone.

From cities and towns of the North a steady stream of men and boys in blue moved south, always south, month by month filling gaps in the ranks. The machinery of the draft was working. Among generals it was commented that the substitutes, bounty men, human material pressed into service by the enrolling officers, were not as good soldier stuff as the earlier recruits of the war. Former recruits, volunteers, "enlisted for patriotism and not for money," said the *New South*, published at Port Royal, South Carolina, for readers in the Union Army and Navy. Its Boston correspondent reported sharp practices by substitute brokers and professional enlisters: "Cripples have been passed off as sound, false teeth have been palmed off on credulous examining physicians as of nature's own dentistry. The other day a New Yorker, who will probably be discharged and enlist again, and who is over sixty years of age, was doctored up with rice-water bandages, paints, hair-dye, a four-dollar wig, and some stimulants, so that he could manifest the greatest agility and did not appear of thirty. After the agent had got his five hundred dollars or so, from the City of Concord, N.H., he told the story himself, and bragged that he had sold the wig for within two dollars of what it cost him."

Frauds so shameless and crazy as this were not common. Such cases worried the President less than the many instances brought to him of Federal judges releasing drafted men through habeas-corpus proceedings. He called a Cabinet meeting on September 14 to consider this. He said these judges were "defeating the draft . . . discharging the drafted men rapidly under *habeas corpus*," Welles noting, "He is determined to put a stop to these factious and mischievous proceedings if he has the authority." Seward and Bates had been consulted and had no doubt of the President's authority to defy the Federal judges and, in effect, to tell those judges their Federal court orders to release drafted men were not worth the paper they were written on. Blair was satisfied that the President had the legal power to do this but Blair didn't like the way it was to be done, through "an order from the President directing the provost marshals to disregard the writ [of habeas corpus], or to make return that the person to be discharged was held by authority of the President. . . .

"Mr. Chase feared civil war would be inaugurated if the privilege of habeas corpus was suspended," wrote Welles. "Mr. Usher had doubts and uncertainties." Welles himself had nothing decisive to suggest. Stanton gave no opinion and, believed Welles, had undoubtedly "prompted the proposed action" for overriding obstructive judges and courts.

The Cabinet saw Lincoln this day in a warlike mood, going so far as to say he might have to arrest a few Federal judges and send them down through the Union Army lines into the sheltering arms of their Confederate friends and allies. "The President was very determined," noted Welles, "and intimated that he would not only enforce the law, but if Judge Lowry [Lowrie] and others continued to interfere and interrupt the draft he would send them after Vallandigham. As considerable discussion had taken place, he was prepared to act, though willing to listen to, and, if mistaken, to defer to, others."

Of another Cabinet session the next morning Chase recorded in his diary that the conversation turned on writs of habeas corpus issued from Federal courts. And it came out that two United States court judges in Pennsylvania—Cadwalader at Philadelphia and McCandless at Pittsburgh—had released more drafted men by far than all the State courts put together. Stanton's view was that these two Federal judges had taken a hand in "some very gross proceedings, under color of judicial authority, manifestly intended to interfere with the recruiting and maintenance of the army."

At another Cabinet session the next morning the President read to the Cabinet the same order that he had read to them the day before, only modified, he explained, so as to apply to the Federal as well as the State courts.

"You, Mr. President," said Chase, "have believed that you have the power to suspend the writ of habeas corpus without being authorized by Congress, and in some cases have acted on this belief. After much consideration I have come to the conclusion that your opinion and mine are sanctioned by the Constitution. Whatever doubt there may have been as to your power to suspend the writ, it has been removed by express legislation." Chase then urged that the order the President had read did not in terms suspend the writ, though it might in effect. "It leaves the suspension open to debate, and will lead to serious collisions probably, with the disadvantage on the side of the Federal authority." He urged the President to make the order a proclamation so bold and direct that it would command public confidence if a collision arose with a State governor or judge. The President acted on this suggestion.

Chase had helped and he seemed justified in telling his diary of his surprise that in a matter of such importance no one but himself seemed to have read the congressional act of March 3 of '63 with reference to powers granted the President in the writ of habeas corpus.

On the same day of September 15 was issued the proclamation as finally drafted by Seward. In a solemn vocabulary it was made known by the President of the United States of America that "the privilege of the writ of *habeas corpus* is suspended throughout the United States" and this suspension would continue till modified or revoked by a later proclamation. The syllables of the document would produce a sonorous pronouncement when read by a provost marshal to a judge, in support of the marshal's saying in effect to the judge, "I'm going to take this drafted man away with me and put him in the army and your court can't stop me because I have the United States Army and Navy backing me."

Hay wrote to Nicolay on August 7 of Washington being "dismal now as a defaced tombstone." Part of the dismal air came from the conscription. On Executive Mansion stationery Hay wrote: "The draft fell pretty heavily in our end of town. William Johnston (cullud) was taken while polishing the Executive boots and rasping the Imperial Abolition whisker. Henry Stoddard is a conscript bold. You remember that good-natured shiny-faced darkey who used to be my special favorite a year ago at Willard's. He is gone, *en haut de la spout*. And the gorgeous headwaiter, G. Washington. A clerk in the War Department named Ramsey committed suicide on hearing he was drafted."

While the President in early October was dealing with habeas corpus, with the committee of radicals from Missouri and Kansas, with Burnside in Tennessee, Rosecrans at Chattanooga, and Meade in Virginia, besides many routine matters, Seward took on the work of writing a Thanksgiving proclamation, which the President signed. Welles noted on October 3: "Mr. Seward called early this morning and read me the draft of a proclamation for Thanksgiving. I complimented the paper as very well done, and him for his talent in the preparation of such papers, which pleased him." The paper began with allusion to the year as "filled with the blessings of fruitful fields and healthful skies," its bounties such that "they cannot fail to penetrate and soften the heart which is habitually insensible to the ever-watchful province of almighty God." It pointed to peace preserved with all nations. "Order has been maintained, the laws have been respected and obeyed, and harmony has prevailed everywhere, except in the theater of military conflict; while that theater has been greatly contracted by the advancing armies and navies of the Union." It cited material progress and population increase. "No human counsel hath devised, nor hath any mortal hand worked out these great things. They are the gracious gifts of the most high God, who, while dealing with us in anger for our sins, hath nevertheless remembered mercy."

And over the signature of A. Lincoln came the pronouncement, "I do, therefore, invite my fellow-citizens in every part of the United States, and also those who are at sea and those who are sojourning in foreign lands, to set apart and observe the last Thursday of November next as a day of thanksgiving and praise to our beneficent Father who dwelleth in the heavens."

Though the proclamation had no one Lincolnian twist or turn, millions of readers took it as an expression from Lincoln. David Homer Bates, the telegraph office chief, commented: "This proclamation is remarkable not only as exhibiting the President's implicit reliance on an 'ever-watchful God' but for beauty of phrase and logical belief in an overruling Providence. . . . No ruler of millions, since King David the Psalmist, has clothed great thoughts in sublimer language."

The changed air of expectation that the Union cause would yet win, the shift from the gloom of the first half of '62, made the basis for thanksgiving. With the Gettysburg and Vicksburg victories, one of them ending Confederate hopes of winning by invasion of the North, the other sending the Mississippi "unvexed to the sea," many considered the war at an end or nearly so. Intangible psychic factors played on both sides. The North wondered why the South didn't quit.

The South dug deeper into itself for new motives and began fighting with despair for honor, for a mystic pennant, for a lost cause that could eventually be looked back on as having had a clean death. "The drums that beat for the advance into Pennsylvania seemed to many of us to be beating the funeral march of the dead Confederacy," later wrote General Daniel H. Hill, one of Lee's ablest lieutenants, now in the West with Bragg. "Duty, however, was to be done faithfully and unflinchingly to the last." Hill took notice that after the shallow victory of Chickamauga never again could he see "the *élan* of the Southern soldier, that brilliant dash which had distinguished him." He saw quitters. "The waning fortunes of the Confederacy were developing a vast amount of 'latent unionism' in the breasts of the original secessionists, those fiery zealots who in '61 proclaimed that 'one Southerner could whip three Yankees.' The negroes and the fire-eaters with 'changed hearts' were now most excellent spies."

Both Lee and Davis, after the July defeats, issued appeals to soldiers to come back to the army. Davis offered pardon to officers and men absent without leave who would return in twenty days. Wives, mothers, sisters, daughters of the Confederacy were beseeched by the Richmond head of their Government, who went so far in arithmetic as to say, "If all now absent return to the ranks you will equal in numbers the invaders." In upper North Carolina, when deserters were halted and asked to show their furlough papers, they patted their rifles and said, "This is my furlough." Governor Joseph E. Brown of Georgia wrote in August to Vice-President Stephens: "There seems to have settled upon the minds of our people a sort of feeling of despondency which is stimulated by the constant croaking of a class of speculators who have made money and are preparing to curry favor with Lincoln if he should overrun the country, with the hope of saving their property. These men put the worst face upon every mishap to our arms, and while they are guilty of no act of positive disloyalty they do all in their power to discourage our people."

Thousands of Confederate deserters in the mountains of Alabama fought off cavalry sent to arrest them. The Confederate Bureau of Ordnance asked for the church bells of Georgia to be melted and remolded for war. Southern women sent carpets to quartermasters for soldiers to use as blankets. Many housewives were using corncob ash for raising dough when bread-making. One gold dollar bought ten paper Confederate dollars. The *Richmond Examiner* cried out against five dancing parties advertised in one week in that city: "Does not all go merry as a marriage bell? If the skeleton comes in, put a ball ticket at five dollars into its bony fingers, a masquerade ball costume upon its back of bony links, and send the grim guest into the ball-room to the sound of cotillion music." Senator Herschel Vespasian Johnson of Georgia, who had opposed secession till it was a fact and then had joined up for it, sounded a tragic bugle song of resistance to the Federal authorities: "We cannot yield if we would. The bleaching bones of one hundred thousand soldiers slain in battle would be clothed in tongues of fire to curse the everlasting infamy of the man who whispers yield. God is with us, because He is always with the right."

A Louisiana father, beginning to doubt the Southern orators, was writing his son in the Confederate Army, "This war was got up drunk but they will have to settle it sober."

In a call for 300,000 more troops issued on October 16, 1863, the President at Washington said that the new men were wanted to follow up and clinch the winning streak of Union armies that summer, "to reinforce our victorious armies now in the field, and bring our needful military operations to a prosperous end, thus closing forever the fountains of sedition and civil war." The President had considered issuing it earlier but held it till three days after the October 13 elections in Ohio and Pennsylvania. It might have affected the votes in those States. The document was headed "Call for 300,000 Volunteers," yet it stipulated that quotas would be *required* from the various States. In reality it was another executive order for a draft. Between provost marshals and various State officials, particularly Governor Seymour of New York, there began discussions and quarrels as to methods of drafting, the basis of credits to districts for troops furnished in the past. Newspapers again carried sections of classified advertising calling for substitutes. Two of twelve similar want ads in the *New York Herald* of October 29 read:

> Three hundred and fifty dollars cash in hand paid for substitutes. $350. Call at 74 Cortland St upstairs near West St. Barker and Spencer.

> $425. Substitutes wanted this day, for the country. The highest cash bounty in the city will be paid down. Call early on Captain Flannagan room 22 Tammany Hall, opposite City Hall.

Rhymers again felt the event called them. *Portland* (Maine) *Advertiser* verses, signed "By a Conscript," hit at the Administration's weakest point:

> We're coming, Ancient Abraham, "severial" hundred strong.
> We hadn't no $300, and so we come along;
> We hadn't no rich parients to pony up the tin,
> So we went unto the provost, and there were mustered in.

The war, the draft, habeas-corpus suspension, were denounced at five overflow meetings in and around Cooper Union in New York City on June 3, 1863, at a Peace Convention. "God did not intend that we should succeed in this war," said the convention's address to the public. "Had He intended it He would not have placed in command a Lincoln with such coadjutors as Butler or Burnside." The war must end if liberties were to be preserved. As the address was read to the convention, "the groans and hisses for the President, and the cheers for Vallandigham and peace were specially vigorous," said the *New York Times*. Bartenders in saloons roundabout served patrons with "Jeff Davis cocktails," "Stonewall punches," "Sumter bumpters," "Charleston cobblers." A fiery antiwar speech of the publisher of the *New York Express* was reprinted by the *Charleston Mercury* with the comment "The reader will be struck with the brave and telling speech of Mr. James Brooks, who entitles himself to our admiration."

By his course in dealing with Vallandigham, Lincoln revealed himself "a trifler and demagogue," said the *Detroit Free Press*. Much was made of the London *Times* saying that Englishmen had all come to the conclusion long ago that it was best that her American colonies should be independent, and it was evident "the Federals will one day come to the same conclusion with regard to the Southern States." Daily and weekly newspapers chimed with the *Chicago Times* "Washington correspondence" written in Chicago: "The substance of liberty is already gone. That I, and you, and your readers are not within the four walls of a dungeon today is solely owing to the gracious forbearance of King Abraham the First. It only needs a nod from him to consign the purest patriot in the land to a living death; and there is no power in the land that can deliver him. If we would recover our lost liberties, the present corrupt administration must be hurled from power."

The *Crisis* of October 14 tore its shirt and made the welkin ring with a rhodomontade doggerel which referred to "Columbia's hated tyrant" who waved "his gory scepter" and supported by "rascals, knaves and traitors, vile renegades from God" proceeded "to shackle the Saxon conscript" in the name of Negro freedom:

> What if great Abe in his providence draft six hundred thousand more,
> What! why sing, sing, ye blood-washed saints and let your voices ring,
> All glory to old Abraham your anointed king;
> O Glory! Glory Hallelujah, come up every man,
> And give your life a sacrifice to Abraham, I AM.

Also under the heading "Lincoln to Be Declared Perpetual President," the *Crisis* on October 7 said, "It is now stated that a bill has been prepared and will be placed before the next Congress declaring Lincoln President while the war lasts." The *Cincinnati Enquirer* printed the same, and wailed, "Thus the mad fanatics are plotting against our liberties, and if we do not speak right soon through the ballot-box, the last vestige of our republican government will have been swept away."

This was part of the fast and furious fall campaign in the Buckeye State, where Vallandigham, sojourning at Windsor, Canada, near Detroit and Toledo, was the Democratic candidate for governor. The Copperhead press reprinted a *Richmond Examiner* article giving a supposed White House conversation. One Dr. Hamblin reported Lincoln as saying: "Do you think my term of office closes with these four years? No, sir; there will be a dispute in regard to the electoral vote, and I shall be President another term as God has directed!" The *Crisis* commented that it was generally believed that Lincoln intended "to hang on to the White House four years more, by some means, fair or foul."

The campaign revolved around Lincoln. Ohio mass meetings at which orators excoriated the President, and with metaphors nailed his hide to the barn door, drew thousands of people. Crowds did not number 30,000 and 40,000 as often as the Democratic press claimed, yet the Copperhead clans did gather in tens of thousands. Likewise the Union-party meetings drew tens of thousands. Not since the Lincoln-Douglas debates had the prairie electorate gathered in such numbers and with so high an excitement. Congressman George Julian, the last of several speakers at an Ashtabula County meeting of mostly farmers, was going to quit talking between sunset and near dark, when from a crowd that had stood four hours in a cold drizzle of rain, came the calls, "Go on! . . . Go ahead! . . . we'll hear you; it's past milking time anyhow."

George E. Pugh, candidate for lieutenant governor, shouted from the campaign platform that if his running mate, Vallandigham, were elected governor there would be "fifty thousand fully armed and equipped freemen of Ohio to receive their Governor-elect at the Canadian line and escort him to the State House to see that he takes the oath of office." The Union-party candidate, John Brough, a War Democrat and a rough-and-tumble campaigner, gave notice that Vallandigham's election would start a civil war in Ohio, "for I tell you there is a mighty mass of men in this State whose nerves are strung up like steel, who will never permit this dishonor to be consummated in their native State."

Leslie's Weekly reprinted mockery and persiflage from the *Boston Evening Transcript:* "Secretary Chase has gone to Ohio, to speak and vote, and the Secretary of War reigns and arraigns, smiling grimly in the War Office. The Secretary of State, as usual, is trying to be 'all things to all men' and the Secretary of the Navy continues to be nothing to anybody. The Secretary of the Interior remains noncommittal, and the Postmaster-General is trying to galvanize himself into a candidate for the next Presidency."

On October 13, election day in Ohio and Pennsylvania, Welles called at the White House, and noted of what he heard, "The President says he feels nervous."

The wires that night clicked off news that the Ohio Copperhead ticket had the votes of 185,000 citizens and 2,200 soldiers of Ohio. However, John Brough of the Union party was elected governor by a majority of 61,920 in the citizen vote and 39,179 in the soldier ballots, a total of over 101,000. Just what happened as between Brough and Lincoln on the night of election in Ohio was not clear. A story not correct in details, yet carrying some of the breath of Lincoln's jubilation, was published:

About ten o'clock, a message clicked on the wires in the telegraph office of Cleveland, saying, "Where is John Brough? A. Lincoln." Brough was at hand, and directly the electric voice inquired, "Brough, about what is your majority now?" Brough replied, "Over 30,000." Lincoln requested Brough to remain at the office during the night. A little past midnight the question came again from Lincoln, "Brough, what is your majority by this time?" Brough replied, "Over 50,000." And the question was thus repeated and answered several times, with rapidly increasing majorities, till five o'clock in the morning, when the question came again, "Brough, what is your majority now?"

The latter was able to respond, "Over 100,000." As soon as the words could be flashed back over the wire, there came: "Glory to God in the highest. Ohio has saved the Nation. A. Lincoln."

Pennsylvania returns gave Governor Curtin re-election by a 41,000 majority. A letter from General McClellan endorsing Curtin's opponent had had little effect. Welles on October 14 found Lincoln relieved of the gloom of the day before. "He told me he had more anxiety in regard to the election results of yesterday than he had in 1860 when he was chosen. He could not, he said, have believed four years ago that one genuine American voter would, or could be induced to, vote for such a man as Vallandigham, yet he had been made the candidate of a large party, their representative man, and has received a vote that is a discredit to the country. The President showed a good deal of emotion as he dwelt on this subject, and his regrets were sincere."

Just before the elections in Maryland, Governor Bradford complained of Union troops instructed to man the polls in his State, arrest all "disloyal persons," and unduly control the voting through requirements as to election judges and oaths of allegiance. The President in a final long letter to Governor Bradford said that General Schenck, in charge in Maryland, gave assurance that violence would be used in the forthcoming election at some of the voting places on election day unless his provost guards prevented it, and furthermore at some of the places Union voters would not attend at all, nor try to run a ticket, unless they had protection.

As to who should vote in Maryland, the President cited an example: "General Trimble, captured fighting us at Gettysburg, is, without recanting his treason, a legal voter by the laws of Maryland. Even General Schenck's order admits him to vote, if he recants upon oath. I think that is cheap enough." The right of voting was assured to all loyal men, and in doubt a man's loyalty was fixed by his oath. "Your suggestion that nearly all the candidates are loyal, I do not think quite meets the case. In this struggle for the nation's life, I cannot so confidently rely on those whose elections may have depended upon disloyal votes. Such men, when elected, may prove true; but such votes are given them in the expectation that they will prove false."

Having rebuked the Governor and stood by his man Schenck, the President revoked the first and most important of three propositions in a general order issued by Schenck, "not that it is wrong in principle, but because the military, being of necessity exclusive judges as to who shall be arrested, the provision is too liable to abuse." The President substituted his own order that the military should prevent all disturbance and violence at the polls by any person whomsoever. Much public squabbling went on between Bradford and Schenck as to whether the order meant anything very different since changed by the President. At the election the Governor's party, Conservative Union, was sunk with a vote of 15,984 as against 36,360 for the candidates of the Unconditional Union or Emancipation party. Four on the latter ticket were among the five new Congressmen elected, and the Emancipationists won a majority in both houses of the legislature.

In the Border Slave States of Delaware and Kentucky the Union party also won, while in Missouri the Union Emancipationist radicals swept into so many legislative seats that the two United States Senatorships were divided between Union-party factions, one to B. Gratz Brown, a leading radical, the other to John B. Henderson, a conservative.

Lincoln was pleased. The event fitted the turmoil. He sent a telegram on November 13 to friends at Jefferson City, Missouri: "Yours saying Brown and Henderson are elected senators is received. I understand this is one and one. If so it is knocking heads together to some purpose."

In all the Northern States except New Jersey, the Union-party ticket swept the field. The summer victories, the policies of the President and his appeals, had been factors, while many other causes had been in play toward political ends. A Chicago newspaper exulted: "Everywhere it has been a slaughter of Copperheads. Springfield, Ill., went Union by 138, a gain of 440 since 1862." In the State House at Springfield sat Governor Dick Yates, who when lit up was a blunt and familiar talker. In the campaign just closed he had made a speech to a Methodist conference at Springfield and was quoted: "I do not endorse everything Old Abe has done. But he has done mighty well generally. He has a backbone. But it is not quite stiff enough for him. I want to deal rigidly with the rebels. I want to see them eternally damned. [Cheers.] Not scripturally but politically damned. [Great cheering.] I have visited Old Abe and urged him to use more radical measures and he has said to me, 'Never mind, Dick, it will be all right yet. Hold still and see the salvation of the Lord!' [Loud and prolonged cheering, stamping of feet, etc.]" The speech had something, and was argued about in the tall-grass weeklies, even the *New York Herald* saying that immense applause from the people had greeted "the above Cromwellian phrase."

CHAPTER 44

LINCOLN SPEAKS AT GETTYSBURG

A PRINTED invitation came to Lincoln's hands notifying him that on Thursday, November 19, 1863, exercises would be held for the dedication of a National Soldiers' Cemetery at Gettysburg. The same circular invitation had been mailed to Senators, Congressmen, the governors of Northern States, members of the Cabinet, by the commission of Pennsylvanians who had organized a corporation through which Maine, New Hampshire, Vermont, Massachusetts, Rhode Island, Maryland, Connecticut, New York, New Jersey, Pennsylvania, Delaware, West Virginia, Ohio, Indiana, Illinois,

Michigan, Wisconsin, and Minnesota were to share the cost of a decent burying-ground for the dust and bones of the Union and Confederate dead.

In the helpless onrush of the war, it was known, too many of the fallen had lain as neglected cadavers rotting in the open fields or thrust into so shallow a resting-place that a common farm plow caught in their bones. Now by order of Governor Curtin of Pennsylvania seventeen acres had been purchased on Cemetery Hill, where the Union center stood its colors on the second and third of July, and plots of soil had been allotted each State for its graves.

The sacred and delicate duties of orator of the day had fallen on Edward Everett. An eminent cultural figure, perhaps foremost of all distinguished American classical orators, he was born in 1794, had been United States Senator, Governor of Massachusetts, member of Congress, Secretary of State under Fillmore, Minister to Great Britain, Phi Beta Kappa poet at Harvard, professor of Greek at Harvard, president of Harvard. His reputation as a public speaker began in the Brattle Street Unitarian Church of Boston. Two volumes of his orations published in 1850 held eighty-one addresses, two more volumes issued in 1859 collected one hundred and five speeches. His lecture on Washington, delivered a hundred and twenty-two times in three years, had in 1859 brought a fund of $58,000, which he gave to the purchase and maintenance of Mount Vernon as a permanent shrine. Other Everett lectures had realized more than $90,000 for charity causes. His wife was Charlotte Gray Brooks, daughter of Peter Chardon Brooks, first of American marine and life-insurance millionaires. Serene stars had watched over their home life and children until tragedy crept in, and Edward Everett's wife was sent to a private retreat, incurably insane. A life-long friendship took root between him and her father; they shared a sorrow; when Peter Brooks died in 1849 Everett wrote a eulogistic biography. No ordinary trafficker in politics, Everett had in 1860 run for Vice-President on the Bell-Everett ticket of the Constitutional Union party, receiving the electoral votes of Virginia, Kentucky, and Tennessee.

The Union of States was a holy concept to Everett, and the slavery issue secondary, though when president of Harvard from 1846 to 1849 he refused to draw the color line, saying in the case of a Negro applicant, Beverly Williams, that admission to Harvard College depended on examinations. "If this boy passes the examinations, he will be admitted; and if the white students choose to withdraw, all the income of the College will be devoted to his education." Not often was he so provocative.

On the basis of what Everett had heard about Lincoln he wrote in his journal shortly before the inauguration in '61 that the incoming President was "evidently a person of very inferior cast of character, wholly unequal to the crisis." Then on meeting the new President he recorded that he found him of better stuff than he had expected. As a strict worshiper of the Constitution and the Union he was drawn toward Lincoln's moderate slavery policy, writing to critics after the Administration had lost in the '62 fall elections, "It is my purpose to support the President to the best of my ability." Speaking publicly as a man of no party, and as the leading founder of the Mount Vernon memorial to George Washington, he trusted he would offend no candid opponent by saying that the main objection against Mr. Lincoln, "that personally he lacks fixedness of purpose," might on precisely the same grounds be brought against George Washington and his Administration. The President's "intellectual capacity" had been proved in his debates with Douglas. "He is one of the most laborious and indefatigable men in the country," said Everett, "and that he has been able to sustain himself under as great a load of care as was ever laid upon the head or the heart of a living man is in no small degree owing to the fact that the vindictive and angry passions form no part of his nature and that a kindly and playful spirit mingles its sweetness with the austere cup of public duty."

In September of '62 Lincoln wrote a note of introduction for Everett's use on a trip to Europe, saying Everett's visit, because of his reputation, was "sure to attract notice, and may be misconstrued." Therefore the President saw fit to say that Everett "bears no mission from this government, and yet no gentleman is better able to correct misunderstandings in the minds of foreigners in regard to American affairs." With a pleasant salutation, Lincoln ended this note: "While I commend him to the consideration of those whom he may meet, I am quite conscious that he could better introduce me than I him in Europe."

Serene, suave, handsomely venerable in his sixty-ninth year, a prominent specimen of Northern upper-class distinction, Everett was a natural choice of the Pennsylvania commissioners, who sought an orator for a solemn national occasion. When in September they notified him that the date of the occasion would be October 23, he replied that he would need more time for preparation, and the dedication was postponed till November 19.

Lincoln meanwhile, in reply to the printed circular invitation, sent word to the commissioners that he would be present at the ceremonies. This made it necessary for the commissioners to consider whether the President should be asked to deliver an address when present. Clark E. Carr of Galesburg, Illinois, representing his State on the Board of Commissioners, noted that the decision of the Board to invite Lincoln to speak was an afterthought. "The question was raised as to his ability to speak upon such a grave and solemn occasion. . . . Besides, it was said that, with his important duties and responsibilities, he could not possibly have the leisure to prepare an address. . . . In answer . . . it was urged that he himself, better than any one else, could determine as to these questions, and that, if he were invited to speak, he was sure to do what, under the circumstances, would be right and proper."

And so on November 2 David Wills of Gettysburg, as the special agent of Governor Curtin and also acting for the several States, by letter informed Lincoln that the several States having soldiers in the Army of the Potomac who were killed, or had since died at hospitals in the vicinity, had procured grounds for a cemetery and proper burial of their dead. "These grounds will be consecrated and set apart to this sacred purpose by appropriate ceremonies on Thursday, the 19th instant. I am authorized by the Governors of the various States to invite you to be present and participate in these ceremonies, which will doubtless be very imposing and solemnly impressive. It is the desire that after the oration, you, as Chief Executive of the nation, formally set apart these grounds to their sacred use by a few appropriate remarks."

Mr. Wills proceeded farther as to the solemnity of the occasion, and when Lincoln had finished reading the letter he understood definitely that the event called for no humor and that a long speech was not expected from him. "The invitation," wrote Clark E. Carr, "was not settled upon and sent to Mr. Lincoln until the second of November, more than six weeks after Mr. Everett had been invited to speak, and but little more than two weeks before the exercises were held."

On the second Sunday before the Gettysburg ceremonies were to take place Lincoln went to the studio of the photographer Gardner for a long-delayed sitting. Noah Brooks walked with him, and he carefully explained to Brooks that he could not go to the photographer on any other day without interfering with the public business and the photographer's business, to say nothing of his liability to be hindered en route by curiosity-seekers "and other seekers." On the White House stairs Lincoln had paused, turned, walked back to his office, and rejoined Brooks with a long envelope in his hand, an advance copy of Edward Everett's address to be delivered at the Gettysburg dedication. It was thoughtful of Everett to take care they should not cover the same ground in their speeches, he remarked to Brooks, who exclaimed over the length of the Everett address, covering nearly two sides of a one-page supplement of a Boston newspaper. Lincoln quoted a line he said he had read somewhere from Daniel Webster: "Solid men of Boston, make no long orations." There was no danger that he should get upon the lines of Mr. Everett's oration, he told Brooks, for what he had ready to say was very short, or as Brooks recalled his emphasis, "short, short, short." He had hoped to read the Everett address between sittings, but the photographer worked fast, Lincoln got interested in talk, and did not open the advance sheets while at Gardner's. In the photograph which Lincoln later gave to Brooks an envelope lay next to Lincoln's right arm resting on a table. In one other photograph made by Gardner that Sunday the envelope was still on the table. The chief difference between the two pictures was that in one Lincoln had his knees crossed and in the other the ankles.

Lamon noted that Lincoln wrote part of his intended Gettysburg address at Washington, covered a sheet of foolscap paper with a memorandum of it, and before taking it out of his hat and reading it to Lamon he said that it was not at all satisfactory to him, that he was afraid he would not do himself credit nor come up to public expectation. He had been too busy to give it the time he would like to.

The armies of Meade and Grant required attention. And there were such unforeseen affairs as the marriage of Kate Chase, daughter of the Secretary of the Treasury, at the most brilliant wedding the new Northern regime had as yet put on in Washington. The bridegroom was Governor William Sprague of Rhode Island, handsome of figure, an heir of wealth, iron and textile manufacturer, railroad and bank president, artillery officer with a record of a horse shot from under him at Bull Run, United States Senator by election in the spring of '63. He was thirty-three years old, had paid $11,000 for one of his string of horses, and his bride of twenty-eight had beauty plus wit and a gift for politics. A wealthy and powerful force in New England business and politics was being allied to the Chase family; it was talked of with reference to the hopes of the Secretary of the Treasury that he might be nominated for President in '64. The wedding at the Chase residence was an affair of which it was said that everybody who was anybody was there. Lincoln, attending alone, and bringing a dainty fan as a present for the bride, probably went because that was better than to let talk run as to why he did not go. He did not stay long. "The President came for a few minutes," wrote John Hay. He may have noticed, as did Hay, that Kate looked "tired out and languid" at the close of the evening, "when I went to the bridal chamber to say good-night. She had lost all her old severity and stiffness of manner, & seemed to think she had *arrived*."

The whirl of dust raised by the bridal barouche, and its escort that saw them off at the railroad depot—this had settled—but endless small talk went on, wrote Noah Brooks. "Who was there and who was not there; how the bride looked in her white velvet dress, real point lace veil and orange flowers; how the President went in solitary state and a white cravat and things; how Mrs. Lincoln did not go because she is yet in black wear and had an opportune chill betimes; how the President stayed two hours and a half 'to take the cuss off' of the meagerness of the Presidential party; how the bride wore a 'tiara' of pearls and diamonds, the like of which was never seen in America since the days of the Aztec 'barbaric pearl and gold'; how Secretary Chase was the first to kiss the newly made wife and say 'God bless you'; how the victuals and drink were lavish; how the newspapers were snubbed, having only curbstone tickets—except the editor of a New York horse paper—and how the Bohemians revenged themselves by refusing to puff the wedding—lo! all of these things are good for Washington gossip, and the National Village is yet agitated."

The gifts to bride and groom, valued at $100,000, "broke the record for all recent American weddings," said newspapers. The presents included ten boxes of Lake Erie Island grapes from Jay Cooke. To Cooke, Secretary Chase had months before written that his daughter and the Rhode Island financier would be married in the autumn "if they both live and don't change their minds." Some recalled that the groom's grandfather had introduced into America the art of color-printing on cloth and had handed on to his heirs what became in reputation the largest print-color mills in the world. Others had heard of the groom as a hard drinker and a man of set ways who might not, after the honeymoon, easily adapt himself to the equally set ways of Kate Chase. Not often did a wedding have so many morsels for the gossips to pick over.

And social functions aside, there were such matters as Thurlow Weed's calling on the President and outlining a plan to end the war more speedily, a plan that Weed said Stanton approved, though Seward was silent on it. Lincoln asked Weed to put it in writing. In that form it proposed that: (1) at the first military success the President should proclaim pardon and amnesty to all who had been making war on the Government; (2) during a 90-day armistice travel should be free and protected North and South; (3) all former Confederates during this armistice returning to Union allegiance should be restored to former rights; (4) at the end of the armistice the President should proclaim that as the war went on for the Union in the future "all territory, whether farms, villages, or cities, shall be partitioned equitably between and among the officers and soldiers by whom it shall be conquered."

So extreme and definite a plan coming from the New York past master of politics and journalism was something to think about, particularly when he added in a letter to Lincoln that before leaving New York he had held a long conversation about it with Dean Richmond, a Democrat and a railway millionaire who had consolidated branch lines into the New York Central trunk road. "Mr. Richmond authorized me to say to you that, in his opinion, this plan, fully and fairly carried out, would make the North a unit in support of the war, that it would immediately give us as many good soldiers as the government wanted, and that the Rebellion would be crushed out within six months after the expiration of the armistice." Weed received an impression the President considered the plan practicable and noted: "Just before he left Washington to deliver the address at Gettysburg he characterized the plan as 'water-tight.' "

Lincoln was examining every current of thought he could get at in the minds of men that gave the slightest hope of engineering a practical course for the Government to steer. Certainly he would have preferred to find this Weed plan watertight rather than leaky and waterlogged. For Weed was his skilled hand as a manipulator of Republican-party machinery in New York, had been no stickler for partisanship. He had joined with Lincoln in the viewpoint that the Republican party alone could not win the war. The door should be open and a ready welcome be extended to all War Democrats. The Union-Republican party in New York had that year overwhelmed an Abolition-Republican ticket. Perhaps the name "Republican" should be dropped and the prowar party of the North designated as the Union party till the war was over. The War Democrats should have the Administration favors rather than the Republican radicals who were lukewarm or hostile to Lincoln. Such counsels from Weed, Lincoln could not be deaf to.

When Weed for a time dropped out of the habit of calling at the White House or of writing to the President, Lincoln in October had written him that he feared somehow he had given a degree of pain to Weed, whereas "I have never entertained an unkind feeling or a disparaging thought toward you; and if I have said or done anything which has been construed into such unkindness or disparagement, it has been misconstrued. I am sure if we could meet we would not part with any unpleasant impression on either side." And Weed's answer had been a personal call and the submission of a drastic, hazardous plan to end the war. It was one of the many interruptions that made sure the Gettysburg address would be, as Lincoln told Brooks, "short, short, short."

Two men, in the weeks just before the Gettysburg ceremonies, had worked on Lincoln, doing their best to make him see himself as a world spokesman of democracy, popular government, the mass of people as opposed to aristocrats, classes, and special interests. John Murray Forbes, having read Lincoln's lively stump-speech letter to the Springfield, Illinois, mass meeting, wrote to Sumner on September 3, "I delight in the President's plain letter to plain people!" Forbes followed this five days later with a letter which Sumner carried to the White House and handed to Lincoln. It began with convincingly phrased praise of the Springfield letter, and proceeded into the unusual question: "Will you permit a suggestion from one who has nothing to ask for himself: one who would accept no office, and who seeks only to do his duty in the most private way possible?" With such an opening it could hardly be doubted that Lincoln read on into the next paragraphs—and read them more than once.

An aristocracy ruled the South and controlled it for war, believed Forbes, pointing to "the aristocratic class who own twenty negroes and upwards" as numbering "about 28,000 persons, which is about the 178th part of 5,000,000" whites. So Forbes urged, "Let the people North and South see this line clearly defined between the people and the aristocrats, and the war will be over!"

Forbes would have the President know that people at a distance had seen this issue clearer than those in the midst of it. "Our friends abroad see it. John Bright and his glorious band of English republicans see that we are fighting for democracy: or (to get rid of the technical name) for liberal institutions. The democrats and the liberals of the Old World are as much and as heartily with us as any supporters we have on this side. Our enemies, too, see it in the same light. The aristocrats and the despots of the Old World see that our quarrel is that of the people against an aristocracy. If our people of the North can be made to see this truth, the rebellion will be crushed for want of Northern support, which it has had from the wolves under the sheep's garments of sham democracy, who have misled large bodies of unthinking and ignorant but generally honest Northern men."

After military successes, believed Forbes, the mass of the Southern people could be made to see this issue, "and then reconstruction becomes easy and permanent." And how could the plain people, North and South, be convinced of it in the shortest time? "Bonaparte, when under the republic, fighting despots of Europe, did as much by his bulletins as he did by his bayonets: the two went on together promising democratic institutions to the populations whose leaders he was making war upon."

"You," Forbes urged the President, "have the same opportunity, and greater; for you have enemies North and South, reading our language, whom you can teach. My suggestion, then, is that you should seize an early opportunity and any subsequent chance, to teach your great audience of plain people that the war is not the North against the South, but the people against the aristocrats."

This same idea Forbes wrote to William Evans, an English liberal, who was to call on the President. "I wish you could make him see and feel," said Forbes, "that you and Bright and others represent the democratic element in Great Britain, and that you look upon him as fighting the battle of democracy for all the world! I wish our people understood this as well as yours do!" And William Evans came away from his visit with Lincoln to write Forbes on November 3: "Your suggestions were duly attended to. . . . I took advantage of the hospitality afforded me to explain my views, which were in accordance with your own. . . . I did not hesitate to tell the President that had it not been for the anti-slavery policy of his government there would have been much greater difficulty in preventing a recognition of the Southern States."

Thus while Lincoln shaped his speech to be made at Gettysburg he did not lack specific advice that when the chance came he should stand up and be a world spokesman for those who called themselves democrats and liberals as opposed to what they termed "the aristocratic classes."

Some newspapers now had it that the President was going to make a stump speech over the graves of the Gettysburg dead as a political play. Talk ran in Washington that by attending Governor Curtin's "show" the President would strengthen himself with the Curtin faction without alienating the opposing Cameron clique.

Various definite motives besides vague intuitions may have guided Lincoln in his decision to attend and speak even though half his Cabinet had sent formal declinations in response to the printed circular invitations they had all received. Though the Gettysburg dedication was to be under interstate auspices, it had tremendous national significance for Lincoln because on the platform would be the State governors whose co-operation with him was of vast importance. Also a slander and a libel had been widely mouthed and printed that on his visit to the battlefield of Antietam nearly a year before he had laughed obscenely at his own funny stories and called on Lamon to sing a cheap comic song. Perhaps he might go to Gettysburg and let it be seen how he demeaned himself on a somber landscape of sacrifice.

His personal touch with Gettysburg, by telegraph, mail, courier, and by a throng of associations, made it a place of great realities to him. Just after the battle there, a woman had come to his office, the doorman saying she had been "crying and taking on" for several days trying to see the President. Her husband and three sons were in the army. On part of her husband's pay she had lived for a time, till money from him stopped coming. She was hard put to scrape a living and needed one of her boys to help.

The President listened to her, standing at a fireplace, hands behind him, head bowed, motionless. The woman finished her plea for one of her three sons in the army. He spoke. Slowly and almost as if talking to himself alone the words came and only those words:

"I have two, and you have none."

He crossed the room, wrote an order for the military discharge of one of her sons. On a special sheet of paper he wrote full and detailed instructions where to go and what to say in order to get her boy back.

In a few days the doorman told the President that the same woman was again on hand crying and taking on. "Let her in," was the word. She had found doors opening to her and officials ready to help on seeing the President's written words she carried. She had located her boy, camp, regiment, company. She had found him, yes, wounded at Gettysburg, dying in a hospital, and had followed him to the grave. And, she begged, would the President now give her the next one of her boys?

As before he stood at the fireplace, hands behind him, head bent low, motionless. Slowly and almost as if talking to himself alone the words came and as before only those words:

"I have two, and you have none."

He crossed the room to his desk and began writing. As though nothing else was to do she followed, stood by his chair as he wrote, put her hand on the President's head, smoothed his thick and disorderly hair with motherly fingers. He signed an order giving her the next of her boys, stood up, put the priceless paper in her hand as he choked out the one word, "There!" and with long quick steps was gone from the room with her sobs and cries of thanks in his ears.

Thus the Kentuckian, James Speed, gathered the incident and told it. By many strange ways Gettysburg was to Lincoln a fact in crimson mist.

At the Cabinet meeting of November 17 the President requested the Secretary of War to arrange for a special train to Gettysburg. Stanton agreed, but excused himself from going, as did Welles too. Secretaries Seward, Usher, and Blair agreed to go. To Chase, who was not present, Lincoln wrote a note as though Chase might go along too, but Chase replied he had important public business. General Meade had written that duty held him with the Army of the Potomac. To Stanton later in the afternoon Lincoln wrote that an early morning train on November 19 would be at the best "a mere breathless running of the gauntlet," and plans were changed for a train to start at noon of the next day, November 18.

Thaddeus Stevens, Republican floor leader in the House, was asked if he were going to Gettysburg and said No. He was a Pennsylvania man, had at one time practiced law in Gettysburg and was then its foremost real-estate taxpayer. There might have been sentimental and practical reasons why he should go. He believed and said, however, in November of '63 that Lincoln was a "dead card" in the political deck. He favored Chase as a more thoroughgoing antislavery man for the next President of the United States, and when he heard that Lincoln and Seward were going to the dedicatory exercises, but not Chase, he clipped his words, "The dead going to eulogize the dead." Dining with the painter Frank B. Carpenter, Chase confided that Lincoln at a meeting of his Cabinet members had told them of Thaddeus Stevens's being asked by someone where the President and Seward were going.

"To Gettysburg," replied Stevens.

"But where are Stanton and Chase?"

"At home, at work; let the dead bury the dead."

William Saunders, landscape gardener and superintendent of grounds in the Department of Agriculture, called at Lincoln's request on the evening of November 17 with the plan of the cemetery he had designed. "I spread the plan on his office table," said Saunders. "He took much interest in it, asked about its surroundings, about Culp's Hill, Round Top, and seemed familiar with the place though he had never been there. He was much pleased with the method of the graves [with uniform headstones and the dead grouped by States], said it differed from the ordinary cemetery, and, after I had explained the reasons, said it was an admirable and befitting arrangement. He asked me if I was going up to Gettysburg tomorrow. I told him I intended to be there and take up the plan. He replied, 'Well, I may see you on the train.'"

Also on the day of November 17 the President issued a little proclamation fixing a township line "within the City of Omaha" as the starting-point for the Union Pacific Railway. Congress had made it his duty to do this. He had called General Dodge from Corinth, Mississippi, and the two men met in Washington who had last shaken hands at Council Bluffs, Iowa, and stood on a high tall bluff looking west. "Dodge, I want you to help me decide the commencement point of the Union Pacific railroad." He told Dodge that Peter A. Dey, in charge of surveys of the railroad, had been at the White House; it seemed that the survey could not begin till an initial point was fixed. Lincoln told Dodge the Government had its hands full, but he was willing to help private enterprises. Dodge spoke for directors of the road in criticizing the wording of the act of Congress, said no one was going to buy second-mortgage bonds at any price, and that capitalists would not invest in the railroad unless the company's bonds became a prior lien to the subsidy bonds of the Government. "Lincoln intimated," said Dodge, "that he was willing to advocate a change in the law so that the government should take the second mortgage and the promoters of the road the first." They took out maps and discussed the various proposed lines for the road. Points from Sioux City to Kansas City were competing for the western terminus. But in the proclamation now issued Lincoln was holding to the same view he had voiced to Dodge on the tall bluff overlooking the Missouri River opposite Omaha as to the starting-point of the Union Pacific.

The Gettysburg speech was shaping at the same time that Lincoln was preparing his annual message to Congress, assembling it in less than three weeks. In that message he would point to "actual commencement of work upon the Pacific railroad," his own act of fixing an initial point being the most tangible part of the commencement.

When Lincoln boarded the train for Gettysburg on November 18, his best chum in the world, Tad, lay sick abed and the doctors not sure what ailed him. The mother still remembered Willie and was hysterical about Tad. But the President felt imperative duty called him to Gettysburg.

Provost Marshal General James B. Fry as a War Department escort came to the White House, but the President was late in getting into the carriage for the drive to the station. They had no time to lose, Fry remarked. Lincoln said he felt like an Illinois man who was going to be hanged and as the man passed along the road on the way to the gallows the crowds kept pushing into the way and blocking passage. The condemned man at last called out, "Boys, you needn't be in such a hurry to get ahead, there won't be any fun till I get there."

Flags and red-white-and-blue bunting decorated the four-car special train. Aboard were the three Cabinet members, Nicolay and Hay, army and navy representatives, newspapermen, the French and Italian Ministers and attachés. The rear third of the last coach had a drawing-room, where from time to time the President talked with nearly everyone aboard as they came and went. Henry Clay Cochrane, lieutenant of Marines, noted:

"I happened to have a 'New York Herald' and offered it to Mr. Lincoln. He took it and thanked me, saying, 'I like to see what they say about us.' The news was about Burnside at Knoxville, Grant and Sherman at Chattanooga and Meade on the Rapidan, all expecting trouble. He read for a little while and then began to laugh at some wild guesses of the paper about pending movements. It was pleasant to see his sad face lighted up. He was looking sallow, sunken-eyed, thin, care-worn and very quiet. He returned the paper remarking among other things that when he had first passed over that road on his way to Congress in 1847 he noticed square-rigged vessels up the Patapsco river as far as the Relay House and now there seemed to be only small craft.

"At the Calvert Street Station Secretary Seward began to get uneasy as we approached Baltimore. Upon reaching the Calvert Street Station in Baltimore all was quiet, less than two hundred people assembled, among them women with children in arms. They called for the President. He took two or three of the babies up and kissed them which greatly pleased the mothers. General Schenck and staff joined us and soon after the President went forward in the car and seated himself with a party of choice spirits, among whom was Mayor Frederick W. Lincoln of Boston, not a kinsman. They told stories for an hour or so, Mr. Lincoln taking his turn and enjoying it. Approaching Hanover Junction, he arose and said, 'Gentlemen, this is all very pleasant, but the people will expect me to say something to them tomorrow, and I must give the matter some thought.' He then returned to the rear room of the car."

An elderly gentleman got on the train and, shaking hands, told the

President he had lost a son at Little Round Top at Gettysburg. The President answered he feared a visit to that spot would open fresh wounds, and yet if the end of sacrifice had been reached "we could give thanks even amidst our tears." They quoted from his unburdening to this old man: "When I think of the sacrifices of life yet to be offered, and the hearts and homes yet to be made desolate before this dreadful war is over, my heart is like lead within me, and I feel at times like hiding in deep darkness." At one stop a little girl lifted to an open window thrust a bunch of rosebuds into the car. "Flowerth for the Prethident." Lincoln stepped over, bent down, kissed her face. "You are a little rosebud yourself."

Nearing Gettysburg, Hay noted the President in a little talk with Wayne MacVeagh (lawyer and chairman of the Pennsylvania Republican Central Committee) about Missouri affairs. "MacV. talked Radicalism until he learned he was talking recklessly." MacVeagh brought up the Edwards case as though it were hardly any credit to the Administration. "The President disavowed any knowledge of the Edwards case." Bates had said to Lincoln, as indeed Lincoln had said to Hay, "that Edwards was inefficient and must be removed for that reason." It seemed, however, to be an uppermost matter in MacVeagh's mind and he thrust at the President about it and enjoyed doing so. It was precisely the sort of matter that professional politicians heading State central committees sought opportunity to bring up.

At sundown the train pulled into Gettysburg and Lincoln was driven to the Wills residence, Seward to the Harper home fronting on the public square. A sleepy little country town of 3,500 was overflowing with human pulses again. Private homes were filled with notables and nondescripts. Hundreds slept on the floors of hotels. Military bands blared till late in the night serenading whomsoever. The weather was mild and the moon up for those who chose to go a-roaming. When serenaders called on the President for a speech, he made again one of those little addresses saying there was nothing to say. "In my position it is sometimes important that I should not say foolish things. [A voice: "If you can help it."] It very often happens that the only way to help it is to say nothing at all. Believing that is my present condition this evening, I must beg of you to excuse me from addressing you further."

The crowd didn't feel it was much of a speech. They went next door with the band and blared for Seward. He spoke so low that Hay could not hear him, but he opened the stopgaps of patriotic sentiment, saying in part, "I thank my God for the hope that this is the last fratricidal war which will fall upon the country which is vouchsafed to us by Heaven—the richest, the broadest, the most beautiful, the most magnificent, and capable of a greater destiny than has ever been given to any part of the human race." What more could a holiday crowd ask for on a fair night of moonlit November? Seward gave them more and closed: "Fellow citizens, good night." It was good night for him but not for them. They serenaded five other speakers.

Something of the excess spirit of the evening was set down in Hay's diary. He with MacVeagh and others went out to the Lutheran Theological Seminary, ate from a chafing dish of oysters, then a real supper, loafed around the courthouse where Lamon was holding a meeting of his marshals, then hunted up John W. Forney, a Democrat born and raised in near-by Lancaster, editor of the *Intelligencer and Journal* there, later editor of the *Washington Union*, defeated for United States Senator from Pennsylvania by Simon Cameron. As a Douglas Democrat editing the *Philadelphia Press*, Forney was credited as much as anyone except Douglas with splitting the Democratic party in 1860 and giving the election to Lincoln. Forney's newspaper, the *Sunday Morning Chronicle* in Washington, had in 1862 become a daily paper, an Administration organ, a defender and expositor of Lincoln.

"Before I ever saw or knew Mr. Lincoln," said Forney to friends, "he wrote me a letter directly after his election in 1860 thanking me for what he was pleased to call my service in resisting the Buchanan administration, and proffering a friendship which never abated. When I was defeated for Clerk of the House in March, 1861, Mr. Lincoln called upon a number of Senators and asked them to vote for me for Secretary of that body. When Stonewall Jackson was killed, and one of my assistant editors spoke kindly, Lincoln wrote to me commending the tribute to a brave adversary. . . . I recommended Horace Greeley for Postmaster-General, because dear old Horace, four years before, without knowing that I had fallen from grace under Mr. Buchanan, recommended me for that office. But as Lincoln had selected Seward for Secretary of State from New York, he could not, of course, appoint Greeley from the same State, and so he replied, and that proposition fell." Trends and manipulations in the Senate often came quickly to Lincoln through Forney, whose information and counsel were freely given when the President asked for it on the hundreds of visits Forney made to the White House. That Forney was a storyteller full of anecdotes, and a philosopher of so wide a tolerance that he was intimate with both the righteous and the wicked, did not lessen his charm for Lincoln. Hay had seen him often at the White House.

"We found Forney," Hay wrote of this Wednesday evening in Gettysburg . . . "and drank a little whiskey with him. He had been drinking a good deal during the day & was getting to feel a little ugly and dangerous. He was particularly bitter on Montgomery Blair. MacVeagh was telling him [Forney] that he pitched into the Tycoon coming up and told him some truths. He [Forney] said the President got a good deal of that from time to time and needed it. . . . He talked very strangely. Referring to the affectionate and loyal support which he and Curtin had given to the President in Pennsylvania, with references . . . to favors shown the Cameron party whom they regard as their natural enemies." The party went out, heard Lincoln, heard Seward speak to the serenaders, "Forney and MacVeagh . . . still growling about Blair." They picked up Nicolay. "We went back to Forney's room . . . and drank more whiskey. Nicolay sung his little song of the 'Three Thieves' and we then sung John Brown. At last we proposed that Forney should make a speech and two or three started out . . . to get a band to serenade him."

And Forney sat growling quietly. The band arrived with a crowd and newspaper reporters. "Hay, we'll take a drink!" said Forney. Somebody commanded prudence. "I am always prudent," said Forney sternly. The crowd shouted as he opened the door. "My friends," said Forney, "these are the first hearty cheers I have heard tonight. You gave no such cheers to your President down the street. Do you know what you owe to that great man? You owe your country—you owe your name as American citizens." Forney blackguarded the crowd for its apathy, diverged to his own record; he had been for Lincoln in his heart in 1860; open advocacy was not as effectual as the course he took in dividing the most corrupt organization that ever existed, the proslavery Democratic party. "He dwelt at length on this question," noted Hay, "and then went back to the eulogy of the President, that great, wonderful mysterious inexplicable man who holds in his single hands the reins of the republic; who keeps his own counsels; who does his own purpose in his own way, no matter what temporizing minister in his Cabinet sets himself up in opposition. . . . And very much of this." Mac-Veagh and another speaker held forth. John Russell Young of the *Philadelphia Press* remarked as to Forney: "That speech must not be written out yet. He will see further about it when he gets sober." They went upstairs with Forney, sang "John Brown" again, went home and called it a night.

At dinner in the Wills home that evening Lincoln met Edward Everett, a guest under the same roof, and Governor Curtin and others. About ten o'clock he was in his room, with paper and pencil ready to write, when he sent a colored servant down for Judge Wills to come up. Still later, about eleven o'clock, he sent the colored servant down again for Judge Wills, who came up and heard Lincoln request to see Mr. Seward. Judge Wills offered to go and bring Seward from next door at the Harpers'. "No, I'll go and see him," said Lincoln, who gathered his sheets of paper and went for a half-hour with his Secretary of State.

Whether Seward made slight or material alterations in the text on the sheets was known only to Lincoln and Seward. It was midnight or later that Lincoln went to sleep, probably perfectly clear in his mind as to what his speech would be the next day. The one certainty was that his "few appropriate remarks," good or bad, would go to an immense audience. Also he slept better for having a telegram from Stanton reporting there was no real war news and "On inquiry Mrs. Lincoln informs me that your son is better this evening."

Fifteen thousand, some said 30,000 or 50,000, people were on Cemetery Hill for the exercises the next day when the procession from Gettysburg arrived afoot and horseback representing the United States Government, the army and navy, governors of States, mayors of cities, a regiment of troops, hospital corps, telegraph-company representatives, Knights Templar, Masonic Fraternity, Odd Fellows, and other benevolent associations, the press, fire departments, citizens of Pennsylvania and other States. They were scheduled to start at ten o'clock and at that hour of the clock Lincoln in a black suit, high silk hat, and white gloves came out of the Wills residence and mounted a horse. A crowd was on hand and he held a reception on horseback. At eleven the parade began to move. The President's horse seemed small for him, as some looked at it. Clark E. Carr, just behind the President, believed he noticed that the President sat erect and looked majestic to begin with and then got to thinking so that his body leaned forward, his arms hung limp, and his head bent far down.

A long telegram sent by Stanton at ten o'clock from Washington had been handed him. Burnside seemed safe though threatened at Knoxville, Grant was starting a big battle at Chattanooga, and "Mrs. Lincoln reports your son's health as a great deal better and he will be out today."

The march of the procession of military and civic bodies began. "Mr. Lincoln was mounted upon a young and beautiful chestnut horse, the largest in the Cumberland Valley," wrote Lieutenant Cochrane. This seemed the first occasion that anyone had looked at the President mounted with a feeling that just the right horse had been picked to match his physical length. "His towering figure surmounted by a high silk hat made the rest of us look small," thought Cochrane. At the President's right Seward and Blair rode their horses, at his left Usher and Lamon. In the next rank were six horses with the secretaries Nicolay and Hay, Provost Marshal General Fry, Lieutenant Cochrane, and military officers. Cochrane rode "a mischievous brute that required much attention to keep him from getting out of line to browse on the tail of the President's horse." The President rode "easily, bowing occasionally to right or left," noted Cochrane, while Seward lacked dignity, his trousers working up over the shoe tops to show his homemade gray socks. Seward was "entirely unconscious" that the Secretary of State looked funny—and nobody really cared. In the town of Gettysburg men with wounds still lingered in hospitals. And many flags along the main street were at half-mast for sorrow not yet over.

Minute guns spoke while the procession moved along Baltimore Street to the Emmitsburg Road, then by way of the Taneytown Road to the cemetery, where troop lines stood in salute to the President.

The march was over in fifteen minutes. But Mr. Everett, the orator of the day, had not arrived. Bands played till noon. Mr. Everett arrived. On the platform sat Governors Curtin of Pennsylvania, Bradford of Maryland, Morton of Indiana, Seymour of New York, Parker of New Jersey, Dennison of Ohio, with ex-Governor Tod and Governor-elect Brough of Ohio, Edward Everett and his daughter, Major Generals Schenck, Stahel, Doubleday, and Couch, Brigadier General Gibbon and Provost Marshal General Fry, foreign Ministers, members of Congress, Colonel Ward Hill Lamon, Secretary Usher, and the President of the United States with Secretary Seward and Postmaster General Blair immediately at his left.

The United States House chaplain, the Reverend Thomas H. Stockton, offered a prayer while the thousands stood with uncovered heads.

"O God, our Father, for the sake of Thy Son, our Saviour, inspire us with Thy spirit, and sanctify us. . . . By this altar of sacrifice and on this field of deliverance—on this mount of salvation—within the fiery and bloody line of these munitive rocks, looking back to the dark days of fear and trembling, and to the rapture of relief that came after, we multiply our thanksgiving, and confess our obligations to renew and perfect our personal and social consecration to Thy service and glory. . . . Bless the efforts to suppress this rebellion. . . . As the trees are not dead, though the foliage is gone, so our heroes are not dead though their forms have fallen—with their personality they are all with Thee, and the spirit of their example is here. It fills the air, it fills our hearts, and long as time shall last it will hover in these skies and rest on this landscape. . . ."

The chaplain prayed as a master of liturgy and a familiar of sacred literature. The *Philadelphia Press* said that with the prayer "there was scarcely a dry eye in all that vast assemblage," while the *Cincinnati Daily Gazette* reporter wrote his observation: "The President evidently united in this adjuration in all the simplicity of his soul, and the falling tear declared the sincerity of his emotions."

Benjamin B. French, officer in charge of buildings in Washington, introduced the Honorable Edward Everett, orator of the day, who rose, bowed low to Lincoln, saying, "Mr. President." Lincoln responded, "Mr. Everett."

The orator of the day then stood in silence before a crowd that stretched to limits that would test his voice. Beyond and around were the wheat fields, the meadows, the peach orchards, long slopes of land, and five and seven miles farther the contemplative blue ridge of a low mountain range. His eyes could sweep them as he faced the audience. He had taken note of it in his prepared and rehearsed address. "Overlooking these broad fields now reposing from the labors of the waning year, the mighty Alleghanies dimly towering before us, the graves of our brethren beneath our feet, it is with hesitation that I raise my poor voice to break the eloquent silence of God and Nature. But the duty to which you have called me must be performed;—grant me, I pray you, your indulgence and your sympathy." Everett proceeded, "It was appointed by law in Athens," and gave an extended sketch of the manner in which the Greeks cared for their dead who fell in battle. He spoke of the citizens assembled to consecrate the day. "As my eye ranges over the fields whose sods were so lately moistened by the blood of gallant and loyal men, I feel, as never before, how truly it was said of old that it is sweet and becoming to die for one's country."

Northern cities would have been trampled in conquest but for "those who sleep beneath our feet," said the orator. He gave an outline of how the war began, traversed decisive features of the three days' battles at Gettysburg, discussed the doctrine of State sovereignty and denounced it, drew parallels from European history, and came to his peroration quoting Pericles on dead patriots: "The whole earth is the sepulchre of illustrious men." The men of nineteen sister States had stood side by side on the perilous ridges. "Seminary Ridge, the Peach-Orchard, Cemetery, Culp, and Wolf

Hill, Round Top, Little Round Top, humble names, henceforward dear and famous,—no lapse of time, no distance of space, shall cause you to be forgotten." He had spoken for an hour and fifty-seven minutes, some said a trifle over two hours, repeating almost word for word an address that occupied nearly two newspaper pages, as he had written it and as it had gone in advance sheets to many newspapers.

Everett came to his closing sentence without a faltering voice: "Down to the latest period of recorded time, in the glorious annals of our common country there will be no brighter page than that which relates THE BATTLES OF GETTYSBURG." It was the effort of his life and embodied the perfections of the school of oratory in which he had spent his career. His erect form and sturdy shoulders, his white hair and flung-back head at dramatic points, his voice, his poise, and chiefly some quality of inside goodheartedness, held most of his audience to him, though the people in the front rows had taken their seats three hours before his oration closed.

The Baltimore Glee Club sang an ode written for the occasion by Benjamin B. French, who had introduced Everett to the audience. The poets Longfellow, Bryant, Whittier, Lowell, George Boker, had been requested but none found time to respond with a piece to be set to music. The two closing verses of the ode by French immediately preceded the introduction of the President to the audience:

> Great God in Heaven!
> Shall all this sacred blood be shed?
> Shall we thus mourn our glorious dead?
> Oh, shall the end be wrath and woe,
> The knell of Freedom's overthrow,
> A country riven?
>
> It will not be!
> We trust, O God! thy gracious power
> To aid us in our darkest hour.
> This be our prayer—"O Father! save
> A people's freedom from its grave.
> All praise to Thee!"

Having read Everett's address, Lincoln knew when the moment drew near for him to speak. He took out his own manuscript from a coat pocket, put on his steel-bowed glasses, stirred in his chair, looked over the manuscript, and put it back in his pocket. The Baltimore Glee Club finished. The specially chosen Ward Hill Lamon rose and spoke the words "The President of the United States," who rose, and holding in one hand the two sheets of paper at which he occasionally glanced, delivered the address in his high-pitched and clear-carrying voice. The *Cincinnati Commercial* reporter wrote, "The President rises slowly, draws from his pocket a paper, and, when commotion subsides, in a sharp, unmusical treble voice, reads the brief and pithy remarks." Hay wrote in his diary, "The President, in a firm,

Edward Everett

From the Meserve collection

Lincoln in '63

Photograph by Brady, from the Meserve collection

Lincoln about the time of the Gettysburg
speech

Photograph by Brady, from the Meserve collection

Andrew Gregg Curtin

From the author's collection

FACES AT THE GETTYSBURG BATTLEFIELD DEDICATION

The best-known of five photographs of Lincoln made on November 8, 1863, eleven days before the Gettysburg speech, by Alexander Gardner in Washington, published by Philip & Solomon in '64

Original photograph in the Barrett collection

free way, with more grace than is his wont, said his half dozen words of consecration." Charles Hale of the *Boston Advertiser*, also officially representing Governor Andrew of Massachusetts, had notebook and pencil in hand, took down the slow-spoken words of the President, as follows:

Fourscore and seven years ago, our fathers brought forth upon this continent a new nation, conceived in liberty and dedicated to the proposition that all men are created equal.

Now we are engaged in a great civil war, testing whether that nation—or any nation, so conceived and so dedicated—can long endure.

We are met on a great battle-field of that war. We are met to dedicate a portion of it as the final resting place of those who have given their lives that that nation might live.

It is altogether fitting and proper that we should do this.

But, in a larger sense, we cannot dedicate, we cannot consecrate, we cannot hallow, this ground. The brave men, living and dead, who struggled here, have consecrated it, far above our power to add or to detract.

The world will very little note nor long remember what we say here; but it can never forget what they did here.

It is for us, the living, rather, to be dedicated, here, to the unfinished work that they have thus far so nobly carried on. It is rather for us to be here dedicated to the great task remaining before us; that from these honored dead we take increased devotion to that cause for which they here gave the last full measure of devotion; that we here highly resolve that these dead shall not have died in vain; that the nation shall, under God, have a new birth of freedom, and that government of the people, by the people, for the people, shall not perish from the earth.

In a speech to serenaders just after the battle of Gettysburg four and a half months before, Lincoln had referred to the founding of the republic as taking place "eighty odd years since." Then he had hunted up the exact date, which was eighty-seven years since, and phrased it "Fourscore and seven years ago" instead of "Eighty-seven years since." Also in the final copy Lincoln wrote "We have come" instead of the second "We are met" that Hale reported.

In the written copy of his speech from which he read Lincoln used the phrase "our poor power." In other copies of the speech which he wrote out later he again used the phrase "our poor power." So it was evident that he meant to use the word "poor" when speaking to his audience, but he omitted it. Also in the copy held in his hands while facing the audience he had not written the words "under God," though he did include those words in later copies which he wrote. Therefore the words "under God" were decided upon after he wrote the text the night before at the Wills residence.

The *New York Tribune* and many other newspapers indicated "[Applause.]" at five places in the address and "[Long continued applause.]" at the end. The applause, however, according to most of the responsible witnesses, was formal and perfunctory, a tribute to the occasion, to the high office, to the array of important men of the nation on the platform, by persons who had sat as an audience for three hours. Ten sentences had been spoken in five minutes, and some were surprised that it should end before the orator had really begun to get his outdoor voice.

A photographer had made ready to record a great historic moment, had bustled about with his dry plates, his black box on a tripod, and before he had his head under the hood for an exposure, the President had said "by the people, for the people" and the nick of time was past for a photograph.

[handwritten first draft of the Gettysburg speech]

Lincoln writes a first draft (above) of the Gettysburg speech, having the sentence "This we may, in all propriety do." In a later draft (below) he changes this sentence to the more meaningful and musical version: "It is altogether fitting and proper that we should do this." He also changes "are met" to "have come." Originals in the Library of Congress.

[handwritten later draft of the Gettysburg speech]

The *New York Times* reporter gave his summary of the program by writing: "The opening prayer by Reverend Mr. Stockton was touching and beautiful, and produced quite as much effect upon the audience as the classic sentences of the orator of the day. President Lincoln's address was delivered in a clear loud tone of voice, which could be distinctly heard at the extreme limits of the large assemblage. It was delivered (or rather read from a sheet of paper which the speaker held in his hand) in a very deliberate manner, with strong emphasis, and with a most business-like air."

The *Philadelphia Press* man, John Russell Young, privately felt that Everett's speech was the performance of a great actor whose art was too evident, that it was "beautiful but cold as ice." The *New York Times* man noted: "Even while Mr. Everett was delivering his splendid oration, there were as many people wandering about the fields, made memorable by the fierce struggles of July, as stood around the stand listening to his eloquent periods. They seem to have considered, with President Lincoln, that it was not what was *said* here, but what was *done* here, that deserved their attention. . . . In wandering about these battlefields, one is astonished and indignant to find at almost every step of his progress the carcasses of dead

for us to be here dedicated to the great task remaining before us,— that from then honored dead we take increased devotion to that cause for which they here gave the last full measure of devotion— that we here highly resolve that these dead shall not have died in vain; that this nation shall have a new birth of freedom; and that this government of the people, by the people, for the people, shall not perish from the earth.

Above is reproduced one of the sheets from which it is believed Lincoln read the address at Gettysburg. Writing this, he omits the words "under God," inserting them orally when reading it, and again scrupulously writing the words "under God" in a copy for Everett and a copy, reproduced in part below, for George Bancroft.

fore us— that from these honored dead we take increased devotion to that cause for which they here gave the last full measure of devotion— that we here highly resolve that these dead shall not have died in vain— that this nation, under God, shall have a new birth of freedom— and that government of the people, by the people, for the people, shall not perish from the earth

horses which breed pestilence in the atmosphere. I am told that more than a score of deaths have resulted from this neglect in the village of Gettysburg the past summer; in the house in which I was compelled to seek lodgings, there are now two boys sick with typhoid fever attributed to this cause. Within a stone's throw of the whitewashed hut occupied as the headquarters of General Meade, I counted yesterday no less than ten carcasses of dead horses, lying on the ground where they were struck by the shells of the enemy."

The audience had expected, as the printed program stipulated, "Dedicatory Remarks, by the President of the United States." No eloquence was promised. Where eloquence is in flow the orator must have time to get tuned up, to expatiate and expand while building toward his climaxes, it was supposed. The *New York Tribune* man and other like observers merely reported the words of the address with the one preceding sentence: "The dedicatory remarks were then delivered by the President." These reporters felt no urge to inform their readers about how Lincoln stood, what he did with his hands, how he moved, vocalized, or whether he emphasized or subdued any parts of the address. Strictly, no address as such was on the program from him. He was down for just a few perfunctory "dedicatory remarks."

According to Lamon, Lincoln himself felt that about all he had given the audience was ordinary garden-variety dedicatory remarks, for Lamon wrote that Lincoln told him just after delivering the speech that he had regret over not having prepared it with greater care. "Lamon, that speech won't *scour*. It is a flat failure and the people are disappointed." On the farms where Lincoln grew up as a boy when wet soil stuck to the mold board of a plow they said it didn't "scour."

The near-by *Patriot and Union* of Harrisburg took its fling: "The President succeeded on this occasion because he acted without sense and without constraint in a panorama that was gotten up more for the benefit of his party than for the glory of the nation and the honor of the dead. . . . We pass over the silly remarks of the President; for the credit of the nation we are willing that the veil of oblivion shall be dropped over them and that they shall no more be repeated or thought of."

The *Chicago Times* held that "Mr. Lincoln did most foully traduce the motives of the men who were slain at Gettysburg" in his reference to "a new birth of freedom," the *Times* saying, "They gave their lives to maintain the old government, and the only Constitution and Union." He had perverted history, misstated the cause for which they died, and with "ignorant rudeness" insulted the memory of the dead, the *Times* alleged: "Readers will not have failed to observe the exceeding bad taste which characterized the remarks of the President and Secretary of State at the dedication of the soldiers' cemetery at Gettysburg. The cheek of every American must tingle with shame as he reads the silly, flat, and dish-watery utterances of the man who has to be pointed out to intelligent foreigners as the President of the United States. And neither he nor Seward could refrain, even on that solemn occasion, from spouting their odious abolition doctrines. The readers of THE TIMES ought to know, too, that the valorous President did not dare to make this little journey to Gettysburg without being escorted by a bodyguard of soldiers. For the first time in the history of the country, the President of the United States, in traveling through a part of his dominions, on a peaceful, even a religious mission, had to be escorted by a bodyguard of soldiers . . . it was fear for his own personal safety which led the President to go escorted as any other military despot might go." In the pronouncement of a funeral sermon Mr. Lincoln had intruded an "offensive exhibition of boorishness and vulgarity," had alluded to tribal differences that an Indian orator eulogizing dead warriors would have omitted, "which he knew would excite unnecessarily the bitter prejudices of his hearers." Therefore the *Chicago Times* would inquire, "Is Mr. Lincoln less refined than a savage?"

A Confederate outburst of war propaganda related to Lincoln and the Gettysburg exercises was set forth in a *Richmond Examiner* editorial, and probably written by its editor, Edward A. Pollard, taking a day off from his merciless and occasionally wild-eyed criticism of President Jefferson Davis of the Confederacy. And the *Chicago Times*, which seldom let a day pass without curses on Lincoln for his alleged suppression of free speech and a free press, reprinted in full the long editorial from the *Examiner*. "The dramatic exhibition at Gettysburg is in thorough keeping with Yankee character, suited to the usual dignity of their chosen chief," ran part of the editorial scorn. "Stage play, studied attitudes, and effective points were carefully elaborated and presented to the world as the honest outpourings of a nation's heart. In spite of shoddy contracts, of universal corruption, and cruel thirst for southern blood, these people have ideas . . . have read of them in books . . . and determined accordingly to have a grand imitation of them. . . . Mr. Everett was equal to the occasion. He 'took down his Thucydides,' and fancied himself a Pericles commemorating the illustrious dead. The music, the eloquence, the bottled tears and hermetically sealed grief, prepared for the occasion, were all properly brought out in honor of the heroes, whom they crimp in Ireland, inveigle in Germany, or hunt down in the streets of New York.

"So far the play was strictly classic. To suit the general public, however, a little admixture of the more irregular romantic drama was allowed. A vein of comedy was permitted to mingle with the deep pathos of the piece. This singular novelty, and deviation from classic propriety, was heightened by assigning this part to the chief personage. Kings are usually made to speak in the magniloquent language supposed to be suited to their elevated position. On the present occasion Lincoln acted the clown."

This was in the customary tone of the *Chicago Times* and relished by its supporting readers. Its rival, the *Chicago Tribune*, however, had a reporter who telegraphed (unless some editor who read the address added his own independent opinion) a sentence: "The dedicatory remarks of President Lincoln will live among the annals of man."

The *Cincinnati Gazette* reporter added after the text of the address, "That this was the right thing in the right place, and a perfect thing in every respect, was the universal encomium."

The American correspondent of the London *Times* wrote that "the ceremony was rendered ludicrous by some of the sallies of that poor President Lincoln. . . . Anything more dull and commonplace it would not be easy to produce."

Count Gurowski, the only man ever mentioned by Lincoln to Lamon as his possible assassin, wrote in a diary, "Lincoln spoke, with one eye to a future platform and to re-election."

The *Philadelphia Evening Bulletin* said thousands who would not read the elaborate oration of Mr. Everett would read the President's few words "and not many will do it without a moistening of the eye and a swelling of the heart." The *Detroit Advertiser and Tribune* said Mr. Everett had nobly told the story of the battle, "but he who wants to take in the very spirit of the day, catch the unstudied pathos that animates a sincere but simple-minded man, will turn from the stately periods of the professed orator to the brief speech of the President." The *Providence Journal* reminded readers of the saying that the hardest thing in the world is to make a good five-minute speech: "We know not where to look for a more admirable speech than the brief one which the President made at the close of Mr. Everett's oration. . . . Could the most elaborate and splendid oration be more beautiful, more touching, more inspiring, than those thrilling words of the President? They had in our humble judgment the charm and power of the very highest eloquence."

Later men were to find that Robert Toombs of Georgia had in 1850 opened a speech: "Sixty years ago our fathers joined together to form a more perfect Union and to establish justice. . . . We have now met to put that government on trial. . . . In my judgment the verdict is such as to give hope to the friends of liberty throughout the world."

Lincoln had spoken of an idea, a proposition, a concept, worth dying for, which brought from a Richmond newspaper a countering question and answer, "For what are we fighting? An abstraction."

The *Springfield Republican* had veered from its first opinion that Lincoln was honest but "a Simple Susan." Its comment ran: "Surpassingly fine as Mr. Everett's oration was in the Gettysburg consecration, the rhetorical honors of the occasion were won by President Lincoln. His little speech is a perfect gem; deep in feeling, compact in thought and expression, and tasteful and elegant in every word and comma. Then it has the merit of unexpectedness in its verbal perfection and beauty. We had grown so accustomed to homely and imperfect phrase in his productions that we had come to think it was the law of his utterance. But this shows he can talk handsomely as well as act sensibly. Turn back and read it over, it will repay study as a model speech. Strong feelings and a large brain were its parents— a little painstaking its *accoucheur*."

That scribbler of curious touch who signed himself "The Lounger" in

Harper's Weekly inquired why the ceremony at Gettysburg was one of the most striking events of the war. "There are grave-yards enough in the land—what is Virginia but a cemetery?—and the brave who have died for us in this fierce war consecrate the soil from the ocean to the Mississippi. But there is peculiar significance in the field of Gettysburg, for there 'thus far' was thundered to the rebellion. . . . The President and the Cabinet were there, with famous soldiers and civilians. The oration by Mr. Everett was smooth and cold. . . . The few words of the President were from the heart to the heart. They can not be read, even, without kindling emotion. 'The world will little note nor long remember what we say here, but it can never forget what they did here.' It was as simple and felicitous and earnest a word as was ever spoken. . . . Among the Governors present was Horatio Seymour. He came to honor the dead of Gettysburg. But when they were dying he stood in New York sneeringly asking where was the victory promised for the Fourth of July? These men were winning that victory, and dying for us all; and now he mourns, *ex officio*, over their graves."

Everett's opinion of the speech he heard Lincoln deliver was written in a note to Lincoln the next day and was more than mere courtesy: "I should be glad if I could flatter myself that I came as near to the central idea of the occasion in two hours as you did in two minutes." Lincoln's immediate reply was: "In our respective parts yesterday, you could not have been excused to make a short address, nor I a long one. I am pleased to know that, in your judgment, the little I did say was not entirely a failure."

At Everett's request Lincoln wrote with pen and ink a copy of his Gettysburg Address, which manuscript was auctioned at a Sanitary Fair in New York for the benefit of soldiers. At the request of George Bancroft, the historian, he wrote another copy for a Soldiers' and Sailors' Fair at Baltimore. He wrote still another to be lithographed as a facsimile in a publication, *Autographed Leaves of Our Country's Authors*. For Mr. Wills, his host at Gettysburg, he wrote another. The first draft, written in Washington, and the second one, held while delivering it, went into John Hay's hands to be eventually presented to the Library of Congress.

After the ceremonies at Gettysburg Lincoln lunched with Governor Curtin, Mr. Everett, and others at the Wills home, held a reception that had not been planned, handshaking nearly an hour, looking gloomy and listless but brightening sometimes as a small boy or girl came in line, and stopping one tall man for remarks as to just how high up he reached. At five o'clock he attended a patriotic meeting in the Presbyterian church, walking arm-in-arm with old John Burns, and listening to an address by Lieutenant Governor-elect Anderson of Ohio. At six-thirty he was on the departing Washington train. In the dining-car his secretary John Hay ate with Simon Cameron and Wayne MacVeagh. Hay had thought Cameron and MacVeagh hated each other, but he noted: "I was more than usually struck by the intimate, jovial relations that exist between men that hate and detest each other as cordially as do those Pennsylvania politicians."

The ride to Washington took until midnight. Lincoln was weary, talked little, stretched out on one of the side seats in the drawing-room and had a wet towel laid across his eyes and forehead.

He had stood that day, the world's foremost spokesman of popular government, saying that democracy was yet worth fighting for. He had spoken as one in mist who might head on deeper yet into mist. He incarnated the assurances and pretenses of popular government, implied that it could and might perish from the earth. What he meant by "a new birth of freedom" for the nation could have a thousand interpretations. The taller riddles of democracy stood up out of the address. It had the dream touch of vast and furious events epitomized for any foreteller to read what was to come. He did not assume that the drafted soldiers, substitutes, and bounty-paid privates had died willingly under Lee's shot and shell, in deliberate consecration of themselves to the Union cause. His cadences sang the ancient song that where there is freedom men have fought and sacrificed for it, and that freedom is worth men's dying for. For the first time since he became President he had on a dramatic occasion declaimed, howsoever it might be read, Jefferson's proposition which had been a slogan of the Revolutionary War—"All men are created equal"—leaving no other inference than that he regarded the Negro slave as a man. His outwardly smooth sentences were inside of them gnarled and tough with the enigmas of the American experiment.

Back at Gettysburg the blue haze of the Cumberland Mountains had dimmed till it was a blur in a nocturne. The moon was up and fell with a bland golden benevolence on the new-made graves of soldiers, on the sepulchers of old settlers, on the horse carcasses of which the onrush of war had not yet permitted removal. The *New York Herald* man walked amid them and ended the story he sent his paper: "The air, the trees, the graves are silent. Even the relic hunters are gone now. And the soldiers here never wake to the sound of reveille."

In many a country cottage over the land, a tall old clock in a quiet corner told time in a tick-tock deliberation. Whether the orchard branches hung with pink-spray blossoms or icicles of sleet, whether the outside news was seedtime or harvest, rain or drouth, births or deaths, the swing of the pendulum was right and left and right and left in a tick-tock deliberation.

The face and dial of the clock had known the eyes of a boy who listened to its tick-tock and learned to read its minute and hour hands. And the boy had seen years measured off by the swinging pendulum, and grown to man size, had gone away. And the people in the cottage knew that the clock would stand there and the boy never again come into the room and look at the clock with the query, "What is the time?"

In a row of graves of the Unidentified the boy would sleep long in the dedicated final resting-place at Gettysburg. Why he had gone away and why he would never come back had roots in some mystery of flags and drums, of national fate in which individuals sink as in a deep sea, of men swallowed and vanished in a man-made storm of smoke and steel.

The mystery deepened and moved with ancient music and inviolable consolation because a solemn Man of Authority had stood at the graves of the Unidentified and spoken the words "We cannot consecrate—we cannot hallow—this ground. The brave men, living and dead, who struggled here, have consecrated it far above our poor power to add or detract. . . . From these honored dead we take increased devotion to that cause for which they gave the last full measure of devotion."

To the backward and forward pendulum swing of a tall old clock in a quiet corner they might read those cadenced words while outside the windows the first flurry of snow blew across the orchard and down over the meadow, the beginnings of winter in a gun-metal gloaming to be later arched with a star-flung sky.

CHAPTER 45

EPIC '63 DRAWS TO A CLOSE

A WEEK after Lincoln's return from Gettysburg, Hay wrote to Nicolay: "The President is sick in bed. Bilious." Newspapers said visitors, Cabinet members, personal friends, were excluded from the President's room. Press reports ran: "At first it was supposed to be a cold, next a touch of bilious fever; a rash then appeared on his body and the disease was pronounced scarlatina; but it has leaked out that the real complaint is small-pox." Still later came definite information. The President had varioloid, a mild form of smallpox.

Owen Lovejoy sent in his name, waited in the reception room, saw a door open just enough to frame Lincoln in a dressing-gown saying, "Lovejoy, are you afraid?" "No, I have had the small-pox; come in." And walking in, Lincoln said: "Lovejoy, there is one good thing about this. I now have something I can give everybody." Press items told of office-seekers suddenly fleeing the White House on hearing what ailed the President.

During days the President lay sick, an epic of action around Chattanooga came to its high point. The legs of men, mules, horses, tugged and hauled at this epic in mud and rainstorms, in fog and moonlight, moving rations, munitions, cannon, laying pontoon bridges, clearing steamboat routes. It was chaos and order, paradox and common sense, at the center of it Grant, of whom it was said, "Where that man goes things always seem to git!" As he had looked over the plans of Rosecrans, Grant said they were excellent; he wondered why they had not been put into action.

Ten thousand animals in a few weeks had perished hauling rations overland to Chattanooga before a river route was opened. Bragg's army had hoped to starve out the Union forces at the time Grant was taking command, when Thomas wired Grant, "We will hold the town till we starve."

Jeff Davis had gone back to Richmond proclaiming fresh faith in Bragg and his army. Bragg, hoped Davis, was to bag Grant at Chattanooga as Grant had bagged Pemberton at Vicksburg.

Grant's army lay south and east of Chattanooga, the Tennessee River at its back. Facing it, in a big half-circle, and high over it on Lookout Mountain and Missionary Ridge, some four hundred feet and higher up, lay Bragg's men with cannon and rifle pits amid rocks, timber, and chasms. From their witness gallery up close to the clouds the Confederates saw Union regiments march out on the plain below as if for drill, review, or parade. Then they saw the troops in blue form into storming columns that soon traded shots with the first line of defense up Missionary Ridge and captured that first line.

The Union troops kept going on up the slopes. It was against orders. They had been told to take only the first rifle pits. On up they went.

Grant at Orchard Knob saw them, turned to Thomas, "Who ordered those men up the ridge?"

Thomas did not know, turned to General Granger, "Did you?"

"No," said Granger, "they started up without orders." Phil Sheridan and others had sent back for orders to go on up and take the crest of the mountain but the orders that came were not clear. "How!" said Sheridan, waving a whisky flask toward the enemy, taking a drink and joining his men. They swept on up.

The killed and wounded fell by scores, hundreds. They fought above the clouds, some columns in rain and mist, past afternoon into evening under clear moonlight. On Missionary Ridge the same drama was enacted of foot troops moving up, dislodging and routing a naturally fortified enemy. It was told afterward as an event where men suddenly smitten with strength hurled themselves upward as smoothly and madly as though plunging downward.

They said they couldn't tell how or why they did it. To some it was a howling, inexplicable jamboree. To others it was a miracle.

Lincoln on a sickbed could read a Grant telegram: "Lookout Mountain top, all the rifle-pits in Chattanooga Valley, and Missionary Ridge entire, have been carried and now held by us," and a dispatch from Thomas: "Missionary Ridge was carried simultaneously at six different points. . . . Among the prisoners are many who were paroled at Vicksburg." And again from Grant on November 27: "I am just in from the front. The rout of the enemy is most complete. . . . The pursuit will continue to Red Clay in the morning, for which place I shall start in a few hours."

For the first time in a large-scale combat, Confederate soldiers had been routed, had run away. They had valor, as they had shown at Chickamauga. What explained their panic? The usual answer was Bragg, upright, moral, irascible, disputatious, censorious, dyspeptic, nervous, so harsh with his corrections and criticisms that the discipline of his army had gone to pieces.

Grant had studied Bragg, knew him as Lee knew McClellan, and gauged his plans accordingly. Bragg had cornered Grant, put his army within gunshot range overlooking the Union army, making retreat for Grant "almost certain annihilation," said Grant. Then the rank and file of Grant's army had thrown orders to the wind and taken mountains away from an army holding the top ridges of those mountains with cannon and rifle pits.

Anger at Jeff Davis, and mistrust of him, arose among some of his best aides because of his not knowing Bragg was second-rate. And Jeff Davis answered by appointing his friend Bragg Chief of Staff of the Confederate armies, with headquarters in Richmond.

"The storming of their ridge by our troops was one of the greatest miracles in military history," wrote Dana to his chiefs in Washington. "No man who climbs the ascent by any of the roads that wind along its front can believe that 18,000 men were moved up its broken and crumbling face unless it was his fortune to witness the deed. It seems as awful as a visible interposition of God. Neither Grant nor Thomas intended it. . . . The order to storm appears to have been given simultaneously by Generals Sheridan and Wood, because the men were not to be held back. Besides the generals had caught the inspiration of the men. . . . Bragg is in full retreat, burning his depots and bridges."

Newspapers of the North spread the story before their readers on the last Thursday of November. More good reason than expected had arisen for the Day of Thanksgiving proclaimed by the President weeks earlier. If he had wanted good news as he lay abed with varioloid in the White House, he had it with running-over measure.

Now Sherman could be released with an army to march on Knoxville and relieve Longstreet's siege of Burnside there—which Sherman did in a clean, fast operation.

Now Grant and Sherman could lay their plans to move farther south— on Atlanta—perhaps drive a wedge and split the Confederacy that lay east of the Mississippi.

General O. O. Howard rode into Knoxville with Sherman, sat at a turkey dinner with Burnside, and wrote of it: "The loyal East Tennessee people had kept him well supplied during all that long siege. I then remembered President Lincoln's words at my last interview with him, 'They are loyal there, general!' During my march of 100 miles I was every day made aware of the truth of Lincoln's declaration."

Minor operations took place, such as General Averell raiding food supplies of Longstreet, cutting telegraph wires, crossing his cavalry over the Alleghenies, feeding his horses in a poor country, burning his own wagons, swimming his men across Jackson's River, capturing 200 prisoners and 150 horses, his own losses figured at 6 men drowned, 1 officer and 4 men wounded, reporting to Washington on December 21, "My command has marched, climbed, slid and swam 350 miles since the 8th instant."

As late as December 12 Lincoln was not easily available to friends. Browning, no longer a Senator but just a prairie lawyer from Quincy, Illinois, had come to Washington on many affairs of business, his diary saying: "Called at War Department . . . and got George Candee appointed a Pay Master. Also called at the White House, but the President was sick, and I did not ask to see him." His one diary entry of the previous day was: "Cowan & I were vaccinated at my room this morning . . . small pox being prevalent."

On December 14, however, Browning did see the President and got Henry Warfield, an eighteen-year-old "rebel prisoner" in Camp Douglas at Chicago released and committed to the custody of the prisoner's brother-in-law, one Dr. L. W. Brown, with whom Browning called at the White House. Lincoln still held Browning as a confidant, for Browning also noted of that day: "The President told me his sister-in-law, Mrs. Helm [half-sister of Mrs. Lincoln and widow of the Confederate general killed at Chickamauga] was in the house, but he did not wish it known. She wished an order for the protection of some Cotton she had at Jackson, Mississippi. He thought she ought to have it, but was afraid he would be censured if he did so"

The next day at Cabinet meeting Welles noted: "The President was well and in fine spirits." More than a week before Lincoln had met the Cabinet with his annual message reporting to Congress on the year 1863, Welles noting: "He would have avoided the interview, but wished to submit and have our views of the message. All were satisfied." Newspapers reported that Lincoln held a consultation about this message with Thurlow Weed and Senator Edwin Dennison Morgan, of New York, chairman of the Republican State Committee. Reading about this in the public prints, Senator Zach Chandler was hot under the collar, and wrote to Lincoln that a million voters were friendly to the Administration "upon Radical measures" and not a Seward, Weed, or Blair man among them. Chandler warned Lincoln to drop the company of conservatives and traitors. "For God's sake don't exhume their remains in your message. They will smell worse than Lazarus did after he had been buried three days."

Lincoln replied to the stalwart and fiery Detroit dry-goods and real-estate millionaire. He had seen Morgan and Weed "separately, but not together" within ten days. Neither had mentioned the message nor said anything that might bring the message to mind. "I am very glad the elections this autumn have gone favorably, and that I have not, by native depravity or under evil influences, done anything bad enough to prevent the good result. I hope to 'stand firm' enough to not go backward, and yet not go forward fast enough to wreck the country's cause."

The annual message to Congress began with "renewed and profoundest gratitude to God" for another year "of health, and of sufficiently abundant harvests." Efforts to stir up foreign wars had failed. Her Britannic Majesty's Government had stopped hostile expeditions from leaving British ports, while the Emperor of the French was showing a genuine neutrality by like proceedings. The treaty between the United States and Great Britain for suppression of the slave trade was working and "It is believed that, so far as American ports and American citizens are concerned, that inhuman and odious traffic has been brought to an end."

Foreign-born persons who had taken out naturalization papers, or who had already become citizens and voted at elections, were found to have denied the facts and evaded military duty. Local officials were advised to send naturalization lists to the Interior Department at Washington. Also foreigners, it was found, had become citizens of the United States merely to evade taxes in their native countries. "Though never returning to the United States, they still claim the interposition of this government as citizens. Many altercations and great prejudices have heretofore arisen out of this abuse. . . . It might be advisable to fix a limit, beyond which no citizen of the United States residing abroad may claim the interposition of his government." Both at sea and on land persons in the Federal service may have inflicted "injuries, unforeseen by the Government and unintended." Existing courts or specially authorized courts should decide claims thus arising. And Secretary Chase was certified as an able public servant: "The operations of the treasury during the last year have been successfully conducted." The national banking law passed by Congress had proved a valuable support to public credit. The troops were being paid punctually.

And the people? The President saluted them. "By no people were the burdens incident to a great war ever more cheerfully borne."

The report of the Secretary of War, "a document of great interest," was too valuable to summarize. The Congressmen must read it for themselves.

The Union Navy was tightening its blockade of the enemy. More than 1,000 vessels had been captured; prizes amounted to $13,000,000. Of the 578 vessels built or being built, 75 were ironclad or armored steamers. New navy yards were wanted. The naval force on interior waters had doubled in two years and now was larger than the entire naval force when the war began. Mechanics and artisans were creating a new form of naval power. Enlisted seamen in 1861 numbered 7,500, now 34,000. When a man went into the navy his enlistment should be credited to his home community as if he had gone into the army. The bounties paid to army recruits affected the naval service and Congress should look to this and be equitable about it.

The post office had taken in nearly as much money as it had spent and might soon become self-sustaining. The Postmaster General had suggested an international conference which had met at Paris in May and June and inaugurated a general system of uniform international charges at reduced rates of postage.

Though a great war was on, 1,456,514 acres of land had been taken up under the new Homestead Law. The President agreed with the Secretary of the Interior that the law should be modified to favor soldiers and sailors of Federal service. The President hoped for permanent and friendly relations instead of frequent and bloody collisions with Indian tribes. They should have anxious and constant attention to their material well-being, to their progress in the arts of civilization, and, "above all, to that moral training which, under the blessing of Divine Providence, will confer upon them the elevated and sanctifying influences, the hopes and consolations, of the Christian faith."

The breath of a new and roaring age, intricate with man's new-found devices, rose at intervals throughout the message. A continuous line of telegraph from Russia to the Pacific Coast was being wrought out under arrangements effected with the Russian Emperor. The proposed international telegraph across the Atlantic Ocean, and a telegraph line from Washington to the seaboard forts and the Gulf of Mexico, deserved reasonable outlay from Congress. The call of a Chicago convention for a waterway between the Mississippi and the northeastern seaboard was "of the greatest respectability." Such a Midwest waterway seemed imperative. "That this interest is one which, ere long, will force its own way, I do not entertain a doubt, while it is submitted entirely to your wisdom as to what can be done now. Augmented interest is given to this subject by the actual commencement of work upon the Pacific railroad."

A system to encourage foreign immigration was recommended. "Although this source of national wealth and strength is again flowing with greater freedom than for several years before the insurrection occurred, there is still a great deficiency of laborers in every field of industry, especially in agriculture, and in our mines. . . . While the demand for labor is thus increased here, tens of thousands of persons, destitute of remunerative occupation, are thronging our foreign consulates, and offering to emigrate to the United States if essential, but very cheap, assistance can be afforded them. It is easy to see that, under the sharp discipline of civil war, the nation is beginning a new life."

The Executive invited a backward look at the war. A year ago it had lasted twenty months, with the "rebellion" pressed into reduced limits. Yet also a year ago the tone of public feeling at home and abroad was not satisfactory, popular elections were uneasy, "while, amid much that was cold and menacing, the kindest words coming from Europe were uttered in accents of pity that we were too blind to surrender a hopeless cause." Foreign trade suffered. The blockade was threatened. The emancipation policy, and with it the announcement that black soldiers would be received, brought dark and doubtful days. The months passed. The "rebel" borders were pressed still farther back, the Mississippi opened, Tennessee and Arkansas cleared of insurgent control, slaveowners "now declare openly for emancipation," Maryland and Missouri disputing now only as to the best mode of removing slavery within their own limits.

Of former slaves 100,000 were now in the United States military service, half of them bearing arms. "So far as tested, it is difficult to say they are not as good soldiers as any." No servile insurrection or tendency to violence or cruelty had marked the emancipation measures and the arming of the blacks. The tone of public sentiment had improved, the latest elections were encouraging. "Thus we have the new reckoning. The crisis which threatened to divide the friends of the Union is past."

Looking to the present and future, the President had thought fit to issue a Proclamation of Amnesty and Reconstruction, a copy of it being transmitted with the message to Congress.

The time had come to project those words "amnesty and reconstruction" across the country into the minds of as many people as possible. Two of the main objectives of the President, now, were wrapped around those words. "Amnesty" was an old word that meant overlooking something as though it no longer were, as though it couldn't be seen, as though it had been wiped out into oblivion, as though it had been pardoned, erased, changed into nothing. To those who wanted it the Union Government would give amnesty, forget what had been. Reconstruction, the bringing together again of the departed brothers into the Union, would begin with amnesty. This was the theory and the hope, not explicitly formulated, that underlay the proclamation and the oath which Lincoln discussed for Congress in his message.

He cited his constitutional pardoning power; through the rebellion many persons were guilty of treason; the President was authorized to extend pardon and amnesty on conditions he deemed expedient; he had already issued several such proclamations in regard to liberation of slaves; and it was now desired by some persons hitherto engaged in the said "rebellion" to resume their allegiance to the United States and to reinaugurate loyal State governments. Therefore full pardon would be granted to each of them, with restoration of property, except as to slaves and where rights of third parties intervened, and on condition that every such person took an oath:

I, —— ——, do solemnly swear, in presence of almighty God, that I will henceforth faithfully support, protect, and defend the Constitution of the United States, and the union of the States thereunder; and that I will, in like manner, abide by and faithfully support all acts of Congress passed during the existing rebellion with reference to slaves, so long and so far as not repealed, modified, or held void by Congress, or by decision of the Supreme Court; and that I will, in like manner, abide by and faithfully support all proclamations of the President made during the existing rebellion having reference to slaves, so long and so far as not modified or declared void by decision of the Supreme Court. So help me God.

The proclamation had no reference to States that had kept loyal governments, never seceded—meaning Missouri, Kentucky, Maryland, Delaware. Also members elected to Congress from reconstructed States would be passed on by the Senate or House, as to whether they could take seats.

The intention of the proclamation was to give a mode by which national authority and loyal State governments might be re-established. "While the mode presented is the best the executive can suggest, with his present impressions, it must not be understood that no other possible mode would be acceptable."

The President's message reasoned for the amnesty proclamation. "The form of an oath is given but no man is coerced to take it. The man is promised a pardon only in case he voluntarily takes the oath. . . . There must be a test by which to separate the opposing elements, so as to build only from the sound; and that test is a sufficiently liberal one which accepts as sound whoever will make a sworn recantation of his former unsoundness. . . . Why any proclamation now upon this subject? . . . The step might be delayed too long or be taken too soon. In some States the elements for resumption seem ready for action, but remain inactive apparently for want of a rallying-point—a plan of action. Why shall A adopt the plan of B, rather than B that of A? And if A and B should agree, how can they know but that the General Government here will reject their plan? By the proclamation a plan is presented which may be accepted by them as a rallying-point. This may bring them to act sooner than they otherwise would."

The proclamation was in danger of committals on points more safely left to further developments. "Care has been taken to so shape the document as to avoid embarrassments from this source . . . it is not said other classes, or other terms, will never be included . . . it is not said it [reconstruction] will never be accepted in any other way." He pointed to the laws and proclamations regarding slavery as put forth to aid in suppression of the "rebellion." To abandon the freed Negroes would be not only to relinquish a lever of power, but would also be "a cruel and astounding breach of faith."

The Executive set at rest all talk that the Emancipation Proclamation would be revoked. "While I remain in my present position I shall not attempt to retract or modify the Emancipation Proclamation; nor shall I return to slavery any person who is free by the terms of that proclamation, or by any of the acts of Congress."

Before this sentence the silence in the hall was "profound," noted Noah Brooks, but with its reading "an irresistible burst of applause" swept the main floor and galleries.

Movements for emancipation in States not included in the Emancipation Proclamation were "matters for profound gratulation." He still favored gradual emancipation by Federal purchase of slaves. "While I do not repeat in detail what I have heretofore so earnestly urged upon this subject, my general views and feelings remain unchanged."

The army and navy, however, were still the main reliance. "To that power alone can we look, yet for a time, to give confidence to the people in the contested regions that the insurgent power will not again overrun them. Until that confidence shall be established, little can be done anywhere for what is called reconstruction."

The careful balancing of issues and interests in the proclamation and message impressed Hay, who on December 10 found Senator Sumner pleased. "It satisfies his idea of proper reconstruction without insisting on the adoption of his peculiar theories."

Noah Brooks in his news letter of two days later contrarily found Senator Sumner "irate because his doctrine of State suicide finds no responsive echo" in the President's message. As a "vent to his half-concealed anger," wrote Brooks, "during the delivery of the Message the distinguished Senator from Massachusetts exhibited his petulance to the galleries by eccentric motions in his chair, pitching his documents and books upon the floor in ill-tempered disgust." Sumner still held to his theory that the seceded States had by secession committed suicide and should be governed as Territories, conquered provinces on trial and under compulsion. Of the President's awareness on this sensitive point, Hay noted that the President "says that he wrote in the Message originally that he considered the decision as to whether a State has been at any time out of the Union as vain and profitless. We know that they were, we trust that they shall be in the Union. It does not greatly matter whether in the meantime they shall be considered to have been in or out. But he afterwards considered that the 4th Section, 4th Article of the Constitution, empowers him to grant protection to States *in* the Union and it will not do ever to admit that these States have at any time been out. So he erased that sentence as possibly suggestive of evil. He preferred he said to stand firmly based on the Constitution rather [than] work in the air."

In this same White House talk with Hay, Lincoln referred to Missouri and the radicals there as absolutely uncorrodible by the virus of secession: "These radical men have in them the stuff which must save the State and on which we must mainly rely. . . . The Conservatives, in casting about for votes to carry through their plans, are tempted to affiliate with those whose record is not clear. If one side *must* be crushed out & the other cherished there could be no doubt which side we must choose as fuller of hope for the future. We would have to side with the Radicals. But just there is where their wrong begins. They insist that I shall hold and treat Governor Gamble and his supporters—men appointed by the loyal people of Mo. as rep's of Mo. loyalty, and who have done their whole duty in the war faithfully & promptly—who when they have disagreed with me have been silent and kept about the good work—that I shall treat these men as Copperheads and enemies to the Gov't. This is simply monstrous."

Lincoln continued to Hay on this snarl of affairs in Missouri: "I talked to these people in this way when they came to me this fall. I saw that their attack on Gamble was malicious. They moved against him by flank attacks from different sides of the same question. They accused him of enlisting rebel soldiers among the enrolled militia, and of exempting all the rebels and forcing Union men to do the duty: all this in the blindness of passion. I told them they were endangering the election of Senator; that I thought their duty was to elect Henderson and Gratz Brown; and nothing has happened in our politics which has pleased me more than that incident."

Lincoln spoke of the newborn fury of some of these men, of Drake [chairman of the committee of Missouri radicals who had called on Lincoln at the White House with peremptory demands] stumping against Rollins in '56 on the ground that Rollins was an abolitionist. "Not that he objected," noted Hay. "He was glad of it; but fair play let not the pot make injurious reference to the black base of the kettle. He was in favor of short statutes of limitations."

To a remark of Congressman Arnold, the President said he had for a long time been aware that the Kentuckians were not regarding in good faith the Emancipation Proclamation and the laws of Congress, but were treating as slaves the escaped freemen from Alabama and Mississippi; that this must be ended as soon as his hands grew a little less full.

While the President's proclamation and message were over the country being praised, discussed, or dragged in the mud, Hay wrote December 13 of the President "very much displeased" at fresh reports from Missouri. Congressman Washburne had been in Missouri and saw, or thought he saw, that Schofield was overplaying his hand in factional politics; when Washburne spoke of electing Gratz Brown and J. B. Henderson as United States Senators, one from each faction, Schofield had replied he would not consent to the election of Gratz Brown. Also Gratz Brown had told the President that Schofield had refused to consent to a State constitutional convention, even though Gratz Brown had promised in that event he would as United States Senator vote to confirm Schofield as a major general. "These things," wrote Hay, "the President says, are obviously transcendent of his instructions to Schofield and must not be permitted. He has sent for Schofield to come to Washington and explain these grave matters. The President is inclined to put Rosecrans in Schofield's place and to give Gen. Curtis the Department of Kansas. But Halleck and Stanton stand in his way, and he has to use the strong hand so often with those impractical gentlemen, that he avoids it when he can."

Schofield journeyed from St. Louis to the White House, heard Lincoln repeat Washburne's story, replied the facts were that he had told Washburne the desired union of conservatives and radicals in Missouri was impossible, for they were more bitterly opposed to each other than either was to the Democrats. According to Schofield, Lincoln promptly dismissed the subject with the words "I believe you, Schofield; those fellows have been lying to me again."

From Congressman James S. Rollins, Schofield heard that one group of Missouri politicians had called on the President and given a version of Missouri affairs. The President had opened a little right-hand drawer of his desk, taken out a letter from Schofield, read it to them and said, "*That* is the truth about the matter; you fellows are lying to me."

To the Secretary of War, Lincoln wrote: "I believe General Schofield must be relieved from command of the department of Missouri; otherwise a question of veracity, in relation to his declarations as to his interfering, or not, with the Missouri legislature, will be made with him, which will create an additional amount of trouble, not to be overcome by even a correct decision of the question. The question itself must be avoided. Now for the mode." The conservative Senator, Henderson, friendly to Schofield, would vote for his confirmation as major general, while the radical Senator, Gratz Brown, hated Schofield sufficiently to be willing to make him major general if he would get out of Missouri. Also, noted Lincoln, "I find it is scarcely less than indispensable for me to do something for General Rosecrans," and both Missouri Senators were agreed that Rosecrans would do for Missouri.

Also Lincoln was suggesting to Stanton a plan given him by Schofield for detaching Kansas from the Department of Missouri and making two departments, because of the fact that in Missouri the Gratz Brown radicals were against Lincoln while in Kansas the Jim Lane radicals were for Lincoln and no department commander could ever reconcile the two and work smoothly with them. For the new department Lincoln would name General S. R. Curtis. "I have received such evidence and explanations, in regard to the supposed cotton transactions of General Curtis, as fully restore in my mind the fair presumption of his innocence; and, as he is my friend, and what is more, as I think, the country's friend, I would be glad to relieve him from the impression that I think him dishonest by giving him a command. . . . Perhaps the first thing would be to send General Schofield's nomination to me." Stanton did. Lincoln sent it to the Senate. There a majority favored it. But by a small minority, controlling the Military Committee, it was hung up against the President's wishes for weeks.

Then one day came word from Grant that General Foster, heading the Department and Army of the Ohio, was leaving on account of ill-health, and Grant, being asked whom to appoint in Foster's place, wired, "Either McPherson or Schofield." Halleck handed Grant's dispatch to Schofield, who carried it to Lincoln saying he would take all chances on the new job. Lincoln: "Why, Schofield, that cuts the knot, don't it? Tell Halleck to come over here, and we will fix it right away." Then Schofield was appointed and transferred, with Rosecrans taking his place in Missouri.

While the Schofield affair took its course the *Detroit Free Press* one day offered its meditation: "President Lincoln has removed General Schofield from command of the Department of Missouri. This was to have been expected for a few weeks ago Mr. Lincoln told the radicals of Missouri that he would *not* remove him." Which was one way of giving a false impression of what the President was actually doing with Missouri and Schofield.

In *Harper's Weekly* "The Lounger" noted that when one of the German radical papers called upon Congress "to protect the Government against the Administration," it was repeating "the silliest Copperhead sophism." And in a paragraph that voiced publicly almost the same points that Lincoln spoke privately to Hay, "The Lounger" wrote: "No sensible man will forget that the faithful men of Missouri have been tried by fire and blood. A few expletives and superlatives may be pardoned them. A stern, implacable determination that slavery, the monster that has spawned civil war, shall be ended and forever, is only natural to them. They feel its fangs every moment, and they can not choose fine phrases. And they are not unjust. The *Missouri Democrat*, the radical organ, says that President Lincoln has made a tragical mistake, but it does not accuse him of the least ill intent. The President, by his declared policy, belongs with the radical loyal

Missourians. A few months more of war will bring him to their side. A few months more will show him that Mr. Postmaster-General Blair is not a wise counselor, and does not represent a Border State policy."

The *New York Times*, under editorship of Henry J. Raymond, was saying that Lincoln's refusal to identify himself with either side in Missouri exhibited broad-souled patriotism, singleness of purpose. "Mr. Lincoln never forgets he is President of the nation and his prime duty is to save the nation from the rebellion which has threatened to destroy it. He knows how to judge every question with reference purely to that great end and consequently can not be drawn into any petty strife." Nor would the Peace Democrats dictate. "The war shall be carried on not in Seymour's way nor in Vallandigham's way but in Mr. Lincoln's way."

One of the first particular grants of amnesty under the new proclamation was made out by the President for his sister-in-law, under the White House roof unbeknown to the public. In her "restored rights of person and property," she was to be "protected as a loyal person." The document began: "Mrs. Emily T. Helm, not being excepted from the benefits of the proclamation by the President of the United States . . ." She had taken and subscribed to the oath according to said proclamation. A postscript read, "Mrs. Helm claims to own some cotton at Jackson, Mississippi, and also some in Georgia; and I shall be glad, upon either place being brought within our lines, for her to be afforded the proper facilities to show her ownership, and take her property." A presidential pass of the same date requested her return to Kentucky, protected "except as to slaves, of which I say nothing."

Representative Foote of Tennessee in the Confederate Congress at Richmond, in behalf of "the eleven millions of enlightened freemen" of the South, presented resolutions denouncing "the truly characteristic proclamation of amnesty issued by the imbecile and unprincipled usurper who now sits enthroned upon the ruins of Constitutional liberty in Washington City." Representative Miles of South Carolina regretted that such a resolution had been presented. "The true and only treatment which that miserable and contemptible despot, Lincoln, should receive at the hands of this House is silent and unmitigated contempt. This resolution would appear to dignify a paper emanating from that wretched and detestable abortion, whose contemptible emptiness and folly will only receive the ridicule of the civilized world."

Mr. Foote was willing that both preamble and resolution should be tabled, with the understanding that it would indicate the unqualified contempt of the House for Abraham Lincoln and his message and proclamation. Mr. Miles said there would be no misunderstanding about that. And the motion to table was unanimously adopted. Representative Miller of Virginia brought up further resolutions of contempt whereby the Representatives of the people, as such and as individuals, would "hereby solemnly and irrevocably utterly deny, defy, spurn back, and scorn the terms of amnesty offered by Abraham Lincoln in his official proclamation." These too were tabled.

Not yet were one-tenth of the people of the South ready for reconstructed States, said the *Richmond Examiner*. "We gratify the curiosity of our readers with the message of Abraham Lincoln. Recovering but recently from an attack of the small-pox, some excuse may be made for the message. It is but another exhibition of his weakness and folly. Why his Cabinet will permit him to make such a fool of himself, can only be accounted for on the supposition that it is the easiest way to get rid of him. They therefore permit him fullest use of his pen."

The *Richmond Sentinel* quoted Benjamin Franklin's reply to a British offer of amnesty: "We, who have committed no offense, need no forgiveness." The Confederate answer would be the same even if Lincoln's offer imitated the humanity of Great Britain's. "Forgive us for having burned our towns and desolated our homes? . . . How impudent it is to come, with our brothers' blood upon his accursed hands, and ask us to accept his forgiveness! But he goes further. He makes his forgiveness dependent on terms. We have only to swear obedience to his will, to his Proclamation of Emancipation. . . . This is the best that Lincoln can think of for us—utter prostration at his feet—a social ruin, horrible to every white man, rich or poor; and our choicest citizens, whose names are our pride, handed over to be hanged!" No British commissioner in all his arrogance had ever put forth so "impudent" a message. The Confederate reply would be new zeal, new efforts. "How he and Seward and Sumner would gloat over the hanging bodies of 'dead rebels.' "

The Richmond War Office clerk, J. B. Jones, was writing in his diary: "It is said the President [Davis] and cabinet have a large special fund in Europe. If they should fall into the hands of Lincoln, they might suffer death; so in the event of subjugation, it is surmised they have provided for their subsistence in foreign lands."

This month of December, 1863, seemed to mark the beginning of a period in which, North and South, extremists more often referred to Confederate leaders ending in the noose on the gallows, treading air. Hanging with rigor, system, ceremonial, lay in the imaginings of the more fiery Republican radicals.

The *Richmond Examiner* editorial writer, Edward A. Pollard, in December quoted from Lincoln's Amnesty Proclamation and set down his judgment as a historian: "In proposing these utterly infamous terms, this Yankee monster of inhumanity and falsehood, had the audacity to declare that in some of the Confederate States the elements of reconstruction were ready for action. . . . This insulting and brutal proposition of the Yankee Government was the apt response to those few cowardly factions which in North Carolina, and in some parts of Georgia and Alabama, hinted at 'reconstruction.' "

Considering Mr. Lincoln's personal behavior, Pollard as a historian saw him a total loss in manners, a peasant upstart. "Mr. Lincoln was jocose again. He snapped his fingers at 'the rebellion.' He attended the theatre nightly. This piece of human jacquerie chattered incessantly over the success of his schemes."

The opposition press of the North tore at the President's proclamation and message. "The document is marked by the usual characteristics of rough rhetoric and defiance of ordinary rules of construction," said the *New York Journal of Commerce*. "Its words and sentences fall in heaps, instead of flowing in a connected stream, and it is therefore difficult reading." The *New York Metropolitan Record* queried: "Ye war Democrats, what do you think of being told that the black soldier is just as good as the white, for this is the amount of the President's message? What next? Shall we look among the black race for the President's successor?" Worst of all, clamored this newspaper, was "the brazen audacity" with which the President claimed the pardoning power. "It is the despot's claim; it is put forth in the spirit of a man who is so used to the exercise of arbitrary power that he acts and speaks upon the presumption that he is addressing a nation of slaves. He, the fourth or fifth rate lawyer—and if there was a lower rate than that he might find place under it—he, the hack politician of a sectional, factious party, pretends to tell the freemen of this country that he will pardon them."

The *Record* saw the oath provided by "Abraham the First" as a tyrant's tool. The taking of such an oath would be "an act of debasement so low, an act of self-degradation so vile, that you cannot be guilty of it without placing yourself on a level with the great criminal who now occupies the Presidential chair."

The President was the writer of his own message, undoubtedly, surmised the *Chicago Times*. "It is in his style, and his is a style that nobody imitates. Slipshod as have been all his literary performances, this is the most slovenly of all. If they were slipshod, this is barefoot, and the feet, plainly enough, never have been shod. . . . The reader will wonder why the fore part was written. And the latter part rests upon an appendix. . . . The conditions of pardon which he offers will further inflame the rebellion. . . . The President appears to be not very firmly committed to his own propositions. He reaches them haltingly. But it has been haltingly that he has reached all the extreme measures which have been pressed upon him." On second reading, and two days later, the *Times* veered slightly: "We must give the President credit for a certain low cunning in framing his proclamation of amnesty. He had to find the dividing line between terms which would, to common minds, have some little semblance of fairness."

The *Charleston Mercury*, now two small pages in size, printed the message and proclamation nearly entire. "Information it contains is important to the right understanding of the present phase of the war." The editor agreed with the *Richmond Examiner* that it was as bare as a leaf from a ledger. "Such derisive laughter has been excited by the Hoosier's [Lincoln's] previous attempts at fine writing, that he has no longer spirit to show himself. The tone is subdued; the language dry and plain; the exposition is brief as arithmetic." The document was important as revealing the decline of the mania for war in the United States. "Lincoln represents his people now as he did two years ago. Then, all was bloody. Confiscation, subjugation, extermination, were the only measures he and they thought or spoke of. . . . The chief hope now rests in a juggle. There is a time for all things. A time for fighting, and that time is nearly past; a time for cheating, and that time has nearly come."

Lincoln was a type of tyrant repeated from age to age, the *Mercury* advised its readers. It quoted from Motley's *History of the Dutch Republic*, Volume II, page 461, the proclamation of Alva to his Flemish subjects in 1573, saying that "with a few verbal alterations and a dash of flippancy and vulgarity, it might be supposed to be the production of Mr. Lincoln in 1863." And the words of Alva read:

But if ye disregard these offers of mercy, receiving them with closed ears, as heretofore, then we warn you that there is no rigor, nor cruelty, however great, which you are not to expect by laying waste, starvation, and the sword, in such a manner that no where shall *remain a relic of that which at present exists*, but his Majesty will strip bare and *utterly depopulate the land*, and cause it to be inhabited *again by strangers;* since otherwise his Majesty could not believe that the *will of God and of his Majesty* had been accomplished.

The *Mercury* showed remarkable good faith with its readers in often printing Lincoln's important letters and addresses correctly and in full text. Once it quoted from a speech where Lincoln was interrupted and again began speaking, the *Mercury* paragraph closing: "The Baboon resumed and finished his remarks." In its report of a group of ministers visiting the President, the *Mercury* said, "Members of the Baltimore Presbyterian Synod called on ABRAHAM (HANKS) LINCOLN," and thereafter referred to Lincoln as "HANKS," this being a byplay on the common talk that Lincoln's parental lineage was clouded and he sprang from the lower "white trash" of the South. Not merely the President but the entire New England tribe were an evil lot, the *Mercury* taught its readers, quoting from a London traveler to Boston in 1699:

In Boston there is more religious zealots than honest men; more parsons than churches, and more churches than parishes. For the town, unlike the people, is subject to no division. The inhabitants seem very religious, showing many outward and visible signs of an inward and spiritual grace. But though they wear in their faces the innocence of doves, you will find them in their dealings as subtile as serpents. Interest is their faith—money their God, and large possessions the only Heaven they covet.

Ready to sacrifice the lives of a million more citizens of the North to win the war, thus stood the Yankee President, said the *Mercury*. "Even then he will only have stepped knee deep into the fathomless ocean of blood which must be shed before the horrid crime can be accomplished." Scores of articles, paragraphs, and squibs thrusting at Lincoln as both tyrant and fool were reprinted from the London *Times*. "The President made a speech that not even the friendly reports could invest with dignity."

Now in December of '63 a darker brooding began to tint the editorials of Robert Barnwell Rhett, whose thirty-year agitation of the doctrine of secession, as received by him from the lips of John Calhoun, had been an immediate factor in bringing on the war. What the Greeks had done under Miltiades, the Prussians under Frederick the Great, the French under Napoleon in hurling back stronger squadrons and heavier artillery, was told in articles that ran three and four columns in length. Any "state of truce" would be miserable, the name of "Union man" a merciless insult. "If it requires every man and every dollar in the Confederacy, we will collect, marshal and use them; but to submit to Yankee ferocity and brutality, never —never! Let no man despair—let no man fail of his duty; for we will sow our land with salt and brimstone, nor leave one rose standing to tell where the garden had been, ere the foe shall possess our goodly heritage! When the hard conflict is won, the results of joy and good will be correspondingly good."

Three months before the President's first proclamation looking tentatively toward reconstruction, the *Mercury* voiced the Cotton States and the Deep South in saying: "The war has shown that no union with the people of the United States can exist, consistent with our liberties or the safety of property. We must be entirely independent of them or perish as a people. The war, and the war only, has probably settled all doubts as to reconstruction."

It was natural that Lincoln should refer with a gesture half of despair to guns and bayonets as the only appeal and arbitrament that could touch "those who are salivated by the *Charleston Mercury*." The *Mercury's* more frequent advertisements of cash rewards for deserters from the Confederate Army, its cut in size from four to two pages, its advance of subscription rates from $10 to $30 a year this December of '63, might be signs of the sunset of the Confederacy—perhaps a long, lurid gloaming.

Democratic politicians and newspapers of the North, in their hue and cry against the Lincoln Administration, aimed partly at keeping their party alive for the '64 campaign. John Hay dined, cracked jokes, and gossiped pleasantly with Samuel S. ("Sunset") Cox, an Ohio Congressman who was part of the organization that had tried to elect Vallandigham governor of the Buckeye State. Cox told Hay it was delightful to be in the minority. "You are not bored by your people for offices." Cox had humor, said he was getting tired of Washington, would like to spend a few years in Europe, would go over there if McClellan was elected President in '64.

Cox knew his crowd did not believe all they were saying of Lincoln. Like the *Detroit Free Press*, he saw no other course as a Democratic-party voice than to howl against the Administration. The *Detroit Free Press* had croaked as to Lincoln's latest, "There never was a message from a President of the United States so weak and puerile as this." The *New York World* led up to its comment on Lincoln's proclamation by saying that the feelings which gave revolutionary impulse to the South might be poetry or might be a madness, which is a sort of diseased poetry. "You can no more control it than a flaxen hand can fetter flame." Yet such control was being attempted. "President Lincoln has shown himself utterly destitute of the statesmanlike tact requisite for dealing with a great people in revolt; he is blind . . . if Mr. Lincoln were a statesman, if he were even a man of ordinary prudence and sagacity, he would see the necessity of touching the peculiar wound of the South with as light a hand as possible." Of the proposed oath and the President's assumed power of pardon, said the *World*, "If there is any lower depth of absurdity, trust to the sure instinct of Mr. Lincoln to find it."

Yet in the same week that the President's message was issued, and while the President yet lay a sick man not recovered from varioloid, both the *New York World* and the *Detroit Free Press* joined in a remarkably human commentary. From those intensely partisan organs came honeyed words, curious discriminations, generous wishes. It was a moment in which to tell their readers of other Republicans to be hated worse than Lincoln. And they editorialized:

We believe we but echo the feelings of the whole country, without distinction of party, in sincerely hoping that the President will soon be restored to health and strength. Men of his habit of body are not usually long-lived, and the small-pox to a man of his age, even when the health is usually good, is a very serious matter. His death at this time would tend to prolong the war.

Until the Presidential election is held we wish to see Mr. Lincoln conduct the government rather than Mr. Hannibal Hamlin, the present Vice-President. Better a plague, better the death of all our Generals, better the loss of the Mississippi and a foreign war combined, than that the furious anti-slavery fanaticism which Mr. Hamlin represents should get complete control of the machinery of the government.

Mr. Lincoln has oftentimes acted wrongly, unwisely, arbitrarily; but still he hesitates before he takes an extreme position, and is willing to obey, although not always quick to perceive, the drift of public opinion. Without elevation of character, he has a self-poise, a reticence, an indisposition to commit himself, which in many a trying crisis has saved him from being the utter tool of the madmen whose folly brought on the war, and who never knew, and can never learn, how to carry it on. But Mr. Hamlin is a very different person. Were he President, people of the stamp of Garrison and Greeley would be called to the Cabinet. Frémont and Butler would be put at the head of our armies, and the whole machinery of the government would be put into play to put down free speech and a free press.

Mr. Lincoln was frank enough to tell Wendell Phillips that his proclamation of emancipation was the most foolish act of his life; but Mr. Hamlin, when this same Phillips was introduced upon the floor of the Senate, ostentatiously gave up his position as presiding officer to greet and welcome that first of orators and worst of fanatics and disunionists. Mr. Hamlin's speech, not long since, at the Cooper Institute, gave the country the measure of his character. It was scurrilous, intemperate; without dignity, breadth of view, or appreciation of the mortal agony of the nation. Such men sometimes help parties, but they ruin governments.

So heaven help Abraham Lincoln, and restore him to his wonted health and strength.

As to literary style and human approach in the December message and proclamation, the *New York Times* said: "Abraham Lincoln is one of the few men who believe that words stand for things; he economizes them accordingly. . . . Those who know best the character of his administration, know that it could never be cruel. The principal danger is from excessive leniency." The *New York Herald* occasionally flung a flower of approval toward Lincoln, but left that chiefly to the *Times*, which had become in effect the Lincoln Administration organ in New York. Neither could the *Herald* join with its other rival, Greeley's *Tribune*, which leaned always to the radicals, nor with the *New York Express*, the *World*, the *Daily News*, the *Metropolitan Record*, which were antiwar, anti-Negro, and proslavery.

So the *Herald* kept public and readers guessing every day as to how far ahead it would go and then back up. Of the December message it said: "The art of riding two horses is not confined to the circus. It is an old trick of the trade and has been practiced by politicians from time immemorial. . . . President Lincoln has been riding two horses with the skill of an old campaigner and the radical horse is a 'leetle ahead.' . . . After having listened to the demands of the radicals for the removal of Mr. Seward and after having excited their wrath and threats of vengeance in the matter of the Kansas-Missouri muddle, he exalts them in his Message to the seventh heaven of Mahomet. Next to a good joke it is evident 'Old Abe' is fond of a rousing sensation."

The *New York Evening Post* under the editorship of William Cullen Bryant took notice that an impetuous part of the public often complained of Mr. Lincoln that he moved months after he ought to, that he was a laggard, a "slow coach." However, Mr. Lincoln, "being the mere servant of a free and somewhat opinionated people," had acted in the main wisely. "He evidently holds it to be the duty of the President of the United States to govern the country according to the will of the majority of the people. . . . Sworn interpreter of that will . . . he has endeavored diligently to first ascertain it, then to put it into execution." Could this be the personal judgment of the same William Cullen Bryant who had favored the Missouri radicals, who a few weeks previous had stood on the Cooper Union platform and joined their speakers in sharp deviation from the Lincoln Administration, who had written extensively that the paper-money policy of the government, particularly in making greenbacks legal tender, was vicious? So it seemed.

And he proceeded: "Mr. Lincoln has seen that to move faster than public sentiment would provoke useless hostility; and he has chosen to go with the people; to let his acts advance parallel with their convictions and thus to secure for every measure the sympathy of the great mass of loyal Americans. If we glance back at the conspicuous events of the last two and a half years we shall see that in every instance he has conducted public affairs upon this theory; and we shall recognize in most of his delays, often unaccountable at the time and vexatious to our own more eager spirits, he was but waiting to discern the real sense of the public mind. The Amnesty Proclamation is another evidence of the care with which the President studies the wishes of the people. His Proclamation is framed to meet the interests and opinions of the Union men of the States affected by it."

This seemed to be the first time that a publicist of importance had dwelt at such length on the merits of Lincoln as a laggard, had seized on the very point that Lincoln wavered, hesitated, waited, before his big decisions, and in so doing had practiced precisely the cool deliberation wanted in the smoke and throaty clamor of a war of brothers.

The author of "Thanatopsis" and "To a Water Fowl" could not have done better to confuse further the minds of Senator Gratz Brown and the Frémont followers in their judgment that Lincoln was a Mr. Facing-Both-Ways. Once had Bryant gone with a delegation to the White House to urge immediate and universal emancipation. And he had since decided that his mind did not work so clearly in the Washington atmosphere and he would make it a habit to stay away from the capital city. It was thirty-one years, a story said, since Bryant had traveled the Ohio and the Mississippi to St. Louis, crossed the prairies to his brother at Princeton, Illinois, and en route met a Black Hawk War company of soldiers with a lank, racy captain who Bryant had later learned was Lincoln. It was only four years since Bryant had introduced Lincoln for a speech in Cooper Union, and he never did find out how the little story arose that Lincoln had said of meeting Bryant in New York, "It was worth the journey to the East to see such a man."

Having studied the Amnesty Proclamation for a week, Bryant wrote an editorial that read as if he had sat to its writing with an intention to read deep into Lincoln's heart. Others were remarking that Mr. Lincoln's proposal to pardon the rebels on condition of their forswearing slavery was very novel. Bryant could see it as novel only in its terms, not in its general design. "It has been usual for the executive powers of states, at the close of great rebellions against authority, to offer pardon to persons implicated in them, with certain exceptions. They might, according to the law, execute the severest penalties upon every man who had taken up arms; confiscate their property, disgrace them or order them to perpetual exile. . . . Mr. Lincoln, in the stupendous case of the slaveholders' rebellion, exhibits a magnanimity beyond greatness. He not only extends to the guilty infractors of their country's laws, the prospect of an entire oblivion of their offenses but makes the condition of the pardon the grandest favor which it is possible to confer upon them and their posterity. He says to them that they have been induced into acts of foul and bloody debauchery and that every man of them deserves the halter or exile but that he will insist upon no vengeance, that he will soften even the requirements of justice if they will give utterance that they will get drunk no more."

Little by little, by word and act, Lincoln had convinced certain sections of the educated classes that he was worth studying, or at least they should waste no time feeling sorry for him. The eminent Boston author and literary critic Charles Eliot Norton, an authority on the New Testament, on Dante,

William Blake, and Michelangelo, had in 1862 written of a Lincoln message: "Could anything be more feebly put, or more inefficiently written? His style is worse than ever; and though a bad style is not always a mark of bad thought, it is at least a proof that thought is not as clear as it ought to be."

A year later Norton wrote to the same friend: "The President's letter struck me just as it has struck you. It is eminently characteristic of his better qualities of mind—those which he shows when pushed hard or really touched." A few months later Norton referred to the stump speech read to the Springfield, Illinois, mass meeting, "the extraordinary excellence of the President's letter." Each new effort had gains. "His letters are successive victories."

From deeper acquaintance with chaos and fiery trial Lincoln, as Norton saw it, was writing more simply and familiarly. It was not unlike the progress of a soul through Dante's Purgatory, on which Norton was author-itative. On reading the December message to Congress, Norton wrote to George William Curtis, "Once more we may rejoice that Abraham Lincoln is President," and of the Proclamation of Amnesty: "As a state paper its naïveté is wonderful. Lincoln will introduce a new style into state papers; he will make them sincere, and his honesty will compel even politicians to like virtue. I conceive his character to be on the whole the great net gain from the war."

The antislavery radicals, as Norton weighed them, usually remembered nothing, learned nothing, and had no gratitude except for future benefits. He quoted Lincoln as saying to someone, "It is very difficult to do sensible things."

A history rather than a biography would be required for recording the life of Lincoln, wrote James Russell Lowell, joint editor with Charles Eliot Norton of the *North American Review*, finishing an article on Lincoln for issue in January, 1864. An eminent Bostonian, author of Yankee dialect verse, a poet whose "Vision of Sir Launfal" and other works had wide appeal, an essayist and a critic who took his Americanism with little con-descension to foreigners, the Harvard professor who had followed Long-fellow in the chair of modern languages and belles-lettres—this was Lowell. His paper on the President's policy during three years was a confession of what had slowly and with gnarled growth entered some of the tougher minds of the country.

Lowell sketched the earlier months of the war, three years of searching and straining, during which he saw a steady purpose and a definite aim given to jarring forces. A popular excitement had been slowly intensified into an earnest national will; a somewhat impracticable moral sentiment had been made the unconscious instrument of a practical moral end; treason of covert enemies, jealousy of rivals, unwise zeal of friends, had been made not only useless for mischief but even useful for good. "All these results," wrote Lowell, "any one of which might suffice to prove greatness in a ruler, have been mainly due to the good sense, the good humor, the sagacity, the large-mindedness, and the unselfish honesty of the unknown man whom a blind fortune, as it seemed, had lifted from the crowd to the most dangerous and difficult eminence of modern times."

A politician of metal, tested by events, Lincoln would admit whatever of truth the opposition had so as to give his own replies to the opposition the force of argument. The politician of proven genius must allow hostile combinations to go so far as by the inevitable reaction to become elements of his own power, "especially . . . by so gently guiding public sentiment that he seems to follow it, by so yielding doubtful points that he can be firm without seeming obstinate in essential ones."

People come in time to see that such a political leader has shaken himself loose and is free from temper and prejudice. "For qualities such as these . . . we firmly believe History will rank Mr. Lincoln among the most prudent of statesmen and the most successful of rulers. If we wish to appreciate him, we have only to conceive the inevitable chaos in which we should now be weltering, had a weak man or an unwise one been chosen in his stead."

A new man as head and hand of the nation could have made costly mistakes with the weapons held by him when men were on fire. "You may make everything else out of the passions of men except a political system that will work," wrote Lowell. "There is nothing so pitilessly and unconsciously cruel as sincerity formulated into dogma. Perhaps the severest strain upon Mr. Lincoln was in resisting a tendency of his own supporters who chimed with his own private desires while wholly opposed to his convictions of what would be wise policy."

Three years of change had brought lessons to lay on the heart. "Never did a President enter upon office with less means at his command, outside his own strength of heart and steadiness of understanding, for inspiring confidence in the people, and so winning it for himself, than Mr. Lincoln. All that was known of him was that he was a good stump-speaker, nominated for his *availability*,—that is, because he had no history,—and chosen by a party with whose more extreme opinions he was not in sympathy. . . . He was to carry on a truly colossal war . . . disengage the country from diplomatic entanglements . . . and to win . . . in the confidence of the people, the means of his safety and their own. He has contrived to do it, and perhaps none of our Presidents since Washington has stood so firm in the confidence of the people as he does after three years of stormy administration. . . . At first he was so slow that he tired out all those who see no evidence of progress but in blowing up the engine; then he was so fast, that he took the breath away from those who think there is no getting on safely while there is a spark of fire under the boilers. . . . Mr. Lincoln . . . has always waited . . . till the right moment brought up all his reserves."

This was Lowell's admission of mistaken judgment when months before he had written in a private letter: "Lincoln may be right, for aught I know, but I guess an ounce of Frémont is worth a pound of long Abraham. Mr. Lincoln seems to have the theory of carrying on the war without hurting the enemy. He is incapable, apparently, of understanding that they *ought* to be hurt."

Lowell now enfigured Lincoln as a logger in a crazy river snatching his way on a shaky raft and trying to hold to the main current through rapids. "He is still in wild water, but we have faith that his skill and sureness of eye will bring him out right at last."

That Mr. Lincoln was neither handsome nor elegant could be learned from certain English tourists who would resent remarks upon the figure of Queen Victoria. British critics, not unfriendly, reproached Mr. Lincoln for his Americanism. "With all deference, we cannot say that we like him any the worse for that."

Rather than proclaiming adhesion to certain doctrines, believed Lowell, Lincoln was achieving their triumph by quietly accomplishing his own ends. "There is no more unsafe politician than a conscientiously rigid doctrinaire, nothing more sure to end in disaster than a theoretic scheme of policy that admits of no pliability for contingencies." Many would have Lincoln fill full the popular image of a ruler in whose plastic hands mankind became wax. "In real life we commonly find that the men who control circumstance, as it is called, are those who have learned to allow for the influence of their eddies, and have the nerve to turn them to account at the happy instant."

Between Henry IV of France moving a course among Protestant and Catholic interests, and Lincoln charting a path between slaveholder and abolitionist, Lowell could see parallels. Each was full of wise saws and modern instances, keeping his own personality amid confusions, neither being so good-looking. The distinction between the two would be: "Henry IV went over to the nation; Mr. Lincoln has steadily drawn the nation over to him. One left a united France; the other, we hope, and believe, will leave a reunited America."

As a lawyer Lincoln had always to deal with the two sides to a question. Debating with Douglas, amid the kind of prejudices and bigotry that turns orderly citizens into mobs of barbarians, he had won his case before a jury of the people. Lincoln had not learned his politics in a rush. He had studied the curious balances of human affairs. Later, more deliberately, Lowell added: "His slow, but singularly masculine intelligence taught him that precedent is only another name for embodied experience, and that it counts for even more in the guidance of communities of men than in that of individual life. . . . Perhaps . . . his want of self-confidence more than anything else . . . won him the unlimited confidence of the people, for they felt that there would be no need of retreat from any position he had deliberately taken. The cautious, but steady, advance of his policy during the war was like that of a Roman army. He left behind him a firm road on which public confidence could follow; he took America with him where he went."

The very homeliness of Lincoln's genius was its distinction, thought Lowell. "His kingship was conspicuous by its workday homespun. Never was ruler so absolute as he, nor so little conscious of it; for he was the incarnate common-sense of the people. With all that tenderness of nature whose sweet sadness touched whoever saw him with something of its own pathos, there was no trace of sentimentalism in his speech or action. He seems to have had but one rule of conduct, always that of practical and successful politics, to let himself be guided by events, when they were sure to bring him out where he wished to go."

Voltaire had said, "A consideration of petty circumstances is the tomb of great things," which, however true of individual men, was certainly not true of governments. A multitude of trifles were thrown into the weight and framing of any policy. Some trifles would seem inconsistent, not properly belonging. "The imputation of inconsistency is one to which every sound politician and every honest thinker must sooner or later subject himself. The foolish and the dead alone never change their opinion."

On the delicate and embarrassing slavery issue the President had kept to a little creed of politics which Lowell phrased as "loyalty to great ends, even though forced to combine the small and opposing motives of selfish men to accomplish them . . . the anchored cling to solid principles of duty and action, which knows how to swing with the tide, but is never carried away by it."

Some ardent and sincere persons had seemed to think presidential emancipation of the slaves as simple a thing to do as to lead off a Virginia reel. They forgot Mr. Lincoln had not been chosen as general agent of an antislavery society, but as President of the United States, to perform certain functions defined by law, whatever his personal wishes. A man of display would have freed the slaves forthwith. An acute and merely bargaining man would have compromised. A prudent and wise man had to take still another course, dull and homely-looking. "Mr. Lincoln dallied with his decision perhaps longer than seemed needful to those on whom its awful responsibility was not to rest, but when he made it, it was worthy of his cautious but surefooted understanding. The moral of the Sphinx-riddle, and it is a deep one, lies in the childish simplicity of the solution. Those who fail in guessing it, fail because they are over-ingenious, and cast about for an answer that shall suit their own notion of the gravity of the occasion, and of their own dignity, rather than the occasion itself."

Lowell set forth an expansion and paraphrase of Lincoln's policy on slavery as given a few months later in a letter of Lincoln to A. G. Hodges of Kentucky, Lowell giving emphasis later to points which Lincoln was confidentially mentioning to Hay and to Lamon but not yet putting into public papers. "Everything has been at work for the past ten years in the cause of antislavery, but Garrison and Phillips have been far less successful propagandists than the slaveholders themselves, with the constantly growing arrogance of their pretensions and encroachments. They have forced the question upon the attention of every voter in the Free States, by defiantly putting freedom and democracy on the defensive."

Every month of the war, every movement of the allies of slavery in the Free States, had been making abolitionists by the thousand. Of this

Lowell was sure; also, "While every day was bringing the people nearer to the conclusion which all thinking men saw to be inevitable from the beginning, it was wise in Mr. Lincoln to leave the shaping of his policy to events. . . . Mr. Lincoln is not in the habit of saying, 'This is *my* opinion, or *my* theory,' but 'This is the conclusion to which, in my judgment, the time has come, and to which, accordingly, the sooner we come the better for us.'"

From his armchair with an outlook on sedate Cambridge elms, from his Harvard eminence, Lowell stressed as "particularly admirable" in the public utterances of President Lincoln "a certain tone of familiar dignity, which, while it is perhaps the most difficult attainment of mere style, is also no doubtful indication of personal character." A profound common sense is the best genius for statesmanship. "In this country, the rough and ready understanding of the people is sure to be at last the controlling power." To break through etiquette of conventional rank, to descend to the level of confidential ease without losing respect, to trust himself to the reason and intelligence of those who have elected him, requires something very manly and essentially noble in an elective ruler.

"No higher compliment was ever paid to a nation than the simple confidence, the fireside plainness, with which Mr. Lincoln always addresses himself to the American people," ran Lowell's compliments. "This was, indeed, a true democrat, who grounded himself on the assumption that a democracy can think. . . . We have never had a chief magistrate who so won to himself the love and at the same time the judgment of his countrymen. To us, that simple confidence of his in the right-mindedness of his fellow-men is very touching, and its success is as strong an argument as we have ever seen in favor of the theory that men can govern themselves."

One secret of Lincoln's success in "captivating the popular mind," hazarded Lowell, was his use of the capital "I" without any suggestion of egotism. "There is no single vowel which men's mouths can pronounce with such difference of effect." Some men in discourse would use the capital "I" with offensive challenge, a dry northeast wind giving goose flesh. "Mr. Lincoln forgets himself so entirely in his object as to give his *I* the sympathetic and persuasive effect of *We* with the great body of his countrymen. Homely, dispassionate, showing all the rough-edged process of his thought as it goes along, yet arriving at his conclusions with an honest kind of every-day logic, he is so eminently our representative man, that, when he speaks, it seems as if the people were listening to their own thinking aloud."

Thus Mr. Lowell anticipated several, many, of his compeers.

The new Congress assembled the first Monday in December of '63, by the *New York Tribune Almanac* classification, had in the House 102 Republicans and unconditional Unionists, 75 Democrats, 9 Border State men; in the Senate 36 Republicans and unconditional Unionists, 9 Democrats, and 5 conditional Unionists.

By a vote of 101 to 81 Schuyler Colfax was elected Speaker of the

House. That Lincoln preferred for Speaker his own ally and Grant's particular friend, Elihu B. Washburne of Galena, Illinois, was indicated in a diary entry of Welles. Montgomery Blair had maneuvered for Washburne although, Welles noted, "Blair tells me his opinion of W[ashburne] is pretty much the same as mine and that he suggested and spoke of him at the instigation of the President, who, while he has not a very high opinion of Washburne, wants confidence in Colfax, whom he considers a little intriguer,—plausible, aspiring beyond his capacity, and not trustworthy." When a few days later Speaker Colfax shifted from what Welles regarded as "an explicit understanding" as to who should be appointed to the House Naval Committee, Welles wrote, "The President has, I see, a right appreciation of Colfax."

Among accomplished politicians sworn in as new members of Congress was James Brooks, editor and owner of the *New York Express*, fiercely anti-Lincoln and truculently antiabolitionist, though oddly enough when Brooks in 1841 had married Mrs. Mary Randolph, a Richmond widow, he had required her to free her three slaves before the wedding. Also among new faces in Congress were James G. Blaine, former editor of the *Portland* (Maine) *Advertiser*, Brutus Junius Clay of Kentucky, George S. Boutwell and Oakes Ames of Massachusetts, and two brigadier generals who had seen field service, James Abram Garfield and Robert Cumming Schenck, both of Ohio, Schenck taking Vallandigham's old seat.

Weeks before Congress met a letter had come to Lincoln from Postmaster Hood at Chattanooga, who was on friendly terms with Emerson Etheridge, clerk of the House of Representatives. Hood wished the President to know that Mr. Etheridge had a scheme up his sleeve to give control of the House to the Democrats. Etheridge had been given his job by the Republicans because as a former Congressman and a Union man in Tennessee he had faced persecution. While in Washington the first two years of the war he had drifted into the ranks of the anti-Administration men, had in June of '63 published a three-column letter in Copperhead newspapers arguing in a curiously blatherskite manner against equality of the races, against the Emancipation Proclamation, with left-hand passes at "Abraham Lincoln, Esq."

Now it came out that Etheridge had sent word to Democratic members that he intended on a technical legal point to leave off the rolls of the House the names of all members whose certificates did not bear the statement that they had been elected "according to the laws of the State or of the United States," as provided in a bill rushed through the last day of the previous Congress.

News of this came to Lincoln who, as quietly as Etheridge, sent word to leading Republicans in all the loyal States that they should have duplicate certificates prepared meeting any objection Etheridge might raise. Some Congressmen nevertheless arrived in Washington without such certificates. And they did not feel easy.

Lincoln called some of the leading Congressmen to the White House, told them the main thing was to be sure that all Union members were present. "Then," said Lincoln, as Nicolay heard him, "if Mr. Etheridge undertakes revolutionary proceedings, let him be carried out on a chip, and let our men organize the House."

Others likewise had thought of this way out. And one Congressman, the broad-shouldered and deep-chested Reverend Owen Lovejoy of Princeton, Illinois, gave word that he felt personally able to carry out Mr. Etheridge on a chip if necessary. However, at the hotels, saloons, and gambling-houses it was now an open secret that Mr. Etheridge would be taken care of; he knew it and it was getting on his nerves; he was saying he did not see why the Republicans should regard him vindictively.

The House on December 7 opened. The Reverend Byron Sunderland prayed, "We Beseech Thee, O Lord, to recover the President from his present illness again to health."

Then Mr. Etheridge did, as he had said he would, leave off the rolls the names of all members not having proper certificates, in his opinion, but he did readily hear a motion to restore such names. Lovejoy of Illinois rose to say that Mr. Etheridge certainly had "brass." Proslavery members protested, but the vote taken showed a majority of 20 for the Government. And by another vote soon taken Mr. Etheridge was thrown out as clerk of the House, and Edward McPherson of Pennsylvania put in.

Chaplain Sutherland again the next day prayed for the President of the United States: "Restore him to health, we beseech Thee, if it please Thee, and so replenish him with heavenly wisdom that in all the difficult and trying circumstances in which he is placed he may faithfully discharge his duty to God and to this great people."

One set of reports about himself that year the President did not bother to answer. Over and again the opposition newspapers large and small said in cold black type that his salary was to be raised from $25,000 to $100,000 a year, as he wished, that he was drawing his salary in gold while the soldiers were paid in greenbacks, that his length of time in office was to be fixed by Congress for a life term, as he wished. These reports were to be met in the next year's campaign, as also the story that Lincoln had asked Lamon to sing a comic song on the Antietam battlefield.

Correspondents of the opposition press were not taken care of as were some of the Republican boys. Under the head of "Office Holding Correspondents," the *Detroit Free Press* itemized on December 22, 1863: "Six correspondents of Republican journals have been appointed to clerkships under the new *regime* of the House and Senate, as follows: House Librarian, Whitelaw Reid, *Cincinnati Gazette;* clerk to Committee on Elections, D. Bartlett, *New York Evening Post;* clerk in office of House, Noah Brooks, *Sacramento Union;* clerk to Committee on Printing Records of Congress, Ben. Perley Poore, *Boston Journal;* clerk to Committee on Military Affairs of the Senate, Horace White, *Chicago Tribune;* clerk to the Senate Committee of Agriculture, J. B. McCullagh, *Cincinnati Commercial.*"

Of these news-writers there seemed to be only one whose methods and tactics were considered so questionable and unjust that a member of the White House staff tried to get the man removed from a rather powerful connection. This was Whitelaw Reid. Young John Hay had seen one newspaper story after another written by young Reid coloring fact and circumstance in favor of Chase and against Lincoln, and sent as news to a group of Midwest newspapers. On December 13, 1863, Hay wrote in his diary: "I talked with Ray [Charles H. Ray, one of the *Chicago Tribune* editors?] this morning to try to get Reid removed from his functions as Correspondent Western Ass^d Press. He is so outrageously unfair to the President and so servilely devoted to Mr. Chase."

Again in November and December the wires had carried speeches of Wendell Phillips, at Augusta, Maine, and in Boston. Again Phillips analyzed Lincoln and called for the creation of a public opinion to move the hesitant President in Washington. The Emancipation Proclamation should be followed by a Constitutional Amendment abolishing slavery in all States. The Government was too indecisive for such action without pressure. Said Phillips: "When Mr. Lincoln was asked to provide for the safety of the officers of colored regiments, he said, 'Don't ask me a word until after the Ohio election.' . . . I ask nothing further of Lincoln in the way of policy, only of action. He has taken the first great step by issuing the proclamation, and if he believed in January last, as he told me, that it was a great mistake, he has changed his mind since then. The man who had the heart to originate that proclamation, and to stand by it, ought to remain in power at least six years longer. Still, Abraham Lincoln was not my first choice. If we could have had Frémont [Applause.], a master and not a servant, a man already intelligent in the point most needful, and not one whose education was to be conducted at an expense of $25,000 a year in the Presidential chair, we should have made better progress."

Immediately opposition newspapers and orators spread it as fact that the President had said the Emancipation Proclamation was "the greatest mistake in my life." Also the report was widely published that the leading abolitionist orator had nominated Lincoln for a second presidential term, the inference being that Lincoln had been swept pell-mell into the extreme antislavery ranks.

In less than three weeks, however, the President had issued his conditional offer of pardons to "rebels," along with his declaration that so long as he were President he would not retract or modify the Emancipation Proclamation nor return any freemen to slavery. This, said Phillips, was throwing the Negro on the mercy of the Supreme Court. "The President's proclamation of last January is to be filtered through the secession heart of Roger B. Taney. If the negro's freedom has no protection but that, God help him! So far as State legislation goes, the President's plan leaves the negro at the mercy of the large landholders, who just now are slaveholders."

Then Phillips set forth the viewpoint that marked the parting of the ways for him and Lincoln, a revolutionary viewpoint approved by the grim Congressional floor leader, Thaddeus Stevens, Phillips saying: "The President's message has two merits. He pledges himself absolutely and forever to Emancipation, and he leaves it possible to save the Old State alive—a measure of first rate value. Otherwise he launches the Emancipation question in the worst possible form; and by setting aside the Confiscation act, he reconstructs the Union in such way as to leave the land of the South in the hands of the Union's foes. Landholders always decide the nature of a Government. Such a South must be, at least for this generation, aristocratic and hostile to Northern civilization. For thirty years the machine would be sure not to work. Peace gained by such reconstruction would be a sham—would, for many years, embroil the nation and grind the negro victim."

In quarters such as the office of the *New York Tribune*, Phillips had a more respectable standing than Lincoln. Greeley in reviewing a volume of Phillips's speeches, just published by James Redpath, estimated Phillips as far more than a great orator. "He is the eminent apostle of a great renovation, silver-tongued, earnest, fervid." The case of the mulatto Margaret Garner was recited by Phillips to rouse public opinion. She with her three children had broken from slavery, and reaching Cincinnati, they were arrested to be held for trial and probably returned to slave life.

While waiting trial, Margaret Garner killed with a butcher knife one of her three children, a little girl almost white in color. A minister asked her why. She answered: "The child was mine, given to me by God to do the best a mother could by it. I have done the best I could; I would have done more and better for the rest. I knew it was better for them to go home to God than back to slavery." Her Kentucky owners proved in court that she was a piece of slave property. And under the Fugitive Slave Law, Margaret Garner, with her two living children holding her hands, and the third child cold in a pine box, were taken back to their owner with armed officers of the law guarding the journey.

The President, urged Phillips, continued to take the position that he was President of the whole people, including such Border State slaveholders as were loyal to the Union; and some of these had made sacrifices. The President seemed to be waiting for the passage of a bill put in by Thad Stevens in the House and Sumner in the Senate. It would repeal the Fugitive Slave Act of 1793 and amend the one of 1850, making it unlawful to send an escaped slave such as Margaret Garner back to her owner. The President might sign that bill if it passed. He might also sign, if they passed, the bills of Ashley of Ohio and Wilson of Iowa in the House, and of Henderson of Missouri and Sumner of Massachusetts in the Senate, to abolish slavery by Constitutional Amendment. Sumner's proposed measure declared "everywhere within the limits of the United States . . . all persons are equal before the law, so that no person can hold another as slave."

Day after day, as an incessant doom that would not down, the question of the black man and his destiny crossed the events of each hour. He was "the inevitable Sambo," "the everlasting nigger," the living interrogation point. To one side he incarnated the slavery issue, to the other the race-equality problem. On both sides were philosophers saying legislation would never smooth out the intricacies of the matter, that the extremists on both sides had always openly or covertly mocked at the regulatory measures.

The trend of feeling against slavery went on deepening. Francis George Shaw of New York wrote to the President, "My only son, Colonel Robert Gould Shaw of the 54th Regiment Massachusetts Volunteers [colored troops] was killed on the parapet of Fort Wagner in South Carolina, and now lies buried in its ditch among his brave and devoted followers." To the request of Colonel Shaw's friends for his corpse came a reply it was "buried under a layer of niggers." The father urged the President to take immediate measures for protection to colored troops. "If our son's services and death shall contribute in any degree towards securing to our colored troops that equal justice which is a holy right of every loyal defender of our beloved country, we shall esteem our great loss a blessing."

That the year of '63 was coming to an end with not one Negro slave revolt, not one scene of killing and plunder, as a result of the Emancipation Proclamation, made the going easier for Lincoln. Any action like a Spartacist uprising in ancient Roman times, or any such episode as the Nat Turner insurrection repeated, would have made the race issue still more complex. The Illinois War Democrat, General John M. Palmer, visited the White House and told Lincoln that at first he and others in the field thought the Emancipation Proclamation might as well have cried to the Negroes, "Arise, Peter, slay and eat."

LINCOLN. You were all opposed to the proclamation when it was first issued, weren't you?

PALMER. Yes.

LINCOLN. Well, don't you see that on the average I am about right?

Negro recruiting came under the President's personal scrutiny. "Please give me, as near as you can, the number of *slaves* you have recruited in Maryland," he telegraphed to Colonel Birney at Baltimore. "Of course the number is not to include the free colored."

Antislavery Roman Catholics declared their convictions in a more positive tone. The Christmas issue of the *Catholic Telegraph*, December 24, 1863, published a paragraph: "It seems that there is a Priest in Kentucky who is still holding forth in favor of slavery. He ought to hide in the Mammoth Cave and associate with the fossils. Let him be careful in concealing his name; by signing himself 'Priest' he divides the odium of his pro-slavery work with all his brethren, for which many, even in Kentucky, do not thank him; but the weight of public censure, if concentrated on his own patronymic, would be overwhelming. A Catholic Priest, in the holy times of Christmas, advocating slavery! Handing over women and children into infamous bondage with one hand and offering incense with the other to the infant Saviour—THE REDEEMER OF ALL! What a subject for meditation before the altar on Christmas morning! If slavery must have its advocates let them be found amongst the laity, and not amongst the Priests. They whose special duty it is to teach the observance of the law of God should not advocate a system by which the law is violated. A Catholic Priest upholding a system which ignores the sacrament of marriage! Shame!"

A Confederate envoy, A. Dudley Mann, Assistant Secretary of State in the Buchanan Administration, had in November presented to Pope Pius IX at Rome a letter from President Davis looking toward greetings and approval of the Confederate States. The Pope did give greetings—and prayers —but instead of issuing approval of the Confederacy, he inquired as to the impression created abroad by the Lincoln Government that it might be judicious for the Davis Government to favor gradual emancipation of the slaves. The envoy, Mann, reported to his chief, Secretary Benjamin, that as the letter of President Davis was being translated from English into Latin for His Holiness:

Every sentence of the letter appeared to sensibly affect him. At the conclusion of each he would lay his hand down upon the desk and bow his head approvingly. When the passage was reached, wherein the President states in such sublime and affecting language, "We have offered up at the footstool of our Father who art in heaven prayers inspired by the same feeling which animated your Holiness," his deep-sunken orbs, visibly moistened, were upturned toward that throne upon which ever sits the Prince of Peace, indicating that his heart was pleading for our deliverance. . . .

The emotion occasioned by the translation was succeeded by a silence of some time. At length His Holiness asked whether President Davis were a Catholic. I answered in the negative. He then asked if I were one. I assured him that I was not. His Holiness now stated, to use his own language, that Lincoln and Company had endeavored to create an impression abroad that they were fighting for the abolition of slavery and that it might be judicious in us to consent to gradual emancipation. I replied that the subject of slavery was one over which the Government of the Confederate States, like that of the old United States, had no control whatever; that all ameliorations with regard to the institution must proceed from the States themselves, which were as sovereign in their character in this regard as was France, Austria, or any other Continental power; that true philanthropy shuddered at the thought of a liberation of the slave in the manner attempted by Lincoln and Company; that such a procedure would be practically to convert the well-cared-for civilized negro into a semibarbarian.

His Holiness . . . then said: "I should like to do anything that can be effectively done or that even promises good results, to aid in putting an end to this most terrible war which is harming the good of all the earth, if I knew how to proceed."

I availed myself of this declaration to inform His Holiness that it was not the armies of Northern birth which the South was encountering in hostile array, but that it was the armies of European creation, occasioned by the Irish and Germans, chiefly the former, who were influenced to emigrate (by circulars from Lincoln & Company to their numerous agents abroad) ostensibly for the purpose of securing higher wages, but in reality to fill up the constantly depleted ranks of our enemy; that these poor unfortunates were tempted by high bounties, amounting to $500, $600, and $700, to enlist and take up arms against us; that once in the service they were invariably placed in the most exposed points of danger in the battlefield; that in consequence thereof an instance had occurred in which an almost entire brigade had been left dead or wounded upon the ground; that but for foreign recruits the North would most likely have broken down months ago in the absurd attempt to overpower the South.

His Holiness expressed his utter astonishment repeatedly, throwing up his hands, at the employment of such means against us and the cruelty attendant upon such unscrupulous operations.

"But your Holiness," said I, "Lincoln & Co. are even more wicked, if possible, in their ways, than in decoying innocent Irishmen from their homes to be murdered in cold blood. Their champions, and would your Holiness believe it, unless it were authoritatively communicated to you?—their pulpit champions have boldly asserted this as a sentiment: 'Greek fire for the families and cities of the rebels, and Hellfire for their chiefs.'"

His Holiness was startled at this information, and immediately observed: "Certainly no Catholic would reiterate so monstrous a sentiment." I replied, "Assuredly not. It finds a place exclusively in the hearts of the fiendish, vagrant pulpit buffoons whose number is legion, and who impiously undertake to teach the doctrine of Christ, for ulterior sinister purposes."

His Holiness now observed: "I will write a letter to President Davis, and of such a character that it may be published for general perusal."

Nearly a month later Mann received from the Cardinal Secretary of State, Antonelli, a letter in Latin, addressed to President Davis. The Sovereign Pontiff referred to his exhortations the previous year to "the venerable Brethren, John, Archbishop of New York, and John, Archbishop of New Orleans" that they because of their exemplary piety and episcopal zeal should employ the most earnest efforts that the people of America might again love each other with mutual charity. Peace and only peace could Jefferson Davis find as a teaching in the message from the Pope reading:

And very grateful was it to us, illustrious and honorable sir, to perceive that you and those people were animated with the same feelings of peace and tranquillity which we so earnestly inculcated in the letters mentioned as having been addressed to the aforesaid reverend brethren [Archbishops of New York and New Orleans]. And would that other people also of those regions, and their rulers, seriously considering how grievous and mournful a thing is intestine war, would be pleased with tranquil minds to beseech and pray God, the omnipotent and all-good, to pour out the spirit of Christian charity and peace upon all these people of America, and deliver them from the evils so great with which they are afflicted. And of the most merciful Lord of compassion Himself, we likewise pray that He may illumine Your Excellency with the light of His grace, and may conjoin you in perfect love with ourselves.

Given at Rome, at St. Peter's, December 3d, in the year 1863, and of our pontificate the eighteenth.

P. P. IX

Envoy Mann's high hopes of this letter were dashed when Secretary Benjamin wrote him that he should have noticed Pope Pius IX termed the American conflict an "intestine" or "civil" and not a "foreign" war. "This phrase of his letter shows that his address to the President as 'President of the Confederate States' is a formula of politeness to his correspondent, not a political recognition of the fact. None of our political journals treat the letter as a recognition in the sense you attach to it."

As early as '61, Archbishop John Hughes of the Catholic diocese of New York had come to Washington, met Lincoln and the Cabinet, indicated that he could not take official appointment from Lincoln. At the President's request, however, joined to that of his old friend Seward, the Archbishop became one of the President's personal agents with full powers to set forth the Union cause in Europe. The Archbishop had interviewed the French Emperor, attended a canonization of martyrs in Rome, laid the cornerstone of a new Catholic university in Dublin built partly from moneys collected in America. In this tour of eight months over Europe the Archbishop spoke the pro-Northern views which he gave in a published letter to the pro-Southern Archbishop of New Orleans.

The American Government, through Seward, intimated to the Holy See at Rome that any honor given to Archbishop Hughes would be appreciated; the action came naturally to Seward, who had in the past been associated with the Archbishop in combating a hostile Masonic movement in New York State. The Archbishop's sermon on the war delivered on August 17, 1862, was resented by Southern Catholics, by Northern antiwar groups; he replied to criticisms of his course printed in the *Baltimore Catholic Mirror*. He broke his connection with the fiercely antiwar and anti-Lincoln *Metropolitan Record*.

The year of 1863 saw glimmering of the last hopes of the Richmond Government for European recognition. The despair of Jefferson Davis as to overseas help, as to ships or money from the England he had often referred to as "the mother-country," was set forth in his December message to the Confederate Congress. Davis dwelt at such length and so bitterly on the point that he was rebuked by some of the Southern newspapers for over-emphasis of it.

Under the flow of words from Davis, from Benjamin, from Confederate spokesmen whose addresses were published in North America and Europe, came no signs of their innermost thoughts as to slavery. They were using language to avoid telling those thoughts. They had given a sign of those innermost thoughts when in the adoption of their Constitution in February of 1861 they had outlawed the African slave trade. That action was a compromise and a ghostly beckoning finger foretelling Lincoln's Emancipation Proclamation. Rhett and Yancey among civilians, and the former slave-trader General Bedford Forrest, a military leader perhaps as great in his own field as Stonewall Jackson, had said, "If we are not fighting for slavery, then what are we fighting for?" They were told that the outlawing of the African slave trade was a gesture for European goodwill with a hope of recognition as a World Power among nations. Yet that recognition had not come. All maneuvers and prayers for it had failed.

Meanwhile the war, the Emancipation Proclamation, the messages of Lincoln, the antislavery propaganda, had sharpened the instinct against slavery among masses of people in all countries. In homes and at work millions in Europe had asked, "What is this slavery in America?" the simplest answer being, "It is where a white man owns a black man like he owns a horse, a cow or a dog," the talk going farther, "What about the black women and children?" "The white man owns them too." "He can breed them, beat them, sell them?" "Yes." "Oh! oh!"

Uncle Tom and Simon Legree, Little Eva, and Eliza crossing the ice pursued by bloodhounds, had been presented on stages of world capitals and in hundreds of smaller cities. A sentiment of horror over slavery spread farther and deeper. Palmerston, Gladstone, Napoleon III, knew this to be a factor interfering with imperialistic schemes. Czar Alexander of Russia knew it. The Pope knew it—and knew also that his church had as a traditional policy always frowned on slavery, chiefly because of its degradation of marriage and the family, and its travesty of all shrines having to do with the Madonna and Child.

Among the reckonably powerful rulers of the earth, Jefferson Davis seemed least aware of this sentiment. Yet it underlay his acrid recital of Confederate failures to win Europe. He writhed at being the spokesman of an outlawed nation.

A thousand folk tales had gone traveling of the mixed bloods of white and Negro races, of fathers selling their children, of lusts and sins and concubines, of fantastic tricks of fate involving those legally proved to have one drop of Negro blood. They were tales that seized men's hearts, stories that could not be forgotten, stories to brood over and pass on to others. Such a one was met by Captain Alonzo Abernethy of the 9th Iowa Infantry when Sherman took Jackson, Mississippi. Abernethy walked into the state prison there, to find all the convicts had been pressed into the Confederate ranks for field service except one old white-haired man, set free after thirty years behind the bars. The old man was born and raised in Fall River, Massachusetts, had gone south to Mississippi City, worked at his trade of carpenter and joiner, boarding with a private family. And as Abernethy caught the story of this old man:

He became enamored of a young woman employed at needlework in the house, of rare beauty and intelligence. Unfortunately, her otherwise aristocratic southern blood was tinctured one-sixteenth African. She was a semi-octoroon, and a slave, though her complexion was fair as that of any woman. To her he was plighted in marriage. They started north, through Alabama, making their way rapidly until he was suddenly prostrated by sickness. He urged her to go on and he would follow. She resolutely refused. The delay proved fatal to their plans.

As they were about escaping into the mountain ranges of East Tennessee where friendly hands would have helped them forward, they were overtaken. She was carried back into slavery, he never knew where. He was thrown into jail, whence he was sent to the Alabama State Prison, for the crime of "Abducting a slave from her master." At the expiration of a twenty year term of imprisonment he was turned over to the state authorities of Mississippi on a twenty year old indictment, for the further crime of "Attempting to marry a slave." Though he had the sympathy of both judge and jury, and was given the lightest sentence allowed under the laws of Mississippi, he was "sent up" for another ten years.

He completed his remarkable story: "In three months more I should have completed thirty years' imprisonment in these two penitentiaries for two offences, neither one of which would have been even so much as indictable in my own native state of Massachusetts."

Seeing that I had become deeply interested in his story, he requested me to go with him to a neighboring cell, where he took the half of a pair of broken hand-cuffs, which had encased his own wrists, and asked me to keep it in remembrance of a heartbroken, homeless old man.

This was only a specimen from a vast collection of dramatic and tragic incidents that became folk talk over the world, that laid the basis for the outlawry of slavery among civilized nations, that also underlay clamor for "the hanging of Jeff Davis and his whole gang." These mixed motives Lincoln had to ponder.

A long letter to the Loyal National League of New York came from "friends of America" in France. The signers were the Count de Gasparin, Protestant, former Minister of Public Instruction and member of the Chamber of Deputies; Augustin Cochin, Catholic, author of *The Abolition of Slavery;* Henri Martin, Catholic, Republican, author of a history of France; Edouard Laboulaye, professor in the Collège de France, "moderate Catholic, moderate Republican, allied to, but not positively identified with, the party of Prince Napoleon."

They gave Lincoln and his Administration approval in a propaganda document of seventeen pages dated October 31, 1863, and reprinted some weeks later in America. "We, gentlemen, are abolitionists; and we declare that we have never hoped nor wished for a more steady, rapid and resolute progress. We have understood the difficulties which surrounded Mr. Lincoln. We have honored his scruples of conscience with regard to the Constitution of his country which stopped his path. We have admired the courageous good sense with which he moved straight on, the instant he could do so without danger to his cause or violation of the law."

These Frenchmen foresaw the rebellion as soon stifled. Then what? From European experience they would advise against the "vulgar tyranny" of death penalty, confiscation, reprisals, vengeance; let slavery alone fall; let those of the South who would take the Union oath come back on the old footing of perfect equality.

Italian republican liberals sent to Lincoln a cadenced address lavish with Latin gestures, its first signer the famous fighting patriot Giuseppe Garibaldi. "If in the midst of your Titanic battles, our voice can yet reach you, let us, O Lincoln, free sons of Columbus, send you a word of good wishes and of admiration for the great work that you have begun. Heir of the aspirations of Christ and of John Brown, you will pass to posterity with the name of the Emancipator; more enviable than any crown or any human treasure." The unshackling of the slaves was to them a vast romantic drama, with Lincoln the overshadowing figure. They spoke for masses of people beginning to venerate a titanic legend shaping in American events.

"Let free men religiously keep sacred the day of the fall of slavery," admonished Garibaldi. "Prosperity to you, Abraham Lincoln, pilot of liberty; hail to all you who for two years have fought and died around her regenerating banner; weal to you, redeemed sons of Ham—the free men of Italy kiss the glorious marks of your chains."

Señor Don Matias Romero, envoy of the Republic of Mexico, presented his credentials at the White House. An army of some 25,000 French soldiers and a fleet were holding a large part of Señor Romero's country. But the fugitive President Juarez had in the field perhaps 27,000 troops. By receiving Señor Romero, Lincoln would be recognizing the old republican government of Mexico and ignoring the new monarchical one established by Napoleon III. Also he would be following the course of Minister Tom Corwin in Mexico, who had refused to hold interviews with the new French government and had made it a point to stay away from a birthday feast for Napoleon III.

As if the affair had been arranged beforehand, Señor Romero delivered his credentials and said that the two neighboring and friendly republican governments of Mexico and the United States had identical interests. "I do not doubt that in the discharge of the mission which has been confided to me I shall meet with the coöperation of the government of your excellency." Lincoln read a response:

Mr. Romero—
You have hitherto resided with us, and for a considerable period have been the chief diplomatic representative of your country at this capital. You know how sincerely and how profoundly during that residence the United States desired that Mexico might always enjoy the blessings of domestic and foreign peace with perfect security, prosperity, independence and freedom. You know also that during the previous residence to which I have referred, you enjoyed the respect and esteem of this Government, and the good will of the people of the United States. I have the pleasure of assuring you that in all things, as well affecting your country as yourself personally, these feelings remain unchanged. Thanking you for the liberal sentiments you have expressed for the United States, and congratulating you upon the renewed confidence which your government has reposed in you, it is with unaffected pleasure that I bid you welcome to Washington.

A Spaniard in New York, D. José Ferrer de Couto, issued *Enough of War!* a book not at all in agreement with the Mexican, Italian, and French friends of Lincoln. Slavery had its origin in the history of war, and the history of war in that of the human race, Señor de Couto expounded. The first property titles were to slaves. At first conquerors killed their prisoners; later they put them to work. Thus slavery was born. Señor de Couto defined his horror over one man's owning other men as property. Then he gently presented a set of compromises by which he would end the American civil war with honor to all, chiefly by protection of the marriage relation among slaves and by guarantees of kinder treatment by masters over slaves.

Couto pointed to civil wars that had destroyed nations, quoted Livy—"Even idiots are taught by experience"—and a Spanish Minister of Finance, Llorente—"Circumstances occur every day which may make us modify the most rooted opinions." Throughout his beautifully written book Señor de Couto was serenely unaware of the rooted opinion and untouchable doctrine of the South that each State is sovereign. And to Señor Couto, Lincoln was just one more embarrassed and hesitating politician.

In Great Britain, with "the mother-tongue," were cross currents as complex and varied as in the United States, as muddled as Missouri. The Emancipation Proclamation, mass meetings of workingmen formulating resolutions and addresses to Lincoln, had roused the active friends of the South, who organized Southern Clubs, gathered in men of influence, and carried on propaganda favoring the Confederacy. The rout of the Union army at Fredericksburg, its losses at Chancellorsville, and the hauling and mauling of Grant's forces at Vicksburg without results, the Northern military failures of the first half of '63, sent Confederate hopes soaring.

In April, in London three days' subscriptions to a Confederate loan amounted to £9,000,000 sterling; later it ran to a total of £16,000,000, subscribers paying 15 per cent down. The last week in June of '63 a motion in the House of Commons for recognition of the Southern Confederacy as a sovereign state was shelved by adjournment and by the speeches and tactics of John Bright and a handful of liberals. When, a little later, news arrived of the victories of Gettysburg and Vicksburg, the motion had lost what chance it ever had. The unrecognized Confederate Minister at London quit that city for Paris, under instructions from Richmond to consider his mission at an end among the British and to await further orders.

The collapse of Confederate credit was wrought partly by the undersized but resourceful and astute Robert J. Walker, who so often did not let his right hand know what the left was doing. Lincoln and Seward had talked with Walker, arranged for his credentials, and sent him as a special financial agent of the Government of the United States to London. There Walker set up headquarters and a personal dignity; he was compared in style to the Austrian Minister. He had an importance of his own, took no back seat to Minister Adams, and Adams did not quite gauge the little man whose wife was a great-granddaughter of Benjamin Franklin.

Walker carried a checkbook. The London *Times* opened its columns to him. He signed *American Slavery and Finances*, the first of his devastating pamphlet attacks on the Confederacy, "the Honorable Robert J. Walker, M.A., Counsellor at Law in the Supreme Court of the United States, Late Senator of the United States, Secretary of the Treasury, Commissioner to China, Governor of Kansas, etc., etc." Walker raked out an old skeleton from the closet of Jefferson Davis's past, quoted a letter in which Senator Davis of Mississippi blamed for the repudiation of $5,000,000 of State bonds (mostly sold in England) fraudulent individuals who had violated the State constitution, Davis writing: "The State of Mississippi has no other question with bondholders than that of debt or no debt. . . . The crocodile tears which have been shed over ruined creditors, are on a par with the baseless denunciations which have been heaped upon the State." The London

MR. BULL (*Confiding Creature*). "Hi want my Cotton, bought at Fi' Pence a Pound."
MR. LINCOLN. "Don't know any thing about it, my dear Sir. Your friends, the Rebels,
are burning all the Cotton they find, and I confiscate the rest. Good Morning, JOHN!"

Harper's Weekly cartoons Lincoln's attitude toward John Bull, the English cotton
famine—and a $15,000,000 loan subscribed to the Confederacy

Times had on July 13, 1849, reprinted this letter six weeks after it was
published in the *Washington Daily Union*—and had made a London *Times*
reply in true form.

Walker had dug out shivering relics and put them on exhibition for all
investors in the British Empire and any European financiers who might be
interested. In 1849, according to the London *Times* of that year, Jefferson
Davis had "openly proclaimed that the Governor and Legislative Assemblies
of his own State deliberately issued fraudulent bonds for five millions of
dollars to 'sustain the credit of a rickety bank'; that the bonds in question,
having been hypothecated abroad to innocent holders, such holders have
not only no claim against the community by whose executive and repre-

sentatives this act was committed, but that they are to be taunted for appealing to the verdict of the civilized world, rather than to the judgment of the legal officers of the State by whose functionaries they have been already robbed; and that the ruin of toil-worn men, of women, of widows and of children, and the 'crocodile tears' which that ruin has occasioned, is a subject of jest on the part of those by whom it has been accomplished." No foreigner, said the *Times* then in 1849, had ever penned such a libel on American character. And Jeff Davis, then in 1849, had replied that "the hypocritical cant" and "calumnious imputation" of "hired advocates" was "very well for the high Tory paper as an attack upon our republican government," yet "with far more propriety might repudiation be charged on the English Government."

These acrimonious remarks of fourteen years before, in which Jeff Davis and the London *Times* stood up in public and politely called each other liars, thieves, and hypocrites, had been hunted out by Walker and were again put into print, in the very columns of the *Times* itself. In publishing this material in the most influential financial and investment journal in the world, and in printing it as a pamphlet and scattering it freely, Walker believed he was battering down Confederate resources as relentlessly as the cannon of Meade or Grant in that summer of '63. He hurled questions:

Is Virginia independent? Why, all her coasts and sea ports are held by us, so is Norfolk, her commercial capital, more than half her area and white population, and nearly half her territory has been organized as a new State of the Union, and, by the almost unanimous vote of her people, has abolished slavery.

Are North and South Carolina, Georgia, Florida, Alabama, and Texas, independent? Why, their whole coast and large portions of the interior are held by our army and navy.

Is Tennessee independent? Two-thirds of her territory, as well as her political and commercial capitals, Nashville and Memphis, are held by us. The same thing is true, to a great extent, as to Arkansas.

As to Mississippi—her whole sea coast, and her whole river coast, for 500 miles, with the exception of a single point, is held by us, and more than half her territory.

As to Louisiana, we hold three-fourths of her territory, all her sea coast, all her river front on both banks of the Mississippi, except one point, and her great city, New Orleans, with four times the population of any other southern city.

How can the so-called Confederacy, claiming to be a league of sovereign and independent States, be recognized as independent, when the States composing that league are not independent?

How is Richmond to be reached by an English envoy, or is the blockade to be broken, which is war?

Having thrown ghastly light on the Confederacy, Walker proceeded with bland illumination on the United States—in a series of geographical, statistical, and fiscal reports on people, products, coal, oil, gold, railways, inventions, the stability of American securities, and the material prosperity that was roaring across the North in spite of the war. No investor could accept his picture of the United States and not believe that the new country was worth putting money into. In elegant coaches with champing horses, Walker went from city to city holding meetings, dining with the influential, spreading information.

In October Walker made a balloon trip from Blackheath, going a mile high with Count Franz Schaffgotsch; who made scientific observations. All Britain read of it. Said the *New York Herald*: "The healths of respective sovereigns were given, viz: Our Queen, the Emperor of Austria, the President of the United States. Then Mr. Walker gave the toast: May England and America always be at peace."

Seward must have smiled on reading in a letter from John Bigelow, dated Paris, October 9, 1863: "Mr. Robert J. Walker dined with the Slidells, who returned to town day before yesterday." Two adroit old Democratic-party politicians, on opposed European missions, sat dining to see what they could glean from each other; two wary foxes held a palaver.

Much more was heard in America of Henry Ward Beecher, who to avoid a scandal involving the veracity of a deathbed confession of Mrs. Henry C. Bowen was vacationing in Europe. The Fourth of July was celebrated by Beecher at London in a speech to temperance leaders from all over England wherein Beecher pointed to failures of Union armies as "owing entirely to the drunkenness of officers," charged Hooker with being "under the influence of liquor" at Chancellorsville.

Not yet had the news of Gettysburg and Vicksburg reached Europe. In Paris Beecher heard those tidings. And though no one in America had been more violently anti-British during the Trent Affair, and though no one in America had requested or commissioned him to do so, Beecher went to England and addressed mass meetings at Manchester, Liverpool, and elsewhere in support of the Union cause. He achieved dramatic effects; in his audiences usually a majority was with him at the start. But there was always a disturbing minority of English hecklers, of Southern sympathizers, or of British patriots who hated Beecher's anti-British outbursts of a year or two earlier.

Beecher's war cry during the Trent Affair, "The best blood of England must flow," with like utterances, was placarded on walls in black and red letters—and Minister Adams did not like it. Facing English audiences Beecher laid all blame for the New York draft riots on the Irish Catholics, as though to say that America had the same Irish problem as England; Beecher did not discuss the $300 clause nor mention that Generals Meade, Rosecrans, Sheridan, Meagher, Sickles, Ord, Gillmore, and scores of brigadiers and colonels in active service were Catholics. In England, as in his homeland, he was dramatist, politician, stump orator.

Of the man whose editorials in the *Independent* had wrenched from Lincoln the reproach "Is thy servant a dog?" the London *Era* said: "The Reverend Mr. Beecher is delivering very showy addresses, which immense crowds flock to hear. . . . As Falstaff says, 'He spoke very wisely, but we regarded him not!'" Had his October and November addresses come in the gloom period of the first six months of 1863 they would have had a different historic value. Beecher's political instinct told him when the news of Gettysburg and Vicksburg came, and when the collapse of Confederate credit had been accomplished by the operations of Robert J. Walker and other forces, that his brilliant platform artistry should be put into action. America would read that the clergyman who had auctioned a mulatto from his pulpit in Brooklyn was now in London and Liverpool twisting the British lion's tail, Brother Jonathan again making John Bull squirm and squeal.

One audience interrupted Beecher incessantly, howled and booed, but he stood his ground, made point after point, delivered flashing arguments in favor of the Union and the antislavery cause. No citizen of the United States had ever before so dramatized himself as an American David combating the British Goliath on British soil. Yet Beecher was rather a leisurely outrider who arrived on a field of verbal conflict after the heavy work had been done by others whom he belittled with omission of names, including Lincoln, Stanton, Adams, Walker, and a Russian war fleet. His results were slight compared with those of Walker—or of Thurlow Weed in England that same year going to seats of power and advising Seward and Lincoln what he saw and heard. "I had done all the talking," wrote one man of an hour's interview with Weed. "He won men as a heartless belle wins lovers, through the use of his ears. What can you do with a man who leads you to a remote corner of a room and, in the most deferential manner, tells you nothing in a low, confidential tone?"

Beecher's own later version of his start for Europe in June of 1863 gave the definite impression that he did not expect at all that he would be called on to prove himself a hero in the act of taming wild audiences. He wrote: "I was not requested, either by President Lincoln nor by any member of the Cabinet, to act in behalf of this government; it was purely a personal arrangement. The government took no stock in me at that time. Seward was in the ascendency, and, as I had been pounding Lincoln during the early years of the war, I don't believe there was a man in Washington, excepting perhaps Mr. Chase, who would have trusted me with anything; at any rate, I went on my own responsibility, with no one behind me except my church. They told me they would pay my expenses and sent me off. I went away wholly for the sake of rest and recuperation. I went simply as a private citizen, and I went with a determination not to speak in Great Britain."

In Britain, Beecher had a tone of voice about Lincoln that he had never used in America. Among the English abolitionists he met a warmth and kindliness toward Lincoln not so common in America, the English leaning to the Garrison rather than the Phillips and Frémont viewpoint of the American President. Explaining to an Edinburgh audience that in the Emancipation Proclamation "it was the President and not the man who spoke," and that the country and not the President was responsible for the proclamation, Beecher said: "The President was very loath to take the steps he did; but, though slow, Abraham Lincoln was sure. A thousand men could not make him plant his foot before he was ready; ten thousand could not move it after he had put it down." To an interruptious Liverpool audience Beecher said:

I will read you a word from President Lincoln. [Renewed uproar.] It is a letter from Theodore Tilton. [Hisses, and cheers.] Won't you hear what President Lincoln thinks? ["No, no."] Well, you can hear it or not. It will be printed whether you hear it or hear it not. ["Hear," and cries of "Read, Read."] Yes, I will read. "A talk with President Lincoln revealed to me a great growth of wisdom. For instance, he said he was not going to press the colonization idea any longer, nor the gradual scheme of emancipation, expressing himself sorry that the Missourians had postponed emancipation for seven years. He said, 'Tell your anti-slavery friends that I am coming out all right.' He is desirous that the Border States shall form free constitutions, recognising the proclamation, and thinks this will be made feasible by calling on loyal men." [A voice: "What date is that letter?" and interruption.] Ladies and gentlemen, I have finished the exposition of this troubled subject.

In Exeter Hall, London, rose a mass sentiment so deeply favoring Lincoln that Beecher went out of his way with compliments such as had never before come from his lips or pen for the American President, praise he would not renew for the living Lincoln on reaching America. English publication of the London speech gave this passage:

The North did not at first go to war to enforce emancipation. She went to war to save the National institutions;—[Cheers.]—to save the Territories; to sustain those laws, which would first circumscribe, then suffocate, and finally destroy slavery. [Cheers.] That is the reason why that most true, honest, just, and conscientious magistrate, Mr. Lincoln—[The announcement of Mr. Lincoln's name was received with loud and continued cheering. The whole audience rose and cheered some time, and it was a few minutes before Mr. Beecher could proceed.] From having spoken much at tumultuous assemblies I had at times a fear that when I came here this evening my voice would fail from too much speaking. But that fear is now changed to one that your voices will fail from too much cheering. [Laughter.]

The same publication recorded that Mr. Beecher and his friends were received with loud cheers when they issued from Exeter Hall and "a call for a cheer for Abraham Lincoln was responded to in a manner that only an English crowd can exhibit."

On his return to America larger audiences than ever flocked to hear Beecher's voice and to see the only American of the generation who had gone to England and twisted the British lion's tail. "We are wonderfully fortunate in our advocate," wrote the editor of *Harper's New Monthly Magazine*. "Our friends in England heard in Mr. Beecher's speeches the voice of this country plainly. . . . When he rose to speak at the Brooklyn Academy of Music, he was, next to Abraham Lincoln, the most honored man in the country."

The open propaganda, secret representations, and partly open and partly secret negotiations that year, by which Confederate credit was destroyed and by which the foremost moneylenders in Europe were led to bet on the North as against the South, would require a shelf of several volumes if all the documents and conversations on international diplomacy and banking were made a matter of record—which they were not.

A minor factor was the entrance into the London financial district of the American international banking house of L. P. Morton, Burns & Company, who ambitiously, some said presumptuously, were challengers in a field dominated by the Rothschilds and the Barings.

At the American Thanksgiving dinner in London, the President's proclamation of that day was printed with the menu, which included *Fricassee de Poulet à la Washington* and *Quenelles de Gibier à la Lincoln*. Walker officiated as chairman, with Mrs. Walker and Miss Walker present, Minister Adams and legation officials at the right of the Chair. Walker's opening speech was primed for British consumption; to those who accepted his points, the Confederacy had no leg whereon to stand. He introduced His Excellency Mr. Adams, whose toast was "The President of the United States."

The American Chief Magistrate had not had any such amount of laudation as would be likely to turn his head, Minister Adams noted; it had become the practice of "our people" to hold the President responsible for any mistake committed by anybody and every misfortune at any time. "There is hardly a single act that he does against which somebody is not found to carp." Even the President's Thanksgiving proclamation was criticized as morally obtuse or savage and vindictive because of its call for thanks to God in time of war and distress. Minister Adams then gave a nutshell history of the war thus far, in order, as he said, to get at the precise blessing for which they were assembled to give God thanks.

The President had come to his post "with less of practical experience in government than any individual since the foundation of the Government." The walls seemed crumbling around him. "He came to Washington and was qualified as President. But President of what?" With departments shaking, with treachery ramified, he had eliminated treason from uppermost to lowermost places. "Is not this something to be thankful for? [Cheers.]" The foreign service had to be rebuilt and confidence inspired abroad. The military and naval organizations had to be reconstructed, many units from the bottom up, and many entirely new branches perfected. Then the emancipation measures had been nursed along, the policy of Negro troops established. The Government, almost disintegrated, had become solid. Instead of being staggered in faith, as at first, the people were now upholding the President with men and means.

As Minister Adams closed his review of each series of events, with asking, "Is not this something to be thankful for?" there were cheers. Adams finished: "We stand now firmly, having every reliance that the Government is able, and the people willing, to go through this trial triumphantly. [Cheers.] And all this change has been effected through the agency of a President, who came into power with less practical political experience than any one man preceding him. ["Hear, hear."] And how has this been done? Has it been by any superior genius on the part of the President?

Not at all. The President has shown ability and capacity, but not above that of most of his predecessors. What is the reason, then, why he has succeeded in all these results? I will tell you the reason. He has succeeded because he has, from the beginning to the end, impressed upon the people the conviction of his honesty and fidelity to one great purpose. [Loud cheers.] I therefore say, Mr. Chairman, in conclusion, that for these reasons I have to thank you for having enjoyed the opportunity of expressing these sentiments as an echo to the toast of the health of the President of the United States. [His Excellency resumed his seat amidst the greatest applause.]"

Chairman Walker took note that many present knew "how strong and deep have been the personal feelings of the Queen, and of her lamented Consort, the good Prince Albert, against slavery, and in favor of the American Union." They would join in the next toast to "Her Majesty the Queen," and there was prolonged cheering. Then came George Thompson, representative of the largest constituency of England in the British Parliament, lifelong opponent of the African slave trade, advocate of England and America allied as mother and daughter. Thompson spoke soberly and familiarly of American affairs, "thanking God for our victories in the cause of Liberty and Union." The American consul at London, Freeman H. Morse, followed with the toast "The Emancipation Proclamation—slavery's epitaph written by the finger of God on the heart of the American President." The first day of January, 1863, would mark an epoch in human history, a chosen time from which to date a great advance in the life and exaltation of a whole race of the human family, the London consul was sure. "To this race it will ever be a holiday, the annual dawn of which will be ushered in with joy and rejoicing, and a grateful remembrance of the far-seeing and good author of the Emancipation Proclamation. His name will be associated with that Proclamation, and go with it to the future, blessed and beloved, as long as liberty and justice shall be revered among men. [Loud applause.]"

Toasts were given to the army and navy, to Washington, to the press, to "the Ladies, their holy influence will break all chains but those which bind our hearts to them." The proceedings, as duly published in Piccadilly, were mailed out as informative material on how Americans abroad might conduct a patriotic celebration. The shrill Yankee Doodle note of the evening had been delivered by Major Z. K. Pangborn of Boston in the toast "The Union—from the Atlantic to the Pacific, from the Lakes to the Gulf, from the source to the mouth of the Mississippi, forever one and insepara-ble." The Major could see a rainbow promise of perpetual peace spanning a continent, one arch resting among the singing pines of the Aroostook, the other sunk in the unvexed wave by the Golden Gate of the Pacific.

The Major had touched a theme that lurked in the unspoken motives of Palmerston, Russell, and the powers behind the London *Times*, having direct connection with the question, If the North wins the war and establishes the American Union as one nation for the future, what place will it take as a

World Power? The *North British Review*, in a long and able treatise, had taken up this question and discussed it more frankly and decently than the London *Times*, which incessantly cried that America had a gorgeous design for world conquest.

"Finding the leaders of the Slave-Power deeply culpable and utterly wrong," said the *North British Review*, "we do not forget that they have a real cause of quarrel with the North. And as to slave-holding individual men, and women too, we have found them to be *such* as to win for themselves a cordial welcome under our roof." As to States' Rights: "When in the calm mood of lookers-on, we enter upon the thorny argument concerning the *right* of secession, asserted on the Southern side and denied on the Northern, we quickly become entangled among legal refinements and constitutional controversies, which show an aspect of endless perplexity. From these, we—the European public—may very properly retire. On this side the Atlantic it might be well not to meddle with matters so far beyond our line."

The *North British Review* writer came then to the nub of the matter for many of the British. He quoted from pamphlets and personal letters of Americans showing their almost barbaric faith that "the hand of God" was shaping America and "we must do what Providence intends us to do for the world at large." How natural for these quasi-religious phrases to come from the conquerors of a vast new continent stored with wealth! What else could be expected from the Anglo-Saxon pioneer than, having set his dominion on one hemisphere, he should move to others? "Upon fresh American soil the germ has indeed germinated and it is now shooting up heavenward with tropical force. Citizens of the United States are born with a giant ambition in their brains; and almost the first syllables they lisp have a sort of trumpet twang, as thus, 'Here I come, ready to grasp a sceptre and to rule the world.'"

Beyond their outspoken phrases "Restore the Union," "Maintain order," Northern leaders mumbled in parenthesis of a future universal empire for the United States. The same world domination was "a darling ambition with the coarse-minded and ignorant masses of the people." The immediate interpretation in England was: "Canada is to be governed from Washington; the British are to be expelled from on both sides; and Russia also is to be driven back across Behring Straits." In effect the *North British Review* writer had guessed precisely what Joe Medill of the *Chicago Tribune* had in May of that year written to a brother: With the South squelched, the next job of the Government at Washington would be to take Canada on the North and Mexico to the Isthmus.

In calmly facing the argument between the North and the South, the *North British Review* writer found that the President of the United States could do nothing less, in accordance with his oath of office, than to make war to maintain his Government. Yet while so doing he might understand points of justice on the side of rebellion. The President would require, so to speak, two consciences. "He need not proclaim his inner belief, but he may silently hold it in all sincerity; and who shall affirm that the actual President Lincoln—who is allowed to be a man of conscience, as well as clear-sighted—does not in fact at this very moment, and in this very manner, harbour two consciences?"

For all the quaffing of toasts to the British Queen and her people, Lincoln and Seward saw that their only dependable well-wisher in Europe, except republican Switzerland, was the land of absolutist monarchy, Russia, the farthest of European extremes from "government of the people, by the people, for the people." A congressional publication mentioned a letter from President Lincoln to the Russian Government, delivery of the letter by Bayard Taylor to Foreign Minister Gorchakov at St. Petersburg, and Gorchakov's declaration to Taylor, "Russia alone has stood by you from the first, and will continue to stand by you." Realistic international politics was in play; Russia had just taken a costly beating in the Crimean War from Britain and France.

Gorchakov advised Taylor that when other nations proposed that Russia join them for interference in America, "She will refuse any invitation of the kind. You may rely upon it, she will not change." Not often in diplomatic conversations were pledges so explicit. In the embassies and chancelleries of Europe it was tacitly understood that recognition of the Confederacy by Britain and France would mean the alliance of the United States and Russia for a war scaled to world size.

Seward arranged secret understandings with Russia so momentous that he must have consulted with Lincoln about them. In America perhaps only Seward and Lincoln knew what conditional assurances were given the Russian Government as to the purchase of the peninsula of Al-ay-es-ka, shortened by Seward to the name of Alaska, a wilderness and "polar bear garden" where a narrow strip of water drew a line between North America and Asia. Estimates ran that it was worth from $1,400,000 to $10,000,000. The United States was to buy it as soon as convenient, the purchase price to include certain naval expenses of the Russian Government—some such understanding was worked out between the Washington and St. Petersburg governments.

Early in October of '63, two Russian fleets lay in American harbors, one in San Francisco, the other at New York with five first-class war vessels, the screw frigate *Alexander Nevski*, carrying fifty-one guns, being Admiral Lessovski's flagship. Officers and crews during a stay of three months went many places, and a good time was had by all. They were taken on the beflagged steamer *Daniel Drew* up the Hudson to Albany, received by the Governor and staff, and with cheers sent on to Niagara Falls, given a concert by Mr. Waters, the Irish harpist. Their stalwart Muscovite frames in gay uniforms, their outlandish whiskers, their excellent Russian, indifferent French, and worse English speech, added merriment wherever they went. They sat for Brady photographs. They visited Meade's headquarters in Virginia, fell from the upper decks of cavalry horses, ate heartily, carried their liquor well, and the Army of the Potomac had a good day off. A grand ball for the officers in the Academy of Music in New York on November 5 of '63 was "in every respect one of the most distinguished entertainments ever given in the city." In December, the Admiral and his officers sent Mayor Opdyke $4,700 for the poor of New York, with thanks for many civic courtesies received. When the first and second masters of the warship *Witzas* complained to the police that in a disreputable house in Greene Street they had been robbed of twenty-nine Russian gold pieces worth $174 in American money, the police helped get the money back. Three sailors locked up as ordinary drunks, booked as Russian No. 1, No. 2, and No. 3, heard a magistrate next morning, "not desiring to do anything calculated to disturb the friendly relations which exist between the Emperor of Russia and the President of the United States," order the Czar's subjects set free.

Special writers filled many newspaper columns with tales of the Russian naval visitors, giving an extra spread to one shipboard reception where United States military officers and Mrs. Lincoln drank to the health of the Czar. The *New York Herald* quipped of Mrs. Lincoln's glass of fellowship, "That toast and that act will be heard with dismay in the palaces and aristocratic halls of Europe, and with joy in the icy North and the steppes of Asia."

The *Richmond Examiner* quoted a French wit, "A cypher well placed is very valuable," and expatiated: "The apparently trivial occurrence of a health being drunk by the wife of an Illinois lawyer should convulse with fear, or elate with joy, the people of Europe and Asia. Plain Mrs. Lincoln would never have made much of a noise in the world. Appendant to that extraordinary freak of nature, the President of the United States, she can not only distinguish herself by the resplendent tints of her silks and possession of her jewels, but can frighten the world 'from its propriety' by simply drinking a glass of sherry."

Then came a parallel between Czar Alexander and President Lincoln: "The Czar emancipates the serfs from their bondage of centuries, and puts forth the whole strength of his empire to enslave the Poles. Lincoln proclaims freedom to the African, and strives at the same time to subjugate free born Americans. In this striking coincidence a similarity of character and feeling is denoted, which accounts for their close friendship, heretofore suspected, and now clearly displayed to the mingled admiration and awe of the world by Mrs. Lincoln's toddy."

The *New York Herald*, the *Chicago Times*, and other newspapers reprinted in full this *Richmond Examiner* comment, nearly a column of fine type. Also many journals gave their readers the verses of London *Punch* on "The President and the Czar," which ran in part:

> ABE.—Imperial son of Nicholas the Great,
>   We air in the same fix, I calculate.
>   You with your Poles, with Southern rebels I,
>   Who spurn my rule and my revenge defy.

ALEX.—Vengeance is mine, old man, see where it falls,
Behold yon hearth, laid waste, and ruined walls,
Yon gibbets where the struggling patriot hangs,
While my brave myrmidons enjoy his pangs.

ABE.—I'll show you a considerable some
Of devastated hearth and ravaged home:
Nor less about the gallows could I say,
Were hanging not a game both sides would play.

ALEX.—Wrath on revolted Poland's sons I wreak,
And daughters, too, beneath my knout they shriek,
See how from blazing halls the maiden flies,
And faithful Cossacks grasp the screaming prize.

English newspapers editorialized on what they set up as Lincoln's threats of war against Great Britain, rousing the *Chicago Times* to comment: "Wicked Old Abe! Who that saw you years ago 'poling' your humble flat-boat laden with hog and hominy down the Ohio, would have imagined you in later years charging like a vicious old Jupiter against the affrighted people of one of the greatest nations on the earth."

The *Missouri Republican* struck an attitude: "The pale corpse of Poland's

EXTREMES MEET.

Abe. Imperial son of NICHOLAS the Great, | You with your Poles, with Southern rebels I, | *Alex.* Vengeance is mine, old man; see where it falls, | Yon gibbets, where the struggling patriot hangs,
We air in the same fix, I calculate, | Who spurn my rule and my revenge defy. | Behold yon hearths laid waste, and ruined walls, | Whilst my brave myrmidons enjoy his pangs.

Punch of London sees the American President and the Russian Czar as good chums, having like viewpoints

murdered liberty" would haunt America. Meanwhile one could laugh at the capers over the Russians. "By-and-by we will doubtless all wear Russian beards, Russian overcoats, and Russian pants; our wives will wear Russian petticoats and hoops, and our little, innocent children will receive daily

"HOLDING A CANDLE TO THE **** " (MUCH THE SAME THING.)

Another *Punch* cartoon which denies that Lincoln cannot hold a candle to the Russian Bear—in reality representing British Tory and imperialist fear of a military and naval co-operation between the United States and Russia

lessons in the Russian system of government, by a due application of the lash."

The essential viewpoint of Seward and Lincoln in bringing the Russian fleets to American shores was probably hit off by *Harper's Weekly*, which noticed English and French ships also riding at anchor in New York Harbor: "England and France have recognized the belligerent rights of the rebels . . . Russia has not . . . if an English pirate, like the *Florida* or *Alabama*, should appear off the bay, the English and French ships would treat her as a commissioned vessel of war, and the Russian ships would treat her as a pirate. These are little things visible to the mind's eye, whatever the excellent John Bull may think of the 'splendor' of the civic reception.

"John [Bull] thinks that we are absurdly bamboozled by the Russian compliments, and laughs to see us deceived by the sympathy of Muscovy.

If one of the Russian officers, he says, were to express in St. Petersburg a tithe of the regard for American institutions which Americans recklessly attribute to them he would soon be in Siberia. But we are not very much deceived. Americans understand that the sympathy of France in our Revolution was not from love of us, but from hatred of England. They know, as Washington long ago told them, that romantic friendship between nations

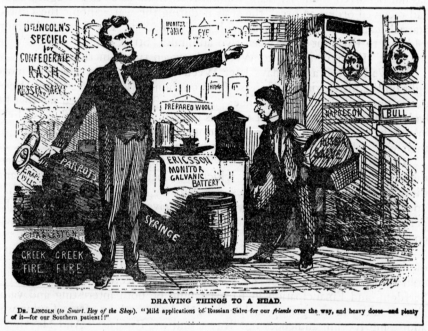

DRAWING THINGS TO A HEAD.

DR. LINCOLN (*to Smart Boy of the Shop*). "Mild applications of Russian Salve for our *friends* over the way, and heavy doses—and plenty of it—for our Southern patient!!"

Harper's Weekly cartoons Lincoln telling Seward to use "Russian Salve" (the goodwill and the fleet of the Russian Government) on "friends over the way," across the street, Napoleon III and John Bull

is not to be expected. And if they had latterly expected it, England has utterly undeceived them.

"Americans do not suppose that Russia is upon the point of becoming a republic; but they observe that the English aristocracy and the French empire hate a republic quite as much as the Russian monarchy hates it; and they remark that while the French empire imports coolies into its colonies, and winks at slavery, and while the British Government cheers a political enterprise founded upon slavery, and by its chief organs defends the system, Russia emancipates her serfs. There is not the least harm in observing these little facts. Russia, John Bull will remember, conducts herself as a friendly power. That is all. England and France have shown themselves to be unfriendly powers. And we do not forget it."

Lincoln and Seward kept to themselves the arrangements with Russia, vague or definite, which operated that year. Not to Nicolay nor Hay nor

Noah Brooks, nor to others to whom the President sometimes revealed secrets of state, did he give any inklings. And not even to his bosom friend Thurlow Weed did Seward give clues.

Weed had asked Admiral Farragut why the Russian fleet was idling a winter in New York Harbor. Farragut answered that the Russian Admiral said, "I am here under sealed orders, to be broken only in a contingency that has not occurred." The Russian Admiral further admitted to Farragut that he had received orders to break the seals if during the war at home the United States became involved in a war with foreign nations. The Russian Admiral told this to Farragut as between two admirals: "Strict confidence was then enjoined." Farragut told it to Weed as between two American patriots.

In Washington a few days later Weed tried to get from Seward more light on the Muscovite warships so far from home. What he gathered Weed put in one close-mouthed sentence: "Secretary Seward informed me that he had asked the Russian Minister why his government kept their ships so long in our harbors, who, while in answering he disclaimed any knowledge of their visit, felt at liberty to say that it had no unfriendly purpose."

The editor of *Godey's Lady's Book and Magazine* noted for his readers that the first Russian railroad, which ran between St. Petersburg and Moscow, some four hundred miles, was built by an American firm that had operated it for the Russian Government twelve years at 2,500,000 rubles per year. "This firm, it is said, netted out of their Russian contracts, 30,-000,000 rubles."

To Bayard Taylor, author of travel books, who had served as secretary of the American Legation at St. Petersburg under Minister Cameron, Lincoln wrote in December of '63: "I think a good lecture or two on serfs, Serfdom, and Emancipation in Russia would be both interesting and valuable. Could you not get up such a thing?" And not long after, Taylor was addressing lyceum audiences on "Russia and the Russians." And Hay mentioned in his diary that the President went one evening to hear Taylor's lecture.

Ben Butler, on his way to Fortress Monroe to resume command of the Department of Virginia and North Carolina, came from a White House visit with what he took to be a hint from Lincoln as to why one department commander had been relieved, the President casually saying, "Let me advise you not to amuse yourself by playing billiards with a rebel officer who is a prisoner of war."

Butler quoted Lincoln: "I wish you would give all the attention you can to raising negro troops; large numbers of negroes will probably come in to you. I believe you raised the first ones in New Orleans." Butler: "Yes, Mr. President, except General Hunter at South Carolina whose negro troops were disbanded by your order." Lincoln, laughing: "Yes, Hunter is a very good fellow but he was a little too previous in that. . . . Don't let Davis catch you, General; he has put a price on your head; he will hang you sure." Butler: "That's a game two can play at, Mr. President. If I ever catch him I will remember your scruples about capital punishment, and relieve you from any trouble with them in his case. He has outlawed me and if I get hold of him I shall give him the law of the outlaw after a reasonable time to say his prayers."

What lay ahead? What further of bitterness and death in the year of 1864 looming?

To James H. Hoes, Esq., Lincoln wrote a letter of thanks for a solid gold watch. Hoes, a Chicago jeweler, had donated the watch to the first Sanitary Commission Fair held in Chicago, as a token to be awarded the one person making the largest contribution of funds to the fair. Lincoln donated his original handwritten draft of the Emancipation Proclamation. It sold at auction for $3,000. A Chicago publisher was assigning territory to canvassers selling lithographed copies of "The Emancipation Proclamation, Genuine Facsimile in President Lincoln's Handwriting."

To Usher F. Linder, Douglas Democrat and storytelling lawyer of the old "orgmathorial" Eighth Circuit, Lincoln sent a Christmas gift. Linder's boy had wandered off into the sworn cohorts of the Confederate Army, had been taken prisoner, and his father sent letter after letter to Lincoln asking a pardon for the boy. Weeks had passed when Linder received a note dated the Executive Mansion, December 26, 1863: "Your son Dan has just left me with my order to the Secretary of War, to administer to him the oath of allegiance, discharge him and send him to you."

The lurid year of '63 drew to a close with Lee and his army south of Mason and Dixon's line, Vallandigham north of the Canadian border. Free speech and a free press operated in the Buckeye State, where in the shadow of the State capitol and the armories of the State guards, old Sam Medary got out a New Year's number of the *Crisis* comparing the inhuman cunning of Mr. Lincoln to that of the fox and the snake, or that of the lunatic whose instinct "frequently outwits the strongest brain in the soundest cranium."

Also for the New Year's season the *Crisis* reprinted a grim lamentation from the *Zanesville* (Ohio) *Aurora:* "The people of the North owe Mr. Lincoln nothing but eternal hatred and scorn. There are 500,000 new made graves; there are 500,000 orphans; there are 200,000 widows; there is a bottomless sea of blood; there is the Constitution broken; there are liberty and law—liberty in chains and in a dungeon; thieves in the Treasury, provost marshals in the seats of justice, butchers in the pulpit—and these are the things which we owe Mr. Lincoln. As the Lord liveth, we shall pay him all we owe him some day—him, and all the bloody band of traitors, plunderers and knaves, who have wrought the destruction of our country."

For the first time since the reoccupation of Norfolk and Portsmouth, Virginia, on November 1 of '63 President Lincoln was "openly prayed for in the churches of those cities," chronicled *Leslie's Weekly*.

The year of '63, almost gone, had seen Yancey pass out moaning his despair that the revolution he and Rhett and a few others chiefly had precipitated, was under the direction of men who had only reluctantly said Yes to secession in '61. The Kentuckian John J. Crittenden, old and full of years, author of the Crittenden Compromise to stop outbreak of war by making slavery constitutional, had in his final illness said to a visiting clergyman, "Mr. Lincoln is an honest man and a true patriot fairly entitled from every Christian man to the favorable construction you are disposed to put upon his conduct."

Old Sam Houston, the foremost historic figure of the State of Texas, had died saying he regarded secession as a grave mistake, but the people had set their hands to the plow and it would be ignominy to turn back; his last prayers would be for the happiness and safety of his people of Texas. This was three weeks after the surrender of Vicksburg, with a bedside gathering of all his family except one son wounded and a prisoner in a Northern camp. The intimates of Sam Houston knew that had he been twenty years younger he would have manipulated and fought to swing his State into the Union.

Another Southern Union man, James Louis Petigru of Charleston, South Carolina, seventy-four years old, had gone as worn and infirm oaks fall, so rare a justice and decency attaching to him that even Rhett said he could not find words to tell what a man this had been. At the first gun of the war Petigru had said, "I never believed that slavery would last a hundred years, now I know it won't last five," and he asked why war, which was a game of kings and a cruel sport, should be taken up with such joy as ran riot then among masses of people. He was an honest lawyer whose name for appointment to the United States Supreme Court to replace Justice McLean or Justice Campbell was seriously laid before Lincoln and by him gravely considered. In the epitaph chosen by Petigru's daughter was the line "Nothing is here for tears, nothing to wail or knock the breast."

This daughter, Mrs. Caroline Petigru Carson, would keep and treasure a letter from her friend George L. Schuyler written early in '62 from Washington: "I had an interview with the President at half past ten last Saturday night—a long social sort of a talk. He in his slippers and feet on the fender—I in dress clothes from a dinner party. He spoke most cordially of your father, for I pressed upon him his appointment as a judge of the Supreme Court. He said it was an excellent idea—he would think of it. But the only thing I feel confident of is this. That if your father would leave Charleston and come to this place he is sure of a warm and hearty reception, and of being offered a position which would not fail to be acceptable to him." Northern money and comfort, however, could not override the love of Petigru for his people. He stayed with them, believing them wrong, stalking out of church when he heard a prayer that omitted the President of the United States. He went to Fort Sumter to say good-by to the Union flag just before surrender, Major Abner Doubleday writing of what was seen, "The tears rolled down his cheeks as he deplored the folly and madness of the time." Doubleday quoted Petigru's answer to the South Carolinian who asked whether he would join the secession movement: "I should think not! South Carolina is too small for a republic, and too large for a lunatic asylum."

Of Lincoln, Petigru had no high opinion, writing in March of '62, "The *Mercury* has thrown off all reserve and proclaims J. D. [Jefferson Davis] is unfit for his place. I am myself afraid that he is but little better qualified for it than Lincoln is for his." Shortly before his death Petigru wrote his free and dispassionate judgment "that the independence of the Southern States or at least some of them will ultimately be recognized by a treaty of peace." This he had believed from the first. "I deplored it then, and deplore it now as much as ever. When that peace will come nobody knows, not even Jeff Davis or Seward; but I suppose the war will not last more than five years more." Now Petigru was beyond the war and his daughter was further to write in his epitaph, "In the great Civil War he withstood his People for his Country, but his People did homage to the Man who held his conscience higher than their praise."

John B. Floyd was in limboland, recorded as a coward by the Confederates who blamed him for the Fort Donelson surrender, excoriated in the North as a traitor Secretary of War who sat in Buchanan's Cabinet and took a hand in shipping arms south for the event of war against the Government in which he was a responsible minister. Stonewall Jackson was becoming a bright legend with an aura. Both sides had laid under earth brigadiers and major generals, the South mourning Van Dorn, Helm, Paxton, Tracy, Tilghman, Pender, both Garnetts, Barksdale, Preston Smith; the North its Reynolds, who had rejected Lincoln's offer of command of the Army of the Potomac, its Berry, Sill, Lytle, Bayard, Sanders, Buford, Corcoran. Their commissions had come to Lincoln's desk and he had signed them; the War Department reports had come to his desk that they were through with commissions.

Buford had led cavalry under Stoneman almost to the gates of Richmond, had repulsed the first gray infantry marching on Gettysburg; as he lay in his last sickness he signed for Lincoln his acceptance of the President's commission as a major general, crying in a final delirium, "Send for the brigade commanders; put guards on all those roads and keep those men from going to the rear."

General Michael Corcoran, who had proved his valor often under fire, had died from the fall of a horse on him, and a comrade of the Fenian Brotherhood in New York had intoned a requiem: "Deep in the green sod let him rest under the starry arch of the Republic he so nobly served and within sight of that city where his name will never sound strange." Captain George W. Vanderbilt, son of a multimillionaire, had graduated from West Point in 1860 and, twenty-five years old, had died from disease incurred in field service. Colleges, societies, lodges, clubs, were treasuring in creped rosters the names of their dead who had not availed themselves of the $300 clause. Aloof from the war, Henry Fitz, who better than anyone else in North America made telescopes for stargazers, had put away his lens-grinders and vanished. Across in Germany Jakob Grimm, language scholar and finder of folk tales, had faded from all thresholds, saying among his later words that he hoped Lincoln and the Union cause would win and the slaves go free. Only minor monarchs had died that year, kings of Madagascar, of the Sandwich Islands, of Denmark.

Younglings were on hand—with hope. The boy Tom Edison was peddling his papers on a dinky railroad from Detroit to Port Huron. Near its right of way was born in '63, in a family named Ford, a baby they christened Henry, whose neighbors were saying he might grow up and make a name for himself, the like being said of many other innocent, wriggling babies in that faded, collapsed, and memorable year of 1863.

Down near Beaufort, South Carolina, a Boston white man, captain of a company of Negro troops, heard one of them pray:

"Let me so lib dat when I die I shall hab manners, dat I shall know what to say when I see my Heabenly Lord. Let me lib wid de musket in one hand, an' de Bible in de oder—dat if I die at de muzzle ob de musket, die in de water, die on de land, I may know I hab de bressed Jesus in my hand, an' hab no fear. I hab lef' my wife in de land o' bondage; my little ones dey say eb'ry night, Whar is my fader? But when I die, when de bressed mornin' rises, when I shall stan' in de glory, wid one foot on de water an' one foot on de land, den, O Lord, I shall see my wife an' my little chil'en once more."

Major General John A. Logan, on furlough from Grant's army and not yet so versed in devious political vocabulary that he used language to conceal thought, had spoken to the people of Duquoin, Illinois: "How do they know we are all abolitionists, regular straight-outs? Did we tell them so? Did we say so? Why is it? Well, I will tell you. It is because we are in the army and Abraham Lincoln is President. That is the reason. These men don't know enough or don't want to know that Abraham Lincoln, because he is President don't own the Government. This is our Government. This war ain't fighting for Mr. Lincoln. It is fighting for the Union, for the Government. . . . I have seen Democrats shot down and buried in the same grave with the Republican and the Abolitionist. They are all fighting for the same country, the same ground. . . . You will again see the great railroads running from the North to the South, from the East to the West."

Another old-time Douglas Democrat wrote to the *Troy* [New York] *Times* that a Peace Democrat was a Judas Iscariot and a Benedict Arnold. "If you have any Copperheads among your readers, tell them we soldiers think the secesh are a little better and a good deal more manly."

The Arkansas swamp ranger, Brigadier General Jeff Thompson, arriving as a prisoner in St. Louis, was interviewed and said, "Some people think we have nothing to eat down South but I will tell you gentlemen privately there are plenty of corn bread and the hill cattle are not half gone yet." In Richmond the War Office clerk J. B. Jones was starting cabbage plants in a glass-covered half-barrel in his back yard; if it turned freezing he would carry his little greenhouse in by the sitting-room fireplace; he was writing that by next summer the Yankee armies would "encompass" Richmond.

The upper classes still fared well as to food, Mrs. Chesnut at the Prestons' on Christmas Day in Richmond partaking of "oyster soup, roast mutton, ham, boned turkey, wild duck, partridge, plum pudding, sauterne, burgundy, sherry, and Madeira. . . . Others dropped in after dinner," she wrote, "some without arms, some without legs; von Borcke, who can not speak because of a wound in his throat. Isabella said, 'We have all kinds now, but a blind one.' Poor fellows, they laugh at wounds."

Every Sunday Mrs. Chesnut heard Mr. Minnegerode cry aloud in anguish his litany "from pestilence and famine, battle, murder, and sudden death," and she on her knees joined with others in "Good Lord, deliver us." She walked the capitol grounds seeing returned prisoners, "men so forlorn, so dried up, and shrunken, with such a strange look in some of their eyes; others so restless and wild-looking; others again placidly vacant, as if they had been dead to the world for years." She stood touching elbows among them while Jefferson Davis made a speech. "They cheered with all their might, and I wept for sympathy, and enthusiasm." She went out to sell some of her old dresses at a store kept by a mulatto woman who bought from rich white women and sold to Negroes. Amid piles of rubbish and occasional Parisian silks and satins, she heard her companions, three young women, flinging talk at each other:

FIRST YOUNG WOMAN. Sally is going to marry a man who has lost an arm, and she is proud of it. The cause glorifies such wounds.

SECOND YOUNG WOMAN. I fear it will be my fate to marry one who has lost his head.

THIRD YOUNG WOMAN. Tudy has her eyes on one who has lost an eye. What a glorious assortment of noble martyrs and heroes!

FIRST YOUNG WOMAN. The bitterness of this kind of talk is appalling.

In a farmhouse near the hardest fighting at Gettysburg, narrated a Sanitary Commission report, was an apple-cheeked country girl baking bread. They had asked if she wasn't scared. "Well, no. You see we was all a-baking bread round here for the soldiers, and had our dough a-rising. The neighbors they ran into their cellars but I could not leave my bread. When the first shell came in at the window and crashed through the room, an officer came in and said, 'You had better get out of this' but I told him I *could not* leave my bread and I stood working in it till the third shell came through and then I went down cellar but (gleefully) I left my bread in the oven!"

In Iowa the Reverend Mr. Shrine, chaplain of the State legislature, had opened the recent session with a prayer: "Bless Thou the young and growing State of Iowa, her senators and representatives, the governor and State officers. Give us a sound currency, pure water and undefiled religion—for Christ's sake. Amen."

The human causes operating in America were many and varied and moving, requiring the brush of chaos to do a mural of the crossed interests of climate and geography, of native and foreign blood streams, of bread-and-butter necessity, of cultural environment, of mystic hopes.

As they passed before Lincoln in their many guises and dialects, he considered, decided, waited, looked often abstracted, seemed more often to have his mind elsewhere than in Washington. Robert E. Lee, Mrs. Chesnut, the country girl baking bread at Gettysburg, Jeff Thompson, Ben Butler, Black Jack Logan, the praying Negro soldier in South Carolina, and the chaplain of the Iowa Legislature—they must all enter into his plans and calculations no less than scores of men as strong and complex as Grant, Chase, Medill, Greeley, Bennett, Raymond, Beecher.

Lincoln at the vortex of the revolution that, if it won, was to break the power of the Southern planter aristocracy and usher in the dominance of the financial and industrial interests centered in New York City, may have seen and taken comfort in what the Paris correspondent of the *New York Times* was writing his paper at the year's end: "The popularity of Mr. Lincoln has much advanced abroad by his late acts. His maintenance of the act of Emancipation in his annual message, his sagacity, straight-forwardness and honesty in the midst of such confusion and excitement called from M. Laboulaye the other day at the Collège de France before an immense audience of the elite of the intellectual world, the exclamation that Mr. Lincoln was 'a greater man than Caesar!' So, too, I heard a leading French politician say lately: 'You Americans don't appreciate Mr. Lincoln at his proper value. No monarch in Europe could carry on such a colossal war in front while harassed by so many factions and fault-finders behind. No, you don't give him his due.' From an European point of view the merit of Mr. Lincoln is, in effect, immense. On every side I hear people begin to say that Mr. Lincoln will merit more than a biography—he will merit a history."

Newspapers were printing a strangely worded psalm of praise for Lincoln the man, spoken in the 1863 Thanksgiving sermon at the Second Presbyterian Church of Auburn, New York, by its pastor, the Reverend Henry Fowler, former editor of *Holden's Magazine*, one-time editor and part owner of the *Chicago Tribune*, and in his versatile career professor of political economy at the University of Rochester for five years. The progress of the President kept pace with the progress of the people, Fowler believed, comparing it with the time in Jewish history when the prophet Samuel was the mediator between a passing and a coming epoch. "Such an epoch of perplexity, transition, change, is not often witnessed. In every such passage of a nation there ought to be a character like that of Samuel. Misunderstood and misrepresented at the time; attacked from both sides; charged with not going far enough and with going too far; charged with saying too much and saying too little, he slowly, conscientiously and honestly works out the mighty problem. He was not a founder of a new state of things like Moses; he was not a champion of the existing order of things like Elijah. He stood between the two; between the living and the dead; between the past and the present; between the old and the new; with that sympathy for each which at such a period is the best hope for any permanent solution of the questions which torment it. He has but little praise from partisans, but is the careful healer binding up the wounds of the age, in spite of itself; the good surgeon knitting together the dislocated bones of the disjointed times."

Samuel was such a man among the Jews, Athanasius among the early Christians. "Such a man is Abraham Lincoln in this day." By word and act Lincoln had evidently haunted the Reverend Henry Fowler, who sought brief and graphic phrases for his portrait of the figure he then saw as a major American prophet:

"The explanation for his every act is this: He executes the will of the people. He represents a controlling majority. If he be slow it is because the people are slow. If he has done a foolish act, it was the stupidity of the people which impelled it. His wisdom consists in carrying out the good sense of the nation. His growth in political knowledge, his steady movement toward emancipation, are but the growth and movement of the national mind. Indeed, in character and culture he is a fair representative of the average American.

"His awkward speech and yet more awkward silence, his uncouth manners, his grammar self-taught and partly forgotten, his style miscellaneous, concreted from the best authors, like a reading book, and yet oftentimes of Saxon force and classic purity; his humor an argument, and his logic a joke, both unseasonable at times and irresistible always; his questions answers and his answers questions; his guesses prophecies, and fulfillment ever beyond his promise; honest yet shrewd; simple yet reticent; heavy and yet energetic; never despairing and never sanguine; careless in forms; conscientious in essentials; never sacrificing a good servant once trusted, never deserting a good principle once adopted; not afraid of new ideas, not despising old ones; improving opportunities to confess mistakes, ready to learn, getting at facts, doing nothing when he knows not what to do; hesitating at nothing when he sees the right; lacking the recognized qualification of a party leader, and yet leading his party as no other man can; sustaining his political enemies in Missouri to their defeat, sustaining his political friends in Maryland to their victory; conservative in his sympathies and radical in his acts; Socratic in his style and Baconian in his method; his religion consisting in truthfulness, temperance, asking good people to pray for him and publicly acknowledging in events the hand of God, he stands before you as the type of 'Brother Jonathan,' a not perfect man and yet more precious than fine gold."

The President took such outpourings to heart. As prose it had a touch of his own flavor. He may have inquired of himself whether while he was alive and a witness there was a process of building a tradition of himself as the titan of a colossal tale, as "a saint and a martyr," also as "a not perfect man and yet more precious than fine gold."

New Year's Day of 1864 came, and Benjamin Perley Poore noted at the morning reception in the White House "Mr. Lincoln was in excellent spirits, giving each passer-by a cordial greeting and a warm shake of the hand, while for some there was a quiet joke." Mrs. Lincoln stood at his right hand, wearing purple silk trimmed with black velvet and lace, a lace necktie fastened with a pearl pin, a white plume topping her headdress. Secretary Seward was there, sphinxlike, rusty-looking. Secretary Chase to Poore seemed perplexed, balancing chances for the next Presidency. Secretary Welles with patriarchal beard and flowing wig was there, but not so many Senators and Congressmen, most of them taking a New Year holiday. The army officers came in from the War Department, headed by General Halleck, some with epaulets and feathers but more in fatigue blue. The navy as usual was spick and span. At noon the doors were thrown open for the people to pour through in a continuous stream for two hours. "A living tide which swept in, eddied around the President and his wife, and then surged into the East Room which was a maelstrom of humanity, uniforms, black coats, gay female attire, and citizens generally."

In shining clothes, with stars, garters, medals of honor, the diplomatic corps outshone all others. "The rush for a glimpse of these gay birds was very great," wrote Noah Brooks for the *Sacramento Union*. As among them he saw the Secretary of State in neglected attire, he noted "Seward looked very much like a molting barnyard fowl among peacocks." His eye took in Mrs. Lincoln lacking mourning garb for the first time in the twenty-two months since Willie Lincoln died.

Since recovery the month before from varioloid "the President looks better," was Brooks's impression. "I don't mean to insinuate that the disease has added any new charms to his features; but his complexion is clearer, his eyes less lack-luster and he has a hue of health to which he has long been a stranger. He stood up manfully against the great crush and bore the handshaking like a blessed old martyr, as he is."

While the President, just after his return from Gettysburg and his speaking there, had lain abed with varioloid, an immense crowd had streamed down Pennsylvania Avenue to the Capitol grounds looking skyward toward the Capitol dome. The bronze legs and torso of the massive heroic figure of a helmeted woman representing the Goddess of Liberty, after years of lying helpless and forlorn on the ground below, had been lifted to the top of the dome. And on this day, precisely at noon, the last section of this 19½-foot high bronze statue, consisting of the head and shoulders of the incomplete goddess, left the mass of material at the foot of the dome and moved serenely upward, drawn by a slender wire cable.

From a chaos of timbered scaffolding the head and shoulders emerged and swung lightly and calmly into place joined to her torso. A workman drove a ringing sledge hammer three times. It was over. The Union banner ran up a flagstaff. Artillery roared a salute.

To one onlooker, Noah Brooks, the prolonged and loud shout of the crowd seemed to say to the azure that day: "Take her, oh, heavens blue and gay, take her to thy protecting arms, with all her bronze and all her charms."

John Eaton of Toledo, Ohio, had talked with Lincoln one day about the statue of Liberty to be hoisted over the Capitol dome, new marble pillars to be installed on the Senate wing, a massive and richly embellished bronze door being made for the main central portal. People were saying it was an extravagance during wartime, Eaton remarked.

Lincoln answered, "If people see the Capitol going on, it is a sign we intend the Union shall go on."

CHAPTER 46

GRANT GIVEN HIGH COMMAND '64

THE war had not uncovered a Napoleon nor a Wellington. There was talk, however, of the North having found a Suwarrow. The record of Suwarrow was looked up. Russia's biggest name in military annals—that was Suwarrow, or Alexander Vasilievich Suvarov—piled his men in and took any slaughters that would give him victory. In Turkey, Poland, Italy, and elsewhere Suwarrow in the eighteenth century starved cities, gave captured towns horror and cruelty, with little mercy for either his own troops or their captives. Yet Suwarrow, the descendant of a Swede named Suvor who emigrated to Russia, Russia's greatest field marshal, had come up from the lowest ranks, lived plainly, in active service slept on straw, ate the black bread of the common soldier, and threw himself into the front-line dangers.

Southern West Pointers saw the North as having realized no Napoleon in McClellan, no Wellington in Hooker or Burnside. The North had its Suwarrow, however, they told Mrs. Chesnut; it would be just like the Yankees to find a merciless, primitive warrior patterned after a Russian tradition. "Grant . . . is their right man, a bull-headed Suwarrow," wrote Mrs. Chesnut on January 1, 1864. "He don't care a snap if men fall like the leaves fall; he fights to win, that chap does. He is not distracted by a thousand side issues; he does not see them. He is narrow and sure—sees only in a straight line . . . from a battle in the gutter, he goes straight up. . . . If General Lee had had Grant's resources he would have bagged the last Yankee, or have had them all safe back in Massachusetts."

In the North were those who agreed with Mrs. Chesnut that Grant won by sheer overwhelming numbers, by cold, brutal, mass sacrifices of human material. This feeling in the North had gone down somewhat as Grant slowly rode into national popularity and fame, out of nothing much to start with. His string of combats and victories had won the imagination of many who wanted the war to end soon in favor of the Union. And Grant, the plain, plodding, short, stoop-shouldered Grant, with no put-on, no show-off about him, seemed to be the hero they had been looking for. He had captured two armies and routed a third, his dramatic actions touched with shock and surprise. Donelson was the first Union shout from early darkness, Vicksburg an engineering and surgical exploit cutting a deep incision, Chattanooga an onrush with slaughter beyond prediction.

From Grant no promises beforehand, no signs of bragging, but suddenly out of rain and mud, long marches and spadework interspersed with skirmish and assault, would come the word of a certain piece of workmanship toward winning the war. Many days his comings and goings, or the mystery of where he was and what doing, crowded out all others as the foremost newspaper items of the hour. On the hazards of Grant hung the anxieties and wonderings of millions of people. When he came out of those hazards with another complete operation of neat and final skill, reporting it in words modest and almost bashful, it took the hearts of those who prefer their heroism plain and unexpected.

As a former Douglas Democrat now for the war and the Union, Grant was accepted and endorsed by an element that could never see Lincoln as their leader. The powerful *New York Herald* spoke for a miscellany of interests when through the winter of '63 and '64 it incessantly rang changes on the cry for Grant as next President of the United States, long editorials headed "Grant, the People's Candidate." Many other newspapers joined in urging that Grant was the one safe and efficient public figure they considered free from the looseness, the vagaries, and the entanglements of Lincoln.

Neither Grant nor his relatives nor his soldiers wanted him to run for President. The *Chicago Tribune* declared in editorial advice to the *New York Herald:* "We claim the right to tell this organ of the Five Points and the Thugs of New York, that it must keep its copperhead slime off our Illinois General. He has no attribute, thought or sympathy in harmony with the *Satanic* [a nickname for the *New York Herald*]. General Grant is an old neighbor and friend of President Lincoln. The latter has stood by him with the strength of iron from the first. . . . In return General Grant has been true as steel to his friend and Commander-in-Chief. For the *New York Herald* to bring out General Grant is a gross libel on him and an insult to his friends. Unless it keeps its unclean and treacherous hands off of him, it may expect to get 'tomahawked.' " The *Herald* could run McClellan or Fitz-John Porter for President. "But it cannot be allowed to paw and slobber over our Illinois General, and if it has any regard for its 'throat' or its 'fifth rib,' it will take warning and govern itself accordingly."

The *New York Herald* replied that the *Chicago Tribune* was "the sewer into which goes everything too dirty for its New York namesake to print." When the *Herald* stopped its Grant editorials for a few days and lambasted the *Chicago Tribune*, Medill wrote: "The people want Old Abe to stay where he is until he has finished *his* big job . . . and General Grant to stay where he is until he has finished *his* big job. . . . Let our Western General alone. . . . Who will be next proposed for President?"

Sherman saw a star of destiny hovering momentously over Grant, shedding the frail light that sometimes turns good men into fool puppets of ambition. Sherman wrote to Grant on December 29 of a conversation they had had. "I repeat, you occupy a position of more power than Halleck or the President. There are similar instances in European history, but none in ours. For the sake of future generations, risk nothing. Let *us* risk—and when you strike, let it be as at Vicksburg and Chattanooga. Your reputation as a general is now far above that of any man living, and partisans will maneuvre for your influence. . . . Preserve a plain military character; let others maneuvre as they will, and you will beat them, not only in fame, but in doing good in the closing scenes of this war."

Sherman had held the thought of army heads such as Grant and himself more than once in European history taking control of governments and setting up dictatorships. Thus far he and Grant had kept discreet silence as to their contempt for advice from Washington. It was a later time that Sherman heard Chauncey Depew tell of Grant's offhand mention of times he cut the wires between his army and Washington. "Did he?" laughed Sherman. "Why, I did that! I never heard before that Grant did it!"

The impressionistic Mary Boykin Chesnut told her diary of Richmond talk not like it used to be about Grant and Lincoln. "As with Lincoln, they have ceased to carp at him as a rough clown, no gentleman, etc. You never hear now of Lincoln's nasty fun; only of his wisdom. Doesn't take much soap and water to wash the hands that the rod of empire sway. . . . Now, since Vicksburg they have not a word to say against Grant's habits. He has the disagreeable habit of not retreating before irresistible veterans."

Grant was taken up as a hero even by antiwar elements such as the *Crisis* at Columbus, Ohio, which saw Grant "unencumbered with the political charlatanism of most other officers," bringing to the country a calm confidence not before witnessed during the war. "The whole people seem relieved from apprehension. . . . He is no mere newspaper general, puffed into place and importance by acts of petty favoritism, and still more petty tyranny over the many to purchase the favor of the few for selfish and ambitious purposes."

Lincoln had never seen Grant. He knew Grant only from what he read in the papers and official reports, and from what he heard in talk about Grant. Not yet had he had a chance personally to size up the man who, on form, was his best fighter. To Congressman Washburne, Grant's home-town Illinois friend, Lincoln said: "About all I know of Grant I have got from you. I have never seen him. Who else besides you knows anything about Grant?" Washburne: "I know very little about him. He is my townsman but I never saw very much of him. The only man who really knows Grant is Jones. He has summered and wintered with him." Washburne referred to a Galena man, J. Russell Jones, a United States Marshal at Chicago who had visited with Grant in Mississippi.

Lincoln wired J. Russell Jones to come on to Washington. Jones packed his valise, stopped at his office and got his letters on the way to the train. The train started and Jones opened his mail to find a letter from Grant answering one that Jones had written urging the General to pay no attention to the newspapers trying to run him for President. Grant was saying that he had as big a job as one man could ask, that he was out to suppress the "rebellion," and everything that reached him trying to push him into politics went into the wastebasket.

Arriving in Washington, Jones sent word to the President that he would be glad to call when convenient. The President set eight o'clock that evening. Then as Jones told it:

When the President had gotten through with the persons with whom he was engaged, I was invited into his room. The President then gave directions to say to all that he was engaged for the evening. Mr. Lincoln opened the conversation by saying that he was anxious to see somebody from the West with whom he could talk upon the general situation and had therefore sent for me. Mr. Lincoln made no allusion whatever to Grant. I had been there but a few minutes, however, when I fancied he would like to talk about Grant, and I interrupted him by saying:

"Mr. President, if you will excuse me for interrupting you, I want to ask you kindly to read a letter that I got from my box as I was on my way to the train."

Whereupon I gave him Grant's letter. He read it with evident interest. When he came to the part where Grant said that it would be impossible for him to think of the presidency as long as there was a possibility of retaining Mr. Lincoln in the office, he read no further, but arose and, approaching me, put his hand on my shoulder and said:

"My son, you will never know how gratifying that is to me. No man knows, when that presidential grub gets to gnawing at him, just how deep it will get until he has tried it; and I didn't know but what there was one gnawing at Grant."

The fact was that this was just what Mr. Lincoln wanted to know.

Among the first acts of Congress that winter was the voting of a medal of thanks to Grant for his victories. The Philadelphia mint began work on a design with Grant's head in profile, wreathed by laurel, encircled by one star for each State; on the other side a figure of Fame seated in the heavens with emblems of prosperity and power.

The country had its first word from Grant, as to running for President, in January of '64. The press gave his reply when bantered about the *New York Herald's* aim to put him in the White House: "I aspire only to one political office. When this war is over, I mean to run for Mayor of Galena [his Illinois home town], and if elected, I intend to have the sidewalk fixed up between my house and the depot." Some comment ran like that of *Leslie's Weekly:* "If General Grant should go on joking in this dry style, he will soon joke Lincoln out of the next nomination."

To his father on February 20 Grant wrote cautioning the old man not to believe all he read in the public prints. "I am not a candidate for any office. All I want is to be left alone to fight this war out."

Grant and his closest friend and adviser, John A. Rawlins, had foresight and could tell a hawk from a handsaw in politics. This was evident in a letter of Rawlins to General James Harrison Wilson early in March. Rawlins was the only man who had on occasion cursed Grant for drinking, almost weeping while he cursed. Rawlins too had expelled from camp at

Vicksburg a relative of Grant's by marriage who was buying cotton and trying to ship it North, against trade regulations. When Grant asked Rawlins to suspend the order of expulsion Rawlins broke out in a flood of oaths at Grant, ending with the declaration that as a commander of 100,000 men Grant ought to hang his relative to the highest tree within five miles of camp. Rawlins stalked out, came back later, apologized for losing his temper. "Of course," smiled Grant, "you were not cursing but merely expressing your 'intense vehemence on the subject matter.' Don't think of it again but now that the storm is over you can destroy that order and tell the gentleman to whom it refers that his health requires him to take the first steamer back to Cairo." From Galena to Vicksburg and on to Washington Rawlins had been at Grant's side, loyal, sleepless, outspoken. And what Rawlins wrote in early March was the sense of the two of them on the point of why Grant would give out no statement on whether he wanted to be President. Rawlins wrote to Wilson:

I cannot conceive how the use of General Grant's name in connection with the Presidency can result in harm to him or our cause, for if there is a man in the United States who is unambitious of such honor, it is certainly he, yet the matter is not in such shape as to justify him in writing a letter declining to be a candidate for the Presidency. The nomination for the office has not been tendered him by the people; nor has it by either of the great political parties or any portion thereof. To write a letter of declination now, would place him in much the position of the old maid who had never had an offer declaring she "would never marry"; besides it would be by many construed into a modest way of getting his name before the country in connection with the office, having, as he always has, avoided public notice or newspaper talk relating to him. . . . The Honorable E. B. Washburne [Grant's foremost friend and advocate in Congress] I am sure is not in favor of Grant for the Presidency. He is for Mr. Lincoln.

The *New York Herald* and other journals kept on week in and week out promoting Grant for President. Grant anecdotes sprinkled newspaper columns; his horsemanship, his licking the officers of his West Point company and offering to take on all comers one by one, his ever present cigar that protruded from his face even at military reviews, his talk with a quartermaster on the evening of the first day at Shiloh. There would not be transportation to carry the defeated army across the Tennessee River, the officer reported. Grant asked how many he could handle. "Ten thousand," said the quartermaster. "Well," said General Grant, "if we are defeated you will be able to carry all that are left."

America had its chuckle over Mrs. Grant's saying to a *New York Herald* interviewer, "I have no doubt Mr. Grant will succeed, for he is a very obstinate man." Lincoln heard of this and thereafter occasionally spoke of "Mr. Grant, as Mrs. Grant calls him."

Early in February bills in House and Senate proposed to revive the rank of Lieutenant General of the Armies of the United States. The House bill provided that Grant should be appointed to the office. In the upper house Senator Howard of Michigan held "it is not indelicate . . . it is necessary" that Grant be named. "I think the President of the United States can have no ground whatever to complain . . . of the Senate in making this respectful request. . . . Give us, sir, a live general . . . who will . . . give us victory . . . and not let us be draggling along under the influences such as have presided over the army of the Potomac for these last many tedious and weary months—an army oscillating alternately between the Rappahannock and the Potomac, defeated to-day and hardly successful to-morrow, with its commanders changed almost as frequently as the moon changes its face. Sir, for one I am tired of this; and I tell . . . Senators here that the country is getting weary of it."

Senator Lane of Indiana had no doubt the President would appoint Grant. The Military Committee of the Senate, Lane was sure, favored appointment of Grant. Yet the committee was opposed to Congress's arbitrarily taking from the President the power to name a lieutenant general. Lane agreed with Senator Wilson of Massachusetts that it would be indelicate for the Senate to insist on naming the chief army head. "To-day we recommend the appointment of General Grant. He is sent in for confirmation. To-morrow we believe he should not be confirmed. Our hands are tied, for the President turns upon us and says, 'Here by a solemn act of Congress you have requested me to appoint this man to office.'" Senator Johnson saw it as a bad precedent for Congress to tell the President who must head the army; the time might come when a majority of Congress, trying to master and control a President, would say to him, "Take our man or take the consequences."

General Garfield advised waiting till the war was over and then awarding the honor of lieutenant general to the most worthy officer. Senator Grimes spouted: "I am unalterably opposed to the passage of this bill in any shape in which it can be presented to the Senate. . . . Is it worth while for us to establish this precedent of creating lieutenant generals for the purpose of giving General Grant an empty honor? I trow not." Fessenden was sure the President would name Grant without Congress's ordering him to. "When the President says to us, as he will say unquestionably, 'I consider that General Ulysses S. Grant is the man of all others, from his great services, to be placed in this exalted position,' and when we as we shall unquestionably unanimously say 'ay' to that and confirm him, have we not given him a position such as any man living or who ever lived might well be proud of, without putting his name in our bill originally, and thus saying to the President, 'Sir, we cannot trust you to act on this matter unless we hint to you that we want such a man appointed'?" Among Republicans who voted against the bill were Ashley of Ohio, Boutwell of Massachusetts, Broomall of Pennsylvania, Henry Winter Davis, James A. Garfield, George W. Julian, William D. Kelley, Thaddeus Stevens.

The bill on February 26 passed both houses, leaving it to the President to appoint by and with the advice of the Senate a lieutenant general from among the major generals of the army. On February 29 the President signed the bill, named Grant for the newly created office. Only two men, George

Washington and Winfield Scott, had hitherto in American history held the rank of lieutenant general. The Senate confirmed the President's appointment. Nicolay and Hay believed "the Administration exercised no influence in the matter, neither helping nor hindering the progress of the bill through the Houses of Congress."

And now Halleck at last was to go. The diatribes of politicians and newspapers against him had never let down; his critics ever sought new ways of saying he did nothing or if he did he blundered. Lincoln had told Hay and others on various occasions, "I am Halleck's friend because he has no others." Also to Hay, Lincoln had said that Halleck was "little more . . . than a first-rate clerk." Hay noted in his diary: "I suppose Halleck is badly bilious about Grant. Grant, the Pres^t says, is Commander in Chief & Halleck is now nothing but a staff officer. In fact, says the President, 'When McClellan seemed incompetent to the work of handling an army & we sent for Halleck to take command he stipulated that it should be with the full power and responsibility of Commander in Chief. He ran it on that basis till Pope's defeat; but ever since that event, he has shrunk from responsibility wherever it was possible.'"

Grant was at Nashville when word came that the President had named him for the Senate to confirm as lieutenant general. Grant had been directing railroad rebuilding, gathering of supplies, minor troop movements, looking toward a spring drive to end the war west of the Alleghenies. He had approved a raid of Sherman's army which made a swift, quiet march across the State of Mississippi to Meridian, burned an arsenal, two large hotels, and gristmills, destroyed railroads within a radius of twenty-five miles. Sherman said as he returned to Vicksburg that the enemy losses were $50,000,000. To Sherman on March 4 Grant wrote that he was ordered to Washington to take office as lieutenant general if the Senate confirmed the President's appointment. His personal success in the war, Grant wrote Sherman, was due to the energy and skill of his subordinates, above all to Sherman and McPherson. "I feel all the gratitude this letter can express, giving it the most flattering construction."

Sherman replied with groaning over the prospect of Grant's leaving. "For God's sake and your country's sake, come out of Washington. . . . Come West; take to yourself the whole Mississippi Valley. Let us make it dead-sure, and I tell you the Atlantic slope and Pacific shores will follow its destiny as sure as the limbs of a tree live or die with the main trunk. . . . Here lies the seat of coming empire." On the same day Sherman wrote in another letter of the Mississippi River as "the grand artery" of America. "I want to live out here and die here also, and don't care if my grave be like De Soto's in its muddy waters." Sherman knew that for Grant, as for himself, the war was for a river and the point of whether that river should belong to one or several nations. Also both of them knew that political forces in Washington could hamstring the best of commanders.

In a letter home just after the Vicksburg surrender, Sherman had written,

"Thank God, no President was near to thwart our plans," but in the same letter he had also written, "I wish Halleck would put a guard over the White House to keep out the committees of preachers, grannies and Dutchmen that absorb Lincoln's time and thoughts, fill up our thinned ranks with conscripts, and then handle these vast armies with the single thought of success regardless of who shall get the personal credit and glory." Half expecting that Grant would stay West yet half in tone of farewell, Sherman told Grant: "I believe you are as brave, patriotic and just as the great prototype Washington; as unselfish, kind-hearted and honest as a man should be . . . the simple faith in success you have always manifested I can liken to nothing else than the faith a Christian has in a Savior. . . . When you have completed your last preparations, you go into battle without hesitation—no doubts, no reserves; and I tell you it was this that made us act with confidence. I knew wherever I was that you thought of me, and if I got in a tight place you would come if alive."

Grant traveled toward Washington with his fourteen-year-old boy Fred, and his chief of staff John Rawlins. His intention was (for Sherman had read him right) to return to Chattanooga and make that his headquarters, unless what he saw and heard in Washington told him he must stay East. Crowds and cheers met Grant as the train moved on to Washington. There on the evening of March 8 he walked into Willard's Hotel and asked for a room. The clerk said he had only a top-floor room. Grant said that would do—and signed the register. The clerk took a look at the name and then jumped fast to assign Grant the best in the house. Grant walked into the dining-room and was ordering food when word passed around among the guests, "It's Grant," and questions: "Where is he?" "Which is he?" Someone stood on a chair and called for three cheers for Grant. Three cheers rang out. The diners pounded on tables, waved napkins, threatened the glassware, yelled various suggestions, and called the name of Grant, Grant, Grant!

After a few minutes, as Noah Brooks noted it, "General Grant, looking very much astonished and perhaps annoyed, rose to his feet, awkwardly rubbed his mustache with his napkin, bowed, resumed his seat and attempted to finish his dinner." The diners at Willard's that evening then seemed slowly to get the idea that Grant had come to the dining-room for a meal. And they let him eat in peace. On his way out Congressman Moorhead of Pennsylvania took him in hand, introduced him to a mob of admirers and curiosity-seekers.

The evening was young yet, however, as Grant was on his way with Senator Cameron to report to the President at the White House, in a tarnished uniform with a major general's stars on the shoulder straps. "He had no gait, no station, no manner, rough, light-brown whiskers, rather a scrubby look," wrote Richard Henry Dana. "He had a cigar in his mouth, and rather the look of a man who did, or once did, take a little too much to drink . . . a slightly seedy look, as if he was out of office and on half pay, nothing to do but hang around, a clear blue eye and a look of resolution, as if he could not be trifled with, and an entire indifference to the crowd about him. . . . He does not march, nor quite walk, but pitches along as if the next step would bring him on his nose."

Perhaps Grant would not have started for the White House that evening had he known it was the night of the President's weekly reception. A buzz and a murmur ran round the big East Room receiving-room, reaching the President with news that Grant would soon step into the room. As the General entered in tarnished blue, a hush fell on the crowd. They moved back and made a pathway for the head of all the armies of the United States to walk up to the Chief Magistrate.

Lincoln saw him coming, put out his long bony hand for the shorter and smaller one of Grant's. "I'm glad to see you, General." The two men stood a moment with struck hands.

Lincoln introduced the General to Seward, who escorted him toward Mrs. Lincoln in the East Room. The buzz of talk became a hullabaloo. The crowd swirled around the short bullet-shaped man who embodied Donelson, Shiloh, Vicksburg, Chattanooga, in his rough frame. They cheered and yelled, jammed toward him, men and women wanting to touch his hands. He "blushed like a schoolgirl," shook hands till sweat poured down his face. Veins on his forehead bulged red. He dropped a remark later that it was a hotter spot than he had ever known in battle.

"Stand up so we can all have a look at you!" came cries. And the shrinking war hero stepped up on a sofa and stood where they could look at him. Then he made a tour of the room with Mrs. Lincoln's arm in his. Lincoln, with a lady on his arm, followed, his fissured face lighted, taking in all the contrasts that appealed to his sense of humor. Ladies of the evening, caught in the crush, had their laces torn and crinolines mashed; many got up on chairs, tables, sofas, to be out of harm's way or to get a better view.

"It was the only real mob I ever saw in the White House," wrote Noah Brooks. . . . "For once at least the President of the United States was not the chief figure in the picture. The little scared-looking man who stood on a crimson-covered sofa was the idol of the hour. He remained on view for a short time, then he was quietly smuggled out by friendly hands."

Grant returned later when the crowd was gone and met Lincoln with Stanton and Nicolay in a small drawing-room. Lincoln had done some careful thinking about the ceremonies next day, when he was to hand formally to Grant the new commission. And at this little conference of two powerful war leaders who met for the first time on this night, Lincoln did nearly all the talking—and all of it bore on the point that the next day each of them should say little, but what they did say should be pat to the occasion. The President explained: "I shall make a very short speech to you, to which I desire you to reply, for an object; and that you may be properly prepared to do so, I have written what I shall say, only four sentences in all, which I will read from my manuscript as an example which you may follow and also read your reply—as you are perhaps not so much accustomed to public speaking as I am; and I therefore give you what I shall say so you may consider it. There are two points that I would like to have you make in your answer: First, to say something which shall prevent or obviate any jealousy of you from any of the other generals in the service; and second, something which shall put you on as good terms as possible with the Army of the Potomac. If you see any objection to doing this, be under no restraint whatever in expressing that objection to the Secretary of War."

Grant put in his inside coat pocket the copy of the President's speech for the next day and, saying good night, left the room with Stanton. The next day at one o'clock the Cabinet, Halleck, Grant's son Fred, Rawlins, Owen Lovejoy, and Nicolay assembled to hear two little speeches that were telegraphed to the wide world.

Lincoln, facing Grant, read four sentences: "General Grant, The nation's appreciation of what you have done, and its reliance upon you for what remains to do, in the existing great struggle, are now presented, with this commission, constituting you lieutenant-general in the Army of the United States. With this high honor devolves upon you also a corresponding responsibility. As the country herein trusts you, so, under God, it will sustain you. I scarcely need add, that with what I here speak for the nation, goes my own hearty personal concurrence."

Grant held a half-sheet of note paper. On it was a hurried lead-pencil scrawl. And he wasn't sure what he had written to read off to the important though small audience. "His embarrassment was evident and extreme," noted Nicolay. "He found his own writing very difficult to read." The speech, however, as he finally made the grade, fitted Grant. He read, facing Lincoln, his three-sentence response: "Mr. President, I accept the commission, with gratitude for the high honor conferred. With the aid of the noble armies that have fought in so many fields for our common country, it will be my earnest endeavor not to disappoint your expectations. I feel the full weight of the responsibilities devolving on me; and I know that if they are met, it will be due to those armies, and above all to the favor of that Providence which leads both nations and men."

The two leaders then had a short talk. Grant asked what special service was required of him. "The President replied," noted Nicolay, "that the country wanted him to take Richmond; he said our generals had not been fortunate in their efforts in that direction and asked if the Lieutenant-General could do it. Grant, without hesitation, answered that he could if he had the troops. These the President assured him he should have. There was not one word said as to what route to Richmond should be chosen."

The news of Lincoln and Grant meeting, their two simple little speeches, their private White House conference, the wonder over what the new high commander would do—this was at once a universal press and sidewalk topic. The North brightened a little.

The South saw Northern morale changed, at least slightly, for the better. "The Yankees say," wrote Mrs. Chesnut, "that at last they have scared up a man who succeeds, and they expect him to remedy all that has gone wrong. So they have made their brutal Suwarrow, Grant, lieutenant-general."

Grant rode by rail to the Army of the Potomac headquarters at Brandy Station, talked with Meade, felt out the spirit of the officers and men, said nothing much. Of intrigue and wirepulling in Washington he had heard and seen not a little in this week the President gave him supreme command. Senators Wade and Chandler had been to the President and called for removal of Meade from command of the Army of the Potomac. Wade had .directed the stenographer of the Committee on the Conduct of the War to enter it on the journal of the Committee that "being asked [by the President] what general they would recommend for the command of the Army of the Potomac, they said that, for themselves, they would be content with General Hooker, believing him to be competent; but not being advocates of any particular general they would say, if there was any general whom the President considered more competent for the command, then let him be appointed. They stated [to the President] that Congress had appointed the committee to watch the conduct of the war."

When the committee had summarily called Meade to testify that week as to how he had fought the battle of Gettysburg, Wade denied there were any charges against Meade, saying that the committee was merely making up a history of the war. Meade wrote to his wife's brother-in-law: "My enemies consist of certain politicians who wish me removed to restore Hooker; then of certain subordinates, whose military reputations are involved in the destruction of mine; finally, a class of vultures who in Hooker's day preyed upon the army, and who sigh for a return of those glorious days." Conspiracies, charges, excuses, perversions, greed for power and favors, gossip filled with half-truths difficult to sift—these blew in the air of this Washington to which Grant had come.

Grant found Meade sincere, generous, open-minded, saying that Grant might want an officer to command the Army of the Potomac who had been with him in the West, possibly Sherman. Meade begged Grant not to hesitate about making a change; the work before them was so vast that the feelings or wishes of no one person should stand in the way of selecting the right man; he would serve to the best of his ability wherever placed. Grant told Meade he had no thought of a substitute for him, and as to Sherman, he could not be spared from the West. "I was much pleased with Grant," Meade wrote to his wife, "and most agreeably disappointed in his evidence of mind and character. You may rest assured he is not an ordinary man."

The congressional gold medal struck off for Grant arrived from the Philadelphia mint. Seward and Washburne called at the White House one evening and showed it to the President and Colonel James Grant Wilson, a dinner guest. On a small center table under a drop light, in a morocco case, lay the medal as Lincoln and Wilson stood looking at it—the medal upside down. After a long pause Colonel Wilson ventured, "What is the obverse of the medal, Mr. President?" Lincoln looked up, turned to Seward, and said, "I suppose by his obverse the Colonel means t'other side." They all laughed, Wilson joining in and noting later, "The President's jocoseness was partly natural, partly intentional; in the sea of troubles that almost overwhelmed him, he affected a serenity he was far from feeling." And whatever the art merit of the medal, they were agreed it was a nice token and remembrance for Grant to have. They expected that after it was handed to Grant he would never adorn his bosom with it. Nor did he.

No other man of high command in Washington had been so completely noncommittal regarding future plans as Grant. He was a good listener, and

of his first interview with Lincoln alone, Grant wrote: "He stated to me that he had never professed to be a military man or to know how campaigns should be conducted, and never wanted to interfere in them: but that procrastination on the part of commanders, and the pressure from the people at the North and Congress, *which was always with him*, forced him into issuing his series of 'Military Orders'—one, two, three, etc. He did not know but they were all wrong, and did know that some of them were. All he wanted or had ever wanted was someone who would take the responsibility and act, and call on him for all the assistance needed, pledging himself to use all the power of the government in rendering such assistance. Assuring him that I would do the best I could with the means at hand, and avoid as far as possible annoying him or the War Department, our first interview ended.

"The Secretary of War . . . and General Halleck both cautioned me against giving the President my plans of campaign, saying that he was so kind-hearted, so averse to refusing anything asked of him, that some friend would be sure to get from him all he knew. . . .

"In our interview the President told me he did not want to know what I proposed to do. But he submitted a plan of campaign of his own which he wanted me to hear and then do as I pleased about. He brought out a map of Virginia on which he had evidently marked every position occupied by the Federal and Confederate armies up to that time. He pointed out on the map two streams which empty into the Potomac, and suggested that the army might be moved on boats and landed between the mouths of these streams. We would then have the Potomac to bring our supplies, and the tributaries would protect our flanks while we moved out. I listened respectfully, but did not suggest that the same streams would protect Lee's flanks while he was shutting us up.

"I did not communicate my plans to the President, nor did I to the Secretary of War or to General Halleck."

After four days in Washington Grant told Lincoln he would go West, be gone about nine days, then return and direct operations from Eastern headquarters. Of his four-day stay in Washington he said to Lincoln, "This has been rather the warmest campaign I have witnessed during the war." Lincoln told Grant, however, that Mrs. Lincoln shared in the universal gratitude and admiration for him and was inviting him to a party at the White House that evening, a dinner gathering arranged especially for Grant.

GRANT. Mrs. Lincoln must excuse me. I must be in Tennessee at a given time.

LINCOLN. But we can't excuse you. Mrs. Lincoln's dinner without you would be *Hamlet* with Hamlet left out.

GRANT. I appreciate the honor Mrs. Lincoln would do me but time is very important now—and really—Mr. Lincoln—I have had enough of this show business.

And that evening Grant started West. He had been formally put in command, Halleck relieved. He had changed his mind about staying West. "When I got to Washington and saw the situation it was plain that here [East] was the point for the commanding general to be." No one else could resist for him the pressure to change plans, to follow other plans than his own. And even before starting West, he saw that orders were issued giving Sherman command of all Western armies, McPherson to take Sherman's department, John A. Logan being given McPherson's corps. He rode to Nashville, talked with Sherman on a campaign plan, huge but simple, as Sherman put it: Grant "was to go for Lee and I was to go for Joe Johnston." That was all. The two of them believed they would start a never-ending hammering, a pressure of irresistible pincers—and close out the war.

Returning to Washington, Grant found himself hailed as the most popular man in the United States. "He hardly slept on his long journey east," said the *New York Tribune*, "yet he went to work at once. Senators state with joy that he is not going to hire a house in Washington, and make war ridiculous by attempting to maneuvre battles from an arm-chair." Senator Sherman wrote to his brother: "General Grant is all the rage . . . subjected to the disgusting but dangerous process of being lionized. He is followed by crowds, and is cheered everywhere. While he must despise the fickle fools who run after him, he, like most others, may be spoiled by this excess of flattery." General Sherman replied: "Let him alone. Don't disgust him by flattery or importunity. Let him alone." The *New York Herald* said one day, "We have found our hero," and on another: "The arrival of the unpretending victor of Fort Donelson, Vicksburg and Chattanooga reminded Mr. Lincoln of nothing he ever saw before, and he has quite lost his senses in consequence. The people at the War Department never had any to lose, while we all know that there never was method in the madness of Chase. Secretary Welles would be crazy had he awakened from his long nap; but he still sleeps."

James R. Gilmore, calling on Lincoln in latter March, believed he saw a load of care lifted off the President by the mere prospect of Grant's taking control of army operations, and mentioned that the President was looking better. The reply: "Oh, yes! I feel better, for now I'm like the man who was blown up on a steamboat and said, on coming down, 'It makes no difference to me,—I'm only a passenger.' " Gilmore had arrived on General Garfield's writing to him, "The President says, 'Let Gilmore show me the light of his countenance as early as convenient.' " They talked over Gilmore's proposed journey to North Carolina to see if he could negotiate with Governor Vance for that State to return to the Union. The plan, according to Gilmore, was for Burnside with 20,000 troops to join a naval force and take Wilmington. It turned out, however, that Grant said he would need the troops against Lee. Gilmore, hearing this, ventured to ask Lincoln if he were not putting too much military control in Grant's hands. Lincoln: "Do you hire a man to do your work and then do it yourself?"

Grant ordered so many troops away from Washington for service with the Army of the Potomac that Stanton showed anxiety, even nervousness, about the small garrisons that would be left to man the forts around the capital. "I have already sent the men to the front," Grant replied to Stanton's questions. Stanton held this contrary to his plans and said he would order the men back.

GRANT. I shall need the men there and you cannot order them back.

STANTON. Why not? Why not?

GRANT. I believe that I rank the Secretary in this matter.

STANTON. Very well, we will see the President about that. I will have to take you to the President.

GRANT. That is right. The President ranks us both.

STANTON (*in Lincoln's office facing the seated President*). Now, General, state your case.

GRANT. I have no case to state. I am satisfied as it is.

LINCOLN (*after hearing Stanton's argument that Grant was exceeding his authority and putting Washington in danger by stripping the garrisons*). Now, Mr. Secretary, you know we have been trying to manage this army for nearly three years and you know we haven't done much with it. We sent over the mountains and brought Mr. Grant, as Mrs. Grant calls him,

Ulysses Simpson Grant, Lieutenant General of the Armies of the United States, 1864

Photograph from the McLellan Lincoln collection, Brown University

Charles Francis Adams, Sr.

Photograph presented to the author in 1928 by A. W. Hannah of Chicago

Charles Sumner

Photograph in McClees, from the author's collection

to manage it for us; and now I guess we'd better let Mr. Grant have his own way.

And there the matter rested. Thus the incident was told and published, many believing it had a quality of the three men partaking. It was evident to Grant at the start that Stanton in the days to come would be more or less troubled about plenty of troops to defend the national capital. It was evident too that a series of situations would develop in which Lincoln would have to steer a delicate course between his War Minister and the high command.

Grant had brought East with him his mail-service officer, Colonel A. H. Markland, who one day brought Lincoln a note from Postmaster General Blair saying that while mail service had been satisfactory with the army in the West, it was not so in the East. General Grant had prepared requisite orders, wrote Blair, "but they remain unacted on in the War Department." The President read this note handed him by Colonel Markland, asked some questions and then: "If I understand the case, General Grant wants the orders issued, and Blair wants them issued, and you want them issued, and Stanton won't issue them. Now, don't you see what kind of a fix I will be in if I interfere? I'll tell you what to do: If you and General Grant understand one another, suppose you try to get along without the orders, and if Blair or Stanton make a fuss I may be called in as a referee, and I may decide in your favor." Months passed and, according to Markland, the orders were never issued and pleasant relations were maintained all around on that particular score.

Lincoln's own way of telling Grant to call on the Administration for troops, but not too many, took the form of an ancient fable. He mirthfully poured it into Grant's ear for Grant alone to hear. "He said he thought he could illustrate what he wanted to say by a story," wrote Grant—and the story ran: "At one time there was a great war among the animals, and one side had great difficulty in getting a commander who had sufficient confidence in himself. Finally, they found a monkey, by the name of Jocko, who said that he thought he could command their army if his tail could be made a little longer. So they got more tail and spliced it on to his caudal appendage. He looked at it admiringly, and then thought he ought to have a little more still. This was added, and again he called for more. The splicing process was repeated many times, until they had coiled Jocko's tail around the room, filling all the space. Still he called for more tail, and, there being no other place to coil it, they began wrapping it around his shoulders. He continued his call for more, and they kept on winding the additional tail about him until its weight broke him down."

Nearly two years before, Orpheus C. Kerr had published the same story with verbose trimmings satirizing McClellan's repeated calls for reinforcements. Grant saw the point, rose from his chair: "Mr. President, I will not call for more assistance unless I find it impossible to do with what I already have."

A say-nothing policy seemed more natural to Grant than to Rawlins, who told of once going to Grant and suggesting that the press be given a statement it requested as to the objectives of the heaving and hauling maneuvers roundabout Vicksburg before the siege began. Grant: "This life is too brief to be frittered away with explanations."

On the way to Washington Grant and Rawlins had to wait over at Louisville and went to see a play. The audience cheered and yelled for Grant. Something about it worried Rawlins. He wrote his wife that night he was afraid Grant was giving way too easily to the audience, that Grant maybe was beginning to feed on applause. Rawlins further wrote to his wife that Grant had made him Chief of Staff and he was afraid that, lacking military education, he might not fill the place in proper style. A humble and loyal aide Grant had at his side. Grant refused to let Rawlins talk about resigning. He wanted Rawlins along and close by even though Rawlins's education had come by reading law in an office in Galena and not by the West Point route. To his wife Rawlins wrote he was pleased that Grant made short speeches at the ceremonies in Washington, stuck close to business, and did well not to miss a night train for the sake of the White House dinner Mrs. Lincoln arranged for Grant. That Mrs. Lincoln was already beginning to harbor dislike for Grant and Mrs. Grant was not then in the thought of John A. Rawlins.

Short Phil Sheridan in Washington early in April did not look the part he was to play. Grant had appointed him to head the combined cavalry of the Army of the Potomac. Sheridan was only five feet five inches high, less than a hundred and thirty pounds in weight—and a total stranger to Washington and service in the East. So young-looking he was—and only thirty-three years old. Cool and guarded he was, refusing to tell anybody how to win the war. Halleck took him to Stanton and it was a meeting of opposite temperaments and no compliments. Halleck took him to the White House. Lincoln offered Sheridan both his hands, said he hoped Sheridan would fulfill Grant's expectations, and added that the cavalry of the Army of the Potomac had not gone so far as it might have.

As byplay Lincoln asked the current question, "Whoever saw a dead cavalryman?" which Sheridan felt was not quite called for.

At Culpeper Court House with Grant the next day Sheridan again felt at home. A black-haired Irish Catholic boy who went from Perry County, Ohio, to West Point, Sheridan had followed soldiering ever since. He seemed made for the army life, and as a fighter leading men against odds had proved his wild and stubborn ways at Murfreesboro, Chickamauga, and Chattanooga. Grant heard doubts spoken in Washington about Sheridan. They would soon find out whether Sheridan could fight, answered Grant.

Lincoln about this time was asked for an opinion of Sheridan and limited himself to saying: "I will tell you just what kind of a chap he is. He is one of those long-armed fellows with short legs that can scratch his shins without having to stoop over."

In snow and rain of the last week in March, Grant and Rawlins set up headquarters at Culpeper Court House with the Army of the Potomac. Into their hands came daily reports and dispatches from troops on a line that ran 1,200 miles from the Atlantic to the Rio Grande, 21 army corps, 18 departments, with 800,000 men enrolled, 533,000 present and fit for duty. On a day soon to come the armies were to move, Butler up the James River, Grant and Meade across the Rapidan, Sigel up the Shenandoah, Averell in West Virginia, Sherman and Thomas from Chattanooga, and Banks up the Red River toward Texas.

Hitherto armies had acted independently, "like a balky team, no two ever pulling together," said Grant, as he explained to Lincoln that each army was to hammer away and keep on with the hammering against the enemy armies, enemy railroads and supplies, "until by mere attrition, if in no other way, there should be nothing left to him." Grant and Meade in the East, and Sherman and Thomas in the West, were to be a giant nutcracker having the South crushed when they should finally meet. Thus Grant outlined the grand strategy to Lincoln.

"The President has been powerfully reminded," wrote Hay in his diary, "by General Grant's present movements and plans, of his (President's) old suggestion so constantly made and as constantly neglected, to Buell & Hooker, et al., to move at once upon the enemy's whole line so as to bring into action . . . our great superiority of numbers. Otherwise by interior lines & control of the interior railroad system the enemy can shift their men rapidly from one point to another as they may be required. In this concerted movement, however, great superiority of numbers must tell; as the enemy, however successful where he concentrates, must necessarily weaken other portions of his line and lose important positions. This idea of his own, the Prest recognized with especial pleasure when Grant said it was his intention to make all the line useful—those not fighting could help the fighting. 'Those not skinning can hold a leg,' added his distinguished interlocutor."

Grant was to hit Lee so hard in Virginia that Lee could send no help to Johnston in Georgia. Sherman was to hit Johnston so heavily in Georgia that Johnston would never shift troops to Lee in Virginia. So they hoped and planned.

Grant's orders to his scattered subcommanders were relayed through Halleck at Washington. Meade as commander of the Army of the Potomac received orders and suggestions from the near-by headquarters of Grant. But the newly arrived corps under Burnside was not under Meade, because Burnside ranked Meade as an older head of the Army of the Potomac; so Burnside was taking his orders from Grant.

The Burnside corps had mobilized at Annapolis, its veterans of Roanoke, the Peninsula, Antietam, Fredericksburg, Chancellorsville, and Knoxville being joined by new recruits that included several Negro regiments. They passed in review before the President standing on the balcony of Willard's Hotel. The black troops cheered, laughed, threw their caps in the air, marching past the signer of the Emancipation Proclamation. A rain blew up and soaked the marchers. Bystanders urged Lincoln to go in out of the rain;

he would be soaked. "If *they* can stand it, I guess I can," he answered as burned and shot-riddled flags swept by on Pennsylvania Avenue.

Burnside called at the White House and talked with Lincoln about the coming campaign, Hay noting, "He gave some interesting reminiscences of the siege of Knoxville (Tad laughing enormously whenever he saw his father's eye twinkle, though not seeing clearly why)." A few days later Hay had "considerable talk" with the President and was told that the date set for the armies to move would probably be changed from May 2 to May 5 on request of Sherman. "The stories of Grant's quarreling with the Secretary of War are gratuitous lies. Grant quarrels with no one." Also that day came to the White House through Granville Moody a story of Andrew Johnson, Governor of Tennessee, wrought up over a report that General Buell was going to surrender Nashville, Johnson crying, "We're *sold*, Moody, we're *sold*," and at last suddenly, "Pray! Moody!" And they knelt and prayed and joined in responses like good Methodists, Johnson saying after it was over, "Moody, I feel better. Moody, I'm not a Christian—no church,—but I believe in God, in the Bible, all of it, Moody, but I'll *be damned if Nashville shall be given up!*" The President was also "much amused" at Hay's quoting the latest from Count Gurowski: "I *de*spise the anti-Lincoln Republicans. I say I go against Lincoln, for he is no fit for be President; di say di is for one term (holding up one dirty finger), bimeby di brat Lincoln, den di for two term (holding up two unclean digits): di is cowards and *Ass!*"

Of the evening of April 30 Hay noted, "The President came loafing in as it grew late and talked about the reception which his Hodges letter had met with." For nearly a month the press, the politicians, and the people had discussed Lincoln's peculiar letter of April 4. It was written to a Kentuckian, A. G. Hodges, who with other Border State men had interviewed Lincoln. Lincoln at Hodges' request put into writing, for the country to read, what he had told them face to face in the White House: "I am naturally antislavery. If slavery is not wrong, nothing is wrong. I can not remember when I did not so think and feel." And he had closed the letter, "If God now wills the removal of a great wrong, and wills that we also of the North, as well as you of the South, shall pay fairly for our complicity in that wrong, impartial history will find therein new cause to attest and revere the justice and goodness of God." It was as though he framed a cause to give impetus to the big drive of the Union armies soon to begin.

Rather gratified was Lincoln that Greeley's *Tribune* took kindly to the Hodges letter. He had hunted out and gave to Hay the letter written by Greeley just after the battle of Bull Run, the *New York Tribune* editor saying he had passed sleepless nights and rather than enter on a long bloody war would give it up and let the South have what it wanted. Though nearly three years had passed, Hay noted of it, "This most remarkable letter still retains for me its wonderful interest as the most insane specimen of pusillanimity that I have ever read." Nicolay said, after Hay had read the letter aloud: "That would be nuts to the *Herald*. Bennett would willingly give

$10,000 for that." Lincoln, tying red tape around the letter and preparing to again put it away: "I need $10,000 very much, but he could not have it for many times that."

That particular evening in the White House was young yet, according to Hay's diary, for a little after midnight the President came into the office laughing, with a volume of Hood's works to show Nicolay and Hay a little caricature, "An Unfortunate Bee-ing," utterly unconscious that he, the President of the United States, "with his short shirt hanging about his long legs & setting out behind like the tail feathers of an enormous ostrich was infinitely funnier than anything in the book he was laughing at." Hay wrote, "What a man he is! Occupied all day with matters of vast moment, deeply anxious about the fate of the greatest army in the world, with his own fame & future hanging on the events of the passing hour, he yet has such a wealth of simple bonhommie and good fellowship that he gets out of bed & perambulates the house in his shirt to find us that we may share with him the fun of one of poor Hood's queer little conceits."

On that same day of April 30 Grant took a six-mile ride to see Meade, talking as he rode with Colonel Horace Porter, a staff man, talking of the blooded Kentucky bay horse Cincinnati he was riding, of how in the start of the war he wanted to command a brigade of cavalry, of commanding officers who wasted time on details they could leave to subordinates, of his favorable impression of Lincoln, of how frankly Lincoln had said he did not want to know Grant's plans because everybody was trying to find out from the President what would be the next movement and there was always a temptation "to leak." One day there had come to the White House a delegation of "cross-roads wiseacres," as Lincoln told it to Grant, and they criticized Grant for paroling Pemberton's army at Vicksburg. They insisted that the Confederate troops would violate their paroles and in less than a month be in the field again. "I thought the best way to get rid of them was to tell them the story of Sykes's dog," said Lincoln. And he asked the spokesman of the delegation, "Have you ever heard about Sykes's yellow dog?" The spokesman had not. "Well, I must tell you about him."

Then Grant as he rode along with Porter told the yellow-dog story as he had it from Lincoln, remarking, however, "No one who does not possess the President's unequalled powers of mimicry can pretend to convey an idea of the amusing manner in which he told the story." As a fable that entertained two eminent American citizens it was a curiosity:

Sykes had a yellow dog he set great store by, but there were a lot of small boys around the village, and that's always a bad thing for dogs, you know. These boys didn't share Sykes's views, and they were not disposed to let the dog have a fair show. Even Sykes had to admit that the dog was getting unpopular; in fact, it was soon seen that a prejudice was growing up against that dog that threatened to wreck all his future prospects in life. The boys, after meditating how they could get the best of him, finally fixed up a cartridge with a long fuse, put the cartridge in a piece of meat, dropped the meat in the road in front of Sykes's door, and then perched themselves on a fence a good distance off, holding the end of the fuse in their hands. Then they whistled for the dog. When he came out he scented the bait, and bolted the meat, cartridge and all. The boys touched off the fuse with a cigar, and in about a second a report came from that dog that sounded like a clap of thunder. Sykes came bouncing out of the house, and yelled, "What's up? Anything busted?" There was no reply, except a snicker from the small boys roosting on the fence; but as Sykes looked up he saw the whole air filled with pieces of yellow dog. He picked up the biggest piece he could find, a portion of the back with a part of the tail still hanging to it, and after turning it round and looking it all over, he said, "Well, I guess he'll never be much account again—as a dog." And I guess Pemberton's forces will never be much account again—as an army. The delegation began looking around for their hats before I had quite got to the end of the story, and I was never bothered any more after that about superseding the commander of the Army of the Tennessee.

In a few days "the greatest army in the world" was to try its luck under Grant. Colonel Theodore Lyman of Meade's staff saw in Grant's face "three expressions: deep thought; extreme determination; and great simplicity and calmness." And further: "He habitually wears an expression as if he had determined to drive his head through a brick wall and was about to do it. I have much confidence in him." Colonel Charles Francis Adams, Jr., wrote to his father at London that he could no longer get any real news at headquarters as to what the army would do next. Grant had brought a new secrecy to the Army of the Potomac operations. Wrote Adams: "The feeling about Grant is peculiar—a little jealousy, a little envy, a little want of confidence—all in many minds . . . ready to crystallize at any moment and only brilliant success will dissipate the elements. All, however, are willing to give him a full chance and his own time for it. If he succeeds, the war is over."

To his father Grant wrote on April 16: "It has rained here almost every day since my arrival. It is still raining. Of course I say nothing of when the army moves or how or where. I am in most excellent health and well pleased with appearances here. My love to all at home."

Lincoln adopted a set form to meet one question and, according to the *Chicago Journal* correspondent, the dialogue always ran:

VISITOR. When will the army move?
LINCOLN. Ask General Grant.
VISITOR. General Grant will not tell me.
LINCOLN. Neither will he tell me.

At a White House reception one evening an important visitor remarked pleasantly, "I suppose, Mr. Lincoln, you expect stirring news over here on the Rapidan in a week or two."

"Possibly," said the President.

"Possibly?!" echoed the guest.

"I don't know much about it," explained the President, "but I heard today that General Grant means to take Richmond from the Charleston side."

Senator Ben Wade came to the Capitol one sunny day and a colleague asked him why he was carrying an umbrella. He said he had heard the Army of the Potomac was in motion and it always began raining twelve hours after that army started to move.

CHAPTER 47

WILL HIS PARTY RENOMINATE LINCOLN?

THE chaplain of the United States Senate, the Reverend Dr. Byron Sunderland, who had been rebuked by various Senators for what he said about them in his prayers for the Senate, was packing his bags to go to Paris, France, as pastor of the American congregation there. Now he could pray as his innermost heart dictated. And one day the first week in April part of his invocation ran: "O Lord, give us that Thou wilt in Thine infinite wisdom vouchsafe to our rulers and legislators in this Congress assembled more brains—more brains, Lord." Many who were listening caught his words, and, wrote Noah Brooks, "dropped their heads to their desks to conceal smiles as an emphatic 'Amen' came from the press gallery."

Early in 1864 the *Janesville Gazette* in Wisconsin was sure that if by military edict President Lincoln should adjourn Congress he would be entitled to the thanks of the country. "They are a set of gaseous, windy blatherskites who do little else but eat, drink, draw their pay, and make buncombe speeches." This exaggeration relieved the country editor's feelings. In the Congress itself, however, were members whose feelings ran with the Janesville editor.

Pendleton of Ohio introduced a House resolution that the President of the United States inform the House why a certain major was ordered to report at Fort Vancouver, Randall of Kentucky following with a resolution that the Secretary of War report on claims for the destruction of salt works at Goose Creek, Kentucky. Thereupon Thad Stevens moved that the House adjourn. "Everybody is offering Buncombe resolutions and I think we had better adjourn." But the House voted refusal to adjourn and a little later Green Clay Smith of Kentucky put in a resolution that the Government should "crush and forever destroy" the wicked rebellion, "thereby establishing perfect and unalterable liberty." Augustus Brandegee of Connecticut rose to confess he was "sick of this miserable political claptrap."

Another day Henry W. Harrington of Indiana brought in a resolution to declare Congress had no power to delegate to the President authority to suspend the writ of habeas corpus. The Speaker ruled debate was not in order, and Owen Lovejoy inquired, "Would it be in order to refer these resolutions to the Committee on Buncombe when it shall be appointed?"

Another day Stevens railed, "Debate is exhausted on the amendment, and everybody here is exhausted with the debate." Later again that day Stevens's dry voice was heard: "I am opposed to the amendment. I do not know what the amendment is but I am opposed to it."

The *New York World* agreed with someone saying that "whoever cracked Thaddeus Stevens' skull would let out the brains of the Republican party." He could talk pointedly and waste no time. He rebuked a colleague's insinuating language in a resolution; it was unfair procedure with "a stump speech in the belly of the resolution." The *Detroit Free Press* held Stevens "an abusive and vulgar blackguard" and quoted his priceless rejoinder to one Congressman: "The gentleman who has just spoken need not fear that I will make any insinuations or sneer or thrust at him. There are some reptiles so flat that the common foot of man cannot crush them."

In a whisky-tax discussion Kelley of Pennsylvania declared excessive use of liquor to be "denounced by divine authority." Grinnell of Iowa held it to be a "dreadful poison damaging many of our soldiers and officers." Stevens said: "It seems there is never to be an end of this matter in this House. Men who are on the temperance side of the question have become as much intoxicated on this question of liquor as if they had been drinking whiskey for a month."

The House had characters diverse as the suave and metropolitan James Brooks, fresh from the office of his pro-Confederate newspaper, the *New York Express*, and the rather plodding rural pioneer Josiah B. Grinnell, founder of the town and college of Grinnell, Iowa. Grinnell had entertained and fraternized in his home with John Brown. Grinnell never forgot that one plank of the Republican platform at Chicago called for a railroad to the Pacific Ocean. Also never forgetful of that plank was Representative John A. Kasson of Des Moines, Iowa, attorney for the Mississippi and Missouri Railroad. Kasson had written the plank, and at a midnight conference joined with other railroad projectors in the decision to throw all votes of the Iowa delegation the next day for Lincoln as their man. Ignatius Donnelly sat in the House representing a Minnesota district and beginning to brood over evidence that Bacon and not Shakespeare wrote the dramas credited to Shakespeare; he would write a thick book on the subject. Ebon C. Ingersoll was there from Peoria, Illinois, brother of a Union cavalry colonel and freethinker, Robert Green Ingersoll. In the Senate was much the same variety of American citizenship, each of them before he voted always considering what the businessmen and solid citizens of his constituency might want. The *Cincinnati Commercial* correspondent at Washington classified Senators:

The best lawyer—Mr. Collamer, of Vermont. The best scholar—Mr. Sumner, of Massachusetts. The best general debater and practical legislator—Mr. Fessenden, of Maine. The "keenest" debater—Mr. Trumbull, of Illinois. The most pleasant speaker to listen to—Mr. Doolittle, of Wisconsin. The best financier—Mr. Sherman of Ohio. The richest man—Mr. Sprague, of Rhode Island. A very sensible old man—Mr. Wade of Ohio. The greatest bore that ever lived—Mr. Davis, of Kentucky. The Knight of the Sorrowful Nigger—Mr. Lane of Kansas. The most violent Copperhead—Mr. Powell, of Kentucky. The most eloquent Copperhead—Mr. Carlile, of Virginia. The most bibulous man in Congress—Mr. Richardson of Illinois. The best looking man when sober—Mr. Saulsbury, of Delaware. The man who has least to say—Mr. Hendricks, of Indiana. The man who comes nearest to being nobody—Mr. Riddle of Delaware.

The little Kentucky Senator rated as "the greatest bore that ever lived" newspapermen alluded to as "Garrulous Garrett Davis." One serious scheme of his would divide the Northern States to make Massachusetts and New Hampshire one State, Vermont, Connecticut, and Rhode Island another, and Maine left to take care of itself. Garrett Davis raised a burst of laughter from the Senate galleries with his proposal to so amend the Constitution that no person whose mother or grandmother had been a Negro should be a citizen of the United States. He could rage with fury, or chuckle with mirth, but most often was dull, platitudinous, tiresome, emptying the galleries first and then the seats of his colleagues till there wasn't a quorum.

Garrett Davis began the year 1864 with a series of resolutions aimed to blast and destroy the amnesty proclamation of President Lincoln. "Verily, the people North and the people South ought to revolt against their war-leaders, and take this great matter into their own hands, and elect members to a national convention of all States to terminate a war that is enriching its hundreds of thousands . . . and threatens . . . indefinite slaughter," gushed Davis. Then without elaborating a plan he argued for the ejection of Lincoln and his Administration from power. Officers, plunderers, spoilsmen, contractors, were building a vast military bureaucracy to be maintained by hordes of "negro janizaries."

In a cadenced style that made a lullaby for his own ears Garrett Davis proceeded: "Under the magic power which I believe the President deduces from military necessity, he is authorized to issue his imperial edict to override the Constitution of the United States, to nullify the decisions of the Supreme Court, and by his word, by his mighty fiat, in the remote absence as well as in the immediate presence of armies, to knock the fetters from the slaves and proclaim them to be free. Sir, if the President of the United States has that imperial power, he is the greatest of living autocrats; the greatest of all autocrats that have ever lived. The Czar of all the Russias and the leaden despot of Austria have tame and impotent powers when contrasted with this imperial emperor of this western world."

Garrett Davis believed he had the gift of tongues and went on talking whether Senators were listening or not. "Weak men have arisen to enforce this inequality on the white race, and measure strength with the Omnipotent upon this great question of races, but their utter discomfiture will prove to them how powerless is puny man when he would interfere with the providence of the Eternal." Suddenly Garrett Davis emerged from his thicket of adjectives with a morsel of gossip. "A distinguished man in the West, who was at one time a member of the other House of Congress, told me that a major-general in the service of the United States now in command, told him that if Mr. Lincoln was defeated at the next presidential election, he would not yield his seat of power to his successor, but would hold on to it, and this he could only do by the Army."

From there Senator Davis went on as though the gossip were true and needed merely to be repeated to be still more true. On and on he went in various speeches against usurpation by the President, talking mostly to empty seats and filling pages of fine print in the *Congressional Globe* for anti-Lincoln newspapers to editorialize on. Editors of such newspapers welcomed Davis's statement from the Senate floor that Lincoln was "a man of weak mind and inordinate vanity, who thought himself a great man and a statesman, as he played his fantastic tricks before high Heaven."

On January 8, 1864, Senator Wilson moved to expel Garrett Davis from the Senate for advising the people of the United States to treasonable and insurrectionary action against the Government. In Davis's declaration that "the people North ought to revolt against their war leaders and take this great matter into their own hands," Wilson urged, the Kentucky Senator had meant "to incite the people of the United States to revolt against the President of the United States and those in authority who support him."

Packed galleries a few days later heard Wilson deliver a speech of prosecution. Davis rose to reply, took off his neckwear, unbuttoned his vest, and began talking and talked till the galleries were empty, till most of the Senators were gone. And then he was not through. For his justification required that he should read extended sections of the Fugitive Slave Act and other statutes and documents. From then on the Senate heard still more from Davis. As weeks and months passed twenty Senators made speeches on whether Davis was an adviser of treason, and the matter dragged along till the press, the public, and the Senate itself lost interest in his case and the *Congressional Globe* failed to index any Yeas and Nays on his expulsion.

Alexander Long of Ohio told the House plainly that he favored acknowledging the independence of the Southern States. Garfield compared Long to Benedict Arnold. Speaker Colfax left his seat for the floor, to move expulsion of Long from the House. Another Peace Democrat, Benjamin G. Harris of Maryland, took the floor to endorse what Long had said and to add that he believed in a peace which could be had only by recognition of the Southern Confederacy. A roar came from the Union members. Harris yelled back, "You've got to come to it," and went on to say he had been a slaveowner before the abolitionists stole all his slaves away from him and added insult to injury. "The South asked you to let her go in peace," he cried. "But no, you say you will bring them into subjugation. That is not done yet, and God Almighty grant that it never may be. I hope that you will never subjugate the South."

Then amid yells of twenty members on their feet calling for the floor, the Speaker finally listened to Washburne's demand that the language of Harris be read from the clerk's desk. The members gradually settled down into their seats. Quiet arrived. The clerk read off the words and Harris somewhat dapperly approved. "That is all right. I endorse every word of that."

Washburne then moved to expel Harris with Long. That would make two expulsions up for the day. Fernando Wood slid in with a little speech that he endorsed what Long had said and the House might as well throw him out with Long. Washburne turned pale, shook a fist at Wood, and shouted, "We'll put you out too."

Weeks of argument came, ending in a vote of 81 to 58 for expulsion, and lacking two-thirds, it was lost. Then by a vote of 93 to 18 Long was "severely censured"—and attempts at expulsion went no farther during the session.

These members who dared their Union colleagues to throw them out were politicians first of all. Their carefully framed speeches timed with an eye on the presidential campaign in the coming autumn. They were trying to project issues and hold their party lines intact. Leaders of their party, such as Governor Seymour of New York and Congressman Fernando Wood, counseled repeatedly that in order not to have their party melt away by fusion with Republicans into a Union party, they must maintain a clear-cut opposition to the President and the Administration. Naturally, however, there was more than political maneuvering in Harris of Maryland asking the House to throw him out; his heart lay with the Richmond cause not merely as a slaveowner but in the deeper bonds that approved of the Southern way of life as against the Yankee. And Fernando Wood's political moves were not merely surface expedients; since the day when as Mayor of New York City he had urged its secession from the Union, his record was almost undeviatingly a help to the Richmond Government.

Voorhees of Indiana resented it at the National Hotel one day when Senator Zach Chandler called him a Copperhead. He sent his right fist into Chandler's face. And according to *Leslie's Weekly*, "the fight then became more general, and a friend of Voorhees' broke a pitcher over Mr. Chandler's head."

Issues cut deeper. The cry for blood came oftener. Again in latter January Stevens pointed to the Confederacy as a recognized belligerent, a distinct and hostile foreign nation. Stevens told what must be done. When the South was conquered, Congress would readjust affairs; protect the innocent and pardon the least guilty; punish the leading traitors, seize their lands and estates, sell them in fee simple, put the money into the United States Treasury to pay the cost of the war and to pension widows, orphans, crippled soldiers; and end slavery, the cause of the war. Thad Stevens coupled these proposals with a compliment to President Lincoln as helping along. "The President may not strike as direct a blow with a battering ram against this Babel as some impetuous gentlemen would desire; but with his usual shrewdness and caution he is picking out the mortar from the joints until eventually the whole tower will fall."

From day to day Stevens operated with the patience of a veteran sharpshooter. His program called for extermination of the ruling class of the South and the advancement of the Negro to citizenship and wider control, if not complete power. In the South Stevens's speeches were often quoted—

and misquoted—by editors and orators. His name was coming to stand for vengeance, obliteration, ashes and death.

As the melancholy and ruthless Republican floor leader kept pushing his program of no mercy, press editorials and street talk of citizens over the country mentioned more often the day when Jefferson Davis and the leaders of secession would be hanged or shot. Wholesale executions of "rebels" were forecast to take place when the South was subjugated. Congressman Godlove S. Orth of Indiana spoke in January of how the oldest lawbooks of all civilizations decreed "The traitor must die." Godlove S. Orth quoted from Blackstone the Anglo-Saxon ritual in punishing treason: (1) that the offender shall be drawn to the gallows and not be carried or walk; (2) that he be hanged by the neck and then cut down alive; (3) that his entrails be taken out and burned while he is yet alive; (4) that his head be cut off; (5) that his body be divided into four parts; (6) that his head and quarters be at the King's disposal. For the leaders of the Confederacy any of these procedures would be satisfactory to Godlove S. Orth. He made it clear. Andrew J. Rogers of New Jersey wished to add that it was also in the old lawbooks that a traitor "could not inherit lands nor transmit them to his posterity."

The Southern people had a right to make a revolution, so the organization Democrats argued from Lincoln's 1848 speech in Congress. They quoted Lincoln—and correctly:

Any people anywhere being inclined and having the power have the right to rise up and shake off the existing government, and form a new one that suits them better. This is a most valuable, a most sacred right—a right which we hope and believe is to liberate the world. Nor is this right confined to cases in which the whole people of an existing government may choose to exercise it. Any portion of such people that can may revolutionize and make their own of so much of the territory as they inhabit. More than this, a majority of any portion of such people may revolutionize, putting down a minority, intermingled with or near about them, who may oppose this movement. Such a minority was precisely the case of the Tories of our own revolution. It is a quality of revolutions not to go by old ideas or old laws; but to break up both, and make new ones.

A fragment from the inaugural address in 1861 was brought up so often in House and Senate that many members could repeat it as part of a credo. This read: "Suppose you go to war, you cannot fight always; and when, after much loss on both sides, and no gain on either, you cease fighting, the identical old questions as to terms of intercourse are again upon you." Thad Stevens grew tired of hearing this quoted by Confederate spokesmen in the United States Congress. Stevens offered his own logic that the ruling class of the South held its cause so holy that it would never surrender any points on "the old identical questions"; therefore all members of that ruling class should be killed off. General Sherman from a military viewpoint had set forth his long memorandum to Lincoln and Halleck holding that the war must go on until enough of the Southern owners, the planter aristocrats of the South, were dead. A policy of ruthlessness in military operations in the field and in the shaping of measures in Congress was becoming articulate.

The tone of Congress had an assurance through most of its transactions, as though the United States would stand for a long time, as though no matter what became of the Southern States, there would be in the North a growing World Power, gigantic in commerce and industry, far-flung in its areas from coast to coast. In the South was a deepening courage of despair over the terrorizing possibility that the Confederacy might die, the old South vanish, with its ruling class sunk. Two hopes still held in the South, one the glimmering that by some twist of events would come recognition, money, ships, from Europe, another that the peace party at the North might so weaken the Lincoln Administration that in time it would give up the war as hopeless.

To combat those Southern hopes and wear them down was Lincoln's set task. As part of that task he could never afford to lose close contact with Congress nor let any serious cleavage arise. A worse deliberative body might have been wished on him. He sought the brains and ability there. Reasonable advice, discussion, and inquiry, and no tone of faultfinding, stood forth in his papers in the *Congressional Globe* pages so often sprinkled with the item, "A message in writing was received from the President of the United States, by Mr. Nicolay, his Private Secretary." He would communicate a report "in obedience to the resolution of the Senate." He would "earnestly recommend" that a law be modified. He would "invite the early attention of Congress" to a subject. Or he would lay before Congress a letter from an important committee representing four large Northern cities not clear on what should be done for their increasing population of free Negroes. "Not having the time to form a mature judgment of my own as to whether the plan they suggest is the best, I submit the whole subject to Congress, deeming that their attention thereto is almost imperatively demanded."

The old Douglas Democrat from Illinois, William A. Richardson, picked up contradictions in what Lincoln did when President in 1864 as against what Congressman Lincoln in 1848 said of President James K. Polk. Lincoln then said that Polk in trying to argue Congress out of one position argued himself into it—and that Polk was "like a man on a hot shovel finding no place on which he could sit down." To Richardson, Lincoln now was the man on the hot shovel.

Early in the year several newspapers agreed with the *Detroit Free Press* correspondent at Washington, who wrote, "Not a single Senator can be named as favorable to Lincoln's renomination for President." Any Senator who might want Lincoln for a second term was not making himself heard. On this the Republican-party organs were mainly silent.

In the House only one Congressman was definitely committed to Lincoln. A Pennsylvania editor visiting Washington said to Thaddeus Stevens, "Introduce me to some member of Congress friendly to Mr. Lincoln's renomination." "Come with me," said Stevens. He took the editor to the desk of Isaac N. Arnold of Chicago and said to Arnold: "Here is a man who wants to find a Lincoln member of Congress. You are the only one I know, and I have come over to introduce my friend to you." "Thank you," said Arnold. "I know a good many such and I will present your friend to them, and I wish you, Mr. Stevens, were with us." Thus the very scrupulous Arnold recorded the incident. The other friends of Lincoln in Congress to whom Arnold referred were not named by him, nor did their wish to continue Lincoln as President show in their speeches.

Mixed motives of Stevens and some of his associates could be gathered from a letter he wrote this year to an intimate, J. B. McPherson, saying in the course of his grumbling: "How little of the rights of war and the law of nations our Pres't knows! But what are we to do? Condemn privately and applaud publicly!"

The only remarks favoring Lincoln's renomination for President delivered in either Senate or House came from Arnold in the first week of the year and in March. In the former he quoted from Lincoln's House Divided speech of 1858, held it prophetic, bold, honest, characteristic of "the man, who, then obscure, has become already to-day, the foremost character in American history." Arnold recited the measures under which chattel slavery was crumbling, paid homage "to that great man who has given to the institution of slavery the hardest blows it has ever received," and counseled, "Let Abraham Lincoln finish the great work he has begun." More than a faint implication stood out, for those listening, that Arnold had talked with Lincoln and was stressing what Lincoln regarded as essentials in saying: "The great objects of his life are to crush the rebellion and eradicate slavery. His ambition is to live on the pages of history as the restorer of the Union, the emancipator of his country. For these great ends he has labored and toiled through difficulties and obstacles known only to himself and God. . . . The great fault of his administration, the too tardy removal of incompetent men, has arisen from a too scrupulous care to be just."

Meek-spoken and mild was Arnold in his deep enthusiasm and loyalty. "He has borne censure and denunciation for acts for which others were responsible, with a generosity which has extorted from his rivals the declaration, 'Of all men, Mr. Lincoln is the most unselfish.' I ask the ardent and impatient friends of freedom to put implicit faith in Abraham Lincoln. If you deem him slow, or if you think he has made mistakes, remember how often time has vindicated his wisdom." Lincoln was a radical, urged Arnold, but not one of those loud, boisterous, intolerant, cruel men who to eradicate one evil would tear up good it had taken ages to secure.

"The masses of the people everywhere trust and love him. They know his hands are clean and his breast is pure. The people know that the devil has no bribe big enough, no temptation of gold, or place, or power, which can seduce the honest heart of Abraham Lincoln. They know that while he is President there is no danger of a *coup d'état* . . . that their liberties and laws are safe in his hands. They sleep soundly, with no disturbing apprehensions, while he holds the reins. . . . You have a Chief Magistrate . . . sagacious, firm, upright, and true. Somewhat rude and rough, it may be, but under this rough exterior you have the real and true hero. If he is a diamond in the rough, he is nevertheless real, with no false glitter or garish pretension. You have in him a man of that sobriety, of that self-command, of that freedom from passion, of that justice and truth, of that rectitude of intention, that has had, in all these attributes, no parallel since the days of Washington. Taking the last five years, and Mr. Lincoln has exerted a greater influence upon the popular heart and in forming public opinion than any other man."

Thus Isaac N. Arnold, forty-nine years old, once a country school-teacher in New York State, city clerk of Chicago in 1837, practicing attorney of Cook County, put into the *Congressional Globe* an estimate of Lincoln as a hero. Not then nor in many months after did any member of the House or Senate stand up and deliver any similar estimate. To that particular Congress Lincoln was no hero. And to many of its members he was rather a slow, bungling, conniving politician guilty of inexcusable shifts. Of course, when the President's party policies were attacked or his personal integrity questioned, party defenders arose. But the party defense was of a negative tone and held usually to an implied view that the President was an honest, plodding mediocrity.

A small minority loyal to the President, distinctly not hostile, had they seen it as vitally important to argue his merits to their colleagues, might have done so. Such was Washburne, who in November of '63 wrote to Lincoln for two executive favors and asking whether the party could count on the President to run for a second term. Lincoln replied that he was enclosing a leave of absence for one of Washburne's brothers from army duty, that to another brother of Washburne he was tendering the customs collectorship of Portland, Maine, giving Washburne all that was asked for. To this Lincoln added thanks for kind words and intentions, and "A second term would be a great honor and a great labor, which, together, perhaps I would not decline if tendered."

Of Owen Lovejoy in early '64 it should be noted that he was a sick man for months, that when he died Lincoln spoke to Frank B. Carpenter the few and only words: "Lovejoy was the best friend I had in Congress." Lincoln had had one note from the sick-abed Lovejoy saying: "I am gaining very slowly. It is hard work drawing the sled uphill." And Lincoln had repeatedly visited Lovejoy's bedside, once telling the veteran abolitionist: "This war is eating my life out. I have a strong impression that I shall not live to see the end."

Several Copperhead editors made peculiar comment when Lovejoy died. They saluted him as a true man holding mistaken ideas. Underlying these salutations it could be seen that these Copperhead editors divided antislavery men into genuine heroes and counterfeit, true crusaders and the bogus, preachers with rare love for all mankind and others in the name of Christ ready for Old Testament vengeance, an eye for an eye and a tooth for a tooth—meaning the type of the Reverend George Barrell Cheever of the

Church of the Puritans in New York City, whose pulpit voice cried for a whirlwind fire to ravage the South.

"The opposition to Mr. Lincoln," wrote the Indiana Republican Congressman George W. Julian . . . "was secretly cherished by many of the ablest and most patriotic men of the day. . . . Of the more earnest and thorough-going Republicans in both Houses of Congress, probably not one in ten really favored it [his renomination]." No writer of the day laid open clearly the springs and motives of this opposition, or the exact extent of it. Of course, Lincoln had gone too far—or not far enough—in his acts and policies; he was the Man Between. Yet this would not explain why Congress was sore, suspicious, jealous, almost completely silent about his hold on the people. For nearly all political forecasters in early '64 saw the deep popular current over the country with the President. The *New York Herald*, the *New York World*, the *Detroit Free Press*, proclaimed it as an unpleasant fact, while the *New York Times* and other newspapers agreed with the *Chicago Tribune:* "So far as can be gathered, the public generally mean to elect Mr. Lincoln, when the time comes for an election. . . . God meant him for President, or the nation is deceived." Count Adam Gurowski, with no goodwill for Lincoln, out of daily contacts with weathervanes of politics in Washington wrote in early '64 many diary entries:

Jan. 3—The radicals, the purest men in Congress, begin to cave in, and to be reconciled to the idea of accepting the re-election of Lincoln as an inevitable necessity. They say that the outward pressure is very great. The masses are taken in by Lincoln's *apparent* simplicity and good-naturedness, by his awkwardness, by his vulgar jokes, and, in the people's belief, the great shifter is earnest and honest. The stern and clearsighted radicals expect to be able to bind Lincoln by pledges to change his Cabinet and his *entourage.*

Jan. 12—Every day I more positively find that Mr. Lincoln is not the choice of a majority in both the Houses. The best men in both the Houses observe Lincoln and his workings. They know his length, his breadth, his mind, his nerve, and his cerebellum. The people at large does not know Mr. Lincoln, but judge him by his nickname, and by what greedy politicians and newspapers write and spread about him. The people is generous and credits to Lincoln what is the result of its own, that is, of the people's sacrifices and devotedness. The same erroneous notion about Lincoln is generally current in Europe.

Feb. 4—Everybody says that the country at large is decidedly for Mr. Lincoln. And I have not yet met one single earnest and clear-sighted man, from whatever State he may come, that avows his preference for Lincoln. How strange!

Feb. 12—It is terrible to think that only a great disaster will cure the people at large from this *Lincoln* infatuation.

Feb. 13—George Thompson, old, good natured [antislavery] Englishman, says Washington founded American independence and Lincoln is the founder of American liberty. . . . Washington believed in final success when the masses desponded and despaired; but Lincoln was, and is, always behind the onward march of the people, and is rather dragged by the people than beckoning it to follow him.

Feb. 26—The good men in both Houses painfully feel now how wrong it was not to have long ago told the people the truth about Lincoln's administration; not to have publicly, officially, warned the President, and with decision attempted to put the administration on the right track. Now it is too late to disabuse the people.

Mar. 5—Many genuine, radical, rational Democrats, Democrats not by party name and discipline . . . assert that Lincoln's re-election will demonstrate the utter failure of self-government. It is not at all so. The immense majority of the people is infatuated with Lincoln because the mass sincerely believes him to be able and true. The masses err, or may err—*errari humanum est;* but no mean, selfish aims and purposes direct and inspire the masses. The people is led astray by those whom it is accustomed to consider as beacons and leaders. The alternative laid before the people is: either Lincoln, *one of themselves,* credited by the people with certain capacities and virtues which he in reality has not, or some Democrat who is a worshipper of slavery. In such a dilemma the people sides with Lincoln.

April 4—The re-election! The re-election overawes and submerges everything, even sound common sense. This people, so quick, so wide-awake in almost every other respect, is easily bamboozled, humbugged, thrown off the track by the lowest stratum in its political life. The people, that is, each district, sends to Congress a man in whose brains and integrity it seemingly has confidence, and nevertheless, in such a grave, mighty question as a Presidential election the people—carried away by all kinds of influences—pays no attention to the opinion of its Congressmen, of whom it is to be supposed, that as they had had so much to do with Lincoln, they are better acquainted with his good and bad qualities, his capacities and incapacities, his peculiarities, his character and the want of it, as can be the politicians, newspaper editors and reviewers, living at a distance, and who only occasionally, and, so to say, on state occasions, come in contact with him. And with all this, the people is for re-election, and the majority in Congress is against it.

April 9—Some of the press—this time not the *Tribune*—not the *Cincinnati Gazette*—worship Lincoln as if the country, the people owed everything to him. The press is mute, as it is always, about Congress. But the two Congresses, the 37th and 38th, have saved the cause. They and not Mr. Lincoln did all the good that was done.

April 23—*The strength of nicknames.* The people is taken in by the nickname, honest Abe.

So from week to week during the first four months of '64 Gurowski kept sounding the same theme. The President had somehow reached the people and won a faith or confidence that baffled the Republican-party leaders in Congress. They would like to break the hold the President had on the people. And so far none of them had been able to think up a way to do this without perhaps losing the war and much else.

So sure was the hold of the President on the people that in February Gurowski heard "everybody says that the country at large is decidedly for Mr. Lincoln." Not yet, however, had Gurowski, who circulated daily in departments, lobbies, clubs, found "one single, earnest and clear-sighted man, from whatever State he may come, that avows his preference for Lincoln." What Gurowski's familiars were saying privately, but not publicly, was in his February entry: "It is terrible to think that only a great disaster will cure the people at large from this Lincoln infatuation." It shocked Gurowski that an English antislavery radical, George Thompson, should be traveling trustfully hand in hand with Lincoln. It was further baffling that

Lincoln, not on issues but on personality, had won the affections of the masses. "The people is taken in by the nickname, honest Abe."

This ran into the point that Lincoln's own party men in Congress, most of them, could not quite hate him; he was neither so evil nor so treacherous that they could come out in the open and fight him. They saw him as slow and hesitant, but they could not prove him incompetent; they too had endorsed McClellan; they too had shaped the dominant issues. Nor could they deny that he had certain curious talents and at times unforeseen patience and strength. The charges formulated against the President, by the little clique that once planned to impeach him, ran off into vague generalities, "poured like molasses in January."

The privilege of being suspicious, however, this the radicals indulged. They were not sure of him—they would hold off and put someone else in the White House. This was why their talk ran like Gurowski's diary entries. *Harper's Weekly* of March 5 valued that diary as "only an extravagant expression of opinions frequently expressed in many circles."

Honest and righteous, doers of good and unabashed proclaimers of their own deeds, certain influential radicals saw nothing directly wrong in Lincoln's off-color stories and careless manners. They wished, however, in dead earnest for more dignity in a Chief Magistrate. Their own quality of mirth, if any, ran otherwise than Lincoln's. A friend of Governor John Andrew of Massachusetts noted that Lincoln's offhand behavior at times had so lowered opinion of the President that it was a factor in the personal secrecy that enveloped the choice of a President in '64. This secrecy, also noted Governor Andrew's friend, "is something marvelous; there were so many concerned in it; when it *all* comes out, it will make a curious page in the history of the time." Then Governor Andrew's friend gave a Lincoln story, told how it did not set well in Massachusetts, pointed up the story as showing that others than Massachusetts men were affected politically by the President's manners. He wrote:

It is only just to say, that the reports from Washington in 1863 did impute a frivolity of language and demeanor in the President, which could not but offend many earnest men, and were artfully used by eminent persons in Washington to create dissatisfaction. There was a characteristic anecdote related, which had no especial tendency to render the President popular at the State House in Boston. The legislature has been famous for passing resolutions against slavery. After the war began, the patriotic spirit of members soon showed itself in the same tendency. But there were some who thought the time for this sort of thing had passed, and everything offered was referred to a committee who brought in a resolve in the fewest words possible.

A friend of the Governor, who also held an official position, desired to present it personally to the President. It was accordingly written on parchment, with the great seal annexed, and plenty of red tape. Arrived in Washington, the messenger by appointment met the President at eleven o'clock the next day, to present this resolve of the Commonwealth of Massachusetts.

The Chief Magistrate of the nation sat in an armchair, with one leg over the elbow, while the emissary of Massachusetts presented the parchment with a little speech.

The President took the document, slowly unrolled it, and remarked in a quaint way, "Well, it isn't long enough to scare a fellow!"

It is not remarkable that the Massachusetts official said as he left the room, "That is certainly an extraordinary person to be President of the United States!"

Thus one incident having a definite effect in drawing John Albion Andrew toward the anti-Lincoln movement. It was ominous. For John Andrew rated as no mere ordinary politician riding the antislavery bandwagon. He was not Governor of Massachusetts for his health nor for money nor favors nor prestige. He had raised troops and funds with a loyalty hardly equaled by any other State governor. When asked about having more of money reward for his work, Andrew said money should not be mentioned, that during blood-red years he had stood "at the horns of the altar" and poured out the young men of his State for sacrifice, and since they had given their lives, why should money be mentioned?

John Andrew was spoken of by friends as a hope for the Presidency because of clean, rugged manhood he carried. Located in the antislavery crusade's center, where the Constitution of the United States had been burned in formal rites and pronounced a covenant with hell, surrounded by good men impatient with the President's slowness on that issue, Governor Andrew was looking elsewhere than to Lincoln for a Chief Magistrate. His outlook was somewhat indicated in his writing just after the President issued the Emancipation Proclamation, "It is a poor document, but a mighty act, slow, somewhat halting, wrong in its delay until January, but grand and sublime after all." Andrew had changed in feeling since the day in 1860 when after visiting Lincoln at Springfield, Illinois, he said, "My eyes were never visited with the vision of a human face in which more transparent honesty and more benignant kindness were combined with more of the intellect and firmness which belong to masculine humanity."

Since then John Andrew had been the first governor to put troops into Washington when Lincoln was groaning, "Why don't they come?" The Bay State boys of Andrew had been the first to drop in a Slave State as war sacrifices. He sat on Beacon Hill now, a square-built, deep-chested man, curly hair topping his round head, a face smooth with kindliness, a face almost boyishly cherubic, his eyes peering from behind spectacles, wanting results, results, out of his loyal toiling. He wanted decisions quicker than Lincoln could give them.

There was a twilight zone of fog shadings where skilled and veteran political leaders of the fiber of Lyman Trumbull put out groping hands. The keen and wary Trumbull was not sure but an undertow lurked in the offing that might sweep Lincoln from power. In early February he wrote to H. G. McPike of Alton, Illinois: "The feeling for Mr. Lincoln's re-election *seems* to be very general, but much of it I discover is only on the surface. You would be surprised, in talking with public men we meet here, to find how few, when you come to get at their real sentiment, are for Mr. Lincoln's reëlection. There is a distrust and fear that he is too undecided and inefficient to put down the rebellion. You need not be surprised if a reaction sets in before the nomination, in favor of some man supposed to possess more energy and less inclination to trust our brave boys in the hands and under the leadership of generals who have no heart in the war. The opposition to Mr. L. may not show itself at all, but if it ever breaks out there will be more of it than now appears."

But a few days before these surmises of Trumbull, the wealthy Boston merchant George Luther Stearns, active in Negro troop recruiting, wrote from Washington to his wife that the political complications in the national capital were "most subtle" and unless you knew the past of a man you couldn't tell his motives. "No one knows where he is or who, or what statement to depend on. President, Cabinet, M.C.s, Senators, all are alike. There is no safe public but outside, with nothing to ask, and nothing to give." Stearns heard talk of "the next battle coming between Lincoln and Chase," of Frémont "working underhand for Butler," though he doubted Butler was in the ring. "Wilson [Senator from Massachusetts] says the whole government is so mean that it would go to pieces were it not for the great cause that underlies and props it up. This is true. We must trust in God, and the great heart of our people that never goes far wrong."

The warm kindliness of the *New York Evening Post,* under editorship of William Cullen Bryant, equally with John Andrew a man of clean hands in muddy politics, had veered into a slight chill toward Lincoln. "We deprecate," said the *Post,* "the agitation of a Presidential nomination as premature . . . a great and important work is yet to be done before we can distinguish the man likely to be approved by the people or who is most worthy to be intrusted with the administration of the government during the next four years." The *Post* did not itself originate disparagement of Lincoln, but it passed on to its readers without comment an excoriation in classical style, written by Doctor Orestes Augustus Brownson, first published in *Brownson's Quarterly Review,* and welcomed with glee in Copperhead journals. It chimed with the Chase-Frémont-Phillips estimate of Lincoln and echoed Senators and Congressmen puzzling as to what manner of hero they might pick to ease out Lincoln. Brownson's word portrait of Lincoln, carrying by implication Brownson's own high pride in his personal attainments, read:

Mr. Lincoln evidently knows nothing of the philosophy of history, or of the higher elements of human nature. He imagines that men act only from low and interested motives, and does not suspect, because he does not feel, the presence of a heroic element, the element, Carlyle would call it, of hero-worship, that makes men admire and cling to, and uphold a bold, daring policy, energetically proclaimed, firmly adhered to, and consistently acted on, though in face and eyes of their interest.

His soul seems made of leather, and incapable of any grand or noble emotion. Compared with the mass of men, he is a line of flat prose in a beautiful and spirited lyric. He lowers, he never elevates you.

You leave his presence with your enthusiasm damped, your better feelings crushed, and your hopes cast to the winds. You ask not, can this man carry this nation through its terrible struggles? but can the nation carry this man through them, and not perish in the attempt?

He never adopts a clean policy. When he hits upon a policy, substantially good in itself, he contrives to belittle it, besmear it in some way to render it mean, contemptible and useless. Even wisdom from him seems but folly. It is not his fault, but his misfortune.

He is a good sort of man, with much natural shrewdness and respectable native ability; but he is misplaced in the Presidential chair. He lives and moves in an order of thought, in a world many degrees below that in which a great man lives and moves. We blame him not because he is mole-eyed and not eagle-eyed, and that he has no suspicion of that higher region of thought and action in which lie the great interests and questions he is called upon to deal with as President of the United States. He has done as much as was in his power to make himself, and should be respected for what he has made himself, and the fault that he is not fit for his position is the fault of us that put him there. His only fault is, the misfortune of being unconscious of his own unfitness for his place.

Brownson's sixty-one years had seen many decisions without hesitation; he rated himself an authority on decision and hesitation. Brought up a Vermont Puritan, Brownson joined the Presbyterian Church, left it to take a Universalist pulpit, dropping that to organize a labor party in New York, shifting then to a Unitarian pastorate, leaving that to form in Boston the Society for Christian Union and Progress, stump-speaking then for Van Buren and taking a Federal job as steward of Chelsea Hospital, gravitating from there into the Roman Catholic communion and so editing *Brownson's Quarterly Review* from New York that he aroused protest from the Catholic clergy, and when his orthodoxy was referred to Rome, Cardinal Franzelin found his opinions not worthy of censure, but recommended him to be more moderate in his language. His style pleased Gurowski, who wrote in his diary: "Brownson, in his *Review*, almost alone upholds the dignity of the American mind. Brownson attacks Lincoln from the patriotic standpoint . . . for being undecided, hesitating."

Personal ambitions figured regularly in the anti-Lincoln movements. Some of these were in the open or might as well have been. Friends of Chase and Frémont groomed their favorite horses. Greeley insisted on someone else than Lincoln.

In a one-column editorial in mid-February Greeley sounded a Joshua ram's-horn blast that he hoped would send Lincoln's Jericho walls toppling. He began with first praising Lincoln as having "well discharged the responsibilities of his exalted station," having been "patriotic, honest and faithful," so that it was sure "the luster of his many good deeds will far outlive the memory of his mistakes and faults." Secondly, Greeley would admit in italics that Lincoln "is the first choice, for the next Presidential term, by a large majority of those who have thus far supported his Administration and the War." It would be strange indeed if this were not true, wrote Greeley, then clarifying: "In the fearful ordeal through which we have passed, his place has necessarily and uniformly been first in the thought of the loyal millions; his name first, after God's, in their prayers. To say that, knowing far more, they think more of and feel a warmer attachment to him than to any other living man, is only saying that he has not proved an utter disappointment and failure." These sentences, read once, read twice, and then a third time, would not lose a peculiar lurking light, perhaps of personal jealousy and malice, perhaps of something else. It amounted to saying that the people would have loved any war President, that what they loved now was not Lincoln but a President who had "not proved an utter disappointment and failure." Greeley wrote his doubt of the value of second-term endorsements given Lincoln by several State legislatures. "The loyal masses, not having begun seriously to think of the prospective Presidential contest, have not yet fixed upon someone else to succeed him in his high position."

Did Mr. Lincoln so overtop all other candidates that no others should be considered? "We answer in the negative," wrote Greeley. "Heartily agreeing that Mr. Lincoln has done well, we do not regard it as at all demonstrated that Gov. Chase, Gen. Frémont, Gen. Butler, or Gen. Grant, cannot do *as* well." Greeley favored "the salutary One Term principle" and summed up: "We freely admit Mr. Lincoln's merits; but we insist they are not such as to eclipse and obscure those of all the statesmen and soldiers who have aided in the great work of saving the country from disruption and overthrow."

In reprinting this one-column blast of Greeley, the *Chicago Tribune* credited "its preliminary remarks" as of no account, "being merely the flourish of Greeley's knife before he stabs." Editorially the Midwestern Republican newspaper estimated Lincoln's ability "at least equal, if not superior to that of any man likely to be elected," and "heated caucus for a successor" would be following "Horace Greeley's wretched reason that no President has been re-elected since Gen. Jackson." Of Greeley, "the man who stabs at our President," there were estimates taken from a book by the austere Theodore Parker in 1858: "Greeley's conduct, I think, is base. I never had any confidence in him. He has no talent for a leader. . . . He is capricious, crotchety, full of whims and wrongheaded. . . . He is honest, I think, but pitiably weak."

The Republicans had five candidates for President whom the *New York World* set down "in the order of their availability and probable chances": Abraham Lincoln, Salmon P. Chase, John C. Frémont, Nathaniel P. Banks, Benjamin F. Butler. Of the three last, major generals, "two have never fought a battle, and the military record of the other [Frémont] is not brilliant." To defeat Lincoln would be simply to nominate Chase, deduced the *World*. "Only the adherents of Chase have any interest in thwarting Lincoln. The impossibility of forming a combination against him makes Mr. Lincoln a very strong candidate." In a March or April convention Mr. Lincoln would be "irresistible," and "the sooner the convention is called the better are Mr. Lincoln's chances." Chase might possibly come to a convention with some strength. Frémont could be seen as "a popular idol" with a personal following, but his "ultra-radicals" could not swing a convention for him. Banks or Butler would come into the picture only in case of a convention deadlock between Lincoln and Chase.

Ben Butler hovered available. Chase men offered him second place with their guiding star, Butler smiling that he might yet take Richmond and come thundering home in first place on the Union ticket. "Many of the best men think of Butler as I do," wrote Gurowski in January. "Butler would have good chances for the White House if leading and influential men would speak out their convictions." And in April, "Even the smallest *coup d'éclat* before Richmond would carry Butler into the White House." Ben Wade considered himself able to handle the Presidency without batting an eyelash, but was almost completely reserved about it. As to Thaddeus Stevens, many agreed with Gurowski's jotting, "Stevens was and is as the immovable rock battered by the hurricanes," but there was agreement also that Stevens was too immovable to be President. Sumner's availability was hinted at slightly. And Sumner's secretary, the studious and scrupulous Edward L. Pierce, recorded "the distrust of Mr. Lincoln's fitness for his place" and the impressions of an insider in the anti-Lincoln movement:

Visitors to Washington in 1863-1864 were struck with the want of personal loyalty to him [Lincoln]. They found few senators and representatives who would maintain cordially and positively that he combined the qualifications of a leader in the great crisis; and the larger number of them, as the national election approached, were dissatisfied with his candidacy. An indifference towards him was noted in the commercial centres and among the most intelligent of the loyal people.

He was thought to be wanting in the style, in the gravity of manner and conversation, which are becoming in the chief of a nation. His habit of interrupting the consideration of grave matters with stories was attributed to levity, and offended soberminded men who sought him on public business. A man of "infinite jest," the underlying seriousness of his nature was not readily observed. But the criticism did not stop here.

He was felt to be too easy-going, to be disposed to give too much time to trifles; to be unbusinesslike in his methods, slow and hesitating where vigorous action was required; and the objection in general was, that in capacity and temperament he was inadequate to the responsibilities of the head of a nation at such a momentous period. This estimate was honestly held by many clear-headed and patriotic men; nor can their sincerity be questioned.

This also is to be said,—that whatever those who came near him thought, the popular instinct was with him; and plain men—the masses of the people—did not admit the limitations apparent to those who were present at the seat of the government. Indeed, the very qualities and ways which repelled public men brought the President near to the people.

Senators and Congressmen joining in this anti-Lincoln movement had nearly all been handed their share of patronage by the President. He had met them more than halfway in policies of emancipation and arming the Negro. This worried Thurlow Weed in New York, who once wrote to Judge David Davis, "They will all be against him in 1864, why does he persist in giving them weapons to defeat his renomination?" Medill of the *Chicago Tribune* felt just the other way about it, and wrote to Congressman Washburne in April of '64 that he favored rejecting the President unless the Cabinet was remodeled on radical lines. "Lincoln has some very weak and foolish traits of character. If he had reasonable political sagacity and would cut loose from the semi-copperheads in his Cabinet and about him, if he would put live, bold, vigorous radicals in their places no human power could prevent his renomination."

Welles wrote of the Cabinet's working rather smoothly, though Chase nursed aspirations to be President while Seward had surrendered any expectations he might have and was giving the President fair support. "Blair and Bates are earnest friends of the President, and so, I think, is Usher. Stanton is insincere but will, I have no doubt, act with Seward." Then on January 2 of '64 Sumner called, and after disposing of some little business matters, told Welles the President was moving for a re-election and had spoken very explicitly to several persons on the subject.

"I told him," Welles wrote, "the President had exchanged no word with me on the subject, but that I had taken for granted he would be a candidate, that I thought all Presidents had entertained dreams of that nature, and that my impressions are that a pretty strong current is setting in his favor. To this Sumner made no response. . . . I think his present thoughts are in another direction, but not very decidedly so. Neither of us cared to press the other. Whether he had in view to sound me I was uncertain, and am still." It was some weeks later that Gurowski, to whom Sumner was always a good deal of a hero, wrote in his diary:

Feb. 22—Sumner spoken of as candidate for the Presidency. Spoken of by some devotees and by—himself. He believes he will be the candidate of the eleventh hour, and that Chase and Frémont will transfer to him their votes. Oh!

The President was tricked sometimes, but not often, by "heartless intriguers," Welles wrote as the undercurrents of the presidential campaign became plainer to see. "The President does not conceal the interest he takes, and yet I perceive nothing unfair or intrusive." Some appointments "secured by mischievous men" would never have been made had the President known the facts. These appointments would rise to plague him. A little mystified Welles noted:

In some respects he [the President] is a singular man and not fully understood. He has great sagacity and shrewdness, but sometimes his assertion or management is astray. When he relies on his own right intentions and good common sense he is strongest. So in regard to friends whom he distrusts, and mercenary opponents, in some of whom he confides. A great and almost inexcusable error for a man in his position.

By mercenary opponents Welles meant, as particularly as any, Stanton and Seward and individuals lurking behind them. Welles's judgments often rested on plain jealousy, on suspicions of those Cabinet members who "got the inside track" with the President.

With a touch of dawn maroon and a faint odor of forget-me-nots Miss Anna Elizabeth Dickinson flitted into the Washington scene as pro-Lincoln and faded out anti-Lincoln. She had won name as a Girl Orator, had developed gifts of swift and withering sarcasm, had nursed and brought along an eloquence that made her a torch of promise to thousands who had heard her on the platform. Her chestnut curls cut close to her clean-shapen head, her virginal beauty, her symmetrical figure, her complete self-possession, her contralto fullness of voice, her discussions of momentous issues beginning gravely and flowing into sudden passionate appeals for the redemption of mankind and the holiness of human freedom—these had brought comparisons of her with the Maid of Orleans who saved France when all others despaired.

"The advent of a Joan of Arc is prophesied," wrote the eminent critic Nathaniel P. Willis. "Is it to be for this time and crisis and is Miss Dickinson the woman on whom the mantle has fallen?" At first sight and hearing she seemed cast for such a role, the critic believed, with "her features well chiselled, her forehead and upper lip of the Greek proportion, and her nostrils thin." The men would call her beautiful, considered Willis, and the women would admit it with a customary reluctance. "She was a beauty but for the look a little too determined of that strongly moulded jaw."

Miss Dickinson's effects wrought upon audiences at Music Hall, Boston, Cooper Union, New York, the Academy of Music, Philadelphia, had seemed so tonic to the cause of Union and Emancipation that a committee of Senators and Congressmen invited her to Washington. She was just twenty-one years and three months old when on January 16 of '64 she spoke in the hall of the House of Representatives, Speaker Colfax sitting on her right hand, Vice-President Hamlin on her left, President Lincoln on a bench farther in the foreground, the affair bringing $1,031 for the Freedmen's Relief Association.

"How, to such youthful lips, flowed so easily such stately language!" wrote Willis. Others called it just another stump speech. She referred to the President as though he should be renominated and re-elected. Said the *Detroit Free Press* one day, "The strong-minded Anna Dickinson has renominated the weak-minded Abraham Lincoln," and another day: "Anna Dickinson, in a speech in Washington, advocated Old Abe's re-election to his face. He went away convinced. Anna should be substituted for the old lady of the Naval Department."

The *Washington Chronicle*, an Administration newspaper owned by Lincoln's political friend John W. Forney, clerk of the Senate, reviewed the performance. "Joan of Arc never was grander, and could not have been better in her mail of battle, than was this Philadelphia maid in her statesmanlike demand that this war do not cease until slavery lie dead and buried under the feet of the North, and its epitaph is traced with the point of a bayonet dipped in the young blood of the nation." Her requirement was that "territory wrenched back from the rebellion be used to underlay the

development of the blacks in America into full citizenship, with the ownership in fee of agricultural land."

The London *Telegraph* correspondent wrote his paper that "some
nursery discipline" might help "young ladies who have a mania for spouting politics." He sniffed and huffed. "If this crazy Jane in a red jacket had
uttered her nonsense in some lecture hall or mechanic's institute, her plea
might hold good. But she comes accredited by persons in authority; the
council chamber of the country is placed at her disposal; she speaks *ex
cathedra;* she is handed to her rostrum by the second personage in the republic, and the Speaker of the House is her gentleman usher." Something
about the performance did not sit well with part of the Union press. A
correspondent of the *Cincinnati Gazette* wrote: "As to Miss Dickinson's
nomination of Mr. Lincoln for the next Presidency, I object to it as the
inauguration of an era of *petticoat* government for which we are not prepared at present. I have no objection to the nomination but the source is
not appropriate."

Two months later Miss Dickinson spoke in Metropolitan Hall in Chicago
before the Young Men's Christian Association. One reporter wrote: "At
first you think of the woman who stands before you, with pale immovable
features and almost *petite* look, and feel inclined to wonder at her audacity.
Soon the words flow out from her lips thick and fast, a torrent of burning,
scathing, lightning eloquence. You forget the frail being who stands on the
platform. Attention is fixed only on the theme and you listen spellbound,
scarcely noting even the close of those wonderfully lengthened sentences
uttered without break or pause."

One of her rushing and lengthened sentences ran on to say that the
President's Amnesty Proclamation was a piece of Northern meanness and a
usurpation of the functions of Congress: "The President is a lawyer, and a
Western one at that; it is a wonder he does not know that the oaths of such
men [reconstructed rebels] are but as idle wind. Let them come back and
what is the result? . . . a state of things worse than before. . . . These
men must be punished. South Carolina should be cut up into twenty acre
lots, and as many negroes settled on them as can be got there."

A month later Miss Dickinson called at the White House, interviewed
the President, then went to Boston and there in a public lecture satirized
the Administration and caricatured Lincoln, his twang and his clothes, as
she reported her interview. He had said to her: "They tell me you are
on my side. I want to know how it is." She told him his emancipation
policy was not moving fast enough and pleaded for justice to the Negro.

The President answered, "That reminds me of a story." She had to reply: "I did not come here to hear stories. I can read better ones in the
papers any day than you can tell me." He showed her his correspondence
with officials in Louisiana and asked her what she thought of his plan of
reconstruction there. She replied, "Sir, I think it all wrong; as radically
bad as can be."

The President then "sugar-plummed" her, as Miss Dickinson phrased it. He told her she could talk better than he, and so forth.

Ending their conversation, he remarked, "All I can say is, if the radicals want me to lead, let them get out of the way and let me lead." And, said Miss Dickinson in full contralto to her Boston audience, "When he said that, I came out and remarked to a friend, 'I have spoken my last word to President Lincoln.'"

Loyal Union Republican newspapers published her report of her interview with Lincoln, the *Chicago Journal* heading it, "A Mighty Self-Important Young Lady" and commenting: "Miss Anna E. Dickinson is rather overdoing the thing. She commenced well but has been spoiled by flattery. She is now engaged in making a fool of herself." But it was not quite so that she was spoiled by flattery. She was merely following the same course as Wendell Phillips, entirely sincere and unfailingly temperamental. She was an agitator, and cared not a whit that the *Detroit Free Press* took its fling: "The idea that President Lincoln should have been nominated for re-election by that she-fanatic Anna Dickinson is itself a disagreeable blot."

Phillips had veered toward the President that winter, so far as to say: "I, for one, have no objection to the Presidency of Abraham Lincoln for four or eight years longer. I told the President himself that the man who would honestly put his hand to the plough of that proclamation, and execute it, this people would not allow him to quit while the experiment was trying. Whoever starts the great experiment of emancipation, and honestly devotes his energies to making it a fact, deserves to hold the helm of government till that experiment is finished." The opposition press headed paragraphs "Abolitionist Orator Favors Lincoln."

Then Phillips swung clean away from Lincoln, and speaking to the Woman's Loyal League in Cooper Union, again flared at the slowgoing President whom he thought "all as God made him." At first the President would not touch the Negro. But at last Abraham woke up and said, "He is either a man and I'll enlist him, or he is a dollar and I'll spend him." So from 1860 through 1861 and 1862, Lincoln kept "morally unrolling" until he got to the height of the Emancipation Proclamation. Lincoln was not of granite, as were Frémont and Butler, whose views were broad as humanity. They spoke of Negro *rights* while Lincoln talked merely of Negro *benefits*.

From speech to speech Phillips went on, graphic and simple, and however mistaken and however heady, with a peculiar joy in being temperamentally stubborn, he was the straightest-shooting orator in the country, though no one could foretell when he would suddenly shift targets. He debonairly justified himself: "Mr. Lincoln is a growing man. And why does he grow? Because we water him."

Harper's Weekly took a hand as friendly umpire between Phillips and Lincoln: "If Mr. Phillips made the point clearer, not the President ought to do this or that, but that the people ought to wish him to do it, and insist upon his doing it, Mr. Phillips would be juster to what we suppose to be his real view. . . . Statesmanship is no more the doing, or the attempt to do, what the statesman may individually think to be abstractly right, without regard to the conditions that surround him, than seamanship is laying a course and persisting in it, spite of the wind. In fact, the wind will control the ship, and public opinion the statesman."

Harper's outlined the everlasting cleavage between the statesman in office and power and the agitator outside looking in. Phillips had a genius consecrated to human progress, stood among the truest Americans, and was not to be disposed of as a scold or a professional caviler. "It is precisely such men as he who have kept the sacred fire of liberty burning in this country, while other men sneered and slept." The President could supply reasons enough for what he had done. When Phillips said that Lincoln was a good man and would do what the people wish and therefore the people must be made to wish the best thing, that was fair enough. But when Phillips added that the President was a growing man, "because, we, the people, constantly water him," then the orator was leading into error. "It is not the conviction of Mr. Lincoln, but the executive action of the President, that we water."

From city to city went Phillips lashing with adjectives and scorn Lincoln, Seward, Blair, Chase, saying that in the President-making of the year, "in that terrible storm of personal ambition," he would never rest till the nation was led by men of sense and courage. "Until such men as Butler or Frémont man the guns or hold the helm, no man with justice to himself, to his children, to the negro, to the Union can give rest to his eyelids or silence to his lips." Anti-Slavery Society members in New York on January 29 heard Phillips: "Either the North must rise in the opinion of unanimously crushing the President into submission, or we must have a different leader the next four years. . . . Perhaps, with Chase for President, Butler in the War Department, and Frémont at the head of our armies, we might close the war in two years; but after all public opinion is what is wanted."

Then the bland, bald, large-mouthed William Lloyd Garrison stood up. He had helped nurse the abolition movement, had gone to jail for it, had in one hour stood with a rope around his neck while a mob howled around him—all before young Phillips had enlisted in the cause. And Garrison referred to a remark of Phillips not so long before which had been taken as Phillips's announcement that he was pro-Lincoln: "The President's character was a sun so bright that we could not see the few spots on its surface." And tonight, went on Garrison, the gentleman spent an hour blackening Mr. Lincoln all over, styling him a hypocrite ready to sacrifice the honor of the North to a sham peace. "Has not the President," asked the old war horse, "gone as fast and as far as the people would sustain him? ["No, no."] Mr. Lincoln has travelled as fast toward the negro as popular sentiment would warrant him. Butler and Grant have sustained the President's policy. ["No, no."] And what about Frémont? Events have occurred within a year greatly to diminish my faith in Frémont. Not a word from him in reference to the President's proclamation of amnesty. What a glorious opportunity was there lost! Then we have had the arming of one hundred thousand blacks, and still not one word of encouragement from Frémont."

Also in stride with Phillips was the blond young giant of Plymouth Church, Theodore Tilton, successor of Henry Ward Beecher as editor in chief of the *Independent*, the leading family newspaper of religious cast in the country. An abolitionist from youth up, an out-and-outer, Tilton carried on Beecher's policy of hitting the Administration. Tilton reported from Washington "the great lack there of a positive faith in God." Tilton pressed his point that the next President should qualify with "a sublime allegiance to God." He recited the vast issues in the face of which the country could not afford to make a "haphazard" choice of its next Administration. "The President about to be chosen must be a man born to command, a man with clean hands, a man whose palms are unvexed with the itch for gain. He must have no old political favorites to reward, no old debts to former place owners, no bargains to settle with balance-holding factions, no consultations to hold with dry, rotten lobbymen in Albany and Washington. Who is that man? Let sober-minded people ponder."

The answer was, plainly, not Lincoln. Also, plainly, to the upper circles of Plymouth Church, Brooklyn, the answer was Frémont and nobody else. As the one idolized public figure of the *Independent*, Frémont had many intimacies with Plymouth Church. One of the triumvirate who had founded that church, helping build it to where it paid Henry Ward Beecher a salary of $16,000 a year, was John Tasker Howard, associate of Frémont in the Mariposa gold mine venture in California, a staff member of the Major General at St. Louis. Another Plymouth Church member of Frémont's staff was Ross Raymond. The letters of Howard and Raymond to Beecher had early brought to Beecher their information and belief that Lincoln was jealous of the Pathfinder. When at last Lincoln had dropped the General and Frémont set up campaign headquarters at the Astor House in New York, Beecher came first with regrets and sympathy. Frémont, wrote Beecher for the *Independent*, was "maligned and mistreated . . . unquestionably the most personally popular man in the country." And Tilton now in writing of how the next President must be free from debts, bargains, lobbymen, was forgetting that Henry C. Bowen, the war-ruined merchant who owned the *Independent*, had by solicitation of Senator Sumner been given a comfortable desk in the customs collector's office in New York. And it was nothing to talk about in Plymouth Church circles that a son of Henry Ward Beecher, not yet of age, had been commissioned an officer in the Army of the Potomac and, caught in conduct unbecoming to an officer, had been forced to resign.

In anxiety and shame Beecher had gone to his handsome young friend Tilton, who in turn went straight to the then Secretary of War Cameron, who heard Tilton beg for a commission in the regular army for young Beecher. From Cameron Tilton went to the White House carrying a commission that needed only Lincoln's signature to make it good. Lincoln signed the appointment of young Harry Beecher, lieutenant of artillery, regulars, and Tilton carried it back to Henry Ward Beecher.

Army life was not going hard for young Beecher in December of '63 when his father wrote to Secretary Chase in reply to Christmas good wishes from Secretary Chase, "I am in a very amiable mood, my own son, Harry, a lieutenant in the artillery, regulars, having brought to my house a charming wife, & they together are ruling both father and mother, & having their own way." He agreed, wrote Beecher to Chase, "with the view which you express of the President's Message and Proclamation." Then came an estimate of the President: "His mind works in the right *directions*, but seldom works clearly and cleanly. His bread is of unbolted flour, & much straw, too, mixes in the bran, & sometimes gravel stones. Yet, on the whole the loaf will sustain life, though it makes eating a difficulty, rather than a pleasure. But will not *the Legislation* of Congress, be of a kind to make up, in some degree? I have been inclined to hope that we could get from Congress what we lack in the President." Beecher gave Chase the comfort that he believed recent attacks of Wendell Phillips on Chase "certainly cannot shake the conviction of the great mass of intelligent men that you have been soundly, consistently & wisely faithful to the doctrines of liberty, thro' good report & evil, in office & out of it."

The matter of young Beecher's dismissal and reappointment had point as to military discipline and the conduct of the war; it was of no particular personal importance to either Cameron or Lincoln; it was chiefly of interest as showing that friends of Frémont could in a pinch get a favor from the Administration and thereafter go on as though nothing had happened. "The people are beginning to distrust their rulers," Beecher had written in the *Independent*. "The President seems to be a man without any sense of the value of time. . . . Our armies have been managed as if they were a body of nurses in a foundling hospital."

Beecher's reiterated low rating of Lincoln's mental quality became proverbial in some quarters, made a peg upon which to hang deprecation or persiflage, the *New York Herald* offering: "President Lincoln gives unmistakable evidence that the small amount of intellect with which Henry Ward Beecher credits him (and what 'loyal' man 'engaged in the interests of God and humanity' will dispute the estimate of Beecher?) is gradually failing under the President's anxiety for renomination."

The *Detroit Free Press* took as a text the *Independent's* reference to the next President's qualifying with "a sublime allegiance to God" and approved: "So Mr. Lincoln don't suit the *Independent*—nor indeed should the smutty joker suit anyone pretending to be decent." To seven sarcastic reasons why Lincoln should be a candidate again the *New York World* added, "He writes worse English than any President we ever had," and he surpassed in stories "from the broad smutty to the diluted Joe Miller." The *Chicago Times* picked up a portrait impression of Lincoln from the *South Carolinian*, published in Columbia, South Carolina, and amused its following with a perfectly sincere hymn of hate:

If the Yankees had searched the length and breadth of their land for a fit representative, they could not have made an apter selection than the man, who, in the
Presidential chair, is now playing fantastic tricks before high Heaven.

Abe Lincoln is a perfect type of the people which he governs. He is the ideal
Yankee—the Yankee as we have seen him in a thousand ridiculous caricatures, and
read of him in a thousand ridiculous stories.

With a physiognomy which seems to have been purposely shaped in all its vulgar
features to express sharpness of intelligence, blended with emotional insensibility, lean,
lank, long, lopsided, awkward, and ungainly in person, we might suppose that warmed
into life by some Pygmalion of a sketcher, he had just stepped out of one of the last
numbers of *Punch*. Thus adapted externally to his representative position, he is not
less so in the whole character of his mind.

He is what his history declares him to be—a Yankee wood-chopper, sublimed in a
Yankee monarch, in which capacity he presents a more ludicrous appearance than
that of Bottom crowned with flowers, fed with apricots and dewberries, and nursed
and tended by gentle sprites and ministering fairies.

As one dwells upon the completeness with which Lincoln, at all points, embodies
the peculiarities of his nation, one can scarcely help attributing a certain grave humor
to those ancient ladies, the Fates, who placed him upon the throne.

In the man's hopeless inability to apprehend the proprieties of time, place or person; in the coarse familiarity with which he at once accosts prince or peasant, foreign
envoy, visitor of distinction, or one of his own dirty constituents; in the usual drawl
with which he tells his absurd and inane stories; in his inapposite and impertinent
questions; in his mere smattering of an education, and in the utter impossibility of
awing or abashing him by any exhibition of dignity or reserve, we recognize without
difficulty the well-known characteristics of the Yankee, as they have been again and
again depicted upon the stage.

We might pursue this topic still further, and show how the policy of Lincoln
toward the South has been identical with that Yankee cunning which makes the
Yankee so dextrous in all the chicanery of trade. But we forbear, lest tragedy should
step in and compel us to assume a graver tone than we care to take on so ineffably
contemptible an object.

Is it written in the book of destiny that this thing, the likeness of which we have
faintly drawn, shall ever rule a people in whom the love of truth and honor, and all
noble and generous feelings, are characteristics which belong to them as well by nature as by education? we do not believe it.

Better cringe under the sternest despotism of Europe—better the dominion of the
fiend himself, even though he should come to us, not in the guise of Milton's mighty
"archangel ruined," but with the hoof, horns, and tail of the old legends—better, a
thousand times better extermination from the very face of the earth, than to own as
a master, for the faintest shadow of a second, this mean, wily, illiterate, brutal, unprincipled, and utterly vulgar creature—in a word, this Yankee of the Yankees!

Early in '64 the *New York World* presented General McClellan as the
one man of worth, dignity, and patriotism for nomination by the Democratic party, to overwhelm Lincoln at the polls the next November. Entire
pages were given to an essay on patriotism read by McClellan at West Point
and long detailed reports and correspondence of the General with the War
Department. These aimed to build up McClellan as a monumental hero and
a much-wronged person. In this effort the *World* served financial, indus-

trial, and transportation interests represented in politics by Erastus Corning and Dean Richmond of the New York Central Railroad; by William Henry Aspinwall of the New York-to-San Francisco steamship lines and the Panama Isthmus 49-mile railway which up to 1859 had netted him a fortune of $6,000,000; and more directly and dominantly by August Belmont, politically and financially the most eminent Jew in America.

Born in a rich landholding family in Rhenish Prussia in 1816, Belmont at fourteen had worked without pay as office boy, swept and dusted in the rooms of the powerful banking firm of Rothschild Brothers in Frankfort while learning finance, serving three years as supervisor of a branch house in Naples. In the panic year of 1837 he set up in New York his own banking house of August Belmont & Company, his great asset being the agency for the Rothschilds in America. Becoming a United States citizen, Belmont served on foreign missions, was United States Minister to Holland, developed into a leader of the Democratic party, championed Stephen A. Douglas at the 1860 Baltimore convention, saw himself chosen chairman of the National Democratic Committee. He wore side whiskers, owned ponies and enjoyed horse races, collected rare porcelains and masterpieces of painting. And Belmont had anger and courage, for in 1841 he had fought, because of a woman, a duel at Elkton, Indiana, with William Hayward of South Carolina, took a bullet wound and thereafter walked through life with a limp.

After an interview with Lincoln and Seward, Belmont had gone to Europe and quietly warned financial circles that the Southern Confederacy was not a good business risk, wreaking more practical damage to the South than Beecher's orations in England, though the work of Belmont was under cover. From England he transmitted to Lincoln a short message he had from an interview with Palmerston: "We do not like slavery, but we need cotton, and hate your Morrill protective tariff." As a Union man in 1860 he wrote a letter to his friend John Forsyth, later a Confederate commissioner refused a hearing by Seward: "I prefer to leave to my children, instead of the gilded prospects of New York merchant princes, the more enviable title of American citizen, and as long as God spares my life I shall not falter in my efforts to procure them that heritage."

Belmont had helped raise and equip the first regiment of German troops enlisted in New York City. As a Union man through the war he had run somewhat the course of Governor Seymour of New York. He had sent on to Washington an extract from a letter written at New Orleans, expecting it would be shown to Lincoln. "The time has arrived when Mr. Lincoln must take a decisive course," it read. "Trying to please everybody, he will satisfy nobody." And Lincoln in a long letter to Belmont had urged that his reconstruction policy was clear for those who would read and understand rather than write complaining letters northward. "Broken eggs cannot be mended; but Louisiana has nothing to do now but to take her place in the Union as it was, barring the already broken eggs. The sooner she does so, the smaller . . . the amount past mending."

Belmont joined with Aspinwall in belief that McClellan was "a genius" and, as President, would manage to save the Union without entanglement on the slavery issue. With Seymour he stood for a party policy of unmistakable opposition to the Republicans in power; otherwise the Democratic party would be swallowed and cease to exist in a proposed new Union party foreshadowed by Lincoln and Weed. The high proportion of Democrats among major generals and brigadiers, also among the powerful civil officials appointed by Lincoln, had brought losses to the regular Democratic organization, so that Belmont, Seymour, and other leaders who wished to hold their ranks together could see no other course than to cry down the Administration at every possible point. Their political strength could only be rooted in the population and voters that naturally hated the war, the Administration, Lincoln and all his works. They believed those voters numbered enough to perhaps give them the Government in November.

Manton Marble, publisher of the *New York World*, was ably meeting the wishes of Belmont, who was credited with financially backing the newspaper. No other newspaper, not even the *New York Herald*, so incessantly cried down Chase and Federal money affairs on its financial page. Columns of perverted news items, rumors, conjectures, accusations, insidious gabblings, were printed. If half-true they could mean nothing else than that Chase was an ignoramus in finance yet a thieving manipulator. They directly insinuated that by advance knowledge of money measures Chase and others were piling up fortunes for themselves. That Chase was in debt, and had to manage carefully to pay small loans from time to time, could never be known to those who believed half they read in the *World's* financial page.

The President naturally took the heavier verbal punishment from the *World*. The President had ended free speech and a free press in America, the *World* said in April, being itself free to say, however, that for months the President had run the Government single-handed, for months there had been no Cabinet meetings. "In the knots of two or three which sometimes gather, Mr. Lincoln's stories quite as often occupy the time as the momentous interests of a great nation, divided by traitors, ridden by fanatics and cursed with an imbecility in administration only less criminal than treason." Any byplay of humor that touched the Administration was welcome. The *World* reported one Colonel Max Langenschwartz at a pro-McClellan mass meeting chuckling that he "would not say that Mr. Lincoln had long legs and that was probably why he had overstepped the Constitution." The Republicans, Langenschwartz quipped, were like the man who burned his house and furniture, his wife asking why and the man answering, "To kill the cockroaches." The Republicans, proceeded Langenschwartz, should add to emancipation, to confiscation, and to miscegenation, a policy of polygamy. "Then a man could have a yellow wife from China, a brown wife from India, a black wife from Africa, and a white wife from his own country, and so have a variegated family and put a sign over the door: 'United Matrimonial Paint Shop.' [Great laughter.]"

McClellan's letter handed to Lincoln at Harrison's Landing, Virginia, in 1862, now nearly two years after its writing was made public in the

World. As a political letter by a military man running for the Presidency it seemed as effective in 1864 as McClellan in 1862 had hoped. On the slavery issue he was not merely reserved but noncommittal: he would not interfere with the institution, it seemed, but he threw no light on what form of compromise could be made with it. Still he held to his declaration. "The Constitution and the Union must be preserved, whatever may be the cost in time, treasure and blood." The *World* was more than satisfied. "The letter is one of the most remarkable documents in the history of the war. It forecasts with a statesman's vision."

Metropolitan dailies and country weeklies had their fling when the Commissioner of Public Buildings at Washington reported formally: "The basement of the White House is left untenanted, except by rats and they have undisputed possession. . . . During the latter part of the past summer, the effluvium from dead rats was offensive in all the passages." This was the signal for various sharpshooters to demand a general cleaning out of rats from cellar to garret of the White House.

Lincoln's April letter to Hodges of Kentucky with its confession—"I am naturally antislavery. If slavery is not wrong, nothing is wrong. I cannot remember when I did not so think and feel"—with its frankness that staggered many readers—"I claim not to have controlled events, but confess plainly that events have controlled me"—this had the opposition hard put for pertinent comment. Something in it was as basic and strange as the House Divided speech. "Now, at the end of three years' struggle, the nation's condition is not what either party, or any man, devised or expected. God alone can claim it. Whither it is tending seems plain. If God now wills the removal of a great wrong, and wills also that we of the North, as well as you of the South, shall pay fairly for our complicity in that wrong, impartial history will find therein new cause to attest and revere the justice and goodness of God." The *New York World* was sure the Hodges letter would be read with curious interest all over the country. "It is an original document in every sense of the word, and could not have been written by anyone on this continent save the present occupant of the White House . . . he has an *affected* common-sense way of putting things." After which the *World* argued that Lincoln was dishonest; the letter revealed it and would ruin him with the people.

The question that winter bothering Senators and Congressmen at Washington found its way into editorials. The *World* on February 11 of '64 headed one: "Ought a President to Re-elect Himself?" By screwing one's eyes fixedly upon a sentence in Lincoln's '61 inaugural address, said the one-term advocates who were becoming vocal, it could be seen that the President had pledged himself to one term and no more. That sentence ran, "I now enter upon the same task [as fifteen previous Executives] for the brief constitutional term of *four* years under great and peculiar difficulty." Entirely aside from this point, Chase held that it had now become an American tradition that the President should not serve a second term; for thirty years no President had served two terms, and the custom was established. Chase wrote this in many letters.

Those favoring the one-term tradition from week to week could glean no satisfaction from Lincoln personally. He had nothing, not even an anecdote, about a second term. Until he should say he was a candidate they were up a row of stumps. The *Chicago Times* Washington correspondent, who often and evidently did his Washington corresponding right at home in good old Cook County, Illinois, wrote in January: "Lincoln himself utterly despairs of election. He is haggard, listless, without hope. Sometimes I think he is becoming what he surely will be in ten years—the victim of remorse." This was interesting, but gave no clue, no more than the *Nashville Times* Washington correspondent who quoted Lincoln as saying, "I have no leanings, I can have none."

Somewhat more credible as late as April was the Washington correspondent of the *Springfield Republican,* who wrote: "Mr. Lincoln feels certain of the nomination next June. I don't believe he has a doubt upon the subject. Nor does he attempt to conceal his pleasure over the prospect. He is no hypocrite, and does not try to make people believe that he is unwilling to be the President for another four years. He wants to be and expects to be."

When in October of '63 Lincoln had written to Washburne, "A second term would be a great honor and a great labor, which, together, perhaps I would not decline if tendered," he had marked the letter "Private and confidential." And since then he had said nothing publicly that could be construed into a readiness for a second term. He was waiting. What he was waiting for he did not say. Swett noted, "Lincoln kept an eye out for the spot where the lightning was going to strike and tried to be on that spot."

Lincoln believed in lightning. That was allied to his belief in luck, to his sleep-visioned nature, to the superstitious element, the will of Providence, the dreaming bones that swayed him in vaster matters. In the Hodges letter he pointed to three years of war, the changeful mystery of the national tragedy, noting: "God alone can claim it."

The grinding drama of drums and blood and agony went on. The lines of boys in blue poured south and ever south, fractions of them returning horizontal and groaning in ambulances; others by thousands in shallow rain-soaked graves where hurried burying squads had shoveled them over, still others by thousands, as at Shiloh, Malvern Hill, Gettysburg, with ribs and skulls picked clean and bare by scavenger birds, rain and sunlight finally giving them an ancient and inviolable dignity.

Three years of these rocking lines of destroyers seeking each other and unable to destroy to an end. Three years of it and no foreteller had foretold it as it happened. "God alone can claim it." Inexorable laws and deep-running forces of human society and national life had operated. Any one man in their midst had better count himself of small moment in the blood and slime of the hour. Could it be an hour to step out and form combinations and huckster a candidacy with an eye on November next? Before November would come terrific decisions of men with snarling guns and plunging bayonets. Beyond and out there where men lay rolled in their gray blankets by the bivouac fire under frost or falling rain or white moon—out there lay the dictates of the November election, the action that would sway the November voters.

When Lincoln was actually in a political campaign, as Swett saw him, he never believed in going out to line up factions and interests in his favor. He kept hands off. "Whether an individual man or class of men supported or opposed him never made any difference in his feelings or his opinions of his own success. If he was elected, he seemed to think that no person or class of persons could ever have defeated him, and if defeated he believed nothing could ever have elected him. . . . He saw that the pressure of a campaign was the external force coercing the party into a unity. . . . All his efforts to procure a second nomination were in the same direction. I believe he earnestly desired that nomination. He was much more eager for it than he was for the first, and yet from the beginning he discouraged all efforts on the part of his friends to obtain it."

Swett, who had worked with David Davis to clinch the Pennsylvania delegation for Lincoln in 1860, who performed confidential errands too delicate to record in telegrams or letters, in Washington in the early months of 1864 noted that for a year and more the adversaries of Lincoln had been at work for themselves. "Chase had three or four secret societies and an immense patronage extending all over the country. Frémont was constantly at work, yet Lincoln would never do anything either to hinder them or to help himself." Swett threw his light on how Lincoln managed campaigns by ignoring men and by ignoring all small causes, but by closely calculating the tendencies of events and the great forces which were producing logical results.

"His rivals," noted Swett, "were using money profusely; journals and influences were being subsidized against him. I accidentally learned that a Washington newspaper, through a purchase of the establishment, was to be turned against him, and consulted him about taking steps to prevent it. The only thing I could get him to say was that he would regret to see the paper turned against him. Whatever was done had to be done without his knowledge. Mr. Bennett of the *Herald*, with his paper, was a power, wanted to be noticed by Lincoln, and he wanted to support him. A friend of his, who was certainly in his secrets, came to Washington and intimated if Lincoln would invite Bennett to come over and chat with him, his paper would be all right. Mr. Bennett wanted nothing, he simply wanted to be noticed. Lincoln in talking about it said, 'I understand it; Bennett has made a great deal of money, some say not very properly, now he wants me to make him respectable. I have never invited Mr. Bryant or Mr. Greeley here; I shall not, therefore, especially invite Mr. Bennett.' All Lincoln would say was, that he was receiving everybody, and he should receive Mr. Bennett if he came."

Swett's impressions here were not entirely correct. He probably over-stressed Bennett's thirst for notice from Lincoln. But his close-up judgment that Lincoln kept a peculiar personal independence toward Bennett and Greeley was correct, and was verified by Hay, Nicolay, Welles, David Davis, and others. Lincoln's conception of the public was at variance with that of Bennett, who when asked if he preferred the *New York Herald* as a newspaper replied, "I do not but the public do—I make a newspaper for the public, not for myself."

Swett's analysis had point in the case of the hard-drinking Governor Dick Yates of Illinois, who swam with the radical current in '63 to the extent of telling a Methodist ministers' conference that on the emancipation issue Lincoln's backbone "tapered" a little. Early in '64 Yates saw that he belonged politically in the deeper-running Lincoln current and he plunged into it; he was coerced into party unity, saying in Bryan Hall, Chicago: "It is no use, as I heard a friend of mine say today; the politicians may try to fix it up, but the people will have Old Abe and nobody else. [Applause.] I must confess I am for him first, last and all the time. [Applause.] It is no time to change fronts when you are in the presence of the enemy. It would be unjust to change fronts because although it is said that Abe is an honest man, yet I stand up here to say that from long acquaintance with him, he is not only one of the honestest men that God ever made, but in clear, cool, statesmanlike judgment, he is without a peer in the history of the world. [Applause.] We might as well make up our minds to it, for this government has been attempted to be destroyed during the administration of Abraham Lincoln, and it will be saved during his administration. [Unanimous applause.]"

One Senator watching the drift had decided it might be well for him to support Lincoln early in the running. His State legislature, which must re-elect him—or someone else—the next winter, would be chosen when the voters elected a President. He arranged for one of his constituents, a *New York Times* correspondent, J. M. Winchell (in confidence so strict that Winchell in writing of it afterward would not give the Senator's name), to meet Lincoln. The Senator told Winchell that by coming out early for Lincoln he would be stronger with the President during the second term. "In fact," wrote Winchell, "if the State could thus be carried, in convention and at the polls, the Senator assured me that a most influential position [naming it] awaited his acceptance in the new Cabinet, and coming plumply to the point, he promised me then and there, if I would enter the canvass for both candidates [him and Lincoln], to give me the choice of a high diplomatic position in Europe or an office in Washington, 'in which (I quote his exact words) the present incumbent *says* he has made a million of dollars and wronged nobody.'"

To Winchell this did not look so good for various reasons. "I was not quite overcome by the brilliancy of this proffer. Not to claim extraordinary philosophy or virtue, I will say that I had no very intense faith in political promises, and especially in those made by the gentleman with whom I was conversing." In short, Winchell did not want to be tied to the Senator's political kite, and on top of that he was not for Lincoln. "I had been a Chase man and had shared with a great many Republicans a profound dissatisfaction with the mode in which Mr. Lincoln had allowed the war to be conducted." And Winchell had suspicions that the Senator lied about having inside information that the President would be a candidate and lied again about a promise of a place in the Cabinet.

Without telling the Senator that he believed him a liar, Winchell did tell the Senator it would be impossible for him to go to the President and say that the Senator was getting busy on a tremendous campaign for Lincoln in his home State and could be counted as one of the sure-enough original second-term Lincoln men. Winchell did, however, propose that if the Senator would arrange an interview he would try to learn from the President whether the President really wanted Winchell or the Senator or anybody to get busy and swing a renomination. Also Winchell explained that a talk with the President might satisfy him, Winchell, as to whether the Senator and the President were as close, like two peas in a pod, as the Senator implied.

The Senator on hearing this from Winchell did some thinking of a sort. He reflected, cogitated. Then he answered. His answer sort of took Winchell's breath away. Yes, what Winchell asked was reasonable and proper. The Senator promised Winchell a private interview with Mr. Lincoln in a day or two—and, wrote Winchell, "to my amazement kept his promise, and I had no alternative on my part but to keep the appointment he had made for me, though with the distinct understanding that it should in no way commit me."

So the Senator took Winchell into the President's office, introduced Lincoln and Winchell to each other, excused himself with a phrase or two of compliments, and with dignity and good order walked out of the room, leaving Winchell alone with Lincoln. This was Winchell's third interview with Lincoln, the first one coming in the week after the battle of Murfreesboro, when he asked the President about news from the bloody work there and the President said he had none, the second one being a call with a committee of newspapermen to ask the President to restore to good standing a *New York Herald* correspondent who had been shushed out of the army lines by General Sherman. Of what he saw and heard in the hour or so spent with Lincoln, Winchell wrote:

Mr. Lincoln received me, as ever, kindly and courteously; but his manner was quite changed. It was not now the country about which his anxiety prevailed, but himself. There was an embarrassment about him which he could not quite conceal. I thought it proper to state in the offset (not knowing what the Senator might have said) that I wished simply to know whatever he was free to tell me in regard to his own willingness to accept a renomination, and also as to the extent to which the Senator was authorized to speak for him. The reply was a monologue of an hour's duration, and one that wholly absorbed me, as it seemed to absorb himself. There was very little for me to say, and I was only too willing to listen.

He remained seated nearly all the time. He was restless, often changing position and occasionally, in some intense moment, wheeling his body around in his chair and throwing a leg over the arm. This was the only grotesque thing I recollect about him; his voice and manner were very earnest, and he uttered no jokes and told no anecdotes.

He began by saying that, as yet, he was not a candidate for renomination. He distinctly denied that he was a party to any effort to that end, notwithstanding I knew that there were movements in his favor in all parts of the Northern States. These movements were, of course, without his prompting, as he positively assured me that with one or two exceptions he had scarcely conversed on the subject with his most intimate friends.

He was not quite sure whether he desired a renomination. Such had been the responsibility of the office—so oppressive had he found its cares, so terrible its perplexities—that he felt as though the moment when he could relinquish the burden and retire to private life would be the sweetest he could possibly experience.

But, he said, he would not deny that a reëlection would also have its gratification to his feelings. He did not seek it, nor would he do so; he did not desire it for any ambitious or selfish purpose; but, after the crisis the country was passing through under his Presidency, and the efforts he had made conscientiously to discharge the duties imposed upon him, it would be a very sweet satisfaction to him to know that he had secured the approval of his fellow citizens and earned the highest testimonial of confidence they could bestow.

This was the gist of the hour's monologue; and I believe he spoke sincerely. His voice, his manner, armed his modest and sensible words with a power of conviction. He seldom looked me in the face while he was talking; he seemed almost to be gazing into the future. I am sure it was not a pleasant thing for him to be speaking in his own interest.

He furthermore assured me that the Senator had his full confidence, and that he should respect any proper promises the latter might make. For himself, he affirmed (gratuitously, for I had not said anything to lead in that direction) that he should make no promises of office to anyone, as an inducement for support. If nominated and elected, he should be grateful to his friends, and consider that they had claims on him; but the interest of the country must always be first considered. Meantime, he supposed he should be a candidate; things seemed to be working in that direction; and if I could assist him and his friend the Senator in my State, he should not fail to remember the service with gratitude.

This was a different picture from that of Lincoln sitting still, doing nothing, preserving a look of calm while political factions raged and threatened to pull him down; that picture did go with his dominant mood. But Lincoln held no mood fixed and frozen. His eye caught light and shadow, color and mass, in the flow and heave of a reality he termed Public Opinion. His moods ranged with those of the People in a democracy that in spite of war kept a wide measure of freedom in personal expression.

Conscience and expediency told him, rightly or wrongly, for weal or woe, that he himself in justice should continue to be the instrument of the American people to finish the war, and if it might be, to bind up the wounds and heal the scars without malice. Anxiety weighed him down in these moods. Deep gongs rang. He referred to himself as well as Chase, Frémont, and Butler in the remark that J. Russell Jones, Provost Marshal

General James Fry, and Congressman John Kasson said they heard from him as to the desire to be President: "No man knows what that gnawing is till he has had it."

Without a doubt, too, Lincoln felt a loyalty due from him to people who trusted him, who saw logic and sense in what he was doing, who were afraid to try some other man as President. It was to them Lincoln's Government and army that held the boys and men from so many homes. Father Abraham was not merely a nickname. He cared. They trusted him as he trusted them. There was this kinship between him and a certain legion of loyalists. He seemed to reason that if they wanted him to go on as President they would have their way—and if they didn't want him, he could stand that if they could.

He heard from his legion often, once in March of '64 when the *Chicago Tribune* carried an editorial paragraph: "A sturdy farmer from Oskaloosa, Iowa, one of the bone and sinew class, called upon us yesterday in relation to business matters. Before leaving, we asked him how Mr. Lincoln stood in Iowa. 'Stands?' said the old farmer, with glistening eyes and raising his brawny fist, 'Old Abe stands seventeen feet higher in Iowa than any other man in the United States!'"

A like enthusiasm was found by a *Cincinnati Gazette* writer who in February interviewed John Bright. He quoted this leading English liberal as saying that the re-election of Lincoln would be the hardest blow the North could inflict on the South that year. Bright refused to worry over what he heard of Lincoln as too slow, though he believed a change of Cabinet should be demanded, adding, "Mr. Lincoln is like a waiter in a large eating house where all the bells are ringing at once; he cannot serve them all at once, and so some grumblers are to be expected."

Other newspapers besides the *National Intelligencer* at Washington reprinted a letter signed by G. C. Eisenmeyer of Mascoutah, St. Clair County, Illinois, saying his "first, second and third choice for President at the coming election" would be Abraham Lincoln. "This letter is running the rounds, and is quite the talk," wrote Bates in his diary of March 19. "This letter of Mr. Eisenmeyer proves that the extreme Radicals cannot control all the Germans."

Mrs. John A. Logan heard an old farmer in Illinois: "There ain't no one else and there never was anyone jest like Abe Lincoln." Others who had never seen nor heard Lincoln agreed with the old farmer who had. Senator John Sherman's allusion to Lincoln as "one of the kindest and honestest men the world affords" was given to his Ohio audience partly because the Senator knew they wanted to hear just that. The opposition caricatures of Lincoln interested many Americans also careless as to looks and manners. They brought up Lincoln's droll stories, made him out a joker, because they hoped it was an almost universal rule, as Tom Corwin said, that only the solemn ass could succeed in politics.

In February of '64 the *New York Herald* in satirically excessive compliments meant to carry barbs: "As a joker Mr. Lincoln is unique. With the caustic wit of Diogenes he combines the best qualities of all the other celebrated jokers of the world. He is more poetical than Horace, more spicy than Juvenal, more anecdotal than Aesop, more juicy than Boccaccio, more mellow than rollicking Rabelais, and more often quoted than the veteran Joe Miller." The idea was that a clown ran the Government.

More justly than the *Herald*, the *New York Evening Post* served Lincoln in April by printing on page one a column and more of Lincoln stories and anecdotes. They rendered none of Lincoln's ease in dialect and of course could not carry his personal mimicry and facial mobility. They included one fable till then little known, of a distinguished New York official at the White House bringing up the subject of emancipation and Lincoln responding: "Well, we have got to be mighty cautious how we manage negro questions. If we are not, we'll be like the barber out in Illinois who shaved a fellow with a hatchet face and lantern jaws like mine. The barber put his finger in the customer's mouth to make his cheek stick out. While shaving away he cut through the fellow's cheek and cut his own finger off. If we aren't smart about negro questions, we'll do as the barber did."

The comic element of Lincoln may have drawn to him those who truly valued laughter. Still others preferred less of his humor and discounted or forgot it in the flow of his solemn messages voicing grief, hope, and assurance. Not yet was there a photograph of a smiling Lincoln. A face "woebegone" the Quaker boy, Sergeant Stradling, saw at the White House and saw again in waking moments between sleeps at night for months afterward.

While the army had its quota always of deserters, stragglers, and malingerers, the mass of sentiment there plainly favored "Old Abe." The surest and quickest way for all to get out of the war was to fight it through under the "Father Abraham" in the White House. Thousands of soldier letters written home told this. Letters of protest and murmuring were few in comparison. Their army was the little end of nothing unless their President was something. It was the country's election of "Old Abe" that had "started the fuss."

A veteran on furlough spoke in Chicago on whether the soldiers wanted Lincoln re-elected. He cocked his eyes with a reckless glint: "Why, of course they do. We all re-enlisted to see this thing through, and Old Abe must re-enlist too. He mustered us in and we'll be damned if he shan't stay where he is until he has mustered us out. We'll never give up till every rebel acknowledges he is the Constitutional President. When they got beat at the election they kicked out of the traces and swore they would not submit to a black Republican President. But by hell they have got to. We will show them that elections in this country have got to stand. Old Abe must stay in the White House until every rebel climbs down and agrees to obey the laws of his country. I don't give a cuss for this country if the beaten side has a right to bolt after an election; it would not be fit to live in."

The Lincoln mass sentiment over the country that puzzled trained metropolitan political observers' centers rested partly on country editors. They walked Main Street and talked personally with their readers. The country editor had local pressure on his self-respect. Usually his paper was him and he was his paper. Readers told him face to face on Main Street or at the post office or in his sanctum sanctorum whether his editorials were grand or rotten. He often talked off his editorials before he wrote them, which was not so easy if he was up to some skulduggery.

Ohio, Indiana, Illinois, were spotted with earnest country editors who each week nearly busted their buttons telling the world Lincoln was a tyrant and a cornucopia of folly. They were outnumbered by equally earnest country editors who threatened them with jail and the gallows. In general, the tall-grass weeklies argued the same points the editor covered while sitting with neighbors and townsmen around a hot stove in a grocery post office.

One of these country weeklies, the *Lansing* (Michigan) *State Republican*, on February 10 of '64 in a long editorial presented the case for Lincoln's re-election more keenly and vividly than any of the metropolitan dailies. Its editor, I. M. Cravath, knew his politics and the Midwest American people. Cravath and his country paper were a sign that rural America was wiser to Lincoln's drift than many of the garrulous sophisticates of the big cities. The American people could not do better than to re-elect Abraham Lincoln for the next four years, urged Cravath. He would be an "unselfish" President, the whole country controlling him. In that respect Lincoln grouped with Washington, Jefferson, and John Quincy Adams, being no party hack like Van Buren, Fillmore, Pierce, and Buchanan.

Would he be a "safe" President? Yes, for he had stuck to Halleck, Stanton, Seward, Chase, against clamor of enemies and friends "with pertinacity, we might almost say obstinacy." No theorizer, the President had offered a plan of reconstruction when called on and then served public notice that he would drop the plan when a better one came in sight. Not a professional politician, no man's creature—the masses of the people would give him "confidence and enthusiasm growing out of his personal history as one of the toiling millions of the nation." Men long in politics "do not thereby become any better men," and when the people find a man they can trust, "they will voluntarily give to him a warmth of personal attachment, and a degree of respect and veneration not attained by political measures or artful courting of the people." Finally, Lincoln should have a chance to carry out policies he had already begun. His career of eight years in the Executive chair would make a chapter of history honorable to any nation. "We hope to live long enough to see this result."

Four months earlier Editor Cravath had urged that Lincoln's "mild and moderate course" had advantages over "a stern and severe one." Why should Lincoln imitate Napoleon or Jackson? It would not do. "He is not Jackson nor Napoleon, but Lincoln, a very different person; and by no force of resolution on his part can he transform Lincoln into either of those eminent persons. By taking this common sense view of things, the President has succeeded largely in the vast undertakings before him."

Cravath and his little one-horse weekly paper out in the tall grass had not been fooled by the Congressmen and Senators of his own State, nor by the adroit and miasmic *Detroit Free Press*, nor by any of the politicians and journals that wished to high heaven they could get Lincoln out of the White House. Never having seen Lincoln nor accepted the general small talk about Lincoln, Cravath had judged his President by letters, speeches, acts, decisions—not merely reading but studying and weighing the President's papers and the main important, undeniable facts of his life. This country editor, like others, had come to be somewhat haunted by the sad, scrawny, intricate character who sat at the helm in the storm center in Washington.

Cravath spoke for those readers Lincoln had meant to reach with words, the editor writing: "Mr. Lincoln is the only President we have ever had who may be said to be from the working class of people. . . . No other President has ever worked with his hands for a livelihood after arriving at the full maturity of manhood. This familiarity with the pursuits and feeling of the great laboring class of his countrymen, has doubtless given him some advantages in conducting public affairs . . . has made his style of writing and speaking unlike that of any other President. His messages and letters abound with Saxon words and phrases, to the exclusion, in a great degree of those of Latin origin. The Saxon words, being in common use, and mostly of one syllable, Mr. Lincoln's style is plain, simple, blunt, forcible, emphatic, direct, easily understood, and carries the conviction to the mind of the reader that he means just that thing which he says, and nothing else. Hence the public letters he has written have raised him in general esteem, because the public find therein good sense and earnest patriotism, put into plain words, which cannot be tortured into any doubtful or overt meaning."

This country editor was sure the people took to heart "the good morals of the President, his evident respect for the institutions of religion, his freedom from all appearances of aristocracy and haughtiness, his readiness, on all occasions, to sympathize with the condition of those who toil for their daily bread." From this foundation the President's popularity had been built up by intellect and will—"a strong good sense, which seems to seize everything by the right handle, at the right time and place, and drive it as fast as is expedient, and no faster: and an iron purpose which waits calmly and patiently, because it knows it will not wait in vain."

Cravath far out on the rolling prairies between Lakes Huron and Michigan, like John Bigelow across the Atlantic in the Paris consulate, sometimes knew more about what was going on under the crazy surface patterns in Washington than many of the free-going commentators in the national capital. A writer on the London *Spectator* from month to month solved Lincoln's motives and intentions more definitely than any member of Lincoln's Cabinet. The London journalist and the country editor in

Lansing, Michigan, as distant spectators, each in his own way read Lincoln as a wizard and a prophet. Cravath wrote:

Whatever deficiencies the President may have in some directions, he seems to have something of that prescience of the future, with which minds of the highest class are often gifted. Such minds, by the study of great principles, obtain a sort of calcium light, which throws its illumination far into the distant future, revealing the forms of things in their shadowy and undefined shape, which are not yet, but are to be! Having thus seen them, they have faith in their reality; and though days, months and years pass away, and all things seem to remain as they were, the prophet waits patiently for the coming events: for he knows that it is on its way, every day assuming more distinct and well defined features, until it finally emerges from the dim twilight of the Future, steps on the stage of human action, before all mankind, under the broad sunlight of the Present, as an actual fact; and then continues its line of march, again to become shadowy and indistinct, in the interminable realms of the Past. Minds which can thus see the march of events, do not waste their energies in vain wishes that they might come, or in murmurs and imprecations that they are so long in coming: but their faith makes the future a present reality: and they "learn to labor and to wait."

To a mass of people for whom this Michigan country editor spoke had come a feeling of mystic and heroic quality in Lincoln. This wove with another feeling: In the chaos of events whoever was to run the government would have to be taken on trust; the confusions were too intricate for any President to make himself clear on all he was doing. These feelings ran deep and sure in the Northwest region whose troops had a record of capturing and destroying Southern armies, the section that had supplied Grant and Sherman—and Lincoln—to the country.

Rural editors and Midwest farmers arrived at the same judgments as James Russell Lowell in Boston, who read stacks of books, newspapers, and magazines, and attended sessions of the Saturday Club. All of this pleased little Harriet Beecher Stowe. With intensified interest in slavery new millions of readers took up her *Uncle Tom's Cabin.* Mrs. Chesnut in South Carolina read it a second time. Russian editions of her novel reached the Caucasus Mountains, the steppes of Tartary. Perhaps the second best-known American over the world, next only to Lincoln, was this little woman who in Cincinnati used to sew her own dresses and mend for the family. Perhaps she was close to what was called the People. She might understand why the people could see Lincoln and partisan politicians and metropolitan editors fail. A frail craft on tidal waves of emotion, having words for what moved her, she wrote for the January number of the *Watchman and Reflector* of Boston, with flow and stride, reckless of adjectives and comparisons:

The world has seen and wondered at the greatest sign and marvel of our day, to-wit, a plain working man of the people, with no more culture, instruction or education than any such workingman may obtain for himself, called on to conduct the passage of a great people through a crisis involving the destinies of the whole world. The eyes of princes, nobles, aristocrats, of dukes, earls, scholars, statesmen, warriors, all turned on the plain backwoodsman, with his simple sense, his imperturbable simplicity, his determined self-reliance, his impracticable and incorruptible honesty, as he sat amid the war of conflicting elements with unpretending steadiness, striving to guide the national ship through a channel at whose perils the world's oldest statesmen stood aghast.

She had something to write about and was sure of it. She wrote on:

The brilliant courts of Europe levelled their opera glasses at the phenomenon. Fair ladies saw that he had horny hands and disdained white gloves. Dapper diplomatists were shocked at his system of etiquette, but old statesmen, who knew the terrors of that passage, were wiser than court ladies and dandy diplomatists, and watched him with fearful curiosity, simply asking "Will that awkward old backwoodsman really get that ship through? If he does, it will be time for us to look about us."

Sooth to say, our own politicians were somewhat shocked with his state papers at first. Why not let us make them a little more conventional and file them to a classic pattern? "No" was his reply, "I shall write them myself. The people will understand them." "But this or that form of expression is not elegant, not classical." "The people will understand it," has been his invariable reply.

And whatever may be said of his State papers as compared with the classic standards, it has been a fact that they have always been wonderfully well understood by the people, and that since the time of Washington, the state papers of no President have more controlled the popular mind. And one reason for this is, that they have been informal and undiplomatic. They have more resembled a father's talks to his children than a state paper. And they have had the relish and smack of the soil that appeal to the simple human heart and head which is greater power in writing than the most artful devices of rhetoric.

Lincoln might well say with the apostle, "But though I be rude in speech yet not in knowledge, but we have been thoroughly made manifest among you in all things." His rejection of what is called fine writing was as deliberate as St. Paul's, and for the same reason—because he felt that he was speaking on a subject which must be made clear to the lowest intellect, though it should fail to captivate the highest.

But we say of Lincoln's writing, that for all true, manly purposes of writing, there are passages in his state papers that could not be better put—they are absolutely perfect. They are brief, condensed, intense, and with a power of insight and expression which make them worthy to be inscribed in letters of gold. Such are some passages of the celebrated Springfield letter, especially that masterly one where he compares the conduct of the patriotic and loyal blacks with that of the treacherous and disloyal whites. No one can read this letter without feeling the influence of a mind both strong and generous.

Lincoln's strength is of a peculiar kind; it is not aggressive so much as passive, and among passive things it is like the strength not so much of a stone buttress, as of a wire cable. It is strength swaying to every influence, yielding on this side and on that to popular needs, yet tenaciously and inflexibly bound to carry its great end; and probably by no other kind of strength could our national ship have been drawn safely thus far during the tossings and tempests which beset her way.

Surrounded by all sorts of conflicting claims, by traitors, by half-hearted, timid men, by Border State men and free State men, by radical Abolitionists and Conservatives, he has listened to all, weighed the words of all, waited, observed, yielded now here and now there, but in the main kept one inflexible, honest purpose, and drawn the national ship through.

Mrs. Stowe joined the Iowa farmer who horselaughed that Lincoln stood "about seventeen feet higher" in his State than any other man in the United States. In January when Mrs. Stowe flung these flowers of approval, Judge David Davis, practical in politics and solid in money matters, making his home in Washington, his ear to the winds of gossip and change, wrote to a brother-in-law in Massachusetts: "The politicians in and out of Congress, it is the current belief, would put Mr. Lincoln aside if they dared. They know their constituents don't back them, and hence they gamble rather than make open war."

Seeing itself in a losing contest to nominate General Grant, the *New York Herald* crawfished. "Mr. Lincoln will be the regular nominee of his party. He is in the field and has the reins of the party in his hand. He will enter the canvass as the embodiment of all the blunders, follies, and corruptions of his administration." Under one banner he would have to rally Phillips, Greeley, Seward, and Frémont. "With this precious freight the great jester will push out into the political current as proudly as when in earlier days he strode an Ohio flatboat freighted with his Lares and Penates and a bountiful supply of hog and hominy." Funny was this, but not entirely funny, as the anonymous scribe of the *Herald* knew when he wrote it before stepping out for a toddy at the Astor House bar and a walk along Broadway in the madding throng.

Henry C. Work of Chicago, whose words and tunes for campaigning soldiers and home folks rivaled those from George F. Root of Chicago, added another song to his "Kingdom Coming," "Wake, Nicodemus," "Corporal Schnapps," "Columbia's Guardian Angels," "God Save the Nation," "Little Major." This new piece Work titled "Washington and Lincoln." One gave the country independence, the other saved the Union and set a people free, said the song. The lines were flamboyant. The cohorts of August Belmont and the *New York World* frowned at it. To them it was flapdoodle. Yet the song strode. Anybody in its way might be shot at sunrise. Anonymous and clever satirists shriveled before it. Lincoln had the best-selling song-writers with him.

> Down thro' the ages an anthem shall go,
> Bearing the honors we gladly bestow—
> Till every nation and language shall know
> The story of Washington and Lincoln.

As poetry it was so-so. As the offering of Henry C. Work, among greatest of popular song-writers, it had import. Crusader Work believed the people wanted a song lifting Lincoln alongside the one American historic character whose fame had a whited sanctity beyond challenge or murmur.

Francis Bicknell Carpenter, portrait-painter, like Henry C. Work had a public, and wished to give his public a momentous historic setting for Lincoln. Carpenter's idea of painting Lincoln came in a vision and with voices. Efforts of Lincoln to free the slaves Carpenter likened to the combat of the Angel Michael against Satan, a fitting subject for a masterpiece of art. The Western Continent had witnessed ninety years before "the immaculate conception of Constitutional Liberty," so Carpenter dreamed, and now a voice came to him saying: "Behold how a Man may be exalted to a dignity and glory almost divine, and give freedom to a race. Surely Art should unite with Eloquence and Poetry to celebrate such a theme."

A rich lawyer friend assured Carpenter a six months' income for work on his vision. Carpenter sent a Washington friend to interest Speaker Colfax and Congressman Lovejoy. They called on the President and talked long about art's serving political ends, the President listening patiently and at last: "In short, if I understand you, you wish me to consent to sit to this artist for the picture?" Yes, said Colfax and Lovejoy. And Carpenter a few days later came to the White House with a letter of introduction from Lovejoy, but could not get to see Lincoln. The next day it was the same. And, as he wrote:

> The following morning passed with the same result, and I then resolved to avail myself of Mrs. Lincoln's Saturday afternoon reception—at which, I was told, the President would be present—to make myself known to him. Two o'clock found me one of the throng pressing toward the centre of attraction, the "blue" room. From the threshold of the "crimson" parlor as I passed, I had a glimpse of the gaunt figure of Mr. Lincoln in the distance, haggard-looking, dressed in black, relieved only by the prescribed white gloves; standing, it seemed to me, solitary and alone, though surrounded by the crowd, bending low now and then in the process of handshaking, and responding half abstractedly to the well-meant greetings of the miscellaneous assemblage.
>
> Never shall I forget the electric thrill which went through my whole being at this instant. I seemed to see lines radiating from every part of the globe, converging to a focus at the point where that plain, awkward-looking man stood, and to hear in spirit a million prayers, "as the sound of many waters," ascending in his behalf. Mingled with supplication I could discern a clear symphony of triumph and blessing, swelling with an ever-increasing volume. It was the voice of those who had been bondmen and bondwomen, and the grand diapason swept up from the coming ages.

Carpenter moved along with the other handshakers till it was his turn. His name and profession were spoken to the President by an assistant private secretary. "Retaining my hand, he looked at me inquiringly for an instant, and said, 'Oh yes; I know; this is the painter.' Then straightening himself to his full height, with a twinkle of the eye, he added, playfully, 'Do you think, Mr. C——, that you can make a handsome picture of *me?*' emphasizing strongly the last word. Somewhat confused at this point-blank shot, uttered in a tone so loud as to attract the attention of those in immediate proximity, I made a random reply, and took the occasion to ask if I could see him in his study at the close of the reception. To this he responded in the peculiar vernacular of the West, 'I reckon.'"

At the appointed hour the President sat digging into bills passed by Congress and signing them. He gave Carpenter a chair, read Lovejoy's note of introduction, took off his spectacles. "Well, Mr. Carpenter, we will turn you loose in here, and try to give you a good chance to work out your idea." In the painting the Cabinet members were to be seated and standing around the President seated at a table, in their midst at the exact center of the design that world-famous parchment, the Emancipation Proclamation. This was the idea Carpenter outlined.

Without paying much attention to the overrunning enthusiasm of the painter, Lincoln went ahead with a short-spoken story of how the proclamation was issued: "It had got to be midsummer, 1862. Things had gone on from bad to worse, until I felt that we had reached the end of our rope on the plan of operations we had been pursuing; that we had about played our last card, and must change our tactics or lose the game!" How it was delayed, slightly revised, and finally issued, he told, and "As nearly as I remember, I sat near the head of the table; the Secretary of the Treasury and the Secretary of War were here, at my right hand; the others were grouped at the left."

Carpenter brought out a pencil sketch, said there would be no tricks nor appliances in the picture. Persons, room, furniture, accessories, were to be painted as "realistic." In a scene second only in historic interest to the signing of the Declaration of Independence he had "no more right to depart from the facts, than has the historian." When Carpenter went away and met friends who said the picture would be too plain, he replied that it was to center on "the immortal document,—its anxious author, conscious of his solemn responsibility, announcing his matured and inflexible purpose to his assembled councillors," listening "with unparalleled eagerness to the momentous sentences uttered for the first time in the ears of men . . . the issues involved:—the salvation of the Republic—the freedom of a Race."

The thirty-seven-year-old painter was given the run of the White House, assigned the state dining-room with its big chandeliers for lighting his night work, which sometimes lasted till daylight. Carpenter sat with his sketchbook in the President's office, worried visitors hearing from the President, "He is but a painter." At Cabinet meetings Carpenter sketched, the President having explained, "He has an idea of painting a picture of us all together." This started talk about art. Mention of the sculptor Jones, who had done a Lincoln bust, drew from Lincoln a trifling anecdote he had from Jones. It was about the final sitting of General Scott for Jones, who worked hard on just the face. The General was not satisfied in the finish with Jones's point that he had been working on "the details of the face." "Details?" cried old Fuss and Feathers. "Damn the details! Why, my man, you are spoiling the bust!"

Seward worried Carpenter by remarking, "I told the President the other day that you were painting your picture upon a false presumption." To Carpenter's surprise Seward went ahead to say that slavery was rung out when Lincoln was elected President; the subject for a painting should be the Cabinet meeting when the news of the firing on Fort Sumter came; that was the crisis. "If I am to be remembered," Seward went on with more excitement than pleased Carpenter . . . "let it not be as having loved predominantly white men or black men, but as one who loved his country."

Nathaniel Hawthorne   Wendell Phillips

Mr. and Mrs. Gerrit Smith

From the Barrett collection

The chamber of the United States House of Representatives

Engraving from the Barrett collection

Schuyler Colfax, Speaker of the House

Chauncey Mitchell Depew

From the Meserve collection

Carpenter argued that slavery was the cause and root of the war and no act compared with emancipation. "Well," said Seward, "you think so, and this generation may agree with you; but posterity will hold a different opinion."

Seward explained on another day that no great man should be put on a horse as in equestrian statues; it was all wrong; the horse always got the best of it and degraded the man. Bates too had views on art for Carpenter, and was sarcastic about sculpture around the Capitol, especially the rearing and snorting wonder horse on which Andrew Jackson sat across from the White House. "Genius conceives; talent executes," said Bates.

Carpenter learned that the speech of the President receiving a foreign Minister was carefully written by the Secretary of State. Such a text was handed the President one day when a half-dozen Senators and Congressmen sat around on chairs and sofas. The clerk in a low voice: "The Secretary has sent the speech you are to make to-day to the Swiss minister." Lincoln laid down a pen, took the manuscript: "Oh, this is a speech Mr. Seward has written for me, is it? I guess I will try it before these gentlemen, and see how it goes." He read it with waggery and ended: "There, I like that. It has the merit of *originality*."

Lincoln led George Thompson, the English antislavery commoner, down to see Carpenter's picture one day, saying in a joking way that Thompson understood: "Your folks made rather sad work of this mansion when they came up the Potomac in 1812. Nothing was left of it but the bare walls."

More than once Carpenter walked the streets of Washington late at night with Lincoln, no escort or guard, walking all the way going and returning. In the temporary studio of sculptor Swayne in the Treasury Building, Lincoln sat for a bust, replying to a query from Swayne that he did not write the verses "Why Should the Spirit of Mortal Be Proud?" though they were often signed with his name. When Carpenter asked for it Lincoln recited the poem. On the way to Swayne's studio Carpenter gave the President a *New York Tribune* account, from a correspondent within the Confederate lines, of an elaborate conspiracy worked out in Richmond to kidnap the President, or if kidnapping failed to assassinate him. An organization, the story ran, of five hundred or a thousand men, had been sworn to put through the business.

Lincoln had not seen nor heard of this story, and asked for the details, which Carpenter gave him. He smiled as though he could not believe it, noted Carpenter, and commented: "Well, even if true, I do not see what the Rebels would gain by killing or getting possession of me. I am but a single individual, and it would not help their cause or make the least difference in the progress of the war. Everything would go right on just the same." Ever since his nomination at Chicago the regular installment of threats came in the week's mail, and they no longer bothered him, he informed Carpenter. This surprised him, said the young painter. "Oh," said Lincoln, "there is nothing like getting *used* to things!"

On the evening of the day Lincoln reviewed Burnside's corps, Governor

Curtin came with a friend to the President's office. And in their talk Curtin referred to the volunteer citizen soldier as "worthy of profound respect." Lincoln gave quiet assent, Carpenter noting a "peculiar dreaminess" creep over his face, as if he could not find words should he try to speak his heart.

Carpenter mentioned a story that had gone the rounds of the newspapers a year or two earlier about the President's convening the State governors at the White House, and presenting grave conditions to them. Curtin, ran the story, stood at a window gazing out and drumming on the window glass. Lincoln broke silence with, "Andy, what is Pennsylvania going to do?" Curtin replied, "She is going to send twenty thousand men to start with, and will double it, if necessary."

As Carpenter repeated this press item both Lincoln and Curtin shook their heads, and Lincoln said: "It is a pity to spoil so good a story but, unfortunately, there is not a word of truth in it. I believe the only convocation of Governors that has taken place during the war was that at Altoona—was it not?"

Later in the evening Lincoln and Curtin went downstairs and looked at Carpenter's painting. On a table edge under the chandelier in the state dining-room, Lincoln sat swinging his legs, running his hand through his hair, half-listening while Carpenter explained the picture, then adding: "You see, Curtin, I was brought to the conclusion that there was no dodging this negro question any longer. We had reached the point where it seemed we must avail ourselves of this element, or in all probability go under." Then he gave the story of the Emancipation Proclamation much as he had given it to Carpenter the first time, also meeting Curtin's remark on the impression in some quarters that Seward had opposed the proclamation with the statement that Seward had merely advised postponement till a battle had been won.

Carpenter made himself at home in the White House, kept busy on his big painting, saw the President and Cabinet on and off parade. He told Lincoln of odd happenings and Lincoln replied with stories, none of which seemed dirty to the conventional Carpenter. Carpenter repeated Lincoln stories, correcting spots in the Lincoln vocabulary at times, making the words nicer. Where Lincoln said "skunks" or "polecats" in a story, Carpenter, in retelling it, said "those little black and white spotted animals which it is not necessary to name."

On one of their walks they talked about penalties great men pay for being great. Lincoln drifted into telling of how old Tom Ewing in President Taylor's Cabinet had the nickname "Old Solitude." And Daniel Webster at an evening party saw Ewing heave into view, and feeling good about it, Webster in his deepest bass tones recited well-known lines:

O Solitude, where are the charms
That sages have seen in thy face?

At a regular Cabinet meeting Carpenter was present and saw Judge Bates come in first and take a package out of his pocket, saying, "You may not be aware, Mr. President, that you have a formidable rival in the field." And Bates unfolded a placard from the morning mail, an announcement in large letters: "I introduce for President of the United States, Mr. T. W. Smith of Philadelphia," reciting in further large black print the merits of a candidate nobody ever heard of, all of it signed "George Bates" as though somebody might have heard of him too. Pinned on a wall of the Cabinet room, this announcement of the unknown Smith endorsed by the unknown Bates, for several days gave merriment.

While Carpenter wrestled with his work of art the *New York Herald* and other newspapers printed a story that Mrs. Lincoln came in one day to watch him with his paints and brushes and saluted him, "Well, Mr. Carpenter, how are you getting along with your happy family?"

Carpenter had been hearing that Republican-party leaders believed Lincoln's chances for renomination "somewhat dubious." The painter sensed a slight aroma of this in the atmosphere one evening:

I dined with Mr. Chase, the Secretary of the Treasury, of whom I painted a portrait in 1855, upon the close of his term as United States Senator. He said during the dinner, that, shortly after the dedication of the cemetery at Gettysburg, the President told this story at a cabinet meeting. "Thad. Stevens was asked by someone, the morning of the day appointed for that ceremony, where the President and Mr. Seward were going. 'To Gettysburg,' was the reply. 'But where are Stanton and Chase?' continued the questioner. 'At home, at work,' was the surly answer; 'let the dead bury the dead.'"

Carpenter in February called on Lovejoy, saw him sit up and take nourishment, saying he was better, not knowing he had only three months to live. Lovejoy saw the Frémont movement against Lincoln would divide the party, thought it "criminal." Carpenter said he had noticed many extreme antislavery men seemed to distrust the President. And Lovejoy, though his once magnificent physical frame was nearly used up, burned with a loyalty to the President, and according to Carpenter, his words ran: "I tell you, Mr. Lincoln is at heart as strong an anti-slavery man as any of them, but he is compelled to *feel* his way. He has a responsibility in this matter which many men do not seem to be able to comprehend. I say to you frankly, that I believe his course to be right. His mind acts slowly, but when he moves, it is *forward*. You will never find him receding from a position once taken. It is of no use talking, or getting up conventions against him. He is going to be the candidate and is sure to be reëlected. 'It was foreordained from the foundation of the world.' I have no sympathy or patience with those who are trying to manufacture issues against him; but they will not succeed; he is too strong with the masses. For my part, I am not only willing to take Mr. Lincoln for another term, but the same cabinet, right straight through."

Twenty-seven years had passed since Owen Lovejoy shook with grief over the mob that came with torches and guns on the night they shot and killed his brother Elijah, an abolitionist agitator allied with William Lloyd Garrison. Since then Lincoln, Garrison, and Owen Lovejoy had moved in various spheres of action and out of it all the dying Lovejoy was writing in a letter to Garrison February 22, 1864, a judgment: "I write you, although ill-health compels me to do it by the hand of another, to express to you my gratification at the position you have taken in reference to Mr. Lincoln. I am satisfied, as the old theologians used to say in reference to the world, that if he is not the best conceivable President he is the best possible. I have known something of the facts inside during his Administration, and I know that he has been just as radical as any of his cabinet. And although he does not do everything that you and I would like, the question recurs, whether it is likely we can elect a man who would. It is evident that the great mass of Unionists prefer him for reëlection; and it seems to me certain that the Providence of God, during another term, will grind slavery to powder. I believe now that the President is up with the average of the House."

CHAPTER 48

CASH FOR WAR—ALMADEN—HARD TIMES

THE Union Government was spending easily more than $2,000,000 a day for the war. Chase had reason to say that while the other departments stood at the spigots he had to worry about the barrel. Lincoln met the wishes of Chase in many delicate particulars of appointments, arrangements, measures, that would bring in the cash to keep the war going. He had let Chase keep one Buchanan Democrat as an assistant on Chase's word that the man knew how to run the office, and had let Chase keep another Buchanan Democrat as Treasury head in New York because financial influences which Chase considered important in New York wanted the man kept in office.

A curious annex to the Treasury Department arose in offices across the street from the Treasury Building where Jay Cooke & Company hung up their sign. In January of '64 this company finished the selling of $513,000,-000 worth of United States bonds, the issue being oversubscribed, so that Congress had to act in order to legalize the millions over the half-billion. The commission of Jay Cooke on these immense sales was ¼ of 1 per cent, out of which he paid the costs of a large sales force and advertising space in hundreds of newspapers. He had persistently refused offers of Chase to appoint him an Assistant Secretary of the Treasury, his title being merely United States Subscription Agent. What Robert Morris, the leading cash-provider for George Washington, had been in the dark days of the American Revolution, Jay Cooke was to this war for the Union, his friends were saying.

For more than a year the best arm and the chief reliance of Chase in raising money had been this Jay Cooke, who privately had no political ambitions for himself and in his selling campaigns praised Chase as the foremost financial genius of the age. Chase and his two daughters often visited Cooke's country mansion amid rolling wooded acres at Ogontz near Philadelphia; Cooke invested small funds of Chase where they paid handsome profits.

When Chase wanted a light one-horse coupé, he wrote to Cooke about it and Cooke took a day off in Philadelphia and found a nice coupé and sent it on to Chase, who drove in it once and then sent it back to Cooke with word that it wasn't quite what he needed. In letters to Chase, Cooke would sometimes get matters of public government business and private one-horse coupés mixed up, and as Chase did not care to have such correspondence on record in the Treasury files, he wrote Cooke please to commence all letters on public matters with "Sir," while "letters on private matters may be addressed dear Governor or dear friend, as you will, but let them contain nothing on public business and vice versa."

Cooke shared the changing moods of Chase as to his work and its relation to the President. In one mood on July 4 of '62 Chase wrote to Cooke of that anniversary day, "How sad the state in which it finds us!" and wrote further that he might have to make his way to a cottage on the Miami River in Ohio "and stay there." When the President revoked General Hunter's emancipation proclamation, Chase wrote to Cooke the kindliest judgment he had ever penned of Lincoln: "The President hates to be harsh even when harshness is deserved. He thinks too that it is wisest not to be harsh, and though I find it hard to acquiesce, yet I must say, I have always found his judgment wonderfully good." More often the Chase mood as to Lincoln ran as reported in a letter Jay Cooke received from his brother Henry, telling of a talk with Chase. Henry Cooke had found Chase annoyed that the President was "closeted all day" and had not consulted his Cabinet members on a message being prepared. "Governor C. says that Lincoln takes his own course in regard to military matters . . . the President is alone responsible or entitled to credit or blame . . . he is not willing to be held accountable for other people's blunders."

The disgust of Chase with the Administration policies cropped out concretely on May of '62 when he wrote to Jay Cooke his pleasure over the Cooke brothers having control of the horsecar street railway they had set going in Washington, with Chase as one of the stockholders. Chase had been telling himself he might be better satisfied as the head of the horsecar line than as head of the United States Treasury, writing to Jay Cooke, "I told Henry D. [Jay's brother] that I was strongly inclined to resign as Secretary and take the office of President of the company but believe I will hold out where I am, till I see my whole scheme of finance realized."

When Pope's broken army reeled back toward Washington after Second Bull Run, Henry Cooke wrote to Jay that it was the evil blundering of jealous generals. "The President should have put it down by a drumhead court martial and instantaneous shooting of all engaged in it . . . these too are Governor Chase's views. I spent nearly two hours with him last evening and we talked freely. He regards the prospect as full of doubt, gloom and uncertainty, and would not be surprised if the worst should happen."

The bond-selling campaigns of Cooke under Chase's authority satisfied Lincoln to the extent that he kept his hands off, seeing Cooke only two or three times during many months. Once was in the summer of '62, when Cooke said he believed "thousands of influential and patriotic men" wished McClellan's removal from command of the Army of the Potomac. "I found," wrote Cooke, "the subscriptions to the loans I had in charge rapidly falling off, so that finally with Mr. Chase's consent and desire, I went to Washington and with my brother, Henry D. Cooke, visited Mr. Lincoln with the design of showing him the absolute necessity of placing some more active and bold warrior in McClellan's place. Mr. Lincoln was at the Soldiers' Home and my brother and I drove out there. We found a large crowd of officers and civilians there paying calls and on business, and were requested by Mr. Lincoln to remain until these people had left for the evening, so it was past ten o'clock before we began our conference. Mr. Lincoln had his youngest son on his lap while we were talking. I began by reminding him that the sole charge of raising the vast sums daily required was committed to me, that I was not a politician, that I desired no office, but under God was trying to do my duty in aid of my country, and that now I came to him to plead for a change of commanders of the army . . . that I came direct from the people, and knew their thoughts, and especially had felt the pulse of finance, and feared with all my efforts a feeble response to my appeals, unless the gloom and doubt occasioned by McClellan's supineness and inactivity could be done away with. I impressed these views upon Mr. Lincoln earnestly and almost pleadingly, and have every reason to know that they accorded with his own; but Mr. Lincoln, it is well known, had a tender heart, and he hated to remove McClellan until satisfied that the people and circumstances compelled him." When within a week McClellan was removed from command, Jay Cooke wrote, "I think my interview and appeal were the immediate cause of Mr. Lincoln's prompt action."

Once Cooke had finished breakfast with Chase and they were at work in the library of the Chase home when a servant announced President Lincoln at the door in a carriage with Attorney-General Bates. The Secretary went out to the carriage and learned that Cabinet members and their ladies were going out that day to a drill review of 10,000 men seven miles beyond Georgetown. Chase begged to be excused, saying that Mr. Jay Cooke had come down from his Philadelphia office on important business.

Lincoln insisted on Chase's going and told him to bring Cooke along. As they rode across the country Cooke noticed the President enjoying the holiday. Cooke got to looking at Bates's head of black hair with white whiskers and mustache and said to Bates that his own father had been just like that, not a gray hair in his head but when he grew a beard it always came out white. Cooke said he wondered what was the philosophical and scientific explanation of the matter. And according to Cooke, Lincoln gave a quizzical look at Bates and said, "Oh, Mr. Cooke, that is easily accounted for."

"I shall be glad to know the reason."

"Well, it could hardly be otherwise. The cause is that he uses his jaws more than he does his brain."

Also, Cooke noted, "We all laughed heartily at this impromptu and original joke at Mr. Bates's expense and, as I gave the substance of it to some newspaper men the next day it was published far and wide as one of Lincoln's original sayings."

Breezy, ingenious, tenacious Jay Cooke was a phenomenon rising out of the American civilization taking shape from the war, a sign of bigger figures consolidated out of smaller ones, a token of the power of finance to control transportation and industry. When he needed a vacation he went fishing and duck-shooting, returning to his work and employing baits, decoys, traps, whenever necessary to bag the fish or game he sought. He was strict as a sober churchman in personal conduct, and rather than a gambler was a speculator with an eye for good risks. One of his direct ancestors, Henry Cooke, came over about 1638 and built one of the early houses in Plymouth, Massachusetts. His father, Eleutheros Cooke, had settled on the shores of Lake Erie when Chief Ogontz of the Wyandotte tribe had a village of his Indians there, Eleutheros Cooke building the first stone house in the new town of Sandusky, Ohio, practicing law, launching a railroad with horse-drawn cars, sitting in Congress at Washington, and never lacking fluency of speech. Eleutheros lost one election to Congress because so many of his constituents misspelled his first name when writing it on the ballot sheet. Young Jay sent many long letters to his father at Washington and with his uncle, Erastus Cooke, postmaster at Sandusky, waited many a time till midnight for the sound of the postman's horn saying at last the mail was arriving in spite of bad roads and deep snow. He read his father's speeches in the *Congressional Globe*, built a 16-inch-long steamboat propelled by power from an old clock spring, organized the Philo Literary Debating Society, took a hand in defending a Negro bootblack from the attacks of other debating-society members who said they could not allow a Negro to listen to their discussions.

Young Jay Cooke clerked in Mr. Hubbard's store, studied bookkeeping, began to see that in business a man must know how to add, subtract, multiply. In 1836 at fifteen years of age he traveled to St. Louis by the nearest route from Sandusky, Ohio, taking a stage to Cincinnati, a steamer to Louisville, another steamer to St. Louis, where he clerked in a store, shot a lot of quail, duck, partridge, possum, coons, practiced penmanship in a night school, learned to waltz at a French dancing school, and took lessons in French so that, as he said, "I could converse quite freely with the ladies who came to our store." He wrote to a brother that "the ladies are hard to deal with here, more so than at Sandusky," that the people were French (almost savages), Spanish, Italian, Mexican, Polish (all noblemen!), Indians, a set of gambling Southerners, and a few skinflint Yankees. "There is but few respectable persons in Saint Louis. It is dangerous to go out after dark, for persons are often knocked down at the corners of the streets and robbed and frequently killed." But he had fun, and once wrote of his dancing school, "Picture to yourself your brother Jay in a spacious ball-room with a beautiful French brunette by his side, skipping along and having fine times, hair dressed and all erect, talking Parley Voo with the beautiful creatures."

When the store crashed in the panic of 1837, young Jay Cooke went back to Sandusky, then to Philadelphia for a few months as passenger booking clerk for a packet line, then back to Sandusky, then to Philadelphia again, this time as a clerk, from which post he rose to be at twenty-one a partner and active manager of E. W. Clark & Company, the largest private banking house in the United States, with branches in four large cities. He married Dorothea Elizabeth Allen, the daughter of a Maryland planter and slaveowner, Richard Nun Allen; with long ringlets of hair, a white plume on her head, in a riding habit with three rows of buttons, she might have stepped out of a Gainsborough painting. She bore him two sons and two daughters.

When the house of E. W. Clark & Company crashed in the panic of 1857, Jay Cooke went in for railroad reorganization, joined up the best canals of Pennsylvania into one system, and went fishing and duck-shooting more than ever. In 1861 he had his own banking house in Philadelphia and introduced himself to the United States Treasury officials by sending on Federal loan subscriptions without compensation. Early that year he won national reputation and the gratitude of Governor Curtin of Pennsylvania by selling at par $3,000,000 in bonds issued by that State, which was almost bankrupt and was regularly cursed out in England as a repudiator of honest debts. Henry D. Cooke, Jay's brother, younger by three years, had done newspaper work on the West Coast, had been financial editor of the *Philadelphia North American* and the *United States Gazette*, later becoming owner of the *Ohio State Journal* at Columbus, where politically and socially he had been close to Governor Salmon Portland Chase and Congressman John Sherman, who had since become United States Senator.

Both Chase and Sherman knew that Jay Cooke at Philadelphia was meeting the deficits of the influential but nonprofitable *Ohio State Journal* which had befriended them. And after Chase took charge of the Treasury Department and Sherman became one of the Senate's specialists in financial measures, there were few big decisions touching Federal finance that the Cooke brothers did not know beforehand, early enough usually for them to anticipate any market fluctuations that might follow. To get past the military censorship of telegrams at Washington a cipher code operated between Washington and the Cooke bank in Philadelphia, one such as that of September 18, 1862—reading: "Sweeny applies for more. Decided change in market and cannot reply positively" meaning, "McClellan applies for help. Tremendous battle going on. Result undetermined." "Belmont" meant "Lincoln" in this cipher code, "discount" meant "retreat," and "will not be paid this week" meant "great loss on our side."

When rumors ran that the President would appoint Edward M. Davis, a Quaker and an abolitionist, Assistant Secretary of the Treasury, Jay Cooke sent a long memorandum for his brother's guidance in a talk with Chase. "I beg and implore the Gov. not to let any influence, however strong it may be, induce the President or himself to listen for a moment to this proposal." Both Lincoln and Chase were responsive to the advice of Jay Cooke transmitted through brother Henry: "I would advise Gov. Chase not to try too much to save the pennies but to keep on the right side of those capitalists who are disposed to dabble in the loans, etc., of the government, and if they do make sometimes a handsome margin it is no more than they are entitled to in such times as these. They can be very useful to the government. I repeat that the Governor should keep on the right side of the capitalists till he gets into smoother water."

Not long after this warning from Cooke the Associated Banks of New York had bought $50,000,000 in "seven-thirty" bonds, which paid $7.30 interest a year on each $100 bond, Chase's idea being that 2 cents a day for a year's loan of $100 would be "attractive." The bankers, however, served notice on Chase that they would expect the Lincoln Administration to be vigorous, honest, economical, and efficient—or it would get no more money. The *New York Herald* soon was saying that the President was not meeting the expectations of the bankers, that a delegation of the bankers had appeared in Washington making no secret of their errand of notifying the President that his management of the war had incurred their displeasure, and as they were paying the costs of it, they had come to recommend to him changes in his policy.

The Washington correspondent of the *Philadelphia Inquirer,* a Cooke organ, wrote, "The fact that these gentlemen represent the fifty million which the banks have subscribed to the national loan gives them no prescriptive right to obtrude their views upon the government." Congressman Kellogg of Illinois stood up to say he was pained to hear members talking about "the sacredness of capital" when the youth of the country was being sacrificed without a blush. "We have summoned the youth; they have come. I would summon the capital; and if it does not come voluntarily, before this republic shall go down or one star be lost I would take every cent from the treasury of the states, from the treasury of capitalists, from the treasury of individuals and press it into the use of the government."

Jay Cooke's plan was to go over the heads of the bankers and reach the small investors, the masses of people who could buy a $100 bond or more, the very ranks from which the bankers got their depositors. His drive got under way in the spring of 1863 to sell $500,000,000 of five-twenties, bonds paying 6 per cent interest for twenty years or redeemable in government gold within five years. He saw that New York City was taken care of by local agents who used their own names in advertising, in this way avoiding the New York jealousy of a Philadelphia house managing the loan. He sent out nine agents with assigned territory who traveled back and forth in every settled area west of the Allegheny Mountains, conferring with bankers, brokers, editors, distributing circulars, posting notices at post offices, courthouses, railroad stations, hotels, reading-rooms, on walls, telegraph poles, fences, trunks of trees. They used the Jay Cooke argument to let "our own people own the national debt."

The newspaper campaign of direct advertising, informative news accounts, and editorial comment on the five-twenty bonds that Jay Cooke set going was the most far-reaching, deliberately organized affair of the sort that America had ever seen. At one time eighteen hundred daily and weekly journals were printing paid advertising. Disloyal sheets that hated the Lincoln Administration and all its works could not bring themselves to hate Jay Cooke's cash to the extent of not printing live news, which he sent them fresh from the hands of his large staff of skilled writers. One observer regarded Jay Cooke as a well-proportioned hero who "subsidized" the press by a system, hired newspapers as Napoleon did. "Editors and publishers to whom patriotic considerations were without appeal were touched at a more vulnerable point, and thus practically the entire newspaper press of the loyal states responded to his masterly direction on financial questions."

Henry D. Cooke invited Washington correspondents to his handsome house in Georgetown for good food, drinks if wished for, and complete information on the five-twenties. From week to week and month to month the totals ran higher of bonds sold, and as the advertising campaign reached out into every nook and corner of the country, newspaper editors had more readers owning bonds, and what Jay Cooke did was live news to these many small bondholders. The earlier news accounts ran in this manner:

The principal office of Mr. Jay Cooke, the subscription agent, is in Philadelphia, with over one thousand five hundred correspondents in all of the principal towns and cities of the Union, who likewise receive subscriptions, and each of whom are responsible to their own customers. At the Philadelphia office Mr. Cooke employs upwards of thirty clerks. Upon our first visit to the office we were shown through the banking department to the 5:20 offices, where we found Mr. Cooke surrounded by his assistants, doing a business of over a million dollars a day.

Up to 11 o'clock that morning over one hundred letters had arrived with orders from $50 to $100,000. But most interesting of all to the correspondents were the personal subscriptions.

An old lady totters into the office, and with her money tied up in the corner of her handkerchief, wishes one of the bonds. She is shown into the back room and given a seat. The assistant receives her money, gives her a certificate, and she leaves, happy in the thought that her little pittance is not only safe but is earning her something.

Next comes a hale old farmer from Berks county, with his $5,000. He has heard of the loan; some of his neighbors have invested; he has read Mr. Cooke's letter, and he has concluded to put his money where he is not only sure of his interest, but he is aiding the Government—a double reason—he asks a great many questions, all of which are answered satisfactorily. The consequence of which is, he leaves his $5,000 and takes his certificate.

The telegraph bill ran over $40 a day. From the first weeks, when subscriptions varied from less to more than $1,000,000 a day, on into later weeks when the daily totals were from $2,000,000 to $6,000,000, the drive of Jay Cooke's vision and bustling energy spread out and animated the philosophy of the country. The *St. Louis Daily Evening News* editor wrote: "Money is the great power in war and will conquer at last, and he who contributes his money to aid his country in her hour of danger may thereby evince as much patriotism as he who marches to the battlefield. The widow's two mites hold more of goodness of heart than the rich gifts of those who cast in only of their abundance."

Foreign-language newspapers were brought in. They too published in German, Italian, Yiddish, Polish, advertisements explaining the five-twenty bonds and declaring them "a profitable mode of investment for Trust Funds, the surplus funds of capitalists, as well as the earnings of the industrial classes." First as a newspaper article and then in circular form in repeated editions there was published a farmer's and mechanic's catechism titled "The Best Way to Put Out Money at Interest," and then Jay Cooke's rousing oration committed to white paper, addressed "To Farmers, Mechanics, and Capitalists!" reading in part:

You have a solemn duty to perform to your government and to posterity!

Our gallant army and navy must be supported by every man and woman who has any means, large or small, at their control. The United States Government, to which we owe our prosperity as a nation, security of person and property of every sort, calls on each individual to rally to its support. . . .

What our Revolutionary Fathers are to us, WE will be to coming generations, if we fail not in our plain and simple duty!

The owner of every foot of ground, of every house and workshop, owes a debt of service in the field, of his means in this noble work!

Talk not of Taxes! they *secure* the Loans. Take the Loans! and the Taxes will fall more lightly—and they supply the ready, *present* and *required* means to strike the death blow at rebellion and the foul disturbers of the Nation's peace!

Talk not of Rulers! They are the ministers of GOD! who rules the world and the destiny of this mighty Nation! Our first duty is to God—our next to our country—fail not of either!

Your nearest patriotic Bank or Banker will supply this loan, on which so much depends!

See advertisement of first page. The Bonds are now ready for delivery at the office of Jay Cooke & Co., Bankers, No. 114 S. 3d St., Philadelphia, Pa.

Thus Jay Cooke—with Chase backing him and Lincoln backing Chase—put the impress of his personality on the country, outranking Greeley,

Beecher, and Barnum in his ability to get action from masses of people. His news-writers were quick to relay the information to editors that in the week after the Army of the Potomac took its heavy slaughter at Chancellorsville no less than $8,000,000 in bonds were bought. In one case a man came into Cooke's office, handed over $660 in cash, and was given bonds for it; he handed the bonds back and said he wanted the $660 sent on to the Treasury Department as a free gift to the Union; in a letter so declaring he signed himself "A War Democrat." Maryland, Kentucky, and Missouri subscriptions went into totals of millions. A single order from Kentucky was paid by $350,000 in gold, which at its current premium bought $500,000 in five-twenty bonds. An Indiana banker sent in $10,400 "from a Copperhead neighborhood" where he doubted a single Union man could be found among the buyers in that order. One newspaper article sent out from Jay Cooke's main office told of a day there:

A lady in Camden orders $300 and there is one from Saint Paul, Minnesota, for $12,500. Here lies one from Pottsville, Pennsylvania, for $1,000 and another from Pittsburgh for $75,000. Along comes a telegram from Norristown for $250 and close upon the messenger's heels comes another with a dispatch from New York for $250,-000. Near one of the desks is a nursery maid who wants a bond for $50 and just behind her placidly waiting his turn is a portly gentleman, one of the "solid men" of Philadelphia. He wants $25,000. . . . The people are at last alive to the value of the investment so long within their reach. They are now laying their treasure on the altar of their country with patriotic confidence and generous hands.

The tumbling river of cash flowing in to Jay Cooke, and from him to the Lincoln Government, for men, guns, horses, mules, hardtack, and beans to carry on the war, was possible partly because of the breezy, valiant, inextinguishable optimism of Jay Cooke as to his country. Behind a thousand phrasings that came from him lay his theory that the war was an incident, a minor circumstance, in a deep stream of economic events crowding the United States forward into a future of dizzy figures in railroad, steamship, mill, mine, and oil financing. Steamers from Europe in 1863 had brought to America 182,808 new laborers and homesteaders, the port of New York doubling its arrivals over the previous year, with 92,000 from Ireland, 35,000 from Germany, 18,000 from England, 11,000 from other countries. A few thousand of these new wage laborers would go into the new and growing petroleum industry, digging "rock oil" for the one hundred and twelve companies organized in that production in 1864 with $333,000,000 in stock sold.

Securities that found their way into Mrs. Lincoln's hands were designated by her in a letter to Noah Brooks as "Nevada claims" and "petroleum claims." Lincoln's friends Swett and Lamon gambled in oil and quicksilver stocks and went flat broke. The New York merchant A. T. Stewart paid a tax on $4,000,000 of income, William B. Astor acknowledging his income as $1,300,000, Cornelius Vanderbilt his as $576,000, J. P. Morgan his as $53,000. Joshua Bates of Boston, American partner of the Barings of London, died leaving an estate of $8,000,000. Vanderbilt had five homes at Saratoga, valued at $175,000, a span of mares for which he had been offered $17,000, and a horse named Post Boy which he considered the fastest in the world and priced at $22,000. August Belmont's elaborate collection of paintings was on exhibition in New York at $1 admission, receipts to go to the Sanitary Fair. A 10 by 15 inch Meissonier painting sold for $3,250.

"The prosperity of the North is great," Senator Sumner wrote to John Bright. "Travel is immense; every conveyance, the largest steamer or the largest train, is crowded." California had dug out $70,000,000 in gold and silver the previous year, and other States $30,000,000. Four out of five white men in California were bachelors, and every steamship from the port of New York for the West Coast held scores of marriageable women sailing to where they would try their luck. In the rush for copper and iron lands in the Lake Superior region entries for 26,000 acres were made in the one month of February, 1864. The *Tribune* of St. Joseph, Missouri, noted on March 10 of '64 that since February 1 four hundred teams and wagons had crossed the Missouri River headed for Western mining regions.

East and West were fortune-seekers who with Jay Cooke could see a future worth gambling on. The Illinois Central Railway announced to those who might buy shares of stock that of its nearly $2,000,000 surplus $1,000,000 was in United States bonds, and of its original government land grant of 2,595,000 acres it had sold 1,300,000 acres at a price exceeding $16,000,000. *Leslie's Weekly* reported that not including gold, silver, and stock sellers, the business failures of 1863 aggregated only $10,000,000 as against $28,000,000 in 1862, indicating "a wonderful state of prosperity" that might have a reaction. In all the large cities were large and small fortunes made out of war contracts. The pro-Southern *New York Express* made an investigation, hoping to set up an amazing and disgraceful list of the profit-takers, and the list turned out not so shocking as expected, the item reading:

Since the breaking out of the war quite a number of our citizens have enriched themselves, chiefly by legitimate business operations. G. C. McGuire & Co., the auctioneers, have cleared $300,000 by a contract for mattresses and iron bedsteads; Savage & Co., hardware dealers, at least $150,000; Sibley & Gray, stove dealers, as much more; C. L. Woodward, in the same business, $100,000. These firms occupy contiguous places of business between 10th and 11th streets. John E. Evans & Co., hardware, $200,000; J. & E. Owen, merchant tailors, $76,000; Mr. Lutz, saddler, $60,000; Mr. Rapier, blacksmith, $100,000, for shoeing Government horses. A poor wheelwright, for putting together wheelbarrows, bought at the North, $30,000—they were transported hither in pieces to save freight. Hudson Taylor & Philip & Solomon, stationers, $50,000 apiece. Mr. Taylor has invested part of his profits in a fine house at Poughkeepsie, New York. The landlords of the three principal hotels have cleared from $30,000 to $100,000 a year since December, 1861.

Small, comfortable fortunes had sprung up by thousands across the Northern and Border States, not to mention the Gulf State of Louisiana. Snug accumulations of wartime profits came out of selling wooden and metal legs and arms to men mutilated in battle, and out of providing substitutes to go forth to battle and take chances on being mutilated. Thousands of the dead not hurriedly shoveled over on battlefields were cared for at profits that ran high to firms of embalmers. Hundreds of neat bank deposits traced back to blockade-running and to forbidden traffic in liquor, medical supplies, and scarce ingredients of war munitions.

Good to look at and all too rare was the instance cited by a son of George Luther Stearns, the Boston merchant and Negro recruiting officer: "A Boston firm for whom Mr. Stearns had obtained a lucrative government contract, from which they probably had derived a larger profit than they deserved, sent him a cheque for two thousand dollars, which he returned with a note saying as politely as possible that to partake in such transactions was as culpable as theft."

General Sherman cursed the merchants of Cincinnati for readiness to trade the enemy anything for a profit. Grant cursed Lincoln's friend Swett for trying to trade in hay at exceptional profits, and when Swett told Lincoln that Grant had threatened to shoot him if he went into hay deals, Lincoln told Swett to beware, for Grant generally kept his word. Yet the ordinarily scrupulous though occasionally obtuse Grant did not see anything wrong in his giving a kinsman by marriage an inside track on cotton-trading profits, until Rawlins exploded and shamed him about it. To a request of Ohio's first war governor, William Dennison, that Lincoln give a letter of recommendation to military and naval authorities in behalf of a cotton-trader, Nicolay wired, "The President thinks he cannot safely write that class of letters."

Personal success in business, a stake that would assure a man comfort for life, was a motive so tangibly in the air that Lincoln, according to Whitney, advised his old law associate that Western land deals could bring him $50,000 in not so long a time. Letters of David Davis, Swett, Lamon, Orme, and the Eighth Circuit orgmathorial lawyers were touched with hopes and groans related to whether this one or that among them would come through with a stake to give him financial security for life. Secretary Welles made the mistake of letting a kinsman by marriage have a rather large-sized fortune as a commission on the negotiation of vessel sales to the navy; he was fiercely satirized in *Leslie's Weekly*, the *New York World*, and the *New York Herald*, but because huge amounts were involved it was generally accepted that Welles took a proper course in letting it be handled at a rather low percentage by a man he considered responsible. Repeatedly in his diary Welles bemoaned the palpable rascals who came trying to sell him worn-out ships at fancy prices.

From Dana and Grant to Stanton and then Lincoln went the cases of several cotton speculators trying to snake out profit-yielding bales of fiber for textile mills. Stanton organized a secret-service force that uncovered corrupt practices and frauds. Dana as Stanton's assistant carried this farther and broke down the game of many a thieving quartermaster and contractor whose tricks and delinquencies in buying and selling fuel, forage, harness, tents, clothing, and horses might otherwise have robbed the Government of many of the hard-earned millions that went into the five-twenty bonds sold by Jay Cooke in the name of God and country.

"It is personally known to me," wrote General James Grant Wilson, who was close to Dana, "that many important persons were involved directly or indirectly in these rascalities. A considerable number were tried by military commissions and punished by fine and imprisonment. Restitution was exacted with a firm hand, and large sums of money were saved or recovered for the Treasury, but for obvious reasons these transactions were concealed from the public as far as possible." Seven contractors bid to furnish horses, had their bids accepted, were notified that a contract was a contract, and when they failed to deliver the horses they were arrested, tried, and sent to prison. Politicians and newspapers howled, but Stanton stood by this procedure of Dana's and there were fewer frauds in horses.

Wilson noted one difficulty was that some of the most competent and most energetic contractors were the most dishonest, could not be content with a fair profit: "In tents, a lighter cloth or a few inches off the size; in harness, split leather; in saddles, inferior materials and workmanship; in shoes, paper soles; in clothes, shoddy; in mixed horse feed, chaff and a larger proportion of the cheaper grain; in hay, straw and weeds; in fuel, inferior grades of coal or wood, and so on through the entire list, nearly every article presented its chance for sophistication and dishonest profit. Every contractor had to be watched . . . and quartermasters and inspectors frequently stood in for a share of the profit."

As if this merely was a repetition of European experience, *Blackwood's Magazine* in England commented, "A great war always creates more scoundrels than it kills."

The higher up the hypocrite and thief uncovered by Stanton's secret service, the louder the howling from some newspapers and the heavier the pressure from politicians to let him go. Wilson noted that Governors, Congressmen, Senators, and even the President himself were pressed into the service of the "best citizens" who had been caught cheating the Government. In the winter of 1863-64 Dana helped supervise the buying of 3,000,-000 pairs of trousers, 5,000,000 flannel shirts and drawers, 7,000,000 pairs of socks, 325,000 mess pans, 207,000 camp kettles, 13,000 drums, 14,830 fifes. The War Department paid out from June of '63 to June of '64 more than $250,000,000.

In drawing up contracts Dana had a colleague, Peter H. Watson, a keen attorney who knew patent law and had an eye for the bogus. Watson turned up a fraud in the army forage supplied to horses and mules of the Army of the Potomac. By dishonest mixtures of oats and Indian corn, the contractors played tricks with the cost, weight, and price per bushel. Watson found out how the cheat was worked, and when his evidence was in, he arrested the men most directly involved. Watson was on a trip to New York when the President of the Philadelphia Corn Exchange, and other respectable Philadelphia citizens interested in the swindle, came to Dana at the War Department. They paid Dana $33,000 to cover what one of the men confessed he had stolen, and nearly the same amount was paid back by another of the Philadelphia callers, who went away with easier consciences, as it were. However, they were back next morning demanding of Dana that the swindlers should be released, and that papers and funds taken from them when they were arrested should be returned. Dana replied to the Philadelphians that in his judgment the forage-fraud experts should be given solitary confinement until they cleared up the entire matter and made complete justice possible. Then Dana telegraphed Watson to come to Washington and help.

Meanwhile the Corn Exchange president and his associate Philadelphians went to work in Washington to see how strong they were politically. They found several politicians who recognized their importance in Pennsylvania politics, among them Senator David Wilmot, author of the famous Wilmot Proviso, who went to President Lincoln and made such representations and appeals that the President consented to go over to the War Department and see Watson. While Wilmot stood outside, Lincoln went in and talked with Watson, who detailed the facts and evidence as between two lawyers, and also expressed his feelings as a citizen. The President, Dana noted, "dwelt upon the fact that a large amount of money had been refunded by the guilty men, and urged the greater question of the safety of the cause and the necessity of preserving united the powerful support which Pennsylvania was giving to the administration in suppressing the rebellion." Watson answered: "Very well, Mr. President, if you wish to have these men released, all that is necessary is to give the order; but I shall have to ask to have it in writing. In such a case as this it would not be safe for me to obey a verbal order; and let me add that if you do release them the fact and the reason will necessarily become known to the people."

Not long after, Lincoln picked up his hat and went out to where Wilmot was waiting in the corridor. "Wilmot," said the President, "I can't do anything with Watson; he won't release them." Wilmot's answer to the President was unprintable, according to Dana. Wilmot was sore and talked sore, but, Dana noted, it did not affect the judgment or the action of the President. The forage experts were kept in jail a long time while their frauds were fully investigated and like swindles in the future made impossible. Dana summarized the end of the affair: "If Watson could have had his way, the guilty parties—and there were some whose names never got to the public—would have been tried by military commission and sternly dealt with. But my own reflections upon the subject led me to the conclusion that the moderation of the President was wiser than the unrelenting justice of the Assistant Secretary [Watson] would have been."

A procession of mouthpieces and fixers twined in and out of Lincoln's office from week to week, and he had to sit not merely as judge and jury passing on their guilt or innocence and the punishment due. Beyond that he had to ask whether the Union cause at the military front, and at the political and economic rear, would be served by his judgment. When a large share of a swindler's stealings had been returned and a Senator of considerable influence interceded for a thief of highly respectable position, Lincoln leaned to what Dana called "moderation," though privately exclaiming to John Eaton that the Senator was "too crooked to lie still." In dealing with various stripes of fox, wolf, and hog caught with a smear of guilt on their snouts, Lincoln was more often blamed for "sympathy and clemency" than for vindictiveness. Heavy files of evidence and many intricate considerations stood in the backgrounds of an item in *Leslie's* in June: "The *New York Tribune* says that Capt. Sam Black, U.S. Quartermaster, who was recently convicted at Louisville of perpetrating enormous frauds on the Government, has been pardoned; and that Hall & Smith, Western horse contractors, who had likewise been found guilty of the same offence, have had their sentence suspended. This makes the *Tribune* fear that Kohnstamm may receive Presidential sympathy and clemency."

In the tanglefooted proceedings of the New Almaden Mine case, Lincoln kept patience after his friend Leonard Swett led him into an initial step—wherein Lincoln slipped, and recovered footing. On the sunrise slope of the Santa Cruz Mountains in Santa Clara County, California, was one of the world's richest mines, its cinnabar ore in one of its yielding years producing $2,000,000 of quicksilver. On the basis of a four-to-three United States Supreme Court decision, Lincoln signed a writ ordering and directing United States Marshal C. W. Rand of the Northern District of California to "enter upon mining property embracing about three thousand varas of land in all directions from the mouth of the mine commonly called and known as the New Almaden Quicksilver mine, and to remove therefrom any and every person who shall be found on the same and deliver the said premises, with all appurtenances of whatsoever kind to the possession of Leonard Swett, an agent who has been duly authorized by me to take possession of and hold the same for the United States." To Halleck, a former president of the New Almaden Company, and to Stanton, a Government attorney in New Almaden litigation, Lincoln said nothing of the writ. Swett took this writ and traveled to San Francisco in the company of Samuel Butterworth, president of the Quicksilver Mining Company of New York, which corporation much wanted the New Almaden mine and its phenomenal production.

Before sailing from New York Swett wrote to his former law partner William W. Orme: "I sail for California this morning. I go there employed by a Corporation here to settle some litigation in the Supreme Court of the United States. They will pay me $10,000 in any event. If successful, they will pay me a large conditional fee." Thus Swett landed in San Francisco in a double role—a personal agent appointed by the President of the United States and a paid attorney for a corporation that wanted the property which the President of the United States in a writ carried by Swett ordered a United States Marshal to seize.

The California mining region went into an uproar when Swett made known the President's writ. To Marshal Rand came word that the 170 miners at the New Almaden were armed and prepared to resist. With a cavalry troop Swett and the Marshal rode out to the mine, found complete resistance prepared, and rode away on Swett's decision to avoid bloodshed. Southern secessionist sympathizers seized the event to spread excitement and fear with rumors that all mining-property titles were in doubt and the Federal Government was moving to gather the richest one by one. A flock of telegrams from California and Nevada to the White House warned the President that he would be taking great risk with the Union cause if he stood by his writ ordering military seizure of the New Almaden. A press statement by Swett denied that the President had issued the order "without a full knowledge of its contents and intention," adding: "In contemplating possession of this mine, the Government desired that the business might be so conducted as not to stop its working. Therefore an arrangement was in contemplation with the Quicksilver Mining Company, by which, under the supervision of the Government, the mine would have been temporarily worked by them."

To this the New Almaden owners replied by discussing the four-to-three United States Supreme Court decision, arguing that Swett had "altogether misrepresented" the minority opinion of Justices Catron, Grier, and Swayne. They quoted Swett as remarking, "after his military attempt had failed," that he had "instructions to turn the mine over to the Quicksilver Mining Company." The New Almaden owners proceeded with points too damaging, too correct as to fact, for Swett to try to answer: "We cannot credit Mr. Swett with much sincerity in this statement. On the contrary, we believe that the warrant was obtained from the President to subserve the private interests of an adverse claimant (The Quicksilver Company, incorporated in Pennsylvania, and of which Mr. Butterworth is President); and we will add, that long before Mr. Swett appeared on this coast, armed with the President's warrant, we were informed on good authority, and believe, that Mr. Swett held a large interest (as much as 3,000 shares) in this adverse Company, into whose possession the mine would have been placed if Mr. Swett had succeeded in wresting it from us. And we believe that Mr. Swett still holds that interest. We are also informed that while the matter of this warrant was pending before the President, who was strongly urged not to issue it, he finally referred it to Mr. Swett, his former law partner, intending to be guided by his advice; and this was done while Mr. Swett held his stock in the Quicksilver Mining Company. We believe the President was ignorant of Mr. Swett's interest."

Halleck, in reply to outcries and alarms from old West Coast friends, telegraphed to the Federal commander at San Francisco: "I am directed by the Secretary of War to say that he has no information of any military order to take possession of the New Almaden mine. If there be any such order, it has been surreptitiously obtained." Swett telegraphed back a copy of this to Lincoln. In a Cabinet meeting Bates referred to Halleck's telegram as "false," adding that "a liar ought to have a good memory." Welles wrote of a warm discussion in which Bates and Usher condemned Halleck. "The President, who had been apprised of the facts, thought Halleck had been hasty and indiscreet but he *hoped nothing worse*."

A cipher message of Lincoln to Swett and Port Collector Frederick Low at San Francisco read: "Consult together, and do not have a riot or great difficulty about delivering possession." Low before receiving this had wired Lincoln that he must suspend his order. "The mining interests are so large and so sensitive that this proceeding will give the secessionists every advantage. Don't, I pray you, let anything be done to involve this State in difficulty."

Swett wired Lincoln that he still hoped for "peaceable possession" in a short time, Lincoln replying: "Many persons are telegraphing me from California begging me, for the peace of the State, to suspend the military enforcement of the writ of possession in the Almaden case, while you are the single one who urges the contrary. You know I would like to oblige you, but it seems to me my duty in this case is the other way."

So the writ of possession was suspended and the *San Francisco Bulletin* headed a long editorial "The Foiled Attempt to Steal a Mine"—and the Quicksilver Mining Company, which had beaten the New Almaden in a long court fight that ended in a four-to-three Supreme Court decision, forced a compromise sale of the New Almaden, getting it for $1,750,000, about the price of a year's average yield of the mine. This compromise was satisfactory to the Government, provided that its rights were reserved, Lincoln telegraphed to Swett. To Port Collector Low, Lincoln wired his summing up of the case:

There seems to be considerable misunderstanding about the recent movement to take possession of the "New Almaden" mine. It had no reference to any other mine or mines. In regard to mines and miners generally no change of policy by the government has been decided on, or even thought of, so far as I know. The "New Almaden" mine was peculiar in this, that its occupants claimed to be the legal owners of it, on a Mexican grant, and went into court on that claim. The case found its way into the Supreme Court of the United States, and last term, in and by that court, the claim of the occupants was decided to be utterly fraudulent. Thereupon it was considered the duty of the government by the Secretary of the Interior, the Attorney-General, and myself, to take possession of the premises; and the Attorney-General carefully made out the writ, and I signed it. It was not obtained surreptitiously, although I suppose General Halleck thought it had been when he telegraphed, simply because he thought possession was about being taken by a military order, while he knew no such order had passed through his hands as general-in-chief. The writ was suspended, upon urgent representations from California, simply to keep the peace. It never had any direct or indirect reference to any mine, place, or person, except the "New Almaden" mine and the persons connected with it.

Thus moved a tangled affair from May 8, 1863, when Lincoln signed the writ his old friend Swett wanted, to August 19, 1863, when the New Almaden at a ridiculously low price passed into the hands of a corporation in which Swett was a stockholder and for which he was a paid attorney.

For Swett, Lincoln had no reproaches. In a way he knew Swett better than Swett knew himself. Swett was not so bad, only too anxious about getting a stake for life—too easily played on by the Quicksilver Company sharpers, who paid Swett not as a lawyer but as one who had access to the President. And in the farther background of the case Lincoln probably believed the Supreme Court majority was right and that the Mexican-grant claims of the New Almaden owners were, as his writ said, "fraudulent and void," and they were "intruders thereon without right." When in his telegram to Low he said, "The writ was suspended, upon urgent representations from California, simply to keep the peace," he implied directly that if there were not a civil war in process, he would have the military enforce the decree of the Supreme Court majority.

And Swett? He went in for stock gambling, on tips and inside information from his quicksilver clients, and lost all he had, some $30,000, writing again to Orme: "I intend to come home and practice law . . . and rather practice with you than any other man. . . . The panic tore me terribly and I am trying to get over its effects. I regard the life of a lawyer as much more respectable than any other I can lead."

Three days after the New Almaden sale Lincoln replied to General Daniel E. Sickles, crippled for life at Gettysburg, who asked for help on a California land claim, "The question presented is a property question, with which I do not think I should meddle as a volunteer." Perhaps Lincoln was saying to himself that in the New Almaden affair he had meddled and volunteered too freely. "It will save me labor," he informed Sickles . . . "if you will first point me to the law which assigns any duty to the President in the case." Not again did he burn his fingers in any land claims.

"In the quicksilver case," wrote Attorney General Bates in his diary of one day's hearing of it in the Supreme Court, besides private counsel of high reputation there were three former United States Attorney Generals, Reverdy Johnson, Caleb Cushing, Jeremiah Black, for the corporation. Three of the Justices of the Supreme Court made free, as human beings, to express privately decided feelings they had about the tactics of Caleb Cushing, who seemed "to have excited the implacable disgust of the whole court." Justice James Moore Wayne, "who is habitually bland, and never forgets that he, himself is a gentleman, said to me privately, that Cushing's effort was a perfect failure," while Justice Noah Haynes Swayne confided to Bates that he held one attack of Cushing to be "a brutal outrage."

A rather unusual proceeding in a Supreme Court hearing was noted in Bates's diary with reference to Justice Robert Cooper Grier's open contempt for Cushing: "Judge Grier said to me, in a loud whisper, that every body in ten feet, must have heard—'Ef you speak, give that damned Yankee hell.' I need not say that I was disgusted at his grossness; but Mr. Justice Grier is a natural born vulgarian, and, by long habit, coarse and harsh." During further progress of the case there were newspapers wanting to know why Jeremiah S. Black, Attorney General and Secretary of State under the Buchanan Administration, whom Lincoln had appointed United

States Supreme Court reporter, should take time aside from his public duties to serve as counsel for the quicksilver corporation at a fee named as $20,000.

These were minor complications of a case that Lincoln found a peculiar labyrinth. The President would probably not have disagreed with Bates's diary entry of March 9: "The demoralising effect of this civil war is plainly visible in every department of life. The abuse of official powers and the thirst for dishonest gain are now so common that they cease to shock[.]"

To Oliver Wendell Holmes the sad feature of the new-made fortunes in most cases was that the owners thereof had silly and apish ways of spending. "Multitudes have grown rich and for what? To put gilt bands on coachmen's hats? To sweep the sidewalks with the heaviest silks the toiling French can send us? To float through life the passive shuttlecocks of fashion, from the avenue to the beaches and back again from the beaches to the avenue?"

New York hotels, theatres, jewelers' retail stores, and women's wear establishments were surpassing all former sales records. The shopping crowds and what they were doing was an endless topic in the newspapers. A class of reckless war-profit spenders were named the "Shoddy," a word from the textile trade where a compound of refuse and sweepings pounded, rolled, glued, and smoothed into the external form and gloss of cloth was known as shoddy. *Harper's Monthly* of July, 1864, in a scornful commentary told of soldiers on the first day's march or in the earliest storm finding their jackets and trousers, overcoats and blankets, scattering to the winds in rags or breaking into scraps and dust under a driving rain. "Shoddy has ever since become a word to represent the fraudulent contractor who makes a display of his ill-gotten gains."

Harper's added that the Government had so organized its commissariat that it was no longer at the mercy of the extortionate; the "good time" of the contractors was gone; fortune-seekers had now taken to stock gambling. It was more than an excitement—it was a rage and a mania that reached all classes and had infected many women with the passion for quick gains from a rise in stocks. " 'What's the price of gold today, my dear?' escapes from the pretty mouth of your wife before she has impressed the kiss of connubial welcome on your lips." And the answer might be happy-go-lucky or growling. The barber, the nursemaid, the peanut-vender, had here and there reaped big returns from a few dollars and were plunging farther.

Only two years since John M. Tobin was just a deck hand on a Vanderbilt boat of the Staten Island line and Tobin had raised $5,000, joined a clique of speculators manipulating stocks that ran up and up till Tobin had a million and the million had grown to eight millions. Once in Erie Railway stocks Tobin had cleared a profit of $8,000 in fifteen minutes. Now he was sitting in railroad directorates, buying real estate, and raising gossip as to what he had as a citizen beyond an amazing gambler's instinct for a winning bet. He and the Shoddy spurred the luxury industries to fresh ingenuity.

"The men," said *Harper's,* "button their waistcoats with diamonds of the first water and the women powder their hair with gold and silver dust," the latter costing $15 a head, while diamond dust, ground from glass, cost much less. "We don't feel this war," was a saying of the Shoddy. *Leslie's Weekly* believed it significant that $2,000,000 in diamonds had been imported the previous year. "No wonder Shoddy glitters in the sunlight of Central Park or the gaslight of its own palatial residence; no wonder the jeweler's hands are full, setting gems, while the soldier's feet blister in his paper-soled shoes, and his bare elbows emerge from his worn jacket sleeves."

The same editor complained of New York given up to the leg drama, "legs, physical and of unpadded proportions, female pedals as necessary to dramatic success as is a prima donna in an opera." The *New York Herald* estimated $30,000 an average night's spending for amusement in its city, or a third more than in Paris, France. Camel's-hair shawls at $1,500 were going briskly, rugs, carpets, tapestries, at unheard-of prices. The man who buttoned his vest with diamonds, accompanied by the woman whose hair shook with the glitter of gold dust, went shopping, saying, "We don't feel this war." The mood of those who had made their pile, and those who hoped their stocks would rise into a pile, was in lines of *New York Evening Post* verse:

> The sun's gone down to take a little sleep.
> I met High Daddy in the morning:
> The moon's come out to take another peep,
> I met High Daddy and I won't go home any more, any more.

Extravagance and luxury were the signs of the times in New York, said the *Evening Post.* Go down Broadway. "Ask Stewart about the demand for camel's hair shawls, and he will say 'monstrous.' Ask Tiffany what kind of diamonds are called for. He will answer, 'As near hen's egg size as possible,' 'price no object.' " The war was far off. 'Twas a nice quiet war. "Who at the North would ever think of war, if he had not a friend in the army or did not read the newspapers?"

When in a slum hut of Columbus, Ohio, the widow of a soldier killed at Chickamauga died lacking food and the decencies of life, the *Mahoning Sentinel* threw a diatribe: "Wealth revels in luxury and worth starves in poverty—shoddy swells in bogus jewelry and like a rotten mackerel emits a dazzling glow from its vulgar splendor—in this paradise of parasites and patriots." This was not a Copperhead political outpouring. It was a cry of the same human pitch as the lamentations of the pro-Lincoln *Harper's Monthly.*

While winter snow blew along the city streets, it troubled Oliver Wendell Holmes that fresh peaches at $24 a basket should be offered in show windows to buyers who had money to throw at the birds. The customers of luxury-dealers made merry over the war. It was a pretty little war and had been good to them, a High Daddy. They found a mirthful arithmetic rather than bassoon notes of woe in the statistics from factories where lathes were turning out eight wooden left legs for soldiers as against two right legs, and about the same proportion of right arms to left ones, showing that in this careless and curious war that had been let loose about four times as many of the boys at the front were losing left legs as right, and four right arms were being forcibly disconnected from the human torso as against one left arm.

"16 Bond Street: wigs made to cover scars" ran one New York newspaper advertisement. Others: "Dr. Eisenstein cures shell deafness and restores sight." "Condemned army horses for sale, fifty cents." "Friends and relatives of the brave sailors and soldiers use Holloway's Pills and Ointments." "Amuse Yourself at Niblo's Garden." "Moth Patches, hides blemishes on the face." The concoctors of Drake's Plantation Bitters announced, "From army hospitals, the bloody battlefield, the mansion of the rich and the humble abode of the poor, from every nook and corner of the civilized world, pour in the evidence of the astonishing effects of Drake's Plantation Bitters." Then came the testimonials of human sufferers made well by a bottle of cheap bitters. Few limits were put on those who wanted to employ false and extravagant statements in order to sell medicines, cosmetics, stocks and bonds that represented little more than wind and water.

The working class, the poor, the masses—both the naturally credulous and those so pressed to earn a living that they had not time to investigate—were considered a field for exploitation. They could be sold anything they could be tricked into buying. Out of the hard-earned dollars of the multitudes of the poor came patent-medicine fortunes and other individual heaps of wealth. The reader who accepted Greeley believed "the public" was an abstract crucified humanity to be saved by schools, inventions, and philosophy. Listening to Barnum, one heard, "The public loves to be humbugged." Out of mining-stock enterprises came the saying "A bonanza is a hole in the ground owned by a champion liar."

Prices of food and clothing soared upward while wages stood still or rose slowly. The very process that brought fortunes to speculators and sure-thing gamblers cut the wages, the buying power, of the workman. His wages might double in money but he was buying at prices that had tripled and quadrupled. "The clerk in a store," said *Leslie's*, "who was getting $1,000 per annum, now gets $1,500 and congratulates himself on the rise, is in reality only getting $500, his money being worth exactly that amount."

Noah Brooks noted a charity organization under way to care "for the more pressing wants of the very poor" in Washington, supplying them food, fuel, and clothes. "The back slums and alleys are full of squalid misery and distress, and none but those who go to look for it know of the poverty which is silently endured here at the National capital by hundreds of homeless and houseless ones."

As if by instinct and with no traditions nor practice for guidance, the working class began using the weapon termed the strike. The very word "strike" was so novel that some newspapers put it in quotes as though it were slang or colloquial, not yet fully accepted in good language. The year

1864 saw more strikes than all previous years in American history. In March the engineers on all railroads entering Chicago were on strike. On the Galena & Chicago Union Railroad the cry was that the company was not meeting an alleged January agreement to pay wages of $3 a day; the strike was broken in two days by engineers who went back to work reinforced by engineers brought on from New York and other Eastern cities.

The Brotherhood of the Foot-Board, born in Detroit in 1863, grew into the reorganized Grand International Brotherhood of Locomotive Engineers in 1864. This was the outstanding labor union of the country, testing the matter of how much it could make a strike cost the capital investors in a railway, *Leslie's* noting of a defeated strike on the Pittsburgh, Fort Wayne & Chicago Railroad in early '64, "The company claims to have crushed out the Brotherhood completely, although at a cost of $100,000." That seemed to be the amount the railroad preferred to spend rather than pay a demanded wage increase from $75 a month to $90—and enter into collective-bargaining relations with its workmen. The Illinois Central Railroad met a like demand by a partial wage increase.

Sharp lines were drawn between all skilled-trades workers and the lesser-paid unskilled laborers, the railroad engineers believing they could fight their cause alone and let the firemen organize their own union, while the pick-and-shovel maintenance-of-way men could also shift for themselves.

Payday dollars would buy so little in May of 1864 that the Chicago newspapers told their readers one day that in desperation the common laborers on every railroad running out of Chicago, except one, were on strike for a wage raise from $1.50 a day to $1.75. The bricklayers went on strike in March for a raise from $2.50 a day to $3.12½. The printers in New York, Chicago, and other cities formed their Typographical Union, the bakers, the tailors, the ironworkers, the coopers, the journeymen cord-wainers, the seamen, each in their own craft, organized a union or "protective association" or "benevolent society," usually meeting behind closed doors.

The conductors and horse-drivers on the New York streetcars walked out on their jobs, calling for higher pay. The store clerks in New York formed an Early Closing Association, and one news item ran, "The merchant's clerks of this city are about to memorialize their employers to increase their salaries." Waiters at the Tremont Hotel in Chicago walked out with demands of $20 a month for single men sleeping at the hotel and $22 a month for married men sleeping at home. New York actors and actresses formed a league and went on strike to raise their pay. The chorus in Max Maretzek's opera troupe in New York said they would not sing till they got more money for singing, and Max said New York would go without opera before he would pay more, and New York went without.

The Have-nots were using the only immediate weapon at hand for pressure on the Haves. In some cases the labor union was recognized and took permanent form. More often there was a confused development out of which came somewhat better conditions for the workers. Among sections of the working class it came to be recognized that the walkout, the with-drawal of labor supply, was the chief immediate method by which those who had nothing to sell but their labor could *strike* at those who buy labor.

Labor journals of influence had not yet arisen, and neither newspapers nor speakers at mass meetings made use of President Lincoln's several pointed and emphatic utterances in 1860 on the right of labor to revolt, his reference at Hartford to the shoe-worker's walkout in New England— "Thank God we have a system of labor where there can be a strike. What-ever the pressure, there is a point where the workman may stop." The only strike where Lincoln seemed to have stepped in with his influence as Presi-dent was but partly told of in his letter of December 21, 1863, to the Secre-tary of War: "Sending a note to the Secretary of the Navy, as I promised, he called over and said that the strikes in the ship-yards had thrown the completion of vessels back so much that he thought General Gillmore's proposition entirely proper. He only wishes (and in which I concur) that General Gillmore will courteously confer with, and explain to, Admiral Dahlgren." General Gillmore had a proposition for meeting the demands of the strikers. Admiral Dahlgren did not agree with Gillmore. Lincoln in effect ordered the two of them to get together and settle the strike, Lincoln concurring with Gillmore.

In St. Louis when newspaper printers went on strike General Rosecrans detailed soldiers to take the places of strikers. The union printers sent in a report to Lincoln on their side of the case. And it became a tradition of the labor movement that the President sent word that servants of the Fed-eral Government should not interfere with legitimate demands of labor— and the strike-breaking soldiers were withdrawn.

The bottom dogs of the working class seemed to be in the textile trades, where either in the factories or the homework system the hours were in-humanly long and the wages so low that respectable newspapers frequently published the figures as though for the amazement of readers that human beings could subsist on so few dollars a week. Shirts that sold at retail for $2, $3, and $4 cost in labor only 5 cents apiece, workingwomen earning from $1.50 to $2 a week at sewing. The strike of factory girls at Paterson, New Jersey, was for higher wages through cutting down the workday from twelve and sixteen to ten hours a day.

The necessities of poor and pretty women were made the means of their debauchery by high government officials, so believed the *Springfield Repub-lican*. An editorial summarized Washington scandals which flashed working-girl melodramas of fact through many newspaper columns, all soberly and sadly confirmed as to fact in House reports of May and June. "A bureau of the Treasury Department made a house of seduction and prostitution. Members of Congress putting their mistresses into clerkships. An honorable Senator knocked down in the street by a woman he had outraged. Whisky drinking ad libitum. The government cheated in contracts and openly robbed by its employés. Writes our most careful correspondent, a long resi-dent at the capital, 'Washington was never quite so villainously corrupt as at the present time. In the palmy days of Southern rule, of slavery, there was not half the corruption there is now.'"

A Senate committee of three, headed by Grimes of Iowa, gave instances of technique in corruption. A contractor who started on a shoestring had sold horses to the Government and reaped his first profits through bribing an inspector and three government clerks. He was, said the report, "a Prussian by birth, an Israelite by descent, a pedler and horse jockey by profession," and later turned up as a shipowner chartering thirteen transports to the War Department for the Banks expedition to New Orleans. The ships cost him $65,000, but at the rate per day of charter the committee estimated that if the engagement lasted a year his net profit would be $293,000. Another contractor sold tin to the Navy Department at 27 cents a pound (the price he had bid), buying his tin from Phelps, Dodge & Co. at 29 cents a pound (the price they had bid), and making his profit by cheating in false weight through corrupting the agent and the master mechanic who were to receive the tin. A special investigator for Stanton inspected many bureaus, examined thousands of witnesses, and reported his deliberate conviction that at least 20 per cent, if not 25 per cent, of government expenditures during the war were tainted with fraud.

Boston women wrote to members of Congress and received official figures that the country had paid on luxuries from Europe in a year $27,000,000 for silks, $5,500,000 for laces and embroideries, $12,000,000 for wines, liquor, and cigars. The Woman's Patriotic Association, pledged to buy no imported luxuries, was formed by 2,500 women in New York. Comment unpleasant to Mrs. Abraham Lincoln followed her direct refusal to join this association and endorse its purposes. The *New York Herald* said no movement for reform could reach those who had reaped millions selling bad beef and bad coffee to the soldiers, and broken-down horses to the Government.

In the brighter view $5,000,000 of privately raised funds was given to the Sanitary Commission for its many-sided help to soldiers in camp, on battlefield, and in hospital. Bedding, clothing, vegetables, supplies, upwards of $15,000,000 worth, went from the people back home to the boys at the front. Endowment funds to colleges ran into millions of dollars.

Of all classes the war was falling most heavily on the soldier, Lincoln remarked in closing a Sanitary Fair in Washington. To the soldier, staking his life and often giving it, went the highest merit. Next perhaps would come the women of America, who had been the chief agents in these fairs for the relief of suffering soldiers and their families. "I am not accustomed to the use of language of eulogy," said the President. "I have never studied the art of paying compliments to women; but I must say, that if all that has been said by orators and poets since the creation of the world in praise of women were applied to the women of America, it would not do them justice for their conduct during this war. I will close by saying, God bless the women of America."

So ran intersecting human streaks across America while Jay Cooke carried on his drive that brought a Niagara of money into the United States Treasury, raising in less than eleven months over $500,000,000, a financial feat that to cold European observers indicated some peculiar unity of purpose in the North, and resources that might yet surpass Great Britain's.

As the vast campaign for cash had closed in January, Jay Cooke had written to his brother at Washington, who was seeing Chase daily, that "our first and best people" had been crowding his Philadelphia office for three days, all speaking of Governor Chase as "the most triumphantly successful financier the world ever produced." Through the advertising and circular literature of the campaign had run a quiet promotion of the idea that Secretary Chase was the most prominent executive at Washington and would make an able President of the United States.

When the *American Exchange and Review* of Philadelphia published an extended biographical sketch of Chase, it was Cooke's doing. And what Cooke did all along was in rather good taste, in line with his loyalty to Chase. The rebuffs that Chase over and again gave to Cooke, when Cooke argued for an increase of his commission from two-eighths to three-eighths, never ruffled Cooke, who understood that Chase was keeping a record so scrupulous that no attack in Congress could dent it. Jay Cooke, the financier, believed in linking his own future to that of the finance Minister in office. He performed operations well calculated to erect Chase as a figure for the masses to cry up as a President, but the acknowledgments from Chase were spare and cold.

Jay Cooke inclined to agree with old Zelotes Fuller, editor of the *United States Journal* of Philadelphia, who wrote to him: "Although I have never seen Mr. Chase I am much prepossessed in his favor and would like to see him on the road to the Presidency. Who knows but that one day Jay Cooke will be a member of his cabinet? . . . There is but one thing in him which I do not like, and that is he seems to care too much for his enemies and too little for his friends, and apparently would go farther to placate an enemy than he would to retain a friend."

Lincoln's estimates of Chase always included high appraisal of heavy labor in a difficult field. The President knew well enough what Chase was telling a New England man in the spring of '64. "What is the national debt now in round numbers?" was asked. Chase replied that it was about $2,500,000,000. "And how much more can the country stand?" was further asked, Chase replying, "If we do not suppress the rebellion, when it reaches three billion dollars we shall have to give it up."

George William Curtis, lavish and loyal friend of Lincoln in his *Harper's Weekly* editorials, wrote to a friend the first week in April, "I have seen Lincoln tête-à-tête since I saw you, and my personal impression of him confirmed my previous feeling." Curtis was fifteen years younger than Lincoln, remembered that Lincoln shook hands with him as they parted in the manner of a father, and said: "Don't be troubled. I guess we shall come through."

Two sentences from Lincoln in early '64 had been picked up and in private conversations and public prints threshed out as significant texts or as silly excuses. One was spoken at the Philadelphia Sanitary Fair: "It is difficult to say a sensible thing nowadays." The other was from the Hodges letter: "I claim not to have controlled events, but confess plainly that events have controlled me."

Though spacious and simple as sky and air, these two sentences were like the kaleidoscopic American scene. They could be read as having any shade or tint chosen to suit the views of any interpreter.

What was dying might be a little better known than two or three years before. What was being born was more of an enigma than ever.

CHAPTER 49

CHASE THIRSTS TO RUN FOR PRESIDENT

THREE California Congressmen called on Secretary Chase in his private office. He had asked them to come. He wished them to know of a report by a special agent of the Treasury Department. Secretary Chase entertained them with a brief summary of the report. Then he told them, in a bland way, as though nothing else could be done about it, that on the basis of the report he had resolved to remove all of the leading Federal appointees of his department at San Francisco. He read to the seated and interested Congressmen a list of the new appointees as he had made it out. He waited with calm dignity to hear if the Congressmen had anything to say about this little surprise party to which he had invited them.

The Congressmen felt there was nothing to say; they knew him to be a man of set ways and he had said his decision in the matter was irrevocable. So they took their hats and walked out of the Treasury Building. They were using emphatic language and taking the name of God in vain.

The three Congressmen stepped into the White House and paid their respects to the President without saying anything about what had just happened to them. Then they went to New York to take steamships for San Francisco and home. While they lingered in New York, Noah Brooks was surprised at a telegram from the President to come at once to the White House. There Brooks, as the correspondent of the *Sacramento Union*, if nothing else, was interested to learn that the President had just heard of the wholesale removals and appointments determined on by Secretary Chase without consulting the President or the three California Congressmen, who had departed angry and disgruntled.

The President tramped up and down the long room swinging his arms.

"Tell me," he demanded of Brooks, "are those California Congressmen angry because the San Francisco mint and custom-house appointments were agreed on without their consent?" It seemed so, replied Brooks. "But the appointments are not agreed on," continued Lincoln. "Nothing is agreed on. I got the impression the California Congressmen were consulted and were satisfied. . . . Were they very mad?" Not very, said Brooks. Still they were sore.

"The President then angrily asked why I had not told him this before," ran Brooks's account. "I replied that it was not my affair; that as long as the Congressmen had seen fit to conceal their feelings of disappointment from the President when they bade him good-bye, it certainly was not my business to tell tales out of school. The President expressed his astonishment that he had been kept in the dark about so grave a matter as the emptying and filling of the most important federal offices on the Pacific coast. Then he anxiously asked if there was any way by which the California Congressmen could be reached and brought back."

One of the Congressmen had sailed and was now on the high seas, Brooks answered, but two of them were still lingering in New York. The President handed a telegraph blank to Brooks and told him to wire the two Congressmen asking them to return to Washington to see the President, making it clear also that Brooks was to sign the telegram and was to collect the charges personally from the President the next time he came to the White House.

The two Congressmen came to the White House and lingered around Washington while the President slowly and carefully broke down the list of appointments fixed up by Secretary Chase. The President told Brooks that Mr. Chase was "exceedingly hurt" by the interference with his plans. In the shift of affairs Chase offered to appoint one of the two California Congressmen who had returned to Washington as collector of the port at San Francisco. The President suggested that all three California Congressmen should get together in San Francisco, agree on a list of appointments, and send it to him for approval. This was not agreed on. However, when the two California Congressmen finally took steamer from New York for the West Coast, one of them, Frederick Low, carried with him his commission as collector of the port at San Francisco.

About the same time the Senate threw out an appointment made by Chase to the office of internal revenue collector at Hartford, Connecticut. Chase sent Lincoln a long letter insisting that the President again send the name of Mark Howard, Chase's man, to the Senate, and if the Senate again threw out the Howard appointment, to let Chase then give the President another name to offer the balky Senate. Equally insistent but much shorter was Lincoln's reply to Chase saying that Senator Dixon of Connecticut and Congressman Loomis, both of Hartford, joined in recommending Edward Goodman for the appointment. "I will thank you therefore to send me a nomination, at once, for Mr. Goodman."

The next day Chase again wrote those words which became familiar to Lincoln: "I respectfully resign"—whatever the "respectfully" might mean. But this resignation Chase did not send to Lincoln, partly because, as Chase explained in a note to Lincoln, Senator Dixon sent him a note "of great personal respect and kindness" and he, Chase, had replied to Senator Dixon likewise with great personal respect and kindness, upon which Senator Dixon had called on Chase, and the entire matter was to go over for further consideration of the President. However, Chase made it clear that his purpose was "to secure fit men for responsible places" without control of appointments by Senators or Representatives. Otherwise "I feel that I can not be useful to you or the country in my present position." From month to month these summary notices were served on the President that any moment his Treasury head was ready to quit. And as Chase saw himself, he was no muttering mutineer but a pillar of righteousness.

Letters of protest and memorials of remonstrance came to Lincoln from Puget Sound citizens who wanted Victor Smith thrown out of the collector's office in that district. Smith had been an Ohio man, a personal and political friend of Chase. He was an abolitionist, a spiritualist, talked his pet "isms" freely and freshly, believed in spirit rappings, and was an "eccentric functionary." He gave to Brooks his view that he had "so intertwined himself in the fibers of the government that his removal from office was an impossibility." While collector of customs at Port Townsend, Washington Territory, Victor Smith managed to induce the Government to move the customhouse to another place named Port Angeles, one of several performances which, combined with Victor Smith's arrogant personal manners, raised an outcry from businessmen, politicians, and ordinary citizens that he was a nuisance and an evil to the West Coast.

Joining in the demands that came to Lincoln for Smith's removal and the return of the customhouse to its first point were, according to Brooks, every other Federal officer and nearly every prominent citizen in the Puget Sound district. Among the prominent citizens seeking Victor Smith's official scalp was Anson G. Henry, formerly of Springfield, Illinois, and personal physician years back to a sufferer from hypochondria named Abraham Lincoln, who as President had appointed Henry surveyor general of the Territory of Washington. Henry was among those who gave their word to the President that Victor Smith was a worthless vagabond and an audit might show Smith a defaulter.

A delegation that seemed to include everybody then in Washington, official and unofficial, from the Pacific Coast called at the White House and filed with the President formal charges against Victor Smith and called for his removal. Lincoln told them Secretary Chase was out of town and to return in a few days, which they did, but Secretary Chase was still out of town. On a Friday then Lincoln sent Chase a note to "please send me at once an appointment of Henry Clay Wilson" to replace Victor Smith. This note was official. To it Lincoln added that same Friday another note beginning, "I address this to you personally rather than officially, because of the nature of the case." He explained to Chase that his mind was made up to remove Victor Smith, yet in so doing he had not decided that the charges against Smith were true but had only decided that the dissatisfaction with Victor Smith was too great. "But I believe he is your personal acquaintance and friend, and if you desire it I will try to find some other place for him."

Chase arrived in Washington Saturday night and learned from an Assistant Secretary of the Treasury that the President had directed that particular Assistant Secretary to make out a commission for a new collector in place of Victor Smith. Chase on Monday wrote to Lincoln, "This information surprised and greatly pained me; for I had not thought it possible that you would remove an officer of my department without awaiting the result." Also on this Monday Chase read a note from Lincoln saying that he had learned that the man, Henry Clay Wilson, he had appointed Friday to replace Victor Smith was dead, and therefore Lincoln would appoint one Frederick A. Wilson.

Again Chase sent to Lincoln his resignation. And according to Maunsell B. Field, Third Assistant Secretary of the Treasury (who wrote that he made notes of the conversation on the day it took place), the President had this to say about the resignation he found on his office table: "I waited until evening, and then ordered my carriage and drove to his house. I found him in the office to the left as you enter the door. I went directly up to him with the resignation in my hand, and, putting my arm around his neck, said to him, 'Chase, here is a paper with which I wish to have nothing to do; take it back, and be reasonable.' I then explained to him what had occurred while he was away. I told him that the man whom I had appointed happened to have been dead several weeks; that I couldn't replace the person whom I had removed—that was impossible—but that I would appoint anyone else whom he should select for the place. It was difficult to bring him to terms; I had to plead with him a long time, but I finally succeeded, and heard nothing more of *that* resignation."

Two days later Lincoln sent Chase a letter giving his approval to several matters and closing, "Please send me over the commission for Lewis C. Gunn, as you recommended, for collector of customs at Puget Sound." Victor Smith besought Chase to have himself reappointed and Chase replied that Smith was mistaken as to the influence of words from Chase to the Administration. "If any word of mine would make you collector again you would be reappointed."

In one phase the Victor Smith affair was a duel of political strength as between Smith and Dr. A. G. Henry, Lincoln's old Springfield medical adviser. Though Smith and Dr. Henry were followers of the spiritualist cult and believed they could talk with the dead and departed of another realm, the two men loathed each other and never spoke as they passed by. On the steamer *Brother Jonathan*, bound from San Francisco to Portland, they were both drowned when that vessel struck a reef and sunk.

In Chase's department were more than ten thousand job-holders high and low, and according to Nicolay and Hay, the President let Chase have his way as to all of these except in rare cases, seldom interfering. "It was impossible to get on with him except by constant agreement to his demands." Chase properly insisted that only men of ability and character should fill the positions in his department, but, noted Nicolay and Hay, "He had an exasperating habit of assuming that nobody agreed with him in this view, and that all differences of opinion in regard to persons necessarily sprung from corrupt or improper motives on the part of those who differed with him." Hay wrote Nicolay of Chase, "a hard nut to crack."

The two secretaries saw him undermining Lincoln at every chance and with his double-dealing over and again treading close to the thin line dividing hypocrites and true men. "It cannot be doubted that his motives were pure, his ability and industry unusual, his integrity, of course, beyond question," they agreed. "Pure and disinterested as he was, and devoted with all his energies and powers to the cause of the country, he was always singularly ignorant of the current public thought and absolutely incapable of judging men in their true relations. . . . He regarded himself as the friend of Mr. Lincoln; to him and to others he made strong protestations of friendly feeling, which he undoubtedly thought were sincere; but he held so poor an opinion of the President's intellect and character in comparison with his own, that he could not believe the people so blind as deliberately to prefer the President to himself."

Still later the secretaries agreed as to Chase, "There never was a man who found it so easy to delude himself." This may have been the key to the wormings and gyrations of Chase toward the Presidency—he was self-deluded. Under the portentous exterior of the handsomest man in the Cabinet was an oversized marionette borne down by delusions of grandeur. This was the year Emerson said of an optical distemper endemic to Washington, contracted by those who once look at the President's chair, "Their eyes grow to it; they can never again take their eyes off it; the virus once in is not to be got out of the system." Two sorry points Nicolay and Hay recorded of Chase. He had what they called, for want of a better word, "self-love." And he had no sense of humor to tell him when he wore misfits and others might be hiding laughter at him.

Chase had for months at his home a house guest, the author of *Neighbor Jackwood, The Drummer Boy, Cudjo's Cave*, John Townsend Trowbridge of Boston, thirty-seven years old. Trowbridge took walks with Chase before breakfast and told himself that while Chase had no remarkable wit, he would "embroider his conversation with playfulness." At breakfast one morning Chase read aloud a ridiculous newspaper account of his being locked in his office writing a report and inaccessible even to President Lincoln. "He strongly disapproved of the President's habit of telling all sorts of stories, to all sorts of people, on all sorts of occasions; yet he himself sometimes repeated a Lincoln story with good effect." One of these, as Chase told it to Trowbridge, came in a new version at the Cabinet meeting in December of 1863 when the President read his message to Congress and invited comment. For some time nobody spoke. Chase broke the awk-

The Treasury Building '61

From the Barrett collection

Pontoon bridge and officials from Washington in carriage

Photograph by Gardner, from the Meserve collection

Katherine ("Kate") Garniss Chase Sprague, daughter of Salmon Portland Chase, wife of Senator William Sprague. She led actively in the movement to nominate her father for President in '64

From the Meserve collection

ward silence by suggesting an amendment, whereupon Seward proposed another change. Lincoln turned to Seward. "Governor, you remind me of a Blue Grass farmer who had a black man and a fine yoke of oxen. One day the black man came running to the house. 'Massa,' says he, 'dat ar off ox, him dead. T'udder too. T'ought I wouldn't tell you bofe to oncet, fear you couldn't stand em.'"

Nearly every day Trowbridge stepped out from the large mansion of Secretary Chase, with its sumptuous furnishings cared for by well-groomed, quiet colored servants, and walked across a quadrangle to a street corner diagonally opposite at E and Sixth streets. There in one back room on the third floor of a shabby frame house lived a man keeping house with a bed, a pine table, two chairs, a sheet-iron stove, and an oblong pine box upended to serve as a cupboard. Ten o'clock of a morning Trowbridge would sometimes find this man fixing his breakfast, cutting bread with a pocket jackknife, toasting the slices while a teakettle simmered. A brown paper bag was the sugar bowl, a piece of brown paper the butter plate. After one of these breakfasts that winter the man threw the butter plate into the sheet-iron stove, as usual, and then brought out a sheaf of manuscripts for a book of poems to be titled *Drum-Taps* by Walt Whitman. One poem was a dirge for two veterans, father and son laid in a double grave by the burying squad as a silver moon moved up the sky.

> O strong dead-march you please me!
> O moon immense, with your silvery face you soothe me!
> O my soldiers twain! O my veterans, passing to burial!
> What I have I also give you.
>
> The moon gives you light,
> And the bugles and the drums give you music;
> And my heart, O my soldiers, my veterans,
> My heart gives you love.

Trowbridge went with Whitman a few times to Armory Square Hospital and went the rounds with Whitman, who gave fruit, paper and envelopes for writing letters, tobacco, newspapers, books, to fellows who lay with swamp fever or dysentery or bullet paths in their young bodies. At some beds Whitman spoke greetings and passed the time as if he were an uncle or a brother just from home and the folks. Trowbridge noticed that Whitman might read from the New Testament or Shakespeare but never from his own works; he did not let on he wrote poetry. To one boy Whitman pointed out Trowbridge as the author of a piece the boy liked to hear read and the boy, said Trowbridge, "talked to me with tears in his eyes of the comfort Whitman's visits had given him." The boy was scheduled to have a foot cut off in an hour and Trowbridge had his heart stirred.

John Burroughs, a Treasury Department clerk, and William O'Connor, head clerk of the Lighthouse Board, were two friends who joined with Trowbridge in believing Whitman among the supreme and original poets of America. The four of them sat with their overcoats that winter up in

Whitman's garret (he was what they called a "fresh-air fiend") and argued about which were the best plays Shakespeare wrote. Trowbridge may have given them his estimates of the two men he saw most of in Washington, living close neighbors: "Chase devoutly believing it his right and likewise his destiny, to succeed Lincoln in the Presidency; Whitman aspiring to be for all time the poet of democracy and emancipated manhood—his simple prayer being, 'Give me to speak beautiful words; take all the rest!' One a conscientious High Churchman, reverencing tradition, and finding ceremonious worship so helpful and solacing that (as he once said to me earnestly) he would have become a Roman Catholic, if he could have brought himself to accept the Romish dogmas; the other believing in the immanent spirit and an ever-living inspiration, and as free from all forms and doctrines as Abraham alone with Deity in the desert. For the statesman I had a very great admiration and respect; for the poet I felt a powerful attraction, something like a younger brother's love; and I confess a sweet and secret joy in sometimes stealing away from the company of polished and eminent people in the great house of Chase and crossing over to Walt in his garret."

Trowbridge asked Whitman one day about his taking a government job. Whitman did not believe one could be landed for him. He had asked Sumner about an office and was promised, but it did not come through. Since March last year Whitman had been carrying a letter from Ralph Waldo Emerson to Secretary Chase. He handed it to Trowbridge. With perfect apologies, the next morning after breakfast Trowbridge followed Chase into his private office and laid before the Secretary Emerson's letter saying that here was a great poet who ought to have some modest clerkship maybe. Trowbridge meanwhile spoke of Whitman as a true man worth helping. But Chase was uneasy. "I am placed," he said, "in a very embarrassing position. It would give me great pleasure to grant this request, out of my regard for Mr. Emerson." Also Chase appreciated what Trowbridge said of Whitman.

"Then," noted Trowbridge, "he went on to speak of *Leaves of Grass* as a book that had made the author notorious; and I found that he judged it by conventional standards of taste and propriety. He had understood that the writer was a rowdy, 'one of the roughs,' according to his description of himself." Trowbridge put in: "He is as quiet a gentleman in his manners and conversation as any guest who enters your door." Chase: "I am bound to believe what you say; but his writings have given him a bad repute, and I should not know what sort of a place to give to such a man."

Trowbridge offered to relieve Chase of all embarrassment in the business by withdrawing Emerson's letter. Chase glanced at Emerson's signature, hesitated, and made an answer that surprised Trowbridge: "I have nothing of Emerson's in his handwriting and I shall be glad to keep this." Trowbridge said nothing but thought it "hardly fair." And Trowbridge went on gathering from Chase the bare facts to be ornamentally presented later that year as a biography of Chase titled *The Ferry Boy*, Chase writing to the author, "Indeed, from information or fancy, you have collected some facts which are quite out of my recollection."

"Chase looks and acts as if he meant to be the next President," Richard Henry Dana had written from Washington to Charles Francis Adams at London in March of '63. A few days after a visit with Lincoln in December, Thurlow Weed wrote from Albany to John Bigelow at Paris: "Mr. Chase's report is very able, and his huge banking machine will make him strong. But how pitiable it is to know that his eye is single—not to the welfare of his country but to the presidency! Mr. Lincoln says he is 'trying to keep that maggot out of his head,' but he cannot."

In scores of letters written to politicians, editors, ministers, support worth having, Chase over a two-year period sought to spread the impression that in the midst of incompetents that surrounded him he was the one man who would know how if given the power. "Had there been here an administration in the true sense of the word," he wrote to the Reverend Dr. J. Leavitt, January 24, 1864 "—a President conferring with his Cabinet and taking their united judgments, and with their aid endorsing activity, economy, and energy, in all departments of public service—we could have spoken boldly and defied the world." To Wayne MacVeagh, Republican State Committee chairman of Pennsylvania, two days later: "Oh, for a vigorous, earnest, thorough prosecution of this war!" To Judge Thomas F. Key of Cincinnati the same day: "Some friends are sanguine that my name will receive favorable consideration from the people in connection with the Presidency. I tell them that I can take no part in anything they may propose to do, except by trying to merit confidence where I am." To Judge William M. Dickson of Washington the next day: "The administration can not be continued as it is. There is in fact no administration, properly speaking. There are departments and there is a President. . . . I have not the slightest idea . . . I can remain . . . in my present position another year." To Thomas Heaton, a Treasury Department agent at Cincinnati the next day: "So far as the Presidency is concerned, I must leave that wholly to the people. . . . Whatever disposition they make of it I shall be content." To Edward Gilbert of New York the next day: "The only and the best service I can render, by those who desire to use my name in the approaching canvass, is to devote myself exclusively to the proper duties of my department so long as I remain at its head."

In twilight hesitations Chase wrote letters saying he would let his conscience be his guide. "Were your temperament mine," he wrote to one of his port collectors, as though he had temperament. Possibly some opera soprano in New York, jealous of another's voice, expressed more shifting and contradictory opinions than did Chase of Lincoln. To the wealthiest man in the Senate, his son-in-law, Chase wrote on November 26, 1863, that he could never be driven into any hostile or unfriendly position as to Mr. Lincoln. "His course toward me has always been so fair and kind." He dwelt at length on his "respect and affection" for Mr. Lincoln. Yet in the same letter he made the point that no President should be re-elected, and "I think a man of different qualities from those of the President will be needed for the next four years." To show his son-in-law how fair he was he noted particularly, "If I were controlled by merely personal sentiments, I should prefer the reëlection of Mr. Lincoln to that of any other man." He wished his son-in-law to believe that he was controlled by public interest and not private ambition.

From his desk where he dipped a pen and scribbled Chase sent out these dozens of curiously stilted self-portraits of the noble and worthy citizen, the man of grasp, dignity, and patience, who against his deeper inclinations would serve his country as Chief Magistrate if called on. He evolved forty ways of saying what he wrote a Wisconsin man in December of '63, "There is certainly a purpose to use my name, and I do not feel bound to object to it."

Letter after letter came to Chase from his friend and appointee, George S. Denison, customs collector at New Orleans, telling Chase of efforts for him in Louisiana. At a largely attended meeting of conservatives, wrote Denison, "Old Jacob Barker was the principal speaker and expressed earnest disapproval of Mr. Lincoln. He then spoke highly and at some length of Mr. Chase, Secretary of the Treasury, and although disagreeing with him politically, expressed an earnest desire, on account of his well known ability, that he might be the next President. I shall send you his speech if it is to be published."

Denison reported for Chase: "Gen. Banks is doing nothing to further Mr. Lincoln's renomination. He tells me he is not and I believe him. That is all we can ask of him, for if he should do anything against Mr. L.s renomination, his head would be taken off without delay. . . . Hahn's paper, the 'True Delta,' is out for Lincoln, as I supposed it would be." This however was incidental to the main tidings from New Orleans: "We are forming a Chase Club here . . . some of the best men of the city of different interests and political affinities. I believe we can control the election of delegates to the National Convention." Then Denison took up the matter of B. Rush Plumly and made out that Chase seemed to be neglecting Plumly and nevertheless Plumly was loyal to Chase, was a good hand at politics, was lucky in money and could throw a big party when he felt it was called for. Denison wrote to Chase:

Plumly has worked hard for you ever since he has been here, and works hard for you now. His commission has not come, and I sometimes fear you have changed your mind about sending it at all. I can only assure you that it will be very bad policy and unjust to withhold it. It would have been much better to send it at the time first designated. Plumly will undoubtedly be a delegate to the National Convention. He has been very fortunate in his finances lately. Some old stock held by him and regarded as nearly worthless, has risen in value enormously, and brought him nearly Thirty Thousand Dollars. His family have been here this winter and he has lived with some show but not expensively. He has been economical except on one occasion, when he gave a party which cost nearly a thousand Dollars. He has done much good here.

The Secretary of the Navy wrote in his diary late in the summer of '63: "Mr. Chase called and took me this evening for a two hours' ride." Not often did one member of the Lincoln Cabinet take another for a ride. And Mr. Welles wrote many pages of what Mr. Chase said to him and what he said to Mr. Chase. There was talk of whether the State of North Carolina if she knocked and asked to be let into the Union would thereupon be let in. "Much would depend on the President," said Chase—"all in fact, for were the President to acquiesce in her return it could not be prevented, but on the other hand, if he planted himself firmly and with Jacksonian will on the Proclamation . . . no doubt North Carolina would be excluded." They rode and talked two hours, Mr. Chase and Mr. Welles, but Mr. Welles wrote that Mr. Chase had not made it clear what he would do with the Southern States if and when they should be laid prostrate and subjugated under Northern feet, except that Mr. Chase was sure he would be firm, decisive, Jacksonian. What Mr. Welles wrote in his diary made it clear that Mr. Chase had hoped he would find one member of the Cabinet to stand with him aggressively against the President. He was sounding out Welles.

"I know not that I clearly comprehend the views of Chase," wrote Welles, "and am not sure that he has fully considered and matured the subject himself. He says he makes it a point to see the President daily and converse on this subject; that he thinks the President is becoming firm and more decided in his opinions, and he wants me to second him. Stanton he says is all right, but is not a man of firm and reliable opinions. Seward and Blair he considers opponents. Bates he says is of no account and has no influence. Usher he classes with himself, though he considers him of no more scope than Bates. Seward he says is unreliable and untruthful. The President he compliments for honesty of intentions, good common sense, more sagacity than he has credit for, but [he thinks he] is greatly wanting in will and decision, in comprehensiveness, in self-reliance, and clear, well-defined purpose."

Over and again Welles's diary entries had one tone: Chase "lamented the President's want of energy and force, which he said paralyzed everything. His weakness was crushing us. I did not respond to this distinct feeler, and the conversation changed." Welles guessed in his diary in mid-February of '64 that "Chase intends to press his pretensions as a candidate, and much of the Treasury machinery and the special agencies have that end in view." The President while fearing Chase also respected him. "He places a much higher estimate on the financial talents of Chase than I do."

"The glue in the Cabinet is snapping and cracking," said the wishful *New York Herald* in February. Conflicts of temperament, the same cross currents of purpose, moved the Cabinet as when months back Lincoln held in his hands the resignations of Seward and Chase. While Carpenter from day to day painted at his picture of the President and the Cabinet, Lincoln often brought visitors down to see the work of art and, said Carpenter, he came by himself sometimes three and four times in a single day. In his many remarks seldom did Lincoln cast any reflections or indulge in any personal comments on his Cabinet members. However, one day, Carpenter noted, "with a sly twinkle of the eye, he turned to a senatorial friend whom he had brought in to see the picture, and said: 'Mrs. Lincoln calls Mr. Carpenter's group *The Happy Family.*'"

From the number of long letters Chase wrote in fixing his political fences, and from the number of interviews and conferences he held toward the same end, it could be estimated that he was giving perhaps half of his time to nursing along his hope of residing in the White House. In January of that year Archbishop Hughes of New York died, and Chase took it on himself to see that the powers at Rome should, if possible, choose a proper prelate for the vacancy. And Chase wrote to the Most Reverend Archbishop Purcell of Cincinnati on February 1 letting that high official of the church know that he, Chase, was not idle: "Deeply impressed with the importance of having a successor to Archbishop Hughes, of clear intellect and earnest sympathy with the poor, the oppressed, and enslaved, I ventured, without consulting you, to ask Governor Dennison, when here some time ago, to name the subject to the President. He did so, as he informed me at the time. Subsequently, I spoke to the President myself. He mentioned that Governor Dennison had spoken to him—seemed pleased with the suggestion—and referred me to Mr. Seward. Today I have had a conversation with Mr. Seward, who expresses himself in relation to the subject, as I would wish."

Often called into consultation by Lincoln was Alexander K. McClure, a founder of the Republican party in Pennsylvania, an editor, head of draft enrollment in his State, and an active Curtin man in politics. "The most irritating fly in the Lincoln ointment" in 1863, as McClure saw it, was the embryonic Chase boom which Republican-party enemies of Lincoln hoped would grow into a combination to break Lincoln's power. McClure later recalled Lincoln as unsettled mentally by the Chase stride toward power. And McClure recorded his impressions both as a practical party worker and as a political reporter: "Lincoln saw that if the disaffected elements of the party should be combined on one strong candidate, his own success would be greatly endangered. It was the only subject on which I ever knew Lincoln to lose his head. I saw him many times during the summer and fall of 1863, when the Chase boom was at its height, and he seemed like one who had got into water far beyond his depth."

In one White House visit McClure heard Lincoln speak with great seriousness about the Chase movement, McClure believing he read in Lincoln a keen feeling of the possibility of defeat, while at times Lincoln brightened with pertinent stories about the Chase attitude and laughed "immoderately." This went on for an hour during which the two men reviewed the situation, McClure assuring Lincoln that Chase could not be the Republican candidate, and that he regarded Lincoln's renomination as reasonably certain. At midnight McClure shook hands with Lincoln and started to go. Lincoln followed him to the end of the Cabinet table nearest his desk, swung a leg over the table corner and began a new presentation of the Chase matter. That finished, McClure again said good night and moved toward the door.

"He followed," wrote McClure, "to the other end of the Cabinet table, again swung his leg over the corner of it, and started in afresh to discuss the contest between Chase and himself. It was nearly one o'clock when I again bade Lincoln good-night, and got as far as the door, but when just about to open it he called me and with the merriest twinkling of his eye, he said, 'By the way, McClure, how would it do if I were to decline Chase?' "

McClure was surprised and said, "Why, Mr. Lincoln, how could that be done?" Then, as McClure heard it, Lincoln rambled on: "Well, I don't know exactly how it might be done, but that reminds me of a story of two Democratic candidates for Senator in Egypt, Illinois, in its early political times. That section of Illinois was almost solidly Democratic, as you know, and nobody but Democrats were candidates for office. Two Democratic candidates for Senator met each other in joint debate from day to day, and gradually became more and more exasperated at each other, until their discussions were simply disgraceful wrangles, and they both became ashamed of them. They finally agreed that either should say anything he pleased about the other and it should not be resented as an offense, and from that time on the campaign progressed without any special display of ill temper. On election night the two candidates, who lived in the same town, were receiving their returns together, and the contest was uncomfortably close. A distant precinct, in which one of the candidates confidently expected a large majority, was finally reported with a majority against him. The disappointed candidate expressed great surprise, to which the other candidate answered that he should not be surprised, as he had taken the liberty of declining him in that district the evening before the election. He reminded the defeated candidate that he had agreed that either was free to say anything about the other without offense, and added that under that authority he had gone up into that district and taken the liberty of saying that his opponent had retired from the contest, and therefore the vote of the district was changed, and the declined candidate was thus defeated.

"I think," added Lincoln, with one of his heartiest laughs, "I had better decline Chase."

McClure wrote it was evident to him that the question of inducing Chase to decline was very seriously considered by Lincoln, that Lincoln did not seem to know just how it could be done but it was obvious he believed it might be done in one way or another, and what Lincoln said in jest he meant in sober earnest. In this interpretation of Lincoln McClure was a matter-of-fact observer like Swett, with Swett having the advantage of longer scrutiny of Lincoln methods. Swett would have insisted that McClure overemphasized Lincoln's personal ambition, and that Lincoln had in mind forces and issues not to be computed and solved offhand.

Swett knew, as McClure did not, that Lincoln would often talk in order to get at his own mind. With McClure, Lincoln talked practical politics. That was where McClure had facts, information, knowledge of doings before they got into the papers. And as a man of facts plain as daylight, rather than one curious and troubled about the toil of tangled roots underground that shove facts up into the plain daylight, McClure wrote: "Lincoln's anxiety for a renomination was the one thing ever uppermost in his mind during the third year of his administration, and, like all men in the struggles of ambition, he believed that his only motive in his desire for his own re-election was to save the country, rather than to achieve success for himself. That he was profoundly sincere and patriotic in his purpose and efforts to save the Union, and that he would willingly have given his life as a sacrifice had it been necessary to accomplish that result, none can doubt who knew him; but he was only human, after all, and his ambition was like the ambition of other good men, often stronger than himself."

Then came McClure's further judgments, correct in the main particulars though lacking stress on the point that Lincoln could not overcome fears of what might be done by the forces in which the Chase movement sought deeper roots. "In this," wrote McClure, "as in all political or administrative movements Lincoln played the waiting game. When he did not know what to do, he was the safest man in the world to trust to do nothing. He carefully veiled his keen and sometimes bitter resentment against Chase, and waited the fullness of time when he could by some fortuitous circumstance remove Chase as a competitor, or by some shrewd manipulation of politics make him a hopeless one. His inexperience in the details of politics made him naturally distrustful and apprehensive as to his renomination. He could not, at that early day, get together the political forces necessary to make him feel safe in the battle, and it was not until about the close of 1863 or early in 1864 that he finally formulated in his mind his political policy, and began the work of consolidating his forces for action. He did this with a degree of sagacity and method that would have done credit to the ripest politician of the age."

A short, thickset man wearing side whiskers and the latest cut of clothes, carrying a monocle in the English manner and sporting a gold-headed walking-stick, came to see Lincoln while the Chase movement was under way. And Lincoln gave this man plenty of time and talked much with him. He was Henry Jarvis Raymond, editor and owner of the most distinctly pro-Lincoln daily organ in New York City, the *Times,* the one morning newspaper that tried to hurl back the daily javelins of Greeley, Bennett, Brooks, Fernando Wood. A Congressman-elect from New York State had pressed Lincoln for official action in an important matter, according to Carpenter, and the answer from Lincoln was: "You must see Raymond about this. He is my *Lieutenant-General* in politics. Whatever he says is right in the premises, shall be done."

Raymond was forty-four years old, born in Lima, New York, a University of Vermont graduate, teacher in a young ladies' seminary, editor of the *New Yorker*, a literary weekly started by Greeley. Later he was a reporter for Greeley's *Tribune*, writing a shorthand devised by himself and earning a special reputation for accuracy in transcribing lectures, sermons, speeches. He left Greeley for the *Courier and Enquirer* and for ten years while still carrying on newspaper work he was an editorial adviser and occasional contributor to *Harper's Monthly*. Raymond founded the *New York Times* in 1851 and edited it for a public that wanted more careful statement of the day's events than was to be had in the diabolically brilliant and slimy *Herald* or in the quirks, oddities, and shifts of the *Tribune*. "That little devil of the *Times*," was Greeley's pet reference to Raymond.

A delegate to the Whig National Convention of 1850, later Lieutenant Governor of New York, Raymond had helped organize the Republican party in 1856, stumped for Frémont, in 1858 independently swung away to support of Stephen A. Douglas for President, but in 1860 swung back to Lincoln. He was close to Weed and Seward; the triumvirate of Seward-Weed-Raymond was often satirized and excoriated. Favoring Seward for the Presidency, he was credited with helping put Seward in the Cabinet. Long letters of Raymond in controversies with Greeley and with Yancey were a nourishment for the tough-minded. Articles of his in the *Times* during the winter of '60-'61 dealt ably with economic factors of the war. In the mountain regions of the South, where the slaveholders were few, he had forecast that the South would get fewer fighters for secession.

And now Raymond worked on the most comprehensive and formidable biography of Lincoln that had ever been attempted, to be published late in the spring and portray a statesman with documents, letters, speeches, bearing on all major decisions and policies. That Raymond in 1861 was so hopeless of the Lincoln Administration that he urged in his newspaper a provisional government and a dictator (George Law) to replace Lincoln would not be told in the biography. That a movement to nominate Chase for President was supported by scores of Republican leaders in Washington early in '64 would not be told. Except for matters of this sort, which Raymond considered political family secrets not worth telling in a campaign year, it would be a first-rate contemporary work, a source document as well as a campaign biography.

From day to day Raymond had implied in the *Times* that many distinguished public men resented Lincoln's rejection of their advice, and many more were sore because their claims to office had not been recognized. "The most violent opposition to Mr. Lincoln," as Raymond saw it, "came from those most persistent and most clamorous in their exactions." In so terrible a crisis, it was unavoidable that "vast multitudes of active and ambitious men should be disappointed in their expectations of position and personal gain," this resulting in powerful and organized efforts against the renomination of Lincoln. They talked about that, did Lincoln and Raymond.

And Lincoln, as a judge of men, knew that he was talking with a friend, though he could not guess this friend was to go away and write that "the President has achieved a wonderful success" in maintaining through terrible trials "a reputation with the great body of the people, for unsullied integrity, of purpose and of conduct, which even Washington did not surpass, and which no other President since Washington has equalled." Raymond elaborated this "unspotted character" as a key point in the national situation. Without it, believed Raymond, there would have been national wreck.

The two men talked of Lincoln's state papers. Raymond thought Lincoln had a remarkable faculty of "putting things" to the common people, that what Lincoln might lose in graces of style he gained in simple language that carried precise ideas. "It gives to his public papers a weight and influence with the mass of the people, which no public man of this country has ever attained. And this is heightened by the atmosphere of humor which seems to pervade his mind, and which is just as natural to it and as attractive and softening a portion of it, as the smoky hues of Indian summer are of the charming season to which they belong." So Raymond wrote.

As to the candidacy of Chase, Lincoln said to Raymond that he did not concern himself much about that. It was important to the country that the Treasury Department should have vigor and energy, and whatever stimulated Chase would be good for the country. For illustration Lincoln gave an anecdote, and as Raymond passed it on to the painter, Carpenter, it ran:

"R[aymond], you were brought up on a farm, were you not? Then you know what a *chin fly* is. My brother and I . . . were once ploughing corn on a Kentucky farm, I driving the horse, and he holding the plough. The horse was lazy; but on one occasion rushed across the field so that I, with my long legs, could scarcely keep pace with him. On reaching the end of the furrow, I found an enormous *chin fly* fastened upon him, and knocked him off. My brother asked me what I did that for. I told him I didn't want the old horse bitten in that way. 'Why,' said my brother, *'that's all that made him go!'*

"Now," added Lincoln, "if Mr. C[hase] has a presidential *chin fly* biting him, I'm not going to knock him off, if it will only make his department *go*."

Of course Lincoln had no brother. The brother in the story was a slip of memory in Raymond or Carpenter. Except for this slip Lincoln possibly told the story much as they gave it. Others heard the story in the same essentials from Lincoln. It carried the kernel of Lincoln's idea about Chase and besides gave the impression that Lincoln still laughed occasionally and was not worried by the Chase movement. The *Detroit Free Press* and the *New York Herald* printed another version that ran smoother as a fable to point a moral:

"It was my business," says His Excellency, "to guide the plow, while my assistant, to the best of his ability, with a two-handed hickory, kept Davy in motion. We were all creeping along, old Davy taking our blows and our abuse, when suddenly he moved off at the pace of a young colt just put in the harness. 'What's the matter?'

I inquired. 'Oh,' said my brother, 'it's a great big horse-fly fastened on old Davy's neck; shall I drive him off?' 'No, no,' said I, 'as long as he keeps old Davy going at this rate, let the horse-fly alone. With his assistance we shall get a heap of work out of old Davy.' So it is with Mr. Chase. The next Presidency is his horse-fly, and it makes the Patriotic Secretary as lively at his work as old Davy. Let the horse-fly alone."

His shirt front burdened with self-importance and himself not aware of it, Chase in pleasant conversation at his home one evening, with the daughter Kate and others listening, rambled on in McGuffey school-reader style to John Hay, "It is singularly instructive to meet so often as we do in life and in history, instances of vaulting ambition, meanness and treachery, failing after enormous exertions; and integrity and honesty march straight in triumph to its purpose." Hay in his diary had to follow with the comment, "A noble sentiment, Mr. Secretary!"

A story got out and was printed and passed on to the effect that Chase had one day given Lincoln a gloomy recital of the financial situation. The other departments all stood at the spigots of the Treasury barrel and it was Chase who had to worry about the inside of the barrel. Gold was going higher and greenbacks sinking. The Secretary implored, "What can be done about it?" Lincoln with a flicker of perplexity and another of amusement on his own worried face: "Well, Mr. Secretary, I don't know unless you give your paper mill another turn." At which Chase almost swore as he flustered out.

Republican and Democratic papers enjoyed reprinting facetious charges of the *New York Herald* that Mr. Chase was "putting his own portrait upon the greenbacks of *small* denominations, which everybody sees, while he sticks Mr. Lincoln's comical phiz upon the *large* bills, in order that he may make himself generally known to the public."

As whispers and mutterings among good Republican-party men kept on, incessantly directed toward a change in the White House, John Hay wrote one day: "I do not know whether the nation is worthy of the President for another term, I know the people want him. There is no mistaking that fact. But politicians are strong yet and he is not 'their kind of a cat.' I hope God won't see fit to scourge us for our sins by any one of the two or three most prominent candidates on the ground."

In the fall of '63 Hay had spoken to Lincoln of Chase's "trying to cut under" the Administration, the President saying the conduct of Chase was "in very bad taste" but he had determined to shut his eyes to all these performances, that Chase made a good Secretary; he would keep him where he was. "If he becomes Pres[t] all right. I hope we may never have a worse man. I have all along clearly seen his plan of strengthening himself. Whenever he sees that an important matter is troubling me, if I am compelled to decide it in a way to give offense to some man of influence he always ranges himself in opposition to me and persuades the victim that he would have arranged it differently. It was so with Gen. Frémont—with Genl Hunter when I annulled his hasty proclamation—with Gen. Butler when he was recalled from New Orleans—with these Missouri people when they called the other day. I am entirely indifferent as to his success or failure in these schemes, so long as he does his duty as the head of the Treasury Department."

Later when Rosecrans was removed from command after Chickamauga and before his appointment to the Department of Missouri, Hay told the President that Chase would try to make capital out of the Rosecrans business. The President laughed. "I suppose he will, like the bluebottle fly, lay his eggs in every rotten spot he can find."

Hay noted also: "He seems much amused at Chase's mad hunt for the Presidency. He says it may win. He hopes the country will never do worse. I said he should not by making all Chase's appointments make himself *particeps criminis*. He laughed on & said he was sorry the thing had begun, for though the matter did not annoy him his friends insisted that it ought to." The President was thoroughly aware what he was doing, Nicolay and Hay believed, in appointing Chase men by the dozens to government jobs. "He allowed himself the luxury of a quiet smile as he signed their commissions." Of gossip not easy to laugh at he said on one occasion: "I wish they would stop thrusting that subject of the Presidency in my face. I do not want to hear anything about it."

In measuring men and reading their hearts Lincoln had the advantage over Chase that Chase seldom if ever laughed at himself. To Chase a fool was a dunce and every day in the week was a dunce. For Lincoln any dunce might have off days and even the wicked were not wicked all the time. Chase more often said he *knew* he was right and correct while Lincoln's habit was to say he *hoped* his head and heart were not misleading him. The tentative and weaving approaches by which Lincoln stalked his game rested on his view of man as a laughing animal who can never be sure he will get what he wants.

Chase could only be mystified by a story the *New York Evening Post* laid to Lincoln about a general who hinted to Lincoln that many people took it as settled that he would accept a renomination for President. Lincoln was reminded of an Illinois State official whom an itinerant preacher asked for a permit to lecture in the State House. "On what subject?" was asked, and the reply was, "On the second coming of our Saviour." "Oh, bosh," said the official, "if our Saviour had ever been to Springfield and got away with his life, he'd be too smart to think of coming back again." This, related the *New York Evening Post*, Mr. Lincoln said was very much his case about the renomination.

A long letter went to Lincoln from Chase on January 13 of '64 starting out "I am to-day fifty-six years old," and then outlining another self-portrait. The President had sent a little note about a biographical sketch of Chase to run in a Philadelphia magazine. And it was clear in Chase's answer about it that Chase knew he had slipped a cog and the President also knew it but Chase would rather the President did not know he had slipped a cog. Chase answered that he could not help it if people came to him wanting to do a biography. "He [the publisher] asked for subscriptions, and obtained them. How could I control or supervise that? . . . I should certainly have objected to any subscription by Mr. Jay Cooke or his brother. . . . Not that any wrong was intended or done; but because the act was subject to misconstruction, and there are so many to misconstrue. . . . What Mr. H. D. Cooke did about the unfortunate biography [in subscribing] was done of his own accord, without prompting from me." In closing Chase mourned as one wronged: "I realize how powerless are the most faithful labors and the most upright conduct to protect any man from carping envy or malignant denunciation."

That Chase—like Lincoln—wanted to keep clear of anything about which bothersome questions could be asked was seen in his returning to Jay Cooke a $4,200 profit that Cooke had earned for him in a railway stock deal, explaining to Cooke that he must "avoid every act which could give occasion to any suspicion." "In order to be able to render the most efficient service to our country, it is essential for me to *be* right as well as to *seem* right, and to *seem* right as well as to *be* right." Whether it was Cooke's money that might seem dirty or Whitman's poetry that also might seem dirty, Chase was taking no chances. That Lincoln was punished so little for telling stories that to Chase seemed dirty was amazing to Chase.

Theodore Tilton in the *Independent* mentioned the need for a believer in God as President, stressed the fact that Lincoln in writing the Emancipation Proclamation forgot to mention God and it was Chase who had suggested the closing phrase which invoked "the gracious favor of Almighty God." A friend went to Lincoln, said he felt it was improper of Tilton to publish such matters at such a time and that Chase had probably seen Tilton and was responsible. Lincoln: "Oh, Mr. Chase had nothing to do with it; I think *I* mentioned the circumstance to Mr. Tilton myself." Thus the man who had it from Lincoln told it to the painter Carpenter.

The matter of Hiram Barney, collector of the port of New York, came along early in '64. Somehow Barney was slipping in the running of that office. Lincoln called Chase in for several talks about it. Besides irregularities and mistakes strictly legal, Nicolay and Hay noted: "Several of Barney's subordinates had been detected in improper and corrupt practices, and after being defended by Mr. Chase until defense was impossible, they had been dismissed, and in some cases, punished." Lincoln saw a scandal coming and spoke of making Barney a Minister abroad and putting another man in at New York. But Chase said No all the time, by word of mouth and on paper.

The affair was very mixed, for Collector Barney's health was bad and he had asked months earlier to be relieved from a thankless job, but neither Lincoln nor Chase would at that time let him quit. That Chase had borrowed money from Barney, small sums, and that he and Barney had had a business acquaintance for more than twenty years, were minor points. That Barney was accused by conservatives of favoring radicals in appointments was more serious. Radical and conservative factions clashed about patronage, and Congress began in February an investigation of the New York customhouse, where searches without seizure and permits to ship certain cargoes were worth many dollars to those who could manage to get them.

A House committee summoned as a witness Joshua F. Bailey, special agent of the Treasury Department at New York, and because of what happened Lincoln had to write Chase that while he did not know that he had ever met or heard of this Bailey, nevertheless Bailey was assuming to be collector de facto, was running the collector's office headed nominally by Barney. And this Mr. Bailey, Lincoln wrote Chase, took occasion to call on the chairman of the House committee in advance, "and to endeavor to smother the investigation, saying among other things, that whatever might be developed, the President would take no action, and the committee would thereby be placed unpleasantly." Further as to this Mr. Bailey, Lincoln wrote Chase, "The public interest can not fail to suffer at the hands of this unresponsible and unscrupulous man." Therefore the President proposed to appoint another man, whom he named, as collector at New York.

Again Chase said No. If his friend Barney was removed he would resign. And as to Joshua F. Bailey, he was "not the fool to have made such a suggestion" as to smother a congressional investigation. Lincoln wrote to Chase: "Mr. Barney has suffered no abatement of my confidence in his honor and integrity; and yet I am convinced that he has ceased to be master of his position. . . . I propose sending Mr. Barney minister to Portugal, as evidence of my continued confidence in him."

The President felt "a very great delicacy" about doing anything "that might be offensive" to his friend Barney, according to a conversation which Maunsell B. Field, Third Assistant Secretary of the Treasury, said he noted down the day it took place. "Something had to be done. There was no use in attempting to bring Chase over to my views. But I tried it and failed. Then I waited for a time. At last I made up my mind to take action, hoping to be able to afterward reconcile Chase to it. So I sent for Seward, and told him he must find a diplomatic position in Europe for Barney. Seward said it was not an easy thing to do; but I told him it must be done. After two or three days Seward came back, and reported to me that he had found the place. Just then Chase became aware of my little conspiracy. He was very angry; and he told me that the day that Mr. Barney left the New York Custom-House, with or without his own consent, he, Chase, would withdraw from the Secretary-ship of the Treasury. Well, I backed down again."

A political journal calling itself the *Whig* referred in latter January to "the mongrel myrmidons of Abraham Lincoln" swarming to the work of renominating their master. Copperhead newspapers and radical antislavery journals pressed their readers to believe that the President was setting in motion a vast bureaucracy of government employees who would lose their jobs and offices unless they obeyed their master's voice ordering his renomination. These newspapers and journals savagely clung to their bureaucracy argument as though it jibed with their other argument that Lincoln's congressional party leaders were overwhelmingly against his renomination. By far the larger part of the bureaucracy, such as it was, had been appointed by Lincoln at the wish of the leaders who were overwhelmingly against him. The arguments became further muddled by the point, seldom denied by any political writer, that the mass of the people, what was usually termed "popular sentiment," favored the President for a second term.

A weekly, the *Spirit of the Times*, fed its readers the garbled information: "The patronage of the Government is not only being squandered at this moment to debauch the legislatures into an illicit nomination of Mr. Lincoln, but he has actually been engaged of late in granting pardons to military rebels . . . in order that they may come within our lines and electioneer to carry out his personal purposes." Self-righteous, hectic, irresponsible George Wilkes, owner and editor of a journal advocating Frémont for President, in a single sentence accused Lincoln of being a squanderer debauching State legislatures for an illicit end, besides trafficking with rebels in a way equivalent to betrayal of the Union soldiers.

Nevertheless the patriotic rhymer George Boker and his cohorts in the Union League Club of Philadelphia declared with feeling that President Lincoln should be renominated. The National Union Club of Philadelphia passed similar resolutions. In New York City the National Conference Committee of the Union Lincoln Association issued an address "To the Loyal Citizens of the United States" declaring that in electing an "occupant for the presidential chair" the people should choose "a true leader," one "tried and not found wanting," naming Abraham Lincoln. "No man in modern times ever worked more diligently to bring discordant elements together and make them move in harmony." On February 22 of '64 this committee proposed that all citizens of the United States, without regard to party, who favored the re-election of Abraham Lincoln, should hold town, county, or State meetings and give public expressions of their sentiments. The chairman of this committee was Simeon Draper, merchant, auctioneer, an old-time Whig, chairman of the Union Party State Central Committee of New York, long a personal and political friend of Secretary Seward, and Seward's favorite choice for collector of the port of New York. Another of the twenty-five signers who made up the committee was Moses H. Grinnell, once a Whig Congressman, a presidential elector of the Republican party in 1856, one-time president of the Chamber of Commerce of New York, and in 1864 a commissioner of charities and corrections in New York City. Formidable in its respectability, the committee including Moses Taylor, merchant, shipowner, president of the City Bank, railroad-promoter, and chairman of the loan committee of the Associated Banks of New York. Also a member was George William Blunt, authority on marine lighthouses, organizer of the pilotage system of New York Harbor, of which he was commissioner.

When some postmasters over the country who favored Lincoln's renomination posted this imposing New York declaration where any and all purchasers of postage stamps could see it, the *New York World* howled that the Administration had issued an order coercing the postal service into peanut politics. Horace Greeley had seen the movement rising a month earlier when at an antislavery meeting he was called on to speak and came forward to say that it was hardly a time to be making Presidents. He had not quite decided that the country was to have another President, though he hoped it would. Often, said Greeley, he had gone to bed at night wondering whether he would wake up in the United States of America or in the Confederate States of Jefferson Davis. He would say, however, that he thought about the largest man in this Government was Governor Chase, a statesman who had been fighting on the hardest ground of all to manage and whose battles had all been victorious. Greeley was thankful to God for safety so far and trusted God's protection would continue. As usual, Greeley wrote and printed a long cool editorial to buttress his short impetuous speech. Hay noted of this: "The Pres^t was greatly amused at Greeley's hasty Chase explosion and its elaborate explanation in the *Tribune*."

Also the President defended Chase against flings of Wendell Phillips that Chase was sending the nation into bankruptcy. The scheme by which the new national banks rested on bonds bought from the Government, plus currency printed by the Government for the banks to issue, the banks drawing interest on their bonds *and* their currency—of this Lincoln spoke to Hay as though it coaxed into use the dominant realistic motive of high profits to draw capital out of its hiding-places into patriotic support of the war. Hay wrote: "The President defended Governor Chase from Phillips' unjust attacks, saying that he thought Chase's banking system rested on a sound basis of principle; that is, causing the capital of the country to become interested in the sustaining of the National credit. That this was the principal financial measure of Mr. Chase, in which he [Lincoln] has taken an especial interest. Mr. Chase had frequently consulted him in regard to it. He had generally delegated to Mr. Chase exclusive control of those matters falling within the province of his Department. This matter he had shared in to some extent."

While Greeley grumbled, muttered, and failed to sway his masses of readers politically, some of the most cunning and ruthless political manipulators in the country began working on an upshoot of expression that would cry the mass sentiment favoring Lincoln for renomination. Simon Cameron and John W. Forney, practiced professional politicians of the Keystone State, at one extreme and swaggering gun-fighting Jim Lane of Kansas at another end, not forgetting the Blair boys and Old Man Blair, besides many political workers who knew left hand from right, pitched in to get results that would tell. The *New York World* probably guessed Cameron's motives as keenly as anyone: "General Cameron has no real friendship for a President who wavered all through the winter of 1860-61 as to whether he would keep the promise he had made to give Cameron a place in the Cabinet; who was forced against his will to appoint him; who compelled him to expurgate his second report of its abolitionism on pain of dismissal; who finally did remove him into distasteful but honorable banishment to Russia. But Cameron harbors a more insatiable grudge against Chase than against Lincoln. It was Chase and Chase's friends who, by their industrious attempt to ruin Cameron, kept Mr. Lincoln in indecision throughout the winter after his election. Cameron has gone into this Lincoln movement to pay off old scores against Chase. No man in the Republican party has more energy of character, and there are in that party but one or two more skillful managers."

Among Union members of the Pennsylvania Legislature early in January a paper was passed around. An address to the President, it was, saying that the voters of Pennsylvania had indorsed his policies generously at the recent election and "We are only responding to their demand when we thus publicly announce our unshaken preference for your reëlection to the Presidency in 1864." Signed by every Union member of senate and Assembly, this paper was sent to Lincoln on January 14 by Simon Cameron with the message, "You are now fairly launched on our second voyage. . . . Providence has decreed your reëlection, and no combination of the wicked can prevent it."

A New Hampshire State convention of the Union party had already met on January 6 to nominate a State ticket, and before the chairman knew exactly what he was doing with so many Treasury Department employees present, the delegates had sent up rockets and declared for Lincoln's renomination. The Union Central Committee of New York unanimously took like action, and in sending the news to Lincoln Senator Morgan said, "It is going to be difficult to restrain the boys, and there is not much use in trying to do so." With only one dissenting voice both houses of the Kansas Legislature endorsed renomination of the President. The Union members of the legislature of New Jersey joined in saying, without disparagement of other true men, "You are the choice of the people."

California legislators, almost unanimously, declared that in Abraham Lincoln they recognized purity of life, singleness of purpose, a farseeing statesman whose wisdom, sleepless watchfulness, prompt action, determined will, had kept public confidence in him unshaken. "While we revere and honor other noble patriots who have performed their parts, the people will look to Abraham Lincoln as the instrument selected by Providence to lead their country in safety through its perils."

In much the same tone the legislatures of Ohio, Maryland, Michigan, Wisconsin, Rhode Island, declared themselves, likewise State conventions in Minnesota, Iowa, Indiana, New Hampshire, Connecticut.

When February of 1864 ended, fourteen States had by official action gone on record speaking their preference for Lincoln for a second term.

As this movement gathered headway Hay noted, "The loud Lincoln men, who are useful only as weather gauges to show the natural drift of things, are laboring hard to prove themselves the original friends of the Pres[t]." Through January and February, Greeley had mildly and persistently urged the Chase and Frémont movements as more important than that for Lincoln. In the last week of February, Greeley in the *Tribune* discounted the State legislatures as "anything but a decisive indication of an unbiased choice." Mr. Lincoln had done his utmost to serve and save the country, yet "he is not infallible—not a genius—not one of those rare great men who mould their age." Moreover it had been well settled "by the deliberate actions of both political parties, that a President in office is not to be reëlected unless under pressure of extraordinary circumstances."

As if Greeley meant well but could not fully express his feelings, the *New York World* reprinted his long article the next day, and added its own comment that "the antecedents of our jocular President" made him impossible, the people had lost all confidence in his ability, and "this vacillation and indecision in the President has been the real cause why our well-appointed armies have not succeeded in the destruction of the rebellion." Besides feebleness of will and want of intellectual grasp, he had that species of cunning which characterizes a certain class of lawyers. The *New York Herald* with its lighter touch queried: "How can Old Abe and Secretary Chase get along in the Cabinet together? Both are candidates for the Presidency—Chase on a platform of greenbacks and Old Abe on one of Jokes."

Also during the first two months of '64 money was spent, political workers hired, and literature, open and secret, was spread by the quietly working Chase organization. The Washington branch of Jay Cooke & Company, through Henry D. Cooke, was involved in expenditures estimated at $20,000, while Senator Sprague's payments were put at $10,000. The Cooke firm made an outright gift of $5,000 to the Chase committee, of which Senator Samuel C. Pomeroy of Kansas was chairman, gave a check for $2,000 for the writing and placing of an article about Chase in the *Atlantic Monthly*, and raised a fund of $13,500 toward buying a newspaper, Senator Sprague looking around for one that would make a good Chase organ. Pomeroy's leadership in the affair brought mention that his unexpected election to the Senate in '61 had not been free from charges of bargain and that his record in money matters was not as spotless as that of Chase. And working modestly and without ostentation, quiet as a church mouse, yet fertile of resource and quick of wit, was the daughter and wife Kate Chase Sprague, swept and driven by ambition, even though her loving father when her name was brought into political matters wrote, "Her own good sense teaches her, and it is my earnest wish, that she should keep entirely aloof from everything connected with politics."

While the Chase band wagon was trying at once to make a noise and be quiet, the mass sentiment favoring Lincoln was exploded and reverberated through the State legislatures. Pomeroy and his committee decided in February on a bold play aimed to gather under their banner a cohesive marching force, a phalanx. So a circular was prepared—for private and confidential distribution. It was said to be a joint product of Sumner, Stevens, Davis, Wade, though signed by Pomeroy only. Chase's secretary, J. W. Schuckers, declared it was written by J. M. Winchell. Printed copies of it were mailed broadcast over the country with emphasis that it was "private and confidential." It was a statement of the most comprehensive case against Lincoln, which his party enemies believed would be effective in rallying a working opposition. From men inside the President's own party, men of high office seemingly endorsed by Secretary Chase, went this appeal to Union men that they must counteract the President's attempt to re-elect himself through using the official machinery of the Government: (1) His re-election was impossible because of the combinations that would be against him; (2) on the face of the President's record his second term would be worse than his first; (3) a second term would give the President more power than was safe for republican institutions; (4) Chase on the other hand would guarantee economy and purity in the Government; (5) the unorganized Chase strength needed only systematic effort to win.

The *National Intelligencer* at Washington spread this document in full over its pages, for newspapers everywhere to reprint, for the country to discuss and try to fathom. And the Chase workers, who had counted on secrecy till they had a strength worth bringing into the open, were all surprised, some shocked, Chase himself aghast. The *New York World* in reprinting it said: "The secret circular of the Chase party will be read with curious interest all over the country, and is likely to prove a bombshell in the rival camps of both Lincoln and Chase factions. We were disposed to believe it bogus at first, but our Washington correspondent assures us it is genuine. It is unusual, even in this age of impudent political canvassing, to see a President and his principal Cabinet minister open rivals for a nomination. It now appears that Mr. Chase has a very powerful organization at his back, and that he intends to compass not only the nomination but the presidency, if organization, money and effort can accomplish it."

Clear and plain to all who read the text of the circular was the shame that the "Committee of Prominent Senators, Representatives and Citizens" who issued the document were so afraid of being caught doing it, were stepping into such peculiar hazards of politics and history, that they wanted to be under cover, their names not known. So they did not sign. In so bold and raw a piece of work it was best to be anonymous. But their work was dragged into the daylight. And they scurried from newspapermen asking, "Who wrote it?" The Democratic press jibed at the Republicans in the words of the *New York World*, "Go on, gentlemen! wash your dirty linen in public." The politely phrased and carefully argued document which became both famous and notorious as "The Pomeroy Secret Circular" read in full:

The movements recently made throughout the country to secure the renomination of President Lincoln render necessary some counteraction on the part of those unconditional friends of the Union who differ from the policy of his Administration.

So long as no efforts were made to forestall the political action of the people, it was both wise and patriotic for all true friends of the Government to devote their influence to the suppression of the rebellion; but when it becomes evident that party machinery and official influence are being used to secure the perpetuation of the present Administration, those who conscientiously believe that the interests of the country and of freedom demand a change in favor of vigor and purity and nationality, have no choice but to appeal at once to the people before it shall be too late to secure a fair discussion of principles.

Those in behalf of whom this communication is made have thoughtfully surveyed the political field, and have arrived at the following conclusion: *First,* that even were the reëlection of Mr. Lincoln desirable, it is practically impossible against the union of influences which will oppose him.

Second, that should he be reëlected, his manifest tendency towards compromises and temporary expedients of policy will become stronger during a second term than it has been in the first, and the cause of human liberty, and the dignity of the nation, suffer proportionately, while the war may continue to languish during his whole Administration, till the public debt shall become a burden too great to be borne.

Third, that the patronage of the Government through the necessities of the war has been so rapidly increased, and to such an enormous extent, and so loosely placed, as to render the application of the "one-term principle" absolutely essential to the certain safety of our republican institutions.

Fourth, that we find united in Hon. Salmon P. Chase more of the qualities needed in a President during the next four years than are combined in any other available candidate; his record, clear and unimpeachable, showing him to be a statesman of rare ability and an administrator of the very highest order, while his private character furnishes the surest available guarantee of economy and purity in the management of public affairs.

Fifth, that the discussion of the Presidential question, already commenced by the friends of Mr. Lincoln, has developed a popularity and strength in Mr. Chase unexpected even to his warmest admirers; and while we are aware that its strength is at present unorganized, and in no condition to manifest its real magnitude, we are satisfied that it only needs systematic and faithful effort to develop it to an extent sufficient to overcome all opposing obstacles.

For these reasons the friends of Mr. Chase have determined on measures which shall present his claims fairly and at once to the country.

A central organization has been effected, which already has its connections in all the States, and the object of which is to enable his friends everywhere most effectually to promote his elevation to the Presidency.

We wish the hearty coöperation of all those who are in favor of the speedy restoration of the Union on the basis of universal freedom, and who desire an administration of the Government during the first period of its new life which shall to the fullest extent develop the capacity of free institutions, enlarge the resources of the country, diminish the burdens of taxation, elevate the standard of public and private morality, vindicate the honor of the Republic before the world, and in all things make our American nationality the fairest example for imitation which human progress has ever achieved.

If these objects meet your approval, you can render efficient aid by exerting yourself at once to organize your section of the country, and by corresponding with the chairman of the National Executive Committee for the purpose either of receiving or imparting information.

As argument this had more dignity than a pamphlet by Pomeroy a year before, *The Next Presidential Election,* calling for "an advanced thinker, a statesman profoundly versed in political and economic science" to occupy the White House, throwing tirades: "The cant about 'Honest Old Abe' was at first amusing, it then became ridiculous, but now it is absolutely criminal. Honesty signifies nothing unless there is capacity to wield power. In the language of Wendell Phillips, who cares for the honesty of the President unless he be capable; it is not honesty but capacity that is wanted."

While the circular was still being mailed out, and read as strictly private and confidential, many copies fell into the hands of Lincoln workers and soon began coming to the White House. The President, according to Nicolay, was absolutely without curiosity in regard to attacks on himself, refused to look at the circulars; they piled up "unread" in Nicolay's desk.

From the Cabinet room Secretary Usher confided to R. W. Thompson of Terre Haute, Indiana, his amazement at the Pomeroy Circular as "a most indecent thing" for Mr. Chase to allow "to go to the public." How Chase in strict honor could still hold place as an adviser to the President was beyond Usher. "Lincoln says but little, finds fault with none and judging from his deportment you would suppose he was as little concerned as anyone about the result. I do not see how we are to keep the family together much longer and you need not be surprised to hear of a disintegration of the Cabinet any day." Usher again and later wrote to Thompson that opposition to Lincoln's renomination "has come from the Treasury Department," and "The truth has been withheld and falsehoods have been told by men in the pay of that department. It will be known some day how perfidiously he [Lincoln] has been treated." On the day when the *National Intelligencer* burst into print with the circular, Chase wrote a sick-at-heart letter saying to Lincoln that it was probable that Lincoln had already seen a letter printed in the *Intelligencer*, "written by Senator Pomeroy, as chairman of a committee of my political friends." Until he saw it in print, wrote Chase to Lincoln, "I had no knowledge of the existence of this letter."

Chase explained to Lincoln that several gentlemen had called on him some weeks before and urged him to allow his name to be used toward election as Chief Magistrate. They said their views were shared by many earnest friends. He had replied that his usefulness as head of the Treasury Department might be impaired. They had come again. "We had several interviews." They gave their judgment that he could still be useful while his name was used. "I accepted their judgment as decisive." However, he requested them to withdraw his name whenever in their judgment the public interest would be promoted by so doing. "The organization of the committee, I presume, followed these conversations; but I was not consulted about it . . . nor do I even know who composed it." He had thought this explanation due to the President as well as himself. "If there is anything in my action or position which, in your judgment, will prejudice the public interest under my charge, I beg you to say so. I do not wish to administer the Treasury Department one day without your entire confidence."

Chase then wrote more warmly toned feelings than had ever before shown in his letters to Lincoln. "For yourself I cherish sincere respect and esteem; and, permit me to add, affection. Differences of opinion as to administrative action have not changed these sentiments; nor have they been changed by assaults upon me by persons who profess themselves the special representatives of your views and policy. You are not responsible for acts not your own; nor will you hold me responsible except for what I do or say myself. Great numbers now desire your reëlection. Should their wishes be fulfilled by the suffrages of the people, I hope to carry with me into private life the sentiments I now cherish, whole and unimpaired."

Lincoln studied this letter with its careful excuses, its blurred justifications, its embarrassed self-portraiture. On the next day, February 23, he wrote a one-sentence note to Chase: "Yours of yesterday in relation to the paper issued by Senator Pomeroy was duly received; and I write this note merely to say I will answer a little more fully when I can find time to do so."

Lincoln waited six more days. Robert Lincoln on this sixth day was home from Harvard on vacation, strolled into his father's room, and was met by something to him rather unusual; his father showed him a long letter replying to Chase. The son was surprised that his father had not read the Pomeroy Circular and said so. The father stopped the son sternly, saying that a good many others had tried to tell him something it did not suit him to hear, and he asked Robert to call a messenger to take a letter to Mr. Chase.

Chase could study the letter, a self-portrait in exchange for the one received from Chase. It read: "I would have taken time to answer yours of the 22d sooner, only that I did not suppose any evil could result from the delay, especially as, by a note, I promptly acknowledged the receipt of yours, and promised a fuller answer. Now, on consideration, I find there is really very little to say. My knowledge of Mr. Pomeroy's letter having been made public came to me only the day you wrote, but I had, in spite of myself, known of its existence several days before. I have not yet read it, and I think I shall not. I was not shocked or surprised by the appearance of the letter, because I had had knowledge of Mr. Pomeroy's committee, and of secret issues which I supposed came from it, and of secret agents who I supposed were sent out by it, for several weeks. I have known just as little of these things as my friends have allowed me to know. They bring the documents to me, but I do not read them; they tell me what they think fit to tell me, but I do not inquire for more. I fully concur with you that neither of us can be justly held responsible for what our respective friends may do without our instigation or countenance; and I assure you, as you have assured me, that no assault has been made upon you by my instigation or with my countenance. Whether you shall remain at the head of the Treasury Department is a question which I will not allow myself to consider from any standpoint other than my judgment of the public service, and, in that view, I do not perceive occasion for a change."

The next day after having this letter from the President, Chase had a call from Henry D. Cooke, and Henry wrote to his brother Jay: "The Secretary has the question of running for the presidency still in abeyance. What do you think are the prospects in Pennsylvania? I ask for information. I think the Secretary would like to have your opinion." Three days later Chase was worried lest Lincoln might give out for publication the interesting letters that had passed between him and the President. He wrote a note for Henry Villard, now of the *New York Tribune*, to carry to the President, who wrote to Chase: "In consequence of a call Mr. Villard makes on me, having a note from you to him, I am induced to say I have no wish for the publication of the correspondence between yourself and me in relation to the Pomeroy circular—in fact rather prefer to avoid an unnecessary exhibition—yet you are at liberty, without in the least offending me, to allow the publication if you choose."

As Chase reread the letters between him and Lincoln he knew he would be the worse damaged by publication. When one of Chase's most loyal friends, Robert B. Warden, read the letters at a later time he wrote that he, Warden, nearly lost his head and was tempted to agree with Tom Corwin's having told Lincoln that Chase was "embodied perfidy." Though on second thought Warden could not see "embodied perfidy" in the matter, he had to recall that Tom Corwin once used that phrase to warn Lincoln against Chase.

With the patronage of the Treasury Department almost exclusively Chase's, with scores of letters and interviews in which he made it clear to possible political workers that he would allow the use of his name toward the Presidency if it would not interfere with his serving the country as Treasury head, Chase during the weeks of January and February in '64 had not been able to set up a single rallying-point for his supporters except a committee in Washington whose membership was not made public except that Pomeroy was chairman, and whose one important statement was issued as private and confidential. Thaddeus Stevens as a Chase worker in Pennsylvania had been powerless against Cameron and Forney delivering an endorsement by all Union legislative members for Lincoln. Jim Lane in Kansas had overridden the Pomeroy forces. The son-in-law Sprague in Rhode Island had not been able to swing that tiny bailiwick. The Blair family, old Frank and young Frank and Postmaster General Montgomery, had put their influence and advice where it counted.

Still Chase hoped on. Ohio might come his way. His home State might say Yes. Surely the Buckeyes would want their old Governor for a White House figure. But the Ohio legislative members plopped one and all for Lincoln. And Chase wrote to the former Ohio Congressman A. G. Riddle, early in March: "I am trying to keep all Presidential aspirations out of my head. I fancy that as President I could take care of the Treasury better with the help of a Secretary than I can as Secretary without the help of a President. But our Ohio folks don't want me enough." On March 5, the day after Lincoln told him there would be no publication of the letters between them unless Chase wished it, Chase seemed to be throwing over all hopes of making a run that year for President, as he wrote James C. Hall of Toledo, Ohio, that since "our friends in Ohio manifest a preference for another," it seemed he should accept their decision. "It becomes my duty, therefore—and I count it more a privilege than a duty—to ask that no further consideration be given to my name." Chase ended the Hall letter with a direct intimation that under circumstances that might arise, or that could be arranged, he would lead the Democratic party for the sake of Union.

Freedom, and Justice. Compared with the cause for which he stood, he wrote, "persons and even parties are nothing."

In such peculiar twilights had Chase run his candidacy that when he requested by letter that "no further consideration be given" to his name, it was not taken that he strictly meant what he said. J. M. Winchell, the journalist whom Chase's secretary, Schuckers, said was the actual author of the Pomeroy Circular, wrote that Chase's letter of withdrawal was accepted by Chase's supporters as a "word of declination diplomatically spoken in order to rouse their flagging spirits."

Senator Pomeroy stood up in the Senate on March 10 to say, "I did issue that circular . . . [as] chairman of the national executive committee . . . composed of members of Congress and citizens from nearly every loyal state in the Union." Pomeroy avowed that so far as he was informed, the Secretary of the Treasury "was ignorant as to the persons composing that committee, as also of its action." The Secretary was drafted, without notice. "We still believe him to be the man" for Chief Magistrate. Pomeroy set forth the issues on which the Chase men were united: (1) suppression of the rebellion "without premature offers of pardon to traitors"; (2) Constitutional Amendments prohibiting slavery and giving the Negroes education and suffrage; (3) maintaining the Monroe Doctrine against Old World despotisms; (4) rigid economy; (5) confiscation of the property of leading rebels; (6) sound currency; (7) a strong hand on the seceded States in bringing about race equality; (8) no second term for Presidents; (9) liberty of speech with safeguards; (10) support of foreign immigration; (11) railways to the Pacific. On these issues, said Pomeroy, earnest men were awakening.

Senator Morton S. Wilkinson of Minnesota replied that Pomeroy and his honorable gentlemen "meeting somewhere in some dark corner," holding a grave conclave where nobody could find them, seemed to be aiming to organize a new political party. Since Pomeroy regarded his "issues" as so important, why should he hide the names of the members of his committee? As to Lincoln's being too conservative on these issues Wilkinson said: "I believe it is correct, that the President of the United States has been too slow; he has been behind the popular sentiment . . . but that, in my judgment, is his only fault. Mr. Lincoln has never taken one step backward since this rebellion commenced. He has been as firm as the everlasting hills, when he has assumed a position in favor of emancipation, or any other measure."

That Pomeroy had bungled in behalf of Chase for President, as he had also bungled for Lincoln a scheme for Negro colonization in Central America, was generally agreed. Months in and out Pomeroy had wrangled with Jim Lane over the Kansas patronage, hating so intensely that once when he asked Lincoln for an interview Lincoln refused to see him and instead wrote: "I wish you and Lane would make a sincere effort to get out of the mood you are in. It does neither of you any good. It gives you the means of tormenting my life out of me, and nothing else."

As the Chase boom wavered and sank early in March, Henry Ward